W9-AOK-593

Physical Education for Elementary School Children

Physical Education for Elementary School Children

Sixth Edition

Glenn Kirchner
Simon Fraser University

wcb

Wm. C. Brown Publishers
Dubuque, Iowa

Book Team

Senior Editor
Edward G. Jaffe

Associate Editor
Lynne M. Meyers

Designer
Catherine Dinsmore

Production Editors
Gloria G. Schiesl
William A. Moss

Photo Research Editor
Faye M. Schilling

Permissions Editor
Mavis M. Oeth

Consulting Editor

Aileene Lockhart

wcb
Wm. C. Brown Publishers,
College Division

Lawrence E. Cremer
President

James L. Romig
Vice-President, Product Development

David A. Corona
Vice-President, Production and Design

E. F. Jogerst
Vice-President, Cost Analyst

Bob McLaughlin
National Sales Manager

Marcia H. Stout
Marketing Manager

Craig S. Marty
Director of Marketing Research

Marilyn A. Phelps
Manager of Design

Eugenia M. Collins
Production Editorial Manager

Mary M. Heller
Photo Research Manager

wcb
group

Wm. C. Brown
Chairman of the Board

Mark C. Falb
President and Chief Executive Officer

Cover Photo
Bob Coyle

To George Longstaff, a good friend and an outstanding physical educator who is always willing to share his talents and ideas.

Contents

Preface

The changes occurring in elementary school physical education programs are exciting and positive. New programs that teach children to understand how their bodies work, how to begin a positive life-style, and how to design exciting new activities, such as creative and cooperative games, are but a few illustrations of the many new ideas being incorporated into elementary programs. These new programs and ideas are present in this sixth edition along with a general updating of each chapter. The text, however, has not departed from its original purpose: it remains a basic text for teachers from kindergarten to grade six.

The reorganization and expansion of several chapters provide a more efficient and effective format from which each teacher can develop her own program. Care has been taken to provide a balance between structured and exploratory teaching strategies. In fact, the reader will note a major attempt to integrate direct and problem-solving methods throughout each chapter. More than two hundred new photographs and one hundred new line drawings have also been added to this edition.

The basic organization of this book consists of seven parts. Part 1 describes the purpose of the contemporary physical education program and outlines the basic characteristics and needs of young children. The purpose of the program and the characteristics of children, in turn, become the guidelines for the arrangement, content, and emphasis of the remaining chapters.

Part 2 provides the reader with an understanding of the mechanics of movement and a description of the basic skills and movements that can be achieved by elementary school children. The hierarchy of movement skills described in this section reflects a general trend within this profession to organize movement concepts and skills in a logical and sequential way.

Part 3 concerns itself with the teacher and how she should teach. Included is information about strategies of teaching, organizational plans, and evaluative techniques. Although many "how to" suggestions appear in this part of the book, each chapter allows the teacher to choose the methods, techniques, and organizational procedures that best fit her style of teaching.

Organized in a sequential manner, part 4 streamlines the process of developing a curriculum for each teaching situation. The first chapter in this section describes how to plan a curriculum. Each succeeding chapter explains and illustrates how to cope with special problems, such as mainstreaming handicapped children, incorporating new ideas or activities, integrating subject areas, or adapting physical activities to the classroom.

Parts 5, 6, and 7 provide basic resource material. Part 5 offers a variety of individual and team game activities for primary and intermediate grades. Part 6 contains comprehensive coverage of gymnastic and movement activities that are performed on the floor, with small equipment, and with large apparatus. Part 7 covers rhythmic activities, traditional and contemporary dances, and creative movement. Throughout these sections are suggestions for teaching these activities through both the direct and the indirect method.

The reader will note throughout the book the general use of the pronouns she and her when referring to the teacher. Feminine references are used for the sake of simplicity and consistency. Likewise, the pronouns he and his are used to describe the student, although feminine pronouns are used, of course, to refer to female students in illustrations.

An expanded glossary and appendixes include new information about supplementary references, audiovisual resources, and equipment and supplies. All films with an asterisk were produced by the author and filmed in typical elementary school physical education settings.

A revised instructor's manual accompanies this text. It provides a summary outline of each chapter, along with teaching suggestions and evaluative techniques. The manual offers a quick overview of each chapter and acquaints the teacher with the updated written and audiovisual resources that are available.

Acknowledgments

Once again, I am indebted to many talented teachers and children who contributed to this book. To the professors who sent their suggestions, I hope this edition reflects most of your ideas. To the teachers, particularly Miss J. Sahli, Mr. Mike McComb, and Mr. Roger Linstrom, I extend my sincere thanks.

Jackie Campbell and Elizabeth Carefoot, two very patient and talented ladies, prepared the new drawings. And, for the second time, I wish to thank Mrs. Shirley Heap for typing the manuscript. Finally, I wish to express a very special appreciation to my wife Diane for her editing suggestions and remarkable patience.

In addition to my colleagues and wife, I also want to thank the following reviewers: Joanne W. Schroll, California State University, Fresno; Susan Wagner Lowy, Texas A & M University; Sue Rollins, Drury College; Elizabeth Ann Arink, Pennsylvania State University; Moira D. Luke, University of British Columbia; Dolores Hellweg, Illinois State University. Each read my manuscript and offered worthwhile suggestions, which helped in the preparation of the sixth edition.

Physical Education for Elementary School Children

1 Physical Education and the Growing Child

Part 1 is designed to provide teachers with a basic understanding of the meaning and purpose of physical education and the characteristics and needs of young children.

1 Physical Education in the Elementary School Curriculum

Historical Development of Physical Education

Factors Influencing the Nature and Direction of Physical Education
Individualized and Personalized Instruction Programs
Equal Opportunity for All Children
Mainstreaming Handicapped Children
Integration of Subjects
Health-Related Fitness
Research Findings and Platform Statements

Meaning and Purpose of Physical Education
The Objectives of Physical Education

Format and Approach of This Book

If we observed a highly qualified physical education teacher teaching a class of children, we would observe some things we have seen before as well as many new things and teaching strategies. We would see familiar equipment such as balls, tumbling mats, and tambourines. But, we would not see children lined up one behind the other, waiting for a turn to kick the ball. Nor would we see separate classes of boys and girls, or watch a child attempt a movement too difficult for him to master. We would observe a teacher guiding children towards the accomplishment of clearly articulated and meaningful goals—within each lesson and from lesson to lesson. We would hear new terms such as *body awareness, space awareness, flow,* and *matching sequence,* and notice the use of direct and problem-solving methods, even within one lesson. In this class we would see handicapped children: one blind and one in a wheelchair. Further observation would show that each child is working at his own rate and level of ability. We would also note, as the lessons progress, that the teacher is consciously monitoring the progress of the students and applying a variety of teaching strategies that enhance each child's self-image, that encourage effective interpersonal relationships and that redirect a few children towards more challenging activities.

These observations are the result of many important research findings from such fields of study as growth and development, motor learning, and special education. Factors outside of education have also caused some of these changes. For example, the shift toward health-related aspects of physical fitness, such as cardiorespiratory endurance and body composition, are the direct result of studies by the medical profession, nutritional agencies, and other groups outside of education. Also, the singular influence of Rudolph Laban regarding movement analysis has introduced a new way of classifying movement skills and concepts, and has had a major impact on indirect, or problem-solving, methods of instruction.

This chapter provides a brief historical perspective of physical education and outlines the major factors influencing it. The meaning and purpose of physical education is presented to provide a basic criteria for the selection of content and instructional methods in subsequent chapters.

Historical Development of Physical Education

The history of education reveals that physical education has always been present, but it has been regarded with varying degrees of importance. Ancient Greeks emphasized harmony of body and mind in the education of citizens. This concept of unity and balance involved the harmonious development of the mental, physical, and spiritual aspects of the human personality. Consequently, physical education was considered an integral component of the educational program, with similar purposes but unique contributions. Plato expressed this idea in his writings and by personal exemplification (Cromford 1941). During Plato's time, such balance of mind and body produced individuals of genius and a culture rarely equaled in subsequent generations (Arnold 1968). The warlike Spartans, however, emphasized physical training of the body for military purposes—a trend repeated in virtually every civilization that followed. One major exception was the aesthetic doctrine, which, throughout the Middle Ages, stressed the spiritual, thus completely neglecting the physical and social aspects of man and society.

From the period of Enlightenment to the twentieth century, education emphasized the intellectual development of man. Physical education, expressed in terms of natural play or such organized activities as gymnastics and games, was emphasized by such writers as Locke, Rousseau, and Spencer. The purposes of such programs, however, were conceived in terms of "training" the body to enhance optimum intellectual development. Only during the twentieth century has the Greek ideal of balance and harmony returned to the philosophy of education.

Since the beginning of the twentieth century profound changes in the philosophy, content, and methods of teaching have occurred at all levels in both public and private schools. These changes toward "education for democratic living" were not brought into existence by chance. New theories of learning, such as those presented by Thorndike, Gestalt, and Piaget have produced significant changes in the way children are taught (Arnold 1968). Dewey and his disciples made their interpretations of the nature of learning chiefly in terms of social and philosophical rationale. The combined influences of philosophers, economists, and educators provided the impetus and rationale for the transition toward a liberal, or general, education for all citizens.

Physical education has also undergone profound changes in the nature of its activities and methods of teaching. At the turn of the twentieth century rigid gymnastic programs were still strongly emphasized, although games were gaining acceptance as a valid part of elementary and secondary school physical education programs. The influence of Dewey, particularly between 1930–40, created major changes in the philosophy and thereby the content of physical education programs. Gymnastics were almost eliminated from the program, while games were given a predominant role. Because the educational emphasis was on "learning by doing," with children determining their own needs and interests, play through games was considered a strong contributor to social adjustment. Only minor emphasis was placed on skill and physical development.

From the early 1940s until the late 1950s, physical education programs changed substantially. Increased attention is now given to the professional preparation of specialists in physical education as well as classroom teachers. State laws requiring physical education programs in schools and certification for instructors have also upgraded the caliber of teaching this subject. Extensive research in such areas as growth and development, motor learning, and physical performance has brought back the rationale for a balanced program of physical activities for all levels of public and private education.

Since 1960, the movement education approach developed by Rudolph Laban has significantly altered the nature and direction of physical education in elementary school. Initially, teachers used Laban's movement analysis to teach gymnastics and creative dance activities. Today, however, many of the movement education concepts and teaching strategies are effectively incorporated into virtually every aspect of the physical education program.

Figure 1.1 Bowling in the Fourteenth Century

Factors Influencing the Nature and Direction of Physical Education

During the past two decades the elementary school physical education curriculum has been profoundly influenced by the changing philosophy of elementary education, by new federal and state laws and regulations, and by new developments in the content and teaching strategies of physical education. A few of the major trends discussed in the following paragraphs illustrate how these factors are shaping the future elementary school physical education curriculum.

Individualized and Personalized Instruction Programs

Perhaps one of the most significant trends affecting every subject area in the elementary school curriculum is the shift towards individualized and personalized instruction. This form of teaching creates an environment for successful personal encounter, fostering the free and open expression of ideas, facts, and feelings. It is an environment in which learning activities integrate the personal interests of the students with the goals of the school (Schmuck and Schmuck 1974). In physical education this means we no longer teach according to our own predetermined goals, exclusively choose the types of physical activities for the program, or only use a formal method of instruction. Rather, we shift from group-paced instruction towards a process of teaching that is a shared enterprise between the learner and the teacher.

Equal Opportunity for All Children

Title IX of the Educational Amendments of 1972 has had a profound effect on physical education in that every child must be given an equal opportunity to participate in physical activities in the instructional, intramural, or interschool program. One implication of this major change is that boys and girls within each elementary grade are now taught together. Hence, the selection of activities, as well as the choice of instructional methods, are determined in no small measure by this nonsexist grouping procedure.

Mainstreaming Handicapped Children

Public Law 94–142 mandates that all children possessing handicaps, ranging from hearing loss to restrictive physical anomalies, are not to be discriminated against and are to be educated at public expense. The implication to education in general is that a handicapped child must, according to the limits of his capabilities, be integrated into the regular instructional

Figure 1.2 A handicapped child can participate in a regular physical education program according to the limits of his capabilities.

program. In physical education this means that handicapped children will be scheduled in regular physical education classes. Within each physical education class, the teacher must be able to individualize her instruction to cope with the limitations of each handicapped child. If the latter cannot be accomplished, special education programs for the handicapped child must be alternately provided.

Integration of Subjects

A growing trend in elementary education is towards more conceptual development through an integrated or interdisciplinary approach to learning (Werner and Burton 1979). Common concepts such as *geometrical forms, stability,* and *rhythm* are no longer viewed as the sole property of one subject or another. Rather, teachers are using a variety of subject areas when teaching a single concept. Physical education is seen as an effective medium for teaching basic concepts from such subjects as math, science, language arts, and music. The fundamental implication is that both the classroom teacher and the physical education specialist must view the process of integration as a two-way street.

Opportunities exist for physical education teachers to emphasize a particular concept arising from another subject area and for classroom teachers to reinforce concepts arising from the medium of physical education in a variety of other subjects, particularly science, health, music, and art.

Health-Related Fitness

During the past few years many elementary school physical fitness programs have incorporated more health-related aspects of human wellness. The excessive number of either overweight or undernourished children has created a need for programs that help children assess their eating habits and plan effective weight-control programs. Problems relating to stress management, and alcohol and drug addiction have also prompted the physical education profession to redefine and emphasize new aspects of physical fitness. For example, AAHPERD's new *Health Related Physical Fitness Test Manual* emphasizes cardiorespiratory function, body composition (leanness/fatness) and abdominal and lowback-hamstring muscular skeletal function (AAHPERD 1980). This new direction and emphasis towards a positive state of well-being has created a need for programs that help children understand how their bodies work, how they can monitor body changes, and how they can design personal fitness programs for improving and maintaining optimum levels of health.

Research Findings and Platform Statements

Other factors directly affecting the nature and direction of elementary school physical education programs have resulted from research findings and statements by influential individuals or groups interested in the education and welfare of children. Numerous studies, for example, have been conducted to determine the effect of exercise on such factors as bone and muscle growth, perceptual-motor efficiency, and academic achievement. These investigations clearly indicate that young children must receive appropriate daily exercise to ensure that their bodies grow and develop in a normal, functional manner.

Long-term studies such as the Vanves program (Albinson and Andrews 1976), in which one-third of the school day was devoted to physical education, have shown dramatically that children with strong and healthy bodies tend to do very well academically. These studies do not imply, however, that increases in strength, endurance, or motor coordination increase a child's intelligence. They simply demonstrate that physically fit

children who possess good motor control do well academically. These investigations also show that strong and robust children can meet everyday personal and social pressures and challenges with relative ease.

The American Medical Association (AMA) and numerous other influential organizations have issued statements supporting the importance of daily physical education for children and youth. Such support has encouraged state and local officials to construct playing fields and facilities for physical education and athletic programs.

Public and private organizations have also influenced the direction and emphasis of instructional and extraclass programs. For example, the efforts of the President's Council on Physical Fitness and Sports, the AMA, and numerous other organizations have encouraged and supported physical education programs emphasizing physical fitness, intramural activities, or specific types of interschool competitive athletics. With respect to the latter, the publication *Guidelines for Children's Sports,* prepared by the American Alliance for Health, Physical Education, Recreation and Dance (AAHPERD 1979) and approved by the American Academy of Pediatrics, has had a major impact on all forms of children's athletics.

The collective influence of the individuals and groups mentioned, combined with our contemporary knowledge of human movement, provides the foundation upon which the elementary physical education program is constructed. The next section translates these trends and influences into the purpose and objectives of a contemporary physical education program.

Meaning and Purpose of Physical Education

The elementary school curriculum is composed of subjects, teaching strategies, and experiences designed to help each child reach his fullest cognitive, affective, and psychomotor potential. The language arts curriculum, for example, expresses its purpose in terms of the content, which includes listening, speaking, reading, and writing skills. Like all other subjects in the elementary school curriculum, language arts also includes in its purpose, reference to attitudes and appreciations of the young learner.

The contemporary meaning of physical education includes the content and teaching strategies of the instructional program as well as all the experiences that occur within the intramural, club, and interschool programs. An all-inclusive purpose of physical education is to help each child reach his fullest intellectual, physical, social, and emotional potential through the medium of physical activities. While this general purpose does not differ from the purpose of any other subject

Figure 1.3 The all-inclusive purpose of physical education is to help each child reach his fullest intellectual, physical, and social potential through the medium of physical activities.

in the elementary school curriculum, what justifies physical education in any elementary school curriculum is its unique contributions to each and every child.

The Objectives of Physical Education

The following objectives of physical education should be used by all teachers as a basic guideline when planning and teaching physical education. They are also used in this book as a basic criteria for the selection and emphasis of activities, for the inclusion of numerous teaching methods and techniques, and for the blending of Laban's movement education concepts with all aspects of contemporary game, dance, and gymnastic activities.

Enhance Physical Growth and Development

Every child is born with certain inherited characteristics that determine his approximate height, weight, and general physique. Such environmental factors as proper nutrition, amount of sleep, exposure to disease, and general parental care also affect the child's growth and development. In addition, substantial evidence has shown that normal growth and development of bone, and connective and muscle tissue occur only when a child receives adequate and continuous exercise throughout his growing period. Regular exercise, for example, increases bone width and mineralization (Rarick 1973). Similarly, lack of exercise can severely limit the potential growth of other bodily systems and organs.

Develop and Maintain Optimum Physical Fitness

Since the release of the Kraus-Hirschland report in 1953, a substantial effort has been made by the medical and physical education professions to convince the public of the importance of exercise and physical fitness to children, youth, and adults. There is now a large body of scientific evidence to support a program that helps each child develop and maintain an optimum level of physical fitness.

We know that children who possess the optimum level of physical fitness will normally reach their maximum levels of growth and development. Physically fit children do not show undue fatigue in daily activities and have sufficient reserve to meet emergencies. Physically active children are less prone to emotional disturbances and are generally well adjusted and outgoing. Proper weight is also adequately maintained by children who are continually involved in vigorous physical activity. And finally, physical fitness is a prerequisite for satisfactory performance in sports, gymnastics, and other vigorous activities.

Factors that demonstrate the importance of physical fitness stress striving for and maintaining optimum levels of strength, cardiorespiratory endurance, and other related fitness components as a means of achieving optimum growth, better health, and maximum performance.

Develop Useful Physical Skills

All movements used in everyday activities, such as walking, dodging, and climbing, as well as those highly complex skills involved in sports, gymnastics, and dance activities, may be classified as "useful physical skills." Other terms, such as *neuromuscular* or *motor skills,* also describe this type of physical performance.

All these skills, however, must be learned. Therefore, our task as teachers is to assist each child in developing and perfecting the wide variety of motor skills that will be used in everyday activities and in future leisure pursuits.

The values of efficient and skillful movements, particularly in sports and dance, are many. A child who demonstrates ease and grace of movement is usually physically fit and well adjusted among his peers. Furthermore, a child who displays skill in an activity such as basketball or swimming not only experiences a great deal of enjoyment through participation, but usually pursues the activity for many years. This lesson should be well understood by adults, for we generally participate in activities in which we show a reasonable degree of skill; rarely do we actively pursue or enjoy a sport that we cannot master at least in part.

Figure 1.4 Game situations requiring loyalty, honesty, and fair play promote desirable behavior patterns only if they are intelligently organized and directed.

Develop in Socially Useful Ways

According to the platform statement of the American Alliance for Health, Physical Education, Recreation and Dance (AAHPERD), a socially mature person works for the common good, respects his peers' personalities, and acts in a sportsmanlike manner. Implicit in this is the fundamental principle that democratic citizens possess a deep sense of group consciousness and cooperative living. Physical education, through team games and other group activities, can foster desirable social behavior. But game situations requiring loyalty, honesty, and fair play promote desirable behavior patterns only if they are intelligently organized and directed. A physically fit and well-coordinated child is a valuable asset; however, the individual who does not possess desirable social traits cannot realize or contribute to the broader ideals of a democratic community.

Develop Intellectual Competencies

Intellectual competency involves the cognitive skills of acquiring a vocabulary, and joining words, phrases, and sentences for expressing meaning and communicating thoughts and ideas. On the highest order, it involves the ability to understand, develop, and communicate concepts and ideas. In elementary school education, the development of intellectual competency has generally been delegated to classroom activities, with physical education seen as a way of developing fitness, motor skill, and a variety of social and emotional traits.

While physical education *should* be predominantly physical in nature, it should not be devoid of vocabulary and concepts, or of a need to exercise and nurture the child's thinking processes. Every physical activity has a rich vocabulary. Games, dances, and gymnastic movements require the child to think, remember, and conceptualize. Developing a movement sentence in gymnastics, for example, requires the child to plan each movement in a sequential pattern, to remember, and to improve by exploring and evaluating new ideas through movement. Likewise, individual and team games provide a medium within which the young performer develops concepts relating to space, gravity, force, direction, and time.

The teacher should not view physical education as an academic discipline. It should be seen as a medium of movement within which vocabulary, concepts, and the thinking processes of each child can be developed through effective teaching strategies and the appropriate selection of physical activities.

Develop Creative Talents

Contemporary public education stresses the development of creativity at all levels. Creativity, however, is a difficult concept to define. A work of art such as a painting, sculpture, or musical score is creative in that it is uniquely different in composition, color, or form. In physical education creativity is defined in terms of the way in which a movement or a series of movements is performed or by the degree of inventiveness of a movement.

According to Gladys Andrews, creativity is what the individual thinks, feels, sees, and expresses in terms of himself and in his own way (Andrews, Saurborn, and Schneider 1960). Since every child has a potential ability to be creative, the physical education program should provide numerous opportunities for each child to explore and express creativity through movement.

Enhance a Child's Self-image

Self-image is essentially the feelings a child has about himself. Each child develops feelings about his intellectual abilities, his popularity among peers, and his ability to perform physical activities. If there is reasonable success in each of these dimensions, the child normally has positive feelings about his personal worth. A child who has positive feelings is generally eager to attempt new challenges.

However, the child who constantly experiences failure in any of these areas will normally have a very

Figure 1.5 Every child has the potential ability to be creative.

Figure 1.6 Children who have positive feelings about their personal worth are generally eager to attempt new challenges.

low opinion of himself. This too often leads to withdrawal or other forms of undesirable behavior. Classroom teachers clearly understand the implications of such a child's problems in learning tasks and in getting along with classmates.

The physical education environment can either foster or impede the development of a child's positive self-image. If the activities are presented so that each child, regardless of physical ability, can achieve a measure of success, the child's feelings about himself are enhanced. One needs only to see a young child perform a successful roll or swim his first few strokes to observe the joy of success and the eagerness to try again. On the other hand, a child who is repeatedly required to attempt movement skills beyond his capabilities generally develops a negative attitude.

Since self-image is one of the most important factors in learning motor skills, physical education activities must be presented in such a way that every child achieves some success. New methods and techniques described in later chapters can assist teachers in providing this type of program for all children.

These objectives indicate what the physical education program should be. Perhaps the unique contributions of physical education are physical fitness and motor skill development. The need for a physically fit

nation, from childhood through adulthood, has been emphasized by presidents of the United States, members of the medical profession, and countless leaders in business and education. The inherent values of motor skill development, for the enjoyment of leisure activities and the positive contributions to long-term mental health must be considered of equal importance.

But, the development of intellectual competencies through physical education should also be emphasized, as with art, music, or any other aspect of the curriculum. All subject areas can and should develop each child's intellectual abilities. Similarly, the development of a child's creativity or the enhancement of his self-image is not the sole responsibility of one teacher or one subject area. Physical education simply is a unique medium within which the personal and creative expressions of children can be developed through movement.

Physical education in the elementary school curriculum must not be considered merely as a means of "training the body." Instead, it must be thought of as an integral part of the total curriculum with similar goals and unique contributions.

Format and Approach of This Book

This book has been organized to provide the reader with the basic knowledge and skills required to teach physical education to elementary school children. Parts 1 through 4 are presented in a sequential manner, beginning with background information, progressing through teaching strategies, and finishing with curriculum design information. The latter three parts contain resource material relating to games, gymnastics, and dance activities. The reader will not find a separate chapter dealing with movement education. Rather, she will find the concepts, principles, and skills of movement education integrated with other contemporary approaches used to teach games, dance, and gymnastic activities.

The appendixes contain bibliographic information arranged according to general topics, and additional ideas relating to facilities, equipment, and supplies.

2 The Child and Movement Experiences

Contemporary education focuses on helping the child develop to his full potential. As teachers of physical education, we must understand children's growth and development stages in order to choose appropriate activities and movement experiences. For example, a cursory knowledge of bone growth during childhood clearly indicates that vigorous daily exercise is necessary for normal development of bone tissue. Such knowledge also shows that excessive weight bearing or severe blows accompanying a sport such as contact football are harmful to virtually every elementary school child. Likewise, knowledge of muscle tissue growth, and heart and respiration rates provide insight into the correct amount and duration of exercise for children in the primary and intermediate grades.

Physiological changes, however, are not the sole criterion for selecting activities or teaching methods. Psychological changes involving self-image and attention span, and motivation and sociological changes relating to peer group importance also have significant implications for the physical education program.

This chapter gives a thumbnail sketch of important physical, psychological, and social changes experienced by young children. A few important implications of these changes for primary and intermediate physical education programs are also provided. A brief discussion of the exceptional child concludes this chapter.

Physical Development of Young Children

The physical growth and development of elementary school children can be described as steady and consistent. During early, middle, and late childhood, unique physical changes and needs dictate the type and intensity of physical activity for each age range. These important changes occurring in the skeletal, muscular, and cardiovascular systems are outlined in this section.

Skeletal System

The functions of the skeletal system are to protect the soft tissues of the body, such as the brain, spinal cord, and internal organs, and to provide the general framework of the body. The bones support the weight of the body and serve as an anchor, or attachment, for the skeletal muscles.

The bones of an elementary school child undergo continuous changes in length, width, and general composition. The long bones, such as the humerus (upper arm) and femur (upper leg), have one center of growth in the middle of the bone called diaphysis and one or more centers at each end of the bone called epiphysis (fig. 2.1). Growth occurs from the center of the bone toward the ends, and from the ends toward the center. When these centers merge into a solid bone, bone maturation is complete.

The bone structure of an elementary school child is relatively soft and flexible, and normally can absorb many jars or blows without fracturing the bones. However, severe blows such as those experienced in contact football and excessive weight bearing on any joint should be avoided. But since the ends of the bones and other connecting tissues around the joints are extremely supple, the child can bend and stretch all parts of his body further than even the most fit adult. The yogalike position shown in figure 2.2 illustrates the potential flexibility of young children.

Boys and girls from age five to approximately eleven show a steady increase in bone growth. During this period, however, the bone structure is still relatively weak and flexible. As a child reaches puberty, bone growth appears to be more rapid; this is quite evident with eleven- and twelve-year-old girls in the fifth and sixth grades.

Sufficient scientific evidence indicates that exercise is necessary during these formative years for normal bone growth. According to Dr. C. S. Houston, "If we are active, our bones will be well mineralized and both bones and muscles will be strong." It has also been shown that long periods of inactivity will cause some decalcification of bones (Albinson and Andrews 1976). The result of this demineralization is a weaker and more brittle bone, and hence one that is more susceptible to fractures and other injuries.

Muscular System

Skeletal muscles of young children undergo rapid changes in size and strength. An initial rapid growth in muscle tissue occurs between ages five and six. However, from ages seven to eleven or twelve, growth of muscle mass is relatively gradual and continuous. By

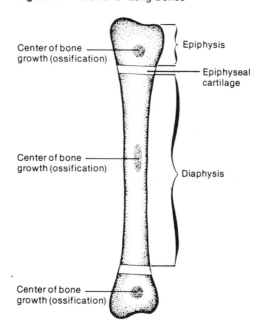

Figure 2.1 Growth of Long Bones

Center of bone growth (ossification)

Epiphysis

Epiphyseal cartilage

Center of bone growth (ossification)

Diaphysis

Center of bone growth (ossification)

age twelve, the average child has nearly doubled the amount of muscle tissue he had at age six. Experts in the growth and development field indicate that increases in the size and strength of muscles, particularly in children in the middle elementary grades (grades three to five), make this a period of restlessness for most children. As with all other systems of the human body, muscle tissue must be exercised if its full potential is to be reached.

The majority of physical fitness norms show that boys are slightly stronger than girls between five and twelve years of age. These differences are not the result of an inherent difference in muscular systems but are normally due to social factors—boys tend to participate in vigorous activities, while girls lean toward less active and physically demanding activities. But this tendency clearly is being reduced by social and cultural changes during the past decades, along with the current policy of giving equal time to both sexes in all publicly supported sport and physical activity programs. In fact, in many contemporary physical education programs, any previously observed differences in strength and general physical fitness levels in this age range have virtually disappeared.

Once they reach puberty, however, boys begin to show significant increases in muscle mass and strength, and physiological changes in girls create proportionately less muscular mass and more fatty tissue. These changes, coupled with other structural changes in both sexes, produce a major difference in the strength of boys and girls as they enter adolescence.

Figure 2.2 This yogalike position illustrates the potential flexibility of young children.

Figure 2.3 Children begin developing basic manipulative skills after their fundamental locomotor and nonlocomotor skills are well underway.

Cardiorespiratory System

The growth of the heart (cardiac muscle) and lungs is almost proportional to the growth of bones and muscles throughout the elementary school years. The pulse and breathing rates gradually decline throughout the primary grades, and by age nine, the pulse rate is rarely above ninety beats a minute. Respiration rate is approximately twenty a minute. Thus, easy fatigue and rapid recovery are characteristic of this age.

By age twelve, the pulse rate is normally between eighty and ninety beats a minute and the respiration rate is between fifteen and twenty a minute. Children between nine and twelve have more endurance, although girls with early signs of puberty may tire sooner.

Implication to Physical Education

The general structural and maturational changes that occur between the ages of five and eleven or twelve are gradual and approximately equal for boys and girls. Normal and optimal levels of development of bone, muscle, and other tissue depend upon daily vigorous physical activity appropriate to each child's age and maturity. Specific recommendations for primary and intermediate physical education programs are provided in the chart on pages 18–21.

Motor Development of Young Children

The development of motor skills follows an orderly sequence through four overlapping age ranges. The first, known as babyhood or infancy, begins about one month after birth and lasts to the end of the second year. During this period, a child displays reflex responses and then proceeds to the rudimentary skills of sitting, crawling, creeping, climbing, standing, and walking.

The next stage, known as early childhood, continues from age two to approximately the end of the sixth year. During this period a child develops the fundamental locomotor and nonlocomotor skills of running,

jumping, leaping, hopping, skipping, sliding, dodging, stopping, swinging, twisting, bending, turning, and stretching. A child also begins to develop the basic manipulative skills of throwing, catching, and striking. Many of these fundamental motor skills are learned prior to kindergarten and, in most instances, through a process of exploration. During the first two years of primary school, the continuing development of these fundamental motor skills should be through a physical education program that emphasizes exploration of movement rather than refinement of skills. This is particularly important when a child is learning the basic manipulative skills of throwing, catching, and striking. The latter skills can be effectively learned through informal and creative games programs.

As children move into middle childhood, they begin to refine fundamental motor skills, and to develop more complex combinations of locomotor, nonlocomotor, and manipulative skill patterns. During third and fourth grades increases in physical size and strength, coupled with improved perceptual and cognitive development, contribute to a child's ability to perform more coordinated movement patterns with greater speed and accuracy.

During the fourth stage, known as late childhood, the more specific movement skills required of games, dance, and gymnastics begin to show some refinement. In game activities, such as soccer, fifth and sixth graders learn to dribble with changing speeds as well as to add feints and other tactics necessary for moving a ball through a variety of complex game situations. Similarly, dance and gymnastic skills become more fluid and creative as the performer acquires greater skill and understanding of the finer aspects of an individual movement or sequence of movements. As children move into adolescence they continue to refine these more specialized game, dance, and gymnastic skills and to acquire new skills that are more related to their social and future leisure activities.

Psychological and Social Development of Young Children

The personal and social characteristics of children, as well as their physical growth and motor development, must be considered when planning a physical education program. This section describes some of the more common personal and social characteristics of children in early childhood (5 to 7 years), middle childhood (8 to 9 years), and late childhood (10 to 12 years). Specific implications of these characteristics for the physical education program are also provided.

Early Childhood (5 to 7 years)

Five- and six-year-old children are still quite egocentric, hence they enjoy playing by themselves or with one or two other children. They have boundless curiosity and enthusiasm, but they tire easily. These children need to explore many types of physical activities and challenges—but without pressure and with generous praise for their accomplishments. As they enter grade two they become much more cooperative, and they display an interest in all types of physical activity, but for relatively short periods of time. Teachers find that seven year olds seek adult approval much more than they did just a year earlier.

Middle Childhood (8 to 9 years)

As children enter middle childhood, their interests shift towards more group activities and group success. They show a keen interest in more complex game and dance activities, and a willingness to practice to improve their individual skills. Although these children seem to display a great deal of group or team loyalty, they tend towards adult supervised activities. It is important that

Figure 2.4 During early childhood, children should explore many types of physical activities and challenges by themselves or with one or two other children, but without pressure.

teachers provide challenging activities with many opportunities for each child to be successful. The importance of the latter comment cannot be overemphasized. Middle childhood is a period during which children begin to test their abilities within a group setting. If all challenges end in failure, the child's self-image reaches a very low ebb, and continued interest in physical activities becomes doubtful. Therefore it is important that instructors provide many opportunities for success in order to provide the child a strong base for coping with the failures that everyone experiences during a lifetime.

Late Childhood (10 to 12 years)

Physical maturation influences the social and psychological development of children in this age group, creating a period of transition and differentiation in the interests and behavior of both boys and girls (Arnold 1968). Both sexes enjoy highly complex team games and, like the previous age range, are willing to practice for long periods to improve their playing ability. They have an intense need to become responsible for their own actions, hence, they enjoy planning, organizing, and

Figure 2.5 During middle childhood, children show a willingness to improve their individual skills so they can participate effectively in more group-related activities.

Figure 2.6 During late childhood, boys and girls enjoy complex team games.

supervising their own activities. The latter has major implications for the daily instructional, intramural, and interschool programs.

Boys tend to be sloppy in their dress and are very concerned about their physical fitness. They are keenly interested in vigorous competitive sports and show a strong concern about their peers and a great deal of confidence in adults. Hero worship, particularly for well-known athletes, is the rule rather than the exception.

There is a changing attitude of girls towards more active participation in all types of vigorous physical activities. More girls are now participating in organized intramural and interschool team sports. Community clubs for gymnastics, swimming, and soccer are also experiencing a major increase in the number of girls wishing to participate in their sports programs. Although the latter is a significant trend, girls of this age level still become increasingly concerned with their personal femininity; therefore, they tend towards less vigorous activities such as body mechanics and social dance.

No magic line separates one age from another; teachers of grades five and six are aware of the tremendous diversity in psychological characteristics of these children. However, as with the younger age range, some basic considerations should be made when planning a physical education program for children in the intermediate grades. (See page 20.)

Characteristics and Needs of Young Children

The choice of an activity, as well as the manner in which children are motivated to learn, must be based upon their developmental characteristics and needs. Although individual variations exist in virtually all phases of growth, certain characteristics and needs are quite dominant in the early, middle, and late childhood years. These characteristics and needs, and their specific and general implications to the physical education program are summarized in table 2.1.

Table 2.1 Characteristics, Needs, and Implications to Program Development

Characteristics and Needs	Implications to the Physical Education Program

Early Childhood (5 to 7 years)

Physical and Motor Characteristics

Height and weight gains moderate and steady.

Boys and Girls	Height	Weight
Boys—5 years	42 to 46 inches	38 to 48 pounds
Girls—5 years	42 to 45 inches	36 to 48 pounds
Boys—6 years	44 to 48 inches	41 to 54 pounds
Girls—6 years	44 to 48 inches	40 to 53 pounds
Boys—7 years	46 to 50 inches	45 to 60 pounds
Girls—7 years	46 to 50 inches	44 to 59 pounds
Average Gain	2 inches a year	4 pounds a year

Continue to provide the same gross motor activities, such as running, jumping, and climbing, for both boys and girls. Attend to postural development; early detection of structural anomalies is important. Children of this age have relatively small bodies, hence, consider the relative size of supplies and equipment.

Proportional gains in weight, primarily attributable to growth in bone and muscular tissue, and a reduced rate of increase in fatty tissue.

Continue to provide vigorous exercise with special attention to developing strength and endurance.

Heart and lungs not fully developed. Pulse and breathing rates are relatively high (pulse rate 80–90; breathing rate 18–20). Easy fatigue and rapid recovery is a particular characteristic of this age range.

Provide vigorous activity, particularly running, climbing, and swimming, with frequent rest intervals. Discourage long periods of inactivity. Encourage recess and period breaks throughout the school day that incorporate vigorous and total body movement.

Eye-hand coordination is not fully developed. Lack precise focus (tendency to farsightedness) and spatial judgment.

Provide for manipulation (catching, throwing, kicking, etc.) of various size balls. Initial instruction should include relatively low speeds of throwing, etc., with short distances. Gradually increase speed, use of small objects, and distance as skill develops.

Reaction time is slow but shows a persistent increase throughout this stage.

Encourage participation in numerous activities involving a change of speed and direction.

Mental and Emotional Characteristics

Gradual increase in attention span. Periods of restlessness in early grades and throughout the age range.

Provide a large variety of activities within the instructional period. Initiate games for the individual and for small groups. Keep them simple in purpose, rules, and directions.

Extremely creative.

Provide method and content that foster creative interests and movements (creative dance and movement education).

Enjoys rhythm and music.

Provide various forms of dance experiences, including singing games and creative dance.

Keen desire to repeat activities they know and perform quite well.

Allow children to choose activities, such as playing the same game each recess period. In dance and gymnastic activities, chronic interest in one activity is characteristic. With patience, children soon run the course and move on to other challenges. Your challenge is to provide more interesting and challenging activities.

Individualistic, but shows a need for adult approval.

In one respect, 5- to 7-year-olds are basically individualistic. Therefore, provide numerous individual activities for all children regardless of ability. Children of this age level also need adult approval.

General lack of fear and an extremely high spirit of adventure.

Encourage the spirit of adventure (climbing, testing one's own ability with other children). At the same time, develop within each child the concern for personal safety and a general awareness and concern for the safety of others. Extensively use the movement education approach with gymnastic activities.

Social Characteristics

Little concern for the opposite sex during the early grades.

Allow children of both sexes to play together. They generally get along quite well during early childhood.

Table 2.1 Continued

Characteristics and Needs	Implications to the Physical Education Program

Middle Childhood (8 to 9 years)

Physical and Motor Characteristics

Height and weight gains moderate and steady.

Boys and Girls	Height	Weight
Boys—8 years	48 to 53 inches	50 to 67 pounds
Girls—8 years	48 to 52 inches	48 to 66 pounds
Boys—9 years	50 to 55 inches	55 to 74 pounds
Girls—9 years	50 to 54 inches	52 to 74 pounds
Average Gain	2 inches a year	4 pounds a year

Provide daily vigorous physical activities. Continue to provide for gross motor activities.

Heart and lungs continue to develop at a slow and steady rate. Pulse rate lowers to about 85, and breathing rate drops to about 15 to 18 times per minute.

Continue to provide daily vigorous physical activities.

Eye-hand coordination continues to improve along with a major improvement in manipulative skills.

Provide numerous individual and team activities involving throwing, catching, and striking.

Early signs of poor posture for both sexes.

Instill a positive attitude toward one's own posture. Use simple screening tests and refer serious cases to family physicians.

Mental and Emotional Characteristics

Continued increase in attention span.

Continue to provide a variety of more complex activities that require closer attention and cooperative behavior.

Improved cognitive development.

Teach the mechanical principles relating to performing movement skills. Encourage children to invent their own games and movement sequences.

Continued high spirit of adventure.

Continue to provide challenging tasks on apparatus and on the playing field. Stress personal and group safety throughout this age range.

Social Characteristics

Gradual trend of mutual antagonism toward the opposite sex.

Plan game, dance, and gymnastic activities that boys and girls can participate in together. When "fierce" antagonism and/or major differences in skill levels exist, particularly in combative activities and ball games, separate the sexes.

Lack of discrimination on the basis of race, color, or religion.

Take care in the methods and techniques used to choose teams, leaders, and various social groupings. The essential teaching characteristic should be fairness to all children.

Accepts just punishment for self and for group.

Do not punish a whole group for the wrongdoings of one child. Children recognize inconsistencies in degrees of punishment, hence, be consistent and fair with the type and amount of discipline and punishment. Because of the "social awareness" and inherent fairness of children, stress group control through self-discipline.

Table 2.1 Continued

Characteristics and Needs	Implications to the Physical Education Program

Late Childhood (10 to 12 years)

Physical and Motor Characteristics

Height and weight gains rapid after the beginning of puberty.

Boys and Girls	Height	Weight
Boys—10 years	52 to 57 inches	59 to 82 pounds
Girls—10 years	52 to 57 inches	57 to 83 pounds
Boys—11 years	54 to 59 inches	64 to 91 pounds
Girls—11 years	54 to 59 inches	63 to 94 pounds
Boys—12 years	55 to 61 inches	70 to 101 pounds
Girls—12 years	56 to 62 inches	72 to 107 pounds
Average gain	2 inches a year	7 pounds a year

Continue to provide vigorous activities, emphasizing strength and endurance for longer periods of time. Although girls, particularly those who have reached the early stages of puberty, may show a general disinterest in vigorous activities, remember that normal growth and development depends upon vigorous and continuous activity.

Postural development for this age group is a particular problem. The problem has been intensified by excessive viewing of television and video games, and general sedentary living. Therefore, observe sitting and walking postures of students, and plan activities for general posture development. Give special attention to girls who have reached puberty and tend toward sloping shoulders to compensate for height and chest development.

Girls normally reach puberty between 10 and 11 years, while boys begin approximately 2 years later. Marked differences in height and weight gains occur in grades 5 and 6.

Heart and lungs are in size and capacity proportionate to height and weight gains. By age 12, heart rate is between 80 and 90 beats per minute. Respiration rate is between 15 and 20. Longer periods of endurance are possible for this age group; however, girls who reveal early signs of puberty will show early signs of fatigue.

Continue to provide vigorous activities for longer periods of time with frequent rest periods for both sexes. Show special consideration for girls who show early signs of fatigue.

Muscle strength continues to increase with boys and girls. Differences in strength between boys and girls during this age level may be due to the type of activities in which they participate rather than inherent structural or physiological changes within each sex.

Provide for strength development of both sexes. Although all muscles of the body need consistent exercise of an overload nature, special attention should be given to activities involving the arms, shoulder girdle, back, and abdominal area. Provide for more self-testing activities that develop strength in these regions of the body. Team games and dance activities are low contributors to developing strength in these muscle groups.

Muscle coordination continues to improve with both sexes.

Provide more highly organized and competitive individual and team sports. If there is a marked difference in level of skill, between boys and girls, separate them when playing team games to allow both sexes to develop according to their own level of skill and interest. Both sexes, however, require extensive practice in the refinement of throwing, catching, and kicking skills. Separate and solid unit construction is appropriate, particularly in the upper grades.

Flexibility decreases, with boys showing greater losses than girls.

Lack of flexibility appears to be due to the type of activity rather than structural or growth reasons. Hence, provide movements that enhance flexibility. Encourage self-testing activities, particularly those involving stretching and the use of apparatus such as stall bars and agility equipment.

Table 2.1 Continued

Characteristics and Needs	Implications to the Physical Education Program
Mental and Emotional Characteristics	
Marked increase in attention span.	Provide more complex and challenging activities. This applies to individual and team games where allowance is made for extensive practice in learning skills, rules, and complex team strategy. Similarly, with dance and gymnastic activities, allow time for developing complex and creative movements.
General increase in intellectual curiosity.	Teach concepts and principles of movement related to the physical and motor skills the children are learning. Through the application of the problem-solving method, test and challenge a child's intellectual ability through movement tasks.
Increased control of emotions in individual and group situations.	Select activities commensurate with the emotional development of each age group. Outbreaks of emotions in tense game situations are normal and, in some situations, desirable. Make provision for each child to experience leadership roles.
General increase toward independence and peer group identity.	The essence of good teaching should be the development of self-direction on the part of each child. Independence is a natural tendency for this age group and must be provided for both in methods and appropriate activities. Teacher-directed approaches should not be completely abandoned but should be blended with other approaches that call for greater freedom and responsibility on the part of the learner. Pay special attention to the kinds of groupings that provide for identification as well as foster team cooperation and loyalty.
Social Characteristics	
Major difference in attitudes toward opposite sex as well as toward different types of activities. Boys and girls alike, particularly during upper grades, show a lack of sympathy and understanding toward each other. Boys tend toward more rough team sports, increased concern for physique and skill, and a dominant interest in competition. Girls begin to show concern for personal appearance, activities involving graceful and creative movements.	Separate sexes within a class for various team games where there is a major difference in skill level. Gymnastic activities when taught through the movement education approach can cope with major interest and skill differences of both sexes. Dance, particularly folk, square, and social, should be coeducational.
Social acceptance is more peer-centered than adult-centered.	Make provisions within the instructional and extraclass program for children to participate in both individual sex and mixed group activities. Allow extensive opportunities for boys and girls to plan and direct activities. The latter not only contributes to the development of cooperation, leadership, and team loyalty, but also allows children to develop other important social traits and personal friendships.
Girls tend to be more self-conscious in the presence of boys as well as when performing within their own sex grouping.	Use discretion when asking girls (particularly 5th and 6th graders) to demonstrate skills or movements in a mixed setting. Although girls are normally more graceful than boys in gymnastic-type movements, they tend to be embarrassed when asked to demonstrate. The reverse, however, is generally true with ball skills where girls are much less proficient than boys. Develop an understanding and appreciation for the differences that exist between boys and girls of this age level.

Figure 2.7 A child who possesses a unique ability in sports, dance, or gymnastics may be described as physically gifted.

The Exceptional Child

The exceptional child is defined in contemporary education as a child who, in one way or another, deviates from the "normal" intelligence, physical health, or behavior of the "average" or "typical" child. This definition includes the intellectually gifted, the physically gifted, the physically handicapped, the slow learner, and the social deviant. Approximately 12 percent of the school population falls within this group, and each type of gifted child requires some form of special attention (Jarvis and Wootton 1966).

In physical education, as in all other subjects, it is necessary first to distinguish the types of exceptional children.

The Physically Gifted Child

Few writers in the physical education field have attempted to define what is meant by a physically gifted child. Yet, by observation of performance and analysis of programs, the contemporary meaning is quite clear. A child who possesses a unique ability in sports, dance, or gymnastics may be described as physically gifted.

In individual and team sports, the gifted child is recognizable as a member of the school team. The gifted dancer, gymnast, or swimmer is a member of a school or community club.

These special talents are also recognized within the physical education program of an elementary school, in both instructional and extraclass programs. If all children are given a well-rounded program, special activities for the physically gifted would appear to be in harmony with the educational philosophy and principles of contemporary elementary school programs. Consider the following when providing special programs for the physically gifted child:

1. All phases of the physical education program should be given fair consideration and emphasis.
2. Gifted children should be expected to do a great deal of planning, executing, and evaluating of classroom activities.
3. Higher standards of achievement are established for gifted children.
4. Gifted children should be encouraged to expand their interests and enrich their experiences through participation in special-interest clubs in the school or community.

5. Specialists in sports, dance, and gymnastic activities should be used within the physical education program. A specialist is defined as a qualified person recognized by the school who is capable of teaching a special talent. For example, a parent who has special talent and qualifications in folk dance would meet this criteria.

The Handicapped Child

A normal, healthy child is defined as one who is free of disease and physical handicaps. Conversely, a handicapped child is one who has an acute or chronic disease, such as rheumatic fever, or is mentally or physically handicapped because of a birth or hereditary malformation. Handicaps of the latter type include Down's syndrome, hearing loss, cerebral palsy, and an extensive list of orthopedic malformations that impair physical performance (Matthews, Krause, and Shaw 1962). A more extensive discussion of handicapped children is included in chapter 10.

Contemporary educational philosophy and practice adheres to the fundamental principle established under PL 94–142 that a child in school is educable. Therefore, whenever it is physically and psychologically feasible, the physical education program will provide desirable experiences for the handicapped child.

The handicapped child's limitations and needs obviously must be determined by such experts as physicians, corrective therapists, and psychiatrists. Furthermore, these authorities should make specific recommendations about the type of physical experiences these children should have. For example, a child who has cerebral palsy but with limited impairment might be permitted to participate in physical activities involving gross motor movement, such as simple games and certain dance experiences. But movements requiring rapid hand-eye coordination, such as are involved in throwing and catching skills, may be too great a task for the spastic child.

Teachers have demonstrated keen insight in virtually all learning experiences involving handicapped children. Within the regular classroom situation, children with sight and hearing losses are placed in more advantageous seats. The epileptic child is no longer kept at home, nor is his condition concealed from his peers. Likewise, the physically handicapped child is integrated into daily physical education activities to the limits of his capacity.

The scope of the handicapped child's program must be based to some degree on the following considerations.

1. The type of exercise should be specified by a competent medical adviser.
2. The type of activities should be appropriate to the child's capabilities and needs.
3. A physical education specialist should be consulted for assistance in developing corrective and remedial programs.
4. The program should allow the child to experience immediate success and enjoyment.
5. Whenever feasible, the extent of a child's handicap should be explained to his peers.
6. The program should include activities that are of long-range recreational value.

The information in this chapter should provide a basic understanding of the nature and importance of a child's growth and development when planning a physical education program. Part 2 presents additional information about the structure and function of movement and the basic skills and movement fundamentals for children in the primary and intermediate grades.

2 Nature and Analysis of Movement

Part 2 concentrates on two important aspects of human movement. Chapter 3 provides a basic understanding of how the fundamental laws of gravity, motion, and force affect a child's movement skills. Chapter 4 describes and illustrates the basic movement concepts and skills appropriate for children in the primary and intermediate grades.

3 Basic Mechanics of Movement

Basic laws, concepts, and principles affect all movements of the body. The laws of gravity, for example, affect balance and the adjustment of position while moving. The human body is a living machine; it converts food into energy and expends the energy in movement. If the human body is kept in optimum condition and is moved in accordance with the principles of force and motion, expenditure of energy will be proportionate to the task. But, if movement is contrary to the laws of motion and force, too much energy will be expended and maximum results will not be achieved.

It is difficult for teachers who have not studied kinesiology (the science of human movement) to understand all the important mechanical principles of human movement. They should, however, understand a few important concepts and principles concerning balance, force, motion, and levers, and be able to apply them when teaching skills and movement patterns.

The information in this chapter provides classroom teachers with a basic understanding of the mechanics of human movement and how these mechanics contribute to the ease and efficiency of all forms of physical movement.

Stability

Stability is the ability of the body to maintain a stationary position or to perform purposeful movements while resisting the force of gravity. Our first consideration then is the "law of gravity," which is the natural force that pulls everything toward the center of the earth. Most important to stability is that gravitational pull always occurs through the center of the weight or mass of an object. Applied to the human body, the center of gravity is that point around which the weight is equally distributed in all directions. The human body is in balance when all forces acting upon

Figure 3.1 The center of gravity (white circle) is in the middle of the body weight.

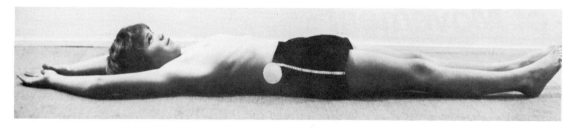

Figure 3.2 The center of gravity is in the middle of the hips.

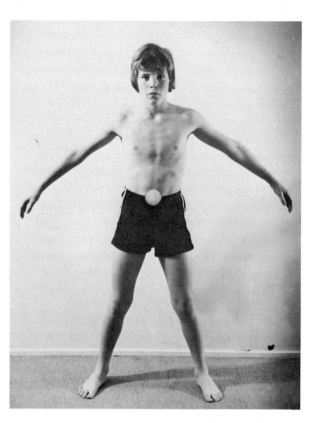

Figure 3.3 The center of gravity rises when the arms are elevated.

it equal zero. The child in figure 3.1 is lying on his back with all his muscles in a state of relaxation. His body is not resisting gravity; therefore, the center of gravity is the point in the middle of his body weight, indicated by the white circle.

In figure 3.2 the center of gravity is in the middle of the hips. The child is maintaining a state of equilibrium, or balance, through the tension he is applying to his antigravitational muscles (the large muscles of the trunk and legs). When the boy raises his arms, as illustrated in figure 3.3, his center of gravity also rises. If the boy relaxes those muscles, he will fall to the ground, obeying the law of gravity.

Principles and Concepts Relating to Stability

The basic principles and concepts relating to stability are important in understanding all stationary and movement skills. When attempting to hold a *static* balance position, a child is concerned with keeping the center of gravity in a stable position. When he is moving, the center of gravity is an important factor in retaining *dynamic balance,* or equilibrium. The ability of the child to maintain stability or balance while in a static position or in motion is governed by the following principles of stability.

Figure 3.4 A wide base of support increases stability.

Figure 3.5 A narrow base of support reduces stability.

Figure 3.6 A wide base of support and a low center of gravity increase stability.

Principles of Stability

1. *The wider or broader the base of support, the more stable the body.* This principle is extremely important in balance stunts. For example, in figure 3.4 the hands and head of the child performing a headstand form a wide triangle, or broad base of support. The center of gravity is located through the hips and head and midpoint between the hands. By comparison, the child's hands in figure 3.5 are almost in line with the shoulders, thus greatly reducing the base of support.

   Teachers will observe that a child performing a headstand this latter way will not hold the position very long, since even a slight movement will cause him to fall sideways, backward, or forward, which can result in a severe strain on the neck muscles, as well as a hard thud.

2. *The lower the center of gravity to the base of support, the greater the stability.* The child in figure 3.6 has assumed the same position as in figure 3.4 but has kept his knees bent, thus dropping the center of gravity closer to his base of support. This example shows that a wide base of support, coupled with a low center of gravity, will help in the performance of numerous balance stunts.

   In sports, a stable position is often required when meeting an oncoming force, such as a large ball. A large utility ball thrown with force could knock a young child off balance if he is standing upright with his feet close together, as in figure 3.7. He has a narrow base of support and a high center of gravity. But in figure 3.8 his legs are spread and his knees are bent, giving him a wider base of support and a lower center of gravity.

3. *The nearer the center of gravity to the middle or center of the base of support, the greater the stability.* Gravity was defined as the natural force that pulls everything towards the center of the earth. The *line of gravity* is an imaginary line that extends through the center of gravity

Figure 3.7 A narrow base of support and a high center of gravity do not provide stability when meeting an oncoming force.

Figure 3.8 A wide base of support and a low center of gravity increase stability when meeting an oncoming force.

directly down towards the center of the earth. In skills requiring a very stable base, the child spreads his arms and legs, lowers his body, and *makes sure the line of gravity* is near the center of the base of support. The child balancing on her hands, knees, and feet in figure 3.9 illustrates this important principle. Notice how the wide base is low to the ground, and the *line of gravity* passes downward through the middle of the body.

There are, however, numerous skills in games, sports, and dance activities where an unstable base of support is desirable—necessary, in fact, to perform the skill correctly. The principles of gravity still apply. Sometimes one must deliberately shift the center of gravity to an unstable position in order to move quickly. When the line of gravity reaches a point outside the base of support, the individual falls in that direction. This happens when we walk or run; we shift our weight forward in order to move. The sprinter in a crouched starting position leans forward considerably, shifting his center of gravity forward (fig. 3.10). He then raises his hips higher than his shoulders to further increase the "unstable" position toward the direction in which he intends to move and to place the strong hip muscles in a position to contract effectively.

Figure 3.9 When the line of gravity is near the center of the base of support, greater stability is achieved.

Figure 3.10 A sprinter shifts his center of gravity to an unstable position for a quick start.

a. Center of gravity (white circle)   b. Center of gravity indicated (white circle)

These principles of gravity are normally taught to elementary school children in the science curriculum. If the following concepts are also explained to children in a meaningful way through the use of their own bodies, they will understand the mechanical advantages of the principles and apply them in sports, games, and other daily activities.

Concepts Relating to Stability

1. To achieve the greatest stability, assume a wide base of support, be low to the ground, and have the line of gravity running through the middle of the base of support.
2. To receive a heavy force or a fast moving object, widen the base of support in line with the direction of the oncoming force.
3. To apply a forceful movement, widen the base of support in line with the direction of the force.
4. To lift or carry a heavy object, keep the object close to the body.
5. To stop quickly, bend the knees and lean away from the direction you are moving.

Motion

Motion is any form of movement that is produced by a force exerted by a push or pull. In the human body motion is produced by muscular contraction. All movements of the human body, whether they change position, slow down, or start another object in motion, are directly influenced by three laws discovered by Sir Isaac Newton in the seventeenth century. These three laws explain how, where, and why the body moves, as well as how to project or receive an object.

Law of Inertia

The law of inertia states that an object will remain in a state of rest and an object in motion at the same speed and direction unless acted upon by a force. Inertia is directly proportional to the size or mass of the object and its velocity. This means that the greater an object's mass and velocity, the more difficult it is to change its direction or motion. The force that changes an object's motion or direction could be gravity, wind, another object, or the contraction of muscles.

Understanding this law is extremely important when performing physical movements. For example, a ball thrown toward a target will move in a straight line and at uniform speed until the force of gravity or wind causes it to change direction (fig. 3.11). Thus, a child must learn to adjust to or compensate for these forces in all throwing and striking activities.

Another example for understanding and overcoming the effects of the law of inertia is dribbling a soccer ball. The ball will not move until it receives an external force—the foot. A force starts the ball moving (overcoming mass); however, so long as the ball is kept in motion, the effect of inertia is minimal. Performing continuous sit-ups and maintaining a steady running or swimming pace are also good examples of overcoming the effects of inertia.

Figure 3.11 Throwing a ball with a high arc allows for the effects of gravity and wind.

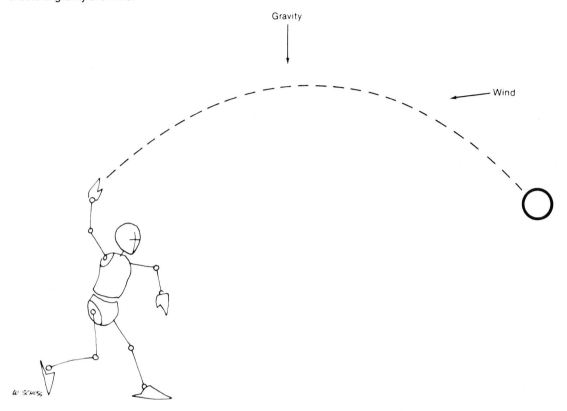

Gravity

Wind

W. SCHOSS

Law of Acceleration

The law of acceleration states that when an object is acted upon by a force, it will move in the direction of that force. The resulting change of speed (acceleration) of the object will be directly proportional to the force acting on it and inversely proportional to the mass. To illustrate this second law, consider a volleyball player executing a high "floating" serve (fig. 3.12a). The force exerted behind the ball is relatively gentle, producing a slow acceleration. The second serve (fig. 3.12b) is a more forceful hit behind the ball, causing a rapid acceleration. In this case, the acceleration is directly proportional to the force. If a player makes the same forceful hit with a tennis ball, its acceleration will be greater because its mass is much less than that of a volleyball. Acceleration in this example is inversely proportional to the mass of the ball.

Law of Action-Reaction

The law of action-reaction states that for every action there is an equal and opposite reaction. Tug-of-war (fig. 3.13) can be used to illustrate this law to elementary school children. The distance that team A moves backward is equal to the distance that team B has been forced to move forward. When swimming, a child moves forward by pushing backward against the resistance of the water. The water is pushing the child forward with a force equal to the force that he is exerting in his backward body movements.

Although this principle is relatively hard to explain to children, and at times to adults, it applies to all movements directed away from a hard surface. For example, when a child jumps up to tip a basketball, the floor pushes back with a force equal to the force the child exerts downward through his feet. There is an equal and opposite reaction. Also, to receive the maximum reaction force, the surface that the force is exerted against must be stable. For instance, a hard surface (fig. 3.14a) allows a runner to push off with maximum thrust because of the equal and opposite reaction between the foot and the hard surface. But on grass (fig. 3.14b), soft mud, or sand (fig. 3.14c), the surface gives and thus decreases the force that propels the runner forward.

Figure 3.12 The acceleration of a volleyball across the net is directly proportional to the force exerted behind the ball.

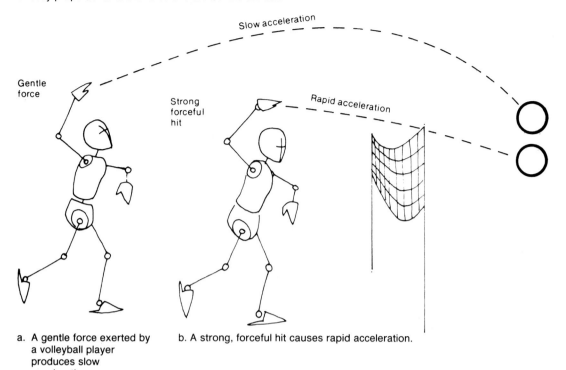

a. A gentle force exerted by a volleyball player produces slow acceleration.

b. A strong, forceful hit causes rapid acceleration.

Concepts Relating to Motion

1. Once in motion a human being or an object continues in motion unless stopped by a force.
2. Once a human being or an object is in motion, the less force required to maintain its speed and direction.
3. The heavier the object, the more force required to move it.
4. The heavier the object and the faster it is moving, the more force required to stop its motion.
5. When an object moves, another object moves in the opposite direction.

Types of Motion

The human body or an object can move in two basic ways—in a linear, or translatory, motion and in a rotary, or angular, motion. All forms of motion, human or mechanical, are linear or rotary, or a combination of the two.

Linear Motion

Linear motion is the movement of a body or an object as a whole in a straight line with uniform speed. Examples are the human body being carried by another object, such as a car or skis. In this type of motion, the

Figure 3.13 Tug-of-war illustrates that every action creates an equal, opposite reaction.

Figure 3.14 Law of Action-Reaction. The force that propels a runner forward is a result of the action–reaction between his feet and the surface on which he is running.

a. Hard road provides a stable surface.

b. Grass field gives, thus reducing force.

c. Soft sand or mud gives even more, with a much greater decrease in force.

Figure 3.15 Rotary Motion during a Forward Roll

a. Large radius, slow rotary speed

b. Short radius, fast speed

c. Large radius, slow speed

body takes on the same motion as the object carrying it. The human body can also move in a linear pathway, as in a walking or running movement; this, however, is a pathway of movement resulting from the rotary action of the legs at the hip joints.

Rotary Motion

Rotary motion is a movement that traces an arc or circle around an axis or a fixed point. As the radius of the circle becomes smaller, the rotary speed increases. For example, in the first phase of a forward roll, the radius is large because the legs and trunk are partially extended (fig. 3.15a). As the performer tucks and rolls, he decreases the radius (fig. 3.15b). When the roll is

completed, the leg and trunk are extended, thus lengthening the radius and slowing the forward motion (fig. 3.15c).

Virtually all physical skills involve a combination of linear and rotary motions. Movements normally begin with a rotary action of the body, then transfer to linear speed. In running, for instance, the rotary action of the legs at the hip joints is converted into linear speed to move the body forward. Similarly, as the ball leaves the thrower's hand, it is converted from the rotary motion of the arm and shoulder into a linear motion. As the ball travels through the air, the motion begins to change into a curvilinear motion because of gravity and air resistance. Curvilinear motion follows a curved pathway, rather than the true arc or circle of rotary motion.

Concepts Relating to Linear and Rotary Motion

1. When performing rotary movements, shortening the radius of the rotation increases speed, and lengthening the radius decreases speed.
2. When performing linear movements, lengthening the radius increases linear speed, and conversely, shortening the radius decreases linear speed.

Force

According to K. F. Wells, force can be felt and its effect can be seen and measured, but force itself, like the wind, is invisible (1971). Force is the effect one body has on another. This can be the movement of one body by another, such as a child throwing a ball, hitting a softball, or volleying a ball. Force can also be the stopping of one body by another, such as the tackler stopping the ball carrier. Finally, force can be resistance against movement, such as that used in isometric exercises or when a wrestler in a defensive position attempts to prevent his opponent from moving him. Force, then, is the push or pull exerted against something.

Teachers should understand several principles relating to the production, direction, and absorption of force to help children execute movement skills with ease, efficiency, and safety.

Production of Force

The total effective force of a movement is the sum of all forces produced by the muscle groups when applied in the same direction and in proper sequence. The jump-reach stunt illustrates this principle as well as related factors that must be considered when executing any forceful movement.

Any muscular action that is intended to move the body weight must have a firm base of action (stability). In figure 3.16a the child's legs are spread reasonably apart and his knees are bent to lower his center of gravity. Strong muscles exert more force than weak ones, and the flexed-knee position allows the boy to begin his jump by contracting his thigh muscles, the strongest muscles of the body. As stated earlier, the total effective force of a movement is the sum of all forces produced by the muscle groups in the same direction. This means that the jump should be executed in a continuous movement, beginning with the extension of the legs, then stretching upward (fig. 3.16b), and finally, fully extending the body (fig. 3.16c).

Achieving maximum results in any forceful movement requires continuity or flow from one part through another and the timing of each muscle group contraction. One only needs to swing a softball bat forward to understand the importance of continuity and the cumulative effect of a properly executed forceful action.

Figure 3.16 Production of Force in a Jump-Reach Stunt

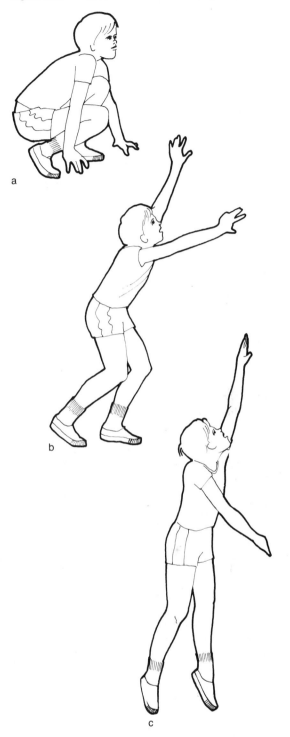

a

b

c

Figure 3.17 The center of gravity (white circle) is too high and too far back to gain maximum force.

Figure 3.18 Shifting the center of gravity lower and in the direction of the intended action increases force potential.

Direction of Force

When initiating a forceful movement, the force should be directed through the center of the body weight in the direction intended. In the jumping procedure illustrated in figure 3.16, the weight of the body is directly over and midway between the feet. When making a forward movement, the force should be applied through the center of weight and in the direction in which it is intended to go. In figure 3.17 the center of gravity is too high and too far back to gain maximum force. By bending and leaning forward (fig. 3.18), the child shifts the weight forward in the direction of the intended forceful action.

Perhaps one of the most important areas of concern is the application of force when lifting heavy objects. "Lift with the legs and not the back" is the overriding principle.

The child in figure 3.19 is attempting to lift the trunk, but his center of gravity is too high and too far forward. When he applies force, it will be upward and backward, decreasing the maximum forces that could have been applied in an upward direction. He is also in a vulnerable position because too much strain may be placed on his back muscles. The potential force of the leg muscles in assisting the upward movement is almost negligible here. But in figure 3.20 the child has moved his center of gravity closer to the trunk and lower by flexing his legs. A forceful movement can now be made by extending the weight upward.

Absorption of Force

When it is necessary to absorb the impact of a forceful movement or object, the shock should be spread over as large an area or as long a distance as possible, or both (Bunn 1955). This principle applies when receiving a blow, landing from a fall, or catching or trapping a ball. The essential point is to gradually decrease the force of the movement or object. In figures 3.21b and 3.21c the gymnast has landed, flexing his knees to absorb part of the downward and forward momentum and using the remaining forward momentum to execute the forward roll. He has gradually and systematically dissipated the forward momentum.

Other examples of gradually spreading the shock of a forceful movement are catching an oncoming ball with arms extended forward, then recoiling the arms; or rolling after falling on a ball when playing football.

Concepts Relating to Force

1. The more fully each working muscle group is stretched, the more force can be supplied.
2. Pushing or pulling an object should be done through the center of the weight of the object and in the direction the object is to move.
3. Maximum force is achieved when each body part is involved in sequential order. Sequence for a throwing action would be trunk rotation, shoulder, upper arm, lower arm, hand, and fingers. Sequence for kicking action would be hip, upper leg, lower leg, and foot.
4. When individual body parts such as arms or legs, or implements such as bats or paddles, are used they should be completely extended at the moment they make contact with the object to be propelled. The longest extension of the arm creates the greatest force.

Figure 3.19 The center of gravity (white circle) is too high and too far forward to gain maximum force.

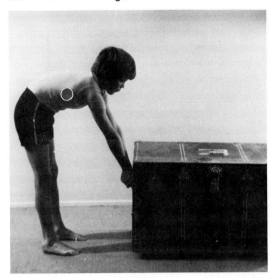

Figure 3.20 Shifting the center of gravity (white circle) lower and closer to the object increases force potential.

Figure 3.21 Absorption of Force. This gymnast executes a forward roll to absorb the force of landing from a stunt.

a

b

c

5. When receiving or absorbing the force of an object, the largest possible area and distance (recoiling) should be used to absorb the force.

6. When landing from a jump, each joint should give (bend) to gradually absorb the force.

7. Once maximum force has been applied in throwing, striking, and kicking movements, the movement should continue in a follow-through action to ensure that maximum force has been applied and to allow for a gradual reduction in force.

8. Force is increased by using more muscles and by increasing the speed of the movement.

Leverage

A lever is a rigid bar that turns around a fixed point called an *axis* or *fulcrum*. It is a simple tool that produces a mechanical advantage in terms of *speed* or *force*. Three different types of levers are each classified according to the location of the fulcrum and the point of application of force and resistance.

First Class Lever

A first class lever has the *fulcrum* between the force and the resistance. The distance between the force and fulcrum is the *force arm* (FA) and the distance between the resistance and fulcrum is the *resistance arm* (RA). In figure 3.22, the force arm is longer, hence, it has the mechanical advantage over the resistance arm. In this type of lever, a longer force arm produces an advantage in terms of force. A longer resistance arm produces an advantage in terms of speed and range of movement.

Second Class Lever

A second class lever has the resistance located between the fulcrum and the force (fig. 3.23). Since this type of lever has a longer *force arm,* it produces *force* at the expense of speed and range of movement. Children should remember that when lifting a wheelbarrow or prying up a heavy object with a plank, the longer the force arm the less force required to move the object.

Third Class Lever

A third class lever has the force between the fulcrum and the resistance. Since this type of lever has a longer resistance arm, it produces speed and range of movement at the expense of force. Most levers of the human body are third class levers. For example, the elbow joint where the movement occurs is the fulcrum (fig. 3.24). The radius bone in the lower arm acts as the lever, and the bicep muscle acts as the force. The resistance is the body segments that are moved as well as any additional weight, such as a ball or heavy object.

Figure 3.22   First Class Lever

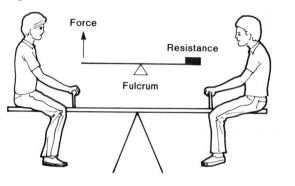

Figure 3.23   Second Class Lever

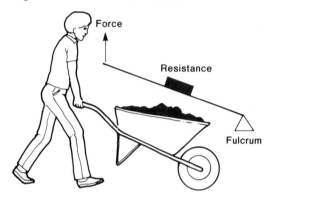

Figure 3.24   Third Class Lever

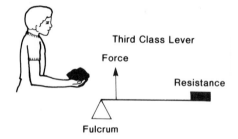

Concepts Relating to Levers

1. The longer the force arm, the greater the force produced.

2. The longer the resistance arm at the moment of release, the faster the action. When throwing a ball, a straight arm at the moment of release produces the fastest thrown ball. Similarly, when implements (bats or racquets) are used, they must be an extension of the lower arm at the moment of contact to propel the object (ball or bird) back in the fastest possible action.

3. The mechanical advantage of any lever is the ratio between the length of the force arm (from fulcrum to force) to the length of the resistance arm (from fulcrum to resistance).

4. Levers are used in the production and absorption of force.

The concepts and principles relating to stability, motion, force, and levers are important considerations when teaching virtually every skill and movement pattern. Children should learn these concepts and principles through their own performances and by the teacher explaining the basic concepts in a meaningful way.

4 Development of Movement Concepts and Skills

Stages of Development

Movement Concepts and Skills
Body Awareness
Space Awareness
Qualities
Relationships

Locomotor Skills
Walking
Running
Leaping
Jumping
Hopping
Skipping
Sliding (Galloping)
Stopping
Dodging

Nonlocomotor Skills
Swinging
Bending
Stretching
Twisting
Turning
Pushing
Pulling

Manipulative Skills
Throwing
Catching
Striking

Basic Rhythmic and Dance Skills
Rhythmic Skills
Folk Dance Skills
Creative Dance

Gymnastic Skills

Numerous attempts have been made during the past few years to provide a simple classification system of the concepts and skills involved in the elementary school physical education program. Before movement education was introduced to the program, skills were usually classified as locomotor and nonlocomotor skills or as basic sport, dance, and gymnastic skills. After movement education was introduced, its concepts and skills were treated as a separate entity, and a movement education unit was taught much like a folk dance or basketball unit. Other teachers virtually abandoned locomotor and nonlocomotor skills and the basic game, dance, and gymnastic skills, and adopted the classification system used in movement education.

The vast majority of elementary school teachers, however, saw merit in both the traditional and movement education approaches and integrated the best of each into their programs. The author of this book, like many of his colleagues recommends the integrated system of classifying movement concepts and skills. This

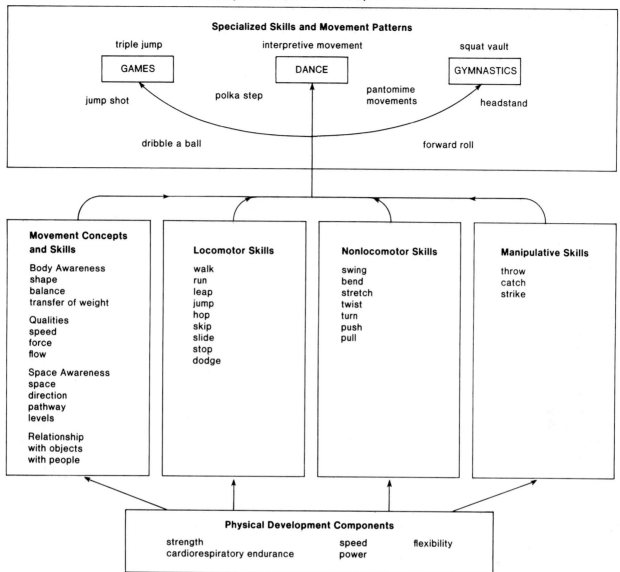

Specialized Skills and Movement Patterns

triple jump   interpretive movement   squat vault

GAMES   DANCE   GYMNASTICS

jump shot   polka step   pantomime movements   headstand

dribble a ball   forward roll

Movement Concepts and Skills

Body Awareness
shape
balance
transfer of weight

Qualities
speed
force
flow

Space Awareness
space
direction
pathway
levels

Relationship
with objects
with people

Locomotor Skills

walk
run
leap
jump
hop
skip
slide
stop
dodge

Nonlocomotor Skills

swing
bend
stretch
twist
turn
push
pull

Manipulative Skills

throw
catch
strike

Physical Development Components

strength   speed   flexibility
cardiorespiratory endurance   power

chapter describes the basic movement concepts and skills that should be taught to elementary school children.

The classification of movement concepts and skills used throughout this book is outlined in the accompanying chart "Physical Development Components." *Strength, flexibility,* and *cardiorespiratory endurance* are the underlying physical development components that provide the foundation of all movement. No movement takes place nor develops without these prerequisite components.

Two basic classifications of movement appear in the chart. One type, "Movement Concepts and Skills," describes what, how, where, and with whom a movement takes place. The other type, including the basic locomotor, nonlocomotor, and manipulative skills, are fundamental motor skills necessary for all specialized skills of the more advanced games, dance, and gymnastic activities.

Stages of Development

During the first two years of life, a child acquires a large number of rudimentary motor skills necessary for dealing with the problems of standing, balancing, moving, and manipulating objects encountered in the environment (Corbin 1973). When and how children acquire these basic motor skills varies; however each child passes through common developmental stages according to his own rate and potential level of motor ability.

Table 4.1 Stages of Motor Skill Development

Babyhood	Early Childhood	Middle Childhood	Late Childhood
Age One Month to 2 Years	*Ages 2, 3, 4, 5, 6*	*Ages 7, 8, 9*	*Ages 10, 11, 12*
Stage One	**Stage Two**	**Stage Three**	**Stage Four**
Rudimentary Skills	*Fundamental Movement Skill Performance*	*Refined Movement Skill Performance*	*Specific Sport, Dance, or Specialized Skill Performance*
Includes:	Includes:	Includes:	Includes:
Rudimentary skills—sit, crawl, creep, stand, walk.	*Movement concepts and skills*—body awareness, space awareness, qualities, relationships.	*Combination and refinement of one or more fundamental skills*—run and jump, slide and stop, land and roll, catch and throw, dribble and kick.	*Advanced and refined versions of sports, dance, or other specialized skills*—running long jump, football pass, Scottish sword dance, hand spring.
	Basic locomotor skills—walk, run, leap, jump, hop		
	Combined locomotor skills—skip, slide, stop, and dodge		
	Basic nonlocomotor skills—bend, stretch, twist, turn, push, pull, swing		
	Basic manipulation skills—throw, catch, strike		

In table 4.1, stage one (babyhood) lasts from one month after birth to approximately two years; stage two (early childhood) begins about age two and ends near the end of the sixth year or overlaps into the seventh year. Stage three (middle childhood) is a period during which fundamental skills are combined and refined into general movement skills. Stage four (late childhood) is an extension of the previous stage. As children enter this stage their interests shift to developing more form and accuracy in individual and team sports, dance, or other highly specialized skills. This latter stage continues through adolescence with greater specialization and increased proficiency.

These four developmental stages, coupled with the tremendous individual differences existing at each grade level, have a very direct bearing on the choice of activities, how these activities are taught, and the learning expectations of every child. The primary program should be a time for acquiring minimal form in the fundamental skills listed under stage two. This program should emphasize exposure to these movement concepts and skills and include numerous opportunities for experimenting with different ways of moving and manipulating balls, bats, and a variety of other small equipment. It is clearly not a time for refinement or specialization.

As children enter stage three (middle childhood), they become interested in improving specific motor skills, hence they devote time and energy to acquiring these skills. They also are keenly interested in playing more organized and challenging games. Teachers of these children should not only show children how to improve their performances and provide interesting and challenging game and dance activities; they should also provide opportunities for exploration and creative expression regardless of the nature of the activity. Children in this age range enjoy competition, but they also enjoy cooperative activities that provide enjoyment and avenues for positive interpersonal relationships.

The fourth stage of motor development is essentially a continuation of the previous stage characterized by a keener interest in improving performance. Differences in physiological maturity, particularly for girls who have entered puberty, present some problems with respect to activity interests and sex preferences in playing or performing some activities. These problems, however, can be dealt with by utilizing more individualized teaching strategies as suggested in later chapters.

Movement Concepts and Skills

Movement education concepts and skills are grouped under the elements of *body awareness, qualities, space awareness,* and *relationships.* Body awareness refers to what the body can do—the shapes it can make, the way it balances, and the transfer of weight from one part of the body to another. Qualities describe how the body can move, and includes skills relating to speed,

Figure 4.1 Stretched Shape

Figure 4.2 Curled Shape

Figure 4.3 Wide and Narrow Shapes

force, and flow of a movement. Space awareness describes the spatial aspects of movement, as well as skills relating to moving in different directions and to different levels. Relationships refer to the connection between the body and other performers or the body and small and large apparatus. The main concepts within each of these four elements are described and illustrated here.

Body Awareness

Body awareness is essentially the ways in which the body or body parts can be controlled, moved, and balanced. This involves three main subelements: shapes the body can make, ways the body can balance, and ways the body can transfer weight from one position to another.

Shapes the Body Can Make

The human body is capable of forming an infinite variety of shapes. Three basic types of shapes form the framework upon which the child learns how he can stretch, bend, and twist his body.

Stretched and Curled Shapes

A stretched shape (fig. 4.1) is an extension of the whole body or a part of it in a variety of directions. For example, a child can stretch upward, to the side, or through his legs. A curled shape (fig. 4.2) results from an action that flexes or bends the body or a part of it.

Wide and Narrow Shapes

Wide and narrow shapes, like curled and stretched ones, are contrasting shapes. A wide shape requires the legs and/or arms to be away from the trunk in some way. In contrast, the arms or legs must be extended close together or in a thin line with the trunk to form a narrow shape. Both are illustrated in figure 4.3.

Twisted Shapes

A twisted shape occurs when one part of the body is held in a stable position while another part of the body turns away from it. A twisted shape can be performed on the floor (fig. 4.4) or in the air (fig. 4.5).

Figure 4.4 Twisted Shapes

Figure 4.5 Twisting—Body in Flight

Figure 4.6 Can you take the weight on three parts of your body?

Balance or "Weight Bearing"

A second important aspect of body awareness is balancing or "taking the weight" on different parts of the body. A child can balance on one foot, his head (as in a headstand), or other parts of the body. Figure 4.6 illustrates how the body can be used to answer specific challenges.

Transfer of Body Weight

The third aspect of body awareness is the transfer of weight from one part of the body to another, which occurs in all human movement. In walking, the transfer of weight is from one foot to another; in a cartwheel, it is from the feet to the hands to the feet; and in movement skills, it is from one part of the body to another (fig. 4.7).

Space Awareness: Where the Body Moves

Space awareness is one element of movement that includes concepts relating to general and personal space, direction, pathways, and levels. The main concepts relating to each area are described in the accompanying paragraphs.

General and Personal Space

All space that a child or group of children can use is divided into two types. General space is the total space that can be used by one child or a group of children. In figure 4.8, the gymnasium floor constitutes the general space the child can use when performing a series of movement skills. Personal, or limited space, is the immediate area a child can use around him. The top of the vaulting box constitutes the personal space available to the child when performing a series of balance skills. As the child moves off the top of the box, she enters the general space.

Figure 4.7 Transfer of Body Weight

a   b   c

Figure 4.8 Levels

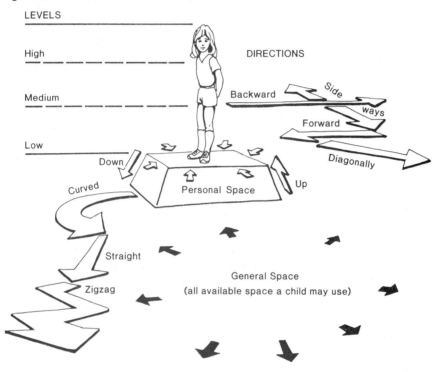

Direction

Direction includes moving forward, backward, sideways, diagonally, and up and down. In figure 4.8, the child moves backwards to the end of the box, downward to the floor, sideways across the floor, and then leaps up and lands and rolls diagonally across the floor.

Pathways

Pathways are the patterns a child makes when moving on or off the floor. The child in figure 4.8 may leap off the box, travel in a curve, followed by a straight, and end in a zig-zag pathway.

Levels

Level refers to the location of the body or body parts to the floor or apparatus. In figure 4.8, the child is high in relation to the top of the box. In figure 4.9, movement is low to the floor; in figure 4.10, movement is at a medium level on all fours; and, in figure 4.11, movement is at a high level in the performance of a cartwheel or leap from the floor.

Figure 4.9 Low Level

Figure 4.10 Medium Level

Figure 4.11 High Level

Figure 4.12 Qualities, or How the Body Moves

SPEED
quick, slow

run. . . .

Qualities: How the Body Moves

Qualities, or effort (the second element of movement education) includes concepts that describe how the body moves from one position to another. *Speed, force,* and *flow of movement* are concepts described within this element.

Speed

Speed describes the rate of a movement. In figure 4.12, the child runs quickly towards the traffic cone, leaps over it, lands, and slowly rolls across the mat to dissipate the forward momentum.

Force

Force describes the effort or tension involved in a movement. A child leaping over a traffic cone, as in figure 4.12, is performing a strong thrusting action to gain enough height and distance to clear the obstacle. But in dance, a child shifts arms lightly from one side to the other to describe something that is very light or gentle (fig. 4.13).

Flow

Flow describes how a movement or a series of movements is linked in a purposeful action. *Bound flow* occurs when a series of movements is stopped with the balance maintained, then continued to another static movement. For example, two children performing a tumbling routine shift from a roll to a shoulder stand and hold this balance position momentarily before lowering their legs and trunks in preparation for another roll (fig. 4.14). Movements that proceed smoothly from one to another are described as *free flow.*

FORCE
strong, light

FLOW
bound, flow

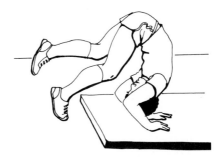

leap. . . .

land and roll

Figure 4.13   Light or Gentle Force

Figure 4.14   Bound Flow

a

b

c

Relationships: Who and What the Body Relates To

The third element of movement involves the relationship of an individual or group to other performers or objects (fig. 4.15). The relationship to an object is described as the relative position a performer is to an apparatus. For example, in figure 4.16, the child on the left side begins *outside* the turret, moves *around,* then *over* stopping *on* the top surface. He is positioned *near* the apparatus. As he moves towards the other turret, he travels *under* the beam.

Concepts describing the manner in which performers relate to each other represent another dimension of relationships. The two performers in figure 4.16 are performing "matching" shapes, with the child on the right turret "leading" his partner. As they continue their sequence they will "meet" and "part."

Figure 4.15   Relationship of Performers

Figure 4.16   Relationship with Objects and Other Performers

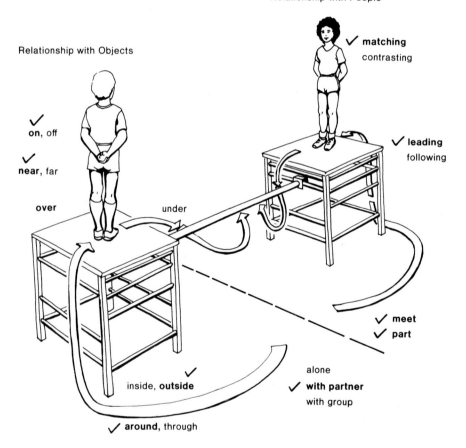

Relationship with People

Relationship with Objects

✓ **matching**
contrasting

✓ **on**, off

✓ **near**, far

over   under

✓ **leading**
following

✓ **meet**
✓ **part**

✓ inside, **outside**

alone
✓ **with partner**
with group

✓ **around**, through

Locomotor Skills

The fundamental locomotor and nonlocomotor skills are the foundation for developing everyday utilitarian and safety skills and are the building blocks for all specialized skills involved in games, dance, and gymnastic activities.

Nine locomotor skills are described and illustrated in this section. The discussion of each skill includes the mechanical principles involved in its proper execution, things to stress, and suggested activities. The nonlocomotor skills will be treated similarly later in this chapter.

The first five locomotor skills described—walking, running, leaping, jumping, and hopping—represent the skeleton upon which the child begins to develop complex movement skills. Although skipping, sliding (or galloping), stopping, and dodging combine several of the first five skills, they are described as separate locomotor skills.

Walking

Walking is the transfer of weight from one foot to the other while moving in a forward or backward direction. In a natural and rhythmical walking action, the body is erect and the eyes focus forwards. The heel of the stepping foot strikes the ground (fig. 4.17a), and the weight of the body is transferred through the ball, then off the toes of the foot. At that moment, the heel of the free swinging leg touches the ground, and the knee of that leg bends, allowing it to absorb the shock of the weight transferred to this leg. In a walking movement, one foot is always in contact with the ground, and the arms swing freely in opposite directions to the feet (fig. 4.17c).

Applying Mechanical Principles
1. *Balance:* Walking has been described as a continuous process of losing and gaining balance. Hence, the inner edges of the feet should move along a straight line to allow the center of gravity to shift directly over the base of support (see diagram in fig. 4.17). This also prevents unnecessary swaying movements.

Figure 4.17 Walking

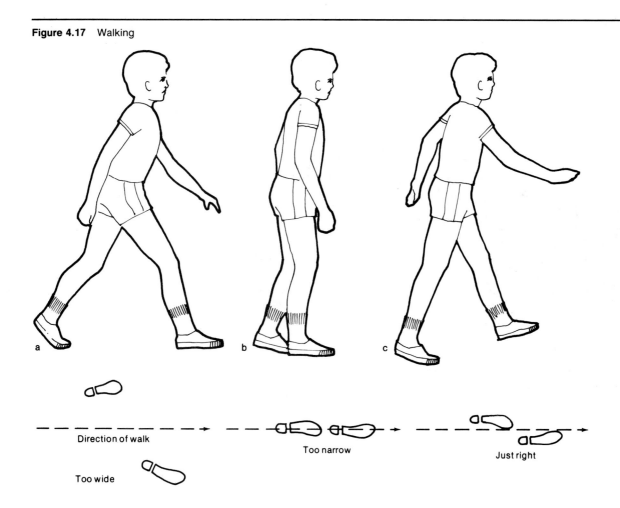

Direction of walk

Too narrow

Just right

Too wide

2. *Production of Force:* Since the total effectiveness of a movement is the sum of all the forces, properly synchronized leg and arm movements are essential.

3. *Direction of Force:* The force initiated from the back leg should be directed forward and upward through the center of the body weight. If the direction of force is too vertical, the walk will be bouncy and inefficient. If the force is primarily horizontal, the walk will be a shuffle.

4. *Absorption of Force:* The force should be gradually dissipated by transferring weight from the heels through the ball of the foot toward the toes.

5. *Momentum:* The forward motion initiated by the backward thrust of the leg is directed forward through the trunk. An unchecked forward movement would carry the trunk beyond the forward base of support too quickly, resulting in a forward fall or a shift to running. To counteract this, the front leg momentarily restrains the forward motion of the trunk, allowing a smooth transfer of weight as the back leg begins to move forward.

Things to Stress
1. Keep body straight and move in a relaxed manner.
2. Swing arms freely and naturally but not too far.
3. Point toes straight ahead and take easy strides to avoid excessive up-and-down and jerky movements.

Walking Activities
1. Walk informally about the room in an easy, relaxed, natural way.
2. Same as activity 1, but walk in a circle.
3. Same as activity 2, but change directions.
4. Walk in different ways—short or long steps, fast or slow, hard or soft, high or low.
5. Change speeds. Start slowly, walk at a moderate pace, then briskly, moderately again, slowly, then stop.
6. Walk on the heels of the feet using exaggerated arm movements.
7. Walk on tiptoes.
8. Walk slowly for balance (use two, three, or four beats per measure).
9. Walk sideways by crossing one foot in front of the other.

10. Do pantomimes of a "happy" or "sad" walk, of carrying a heavy or light load, of a young man or old man, of walking through mud or wet cement.
11. Combine walking with other locomotor skills. Begin with a walk, shift to a run, then shift back to a walk. Repeat with another locomotor skill, such as a skip or a slide.
12. Gradually lower and raise the body while walking.
13. Change arm positions and movements while walking (e.g., hands swinging forward and backward above the shoulders).
14. Walk on painted lines, balance benches, planks, and other available apparatus.
15. Walk in step with a partner. Begin walking together slowly, then increase speed, change direction, or use other locomotor movements.

See chapter 27 for additional ideas.

Running

Running is the transfer of weight from one foot to the other with a momentary loss of contact with the ground by both feet (fig. 4.18). In a slow run, such as jogging, the body leans slightly forward; arms, bent at the elbows, swing forward and backward from the shoulders. The knees are bent and the heel of the foot contacts the ground followed by a shift of the body weight through the ball, then off the toes of the foot. As the speed of the run increases, so does the forward lean and arm action. In a fast run, the ball of the foot touches the ground first.

Applying Mechanical Principles
1. *Inertia:* Overcoming inertia is most difficult at the takeoff and decreases as the child gains speed. Therefore, take off from a crouched position to gain maximum speed in the shortest period of time; this allows maximum force to be exerted in a horizontal direction.

2. *Momentum:* Any increase in momentum is directly proportional to the force producing it. In running, the greater the power of the backward leg drive, the greater the forward acceleration.

3. *Direction of Force:* In running, the body should lean forward about twenty degrees from vertical. This slight forward lean keeps the center of gravity ahead of the forward foot as it contacts the ground and allows the backward extension of the leg to propel the body in a nearly horizontal direction, producing the greatest forward speed and minimizing the inefficient upward

Figure 4.18 Running

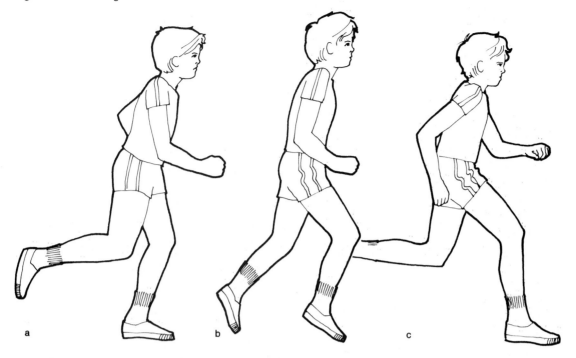

a   b   c

movements of the body. To avoid lateral movements of the body, which restrict forward momentum, move the knees directly forward and upward and swing the arms forward and backward.

4. *Absorption of Force:* In long-distance running, the heel of the foot touches the ground first, and the force is gradually dissipated through the outer edge of the foot toward the toe. In sprinting, the ball of the foot contacts the ground first. This permits the force to be absorbed by slightly flexed hips, knees, and ankles.

5. *Levers:* By shortening the lever arm the speed of a movement is increased. Bending the knees and elbows shortens the lever arms to increase running speed.

Things to Stress

1. In jogging, run in a relaxed and rhythmical manner with a slight forward body lean, gently swing arms with elbows bent and land lightly on the heels.

2. In fast running, increase knee and elbow flexion, swing arms forward and backward and land on the balls of the feet.

3. In all types of running, breathe naturally; never hold your breath.

Running Activities

1. Run informally around the gymnasium.

2. Run with short or long steps.

3. Run with a high knee lift.

4. Run backwards and sidewards.

5. Change speed—begin slowly, run at a moderate speed, then run fast.

6. Run on the heels or tiptoes.

7. Run and change directions.

8. Run and keep in time with a partner.

9. Combine running with other locomotor skills—run, walk, run, slide, and so on.

10. Run around obstacles, such as other children, chairs, or beanbags.

11. Do pantomime running—run like a tall man, a dog, an elephant.

12. Run and jump rope on each or alternate steps.

13. Play running games (chapter 14) and relay activities (chapter 15).

14. Perform individual and partner running sequences to musical accompaniment (chapter 27).

Figure 4.19 Leaping

a   b   c

Leaping

Leaping, like running, is the transfer of weight from one foot to the other. The toe of the takeoff foot leaves the floor last, while the ball of the landing foot contacts the floor first (fig. 4.19). In leaping, however, contact with the ground is lost for a longer period, and greater height and distance are achieved. Also, a leap is usually preceded by a few running steps in order to achieve a maximum lift through the air.

Applying Mechanical Principles

Since leaping is essentially the same as running, the same mechanical principles apply. In addition, the following principles are important in producing a maximum leap.

1. *Momentum:* Since momentum is directly proportional to the force applied, the performer should take several running steps before leaping. The increased momentum gained by the run produces a higher and farther leap.

2. *Direction of Force:* The height of the leap is directly proportional to the angle of takeoff, as well as to the backward force of the takeoff leg. To gain maximum height, decrease the angle of takeoff and exaggerate the forward and upward movement of the arms.

Things to Stress

1. To gain maximum height, stretch upward with the hands and forward with the lead foot.
2. Execute a short and fast run before leaping.
3. To absorb the shock, flex the knee as soon as the ball of the foot touches the ground.

Leaping Activities

1. Run a few steps, then leap. Alternate the takeoff foot.
2. Leap for height and distance.
3. Hop in place a few times, then leap forward or sideward.
4. Leap in different directions.
5. Combine leaping with other locomotor skills—run, leap, walk, and so on.
6. Leap over obstacles—rope, beanbag, hoop.
7. Perform a series of consecutive leaps without breaking stride.

Jumping

Jumping is the transfer of weight from one foot or both feet to both feet (fig. 4.20). For example, a high jump begins with a one-foot takeoff and ends with a two-foot landing action. Other jumping movements, such as the standing broad jump or the jump–reach, start and land with two feet.

Figure 4.20 Jumping

a. Broad jump   b. High jump   c. Jump-reach

Applying Mechanical Principles

There are two types of jumping movements: one for height, such as the vertical or high jump; the other for distance, such as the standing or running broad jump. The basic mechanical principles for leaping also apply to jumping movements; specific principles follow.

1. *Jumping for Distance:* To gain the greatest distance, the jumper should take off with the greatest forward speed and upward thrust. The running broad jump requires maximum speed prior to takeoff; the standing broad jump requires a maximum forward and upward swing of the arms. The angle of takeoff should be about forty-five degrees. As the jumper begins to descend, the arms and body are brought forward, with the knees bent and the feet parallel. The resulting forward momentum prevents the body from falling back upon landing and allows the forward momentum to gradually dissipate through the flexed knees and forward arm movements.

2. *Jumping for Height:* Maximum height depends upon several important factors. The angle of takeoff must be as close to vertical as possible. The hips, knees, and ankles should be flexed in the starting position to permit maximum force to be directed upward by the forceful extension of the strong leg muscles. Additional height is also attained by forward and upward movement of the arms.

3. *Production of Force:* To gain maximum height or distance, the movement must be smooth and synchronized—the sum of all forces.

Things to Stress

1. To gain maximum height or distance, make a few preliminary swings of the arms, then a ballistic but synchronized movement of the various segments of the body through the proper angle of movement.

2. To gain maximum force, flex the ankles and knees prior to initiating the movement.

3. To absorb shock, land on the toes and flex the knees.

Figure 4.21 Hopping

a   b   c

Jumping Activities

1. Jump with feet together and gradually spread legs with each jump.
2. Jump forward, sideward, and backward.
3. Begin jumping from a crouched position and gradually increase the height of each jump.
4. Jump over small equipment, such as ropes, beanbags, and hoops.
5. Jump up and mark the wall with chalked fingertips.
6. Combine jumping with other locomotion or locomotor skills—run, twist, turn, stretch, etc.
7. Skip rope (see pp. 444–47 for suggestions).
8. Jump from various heights—from a box, bench, or other apparatus. Combine this jumping activity with a roll to allow for a gradual dissipation of force.
9. Jump with a partner—with or without a skipping rope.
10. Jump in time to a musical accompaniment.
11. Pantomime jumping skills in sports (jump shot), dance (seven jumps) and gymnastics (two-foot takeoff).

Hopping

Hopping is the transfer of weight from one foot to the same foot. In the upward phase, the toe leaves the floor last; on the way down, the toe contacts the floor first, then the weight gradually shifts to the ball and heel of the foot (fig. 4.21). Throughout this movement, the arms help to maintain balance and to assist in the upward movement.

Applying Mechanical Principles

1. *Balance:* Since the hop is performed on one leg, the body should lean slightly in the direction of the jumping leg, allowing the center of gravity to shift slightly away from the midline of the body.
2. *Force:* For maximum height, the angle of takeoff should be as close to vertical as possible. Additional height is gained by moving both arms upward simultaneously.

Things to Stress

1. To gain maximum height, swing arms backward, then vigorously forward and upward.
2. To apply force in the right direction, lean slightly towards the support leg to allow the force to be directed through the body's center of gravity.
3. To absorb shock, land first on the toes then on the ball of the foot while gradually bending the knee.

Hopping Activities

1. Hop in place. Clear the floor on the first hop, then gradually increase the height of each successive hop.
2. Hop forward, sideward, and backward.
3. Hop in place and make a quarter turn on each hop.

Figure 4.22 Skipping

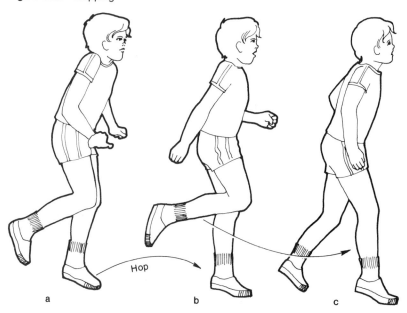

Hop

a   b   c

4. Hop in place to a 4/4 rhythm. Perform different positions in the air on ascent, such as right leg forward, arms sideward or overhead.

5. Hop several times on one foot, then switch to the other foot without losing rhythm.

6. Combine hopping with other locomotor skills—run, hop, skip.

7. Hop over floor lines or small equipment, such as beanbags or ropes.

8. Hop in time with a partner.

9. Hop and change position of body from high to medium to low.

10. Hop in place or on the move and keep changing arm position.

Skipping

A skip is a combination of a long step and a short hop, alternating the lead foot after each hop. In figure 4.22, the child hops on the left foot and swings the right leg forward, stepping on the ball of the right foot. The next sequence would involve a hop on the right foot, followed by a step on the left foot.

Applying Mechanical Principles

Since skipping combines a step and a hop, the mechanical principles that apply to these skills also apply to the skip. The following additional principles are important.

1. *Balance:* Since the base of support is narrow and alternately shifts from one foot to the other, the arms should extend sideward to help maintain balance.

2. *Force:* Since the extension of the leg on the hop produces the upward movement, the angle of takeoff should be nearly vertical. An exaggerated forward lean on the hop causes too much forward movement and makes it difficult for the child to freely swing the opposite leg forward.

Things to Stress

1. Step and hop on the same foot.

2. Since dance style and rhythm are normally emphasized more than distance or height, keep the length of the step and the height of the hop relatively short and small, and maintain smoothness.

Skipping Activities

1. Skip forward, backward, in a circle, or in different directions.

2. Cross hands with a partner and skip together, or skip in other dance positions.

3. Skip four long steps forward, then four short steps backward.

4. Skip four steps beginning with the right foot, then four steps beginning with the left foot.

5. Skip diagonally right for three steps (right–left–right) and bring feet together on the fourth count. Repeat to left.

6. Combine a skip with other locomotor skills—run, skip, walk.

7. Skip and change directions on the step phase of the movement.

8. Combine a skip with other body movements, such as, change arm movements, snap fingers, or clap in time to musical accompaniment.

9. Skip and change body position from high, to medium, to low.

Sliding (Galloping)

A slide combines a step and a short leap and can be performed in a forward, sideward, or backward direction. When the direction is forward or backward, the slide is called a *gallop;* when sideways, it is known as a slide. The movement is performed by stepping with one foot, then sliding with the other foot. The weight is transferred from the lead foot to the back foot. Once the sliding or galloping action begins, the lead foot is always the same foot (fig. 4.23).

Applying Mechanical Principles
Sliding employs many of the mechanical principles listed under walking, running, and leaping. Of these, the following are important for the proper execution of the slide.

1. *Balance:* The center of gravity should be kept within the base of support. When moving to the side, the body should not lean too far, or the center of gravity will fall outside of the body. Similarly, when moving forward, the angle of takeoff for the leap should be close to vertical.

2. *Force:* Forward or sideward momentum is generated by the forceful action of the leap. In dance and sport activities, control rather than height is normally desired. Therefore, the force is controlled or adjusted by the extension of the back leg movement.

Things to Stress
1. Encourage movement in a variety of directions.
2. Emphasize light, smooth actions rather than long, forceful leaps followed by a heavy sliding movement of the following foot.

Sliding Activities
1. In a circle or line formation, slide forward, backward, and sideward.
2. Slide four steps to the right, make a half turn, then slide four steps to the left.
3. With partners slide four steps right, then four steps left.
4. Slide and vary the height of the leap.
5. Slide with the left foot forward, stop, then slide with the right foot forward.

Figure 4.23 Sliding

a. Step

b. Short hop and slide

c. Step

6. Slide in different directions.

7. Combine the slide with other locomotor movements—run, slide, skip.

8. Slide and gallop, changing levels and other body movements.

9. Pantomime sports skills that require a sliding action.

10. Develop sliding routines for partners or small groups.

Stopping

Two basic types of stopping action are used in many sports and daily activities. In the forward stride stop (fig. 4.24), the runner simultaneously bends the knees and leans backwards while moving the arms sidewards. In the skip stop, the performer takes a step and a hop which allows him to shift upwards and lean backward to slow down his forward movement; he then lands in a stride position with the weight over the balls of the feet.

Applying Mechanical Principles

1. *Absorption of Force:* Initiating a preliminary skip and landing in a stride position with knees bent spreads the force over a maximum distance.

2. *Balance:* Landing in a stride position with knees bent and trunk leaning backwards provides a low, stable base of support.

Things to Stress

1. Land with feet apart (stride or parallel) and bend the knees as contact is made.

2. Lean backward from the waist and away from the direction of the movement.

3. Keep your head up.

Stopping Activities

1. Run forward and stop when the whistle blows.

2. Select a line or spot on the floor. Run and stop with front foot on the line.

3. Run forward, sideward, diagonally, and stop when the whistle blows.

4. With a partner; follow the leader with back player stopping when leader stops. Run side by side with one player calling "stop."

5. Run, jump over small equipment, and stop.

6. Repeat activities 1 to 5 using a skip stop.

7. Repeat activities 1 to 5 backwards.

Dodging

Dodging is a quick shifting of one part or all parts of the body away from a stationary or moving object. A dodge is normally executed after a momentary stop by bending the knees and then thrusting the body vigorously towards the side. One or both feet may leave the ground as a performer executes a dodging movement.

Applying Mechanical Principles

1. *Balance:* Since dodging requires a quick shift in position, the center of gravity should be low and close to the center of the base of support just before the shift is made.

2. *Production of Force:* To gain maximum force, the knees should be flexed to allow a maximum extension of the powerful muscles of the legs.

3. *Direction of Force:* By keeping the body relatively low, the force can be directed through the body in a sideward direction. If the player is standing erect, the direction of force will be directed upwards and only slightly towards the side.

Figure 4.24 Stopping

Things to Stress

1. Keep body low with the weight over both feet and the arms to the side.
2. Always lean in the direction of the dodge.
3. Once a dodging movement is made, keep low and shift the center towards the middle of the body in order to prepare for another movement.

Dodging Activities

1. Run, stop, and move right, then left.
2. Run to a partner, stop, and change direction.
3. Run around obstacles—beanbags, balls, chairs.
4. Bounce or dribble a ball, stop, and change direction on command.
5. Bounce or dribble a ball around obstacles.
6. Play relay or tag games involving dodging movements (see chapters 14 and 15).
7. Combine dodging with other locomotor skills— slide, stop, dodge, run.

Nonlocomotor Skills

Nonlocomotor, or axial movements (swing, bend and stretch, rise, fall, twist and turn, push and pull), are performed from a relatively stable base of support. These movements are usually performed while standing, kneeling, sitting, or lying; however, they can be combined with locomotor skills.

Swinging

A swing is a pendular or circular movement of the body or its parts around a stationary center.

Applying Mechanical Principles

The following principles apply to the swinging movements of parts of the body while the body as a whole maintains a stationary standing or sitting position.

1. *Lever:* In movements of the arm, the hand will have greater speed when the elbow is kept straight. Similarly, the foot has greater speed when the knee is kept straight.
2. *Momentum:* The momentum of any part of a supported body can be transferred to the rest of the body. For example, swinging an arm sideward and upward will move the whole body in those directions. This transfer takes place only when the body is in contact with a supporting surface.
3. *Gravity:* The movement of a pendulum is caused by the force of gravity. As the pendulum swings downward, its speed increases; as it swings

Figure 4.25　Dodging

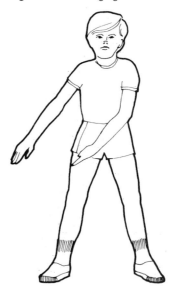

Figure 4.26　Swinging

upward, its speed decreases until it stops at the top of the swing. The speed of pendular movement is not increased by body weight; it is increased only by the application of additional muscular force.

Things to Stress

1. Keep swinging movements relaxed, smooth, and rhythmical.
2. Keep swinging movements equal on both sides; hence do not apply additional muscular force to one side.
3. Dismount swinging bars, rings, or swings at the top of the swing.

Swinging Activities

1. Swing arms forward and backward and from side to side.
2. Swing arms overhead, forward and backward, and sideward.
3. Lie on back and swing arms and legs.
4. Repeat activity 1 with legs.
5. Swing head forward and backward and from side to side.
6. Ask the children how many parts of the body can swing or sway from standing or sitting positions. Allow them to experiment.
7. Swing or sway parts of body in pantomime. Tell the children to sway like a tree, swing like a windshield wiper, and so on. Change tempo with each pantomime movement.
8. Swing arms or legs with moderate speed, then shift to slower or faster speeds.
9. Stand on a box, step, or other apparatus and swing the leg.
10. Grasp chinning bar and swing body forward and backward. Flex arm and repeat.
11. Swing on a rope and release it at different points on the forward and backward swing. Note that the top of the backswing is the best point to release a rope.
12. Combine swinging with other locomotor skills such as a jump or slide.
13. Hang from a bar or rings, then swing.

Bending

A bend is a flexing movement around one or more joints.

Things to Stress

1. To increase flexibility, bend in a slow and sustained manner.
2. Encourage children to find, test, and extend different parts of the body that bend. Also, use terms such as *tuck, curl,* and *coil* in place of *bend* or *flex*.

Bending Activities

1. Bend different parts of the body—arms, legs, trunk.
2. Imitate things that bend—tree, snake, dog, ostrich, giraffe, and so on.
3. Bend one part of the body while keeping another part straight.
4. Combine bending with other locomotor or nonlocomotor movements—bend while stretching, swinging, or jumping.

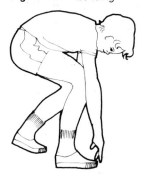

Figure 4.27 Bending

5. Lie or balance on different parts of the body and see how many different parts and ways you can bend.
6. Run and jump, and bend one or more parts while in the air.
7. Balance on different parts of the body and see how many ways or parts you can bend or flex.
8. Make the body into different bent or curved shapes.
9. Make curved shapes with a partner.
10. Make up a series of curved shapes moving from low to high or while moving in different directions.

Stretching

A stretch is an extension of one or more joints of the body. A light or gentle stretch moves the joint partially through its range of movement. A strong forceful stretch, such as a stretch upward and backward, requires maximum extension through many joints.

Things to Stress

1. Initial stretching movements should be light and gentle; discourage ballistic movements.
2. Encourage children to stretch through the full range of movement.
3. Where possible combine stretching and bending movements.
4. Encourage stretching movements from a variety of positions and in a variety of ways.

Stretching Activities

1. Stand and stretch trunk, then arms, wrists, and fingers in a slow upward movement. Repeat moving in other directions.

2. Repeat activity 1, from a front or back lying position.

3. Find different balance positions and see how many different ways and directions you can stretch.

4. Slowly stretch in one direction and slowly curl back to the starting position. Repeat and move quickly back to the curled position.

5. Stretch one arm slowly and bend it back rapidly; reverse movement. Do the same with other parts of the body.

6. Bend one part of the body (arms) while stretching another (legs).

7. Stand on a box or step with toes touching near the edge. Keep legs straight and bend forward and down; try to extend the fingers beyond the toes.

8. Bend and stretch different parts of the body with varying speeds. Stretch arm up slowly, then bend it back to the original position slowly. Repeat with other parts of the body.

9. Pantomime sports movements that require strong sustained stretching movements.

10. Stretch while holding individual ropes, wands, or hoops. Use small equipment to stretch against.

Twisting

A twist is a rotation of parts of the body around its own axis. Twisting movements usually occur at the neck, shoulders, spine, hips, and ankle and wrist joints.

Things to Stress

1. A twisting movement can take place on or off the ground.

2. The range of the twisting action is determined by the type of joint (hinge joint, ball-and-socket joint, etc.).

3. Keep the part of the body around which the twisting action occurs stable.

Twisting Activities

1. Twist to pantomime movements—trees and wind.

2. Combine twisting with other locomotor skills— walk, stop, leap, and jump.

3. Let children experiment: See how many parts of your body you can twist, as well as how many combinations you can make.

Figure 4.28 Stretching

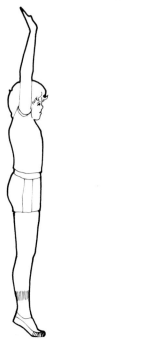

Figure 4.29 Twisting

4. Repeat activity 3 from different positions—lying on side, balancing on knees or hands or on one foot, and so on.

5. Twist part of the upper body one way while twisting part of the lower body the opposite way.

6. With a partner, make up twisting routines— together and against each other's body parts.

7. Pantomime athletic and mechanical movements that involve twisting.

Figure 4.30 Turning

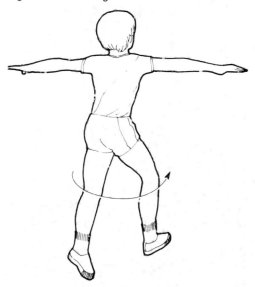

Figure 4.31 Pushing

Turning

A turn is a partial or total rotation of the body accompanied by a shift in the base of support. A pivot towards one side illustrates a turning movement involving a partial rotation and a shift in the base of support. A jump followed by a full rotation in the air illustrates a total rotation and complete change in the base of support.

Things to Stress

1. To increase the speed of a turn, pull the legs and arms close to the body.
2. In activities requiring a quick change of direction, keep the body weight low and the feet about shoulder-width apart.
3. To increase force or speed, twist lightly in the opposite direction prior to starting the turning movement.

Turning Activities

1. Turn the body a quarter, half, or full turn to the right, then to the left.
2. Turn the body to music.
3. Turn to pantomime movements—tops, doors, sport skills.
4. Combine twisting and turning movements.
5. Face partner and pivot toward and away from each other.
6. Begin a turn with arms outstretched, then quickly draw in the arms as the turn is made. Repeat with legs, or legs and arms.

7. Let children experiment: See how many different parts of your body you can turn on—and from different positions.
8. Combine turning movements with a walk, run, jump, skip, or slide.
9. Combine a turn with small equipment such as individual ropes, hoops, wands, and traffic cones.
10. Have partners make up sequences involving twisting and turning movements. These can be performed standing, walking, and from different positions.

Pushing

A push is directing a force or object away from the base of support, such as pushing a door open or pushing against an imaginary object with hands or feet.

Things to Stress

1. For movements requiring excessive force, lower the body to direct the force through the center of weight.
2. Start strong pushing movements with a wide base of support.
3. Keep the back straight during strenuous pushing movements.

Pushing Activities

1. Push in pantomime—push a box or a wheelbarrow.
2. Push objects of various weights and sizes. Begin with small objects and gradually increase weight and size.

3. Push objects with the hands, feet, and back.

4. Do partner activities—from a standing position, one partner assumes a good base of support and the other attempts to push the other backward. Experiment in various positions with different parts of the body. For example, have both partners face each other on the floor and push their legs or arms against each other. From back-to-back position, one partner pulls the other over his head.

5. Begin in different positions, such as lying on the back, side, or stomach, and see how many different ways and directions you can push the body.

6. Balance on one foot and push a box against a wall or partner. Try same movements but balance on two feet. Repeat movements, lowering the body and widening the base of support.

7. Pantomime sport skills that require a pushing action.

8. Perform five or six calisthenic exercises or stunts that require a pushing action.

Pulling

A pull is directing a force or object towards the body. A pulling action is normally initiated by the hands and arms; however, other parts of the body, such as the foot, knee, or trunk, can also initiate a pulling movement.

Things to Stress
1. When lifting or pulling heavy objects, start with a wide base of support, bent knees, straight back, and pull the object upward towards the body.

2. Keep the pulling action smooth; use a controlled sequence of muscular contractions rather than rigid, ballistic-type movements.

Pulling Activities
1. Pull in pantomime—pull a wagon or row a boat.

2. Pull objects of varying weights and sizes towards the body. Start with light objects and progress to heavier ones, gradually adjusting the base of support and angle of pull as the weight increases.

3. Use different parts of the body to pull an object, such as a leg, the trunk, or head.

4. Repeat activity 3 but from different positions, such as lying on your back and pulling an object towards your body with the lower leg.

5. Pull an object with different rates of speed—begin pulling slowly, then gradually increase speed.

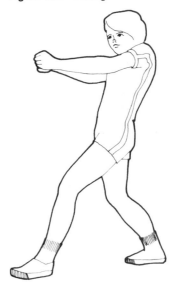

Figure 4.32 Pulling

6. Play tug-o-war with two players. Play as usual beginning in a standing position; then vary the starting position, and begin by kneeling, lying on side, back, and so on.

7. Repeat above with four or more players.

Manipulative Skills

The basic manipulative skills of throwing, catching, and striking represent the foundation of all major individual and team sport activities. These skills should be taught to primary children in a systematic manner through a variety of running, tag, and simple team and creative game activities. As children progress to the intermediate grades, skills are organized in a sequential way within each major sport. Thus the following skills should be acquired by boys and girls before they enter the fourth grade.

Throwing

Primary children normally begin with a two-hand side throw. They progress to a one-hand underhand throw, and finally tackle the one-hand overhand throw.

Two-Hand Side Throw
The child stands with her left foot forward and her weight evenly distributed on both feet. The ball is held in front of the body with the elbows slightly bent and the fingers spread around the sides of the ball (fig. 4.33a). She swings her arms back to the right side until the ball is opposite her right hip, and shifts her weight to her right foot. At this point, her right hand is behind the ball, her left elbow is bent, and her left hand is on

Figure 4.33 Two-Hand Side Throw

a   b   c

the front of the ball (fig. 4.33b). She then swings her arms forward as her body weight shifts to her left foot, and she simultaneously releases the ball (fig. 4.33c). Note that the ball should be released from both hands at the same moment.

Applying Mechanical Principles

The following mechanical principles apply to all three basic throwing skills.

1. *Momentum:* The momentum of any part of the body can be transferred to the ball. To apply this principle, rotate the body toward the side while shifting the weight to the back foot. Bring back the throwing arm as far as possible. If the forward swinging action is smooth, maximum force will be transferred to the ball as it leaves the hands.

2. *Speed:* Greater speed can be gained by increasing the distance over which the force is applied. This is particularly important in the one-hand underhand and overhand throws. The straighter the arm in the forward throwing movement, the greater the force that is generated and the greater the speed of the ball.

Things to Stress

1. Use a large ball (beach ball or 8½ to 12 inch utility ball) with young children, particularly five and six year olds.

2. Begin a throw with legs far enough apart to provide a good base of support.

3. Rotate the body in the same direction as the ball during the preparatory movement.

4. Keep arms straight on the forward swing, and follow through after the ball has been released.

Throwing Activities

1. Use large balls (beach balls, playballs) and large targets (walls, lines on floor, colorful targets painted on plywood). Have children begin by throwing a few feet from the target, then gradually increase the distance.

2. Throw and catch with a partner.

3. Have children experiment with different ways of throwing a two-hand side throw (from either side, while kneeling, or while lying on back, etc.)

4. Play simple throwing games. Refer to Classroom Games (p. 183), Inventive Games Approach (p. 217), and the following chapters for appropriate two-hand side throwing activities:

   Chapter 14: "Running, Tag, and Simple Team Games"
   Chapter 15: "Relay Activities"
   Chapter 16: "Individual and Partner Games"

One-Hand Underhand Throw

The child stands facing the target with her legs slightly apart and her weight evenly distributed on both feet. She holds the ball in front of her body with both hands slightly under the ball (fig. 4.34a). Her right hand swings down and back as her body twists to the right and her weight shifts to her right foot (fig. 4.34b). As her right arm swings forward, she steps forward onto her left foot and releases the ball off the fingertips (fig. 4.34c).

Figure 4.34 One-Hand Underhand Throw

a   b   c

Things to Stress
1. Use a large ball (beach or utility ball).
2. Begin with a wide base of support and extend arms far enough in the initial backswing.
3. Emphasize a smooth forward swing and follow through after the ball is released.

Throwing Activities
1. Adapt two-hand side throw activities to the one-hand underhand throw.
2. Adapt two-hand side throw activities using a beanbag or fleece ball.
3. Roll a ball towards a target or partner.
4. Throw various size balls into the air and catch them on the volley or after one bounce.
5. Repeat 2 to 4 using your other hand.
6. Run, change direction, and throw at a target.
7. Run, stop, turn, and throw at a target.
8. Make up games for individuals or partners that require a one-hand underhand throw.

One-Hand Overhand Throw

The player begins with his left foot forward and his body weight evenly distributed over both feet. He holds the ball with both hands in front of his body (fig. 4.35a). In the first part of the backswing, he raises his upper arm, and flexes his wrist so the hand points backward. At this point, his left side faces the direction of the throw; his left arm extends forward; and his weight is on the rear foot. In a simultaneous movement, his upper arm lifts up and forward and his left arm moves down and back as his weight shifts to the front foot (fig. 4.35b). The ball is released off the fingertips. The follow-through should be in a downward direction, ending with the palm of the throwing hand toward the ground (fig. 4.35c).

Things to Stress
1. Hold the ball with tips of fingers and thumb.
2. Raise upper arm and forearm well above the shoulder on the backward swing.
3. Keep elbow away from the body on the forward throwing action.
4. Snap the wrist and release the ball off the fingertips.
5. Follow through after the ball is released and take a step on the right foot.

Throwing Activities
1. Adapt the two-hand and one-hand underhand activities to the one-hand overhand throw.
2. Refer to practice activities and lead-up games in chapter 22, "Basketball Activities."
3. Refer to practice activities and lead-up games in chapter 23, "Softball Activities."

Catching

A ball can be caught with one or two hands from virtually all angles. In the primary grades, however, the two-hand underhand catch and the two-hand overhand catch should be stressed.

Figure 4.35 One-Hand Overhand Throw

a

b

c

Figure 4.36 Two-Hand Underhand Catch

Figure 4.37 Two-Hand Overhand Catch

Two-Hand Underhand Catch

Use the two-hand underhand catch when the ball approaches below the waist. The player stands with feet about shoulder-width apart, elbows bent, and fingers pointing down. As the ball approaches, the player steps forward, extends his arms, and brings his hands close together. The ball is caught with the tips of the fingers and thumbs (fig. 4.36). The pinkies (baby fingers) should be close together when the ball is caught. As the ball is caught, the hands recoil toward the body to soften the force.

Two-Hand Overhand Catch

When the ball approaches above the waist, the two-hand overhand catch should be used. The elbows are bent and held high, and the fingers and thumbs are spread. As the ball approaches, the arms extend forward and up. The ball should be caught with the tips of the fingers and thumbs; the thumbs are close together (fig. 4.37). As the ball is caught, the hands recoil toward the body to deaden the force of the oncoming ball.

Applying Mechanical Principles

1. *Center of Gravity:* The body should be kept in line with the ball. The legs should be comfortably spread or in a stride position to provide a firm base of support. With the underhand catch, a slightly crouched position lowers the center of gravity, providing an even firmer base of support.

2. *Absorption of Force:* To absorb the impact of the oncoming ball, the force should be spread over as large an area as possible or as long a distance as possible, or both. Catch the ball with the arms extended and the fingers spread and cupped, then recoil the arms toward the body to provide the greatest surface and distance for absorbing the force.

Things to Stress

1. Move into a "ready" position where the body is in line with the oncoming ball.

2. Meet the ball with cupped hands and slightly bent elbows, then recoil back towards the body.

3. Keep feet in a comfortable stride position; for low catches, bend the knees and lean forward in the direction of the oncoming ball.

Catching Activities

See activities listed under one-hand overhand throw.

Striking

Two basic types of striking skills are used in individual, partner, and group games. These striking skills include hitting a ball with the hand or foot and hitting an object with a bat, racquet, or other implement. The basic skills within each of these general areas are described in this section. The more specific sport skills are detailed in chapters 14 to 20.

Striking with the Hand

When striking a ball with the hand or fist, the player stands in line with the oncoming ball. The feet are in a stride position, with the weight on the back foot. If the ball is hit with an underhand striking action (fig. 4.38), the striking arm extends straight back, then forcefully moves forward to contact the ball when it is opposite the front foot. The hand of the striking arm is held firm as the ball is contacted. Follow-through is forceful in the direction of the hit. When a ball is hit with a two-hand overhand striking action, the elbows are bent slightly, the fingers are spread apart, and the thumbs face each other (fig. 4.39). As the ball drops,

Figure 4.38 Hitting the Ball with an Underhand Striking Action

the body and arms extend upward and slightly forward, and the ball is hit with "stiff" fingers. Follow-through is an upward and forward motion in the direction of the ball.

When dribbling with the hands, the striking action is downward. The body leans forward slightly and the knees are bent with the weight evenly distributed over both feet. The wrist of the dribbling hand is flexed, with the fingers cupped and spread (fig. 4.40). The forearm extends downward and the ball is "pushed" toward the ground. As the ball rebounds, the fingers, wrist, and arm "ride" back with it.

Applying Mechanical Principles

1. *Stability:* In all striking skills, the legs should be comfortably spread to provide a wide, stable base of support from which to hit the ball. Standing with the knees slightly bent also lowers the center of gravity, further increasing stability.

2. *Action-Reaction:* Every action causes an equal and opposite reaction. When a player begins to swing his arm toward the oncoming ball, he is building up force. If he maintains a steady forward momentum at the moment of contact, the ball will recoil with an equal force.

3. *Production of Force:* Hitting a ball is basically the transfer of rotary force to linear force. More force can be gained by increasing the distance of the backswing and by cocking the wrist at the top of the backswing. Additional force is also gained by extending the arms as the bat is moved toward the ball.

Figure 4.39 Hitting the Ball with a Two-Hand Overhand Striking Action

Figure 4.40 Dribbling with the Hand

a

b

4. *Direction of Force:* The direction in which an object moves is determined by the direction in which the force is applied. If the force is applied in line with the ball's center of gravity, the ball will travel in a straight line. But if the bat hits the ball above or below the center of gravity, the ball will travel in a rotary motion, losing distance and speed.

5. *Inertia:* An object has its greatest inertia when it is not moving. Once dribbling begins, it should be continued by easy, sequential pushing actions. Each time the ball comes to rest, more force must be applied to overcome the initial inertia.

Things to Stress

1. Keep your eye on the ball.
2. Get in line with the ball.
3. Strike and follow through.
4. When dribbling, push the ball and ride back with the rebound.

Striking Activities

1. Strike a balloon with the hand or the elbow, then with different parts of the body.
2. Repeat Activitiy 1 with either hand and with both hands.
3. Strike different size balls towards a target or to a partner.
4. Attempt to strike a balloon or light nerf ball into the air three or more times.
5. Make up a sequence of striking, throwing, and catching a balloon or ball.
6. Run, change direction, then strike a nerf ball towards a target.
7. Strike a ball into the air, perform a stunt, then catch the returning ball.

8. Make up a game for one person or partners that requires a strike.

9. Adapt games from the following chapters that stress striking skills with one or two hands.

Chapter 12: "Adapting Physical Education Activities to the Classroom"
Chapter 14: "Running, Tag, and Simple Team Games"
Chapter 15: "Relay Activities"
Chapter 16: "Individual and Partner Games"
Chapter 21: "Volleyball Activities"

Striking with the Feet

The majority of kicking games played in elementary school involve kicking a stationary or moving ball with the top or side of the instep. Just before the ball is kicked, the nonkicking foot is even with the ball, the head and trunk lean forward slightly and the kicking leg is well back, with the knee slightly bent. The eyes are focused on the ball, and the arms extend sideways. The kicking leg is then brought downward and forward, and the top of the instep contacts the ball (fig. 4.41). The kicking leg continues forward and slightly upward.

Many kicking games also involve a controlled striking or dribbling action of both feet (fig. 4.42). In this type of striking action, the body is bent slightly forward with the head over the ball. The ball is moved with short controlled pushes.

Applying Mechanical Principles

The mechanical principles listed under "Striking with the Hand" also apply to "Striking with the Feet." The following principles apply to kicking a ball.

1. *Acceleration:* A ball that is kicked moves in the direction of the force, and the resulting change of speed is directly proportional to the force acting upon it. It is important that the force applied by the kicking foot be directly behind the ball and moving in the direction in which the ball is intended to move.

2. *Increasing Linear Velocity:* Kicking a ball involves the conversion of angular velocity to linear velocity. Linear velocity can be increased by taking more steps prior to the kick or by extending the lower leg more to create a longer lever and thus more force when the ball is contacted.

Things to Stress

1. Never kick with the toes.

2. Bend the knee prior to kicking, and follow through in the direction of the kick.

3. When dribbling, push the ball and maintain a steady rhythmical dribbling action.

Figure 4.41 Kicking

Figure 4.42 Dribbling with the Feet

Kicking Activities

1. Adapt the striking activities listed under Striking with the Hands to kicking or dribbling.

2. Adapt practice activities and lead-up games provided in the following chapters to kicking or dribbling a ball.

Chapter 18: "Soccer Activities"
Chapter 20: "Flag or Touch Football Activities"

Striking with an Implement

When striking with a racquet or paddle, the player stands with feet comfortably apart, knees slightly bent and elbow flexed and away from the body. Young children begin with lightweight objects such as balloons, or nerf or sponge balls (fig. 4.43). The striking action for these objects involves light elbow and wrist movements.

When striking a ball with a bat, the player stands with feet parallel about shoulder-width apart. His left side faces the pitcher. He grips the bat comfortably, shifting it to the back of his head about shoulder high. His arms, bent at the elbows, are held away from his body. As the ball leaves the pitcher's hand, the batter shifts his weight to his rear foot, then swings the bat forward as he shifts his weight to his front foot (fig. 4.44). He keeps a firm grip on the bat as the ball is hit. After the ball is hit, the bat continues to swing around the left shoulder.

Applying Mechanical Principles

The mechanical principles listed under Striking with the Hand apply to "Striking with an Implement."

Things to Stress

1. Keep your eye on the ball.
2. Start with feet spread apart and the knees slightly flexed.
3. Maintain a firm grip through the forward swing and follow-through.

Striking Activities

1. Adapt striking activities listed under "Striking with the Hand" to striking with an implement.
2. Adapt practice activities and lead-up games provided in the following chapters to batting an object:

   Chapter 19: "Hockey Activities"
   Chapter 23: "Softball Activities"

The basic throwing, catching, and striking skills are the foundation for a wide variety of more advanced skills that are learned during the intermediate grades. A suggested sequence for introducing the more advanced skills and practice activities and lead-up games for each sport are included in the following chapters:

Chapter 18: "Soccer Activities"
Chapter 19: "Hockey Activities"
Chapter 20: "Flag or Touch Football Activities"
Chapter 21: "Volleyball Activities"
Chapter 22: "Basketball Activities"
Chapter 23: "Softball Activities"
Chapter 24: "Track and Field Activities"

Figure 4.43   Striking a Lightweight Object with an Implement

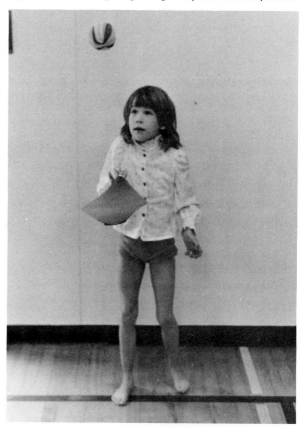

Figure 4.44   Batting

Basic Rhythmic and Dance Skills

Rhythmic and dance skills for elementary school children can be described under the broad categories of rhythmic skills, folk dance skills, and creative dance.

Rhythmic Skills

The fundamental difference in the rhythmical ability of primary and intermediate children is the progressive ease of moving in time or in harmony with a rhythmical accompaniment. Following are the basic rhythmic skills that primary and intermediate children should acquire; each is described in chapter 28, "Rhythmic and Movement Activities."

1. Moving in time to a rhythmic beat.
2. Changing movement patterns in harmony with the musical accompaniment.
3. Varying the speed of a movement according to the tempo of the musical accompaniment.
4. Changing or emphasizing the force of movement according to the varying intensity of a musical accompaniment.

Folk Dance Skills

All singing games and traditional folk dances involve one or more of the locomotor and nonlocomotor skills described at the beginning of this chapter. The dance activities in chapter 29, "Traditional and Contemporary Dances," begin with primary singing games, which normally involve a walk, run, skip, or gallop step performed in a simple dance pattern or movement. The intermediate folk and square dance activities involve more complex locomotor and nonlocomotor movements and more style and finesse in the movement patterns.

Creative Dance

It is extremely difficult to classify the skills used in creative dance activities. The pantomime movements of primary children are essentially combinations of locomotor and nonlocomotor skills. However, since these movements are creative or interpretive, no common standards are involved. The movement concepts and skills described under the categories of body awareness, qualities, space awareness, and relationships (earlier in the chapter) are also used as a medium of expression in creative dance. Chapter 30, "Creative Dance Activities," illustrates how a variety of creative dance activities can be developed for primary and intermediate children.

Gymnastic Skills

The basic skills of traditional gymnastic activities are classified as balance, vaulting, climbing, and agility skills. These skills are organized within each category according to their difficulty. Chapter 25, "Stunts, Tumbling, and Movement Skills," includes the basic stunts and tumbling skills appropriate for primary and intermediate grades and describes how the movement concepts and skills of body awareness, qualities, space awareness, and relationships can be integrated with these structured skills. Chapters 26 and 27 follow a similar pattern, combining the structured and movement skills used with small equipment and large apparatus.

Part 3 Teaching Strategies for Physical Education

Chapter 5
Teaching Strategies and Techniques

Chapter 6
Organizing for Physical Education

Chapter 7
Observation and Evaluation

The process of teaching young children through the medium of physical activities involves a wide variety of teaching strategies, organizational techniques, and evaluative procedures. Chapter 5 provides a basic understanding of how and why children acquire skills, understandings, and appreciations in physical education. This chapter also describes a variety of methods and techniques that each teacher can incorporate into her own style of teaching. Chapter 6 describes the basic organizational patterns for teaching physical education, safety procedures, and standards relating to facilities, equipment, and supplies. Observational techniques and evaluative procedures are discussed in chapter 7.

5 Teaching Strategies and Techniques

Theories of Learning
Association Theory
Cognitive Theory
Cybernetic Theory

Principles of Learning Motor Skills
Principle of Interest
Principle of Practice
Principle of Distributed Practice
Principle of Skill Specificity
Principle of Whole-Part Learning
Principle of Transfer
Principle of Skill Improvement
Principle of Feedback

Teaching Strategies
Individualized Learning
Personalized Learning

Qualities of Good Teaching

Methods of Teaching
Direct Method
Limitation Method
Indirect Method

Techniques of Teaching
Creating an Effective Learning Atmosphere
Teaching Motor Skills

Effective Class Organization
Use of Time before a Lesson Starts
Individualized Teaching Patterns
Teaching Formations
Grouping Procedures
Routine Procedures

Contemporary teaching in the elementary school emphasizes concept development rather than the simple acquisition of facts and knowledge. Accompanying this emphasis is an effort to individualize and personalize the learning process in order to respond to individual differences and to provide a learning atmosphere that will enhance positive relationships. Helping the child achieve his full intellectual, physical, and creative potential can be reached only through an informal learning atmosphere where the responsibility for learning is shared by the teacher and the child.

A child learns new skills and concepts when he is capable of exploring alternatives. This means he must have a goal, some uncertainty as to how to reach it, and the ability and motivation to attempt to reach it. The essential duties of the teacher of physical education, as with all subjects, are to provide learning tasks that are within each child's reach and to give continuous encouragement and assistance through the learning process.

The many skills and movement concepts of physical education cannot be learned through one approach, however. Each new learning situation must be tailored to the varying degrees of interest and skill found in a class of twenty-five or more young learners. There is no ideal type of teaching, no single set of concepts or learning principles, no one best method that will guarantee success. The teacher should draw from the areas discussed in this chapter and develop her own teaching style or approach.

Theories of Learning

A theory of learning is a theoretical assumption of how an organism learns. In physical education, the theory must provide a reasonable basis for understanding motor learning and a list of principles of learning that can be applied to the teaching and learning of physical activities. Brief descriptions of three major theories of learning provide a framework for understanding motor learning and the important principles that should be considered in teaching physical education. Since it is impossible to include an extensive coverage of each theory here, such treatment can be found in the selected references listed in appendix A.

Association Theory

The association theory developed by Thorndike in 1906 was an attempt to describe how a person learns and adjusts to his world. Thorndike's hypothesis was that learning is the strengthening of the "bond" (connection) between a stimulus and a response. Accordingly, his conception of learning was that a person is acted upon and then initiates an act in response. In brief, his "laws" of learning, which are still highly influential in teaching today, are:

1. *The Law of Readiness:* Learning depends upon readiness to act, which, in turn, facilitates the response.
2. *The Law of Effect:* Learning is facilitated or retarded according to the degree of satisfaction or annoyance that accompanies the act.

3. *The Law of Exercise:* The more often a connection between bonds is repeated, the more firmly the connection (pairing of bonds) becomes fixed (learned).

Thorndike modified his laws in later years on the basis of additional findings. He found that greater effects result from satisfaction than displeasure. The results of Thorndike's pioneer work, coupled with the contributions of later associationists (Guthrie, Watson, and Skinner), who became known as behaviorists, have greatly affected the nature of instructional theory and teaching methods.

Principles of teaching physical education based on the association theory appear to be helpful, but incomplete. They are helpful in recognizing the importance of repeating motor skills and making the learning task satisfying to the learner. This theory has at least partial application to learning such skills as throwing, kicking, swimming, and gymnastic movements. But since the theory fails to recognize the fundamental concept (from a cognitive or field theorist's viewpoint) that a learner is a purposeful and holistic organism capable of thinking, it is limited in providing a basis for understanding other types of learning and behavior. For example, the theory falls immeasurably short when used to explain social behavior, individual and team strategy, or creative movement in dance or gymnastics.

Cognitive Theory

The cognitive theory, developed by Wertheimer and refined by Combs, Lewin, and Roger, assumes that the learner has a personality and reacts as a whole from the very beginning. It maintains that the human organism possesses a certain order from the beginning. All attributes are considered integral and indivisible parts of the whole personality; they may be differentiated but cannot be separated from the organization of the whole being (Knapp 1967). Learning proceeds from the comprehension of the whole to the identification of the smaller parts. Therefore, learning is not considered an additive process, as it is with the association theory. Rather, it consists of a continuous reorganization of new learnings with previous ones, resulting in new insights.

The cognitive theory stresses that the fundamental importance that any learning experience has on the learner depends upon his unique perception of the experience in relation to his previous experiences, abilities, and personal desires. From this point of view, learning is "process oriented, emphasizing the means as well as the end product" (Leitmann 1976).

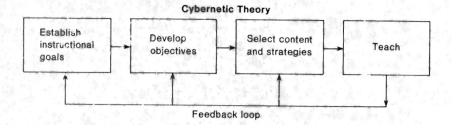

Cybernetic Theory

Establish instructional goals → Develop objectives → Select content and strategies → Teach

Feedback loop

Cybernetic Theory

The cybernetic theory uses a feedback model similar to the one shown above. Proponents of this theory, such as Weiner (1961) and Fitts (1967), recognize the importance of the individual's capabilities and experiences, but they tend to emphasize the way experience is processed. For example, the goals, objectives, content, and teaching strategies of a particular unit of instruction are identified and then put into operation. Once the program begins, however, a continuous feedback process may, at any time, create a change in the nature or direction of any part of the instructional unit. This theory is a reaction against the more random "shotgun" approach of the cognitive theorist as well as a disbelief in the associationist's contention that a learner tends to repeat a learning act because it is satisfying (Leitmann 1982).

Principles of Learning Motor Skills

Theories of learning are just theories; that is, they are assumptions about how individuals learn. Nevertheless, each of the theories just discussed have provided a basis for organizing content, developing methods, and stressing evaluative techniques. Some of the following principles are derived from the association theory, while others are the direct application of the cognitive or cybernetic theories. Thus, these principles represent an eclectic point of view. Since knowledge of the learning process is still incomplete, these principles should be used only as guidelines. The teacher should apply her own common sense to every learning situation.

Principle of Interest

Any skill, whether it is climbing a rope or throwing a softball, will be acquired more efficiently if the child has a motive for learning it. A child's attitude toward learning a skill determines for the most part the amount and kind of learning.

It is inherent in this principle that the teacher foster in the child a desire to learn motor skills. Learning will generally take place if the child experiences immediate satisfaction, if he sees the necessity of building

Figure 5.1 The attitude of children toward learning a skill affects their subsequent performance of the skill.

a strong, healthy body, or if he values the skill as something he can use during leisure activities. Learning can also occur out of fear or because of some extrinsic reward, such as a star or check put beside one's name.

Implications for Physical Education
1. Select activities appropriate to the child's interests, needs, and capacities.
2. Stress the intrinsic value of the activity.
3. Present activities so that each child achieves some degree of success.

Principle of Practice

Research in motor learning strongly suggests that practice is necessary for the acquisition of a motor skill. The child must practice the skill correctly until it becomes overlearned or automatic. Once a child has learned to swim, several months may elapse without practice, yet he will still be able to swim. In general, the more the skill is overlearned, the longer the time before it is lost. But when a skill is practiced incorrectly, it will not lead to improvement and might even lead to regression (Arnold 1968).

Implications for Physical Education
1. Select skills appropriate to the group's interests and maturation level.
2. Stress proper form while the skill is being learned. After the skill has been learned, stress other factors, such as speed and distance.
3. Repeat drill activities after several months to insure retention.

Principle of Distributed Practice

A motor skill is learned more effectively with distributed practice periods than with massed practice periods. The length of the practice period, as well as the time between practices, depends upon the difficulty of the skill, and the child's ability and background. However, as a general rule, a short period of intense effort and attention is better than a halfhearted longer period (Knapp 1967).

This principle generally applies to all age levels and virtually all skills. But there are certainly times, depending on the interest of the children and the amount of effort required, when the practice period might be longer or shorter than normally considered wise. For example, if children are permitted to practice a forward roll until they become dizzy and fatigued, the practice period is too long and too strenuous regardless of student interest. Self-testing activities for any age group should have a variation so that one part of the body is not overworked.

A teacher working with fifth- and sixth-grade children in an activity such as volleyball lead-up games may find that the students remain interested and enthusiastic for ten or fifteen minutes or even longer. So long as interest is high and skill development is fostered, it is not only permissible, but desirable, to extend the practice period. On the other hand, when the children are indifferent and are not attaining the skill, a change in the lead-up activity or a shorter practice period is suggested.

Implications for Physical Education
1. Adjust the length of the practice period and the spacing of rest periods for the class to the material being taught.
2. Change an activity whenever the children show fatigue, boredom, and poor skill development.

Principle of Skill Specificity

A child's ability to acquire a particular skill depends upon his unique characteristics. A child may excel in one skill but be awkward in others that require about the same maturity and physical effort (Cratty 1967). A nine-year-old boy may be able to throw, catch, and hit a softball with ease and accuracy, but still show a subpar performance in volleyball activities, which require about the same effort and physical attributes.

This principle also applies to children who have reached the same psychological and physiological maturity level. After a single demonstration of a skill, one child may be able to perform it in its entirety, while another child may need more demonstration and practice to perform even a part of the skill. This is seen in such sports as swimming, basketball, and track and field.

Implications for Physical Education
1. Provide varied activities at all grade levels.
2. Allow for individual differences in the standards of performance.
3. Allow for variations in the speed at which children acquire the same skill.
4. Develop standards based upon the individual's level and rate of development rather than the class average.

Principle of Whole-Part Learning

According to Knapp, material is learned in the *whole method* by going through it completely again and again. In the *part method,* the material is divided into portions, which are practiced; and eventually the parts are joined as a whole. In physical education, it is difficult to define what is whole and what is a part of the skill or game. Recognizing this difficulty, the available evidence indicates that the whole method is superior to the part method in teaching motor skills (Knapp 1967).

A teacher must decide whether to teach a movement in its entirety or break it into parts. The choice depends first upon the complexity of the skill and second upon the learner's amount and speed of skill development. For example, a teacher demonstrates to her third-grade class a one-foot hop-skipping skill using a single rope. The children then attempt to do the skill in its entirety; this is practice through the whole method.

But if only a few children learn the skill after repeated attempts, it would be better to break down the skill into simpler movements. The children could do a one-foot hop over a long rope turned by two people, then attempt the one-foot hop with a single rope, using a half swing. Finally, with a full turn of the rope, the hopping movement could be integrated into the rhythmic turning of the rope.

Implications for Physical Education

1. Use the whole method whenever the skill represents a single functional movement.
2. It may be desirable to break complex skills into smaller parts. Complexity depends upon the skill as well as the learner's ability.
3. Generally, the rate and amount of learning indicates the effectiveness of the method used.

Principle of Transfer

Transfer in physical education can be defined as the effect that practice of one motor task has upon the learning or performance of a second, closely related task (Cratty 1967). Underlying this principle is the assumption that a learner will take advantage of what a new situation has in common with a previous experience, such as applying the knowledge of an underhand throwing motion in learning to serve a volleyball. Although it has been contended that transfer occurs between identical skills or movements, no conclusive evidence supports this. Instead, the evidence seems to support the principle of specificity discussed earlier.

Implications for Physical Education
Proponents of the movement education approach, including its originator, Rudolph Laban, have said that movement education has a strong carry-over to other skill learning, but no evidence indicates a common motor skill factor. Current research indicates that transfer depends upon the degree of resemblance between the skills.

There are, however, many other reasons for incorporating the movement education approach. One important reason is that a carry-over does occur with movement education in the form of a positive attitude toward other activities.

Principle of Skill Improvement

A child does not always learn every physical skill in the same way. Too many factors affect the learning curve, including the complexity of the skill, the child's motivation and physical ability, and the adequacy of instruction.

Figure 5.2 The practice time needed to master a skill varies from individual to individual.

Generally speaking, however, the initial phase of learning is usually quite rapid. This may be due to the child's enthusiasm for a new activity and the fact that he learns the easy parts first, utilizing previously acquired skills. But progress slows down gradually, even as practice continues, to a period of almost no overt improvement. Numerous explanations have been given for these learning "plateaus," such as lack of motivation, failure to learn a prerequisite skill, and improper instruction. However, with proper analysis and correction an increase in skill attainment should result.

Implications for Physical Education

1. Teachers should recognize children's individual differences in the learning curve for the same activity.
2. After a new skill is introduced, allow sufficient practice time for mastery.
3. Be aware of physiological limitations that hinder or prevent additional improvement.

Principle of Feedback

Feedback is defined as the information a learner receives from internal or external sources (Drowatzky 1975). Such information, whether it comes from an internal "feeling" about a movement, or an observation made by the teacher, is used to direct or redirect the learner towards his goal. When the learner is informed through a process of continuous feedback, it acts as a positive motivator as well as a strong reinforcer of behavior.

Implications for Physical Education

Feedback is an indispensible aspect of learning any cognitive, affective, or psychomotor skill or concept. Virtually all learning involves some form of internal feedback through the visual, auditory, or kinesthetic senses. The following implications apply more generally to external feedback methods and techniques.

1. Structure the teaching situation to allow time for the learner to practice alone as well as while being observed by the teacher or classmate.
2. When observing and guiding a performer, make sure he has a clear understanding of his goal. Closely related to this point is not to set the goal too high for the performer.
3. Provide guidance or teaching cues while the student is performing a motor skill. Assistance, such as auditory clues or touching (spot belts, etc.) as the performer is executing a movement is a very effective form of feedback.
4. Terminal feedback techniques using videotape or individual photographic sequences should be commonplace in elementary school physical education programs.

Older concepts of teaching methods were based upon the premise that the teacher was the sole authority of what was correct and desirable for children. Children were expected to learn, regardless of their limitations and interests or the inadequacies of the learning situation. Contemporary education has replaced these concepts with principles of learning that are based upon tested thinking and experimentation.

All principles of learning are applicable to physical education. Those stated in this chapter, however, are extremely important for selecting physical activities, choosing appropriate methods, and understanding how motor skills are learned. When these principles are considered in relation to the goals of the physical education program and the characteristics of the learner, the scope and direction of the program and the way it should be taught should become abundantly clear.

Figure 5.3 The learner, not the subject, is the center of the curriculum in an individualized instructional program.

Teaching Strategies

The broad goals of physical education, the characteristics of children, and our knowledge of how and why children learn through the medium of physical activities have significantly changed our approach to teaching. Teaching is no longer considered a simplistic form of cohort instruction (AAHPERD, Personalized Learning, 1976) with the teacher teaching the same material to all children in the same way. Differences in each child's maturation, potential ability, and interests have shifted our teaching strategies towards more individualized and personalized forms of learning.

Individualized Learning

Individualized learning is based on the premise that teaching should be adapted to the unique abilities and special needs of the learner. This places the learner, not the subject, at the center of the curriculum and teaching. It must be understood that a teacher who provides individual assistance to one or more children in a class of thirty or more is applying a technique and is in no way teaching an individualized instructional program.

Individualized learning occurs only when there is a sequential plan for every child, including a diagnosis of the child's potential ability and a teaching prescription to develop that potential. True individualization is possible when there is a ratio of one teacher to one child. However, for groups of two or more children with varying degrees of ability, rarely is a true individualized instructional program ever achieved.

When we use the term *individualized instruction* in physical education, we are really talking about a process that adjusts the learning to the student. Such a program usually takes two approaches. The first is to vary the time it takes the children to achieve a specific movement task. For example, we can ask three children with varying levels of ability to walk across a narrow balance beam, allowing each child to complete the task in his own time. However, when the task is a structured one, and the child does not possess the ability to accomplish it regardless of the time given him, we have a nice example of an exercise in futility.

The second approach is to vary the task, and, if necessary, the time. Allowing each child to cross the length of the balance beam in any way possible would be varying the task. If a teacher can vary the task, she has a very real possibility of providing an individualized program.

Personalized Learning

Personalized learning is a version of individualized learning in which the student's involvement with others in the learning environment is used or emphasized. This may involve the learner in a guider-learner relationship with the teacher, or it may involve learner with learner in a shared experience characterized by mutual trust and respect. Personalizing the learning process enhances the dignity and self-image of each child and creates a learning atmosphere that increases the efficiency of learning by each child.

Primary and intermediate teachers can individualize and personalize their teaching in several ways. The following two approaches allow the task to be varied and provide a learning environment that encourages children to share their ideas and creative talents. These approaches also allow each child to progress at his own rate and level of ability, to feel at ease, and to experience success with the task at hand.

Movement Education

Movement education meets the criteria for individualized learning in two fundamental ways. First, there are no standardized skills. Rather, four categories of movement describe what the body is capable of doing, how the body can move, where it can move, and its relationship to apparatus or other performers. Each child attempts to answer a movement challenge according to his ability and interest. Second, each child can vary the task in an infinite number of ways, and the teacher can vary the time it takes to complete the task. This approach was introduced in chapter 4 and is applied in a sequential way in part 6, "Gymnastic and Movement Activities." A further application is also found in chapter 30, "Creative Dance Activities."

Inventive Games

The inventive games approach, introduced in part 5 (p. 215) is an effective way of individualizing the teaching of individual and group games. By changing

Figure 5.4 The teacher's genuine enthusiasm for the value of physical education is the most critical factor in making physical education a true educational experience.

the number of players, playing space, rules, skills, and equipment, the task is automatically varied. The inventive, or creative, games approach is incorporated into each chapter of part 5.

Qualities of Good Teaching

The general qualities of "good" teaching have been presented by numerous authorities and apply to physical education as well as any other subject. It is the writer's personal feeling that genuine enthusiasm by the teacher for the value of physical education is the most critical factor in making this subject a true educational experience.

There are many other desirable and sometimes necessary characteristics for teaching physical education. Although the following list is incomplete, if a teacher possesses these qualities, there is more than a reasonable chance that the physical education period will be enjoyable and educational.

1. A teacher should want to acquire more competence in teaching physical education.

Classroom teachers are normally required to take one or two professional courses in physical education. This, of course, is inadequate preparation for teaching all the areas of this subject, so it is necessary for teachers to gain new skills and insights through additional courses, texts, films, and other in-service media. Probably of equal importance is that the teacher "have the courage to be imperfect and enjoy it." No teacher can be an expert in every subject. What is more

Direct Method	Limitation Method	Indirect Method

←———— Toward teacher control — — — — — — — — — Toward student choice ————→
of movement and use of   of movement and use of
equipment or apparatus   equipment or apparatus

important is the courage to try new ideas and teaching methods, however insecure one might feel. A child's attitude toward a teacher is not based entirely on the teacher's overall competence; it is based on the very simple premise that the child and the teacher are jointly engaged in the search for knowledge and understanding. It is, in essence, a mutual respect for each other's abilities and efforts. When children know the teacher is trying something new for their benefit, they, in turn, will respond in a mature and understanding way.

2. A teacher should possess a sense of humor.

Teaching is very hard work, but it is also a very rewarding profession. The ability to laugh at one's own inadequacies and "gentle" errors is vitally important for the maintenance of sanity and perspective in the day-to-day task of teaching. This is particularly important to classroom teachers who work long hours in confined quarters with children who are extremely demanding of one's patience and understanding.

3. A teacher should possess an optimum level of health.

Teachers obviously need to maintain good physical and mental health. Otherwise, the pressure of teaching becomes too demanding, with serious consequences to both teacher and student. Because physical education is physically demanding, a teacher who lacks strength and stamina will tend to neglect this area of the curriculum, with a loss to both the teacher and the class. New teaching methods do not require a high level of motor skill on the part of the teacher. They do, however, require physical effort and enthusiasm.

Methods of Teaching

An *approach to teaching* can be defined as a comprehensive way of utilizing content and method. For example, a *teacher-directed* approach emphasizes the direct method of instruction (described in this section); but also includes other methods and a unique arrangement and emphasis of content. Similarly, such terms as *individualized, student-oriented, movement exploration,* and *movement education* refer to approaches because they, too, involve a unique arrangement of content and special use of one or more instructional methods and techniques.

A *method,* as distinguished from an approach or technique, is a general way of guiding and controlling learning experiences. There are, in turn, various ways of classifying methods, such as *lecture, tutorial,* or *problem solving.* And each of these can be subdivided into more specific methods.

Attempting to distinquish between an *approach* and a *method,* however, often leads to confusion rather than clarification. Recognizing the limitations of any definition, then, the following classification, based upon the amount of freedom or choice given to students in a particular learning task, will provide a basis for understanding and applying one or more "methods" of instruction.

Direct Method

A teaching method is direct when the choice of the activity and how it is to be performed are entirely the teacher's (Bilborough and Jones 1969). The teacher arranges the class in lines or a circle, chooses the activity, such as practicing a basketball chest pass, and prescribes how and where each child will practice the movement. Use of the direct method is illustrated here in teaching the forward roll (fig. 5.6).

1. *Class Organization:* The class is scattered or arranged in parallel lines facing a mat, with each child working within his own area. The essential aspect is that all children watch a demonstration and then practice the skill.
2. *Choice of Activity:* In this example, the children are restricted to practicing the forward roll. The choice is the teacher's.

Student participation in choosing the activity and how it should be practiced is limited in the direct method. However, it is the most effective and efficient way, for example, to teach a specific movement skill, safety procedure, or the rules of a game. And when the general level of skill is low, such as for heading in soccer or performing a headstand in gymnastics, the direct method is appropriate for illustrating, clarifying, and practicing various aspects of a skill or movement. In addition, this method can be used to regain control and direction when class discipline is low.

Figure 5.5 How methods are applied when teaching content determines the approach to teaching.

Figure 5.6 Teaching the forward roll is a direct method because the choice of the activity and how it is performed is controlled by the teacher.

Figure 5.7 Limitation Method. Can you balance on three parts of your body?

Limitation Method

The limitation method is actually a compromise between the direct and indirect methods of instruction. The choice of the activity or how it is performed is limited by the teacher in some way. For example, when teaching a forward roll, the teacher might limit the performance by indicating that the forward roll be practiced on the floor or on mats. But by posing a challenge, such as "practice the forward roll and see how many variations in leg positions you can make," some freedom of interpretation is provided. This freedom is a basic characteristic of the limitation method. Figure 5.7 illustrates this freedom of interpretation as the children answer another challenge.

Since the limitation method possesses the best aspects of both the direct and indirect methods, it has the greatest application and value in virtually all areas of the physical education program. For example, when teaching dance, a primary teacher might use the direct method initially to teach a skip or gallop step. Once the step has been learned, the limitation method may be applied by providing musical accompaniment and allowing the children to move in any direction to create individual or dual patterns. The single limitation might be that the children use a skip movement.

A few of the more obvious advantages of this method follow:

1. It allows the teacher to give some direction without restricting the free or creative expressions of the children;
2. It allows for physical differences and varying interests of the children;
3. Through a careful choice of activities, it allows the teacher to develop all aspects of movement rather than what might become a "one-sided" development if left solely to each child;
4. Analysis and correction of movements by the teacher is simplified because one type of movement is to be practiced.

One problem that virtually all teachers must overcome when using the limitation method is being able to shift from *directing* children to perform a movement to *guiding* them through suggestions and challenging questions. Although each teacher develops her own style of asking questions, the following phrases and words have proved quite successful:

Can you make a . . . ?
Can you discover a new . . . ?
Can you add to this by . . . ?
Can you find another way of . . . ?
Can you add a different way to . . . ?
Can you vary your . . . ?
Can you improve on the . . . ?
Could you move from . . . ?
Could you shift . . . ?
Could you change . . . ?
Try to add on to . . . .
Try to vary . . . .
How many different ways . . . ?
Are you able to . . . ?
See if you can . . . .
Attempt to do . . . .
Is it possible to . . . ?
Discover a new way to . . . .

Avoid the words "I want you to do. . . ." The key words should stimulate a creative interpretation of a task or challenge. Once you have posed the question, it is usually necessary to give some command to start. Probably the most common, and informal, beginning is "off" or "away you go." Children react extremely well to this type of comment. Other expressions are "and begin" or "start."

Indirect Method

The indirect method allows children, individually or collectively, to choose the activity and decide how they wish to use their time. Obviously, guidelines must be given to younger, unskilled children. To allow six- or seven-year-olds complete freedom of choice in a well-equipped gymnasium without prior instruction in skill and safety would be unfair to students and teacher.

However, when children have been taught a basic movement "vocabulary," as well as to progress according to their own ability, the indirect method has value. Once children have developed the ability to work independently and have respect for the safety and interests of other children, they should be given freedom to develop leadership, creative movements, and group cooperation without the direct assistance of the teacher. The indirect method can thus be used in game, dance, and gymnastic activities to develop and foster these skills and characteristics.

The direct, limitation, and indirect methods of instruction should not be considered separate entities, even within a single lesson. The selection and emphasis of any method should depend upon how a particular movement skill or understanding can best be learned by the children. Also to be considered are the teacher's philosophy and ability, the facilities, and the ability grouping of students.

Techniques of Teaching

A *method* has been defined as a general way of guiding and controlling the learning experiences of children. A *technique,* in a restricted sense, is a small part of a method. For example, a demonstration by the teacher of a throwing or kicking skill is clearly a part of the direct teaching method. A carefully worded question or a unique movement challenge is one technique of the limitation method.

Other types of techniques, such as variations in voice inflections, ways of using equipment and apparatus, and unique applications of audiovisual materials do not belong to any particular method but are used in varying ways and degrees by each teacher. The emphasis the teacher gives to such techniques produces her "style" of teaching. Hence, there is no set number of techniques that one must master to be an effective teacher. It takes the teacher years to develop her style of teaching, and she retains or discards each technique on the basis of its efficiency in the learning process.

Creating an Effective Learning Atmosphere

The atmosphere for a physical education lesson should be the same as for any other classroom situation—a setting where all children are actively engaged in learning skills with the teacher assuming the role of guider or helper. The atmosphere should be friendly with a minimum amount of noise. Children should be able to work in the gymnasium and hear the teacher's voice at any time. A teacher who consistently has to raise her voice to be heard will find she is competing with, rather than controlling, the noise of her class.

Because classroom teachers in most elementary schools are responsible for their own physical education programs, they rarely have time to change clothes for gym period, except for tennis shoes. In fact, it is no longer considered vitally important anyway. "Spotting" by the teacher is used to a limited degree, since each child is taught to progress at his own rate and to be concerned with his own and others' safety. And, although teachers can demonstrate skills, it is preferable from both practical and educational points of view for children (who normally possess greater skill than the classroom teacher) to demonstrate. Of course, teachers who wish to change into gym clothes may do so, particularly if they are assigned to physical education for a large percentage of their time.

Teaching Motor Skills

Motor skills can be taught in many ways, but the best technique is usually the one that works. To learn any skill a child must have the inherent ability, a clear understanding of the movements involved, a reason for learning it, and an opportunity to repeat the skill until it is learned. Generally speaking, a skill is learned through a process of explaining, demonstrating, discovering, and perfecting. But this in no way indicates a simple progression from demonstration of a skill to practice and analysis; each child acquires a skill in his own way. However, to help children learn *standardized* skills, which are those that are performed in much the same way by all children, we usually follow a pattern—explaining and demonstrating, then allowing time for individual practice and analysis.

Following are basic suggestions to assist the teacher in developing her own effective techniques:

1. Arrange the class so that every student has a clear view of the demonstration. Eliminate unnecessary interference, such as equipment, poor lighting, and excessive noise.
2. Explain the skill clearly and concisely. Allow time for the class to digest each important part of the skill.
3. Pause repeatedly during the explanation and check to see if the class understands; when necesssary, repeat parts of the demonstration.
4. Use vocabulary that is appropriate for the group.
5. Provide an accurate demonstration of the skill. If you cannot demonstrate it, use a pupil or visual aids.
6. Demonstrate the skill at a slower speed than it is normally performed.
7. Repeat the demonstration several times, including explanations of one or more key parts.
8. Keep the demonstration short and to the point.
9. Be patient and sympathetic; a child acquires skills according to his own readiness and capacity.
10. If a child is not learning a skill in its entirety, break it down into simpler parts.
11. Give encouragement and praise, rather than scorn and punishment, regardless of how small or large the task.

Figure 5.8 The period of time before the lesson begins should be used constructively.

Effective Class Organization

Once a teacher has decided upon the basic approach and methods she will stress in her program, several important teaching patterns and formations will assist her in creating an informal and efficient learning environment.

Use of Time before a Lesson Starts

Normally children change into physical education uniforms, or at least into tennis shoes, and begin the lesson when everyone is present. The following procedure has been adopted in numerous schools and has proved to be extremely effective in utilizing the time before the lesson officially begins. Although the type of activity and the time available vary from class to class, this procedure can be applied to every physical education lesson, whether in the gymnasium or on the playing field.

Procedure

Each child should constructively use the free time before the lesson begins. Thus, simply provide children who enter the gymnasium or go out on the playing field early an opportunity to practice any skill or movement pattern while waiting for the lesson to begin.

The procedure varies slightly depending upon the type of instructional unit, of course. In a game-type lesson, a variety of balls are made available when the children enter the instructional area. A few instructions are given, such as "practice bouncing and catching by yourself or with a partner as soon as you come into the gymnasium." In a gymnastic unit, place a variety of small equipment—hoops, beanbags, skipping ropes—are placed on the floor. As the children enter the gymnasium, they are instructed to choose equipment and practice any skill they learned in the previous lesson or to explore any movement they want. Practice with large apparatus, such as climbing ropes, vaulting box, or springboard, should be avoided during the free practice time. Free practice activities prior to a dance lesson could involve ball or other small equipment activities, rather than practice of a specific dance step or movement pattern.

This procedure cannot be initiated however until the class as a whole has demonstrated its understanding and ability to work independently without the teacher determining the skill to practice. Primary children who have not been taught with a teacher-directed type of program usually adapt to this procedure within a few lessons. But older children who are accustomed to moving from a well-established squad or line formation only when permitted to do so by the teacher may have difficulty adjusting to such a procedure. The time and patience required by the teacher to institute constructive free time will be worth it in the long run.

The following suggestions show how this procedure can be used effectively even in the first few lessons. After the children have been instructed how and where to change their clothing, use one or more of these ideas while they are changing:

1. *Balls:* Tell the children that as soon as they have changed they may choose a ball and practice bouncing it (or throwing and catching it, jumping over it, or playing catch with a partner).
2. *Beanbags:* Same as above.
3. *Hoop:* Place on the floor and practice jumping over it, jumping in and out of it, or hopping around it.
4. *Skills:* As skills are taught, indicate one or two that can be practiced during this free practice time.

Since children in the intermediate grades have acquired many gymnastic skills, you need only to require that the children practice one or more of them as they enter the gymnasium. Some examples are:

1. *Balance Stunts:* Practice a handstand, cartwheel, one-foot balance, and so on.
2. *Balls:* Require bouncing and change of direction (bounce, throw into air, and make a full turn of body before bouncing again).
3. *Partners:* Do not suggest free practice with partners until the class has demonstrated its ability to work independently in this type of atmosphere.

Individualized Teaching Patterns

The following two individualized teaching patterns allow the teacher to set challenges to meet the level of ability and interest of each member of the class. Task or challenge cards are extremely helpful to beginning teachers since they can be prepared prior to each lesson. Further, once the class is working on their tasks, the teacher can move about the instructional area providing assistance and encouragement where needed. The second teaching pattern, known as station work, not only allows for a variety of individualized teaching patterns but, in addition, is an effective method of using all available equipment.

Task or Challenge Cards

Task or challenge cards are an enjoyable way of individualizing games, dance, and gymnastic activities. The value of this technique is that the teacher can prepare a series of tasks, varying from simple to complex movement challenges, to adapt to the differences in ability that exist within a class of thirty or more. The examples provided illustrate how this technique can be applied to game, dance, and gymnastic activities.

Several examples of the application of tasks or challenges are found in later chapters. Refer specifically to chapters 26 and 27 for additional ideas.

Station Work

Station work is the establishment of a number of practice areas within the available instructional space. Students work at one assigned area for a set period of time, then rotate to the next station. Five or six children are assigned to a station for a few minutes to practice the preassigned skill, as shown in the diagram. When the whistle blows, each group rotates clockwise to the next station. This basic form of station work can be used to teach all game, rhythmic, and gymnastic activities. It is also particularly useful in developing physical fitness stations in the gymnasium or out-of-doors. Station work can also be combined with task cards. Combining these two teaching patterns is an excellent way to individualize the tasks for each child and provides valuable time for the teacher to move freely to stations where special help or praise may be needed.

Teaching Formations

Basic formations for organizing physical education activities are the *line, circle,* and *shuttle.* These patterns, shown in table 5.1, are used to divide classes into smaller groups for relays, team games, and drill exercises. Once learned, the patterns can be formed quickly and in an orderly manner at a simple command by the teacher. They save valuable practice and play time, eliminate confusion, and minimize the potential for accidents.

Challenge Cards

Inventive Games
(Partner Activities)
Make up a game with your partner that
includes one ball, a bounce, and a catch.

Gymnastics
(Individual Sequences)
Make up a sequence that includes a stretch, a
curl, and a change of direction.

Dance
(Rhythmic Activities: Group Work)
In your group of four, develop a routine that
includes clapping, walking, hopping, and two
changes in direction. (Music: ''Pluma Blanca'')

In many cases, the selection of a formation is determined by the activity itself. Running and tag games require a specific formation, and many folk dances begin with the children in a circle or line. Activities such as warm-up exercises, apparatus activities, and low-organization games can be performed from a variety of formations. However, two basic principles should be applied when selecting a formation. First, each squad should be aligned so that all members can see the performer. Second, the activities of one squad should not interfere with those of another.

Grouping Procedures

Grouping children in physical education classes is done by arranging them in squads according to their age, height, ability, or some other criterion. The type of grouping technique a teacher selects depends upon the activity and the performance levels of her class. For example, a third-grade teacher who wishes to organize her class into four teams for a relay could (1) arrange them into groups of two boys and two girls, (2) number the children from one to four, or (3) have four captains choose their own teams. Since the latter is a common method for organizing equal teams, as well as fostering leadership and team loyalty, it is explained here in detail.

The teacher or the class selects four captains. To preclude favoritism, sex preferences, and emotional-social problems stemming from the order in which children are selected, the captains should meet with the teacher away from the class to select teams in private.

Station Work

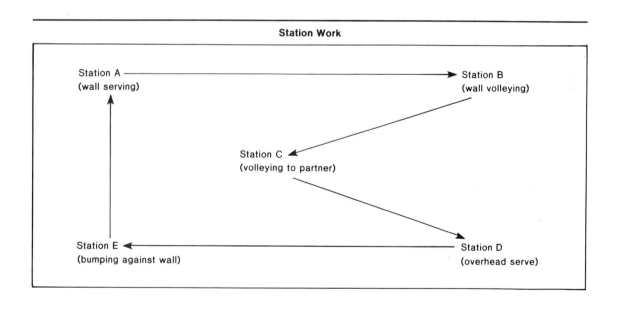

Table 5.1 Basic Formations

Formation	Explanation	Uses
Circle X X X X X X X X X X	Children may form a circle by following the teacher as she walks around in a circle. Other methods include all joining hands and forming a circle, or having the class take positions on a circle printed on the floor or play area.	Simple games Warm-up exercises Circle relays Teaching simple stunts Teaching basic dance steps Teaching throwing and kicking skills Marching Mimetics
Line X X X Ⓧ Teacher or Leader X X	Place one child for each line desired equidistant apart, then signal the class to line up behind these children. The first child in each line may move out in front of his line or shift to the side as illustrated.	Relays Simple games Marching Teaching stunts on floor or mats Roll taking Teaching basic skills

Fan
  X
 X
X
X   Ⓧ Teacher or Leader
X
 X
  X
	The fan formation is used for small group activities. Arrange children in a line facing their leader, then have them join hands and form a half-circle.	Throwing and kicking drills
		Relays
		Mimetics
		Simple floor stunts
		Teaching dance skills

Shuttle 1 X 6 X 4 X 3 X 5 X 2 X	Arrange children in two, three, or more equal lines, then separate lines the distance required for the activity. Player 1 performs his skill, then shifts to the rear of the opposite line; player 2 performs and shifts to the rear of the opposite line, etc.	Throwing and kicking drills Relays Tumbling activities from opposite ends of mat Activities requiring close observation by teacher
Zigzag 1 X → X 2 3 X → X 4 5 X → X 6	Arrange class or squads into two equal lines, with partners facing each other. Player 1 passes to 2, 2 passes to 3, 3 passes to 4, until the last player is reached.	Throwing, catching, and kicking skills

Scattered
  X
X   X
  X
X   X
  X
X   X
  X
  X
	Allow children to find a spot in the play area. Have each child reach out with his arms to see if he can touch another person. Require the children who can touch others to shift until they are free of obstructions.	Warm-up exercises
		Mimetics
		Tag games
		Simple floor stunts
		Creative activities

Table 5.2 Order of Team Selection by Captains

Round No.	Squad Leaders			
	A	B	C	D
1	1st Choice	2nd Choice	3rd Choice	4th Choice
2	8th Choice	7th Choice	6th Choice	5th Choice
3	9th Choice	10th Choice	11th Choice	12th Choice
4	16th Choice	15th Choice	14th Choice	13th Choice
5	17th Choice	etc.		

As illustrated in table 5.2, squad leader A is awarded first choice; B, second; C, third; and D, fourth. At this point, tell each squad leader that if his first choice is a boy, the next choice must be a girl; alternate boy and girl until the last member is chosen. Let us assume captain D selected a boy in round one, and that captain D also has the next selection, which must be a girl.

Other methods of organizing children into squads should be used throughout the year to provide opportunities for children to work with different groups, as both leaders and followers. The method chosen will depend upon the activity, the space, and the age of the children. Following are some methods:

1. Skill tests or observation of skill ability.
2. Numbering off in twos, fives, or whatever other number of teams is desired.
3. Arranging the class in a circle, then dividing it into the desired number of squads.
4. Selecting teams on the basis of birth dates.
   For example:
   Team 1: Children born between January and March
   Team 2: Children born between April and June
   Team 3: Children born between July and September
   Team 4: Children born between October and December
5. Administering a classification test such as McCloy's Index, which places the heavier and older children in one group and the lighter and younger children in another group. The formula, 10 times age plus weight, may be used for ages fifteen and below.

Once children can effectively move into squads (or teams, groups, section places, or units), such groupings can be highly profitable to both the students and the teacher. From the teacher's point of view, the children can be organized quickly according to a particular criterion selected either by the teacher or jointly with the class.

The duties of the elected or assigned leader should include the following:

1. Maintaining order and general control of the squad.
2. Checking routine procedures such as attendance, uniforms, and tardiness.
3. Assisting the teacher in daily planning and lesson organizing.
4. Setting an example of leadership.

The inherent value of squads from a purely organizational standpoint cannot be overemphasized. However, maximum opportunity should be provided so that every child can experience a leadership role. While some students develop leadership ability in the early primary grades, others need encouragement and subtly planned experiences as leaders. Consequently, squad leaders should be selected on a temporary basis so that each child can test his ability as a squad captain. There will always be moments of frustration when young children are given leadership roles, therefore both teachers and children must develop tolerance, understanding, and patience.

Routine Procedures

The success of any physical education program depends to a large extent upon the simple routine procedures a class follows in going to, participating in, and returning from a physical education activity. Primary teachers usually are not confronted with the problems of showering; however, they are concerned with problems relating to changing clothes, class excuses, and class control. At the intermediate level, the teacher must solve problems of changing clothes, showering, and individual excuses.

Physical Education Apparel
Elementary school children usually are not required to wear special uniforms for physical education. The time required to change in relation to the time available,

particularly for five-, six-, and seven-year-olds, does not justify a complete change. However, tennis shoes should be worn for games and some dance activities. For gymnastic activities, the teacher should seriously consider letting the children participate in bare feet if the floor is clean and free of hazards. Bare feet assist in balancing activities and encourage freedom of movement. However, this should be a gradual process to allow the children to get used to running, balancing, jumping, and landing on their bare feet. If the children enjoy participating in gymnastic activities with bare feet and there are no adverse effects (plantar warts or excessive bruising), continue the practice. Students should not be allowed to participate in physical activities wearing only socks. Socks are very slippery on the floor or approaches and may lead to accidents or unnecessary injuries.

Roll Call

Since physical education periods are usually all too short anyway, don't lose time in the routine procedure of checking attendance. In most cases, roll call is not necessary in the primary grades. And the classroom teacher, regardless of grade, who is responsible for her own physical education program will know if any child is absent. However, when the use of specialist teachers or team teaching requires a roll-call procedure, the following methods can be used:

1. A line formation based upon alphabetical list in the roll book.
2. Line formation based upon the tallest to the shortest child, with each child assigned a number.
3. Squads, with one member assigned to take roll.

Class Excuses

Excuses for physical education range from permanent waivers because of chronic health conditions to temporary waivers because of colds or other illnesses. It is imperative that the principal, the school nurse, and the teacher establish policies covering problems encountered in this area. The following situations should be included in the policies:

1. A temporary excuse should be authorized by the school nurse.
2. The school nurse should authorize children to return to physical activity after any illness.
3. Children with physical handicaps should be encouraged to participate in physical education classes. The amount and type of participation, of course, should be indicated by the parents and/ or family physician.
4. On the recommendation of the teacher, a child may be excused from participation in a physical education class because of a detectable illness or injury.

6 Organizing for Physical Education

The quality of any physical education program depends primarily on the interest and competence of the teacher, and the time and facilities available. Although these components vary from school to school, some organizational problems are common to all schools. This chapter discusses the effective use of teachers in the physical education program and problems concerning equipment, supplies, and the safety of the instructional area.

Responsibility for Teaching Physical Education

Several methods are used in assigning the responsibility for teaching physical education. The most ideal method is for each school to employ a trained physical education specialist to teach and supervise phases of the physical education program. Another is to employ rotating specialists or consultants to assist classroom teachers in such areas as program development, equipment and facility planning, and general instruction. The third and most common approach is to assign all responsibility for physical education to the classroom teacher. Paraprofessional assistance through paid teaching assistants, volunteer parents, and student leadership programs are also support programs that are currently in operation in many school districts. The various advantages and disadvantages of each method are discussed under the following headings.

Full-Time Physical Education Specialist

Opinions vary with respect to how a full-time physical education specialist should be used in an elementary school. Several school districts throughout the United States and Canada hire full-time physical education specialists. Initially, these specialists were assigned to teach the intermediate grades with the primary programs left to the classroom teachers. Contemporary research showing the contributions of physical education to academic, physical, and neuromuscular development (Albinson and Andrews 1976) has changed the priority of this teaching assignment. Now, a specialist hired to teach physical education will normally teach all grades in the elementary school.

When physical education specialists have been assigned to elementary schools as full-time teachers, the quality of the program significantly improves. However, several problems arise. First, the health of the physical education specialist must be considered. Teaching young children physical education is an enjoyable and immensely satisfying profession. It is also physically and psychologically demanding on the men and women who must teach all instructional classes and normally supervise the intramural and interschool programs. When these specialists become ill, the whole program virtually comes to a standstill. Principals have also voiced another concern, which is simply that their specialists become isolated from the rest of the staff. Such isolation is due to the nature of the workload as well as the classroom teacher's lack of understanding physical education, and the physical education teacher's lack of understanding academic subject areas. The solution to this problem would seem to be a compromise: allow the physical education specialist to teach physical education approximately half of the time and spend the remaining time as a classroom teacher. This divided workload keeps the physical education teacher in the mainstream of the total school program and allows the teacher to use her special talent—as a teacher and as a resource specialist to other teachers. It also provides the physical education specialist an opportunity to work with the same children in the classroom and the gymnasium.

Consulting Physical Education Specialist

Because of the increased demands on the classroom teacher in all areas of the curriculum, administrators have attempted to alleviate their teaching load by employing consultants or teaching specialists. This is particularly the case in larger school systems, where music, speech, and physical education specialists provide classroom teachers with up-to-date materials, methods, and techniques, and conduct classroom demonstrations and in-service sessions. The responsibility for these subject areas, however, still rests with the classroom teacher.

A classic example of how a teaching specialist is used in a large school is the Blair Elementary School near Spokane, Washington. This is the largest elementary school in the state of Washington with nearly twelve hundred students from kindergarten through grade eight. Recognizing the need for qualified physical education instructors, the administration hired a teaching specialist to assist classroom teachers.

Figure 6.1 Teaching young children physical education is an enjoyable and immensely satisfying profession; it is also physically and psychologically demanding.

Since it was virtually impossible for the specialist to meet with every teacher on a daily basis, a modified approach was taken. During the first three months of the school year, the specialist and each teacher developed instruction units and daily lesson plans. This procedure gave the specialist an opportunity to evaluate the teacher's ability to use her physical education guide, as well as her general competence in handling the physical education program. At the end of the three-month experimental period, a policy was established by the school administration requiring any teacher needing help to submit a lesson plan three days before the lesson. This not only motivated the teacher to develop lesson plans, but it also assisted the specialist in his own preparation for the classroom teacher. Within several months the specialist was able to put many teachers "on their own."

Generally speaking, the mutually developed program provided the assistance the teachers needed to develop their own programs. With additional "free" time, the specialist was able to enrich the program by providing in-service sessions for specific grades in such activities as basketball skills, gymnastics, and track and field activities.

Self-Contained Classroom Teacher

Although administrators and teachers alike recognize the need for physical education specialists, the fact remains that elementary schools are predominantly self-contained, meaning that a classroom teacher, regardless of grade level, must be able to teach as many as eight or nine subjects. The majority of classroom teachers have had approximately one general course in physical education during college. Obviously, this preparation is inadequate, indicating a definite need for in-service workshops, better teaching guides, additional audiovisual aids, and summer school courses. These should provide assistance in content, organization, methods, and evaluative devices for all levels in the elementary school.

To say the current situation is hopeless or to consider physical education as a period of free play does disservice to both the intelligence of the classroom teacher and the needs of growing children. Research, educational philosophy, and automation in its broadest meaning indicate the need for a daily physical education program. The program must include a variety of activities to enhance normal growth and development and to provide opportunities that will foster emotional growth, social adjustment, and permanent leisure-time pursuits.

Many school districts, large and small alike, have attempted to provide physical education programs without the assistance of physical education specialists. In Holt, Michigan, for example, the school board had no official physical education policy in its four elementary schools, yet a program was initiated. According to the director of elementary education, teachers were encouraged to attend workshops, summer sessions, and other in-service sessions. Their efforts led to the writing of a guide for kindergarten through grade six that covered physical education, health, and safety. Since most schools in the district were equipped with all-purpose rooms, each teacher was scheduled for one forty-five minute physical education period each week in such a facility. In addition, all teachers could devote thirty minutes a day to classroom or outdoor activities. As a follow-up, the administration hired adults to supervise noon-hour activities on the playing field and indoors during inclement weather.

Team Teaching

Team teaching is the organization of teachers and students into instructional groups that permit maximum utilization of staff abilities and enhance optimum growth of students. Team teaching may range from two teachers exchanging classrooms for one subject to the pooling of all teachers into a unified effort. The latter may involve regrouping of children, major curriculum changes, and extensive use of outside experts. Obviously, some form of team effort in handling physical education in the elementary school is worthy of consideration. The self-contained classroom structure, particularly for the intermediate grades, is not flexible enough to permit or encourage utilization of the special abilities of all teachers.

Since there are many forms of team teaching, it is difficult to present a list of advantages that apply to every situation. However, it can be said that even the simplest form of team teaching provides the following:

1. A means whereby the most effective use of teacher skill and talent is utilized;
2. More complete and detailed lesson preparation and presentation;
3. An opportunity for students to be exposed to a larger number of capable teachers;
4. An opportunity for more flexible grouping of students;
5. A means of in-service experiences for all teachers;
6. An opportunity for teachers to investigate the effectiveness of new methods, materials, and techniques;
7. An opportunity for teachers to experience greater personal and professional satisfaction.

The simplest form of team teaching is for teachers to exchange classes for an assigned subject. When facilities are limited, such as one gymnasium, and when two or more teachers are willing to share their talents, team teaching can be established. For example, a fourth-grade teacher who is extremely qualified in music may exchange classrooms with a fifth-grade teacher who is equally competent in physical education. In this situation, both the teachers and the students benefit.

Another type of team teaching is two or more teachers pooling their talents to instruct several classes in one subject area. Applied to physical education, this would mean dividing two or more classrooms into groups based upon such criteria as skill performance or physical fitness levels, or a classification index based upon age, height, and weight.

The writer studied such a program in the Eastern Elementary School near San Juan, California. The school was experimenting with this type of team teaching in physical education, using a classification index as a means of grouping children from grades three to six. Four teachers formed the instructional staff for the team approach. In their planning sessions, it was found that one teacher was strong in gymnastics, one in dance, and one in track and field. The fourth teacher, not too strong in any area, was assigned games as an area of emphasis. Since the climate permitted outdoor activities virtually year-round, and since the playground area had sufficient teaching stations, a half-hour in the afternoon was set aside for physical education for grades three through six. The children were assigned to one of four groups based upon the classification index.

A three-week instructional schedule for the four groups was then established. The gymnastics teacher was assigned group one for a three-week block of stunts and tumbling activities in the gymnasium. Each of the other teachers was assigned one of the remaining groups for a similar period. At the end of the three-week period, each student group rotated to a different instructor, who taught her specialty to the new group.

This type of team effort encourages the teacher to develop more detailed lesson plans. Throughout the rotation system, better understanding of student performance was obtained, as well as a greater effort by the equated groups of students. With a limited area of preparation, each teacher found time to experiment with new methods and techniques of learning. And because of the equalizing classification system, students could compete realistically for the same goals, thus deriving more satisfaction and enjoyment in physical activities.

Paraprofessional Activities

The term *paraprofessional* includes a wide variety of voluntary or paid assistants who have special qualifications but do not normally possess a teaching certificate. A few of the more common types of paraprofessionals used in the elementary school physical education program are described in the following paragraphs.

Teaching Assistants

Each state and local school district varies with respect to the certification requirements and the types of duties that can legally be assigned to a teaching assistant. Normally, a teaching assistant has completed a special program in a community college and may be assigned to assist regular teachers or supervise recess, noon hour, and intramural activities. This type of teaching assistance and supervisory help has been very popular in virtually all school districts that have hired these paraprofessionals.

Contracted Recreation Specialists

During the past ten years, the trend towards contracting local recreational specialists in such activities as swimming, skiing, and skating has grown in a number of geographical areas. Perhaps the most popular program has been with local YMCA or recreational centers to teach a basic or survival swimming program to a particular grade. In most cases these specialists have a similar philosophy and instructional approach to teaching young children. These factors should, however, be checked before entering into a contractual agreement with any nonschool agency.

Figure 6.2 Recreational specialists oftentimes have a similar philosophy and instructional approach to teaching young children.

Volunteer Assistance Programs

Under the umbrella term of *volunteer assistance* is a large number of interested and talented parents and neighbors who willingly donate their time and talent to the elementary school physical education program. For example, in the city of Nanaimo on Vancouver Island, over seven hundred parents have volunteered their time to help teach, supervise, and administer physical fitness tests. Special in-service sessions are given to these volunteers to prepare them for specific tasks within each school program. This program has been in operation for several years and has not only enhanced the quality of the physical education offerings but, in addition, has created a positive relationship between parents and school officials.

Student Assistance

Two types of student assistance programs appear to be emerging in a large number of school districts. The first utilizes high school students to assist classroom teachers in the regular instructional program or as supervisors and assistant coaches in the extraclass program. Many teenagers who have worked in this program have received excellent recommendations from principals, teachers, and parents. This early practical experience has also proven a positive method of recruiting mature, talented, and enthusiastic young men and women into the teaching profession.

The second type of student assistance program uses upper grade students to help classroom teachers and to

Figure 6.3 A special rapport between older and primary grade children makes student assistance an asset in the regular instructional program.

act as coaches, managers, and referees in the intramural program. Studies of these programs seem to indicate that older children work exceptionally well with kindergarten and first-grade children. The writer's observation of these programs would agree. Fifth and sixth graders who are not always the most highly skilled but enjoy working with primary children can develop a strong rapport with young children. In numerous cases the younger children, through this program, develop motor skills as well as demontrate a very positive self-image and a respect and appreciation towards their older "idols." It is a program that should be encouraged in virtually every elementary school.

Organizational Details

Once the physical education program has been designed and teaching responsibilities have been assigned to the teaching staff, a number of other important organizational details must be completed. Policies and procedures should be established for the following areas before any instructional program begins.

Class Size and Composition

Prior to the enactment of Title IX of the Education Amendments Act of 1972, elementary school physical education classes were normally scheduled in two ways.

Primary classes were almost exclusively coeducational and, of course, taught by the classroom teacher. Intermediate classes, however, were either segregated into boys and girls classes or taught on a coeducational basis. Regulations within Title IX have created coeducational physical education in all grades. And, P.L. 94-142 has added many atypical children to each physical education class. While there is unquestionable value in both laws, there is also major implications to class size. On the basis of these imposed changes, class size in physical education should never exceed the regular number of children within each respective classroom. Assigning two classes to one physical education class is educationally unsound and may create an extremely unsafe teaching environment. Also, if two or more severely handicapped children are enrolled in a physical education class, extra assistance is warranted.

Time Allotment

The recommended amount of time for physical education varies from a minimum of 20 minutes to one hour per day. The most common figure is 150 minutes per week, which translates into daily 30-minute classes. Within the intermediate grades, the 150 minutes may be arranged into three 50-minute classes per week to provide for showering and longer periods of instruction. However, the 150 minutes per week does not include recess, supervised free play or other intramural or interschool activities.

Scheduling

The problems of scheduling physical education vary from school to school. If the principal and staff are cooperative, it is wise to schedule all physical education classes first. This is not favoritism; it simply permits the most appropriate scheduling of a limited number of physical education facilities. Whenever limited facilities exist for the number of classes, equal access should be given to primary and intermediate classes. In previous years, intermediate classes were normally scheduled into the gymnasium first, leaving the remaining time to primary classes. This also included specialist help if it was available. Today all classes, regardless of grade level, must be given equal access to facilities and specialist assistance.

With respect to whether a class should be scheduled for the first or last period of the instructional day, there is no evidence to support one or the other time periods. If personal preferences can be accommodated within the schedule, the principal should receive this information before classes are scheduled. When several teachers request the same time slot, provisions should be made to rotate their time schedules throughout the school year.

Responsibility for the Welfare and Safety of Students

In virtually every school situation the teacher acts *in loco parentis,* in place of the parent. Whether in the classroom, on the playground, or on a class trip, the teacher is responsible for the students' welfare and safety. The teacher of physical activities must plan and supervise in ways that are not negligent. Since teachers can be held legally liable for acts of negligence, an understanding of this problem and its implication for the physical education program is extremely important.

Negligence

The National Education Association has defined negligence as any act—or its absence—that falls below the standard established by law for the protection of others against unreasonable risk or harm. Negligence, therefore, may be (1) an act that a reasonable person would have realized involved an unreasonable risk of injury to others or (2) failure to do an act that is necessary for the protection or assistance of another and that one is under duty to do. According to this definition, teachers can be held liable if their behavior is proved negligent in the following circumstances:

1. If a pupil is injured on school premises (playground, buildings, or equipment) that are judged defective.

Safety standards for all facilities and equipment are usually set by the school district, and they must be maintained. Consequently, for the protection of the children, any facility or piece of equipment that does not meet these standards (excessive damage to a field, such as large rocks showing; extensive holes caused by flooding; or broken gymnastic equipment) should be reported and *not used* until competent authorities have certified that it meets all safety requirements.

2. If an injury occurs while the teacher has left an assigned instructional or supervisory group for any period of time.

In virtually every teaching situation in the public schools, only a qualified teacher—usually defined as one holding a teacher's credential and under contract with a school district—can assume responsibility for the pupils' instruction and safety. Classroom teachers, therefore, should seek clarification about delegated authority to student teachers and paraprofessional assistants (part-time helpers, parents, etc.). Certainly, a teacher who leaves a student in charge while she leaves the instructional area, regardless of the reason or duration of time, is negligent.

3. If a pupil is injured while attempting to perform an exercise or movement that is beyond his ability.

This is probably the most vulnerable area for a teacher, particularly within gymnastics, where the performance of stunts is potentially hazardous. If a child has been taught according to a normal progression of skill and has been given adequate instruction in form and safety, an accident probably will not occur. If an accident does happen, the teacher is usually not considered liable if adequate teaching has been provided and safety precautions taken.

The important point is that teachers follow the recommended programs and provide adequate instruction and safety for all participants. The gymnastic program recommended in this book adheres to the principle that each child should progress according to his demonstrated ability, not according to some arbitrary standard set for all participants.

4. If a pupil is injured as the direct result of another pupil's negligence.

The teacher should be able to foresee and prevent malicious conduct by any child under her care. The class must adhere to a standard of conduct that includes respect and consideration for the safety of every class member. This is usually stated by the teacher (and better yet, agreed upon by the pupils) in the form of "rules of conduct" that the children must follow. When one child's malicious behavior causes injury to another, the "case" against the teacher would depend upon an evaluation of the teacher's ability, the situation, and a thorough investigation of the incident.

Liability Insurance

Who should purchase liability insurance varies from district to district. Policies are normally held by local school districts, teacher associations, or individual teachers. Since the costs incurred in this area of responsibility are excessive, each teacher should consult with local school officials regarding the extent of liability coverage. If no policy exists to cover teaching responsibilities, particularly in the area of physical education, a personal policy is warranted.

Accidents and Preventive Safeguards

An accident is an unforeseen event that occurs without the will or design of the person whose act caused it; it is an event that occurs without fault, carelessness, or lack of proper circumspection for the person affected or that could not have been avoided under the existing circumstances (Bucher 1963). An accident, therefore, excludes negligence. If the following basic standards are followed, optimum safety will be guaranteed:

1. Maintain playground and gymnasium equipment in proper working order. Repair defective equipment immediately or remove it from the play area.

2. Introduce activities that are appropriate to the child's skill level. Follow educationally acceptable textbooks or physical education guides, and never require a child to perform a stunt or skill beyond his capability. Also, the care exercised by the teacher must increase as the risk involved in the activity increases (Drowatsky 1978).

3. Provide continuous supervision for any scheduled physical education activity. Recess and noon-hour activities also must be adequately supervised according to a desirable pupil-teacher ratio. This ratio should be stated in a written policy agreed upon by the school board, principal, and teachers.

4. Provide safe instructional play areas. The size of the area should meet the standards established by national, state, or local authorities and be free of physical hazards and known nuisances. When it is virtually impossible to remove potential hazards, safety rules should be established and followed.

5. Provide competent, periodic health and physical examinations to determine whether the child should participate in regular or remedial physical education activities.* Establish adequate follow-up procedures for children returning to physical activities after illness, and provisions for detected physical deficiencies.

6. Employ only certified personnel for teaching or supervising physical education activities.

If a child has an accident during any official school activity, teachers should have a standard procedure to follow. This procedure should be established by the district office in concert with principals, teachers, physicians, and school nurses. Part of the procedure should include completing an accident form similar to the one on page 98. This form should be filled out in triplicate and sent to the principal's and superintendent's offices.

Physical education by its very nature is susceptible to accidents. And, because activity is vital to the normal growth and development of the child, teachers should not eliminate vigorous activities from their program for fear of accidents. They should, however, use wisdom and prudence in the selection, instruction, and supervision of the physical education program.

*The interpretation of *competent* should be made by the principal or superintendent. Generally speaking, a competent health and physical examination is one that is administered by a licensed medical practitioner.

Facilities, Equipment, and Supplies

One of the most important considerations in the development of a comprehensive physical education program is the adequacy of facilities, equipment, and supplies. National standards regarding the size of the school property, outdoor play areas, gymnasiums, and swimming pools provide guidelines for local districts and individual schools (Athletic Institute 1979). Beyond this point, however, it is the local community's responsibility, along with each school within its jurisdiction, to provide the facilities, equipment, and supplies required to meet the goals of the program. The following provides a basic coverage of these important considerations.

Playground

The size of the school facility, including the gymnasium and outdoor space, is dependent upon the number of children in the school. National standards recommend a minimum of ten to thirty acres for a neighborhood park-school (Athletic Institute 1979). Beyond this minimum standard, the dimensions of a school site depend upon such factors as climate, economic conditions, and the attitude of the school and community toward physical education.

The primary consideration, however, of any play area is safety. School playgrounds in urban areas should be surrounded by heavy wire fences, and entrances should have double fences rather than gates. If the playground is used by both primary and intermediate children, separate areas should be designated for age groups. If space is limited, a fence around the kindergarten-primary area may be necessary. Part of the playground should be set aside for permanent equipment such as climbing cubes, horizontal ladders, obstacle courses, and adventure playground areas. This apparatus should be permanently anchored in cement casings. The area immediately under and around each apparatus should be loose dirt, sawdust, or sand. A portion of the playground, preferably close to the school, should be blacktop and large enough for such activities as running and tag games. The remaining playground area should be grass turf, when water supply permits. Other types of surfaces used are oil-treated dirt, mixed sand, dirt and sawdust, and asphalt.

Following are the basic recommendations for the playground:

1. Remove any physical hazard.
2. Restrict children to specific play areas.
3. Choose equipment on the basis of proven safety and practical value.
4. Provide adequate room within each area for additional equipment.

```
┌─────────────────────────────────────────────────────────┐
│                                                         │
│              Student Accident Report Form               │
│                                                         │
│  Name of injured student: _____  Phone: _____ │
│                                                         │
│  Age: _____           Address: _____          │
│                                                         │
│  P.E. class: _____    _____                   │
│                                                         │
│  Homeroom: _____      _____                   │
│                                                         │
│  School: _____                                     │
│                            A.M.                         │
│  Date of accident: _____ P.M. _____           │
│                (time)      (day)     (month)            │
│                                                         │
│  Place of accident: _____                          │
│                                                         │
│  Date reported: _____                              │
│                                                         │
│  Location and description of accident: _____       │
│  _____           │
│  _____           │
│  _____           │
│  _____           │
│                                                         │
│  Nature of injury: _____                           │
│  _____           │
│                                                         │
│  Condition of environment: _____                   │
│  _____           │
│                                                         │
│  Supervising person: _____                         │
│                                                         │
│  Type of activity: _____                           │
│                                                         │
│  First-aid treatment: _____                        │
│  _____           │
│                                                         │
│  Where taken: _____                                │
│                                                         │
│  Comments: _____                                   │
│  _____           │
│  _____           │
│                                                         │
│                   Signature _____                  │
│                                                         │
│                   Date _____                       │
│                                                         │
│  White copy: Superintendent's office                    │
│  Pink copy: Principal's office                          │
│  Green copy: Teacher's copy                             │
└─────────────────────────────────────────────────────────┘
```

5. Establish a list of safety rules and make sure each child follows them.

6. Teach children to think in terms of safety for themselves and their classmates.

7. Inspect all equipment regularly.

8. Provide competent supervision within the playground area during regular class time, recesses, and the noon hour.

Creative Playgrounds

Teachers who are serious about helping children become self-directing individuals capable of expressing themselves creatively not only must practice creative teaching strategies; they must also see that the physical environment stimulates the creative process. In many schools, boxlike gymnasiums and flat, unobstructive playing fields constitute the physical education facilities. Playground equipment normally includes swings, slides, and unattractive steel climbing apparatus encased in concrete and surrounded by asphalt, cement, or sand. Although these apparatus may be easy to keep tidy, they are unimaginative and lack educational value.

Basic Criteria for Creative Playgrounds

The following ten criteria (Ledermann and Trachsel 1968) for creative playgrounds provide a guideline for evaluating existing playground facilities and constructing new ones. Several photographs of commercial equipment, as well as "homemade" and "natural" equipment, show how schools in urban and rural areas have utilized available, inexpensive equipment (fig. 6.4). An extensive list of references is also provided in the appendixes.

1. Playgrounds must be designed and equipped with their function for play foremost in mind.

The playground should not be designed purely from the landscape gardener's aesthetic conception or the educator's concern for children's play habits and needs. It must serve the play characteristics of children and, at the same time, be aesthetic in the selection and arrangement of apparatus, pathways, and shrubs and greenery.

2. Architects, landscape designers, and educators must work together to produce good solutions to playground problems.

Architects, landscape designers, and educators tend to visualize the creative playground from their own points of view. The architect injects his bias toward artistic creations; the landscape gardener is more concerned with tree and flower arrangements than children's play activities; and educators often see the creative playground as an extension of the classroom. All three specialists must recognize the contributions of the others, so that each plan is seen as a cooperative effort.

3. The playground is not meant for passive entertainment. It must encourage active, spontaneous, and creative play.

The creative playground should not be a simple collection of commercial equipment, old cars, or concrete tunnels arranged in parallel rows. The apparatus, whether natural or commercial, should be selected and arranged to stimulate the child's imagination and enhance continuous exploration.

4. Half-finished components and materials for play are more valuable than mechanical equipment.

Most playgrounds are dominated by inflexible apparatus such as slides, swings, and a variety of rotary-type equipment. It is not suggested that slides and swings be removed but that consideration be given to including more creative and, if possible, natural equipment such as large roots or trees or other materials that are available in the local area.

5. Playground design and equipment must conform to the typical games of the age group for which the playground is intended.

In the majority of cases, creative playgrounds are first seen as an addition to the primary school playground area. Children from age five to eight thoroughly enjoy playing on or around a creative playground. Intermediate children appear to be more sophisticated; however, experience shows that children of this age level are equally interested in using creative equipment. Thus plans should consider the full age range in the elementary school.

6. The playground must offer a variety of possibilities for play.

A set of swings, a slide, and possibly a climbing tube or an unobstructed playing area do not constitute an adequate play area. Swinging for hours is similar to an adult playing a slot machine for hours. Neither activity is inherently creative. The playground should be arranged to stimulate creative movements both on apparatus and on the play surface.

7. The playground design must reflect the functions and movements of different games.

This involves the total play area of the school. For example, an elementary school playground services both primary and intermediate children. Consequently, the creative playground area should be away from the main ball game areas. If the school is near an area with trees, a ravine, or any type of natural area, the creative playground should be put near this site. Of course safety must be considered; natural areas that are potentially hazardous should not be considered as desirable locations.

8. The games of fantasy should not be overlooked.

Some children enjoy playing by themselves. Therefore, the creative playground, particularly for primary children, should provide small individual areas on or near apparatus where the child can absorb himself in fantasy or other forms of individual self-expression.

9. Architects and landscape designers should "play" a little while designing the creative playground.

The specialists should observe children at play and attempt to visualize the potential area through "the eyes of a child." The designer who does this would not build a square sandbox, place a slide in the middle of an area with slopes and contours, or place equipment in straight lines. Relevance, too, is important. A creative playground near a coast should be representative of the area, with "ships" and "trees"—natural or man-made—in the general play area. Similar themes for the South and Midwest should be present in the creative playground.

Figure 6.4 Imaginative playground equipment is planned on the basis of its safety and the practical value it has for the children.

10. Interested groups of people should cooperate in designing, equipping, and maintaining a playground.

The majority of creative playgrounds that have been constructed in Canada and the United States are the results of cooperative parent-teacher groups that wished to do something for local school children. Initially such projects were undertaken because of the lack of tax money to construct this type of outdoor facility. This cooperative action has given the parents an understanding of the value and purpose of such playgrounds and has also significantly reduced the amount of vandalism, as parents and children alike consider these jointly built facilities community property, and not just for use during school hours.

Gymnasium

The location, size, and special features of the gymnasium should be determined by the philosophy and activities of the physical education program. All too often, however, incorrect planning results in inadequate court dimensions, low ceilings, and, in many cases, avoidable hazards or obstructions. To help eliminate mistakes in the planning and construction of future elementary

school gymnasiums, national leaders in the field of health and physical education have developed a guide, *Planning Facilities for Athletics, Physical Education and Recreation* (Athletic Institute 1979). Included in this guide are standard recommendations for floor construction, playing space, storage facilities, and numerous other aspects of a well-planned gymnasium. When planning new facilities use of this publication is advisable as a basic reference for nationally acceptable standards of gymnasium construction.

There are, however, basic recommendations relating to floor dimensions, placement of equipment, and general safety that apply to any gymnasium or multipurpose room that is used for physical education. The following suggestions will assist teachers in organizing an indoor facility for maximum use and optimum safety:

1. Maintain gymnasium temperature between sixty and sixty-five degrees.
2. Paint permanent boundary lines on the floor for activities held most often. Use different colored lines for each—black for basketball, red for volleyball, and green for a large center circle.
3. Provide adequate safety margins for all games. The standard basketball dimensions for elementary school children are seventy-four by forty-two feet. If the facility is only seventy by forty feet, the actual court dimensions should be sixty-seven by thirty-seven to provide a minimum three-foot safety zone around the court.
4. Remove all equipment that is not being used during the physical education class.
5. Request that any hazardous fixtures, such as floor level heating ducts and lighting fixtures, be covered with protective screens.
6. Establish a standard procedure for obtaining and returning equipment to the storage room.

Classroom

In many elementary schools throughout the country the only available space indoors for physical education is the classroom. Although this is inadequate, some minor furniture adjustments can make the classroom suitable for many different physical activities (see chapter 12). By shifting movable desks and tables, one area of the classroom can be made free of obstructions. Since most lighting and window fixtures in the classroom are not screened, do not permit activities that in any way create a potentially hazardous situation. Adjustable and movable bars may be placed in doorways, mats can be used for tumbling activities, and short four-by-four beams and chairs can be used for balance activities.

Basic Equipment and Supplies

Physical education equipment refers to the more permanent apparatus such as balance beams and outdoor play apparatus. Generally speaking, these materials will last from five to twenty years, even with repeated use. Supplies, on the other hand, are expendable items such as balls, whistles, and records. These items will last one to two years. Each teacher should list the proper equipment for her grade level and, where budgets are limited, suggest how to make various types of equipment. (See appendix B for diagrams of inexpensive equipment. See appendix C for a list of commercial manufacturers and distributors of equipment and supplies.)

The type of physical education program, the geographic area, and economic conditions, among other things, determine the type of equipment a school will buy. The following lists of suggestions will assist in ordering the proper type and size of equipment and supplies.

Recommended Playground Equipment

Climbing apparatus: Climbing cubes, Big Toy apparatus, etc.
Horizontal bar: "Chinning" or "turning bar" at three levels—48, 54, and 64 inches—all 5 feet wide
Monkey rings
Horizontal ladder: 6½ feet high, length optional
Slide: 8 feet high, with safety platform
Balance beam: 8 to 12 feet long, three levels—18, 24, or 48 inches
Tether ball standards: Minimum of three
Basketball standards: Minimum of two; 8 feet high (Heavy duty construction)
Volleyball standards: Minimum of two
Softball backboards: Minimum of two
Soccer goalposts: Minimum of two
Creative playground apparatus: See chapter 6
Sandbox: 6 × 10 feet, with cover
Track and field equipment: Long jump pit, high jump pit and standards, hurdles

Optional and Homemade Equipment

Automobile tires: Suspended on rope or chain, with bottom of line 12 to 14 inches off ground
Movable barrows and kegs
Movable planks: 8 to 12 feet long, with planed edges
Sawhorses: Different heights; see appendix B
Tug-of-war rope
Concrete sewer pipes: Arranged in units of three or four
Obstacle courses: Permanent or portable; type and construction should complement the climate and geographic area; see chapter 9

Recommended Indoor Equipment

Tumbling mats: Minimum of four; light synthetic material; sizes are optional, although 4 × 6 feet mats are easy to handle and store
Individual mats: 18 × 36 × ¾ inches; minimum of forty, or one per child
Record player (three speeds)
Dance drum
Balance beam: 1 to 4 feet high, depending on general use, and approximately 12 feet long; see appendix B
Balance benches: Reversible for optional use, plus hook attachment on one end; see appendix B
Horizontal bar: See appendix B
Scooters: 12 × 12 inches with four casters; see appendix B
Volleyball net and standards: adjustable heights
Basketball standards: Rims 8 feet from floor
Climbing ropes: 15 to 20 feet high; 1½ to 2 inches in diameter
Vaulting box: See appendix B
Set of jumping boxes: See appendix B
Springboard or mini-tramp
Sawhorses: Minimum of six; see appendix B
Portable agility apparatus: See chapter 27
Hockey nets: 2
Cargo nets
Optional equipment: Trampoline and spotting apparatus, pegboards, parallel bars

Recommended Supplies for Gymnasium and Playground

The number of items listed here is a suggested minimum based on a maximum of thirty children using the supplies during one physical education period. If two or more classes meet at the same time, double or triple the number.

Supplies	Minimum Number
Long skipping ropes: ⅝ inch sash, nylon or plastic; 13, 14, and 15 feet	2 of each length
Individual skipping ropes: ⅜ inch sash, nylon or plastic; ten each of 6, 7, 7½, and 8 feet	1 set or 40 ropes
Utility balls (6½, 8½, 10½)	6 each size
Repair kit for balls	1
Beach balls (12 inches, 16 inches)	6 each size
Cage balls (24 inches)	6 to 8
Soccer balls (rubber cover)	30
Volleyballs (rubber cover)	30

Supplies	Minimum Number
Softballs	10 to 15
Softball mats	10 to 12
Beanbags (6 by 6 inches)	30
Wands: ten each at 3, 3½, 4, and 4½ feet	1 set of 40 wands
Indian clubs or bowling pins	24 to 30
Measuring tape (50 feet)	1
Ball inflater with gauge	1
Earth ball	1
Rhythm drum	1
Records (see part 7)	
Colored arm bands	2 sets of 15
Whistles	10 to 12
Stopwatches	6
Hoops	30
Jacks	60
Softball bases	4 sets
Softball catcher's mask, mitt, and body protector	2 each
Softball batting tee	2 to 6
Footballs (junior size)	10 to 15
Basketballs (junior size)	30
Plastic tape (1, 1½, and 2 inches in assorted colors)	2 rolls of each
Horseshoe sets	4
Clipboards	4
Braids (cloth)	30
Blocks (4 inches by 4 inches by one foot)	30
Deck tennis rings	10 to 15
Paddles (paddle tennis)	30
Dance supplies (castanets, tambourines, bells, etc.)	4 of each
Sponge or tennis balls (assorted colors)	40 to 50
Fleece balls	40
Traffic cones	10 to 15
Lummi sticks	60
Scoops	30 to 40
Tinikling poles	12 to 16
Tote bags	10 to 15
Floor hockey sticks	30 to 40
Field hockey sticks	30 to 40
Parachutes	2
Juggling scarfs	90
Juggling bags	90

Optional and Homemade Supplies

Rhythm and dance supplies (see chapters 28–30)	
Shuffleboard supplies	3 sets
Stilts	12 pairs
Automobile tires	6 to 8
Frisbees	12 to 24

Care and Maintenance of Equipment and Supplies

Because equipment and supplies represent a large expenditure of money, they should be stored, used, and maintained in an effective and prudent manner. The following list of suggestions should be incorporated into each school's policies and procedures for handling equipment and supplies.

1. All apparatus, equipment, and supplies should be permanently marked with a number and school identification.
2. Each school should establish a set of rules and procedures for handing out and returning equipment and supplies.
3. All apparatus, equipment, and supplies should be checked before they are issued. Any broken equipment should not be issued; it should be repaired as soon as possible and returned to the storage room. Worn out equipment should be discarded as it leads to poor skill development and potential accidents.
4. Inflate all balls according to the recommended pressure. Place a chart near the ball inflator and adhere strictly to the recommended pressure for each inflated ball. Store balls during the off-season in a partially inflated shape.
5. Store all materials according to recommended standards.
6. Design your equipment room to permit easy and efficient access to all materials.
7. Each school should make a complete inventory of all physical education materials at the beginning and end of each season. Records of how well such items as rubber volleyballs, mats, and skipping ropes perform will aid in future replacement or purchase policies.
8. When ordering materials, always write out the specifications such as brand name, size, and required options. If materials are ordered through a central purchasing department it is extremely important to state the specifications and add "or its equivalent." The latter will guarantee the purchase of a quality item rather than a cheaper, but inferior, second or third choice item.

7 *Observation and Evaluation*

Observation
Periodic Class Observations
Lesson Focus Observations

Evaluation
Formative and Summative Evaluation
Evaluating Student Progress
Grading and Reporting
Evaluating the Program

Evaluation is essential to all phases of the physical education program. A teacher uses the techniques of observation to assess the strengths and weaknesses of her daily lessons in order to make appropriate changes in her teaching strategies. She also uses a variety of objective and subjective evaluational tools to assess performance, to motivate children, or to communicate information to parents and interested citizens.

The value and practical application of a variety of observational skills and evaluative tools and procedures are discussed in this chapter.

Observation

Observation is a very important technique used in the total process of evaluation. It sometimes involves periodic class observations for assessing the general safety and tone of the class, or a series of specific lesson focus observations of individuals or groups of children. Both types of observations, however, assess what is happening in the learning environment so that appropriate changes can be made in the content or teaching strategy. Observation is an ongoing process of assessment, change, and assessment, and is always based upon the progress children are making towards the stated goals of the program.

Periodic Class Observations

The success of any physical education lesson, regardless of its content, depends upon several general and observable factors. The safety of the children, including the care and concern for one another, the condition of the apparatus or equipment, and the manner it is used during the lesson are of foremost concern. Next, the tone of class, including the noise level, the effort the children are making, and the children's behavior towards one another should be periodically monitored throughout each lesson and from different

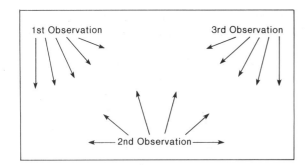

1st Observation   3rd Observation

←——— 2nd Observation ———→

Figure 7.1 Observational skills can be developed and improved.

vantage points. To illustrate this process, let us assume the diagram above represents a soccer lesson. The lesson emphasis is dribbling and passing the ball. The first observation is made from a corner of the field a few minutes after the children begin dribbling the ball within the instructional area. As the teacher quickly scans from left to right, she makes a mental note of spacing, colliding, and individual effort. If the pace and tone of the class appears satisfactory, she begins observing the main focus points of the lesson. As the lesson progresses, she periodically scans the class from a variety of vantage points and makes appropriate adjustments to alleviate any problem areas.

Lesson Focus Observations

Within each lesson one or more skills or movement patterns are considered the main focus of the lesson. In the previous example, dribbling and passing the ball was the main emphasis of the lesson. The almost universal question that arises is "What and who do I observe within my class of thirty children?" The answer to this question is based upon the teacher's knowledge of the activity and the potential level of ability of each child in the class. For example, teaching dribbling and passing requires a basic understanding of mechanical principles, progression of skill development, and alternate teaching strategies for enhancing the development of these skills. The teacher must also have a reasonable idea of each child's level of maturity, interest, and motivation. With this general background information, the teacher assesses the child's or group's performance and, where indicated, changes the task or teaching technique to improve performance. Most classroom teachers, however, do not possess this background information, hence feel frustrated with respect to applying observational skills in a productive manner. The following guidelines will assist each teacher in using her observational skills according to her own general background in physical education.

Guidelines for Effective Observation

1. Before the lesson begins, select one or two *key focus points* and, where appropriate, assist individual children or change the direction of the whole class. For example, the two key focus points in dribbling and passing are keeping the ball close to the feet while dribbling, and passing the ball with either foot. As the lesson progresses the teacher is satisfied with the children's ability to keep the ball close; however, she notes most children only pass the ball with their right foot. She stops the class (while they are practicing with partners) and stipulates that every second pass has to be with the left foot. As a teacher's observational skills and competence in an activity improve, she gradually increases the number of key focus points.

2. Make the observation very brief.

3. If the observation is for the benefit of the whole class, make sure each child has a clear view of the performance.

4. Limit the number of observations for the class's benefit to a few demonstrations.

5. When choosing an individual or a group to perform, do not always select the best performers. Every child, regardless of ability, has something to offer and something to gain when demonstrating a skill or movement idea to peers.

6. When observing a demonstration provide constructive comments and praise. A child gains from positive, not negative, criticism.

7. When children are asked to observe a performance, specify one or two aspects for them to comment upon. Children, like teachers, learn to observe. Asking them to observe one or two aspects, such as "the follow-through action" or "the number of different shapes a child included in his sequence," sharpens the child's power of observation.

Observational skills are not restricted to teachers; they are equally important to every child in the class. When a child can observe another child's performance he may gain insight into his own performance, acquire another idea, or learn to appreciate the individual differences that exist in each child whether performing the same skill or answering a movement challenge in a creative way.

Evaluation

Evaluation in physical education is a process of determining whether the objectives of a single lesson, a unit, or a total program are being accomplished. Although evaluation is usually applied to the learner, it should also apply to the program, the facilities, the equipment, and the teacher.

Formative and Summative Evaluation

Two types of evaluation are used in the physical education program. *Summative evaluation* occurs at the end of an instructional activity, for example at the completion of a lesson, unit, or yearly program. The results of this form of evaluation normally produce a cummulative score for determining the achievement of each child or the whole class. This form of evaluation assesses individual levels of achievement, compares individuals or groups, establishes standards of performance, or provides a basis for establishing a grading system.

The second type of evaluation, *formative evaluation,* is used within each lesson to assess the progress each child is making towards the goals of the lesson. Since the current emphasis in elementary school physical education stresses exploratory ways of learning and unstructured skills and movement patterns, formative evaluative techniques, such as subjective ratings and checklists are extensively used. Objective tests for game skills and physical fitness appraisals also have an appropriate use within this form of evaluation.

Evaluating Student Progress

Both subjective and objective measuring devices for evaluating student progress in physical education must be judged upon their ability to measure accurately the extent to which the objectives of the program are being realized. As previously stated, these objectives include health and physical development, motor skill development, knowledge, and social adjustment. Factors involved in these objectives can be measured, to some degree, by subjective judgment or objective tests. Most teachers rely heavily upon subjective ratings of student progress in such areas as movement concepts and skills and social development. However, within all grade levels, some aspects of the child's performance can be measured by objective tests.

Health and Physical Development

Continuous concern for each child's health and physical development is the responsibility of teachers and school health officials. Physical education provides a special avenue to detect possible anomalies and to refer children with them to more competent authorities. A teacher who understands posture, nutrition, and physical fitness can correct or prevent problems, in certain situations. It is also the teacher's responsibility to detect early signs of illness and to refer these problems to the school nurse or physician.

In most school districts, physical examinations are required annually or at other scheduled times throughout the elementary school program. The results should be made known to the classroom teacher, particularly for children requiring special treatment in the physical education program because of rheumatic fever, birth anomalies, and so on.

The teacher can make other evaluations that will help her plan for the growth and development needs of each child. Several of the more important evaluative techniques relating to physical development, posture, and perceptual-motor abilities are described in the following pages of this book:

Posture: Simple plumb line test, page 141.
Physical Fitness: Description of standardized test batteries for elementary school children, page 143.
Perceptual-Motor Screening Tests: Page 168.

Fundamental Skills

Table 7.1 is an example of a teacher subjectively rating a child's performance of fundamental skills at the beginning of the school year. Each skill is rated as initial, elementary, or mature. Under correction indicated, comments are included for helping the teacher plan activities to correct the child's weaknesses. This type of evaluation sheet can also be developed for specific sports skills and gymnastic activities, and is especially useful in explaining a child's level of performance to parents and in pointing out corrective measures that can be undertaken at home.

Table 7.1 Subjective Rating for Fundamental Skills

Name: Jim Adams
Date: September 1985   **Performance in Fundamental Skills**

Name of Skill	Developmental Sequence			Correction Indicated
	Initial Stage	*Elementary Stage*	*Mature Stage*	
Walking			X	Toes inward
Running			X	Toes inward
Skipping	X			
Leaping	X			
Jumping		X		
Sliding	X			Changes lead foot
Hopping	X			
Swinging and Swaying		X		
Rising and Falling		X		
Pushing and Pulling		X		
Bending and Stretching		X		
Striking and Dodging		X		

Game Skills

Very few standardized tests measure specific game skills of elementary school children, so teachers often must rely on their own test batteries. Each test, whether standardized or homemade, should have the following characteristics:

1. Each item in the test battery should accurately measure one important skill (for example, an underhand catch).

2. The test battery should be inexpensive and easy to administer, and should yield scores that can be totalled.

3. Each test item should accurately measure the skills and movements of the activity. A dribbling test item in basketball or soccer should include such factors as speed, change of direction, and ball control.

4. Each item in the battery should distinguish between low and high levels of ability. If all children score eight or ten points out of a possible ten on an accuracy test—throwing at a large target from ten feet away—the test would be of little value. The results would indicate the distance was too short or the target too large.

Table 7.2 is an example of a teacher-made battery test for measuring throwing and catching skills; it is simple, inexpensive, and easy to administer. Each test item can be modified to meet the skill levels of several grades. The first four tests measure form and accuracy; the fifth measures distance.

Test 1: Underhand Catch. The teacher stands twenty feet from the child and throws him ten balls, which the child must catch with an underhand catch. One point is awarded for each successful catch.

Test 2: Overhand Catch. Repeat test no. 1, but require an overhand catch.

Test 3: One-hand Underhand Throw. The child stands fifteen feet from a wastepaper basket and attempts to throw ten softballs into it. The underhand throw must be used. One point is awarded for each successful throw.

Test 4: Two-hand Chest Throw. Repeat test no. 3, but with a two-hand chest throw and a larger utility ball.

Test 5: Throw for Distance. The child throws a softball three times. The total distance is divided by three and recorded in the appropriate column of the chart.

Other examples of teacher-made skill tests are found in part 5, the games section. Teachers should use these sample test batteries as guidelines in developing their own tests.

Soccer skill test: page 293
Field hockey test: page 303
Flag football test: page 315
Volleyball test: page 330
Basketball test: page 349
Softball test: page 367

A teacher-made skill test should be devised so that the individual scores can be totalled to provide a means of ranking children, as well as indicating where additional emphasis should be placed in the selection of practice activities and lead-up games.

Table 7.2 Objective Skill Test

Name of Student	Throwing and Catching Skills					Total	Grade
	Test 1: Underhand Catch	Test 2: Overhand Catch	Test 3: One-hand Underhand Throw	Test 4: Two-hand Chest Throw	Test 5: Throw for Distance		
1. John Smith	7	5	6	5	38'	61	B
2. Mary Able	6	4	5	5	26'	46	C
3.							
4.							

The American Alliance for Health, Physical Education, Recreation and Dance has recently produced a number of standardized test batteries with accompanying norms for boys and girls, ages ten to eighteen. A series of manuals covering such sports as basketball, football, softball, and volleyball may be purchased through AAHPERD Publications, (Dept. V), P.O. Box 704, 44 Industrial Park Circle, Waldorf, Md., 20601.

Dance Skills

The structured locomotor and nonlocomotor skills of dance can be checked easily by the classroom teacher; the checklist presented in table 7.1 is an example. However, performing skills in rhythmic activities, folk dance, and creative dance involves style, grace, and creativity—all of which must be evaluated subjectively.

Gymnastic and Movement Skills

Evaluation of a student's progress in gymnastic activities, as in dance, is relatively easy when teaching standardized skills, but difficult when teaching movement concepts and skills. In gymnastics, all skills are performed the same way, thus providing a standard performance. And since these skills are arranged from simple to complex, evaluation becomes an assessment of how many skills are performed and how well.

Evaluation of the child's progress using a cumulative number of stunts should be based on individual achievement, with room for individual choice of stunts. There are simply too many variations in skill and maturity to demand the same of all children.

When teaching movement concepts and skills there is no common standard by which to judge progress. The essential purpose of these skills is to help the child use his body in a variety of ways on and off apparatus; thus each movement task should produce different shapes and movement patterns for each child. Thus performance is an individualized matter and must be evaluated on that basis. Nevertheless, the teacher must observe and evaluate each child's progress according to some criteria, no matter how subjective and personal they may be.

Figure 7.2 Judging standardized gymnastic skills is a far easier task than evaluating movement concepts and skills.

The evaluation can be made jointly by the teacher and the child. Since each child learns to progress at his own rate and according to his potential ability, the teacher's assessment is based on whether the child is sufficiently challenged and is continually improving his ability to produce more difficult shapes and movements. Progress, then, is as much concerned with the quality of movement as with the individuality and variety of movements the child performs.

Knowledge

One objective of physical education is to acquire a knowledge and understanding of physical activities and their contribution to physical and mental health. When children know the team positions, rules, and strategy of a game, there is less chance of misunderstandings and fighting. Furthermore, knowing the rules of a team sport, the verses in a singing game, or the parts of a complex gymnastic skill enhances motor learning.

In the primary grades, verbal questions are used to teach simple rules and verses in singing games and to stimulate creative thought through interpretive movements. Written tests can be used in the upper grades in all phases of the physical education program. The choice of true–false, multiple-choice, or short-answer tests depends on the teacher and the capabilities of her students. Regardless of the type of test chosen, care should be taken to pose questions that are clear and appropriate to the physical activity.

Social Development

The traits represented in the term *social adjustment* do not lend themselves readily to either subjective or objective measurement. For example, the ability to get along with others, team loyalty, and sportsmanship cannot be measured accurately by a rating scale, an anecdotal record, or even an expert's judgment. Nevertheless, these are extremely important qualities that we profess to develop within the physical education program. Consequently, some attempt, however meager, should be made to evaluate the development of these qualities. Some of the more practical techniques follow.

Teacher Observations   Probably the most commonly used technique for assessing individual social growth is the daily observation a teacher makes while the children are playing in a structured situation or during free-play activities. Behavioral problems such as cheating and poor sportsmanship may be noted by the teacher. The manner of coping with adjustment problems varies from a change in the method of instruction to a complete change in activities.

Interview   A personal interview between the teacher and the child and/or parent is another technique used to gain a better understanding of a child's general behavior. Usually, specific adjustment problems are discussed with the child or, when appropriate, the parent to determine the reasons behind certain behavioral problems. The teacher should take care, however, not to lecture but to win the child's confidence and show genuine concern for the child. When a child respects and trusts the teacher, chances are he will gain an understanding of his problem and make appropriate changes.

Sociogram   The sociogram is a technique used to study the relationships within a group. By posing key questions such as "With whom would you like to practice catching skills during recess?" or "Who would you like to have on your team?" it is possible to identify children who appear to be well adjusted within the group and those who are isolated and rejected. To obtain the best results from this technique it is wise to keep the following procedures in mind when asking students such questions (Kozman, Cassidy, and Jackson 1967):

1. Make sure the situation for which students are asked to make choices is a real one.
2. Make use of the choices to group students according to their preferences.
3. Make sure that the atmosphere is informal and friendly.
4. Let the students understand that their answers will be confidential.
5. Give no cues to the students about how to choose.

The results of the sociogram can help identify children who need assistance. By drawing circles on a sheet to represent each child and lines to each child as the answers dictate, it becomes quite clear who are the popular children and the rejected children in a particular social group. By a simple regrouping, the shy and retiring child can be brought into a more favorable group without making the reasons for such a change obvious. Furthermore, undesirable group situations can also indicate possible variations in methods of class organization, selection of team captains, and the type of group activities.

Grading and Reporting

The purpose of grading in physical education is identical to that in all other subjects—to report the child's progress. Although the majority of elementary school report cards require only an S or U, or P or F, additional information relating to skill performance, physical fitness, and social adjustment should be available in the form of a cumulative record. When the parent asks, "How is my child doing in physical education?" and the answer is, "He is well adjusted in his group" or "He is doing fairly well in physical skills," very little insight has been gained and the parent may come away with an unfavorable impression of the program.

To overcome the weakness of the P or F grading and reporting system, many schools require a cumulative record in physical education (see chapter 9). This is particularly true in districts where children are given physical fitness tests in the fall and spring. After the spring test has been given, the physical fitness scores are reported to parents or passed on to the next grade to assist the new teacher in setting reasonable limits for the child. Additional information about skill performance in rhythmic, game, and gymnastic activities should be recorded within the cumulative record. The child's evaluation should then be based on his improvement rather than how he ranks with others in the class.

Table 7.3 Physical Education Program Evaluation Form

Program Area	Excellent Compliance	Adequate Compliance	Needs Improvement
1. Objectives of the program are clearly stated.			
2. Objectives of the program are used as a guideline for selecting and emphasizing program content.			
3. The written curriculum is an up-to-date program that provides adequate scope and sequence for each grade level.			
4. The curriculum contains a variety of activities appropriate for children in the primary or intermediate grades.			
5. Provision is made for periodic revisions of the physical education curriculum.			
6. Program content reflects a consideration for the needs and interests of both sexes.			
7. Program content reflects a consideration of physically handicapped children.			
8. Provisions are made to integrate program content of physical education with other subject areas in the elementary school curriculum.			
9. Time allotments for physical education meet school district, state, or national standards.			
10. Provisions are made for student involvement in the selection of activities.			
11. Provisions are made for the involvement of parents and interested citizens in the selection of activities.			
12. Children are required to have a physical examination by a qualified physician on a scheduled basis. The actual schedule is a written policy of the school.			
13. An up-to-date professional physical education library is available within the district.			
14. Flexible plans are followed with respect to the nature and length of instructional units.			
15. An evaluation of the program content is made on a yearly schedule by the classroom teacher and/or other school personnel.			

Evaluating the Program

The physical education program in its broadest meaning includes all the organized experiences, the facilities, and the teachers involved in teaching and supervisory roles. Evaluative techniques for measuring all these factors are simply not available. Even if they were, the time element alone would prohibit extensive assessments. There are, however, periodic evaluations teachers should make about program content, daily lessons, facilities and equipment, and their own effectiveness. Most of the following suggestions apply to each teacher; however, joint evaluative programs, involving the principal, supervisors, or other teachers should be encouraged for providing greater expertise and support to areas of the program where improvement or redirection is indicated.

Program Content

The content of a physical education curriculum can be effectively and formally evaluated by external organizations, such as a state department of instruction or an official accrediting agency. Such evaluations normally utilize highly refined evaluative instruments and include many items of a physical education program. Another way of evaluating the program content is for each classroom teacher to develop her own self-appraisal scale that covers key elements in her instructional program. The sample scale shown in table 7.3 will help the teacher judge how well she is meeting a particular goal or providing a particular service to her students.

Daily Lesson

Perhaps the most important evaluative procedure that teachers make is the ongoing assessment of each physical education lesson. If the following areas are checked on a routine basis, teachers can gauge whether the objectives of the lesson are being reached and where specific changes in content and teaching strategies are needed.

Participation   Since the time available for physical education is usually quite short, each lesson must be planned carefully to encourage maximum participation. The teacher should, therefore, assess the following:

1. The time children take to change and enter the gymnasium.
2. The amount of time devoted to explaining and demonstrating skills. Most teachers spend so much time explaining that they allow too little time for actual practice.
3. The time available for each child to practice each skill or movement.

Effective Routine Procedures   Many unnecessary problems and wasted time can be avoided when children know what is expected of them in the gymnasium. Simple routine procedures should therefore be established and followed from the first lesson. These should include the following:

1. Arrangement of apparatus—who should be responsible.
2. Rotation procedure—moving from one piece of equipment or apparatus to another.
3. Carrying and putting away equipment and apparatus.

Sufficient Challenge to Children   When teachers are continually confronted with disciplinary problems, the reason could be lack of challenge in the tasks given. The teacher should constantly observe the amount of concentration and effort the children are giving to the task. Specific things to look for are:

1. After introducing a new skill, game or challenge, is there a demonstration of general boredom or a general rise in noise.
2. Are various children moving away from their assigned working area to be with friends or to irritate other children.
3. Is there a marked increase in irrelevant questions and comments by the children.

Individual Observation and Guidance   In any learning situation, each child needs some guidance and encouragement, regardless of ability. Too often the outstanding performer is selected for demonstrations and praise, while the low achiever, who really needs attention and encouragement, is neglected. Hence, consideration should be given to—

1. Observing, correcting, and encouraging as many children as possible.
2. Selecting many different children for demonstrations.
3. Recording important and successful techniques that will assist in future lessons.

Facilities and Equipment

The majority of school districts have established policies for the allocation of funds for physical education. Normally, each school receives an annual equipment and supplies grant based upon the number of children in the school. Teachers should refer to the list of suggested equipment and supplies in chapter 6 as a basic guideline. It is extremely valuable for each school district to establish its own recommended list so teachers have a reasonable idea of the quantity and quality of equipment they can expect to receive.

Facilities and equipment should also be inspected prior to and during each lesson for the following:

1. Safety of playing space and equipment.
2. Appropriateness of space and equipment. For example, if the instructional space is too large for good control, reduce its size by markers, or some other device. If balls, bats, or the size and height of equipment or apparatus is too small or too large for the learners, make immediate and appropriate adjustments. Finally, is there equipment in the gymnasium or outdoor playing area that is not recommended for use in the elementary school program? Serious consideration should be given to such apparatus as merry-go-rounds, swings with steel or wooden seats, and such gymnastic equipment as the trampoline and minitramp. The latter two pieces of equipment are desirable for upper elementary, provided competent teachers are present to teach skills on them.
3. Adequate supply of equipment. If the number of balls or other pieces of small equipment are insufficient for the number of children, introduce other techniques such as "station work," to provide for maximum participation.

Teacher Effectiveness

Every teacher should appraise her teaching to determine how she can improve her effectiveness in the classroom and gymnasium. Since the physical education program is undergoing extensive changes, both in content and methods of instruction, teachers should assess whether they are as up to date in this area as they are in other subjects. Consideration should be given to the following areas:

1. New developments in health-related physical fitness tests, movement education, and cooperative and creative games.
2. New textbooks in the general field of physical education and specialized texts in game, dance, and gymnastic activities.
3. New developments in audiovisual materials for physical education (films, filmstrips, and videotapes).
4. New developments in equipment and apparatus, particularly the new agility apparatus.
5. Related research in motor learning, teaching academic concepts through movement, perceptual motor development and physical education.
6. New program developments, particularly programs supported by federal and state funds.

Information and general assistance in these areas can be secured from state and local district supervisors of physical education. Numerous other national organizations, such as the American Alliance of Health, Physical Education, Recreation and Dance (AAHPERD), the Office of Education, and the Athletic Institute will provide information on request.

Evaluation should be an ongoing process of assessing whether goals are being achieved. Adequate program evaluation primarily involves the day-to-day assessment of each lesson in order to make modifications in activities and methods of instruction. Contemporary programs also include student evaluation of the program. Although the children cannot always see the value and reason for all activities, they can provide valuable assistance with respect to their needs and interests. Provision should be made for children to participate actively in program evaluation. When children are respected for their contributions, they, in turn, will generally provide the effort and enthusiasm to make the program a success.

The contemporary definition of an elementary school curriculum includes all the experiences of children for which the school accepts responsibility. In physical education, this encompasses all the learning experiences relating to the physical activities provided within the regular instructional period and out of class. How the school or teacher organizes the physical education curriculum can take several forms. But the fundamental purpose of such an organization is to provide an effective means of choosing activities, teaching strategies, and experiences that best meet the goals of the program.

Contemporary educational practices such as individualized teaching strategies, team teaching, and concept development all directly affect the nature and structure of the physical education program. Teachers must also consider the unique characteristics and needs of children within each grade of the elementary school when selecting the length, type, and nature of each instructional unit. In addition, new federal laws such as PL 93–380 (1974) and PL 94–142 (1975) require that equal opportunities are provided for all children who possess physical, psychological, or social handicaps. Each of these factors are considered, weighed, then translated into broad goals of an elementary school physical education curriculum.

The process of developing an elementary school physical education curriculum is outlined in the chart on page 116. To accomplish the broad goals, the physical education curriculum is divided into two types of programs: the instructional program and the extraclass program. The instructional program is the central core within which children acquire knowledge, skills, and understandings relating to human movement. Chapter 8 describes how to develop yearly, unit, and daily instructional programs. Chapter 9 explains how to incorporate the principles, concepts, and activities relating to posture and physical fitness within each unit of instruction.

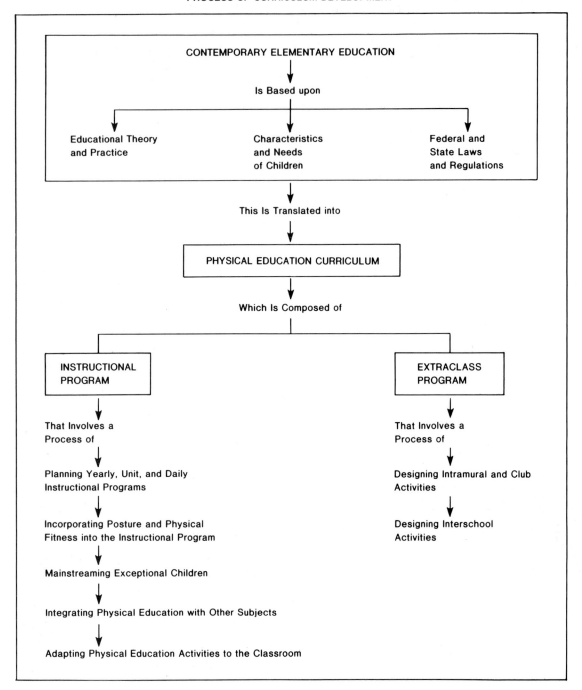

Chapter 10 outlines the importance of PL 94–142 and how to integrate exceptional children into the mainstream of the instructional and extraclass program. The importance of integrating physical education with other subjects is the theme of chapter 11. Numerous ideas are provided in this chapter to illustrate how a variety of language arts, arithmetic, science, and other subject area concepts and skills can be taught through the medium of human movement. Chapter 12 describes the ways physical education activities can be taught in a typical classroom setting. Chapter 13, the last chapter in part 4, explains the nature and scope of the intramural and interschool program.

8 Planning Yearly, Unit, and Daily Instructional Programs

Types of Activities
Posture and Physical Fitness
Locomotor and Nonlocomotor Skills
Movement Concepts and Skills
Game Activities
Gymnastic Activities
Dance Activities

Developing a Yearly Program
Step 1: Establish the Basic Goals of the Program
Step 2: Select General Activity Areas
Step 3: Developing an Instructional Unit
Step 4: Developing Flexible Lesson Plans

The instructional program is more than the physical activities that are taught to the class. Rather, it is the total experience of activities, methods, and teaching strategies.

The activities themselves serve two very basic functions. First, through the activities the child learns the basic movement skills and concepts involved in games, dance, and other organized activities. Mastering these skills, in turn, helps the child maintain an optimum level of physical fitness, move his body easily and efficiently, and express himself creatively. And second, the physical activities provide a medium within which the child learns many intangible, yet important, lessons of life. The child learns, for example, to share experiences, to give and take, and to control emotions under a variety of cooperative and competitive situations.

This chapter describes types of activities and outlines the process of developing yearly, unit, and daily lessons. Sample programs are provided as guidelines for helping teachers develop their own programs. The latter must always be based upon the stated goals, teaching competence, characteristics, and needs of children, and available time, facilities, and equipment. Before movement education concepts and skills were introduced to the elementary school physical education program, activities were arranged according to three levels of contribution, as shown in the pyramid on page 118. The foundation of all movement included the basic components of physical fitness—strength, endurance, power, flexibility. The next level included the basic locomotor and nonlocomotor movements, and manipulative skills. The highest level incorporated the specialized skills involved in individual and team games, folk and creative dance, stunts, tumbling, and other gymnastic activities.

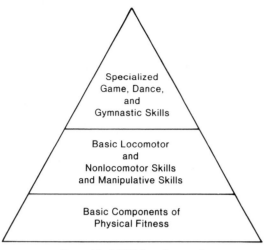

Pyramid of Skill Development

Types of Activities

Generally speaking, primary school children spend time in such areas as locomotor and nonlocomotor skills and low-organization games, dance, and gymnastic activities. As children progress through the intermediate grades, they devote more time to individual and team sports, folk dance, and gymnastic activities. The concepts and skills of the movement education approach have become an integral part of games, dance, and gymnastic activities rather than a separate activity area. Parts 5, 6, and 7 describe these concepts and skills and illustrate how movement concepts and skills can be effectively integrated within these activities.

This chapter includes brief descriptions of activities included in the instructional program and references to detailed discussion elsewhere in the book.

Posture and Physical Fitness

Posture and physical fitness activities include methods of assessing and improving fitness and posture. Special activities such as circuit training, obstacle courses, and yoga exercises are provided in chapter 9, "Incorporating Posture and Physical Fitness into the Instructional Program."

Locomotor and Nonlocomotor Skills

Activities involving locomotor and nonlocomotor skills stress such fundamentals as walking, running, skipping, and dodging. Chapter 4, "Basic Skills and Movement Fundamentals," describes each of these movements, including the basic mechanical and movement principles involved.

Movement Concepts and Skills

The movement concepts and skills integrated into the game, dance, and gymnastic activities included in this book are grouped under the elements of body awareness, qualities, space awareness, and relationships. These elements form the basis of the unstructured movements used to describe what the body can do, how it moves, where it moves, and the relationship of the body to the floor, apparatus, or other performers.

The basic movement concepts and skills are described in chapter 4, "Basic Skills and Movement Fundamentals." An extensive application of these movement concepts and skills appears in part 6, "Gymnastic and Movement Activities;" chapter 28, "Rhythmic and Movement Activities;" and chapter 30, "Creative Dance Activities." And within part 5, "Game and Movement Activities," there are numerous examples of the application of the concepts and skills of movement education to individual, partner, and group games.

Game Activities

Game activities have always constituted a major portion of the physical activities for children in both primary and intermediate grades. The basic game skills of throwing, catching, and striking for primary grades are described in chapter 4, "Basic Skills and Movement Fundamentals." Chapter 14, "Running, Tag, and Simple Team Games," has a variety of low-organization games that enhance these skills. Chapter 15, "Relay Activities," and chapter 16, "Individual and Partner Games," also contain numerous activities that contribute to the development of basic game skills and concepts. These chapters also include activities appropriate for boys and girls in grades four through six.

The more organized individual and team sports taught in the intermediate grades are presented in separate chapters (chapters 18 to 24). Each includes a suggested sequence for presenting skills, descriptions of the main skills, and a variety of practice activities and lead-up games. The activities included progress from simple to more complex activities. Each chapter also includes suggestions for incorporating the problem-solving method, or what is becoming known as the inventive, or creative games, approach. A teacher can either emphasize the structured games approach or adopt a more exploratory method. Whichever route is taken depends on the age of the children and their background in game-type activities.

Gymnastic Activities

Gymnastic activities for elementary school children commonly include three basic types of self-testing skills and movement patterns. The first category, stunts and tumbling (chapter 25), includes basic animal walks and balancing and tumbling skills. The second category includes a wide variety of skills and movement patterns performed on or with small equipment, including beanbags, hoops, individual ropes, and wands (chapter 26). The third type of gymnastic activities involves skills and movement patterns performed on or over large apparatus (chapter 27), including the vaulting box, climbing rope, trampoline, and a new series of agility apparatus designed primarily for elementary school children.

Within each of the three chapters devoted to gymnastic activities, all skills are organized from the simple to the more complex. Each chapter also includes numerous illustrations and suggestions for the sequential introduction of movement concepts and skills.

Dance Activities

Dance activities for primary and intermediate children include basic rhythmic skills, singing games and folk dances, and creative or interpretive movement. Chapter 28, "Rhythmic and Movement Activities," describes how the basic rhythmic skills can be taught to children in the primary and intermediate grades. Chapter 29, "Traditional and Contemporary Dances," includes the more popular singing games for early primary children and a selection of folk and square dances for the late primary and intermediate grades. And chapter 30, "Creative Dance Activities," provides basic approaches for teaching creative dance.

Developing a Yearly Program

In the majority of elementary schools in this country, the classroom teacher is mainly responsible for planning the yearly physical education program. Her task is to translate the goals expressed by school officials, parents, and herself into a broad-based activity program that meets the needs and interests of the children.

If every class was assigned thirty to forty-five minutes a day for physical education, if the interests and abilities of each class were equal, or at least similar, and if all facilities, equipment, and supplies were available for any activity selected, then a basic program with specific percentages of time allocated for specific activities would be suggested for each class. This ideal situation simply does not exist in elementary schools in this country. Therefore, the following four-step plan provides a framework upon which the classroom teacher can develop her own program.

Step 1: Establish the Basic Goals of the Program

The basic goals of an elementary school physical education program discussed in chapter 1 can be used as a starting point for the classroom teacher. Of course, these goals may be modified or others may be added to reflect the philosophy of the local school district or the wishes of parents and school officials. However, these goals should provide a basis for selecting appropriate activities.

1. Enhance physical growth and development.
2. Develop and maintain maximum physical fitness.
3. Develop useful physical skills.
4. Develop socially useful behavior.
5. Develop wholesome recreational skills.
6. Develop intellectual competencies.
7. Develop creative talents.
8. Develop the child's self-image.

Step 2: Select General Activity Areas

Selecting and allocating a percentage of time to games, dance, and gymnastic activities is a difficult task for the classroom teacher. In the first place, classes are usually organized according to age rather than ability. Ability in physical education, as with other subject areas, varies immensely within any age level. For example, a class of second graders, ranging in age from late six to early eight, may vary as much as five years in physiological maturity. In addition, differences occur in prior experience of children, teacher competence in each activity area, and available facilities and equipment. On the basis of these factors, the percentage of time listed for each activity in table 8.1 should be used as a basic guideline.

In the primary physical education program, equal time is allocated to game, dance, and gymnastic activities. And within each of these major areas, the concepts and skills of movement education, locomotor and nonlocomotor movements, and posture and physical fitness are integrated into each lesson. The amount of time devoted to the main activity and to other concepts and skills is based on the characteristics and needs of the class.

The intermediate physical education program shows the changing characteristics and needs of children in these grades. Games are allocated 40 percent of the instructional time, gymnastics 30 percent, and dance activities, the remaining 20 percent. The time and emphasis given posture and physical fitness remains about the same. However, proportionately less time is given to locomotor and nonlocomotor skills.

Table 8.1 Percentage of Time for Activities

Type of Activity	Percentage of Time per Grade						
	K	1	2	3	4	5	6
Game Activities	30	30	30	30	40	40	40
Running, Tag, and Simple Team Games	20	20	20	15	10	5	5
Individual and Partner Games	10	10	10	10	5	5	5
Team Games				5	25	30	30
Gymnastic Activities	30	30	30	30	30	30	30
Stunts and Tumbling	15	15	10	10	10	10	10
Small Equipment	10	10	10	10	10	10	10
Large Apparatus	5	5	10	10	10	10	10
Dance Activities	30	30	30	30	20	20	20
Rhythmic Skills	5	5	5	5	5	5	5
Singing Games	10	5	0	0	0	0	0
Folk Dance	0	5	15	15	10	10	10
Creative Dance	15	15	10	10	5	5	5
Other Activities	10	10	10	10	10	10	10

Includes: Testing, Swimming, Special Programs, or Additional
Time for Games, Dance, or Gymnastics

Table 8.2 indicates the type of activities appropriate for each grade level. The next task within Step Two is to determine the approximate percentage of the school year that will be devoted to one or more of these activities. The following situation illustrates how this is accomplished.

Example Situation

This example illustrates how Ms. Brown, a third grade teacher, used the "Yearly Program Planning Sheet" shown in table 8.3 to develop a balanced program of activities. Her teaching situation included 180 teaching days each having a daily 30-minute physical education class with access to indoor and outdoor facilities.

Ms. Brown's first decision was to allocate equal time to games, dance, and gymnastic activities. This was accomplished by allocating the recommended 30 percent, or fifty-five lessons, to each activity, as suggested in table 8.1. The remaining 10 percent, or fifteen lessons, was reserved for other activities. According to Ms. Brown's checks and written comments on the planning sheet, she reviewed each activity and indicated where problems might arise. For example, she

was concerned about the high risk of gymnastic activities and her general low level of teaching competence in these activities. Consequently she would need to participate in in-service programs and perhaps eliminate the more high risk gymnastic skills that she felt unsure of teaching. She also saw the importance of creative dance activities but noted the low interest of her class. The latter will require a review of more creative and appropriate teaching strategies for this activity. After reviewing the teaching and administrative considerations, she decided to teach four units within each activity area.

The Yearly Program Planning Sheet provides a means of allocating the available instructional time to various activities. It does not, however, indicate what should be emphasized within each activity area, nor the month of the year when each activity should be taught. Table 8.4, a general outline of a yearly program provides a guideline for selecting and scheduling each type of activity. Step Three explains how each unit can be organized and taught to meet a variety of teaching situations.

Table 8.2 Physical Education Activities

		Primary Program				Intermediate			
	Chapter	K	1	2	3	4	5	6	Pages
Physical Fitness Activities									
Posture Activities	9	x	x	x	x	x	x	x	151
Conditioning Exercises	9	x	x	x	x	x	x	x	151
Circuit Training	9				x	x	x	x	148
Obstacle Course	9			x	x	x	x	x	149
Isometric Exercises	9					x	x	x	191
Jogging	9			x	x	x	x	x	148
Yoga Exercises	12	x	x	x	x	x	x	x	193
Games Activities									
Basic Game Skills	4	x	x	x	x				62
Running, Tag, and Simple Team Games	14	x	x	x	x	x	x	x	222
Relay Activities	15	x	x	x	x	x	x	x	240
Individual and Partner Games	16	x	x	x	x	x	x	x	247
Cooperative Games	17			x	x	x	x	x	260
Classroom Games	12	x	x	x	x	x	x	x	183
Soccer Activities	18					x	x	x	272
Hockey Activities	19					x	x	x	295
Football Activities	20					x	x	x	305
Volleyball Activities	21					x	x	x	317
Basketball Activities	22					x	x	x	331
Softball Activities	23					x	x	x	350
Track and Field Activities	24					x	x	x	369
Gymnastics Activities									
Stunts and Tumbling Skills	25	x	x	x	x	x	x	x	390
Movement Skills	25	x	x	x	x	x	x	x	423
Pyramid Building	25					x	x	x	423
Beanbag Activities	26	x	x	x	x	x	x	x	436
Individual and Long Rope Activities	26	x	x	x	x	x	x	x	439
Hoop Activities	26	x	x	x	x	x	x	x	451
Wand Activities	26	x	x	x	x	x	x	x	453
Parachute Activities	26		x	x	x	x	x	X	456
Chair Activities	26		x	x	x	x	x	x	459
Indian Clubs, Traffic Cones	26	x	x	x	x	x	x	x	462
Juggling Activities	26			x	x	x	x	x	463
Balance Beam and Benches	27	x	x	x	x	x	x	x	467
Climbing Ropes	27	x	x	x	x	x	x	x	472
Springboard, Vaulting Box	27		x	x	x	x	x	x	476
Horizontal Bar, Ladder, Stall Bars	27	x	x	x	x	x	x	x	481
Agility Apparatus	27	x	x	x	x	x	x	x	484
Outdoor Apparatus	27	x	x	x	x	x	x	x	486
Dance Activities									
Elements of Rhythm	28	x	x	x	x	x	x	x	493
Rhythm Activities	28	x	x	x	x	x	x	x	498
Singing Games	29	x	x	x					504
Folk Dance	29					x	x	x	524
Creative Dance	30	x	x	x	x	x	x	x	537

Table 8.3 Yearly Program Planning Sheet: Ms. Brown's Third Grade Class

Activities   **Teacher-Learner and Administrative Considerations**

Activities	Chapter	Value High	Value Low	Student Interest High	Student Interest Low	Safety Risk High	Safety Risk Low	Teacher Competence High	Teacher Competence Low	Facilities	Equipment	No. of Lessons
Game Activities												
Unit 1: Ball Skills (hand-eye)		x		x			x	x		Adequate	Class sets of balls	15–20
Unit 2: Ball Skills (foot-eye)		x		x			x	x		Adequate	Class sets of balls	15
Unit 3: Cooperative Games		x		x			x	x		Adequate	Class sets of balls	10
Unit 4: Ball Skills		x		x			x	x		Adequate	Class sets of balls	15
Gymnastic Activities												
Unit 1: Gymnastics		x		x		x			x	Adequate	Small equipment sufficient	15
Unit 2: Gymnastics		x		x		x			x	Adequate	Large equipment limited	15
Unit 3: Gymnastics		x		x		x			x	Adequate	Large equipment limited	15
Unit 4: Gymnastics		x		x		x			x	Adequate	Large equipment limited	10
Dance Activities												
Unit 1: Rhythmics		x			x		x	x		Adequate	Tapes	10
Unit 2: Creative Folk Dance		x			x		x	x		Adequate	Tapes	15
Unit 3: Folk Dance		x			x		x	x		Adequate	Tapes	15
Unit 4: Creative Dance		x			x		x	x		Adequate	Tapes and instruction	15
Other Activities												

Column notes (indicated by arrows):

- Value: In terms of your stated goals.
- Student Interest: In terms of class's needs and interests.
- Safety Risk: Consider class's age in relation to nature and activity.
- Teacher Competence: Consider teaching skills and experiences in each activity.
- Facilities / Equipment: Consider quality and quantity of facilities and equipment: Describe situation for each unit.
- No. of Lessons: Attempt to provide a balanced program of activities.

Table 8.4   General Outline of a Yearly Program

	Fall	Winter	Spring
Kindergarten			
Games	Throwing and catching skills.	Throwing and catching skills.	Kicking skills.
	Individual and partner games.	Simple games.	Individual and partner games.
	Locomotor skills.	Movement skills.	Tag activities.
		Classroom games.	Locomotor skills.
Gymnastics	Animal walks and simple stunts.	Animal walks and simple stunts.	Simple stunts.
	Movement skills.	Movement skills.	Movement skills.
	Small equipment.	Small equipment.	Small equipment.
	Outdoor apparatus.		Outdoor apparatus.
Dance	Singing games.	Singing games.	Singing games.
	Locomotor and nonlocomotor skills.	Locomotor and nonlocomotor skills.	Locomotor and nonlocomotor skills.
	Creative dance.	Creative dance.	Rhythmic skills.
			Pantomime activities.
Grade 1			
Games	Throwing and catching skills.	Throwing, catching, and hitting games.	Kicking games.
	Individual and partner games.	Individual, partner, and simple team games.	Individual and partner games.
	Classroom games.		Simple team games.
		Classroom games.	Relay and tag games.
Gymnastics	Animal walks and simple stunts.	Simple stunts.	Movement skills.
	Movement skills.	Movement skills.	Small equipment.
	Small equipment.	Small equipment.	Large apparatus.
	Outdoor apparatus.	Large apparatus.	Outdoor apparatus.
Dance	Singing games.	Singing games.	Singing games.
	Movement skills.	Movement skills.	Rhythmic activities.
	Pantomime activities.	Rhythmic skills.	Creative dance.
		Creative dance.	
Grade 2			
Games	Throwing, catching, and kicking skills.	Throwing, bouncing, and catching games.	Kicking, dribbling, and hitting games.
	Individual, partner, and simple team games.	Simple team games.	Individual, partner, and simple team games.
	Classroom games.	Relay activities.	Relay and tag games.
Gymnastics	Simple stunts and tumbling skills.	Simple stunts and tumbling skills.	Movement skills.
	Movement skills.	Movement skills.	Small equipment.
	Small equipment.	Small equipment.	Large apparatus.
	Large apparatus.	Large apparatus.	Outdoor apparatus.
Dance	Folk dance activities.	Folk dance activities.	Folk dance.
	Rhythmic skills.	Rhythmic skills.	Rhythmic skills.
	Creative dance.	Creative dance.	

Table 8.4 Continued

	Fall	Winter	Spring
Grade 3			
Games	Kicking and dribbling skills. Individual, partner, and simple team games. Running and tag games.	Throwing, dribbling, and catching games. Individual, partner, and simple team games. Relay activities.	Throwing, catching, and hitting skills. Simple team games. Running and tag games. Track and field activities.
Gymnastics	Stunts and tumbling skills. Movement skills. Small equipment. Large apparatus.	Stunts and tumbling skills. Movement skills. Small equipment. Large apparatus.	Movement skills. Small equipment. Outdoor apparatus.
Dance	Rhythmic skills.	Folk dance. Rhythmic skills. Creative dance.	Folk dance. Rhythmic skills.
Grade 4			
Games	Simple team games. Soccer activities. Volleyball activities.	Individual and partner games. Basketball activities. Classroom games.	Relay and tag activities. Softball activities. Track and field activities.
Gymnastics	Stunts, tumbling, and movement skills. Small equipment. Large apparatus.	Stunts, tumbling, and movement skills. Small equipment. Large apparatus.	Outdoor apparatus. Obstacle course.
Dance	Rhythmic skills.	Folk dance. Creative dance.	Rhythmic skills. Folk dance.
Grade 5			
Games	Individual and partner games. Flag football activities. Volleyball activities.	Individual and partner games. Basketball activities. Floor hockey activities.	Field hockey activities. Track and field activities. Swimming activities.
Gymnastics	Stunts, tumbling, and movement skills. Small equipment: ropes, skipping, wand, and chair activities.	Stunts, tumbling, and movement skills. Pyramid building. Small equipment. Large apparatus.	Stunts and tumbling. Pyramid building. Large apparatus. Outdoor apparatus. Obstacle course.
Dance	Rhythmic skills.	Rhythmic skills. Folk dance. Creative dance.	Folk and square dance. Creative dance.
Grade 6			
Games	Soccer activities. Individual and partner games. Flag football.	Individual and partner games. Basketball activities. Volleyball activities.	Individual and partner games. Field hockey activities. Track and field activities.
Gymnastics	Stunts, tumbling, and movement skills. Large apparatus. Outdoor apparatus.	Stunts, tumbling, and movement skills. Pyramid building. Small equipment. Large apparatus.	Outdoor apparatus. Obstacle course.
Dance	Rhythmic skills.	Folk and square dance activities. Rhythmic skills. Creative dance.	Folk and square dance. Creative dance.

Note: A few minutes of each session throughout the year should be spent on physical fitness activities (see chapter 9) for every grade.

Step 3: Developing an Instructional Unit

An instructional unit is one segment of the yearly program, which normally emphasizes one type of activity, and lasts for a set period of time. Although there is no standard format for a unit plan, it usually contains the following seven items:

1. Objectives.
2. Sequential list of concepts and skills to be learned.
3. Activities.
4. Organization and teaching strategies.
5. Equipment and facilities.
6. Evaluation.
7. Resources.

A clarification of each item is provided along with suggestions to help each teacher construct her own unit plans.

Objectives

The objectives of a unit are normally expressed in terms of general goals, then broken down into specific learning outcomes. For example, a fifteen-lesson soccer unit for a fifth-grade class might have the following general objectives:

1. To teach children to play soccer.
2. To teach children to appreciate the rules and strategies of soccer.
3. To provide for positive interpersonal relations.
4. To enhance leadership qualities, fair play, and sportsmanship.

While these objectives are global in nature and, at times, difficult to evaluate, they are extremely important guidelines for selecting activities, teaching strategies, and other related parts of an instructional unit.

Once the general objectives for a unit are established, a specific list of objectives for each learner must be stated. These are generally referred to as "learning outcomes." For example in the soccer unit cited, the learning outcomes would be as follows:

1. Kick a stationary and moving ball with the instep and side of foot.
2. Trap a ball with the chest, leg, shin, and foot.
3. Dribble and pass with reasonable accuracy.
4. Head a ball with reasonable accuracy.
5. Demonstrate positional play and team strategy.
6. Understand one's own level of ability prior to and after a unit of soccer.

Sequential List of Concepts and Skills

Learning outcomes help identify the skills and concepts for each unit of instruction. However, listing these concepts and skills in a sequential teaching order is generally the biggest problem because the activity itself may not have a specific sequence. Such is the case in creative dance, movement sequences in gymnastics, and creative games. In these activities, the teacher lists a set of outcomes that need not be followed in sequential order. However, activities such as game skills, stunts and tumbling, or track and field events adhere more readily to a sequential listing of concepts and skills. The previous soccer unit can be used to illustrate the sequential listing of introductory skills, rules, and strategies. After referring to the "Suggested Sequence of Presenting Soccer Skills" the teacher would (page 274) make the following tentative list:

1. Instep kick.
2. Heading.
3. Corner and penalty kicks.
4. Pass and trap.
5. Throw in.
6. Positional play.

After administering a skill test and observing the children play a few lead-up games, the teacher would be able to properly sequence the selected activities to meet the level of interest and ability of her class.

Activities

The activities for a unit are the medium through which the learning outcomes are accomplished. In the soccer unit, appropriate activities would include

1. A list of practice activities, page 283.
2. A list of lead-up games, page 288.
3. Rules and regulations of soccer, page 291.

Organization and Teaching Strategies

This part of the instructional unit outlines the various organizational techniques and teaching strategies used throughout the unit. The fifth-grade teacher of the soccer unit might outline the methods and techniques she will employ throughout the unit as follows:

Organization	*Teaching Strategies*
Station work	Modified unit
Rotational team or group leaders	Stress progression from individual to partner to group activities
Reduce size of outdoor instructional area	Stress balance between structured drills and lead-up games with inventive activities
Improvise	
1. Size and type of balls	Stress individual progress and self-evaluation
2. Location and number of goals	

Table 8.5 Sample Weekly Plan for Kindergarten (Multiple Unit)

Monday	Tuesday	Wednesday	Thursday	Friday
Game Skills	*Floor Stunts*	*Rhythmic Activities*	*Singing Games*	*Classroom Games*
Bouncing practice activities— 1. Bounce and catch 2. Bounce several times 3. Bounce to partner	Camel walk, elevator, tightrope walk	Pantomime animal walks, such as bears, lions, dogs, and horses	"London Bridge"	"Ringmaster"

Table 8.6 Dance Unit for Grade Three (Modified Unit)

Week	Monday	Tuesday	Wednesday	Thursday	Friday
1st Week	*Introduce:* "Paw Paw Patch"	*Review:* "Paw Paw Patch" *Introduce:* "Bleking"	*Games:* Stunts Relay Pinch-oh	*Review:* "Bleking" "Skip to My Lou"	*Review:* "Paw Paw Patch" "Bleking" "Skip to My Lou"
2nd Week	*Review:* "Skip to My Lou" *Introduce:* "Pease Porridge Hot"	*Review:* "Pease Porridge Hot" "Skip to My Lou"	*Gymnastics:* Stunts Balance beam Rope skipping	*Review:* "Bleking" "Pease Porridge Hot"	*Review:* "Skip to My Lou" *Introduce:* "Heel and Toe"
3rd Week	*Review:* "Heel and Toe" *Introduce* "Shoo Fly"	*Review:* "Heel and Toe" "Shoo Fly"	*Review:* Games or stunts	*Review:* "Paw Paw Patch" "Bleking" "Skip to My Lou"	*Review:* "Pease Porridge Hot" "Skip to My Lou" "Heel and Toe"

Selecting the appropriate type of instructional unit is one of the most important tasks within this area. Following are three basic types of units that can be used in the primary and intermediate grades. Each teacher should select the unit that most readily meets the needs of her class and is in harmony with her basic teaching approach.

Multiple Teaching Unit

The multiple teaching unit is actually two or three units taught concurrently throughout the year. In other words, games, dance, and gymnastic activities are taught on alternate days for an indefinite period. For illustrative purposes, see table 8.5. Kindergarten activities might include games on Monday, gymnastics on Tuesday, dance on Wednesday, and singing games (representing dance) on Thursday to start the second rotation. In this case, the rotation system has been modified by having similar activities two days in a row.

Advantages of this approach are its variety of activities and its flexibility; therefore, it can be used in kindergarten and first grade classes to cope with the short attention spans of five- and six-year-olds. The facilities and equipment available may determine whether this method can be adopted. Whatever the reasons for selecting the multiple unit, the teacher should make sure that games, dance, and gymnastic activities are given the appropriate amount of emphasis.

Modified Teaching Unit

The modified teaching unit is a block of time allocated primarily for the instruction of one type of activity. For example, dance might be emphasized 90 percent of the time during a three- or four-week period, while the remaining 10 percent is devoted to games and gymnastic activities. Table 8.6 exemplifies a third-grade class with a thirty-minute physical education period scheduled every day in the gymnasium. During the first week of the unit, dance activities are taught on Monday, Tuesday, Thursday, and Friday. Wednesday is set aside for gymnastics or outdoor games.

This method provides both continuity and variety. For example, "Paw Paw Patch" is introduced on Monday and repeated on Tuesday so that the basic skills and dance patterns are learned. Later in the Tuesday lesson, "Bleking" is introduced. To provide variety, Wednesday is set aside for vigorous running and tag games, which could be played in the gymnasium or outdoors. The remaining two days are devoted to dance activities. This pattern continues throughout the second and third weeks.

Table 8.7 Softball Unit for Grade Six (Solid Block Approach)

	Monday (40 min.)	Tuesday (15 min.)	Wednesday (40 min.)	Thursday (15 min.)	Friday (40 min.)
1st Week	*Explain:* Underhand throw (pitching) *Practice:* Zigzag passing *Lead-up:* Center ball	*Practice:* Throwing *Lead-up:* Shuttle throw	*Explain:* Bunting *Practice:* Swing at four *Lead-up:* Twenty-one softball	*Review:* Shuttle throw Twenty-one	*Explain:* Grounders *Practice:* Zigzag passing *Lead-up:* Bat ball

Note: Continue the above pattern during the second, third, and fourth weeks.

The modified block, unlike the multiple unit, provides continuity in learning skills, and has certain desirable instructional features. It permits the teacher to plan one type of activity for an extended period, rather than three different types each week. Furthermore, planning a one year program is much easier using the modified unit than the multiple approach.

Solid Teaching Unit
A solid teaching unit is an extended period of instruction—from one to several weeks—devoted exclusively to one type of activity. Its value lies in its continuity, as there is no disruption in the type of skill development. Perhaps the solid unit has its greatest application in team teaching, where the most qualified teacher is used to maximum effectiveness. However, fifth- and sixth-grade teachers who are responsible for their own physical education programs may find this type of unit applicable in teaching activities that are of great interest to their students.

To illustrate this method refer to table 8.7. A solid four-week unit of softball has been organized for a sixth-grade class. Note that the physical education period is scheduled for forty minutes on Monday, Wednesday, and Friday, but for only fifteen minutes on Tuesday and Thursday. New skills are explained and demonstrated, drills are practiced, and lead-up games are played during the longer periods. The shorter periods are just long enough for a short drill and possibly a lead-up game.

It is suggested that the first week be planned in detail. After four or five days of instruction the teacher may note that certain skills require additional concentration, or that students are ready for more advanced skills and lead-up games. The remaining three weeks should be planned around the skill level and interests of the class.

It is possible to use both the modified and solid units during the year. Early fall and spring activities are particularly adaptable to the solid unit, while the modified unit may be the only feasible approach for activities requiring use of indoor facilities.

Equipment and Facilities
The success of any instructional unit depends upon adequate facilities and sufficient equipment for all participants. In the games program, balls and related small equipment should be procured for each games unit. Different-sized balls and improvised equipment should be acceptable in schools having budget limitations. Gymnastic units involving large numbers of small and larger equipment may require the use of "pooled" apparatus or a revamping of the gymnastic units of instruction to cope with limitations in the type and number of apparatus. Finally, dance units normally require tedious hours of selecting and taping musical accompaniments. If all teachers in school agree on a standardized procedure of copying and storing tapes, many hours can be saved by each teacher. The construction of improvised instruments shown in appendix C can also be used in most creative dance programs.

Evaluation
Formative and summative evaluative procedures should be established for every instructional unit. A list of appropriate subjective and objective evaluative instruments are provided in chapter 7.

Resources
Two basic types of resources should be listed in each unit plan: (1) written materials such as textbooks, individual activity units, and other printed materials, and (2) audiovisual materials such as films, videotapes, or demonstration charts. It is wise to include order forms for films and tapes to confirm their availability before the instructional unit begins.

The above type of instructional plan is appropriate for most structured activities within the game, dance, and gymnastic programs. Instructional units involving creative dance or the movement education approach in gymnastics must adapt this type of unit plan to meet the unique conditions relating to a theme approach to sequencing as well as to methods of evaluation.

Table 8.8 Structure of a Lesson

Part One *Introductory Activity*	Part Two *Skill Development*	Part Three *Group or Final Activity*
Stress vigorous warm-up activities.	**Games:** Stress acquisition of skills and concepts through individual and partner activities.	**Games:** Stress group games.
Standard for all types of physical education lessons.	**Gymnastics:** Stress acquisition of stunts and movement skills and concepts through individual, partner, and small equipment activities.	**Gymnastics:** Stress application of previously learned skills to large apparatus.
	Dance: Stress acquisition of skills and movement ideas and concepts through individual and partner activities.	**Dance:** Stress group activities.

Sample Lesson Plan—Grade Three

Lesson Emphasis: Chest pass

Materials: 30 balls, 15 hoops, box of beanbags

Free Practice Activities

Instruct children to get balls and practice dribbling or catching with a partner.

Introductory Activities (5 minutes)

Circle formation. Begin running in place. Shift to conditioning exercises, stressing arm and shoulder girdle exercises.

Skill Development (7 to 10 minutes)

Keep circle formation.

—Explain and demonstrate chest pass.

—Move to center of circle and pass to each child. Check skill level.

Arrange in partners with a ball.

—partner passing, 10 feet apart

—vary distance

—one stationary; one on move

Group Activities (7 to 10 minutes)

Arrange in groups of six.

Game: "Keep Away"

Inventive Game: Make up a game that includes the following:

1. Use only a chest pass.
2. Every player must be moving.
3. Must use two hoops in the game.

If time remains, change two hoops to three beanbags.

Notes and References

Place four bags of balls in four corners of gymnasium.

```
      X   X
  X           X
      X   X
```

Step 4: Developing Flexible Lesson Plans

A physical education lesson plan should be considered a flexible guideline that includes a brief summary of objectives, activities, methods, and organizational procedures. Although each teacher eventually develops her own abbreviated lesson plan, the basic structure shown in table 8.8 can be used when teaching game, dance, and gymnastic activities.

The first part of a game, dance, or gymnastic lesson is the introductory activity, lasting about three to five minutes. This activity should be vigorous and somewhat related to the main focus of the lesson.

The second part introduces one or more skills or movement concepts, and sets the focus and direction of the lesson. In a game lesson, for example, previously learned skills or concepts are introduced. Similarly, in gymnastic lessons, movement skills are introduced through individual, partner, and small equipment activities. In folk or creative dance lessons, this part is used to set the focus and direction of the lesson.

The third part of a game or dance lesson normally involves a group activity. For example, in dance a Scottische step might be introduced in part two, using individual and partner activities. Then, in part three, groups of four or more might do a Scottische dance. The third part of a gymnastics lesson is used to apply movement skills and concepts to large apparatus.

The sample lesson plan on page 128 illustrates how a third-grade teacher has planned a thirty-minute games lesson. Approximately ten minutes are spent in changing clothes and free practice activities, leaving twenty minutes of instructional time.

The amount of detail that a teacher records on her lesson plan depends, of course, upon her professional background and experience. Beginning teachers tend to write down more detail. Abbreviated notes under each of the main parts of the lesson usually suffice for the more experienced teacher.

Variations in Lesson Plans

The previous lesson plan was based on a thirty-minute physical education period. But in many schools, particularly for the primary grades, the period may last only ten to twenty minutes. Since it is virtually impossible to cover three main parts of a lesson in such a short period, the lesson can begin on one day and continue on the next without any major loss in the continuity of learning. The previous lesson will be used to illustrate such a modification. The first two parts of the lesson are covered in the fifteen-minute instructional period on Monday. On Tuesday, the lesson starts with a five-minute warm-up, then moves directly to part three.

Changing Lesson Emphasis as the Unit Develops

When a new unit of instruction is introduced, more time is usually needed during the first and second parts of the lesson to introduce and practice skills and movement concepts. This leaves less time for the third part of the lesson. If the instructional period is thirty to forty minutes long, the transition normally occurs in the instructional unit as shown in the accompanying diagram.

Regardless of the time available during the first five or six lessons, a considerable amount of it must be devoted to skill development. As the children acquire skill and movement understanding, more time can be devoted to group activities. The best guideline for determining the emphasis of the lesson plan is the children's progress. If the skill level appears to be quite low, continue to emphasize part two. If there is marked improvement, increase the difficulty of individual and partner activities and give more time and emphasis to group activities.

A Three-Part Instructional Unit for Two Class Periods

|◄————————————— 15 minutes —————————————►|

Monday	PART ONE *Introductory Activities* (5 minutes)	PART TWO *Skill Development* (10 minutes)	PART THREE *Group Activities* Leave until Tuesday
Tuesday	(5 minutes)	Leave out	Cover part three of previous lesson

Adjusting the Three-Part Instructional Lesson

	Length of physical education period		
	PART ONE *Introductory Activities*	PART TWO *Skill Development*	PART THREE *Group Activities*
First Part of Unit		Devote more time to this part during the initial stages and gradually decrease as skill and movement ideas develop.	
Latter Part of Unit	Devote approximately three to five minutes to this activity throughout the unit.		Devote less time to this section during early part of the unit and gradually increase time as skill and movement ideas develop.

9 Incorporating Physical Fitness into the Instructional Program

Understanding the Human Body
Skeletal System
Muscular System
Cardiorespiratory System

Developing Good Posture
Common Posture Problems
Methods of Assessing Posture
Methods of Improving Posture

Improving Physical Fitness
Methods of Assessing Physical Fitness
Methods of Improving Physical Fitness
Special Programs for Improving Health-Related
  Components of Physical Fitness

Relating Good Nutrition to Physical Fitness
Balanced Diet
Weight Control
Teaching Suggestions

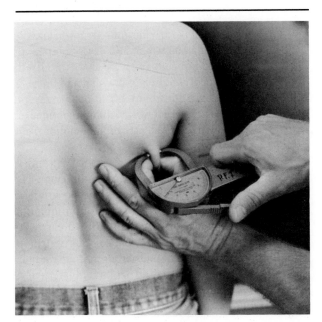

During the past three decades much has been written and said about the importance of raising and maintaining a high level of physical fitness among our citizens. The results of all this interest and improved services and programs has not been very promising. For example, a survey using the *AAHPERD Youth Fitness Test* showed that in virtually all test item comparisons, the 1975 test results showed no significant improvement over the 1965 norms. In fact, a few age groups in the 1975 survey produced lower performance levels on selected items. Numerous explanations have been given for low levels of physical fitness as well as for the significant increase in postural problems among elementary school children. Among the most significant are chronic television watching, lack of proper nutrition leading to malnutrition or obesity, and a major percentage of elementary students throughout the country who are not offered a well-balanced daily physical education program.

The publication of AAHPERD's *Health Related Physical Fitness Test Manual* (1980) represents a major shift in the purpose and direction of elementary school physical fitness programs. This new test emphasizes the importance of an active life-style to achieve and maintain low amounts of body fat, high levels of cardiorespiratory function and sufficient muscular strength, muscular endurance, and flexibility in the lower trunk and posterior thigh areas for healthy low back function.

Parents and teachers have also realized that for children to develop an active and positive life-style, they must understand how their bodies function, and what affect various types of activities have on their appearance or physical prowess. Once children are personally convinced that exercise is important to their own well-being, there is a good chance that physical activity will become a permanent part of their daily lives. It also appears that once a child's life-style moves in this direction, he will begin to modify his diet and other health factors to complement this positive and healthy way of living.

The first part of this chapter provides a basic understanding of three important systems of the body. The next two sections describe ways of improving posture

Figure 9.1 The Human Skeleton

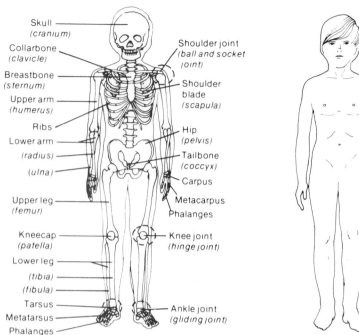

Skull
(cranium)

Collarbone
(clavicle)

Breastbone
(sternum)

Upper arm
(humerus)

Ribs

Lower arm

(radius)

(ulna)

Upper leg
(femur)

Kneecap
(patella)

Lower leg

(tibia)

(fibula)

Tarsus

Metatarsus

Phalanges

Shoulder joint
(ball and socket
joint)

Shoulder
blade
(scapula)

Hip
(pelvis)

Tailbone
(coccyx)

Carpus

Metacarpus

Phalanges

Knee joint
(hinge joint)

Ankle joint
(gliding joint)

Cervical
vertebrae

Thoracic
vertebrae

Lumbar
vertebrae

Sacrum

Heel bone
(calcaneus)

and physical fitness. The last section covers the relationship of good nutrition to a positive and healthy lifestyle.

Understanding the Human Body

The human body is made up of numerous interdependent systems. In physical education, we are very concerned with the skeletal, muscular, and cardiorespiratory systems. Through exercise, we can contribute to normal growth and development of bones and muscles, enhance physical fitness, and improve neuromuscular efficiency.

Once children understand the structure and function of the skeletal, muscular, and cardiovascular systems, they can see the reasons for continuous vigorous exercise throughout their lives.

Skeletal System

The human skeleton consists of 206 bones that work together with the muscles and connective tissues to move the body, to support it, and to protect the internal organs (fig. 9.1). Bones are divided into two broad groups, known as axial and appendicular bones. *Axial bones* consist of the skull, spine, and ribs, and provide the basic structure on which the *appendicular bones* are attached.

A joint is a meeting point between bones. For example, the knee joint (fig. 9.2) is a "hinge" joint, which allows the leg to bend in one away. The shoulder and

Figure 9.2 Bones Forming the Knee Joint

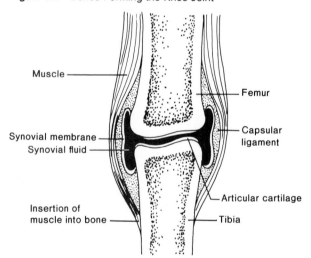

Muscle

Synovial membrane

Synovial fluid

Insertion of
muscle into bone

Femur

Capsular
ligament

Articular cartilage

Tibia

hip joints are ball-and-socket joints, which allow rotary movements in several directions. And, the ankle and thumb joints are "saddle" joints, which permit movement in two directions but without rotation.

The ends of the bones forming a joint, such as the knee joint (fig. 9.2), are covered with a smooth protective layer of cartilage that acts like a shock absorber between bone surfaces. The space between the bones in a joint is filled with a lubricating fluid known as synovial fluid. This fluid works like the oil in an engine; it reduces friction between the moving parts. These moving joints have strong nonelastic stabilizing ligaments that bind the joint together.

Muscular System

The muscular system of the human body represents about 35 to 45 percent of the total body weight. It consists of 650 muscles that are grouped in three categories according to their structure and function. Involuntary or smooth muscles (about 30) form the muscle portion of the internal organs and function automatically rather than under the direct control of the brain. The cardiac, or heart, muscle performs its unique function while under the involuntary control of the brain. The voluntary, or skeletal, muscles (about 620) are attached to the bones and are directly controlled by the brain. All three types of muscles however, operate in the same general way by contracting and relaxing their muscle fibres.

In physical education, we are mainly concerned with the skeletal muscles although all muscles are indirectly affected through movement. A skeletal muscle is composed of bundles of muscle fibers enclosed in a sheath or fibrous tissue called fascicle (fig. 9.3). At the end of the muscle is a noncontracting fibrous tissue called a tendon. The tendon normally is attached to a bone or ligament. When a nerve impulse is received by a muscle, the fibers contract, causing the muscle to become shorter and thicker. As illustrated in figure 9.3, when the arm is flexed, the biceps become shorter and thicker. Since muscle fibers can only contract, the antagonist tricep muscle relaxes as the biceps flex. When the arm is extended, the triceps contract and the biceps relax.

Figure 9.4 will help teachers locate the main skeletal muscles. The muscles of the anterior view (fig. 9.4a) and posterior view (fig. 9.4b) are arranged in pairs. As

Figure 9.3 Muscle Fibers Enclosed by the Fascicle

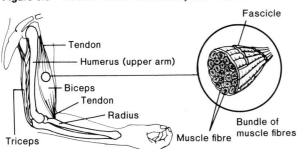

Figure 9.4 Main Skeletal Muscles

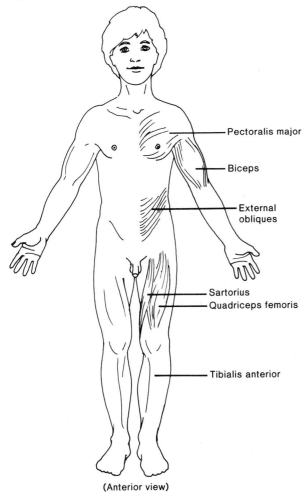

(Anterior view)

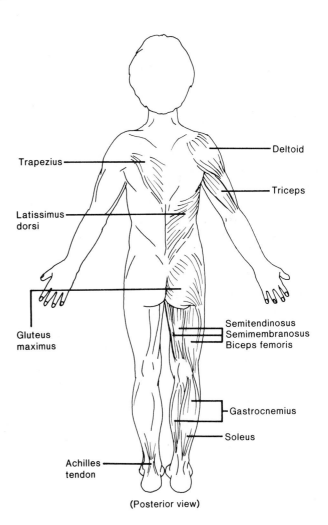

(Posterior view)

Figure 9.5 Blood Flow through the Body

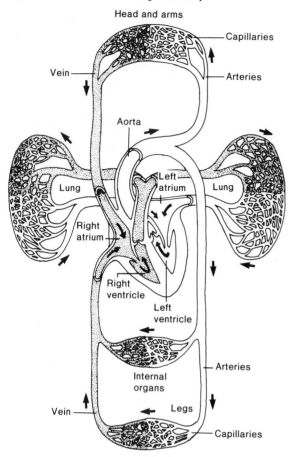

Figure 9.6 Blood Flow through the Heart

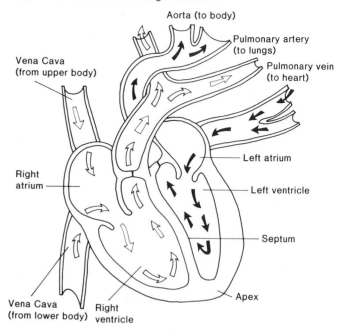

The ends of the smallest arteries branch out into a tiny network of vessels called capillaries. Capillary walls are so thin oxygen and nutrients pass through to the surrounding tissue cells, while carbon dioxide and other waste products move into the capillaries. The capillaries then join small viens, becoming bigger until they reach the upper right chamber of the heart.

Blood Flow Through the Heart

The heart is a very powerful four-chambered muscular pump. Two separate organs sitting side by side work in exact harmony with each other.

Blood flows from the body into the upper right chamber. It then moves down into the lower chamber and is pumped through the pulmonary artery into the lungs. While in the lungs, the blood gets rid of waste gas called carbon dioxide and picks up oxygen before returning to the upper left chamber. It flows down into the lower chamber where it is pumped out of the heart through the aorta to all parts of the body.

Pumping Action of Heart

The pumping action or cycle of the heart is actually a series of very rapid contractions, like squeezes, beginning in the upper chambers and moving in a wavelike action down through the lower chambers. The cycle includes the following three steps.

Step 1: The heart relaxes. While the heart is relaxed the valves between the upper and lower chambers are open so blood flows into the upper chamber and down into the lower chamber.

one (hamstrings) contracts, the antagonist (quadriceps) gradually relaxes to give a smooth and controlled movement. Throughout any movement however, the antagonist muscle never completely relaxes. The feeling of firmness of a relaxed antagonist muscle is known as muscle tone. When muscle groups, such as the hamstrings and quadriceps or abdominal and lower back muscles, are exercised vigorously and routinely, they show firm muscle tone and good posture.

Cardiorespiratory System

The cardiorespiratory system is composed of the heart, arteries and veins, and the lungs. This section explains how the blood is pumped out of the heart, to the lungs to be oxygenated, and to all parts of the body to supply every living cell with the nutrients of life.

Circulation Through the Body

The circulatory system is composed of over 50,000 miles of large and small hollow tubes called blood vessels. Blood carrying oxygen and other nutrients leaves the heart through the aorta which branches into smaller vessels called arteries. Arteries keep branching and getting smaller until they reach every part of the body.

Figure 9.7 Pumping Cycle of the Heart

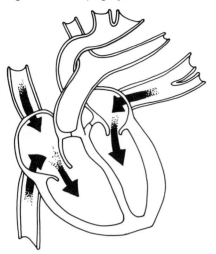

a. Relaxed

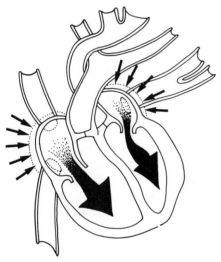

b. Upper chambers contract

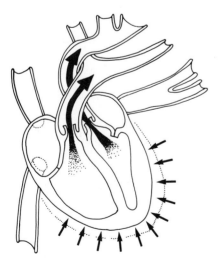

c. Lower chambers contract

Figure 9.8 Heart Rate

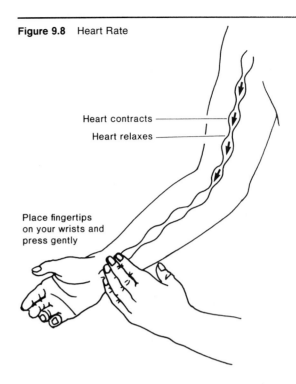

Heart contracts
Heart relaxes

Place fingertips
on your wrists and
press gently

Step 2: The upper chambers contract, forcing more blood into the lower chambers.

Step 3: The thick walled ventricles contract, causing the valves between the upper and lower chambers to close, and the valve in the aorta and pulmonary artery to open, allowing the blood to flow to the lungs and then to the rest of the body. (The heart relaxes again to begin the next cycle.)

Heart Rate

If you place your fingertips on different parts of your body where an artery is close to the skin, you will feel a rhythmical beating. A good place is on the inside of your wrist near the thumb. What you are feeling is the pressure against the wall of the artery every time the heart contracts to send out new blood to the body. When the left ventricle contracts, it forces a large volume of blood into the aorta causing the wall to expand. The ventricle relaxes and the wall of the aorta returns to its normal size. This expansion and contraction of the aorta is sent along the artery in a wavelike motion. The number of times the ventricle contracts in one minute is called *heart rate*. The heart rate of a child is somewhere between 80 and 100 beats per minute. As a person grows older, heart rate slows down until it is about 60 to 80 beats per minute for an adult.

An individual's heart rate is affected by many things such as, fear, excitement, diet, and exercise. For example, vigorous exercise, such as jogging and rope skipping, improve the heart's efficiency in two important ways. First, strenuous exercise performed on a regular basis increases the amount of blood pumped out of the heart on each beat. Second, the heart rate gradually slows down as the individual continues a cardiovascular exercise program. As a result the performer's heart rate becomes more efficient in that it pumps fewer times per minute, forcing more blood out of the heart with less effort.

The following cardiovascular activities can be used to illustrate how the heart and circulatory system are affected by a variety of physical and psychological activities. Additional activities appear in the references listed in appendix A.

Experiment 1: Location and Size of Heart
Divide class into partners and give each twosome one large piece of wrapping paper and marking pens. One partner lies down on the paper with arms extended sideways, while the other partner traces his body. Partners draw and cut out a fist-size heart and tape it to the correct location. (Keep silhouette cutouts until you have covered circulation through the heart and body.) Have each child trace an outline of the heart and place it on the silhouette. Then, draw in arteries to feet, hands, and head, then back through the veins to the heart. Draw in lungs to complete the circulation system.

Experiment 2: Comparative Heart Rates
Have children measure each other's heart rates. Group results according to age and sex. Compare heart rates of various children in the class and with that of the teachers. Make further comparisons with parents, grandparents, high school athletes, and so on.

Experiment 3: Heart Rate Recovery
Each child records his resting heart rate, then runs in place for three minutes. Immediately after running, each performer takes his pulse and records it in the appropriate column. Retake and record heart rates after resting two, four, and six minutes. Use test results to discuss the individual's recovery rate and how cardiovascular fitness can be improved.

Experiment 4: Effects of Different Activities
Divide class into partners. Partners rotate to each of the three activities listed in the chart. Partners cannot start any activity, however, until their heart rates have resumed the resting heart rate. Repeat the experiment at a later date but change the three activities.

Effects of Different Activities

Physical Activity	Resting Rate	Activity Rate	Difference
1. Resting Heart Rate	_____	....	....
2. 3 Minutes Tic-Tac-Toe	....	_____	_____
3. Rest and Record	_____	....	....
4. 3 Minutes Playing Catch		....	_____	_____
5. Rest and Record	_____	....	....
6. 3 Minutes of Rope Skipping (or Run in Place)	....	_____	_____
7. Rest and Record	_____	....	....

Experiment 5: Excitement and Fear
Divide class into partners. One partner repeats the rhyme "Peter piper . . ." twelve times as fast as possible while the other partner attempts to distract him in a funlike manner. (Make faces, count out loud, . . . maybe tickle.) Use this experiment to discuss effects of stress and excitement on cardiovascular fitness. Also, design other similar experiments involving stressful situations.

Excitement and Fear

Resting Heart Rate (Take for 15 Secs x 4) =
Heart Rate after Repeating Rhyme (Take for 15 Secs x 4) =
Repeat the following Rhyme 12 Times: "Peter Piper picked a peck of pickled peppers. How many pecks of pickled peppers did Peter Piper pick?"

Heart Rate Recovery

Activity	Rate 15 Secs	Rate 1 Minute
Resting Heart Rate		x4 =
Immediately after Running On the Spot, as Fast as Possible, for Three Minutes		x4 =
After 2 Minutes		x4 =
After 4 Minutes		x4 =
After 6 Minutes		x4 =

Figure 9.9 Circulation of Blood through the Lungs

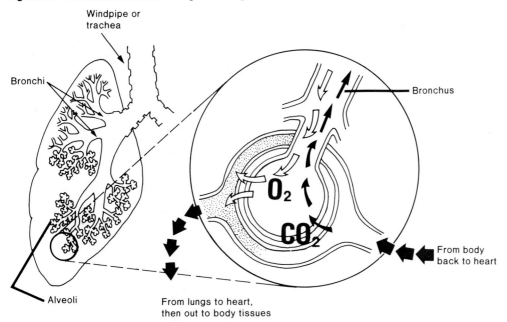

Circulation through Lungs

The lungs of a young child contain over fifty million tiny air sacs called *alveoli*. Air sacs connect to larger tubes called *bronchi* and finally to the large windpipe called the *trachea*.

Blood coming from the pulmonary artery releases carbon dioxide through the capillary wall into the open space between the capillary and the air sac. Carbon dioxide then travels through the bronchi and out the windpipe. At the same time, oxygen moves through the wall of the air sac, across the open space and into the capillary. The blood then travels through the small and large veins until it reaches the upper left chamber.

Respiration, a chemical process that occurs in every living cell of our body, involves the absorption of oxygen, the release of energy, and the elimination of carbon dioxide. The exchange of these gases in the lungs is the breathing part of respiration. Breathing in is caused by the contraction of the muscular diaphragm, moving it downward (fig. 9.10a), and the contraction of the rib muscles, pulling them upward and outward. After the lungs expand and fill with air, the diaphragm and rib muscles relax, allowing the diaphragm to move upward and the ribs to move closer together (fig. 9.10b), thus forcing air out of the lungs.

A normal breathing cycle occurs about twelve to sixteen times per minute. However, during vigorous exercise, the demand for oxygen increases in the body tissues, particularly in the muscle cells. When an individual is in good physical condition, his breathing rate increases the supply of oxygen to the muscle cells. When the oxygen is supplied to the muscle cells to produce

Figure 9.10 Expansion and Contraction of the Diaphragm during Breathing

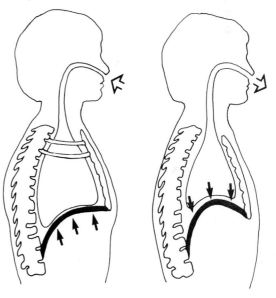

energy during vigorous exercise it is called *aerobic exercise*. If the exercise is too strenuous, the muscle cells cannot get enough oxygen from the lungs. When this occurs, the muscle cells begin to produce energy without oxygen, which is called *anaerobic exercise* and can last for a few minutes. During anaerobic exercise, the cell builds up an oxygen debt that must be paid back during the recovery or rest period.

Vigorous exercise performed in a regular and systematic manner helps to increase the efficiency of the lungs. Inactivity particularly for long periods of time substantially lowers this efficiency. And, other factors such as being overweight and smoking also lower the efficiency of the respiratory system.

Developing Good Posture

Parents, teachers, and school officials have always been concerned about children's posture, particularly since there appears to be a strong relationship between posture and such factors as perceptual acuity, emotional health, and general fitness. Slanting desks, adjustable chalkboards, and improved lighting were all installed to enhance and maintain correct posture. But chronic television viewing and inadequate daily exercise for many children have continued to produce numerous postural problems, which are readily detectable and can be corrected by vigorous exercise.

There is no clear definition or standard of "good" posture that can be applied to all children, whether they are standing, sitting, or moving. Standing posture is judged by the alignment of body segments. The child in figures 9.11 and 9.12 has good posture because his body segments are evenly balanced over the base of support. Viewed from the side, the plumb line runs from a little in front of the ankle through the knee, pelvis, shoulders, and ear. In this position the natural curves of the body are moderate, with the head, shoulders, pelvis, knees, and feet balanced evenly on each side of the line. Viewed from the back, the plumb line runs midway through the head, vertebrae, and hips, and equidistant between the feet.

A child with good posture requires a minimum contraction of antigravity muscle groups to keep his body erect and balanced. But when a child slouches, his upper back muscles must contract to shift the body to the correct posture. If he continues to slouch, his muscles gradually adapt to that position and he might have chronic poor posture if it is not corrected.

Common Posture Problems

Most of the typical posture deviations of young children can be observed and corrected with proper exercise. The following deviations can be observed when the child is standing beside a plumb line.

Round Upper Back (Kyphosis)

Round back, or kyphosis, is a marked increase in the curve of the back (fig. 9.13). The head and shoulders are usually held in a forward position, and the backward curve of the upper body causes the pelvis to tilt

Figure 9.11 Good Posture (side view). Natural curves of the body are moderate.

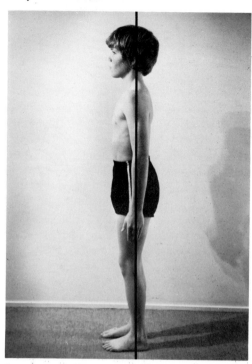

Figure 9.12 Good Posture (back view)

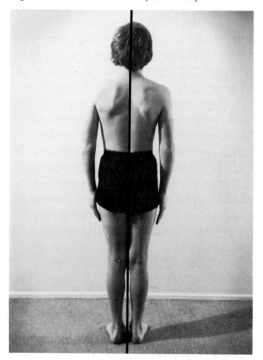

Figure 9.13 Round Back (kyphosis)

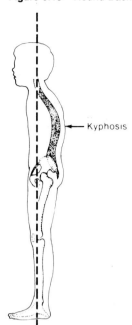

Figure 9.14 Hollow Back (lordosis)

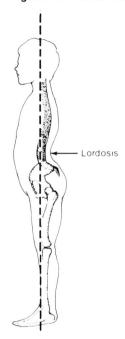

forward slightly and the knees to bend somewhat. This condition increases the strain on the upper back muscles and shifts the weight of the body to the front of the foot.

Hollow Back (Lordosis)

Hollow back, or lordosis, is an exaggerated forward curve of the lower back (fig. 9.14). The most common signs are a protruding abdomen, a swayback, and hyperextension of the knees.

Lateral Curvature (Scoliosis)

Lateral curvature, or scoliosis, can be C-shaped, extending the length of the spinal column, or S-shaped, with a small curve on the upper back and a compensating curve on the lower back (fig. 9.15). The C-shaped curve is normally toward the left since most children are right-handed and tend to lean to the weaker side. This comes from the constant elevation of the right arm and the tendency to lean toward the left side of the desk while writing and performing other sitting activities.

Methods of Assessing Posture

The classroom teacher is generally in the best position to assess her students' postures. Most teachers are genuinely concerned about the way a child sits at his desk and how he moves in his daily activities. For most teachers, the evaluation of posture is primarily one of continual subjective observation. When she notices a major change in a child's posture, the teacher brings

Figure 9.15 Lateral Curvature (scoliosis)—(a) C-type curve and (b) S-type curve

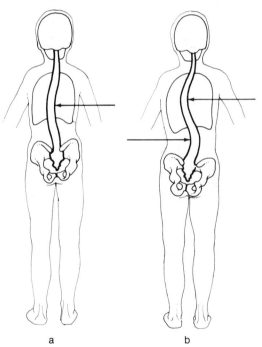

a   b

in the school nurse or parent to determine whether the change is due to a muscular weakness or to other factors, such as nutrition, eyesight, or an emotional disturbance.

If a teacher wishes to use a simple screening test, she might consider the side- and rear-view plumb line test and the posture chart shown in figure 9.16. The chart can be used in various ways, depending on the interests of the teacher, the ages of the children, and the time available. Most teachers can complete the test in the classroom.

Methods of Improving Posture

The plumb line test is designed as a basic screening device. It can detect major postural problems and, perhaps more important, make the child more conscious of his posture when standing, sitting, or moving through a variety of movement patterns. The foundation of good posture, however, is the possession of optimum levels of muscular strength, endurance, flexibility, and efficient motor skill patterns. The following exercises will assist in correcting functional postural defects as well as enhance general muscular strength endurance and flexibility.

1. *Exercises for Improving Head and Neck Position:*
   Head pull, page 153
   Head circling, page 153
   Neck flattener, page 154
   Head lift, page 154

2. *Exercises for Improving Round Shoulders:*
   Hanging, page 155
   Wall push, page 155
   Head and arm raisers, page 156

3. *Exercises for Improving Lower Back:*
   Cat stretcher, page 156
   Trunk stretcher, page 156
   Back arch, page 157

4. *Exercises for Improving Abdominal Muscles:*
   Curl-ups, page 157
   Elbow-knee touch, page 157
   Hip raisers, page 157

5. *Exercises for Improving Functional Scoliosis:*
   Hanging, page 155
   Side stretch, page 156

Improving Physical Fitness

Since the original Kraus survey in 1953, the physical education profession has been plagued with the problem of defining *physical fitness*. One of the most all-inclusive definitions was given by a representative group of the American Alliance for Health, Physical Education and Recreation (AAHPERD 1976) and is generally agreed upon by members of the physical education profession.

Fitness is that state which characterizes the degree to which a person is able to function. Fitness is an individual matter. It implies that ability of each person to live most effectively with his potential. Ability to function depends upon the physical, mental, emotional, and social components of fitness, all of which are related to each other and mutually interdependent.

Many elementary education teachers would agree with this definition and would say that they contribute to one or more of these general areas of fitness in the classroom. But there is also general agreement in physical education that "physical fitness" is just one aspect of total fitness. This definition, however, gives little guidance as to what aspects of fitness should be stressed in the physical education program. So we describe a physically fit child as one who possesses adequate strength and endurance to carry out daily activities without undue fatigue and still has sufficient energy to enjoy leisure activities and meet emergencies. This definition must be interpreted on the basis of each child's genetic structure, which sets the optimum level of physical fitness he is capable of reaching. It must also consider the child's nutritional status and other personal health habits that determine the potential level of improvement the child is capable of reaching.

Methods of Assessing Physical Fitness

Although opinions differ about which basic components of physical fitness should be measured, the majority of contemporary test batteries for children include a combination of health-related and motor fitness elements. Health-related components include strength, cardiorespiratory endurance, flexibility, and body composition. Motor fitness and performance-related components include agility, speed, balance, and power. A low score on a test battery containing health and motor fitness related components indicates that a child does not possess the strength and vitality to carry out everyday experiences and respond to emergencies. It can also reveal a lack of exercise and possible nutritional deficiencies or temporary illness.

AAHPERD's *Health Related Physical Fitness Test* is designed to measure the health aspects of fitness. All other test batteries, including AAHPERD's *Revised 1976 Test* and the *Washington State Physical Fitness Test* include both health and motor fitness components. It appears most school districts will continue to use their existing test batteries and gradually include the testing of more health-related components, particularly those relating to cardiovascular efficiency and body composition.

Figure 9.16   Posture Chart Using the Plumb Line Test

Name: _____

Date: _____
First evaluation: _____
Second evaluation: _____
Third evaluation: _____

Key to score:
Note: Use figure a and b as a Normal (0) rating. Children should assume a relaxed, "normal" posture when taking this test.

Normal	0
Slight	1
Moderate	2
Severe	3

	Side View	First Evaluation	Second Evaluation	Third Evaluation
A	Body Lean: Forward			
	Backward			
B	Forward Head			
C	Round Shoulders			
D	Round Dorsal Curve			
E	Protruding Abdomen			
F	Hyperextended Knees			
	Back View			
G	Head Tilt:			
	to right			
	to left			
H	Shoulder:			
	lower on right			
	lower on left			
I	Bow Legs			
J	Knock Knees			
K	Feet pointing out			
	Feet pointing in			
L	Curve of Vertebrae:			
	C-curve			
	S-curve			

a. Side view

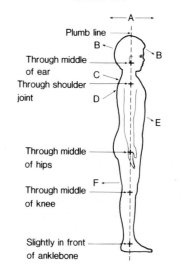

Plumb line

Through middle of ear
Through shoulder joint

Through middle of hips

Through middle of knee

Slightly in front of anklebone

b. Back view

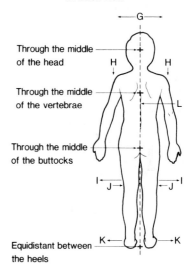

Through the middle of the head

Through the middle of the vertebrae

Through the middle of the buttocks

Equidistant between the heels

Figure 9.17 The Skinfold Test

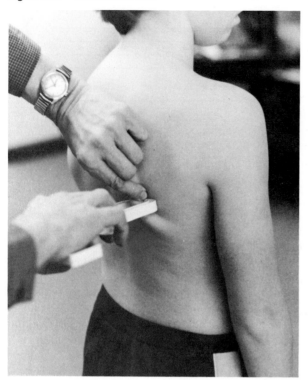

Figure 9.18 Sit-ups

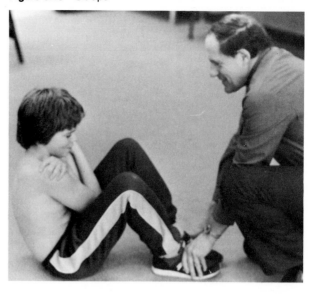

Figure 9.19 Sit-and-reach

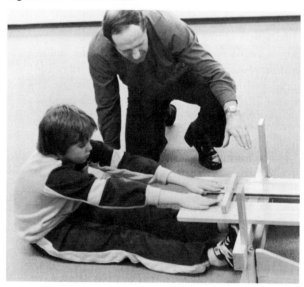

Health Related Physical Fitness Tests

The new *Health Related Physical Fitness Test* developed by AAHPERD represents a major change in the philosophy and direction of elementary school physical fitness programs. The items in this test battery measure the elements of health that are important throughout life. To instill a lifelong positive attitude towards these important aspects of health, a child must understand how his body works and what effect various types of exercise programs have on his own health. This can be accomplished by testing children with this type of test battery, then provide them with appropriate exercise programs along with the knowledge of how the systems of the body are positively affected by these programs.

Four items of this new test battery are described briefly here. A detailed description of this test, along with norms, can be purchased from AAHPERD.

1. *Distance Run:* This test measures maximum function and endurance of the cardiorespiratory system. Two options are available: the mile run (1609.76 m) for time, or a nine minute run for distance.

2. *Sum of Skinfolds:* This test evaluates the level of fatness in school-age boys and girls. The subcutaneous adipose tissue in various regions of the body can be lifted with the fingers and thumb to form a skinfold (fig. 9.17). The

thickness of this skinfold, which consists of a double layer of subcutaneous fat and skin, can be measured with a skinfold caliper. Two skinfold sites (triceps and subscapular) are typically used for this test because they are easily measured and highly correlated with total body fat.

3. *Sit-ups:* This test measures abdominal strength and endurance. The performer lies on his back with knees bent, feet on the floor, and arms crossed. His feet are held down on the floor throughout the exercise. Keeping the elbows against his chest, the performer raises up and touches elbows to thighs.

Table 9.1 Physical Fitness Tests for Elementary School Children

Name of Test	Age or Grade Level	Items in Test Battery	Source
President's Council Youth Physical Fitness Screening Test	Ages 6–17	Pull-ups Sit-ups Squat thrusts	Youth Physical Fitness, U.S. Government Printing Office, Washington, D.C. 1967
New York State Physical Fitness Test	Grades 4–12	Posture test Target throw Modified push-up Side-step 50-yard dash Squat stand Treadmill	Department of Education, Albany, New York
Revised Washington State Elementary School Fitness Test (1980)	Ages 6–12	Standing broad jump Bench push-ups Curl-ups Squat-jump 30-yard dash	Copies of this test battery have been sent to every state department of public instruction. For additional information write to State Department of Public Instruction, Olympia, Washington
Oregon Motor Fitness Test	Grades 4–6	Push-ups (boys) Knee touch sit-ups (boys) Flexed arm hang (girls) Curl-ups (girls) Standing broad jump	State Department of Education, Salem, Oregon
Canadian Physical Performance Test Manual	Ages 7–17	Sit-up Standing broad jump Shuttle run Flexed arm hang 50-yard run 300-yard run	Canadian Association for Health, Physical Education, and Recreation, 333 River Road, Vanier City, Ontario, Canada

4. *Sit and Reach:* This test measures flexibility of the lower back and posterior thigh. The performer assumes a sitting position with knees fully extended and feet resting against the apparatus. The arms extend forward with the hands on top of each other. The performer reaches directly forward, palms down along the measuring scale.

Combined Health and Performance Related Physical Fitness Tests

A wide variety of combined health and performance physical fitness test batteries are available. Some of the more commonly used ones are listed in table 9.1. Each teacher should consult the local supervisor of physical education or the respective state department of public instruction when selecting a test battery.

If no standardized test is recommended, the teacher should evaluate the tests on the basis of the following considerations. The test should be a reliable and valid measure of the basic components of physical fitness. Each test item should be readily acceptable to the varying, and sometimes unique, conditions existing in many elementary schools. Available facilities, the ages of the children, and the size of the class should also be considered. Finally, each test item should be highly motivating and, so far as possible, free of elements that could cause accidents or injury.

The *Revised AAHPERD Youth Fitness Test* (ages nine to seventeen) should be strongly considered on the basis of these criteria. A description of this test battery follows; or you may purchase the complete test manual from AAHPERD, 1900 Association Drive, Reston, Va. 22091. Since the AAHPERD test is not designed for children below nine years, the Revised (1980) Washington State Elementary School Physical Fitness Test is recommended for ages six through twelve. (See table 9.1 for address.) This test battery has a new set of norms for children six to twelve years of age.

Revised AAHPERD Youth Fitness Test (1976)

The following six-item test battery does not require expensive equipment with the possible exception of a horizontal bar. In addition, it is suggested that the test battery be administered in two successive physical education periods.

Test 1: Pull-ups (Boys). This test measures arm and shoulder girdle strength. The performer attempts to complete as many pull-ups as possible. No time limit is stipulated.

Test 1: Flexed-arm Hang (Girls). This test measures arm and shoulder strength. The performer attempts to hold a chinning position for as long as possible.

Test 2: Sit-ups—Flexed Leg (Boys and Girls). This test measures abdominal strength. The performer begins in a back lying position, hands clasped behind head, knees bent, feet flat on the floor, and heels not more than twelve inches from the buttocks. A partner holds the performer's feet close to the floor throughout this test. This test requires the performer to do as many sit-ups as possible in sixty seconds.

Test 3: Shuttle Run (Boys and Girls). This test is designed to measure speed and agility. Two parallel lines are marked on the floor thirty feet apart. Two blocks of wood are placed behind one line. This test requires the performer to run from one line to the opposite line, pick up one block, return it to his starting line placing the block behind the line, then repeat the same action with the second block. Two trials are allowed with the best score recorded.

Test 4: Standing Long Jump (Boys and Girls). This test is designed to measure leg power. The performer stands in a partially crouched position behind a starting line, with feet approximately shoulder width apart. He then attempts to jump as far as possible. Three trials are allowed with the best score recorded.

Test 5: 50-yard Dash (Boys and Girls). This test is designed to measure speed. The performer attempts to run as fast as possible from behind a starting line through a fifty-yard distance and across the finish line. The score is measured to the nearest tenth of a second.

Test 6: 600-yard Run (Boys and Girls). This test measures endurance. A square track with sides measuring fifty yards is laid out in the playing field. The performer attempts to run (or run and intersperse walking) around the square track in the shortest time possible. The score is recorded in minutes and seconds.

Mary Smith, Sept. 1984	Raw Score	Percentile
Flexed Arm Hang	5 seconds	30
Sit-up	28	45
Shuttle Run	11.1 seconds	60
Standing Broad Jump	4 feet, 4 inches	25
50-yard Dash	8.3 seconds	50
600-yard Run	3 minutes, 24 seconds	20

Recording and Interpreting Individual Test Scores The percentile scale is used in the AAHPERD norms to compare the relative performance of test items and to add up individual scores. An example illustrates how raw scores are recorded and transferred to a new percentile score. The table above is an example of an eleven-year-old girl tested in September 1984.

When the raw scores are transferred to the percentile scale and then plotted on the individual profile sheet (p. 145), a clear picture of Mary's current level of physical fitness can be easily interpreted. With the exception of the shuttle run, her performance on all other test items was at or below the fiftieth percentile. Her performance on the remaining items below this line is generally subpar for her age level.

Methods of Improving Physical Fitness

As defined earlier, physical fitness is the possession of adequate strength and vitality to carry out daily activities and meet emergencies. In its broadest meaning, then, physical fitness should be considered a means to an end rather than an end in itself.

Playing a vigorous game such as basketball or soccer requires a high level of endurance. If a child, or the class, does not possess sufficient endurance to play the game, the teacher should take appropriate remedial measures—longer warm-up periods involving continuous movements. Likewise, a boy who cannot perform the "skin-the-cat" on the horizontal bar may well need additional shoulder girdle strength rather than a correction in his motor skill pattern.

Not only is physical fitness important for performance of motor skills, but a high level of physical fitness also is usually indicative of optimum physical and mental well-being. Children with abundant physical vitality generally are organically sound, mentally alert, and socially well adjusted. For these reasons, classroom teachers should test children early in the school year to determine general and specific areas of weakness and then select appropriate activities to correct these deficiencies.

PROFILE RECORD

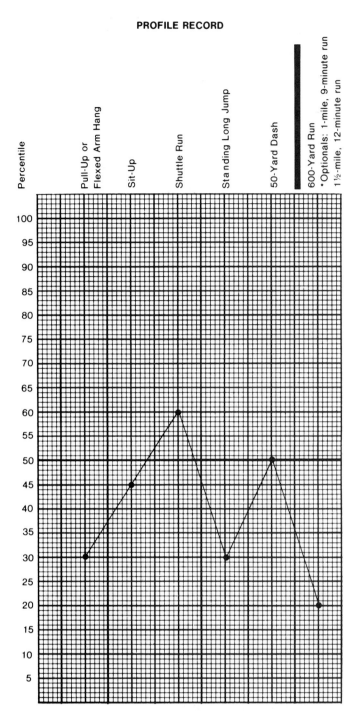

Determining Areas of Need

Each class should take a physical fitness test during the first few weeks of the school year. Once the scores are recorded on a class score sheet, a general diagnosis of the class can be made. As shown in table 9.2, both boys and girls scored well above average in the standing broad jump, shuttle run, and the fifty-yard dash, so activities that improve power, speed, and agility would not require emphasis.

On the other hand, the poor results of the other three tests involving strength and endurance reveal a definite need for activities that increase the strength and endurance of the arm and shoulder girdle, and the abdominal and leg muscles. When the scores of these test items are low, the total physical fitness score is also generally low. By increasing the performance of these three items, the total fitness score obviously will show a proportionate increase.

An individual analysis can also be made of each child to determine specific areas of weakness. Any child who has extremely low scores on all the test items should be referred to the school nurse or family doctor for additional diagnosis. Low scores, particularly for a child who appears to be healthy, often indicate that the child could be suffering from nutritional deficiencies or a temporary illness. If competent medical authorities say the diagnosis is simply lack of adequate exercise, appropriate remedial steps can be taken by the teacher and parents.

The plumb line test for posture (fig. 9.16) can also be used in conjunction with a standardized physical fitness test. A basic screening test for posture determines general areas of weakness and detects children who should be referred to their family physicians.

Selection of Appropriate Activities

Physical education teachers face the multiple purposes of providing vigorous physical activities, teaching motor skills, and providing experiences that foster intellectual and social development. No single activity can accomplish all these goals. Furthermore, no single activity can contribute to all of the basic components of physical fitness described earlier. The value of table 9.3 is that it shows how various activities contribute to these basic elements.

Let us assume we have tested a fifth grade class in September and found results similar to those shown in table 9.2. The class definitely needs activities that will increase the strength and endurance of the arm and shoulder girdle, and the abdominal and leg muscles. During the first few months of the school year, pleasant weather and student interest indicates that an outdoor activity would be the most suitable choice. The teacher had decided to begin with a four week unit on soccer

Table 9.2   Average Class Scores for AAHPERD Test Items

	Arm/Shoulder Girdle Strength	Abdominal Strength	Speed and Agility	Leg Power	Speed	Endurance	Total
	Pull-ups	*Sit-ups*	*Shuttle Run*	*Standing Long Jump*	*50-yard Dash*	*600-yard Run*	*Physical Fitness*
Boys	50% below average	90% below average	70% below average	70% above average	75% above average	65% below average	65% below average
Girls	75% above average	92% below average	70% below average	95% below average	80% above average		70% below average

Table 9.3   Activities for Posture and Physical Fitness

	Strength High	Strength Low	Endurance High	Endurance Low	Power High	Power Low	Speed High	Speed Low	Agility High	Agility Low	Flexibility High	Flexibility Low	Posture High	Posture Low
Game Activities														
Relays	x	x			x		x		x			x	x	
Tag Games	x	x			x		x		x			x		x
Simple Team Games	x	x			x		x		x			x		x
Individual and Team Games	x	x			x		x		x			x		x
Dance Activities														
Fundamental Skills		x		x	x		x		x		x		x	
Singing Games		x		x	x		x			x		x		x
Folk Dances		x		x	x		x		x			x	x	
Creative Rhythms		x		x	x		x		x		x		x	
Rhythmics	x	x			x		x		x			x		x
Gymnastic Activities														
Conditioning Exercises	x			x	x			x	x		x		x	
Vaulting Box	x			x	x	x			x		x			x
Balance Beam		x		x		x	x		x		x		x	
Rope Skipping	x			x	x			x	x		x		x	
Horizontal Bar	x			x	x			x	x		x		x	
Climbing Rope	x			x	x			x	x		x		x	
Stunts and Tumbling	x			x	x		x		x		x		x	
Swedish Gym	x			x	x			x	x		x		x	
Climbing Cube	x			x	x			x	x		x		x	
Overhead Ladder	x			x	x			x	x		x		x	
Agility Apparatus	x			x	x			x	x		x		x	

activities, but table 9.3 indicates that soccer as a "team game" is a low contributer to strength. Recognizing this inherent weakness of the soccer activity and the need for activities involving strength, the teacher emphasizes warm-up exercises that develop strength in the arm and shoulder girdle and abdominal and leg muscles.

Other units of instruction involving games, dance, and gymnastic activities should be analyzed for their potential contribution to physical fitness (table 9.3). Once the inherent limitations of the activity are known, supplemental activities can be included to meet special posture and health-related physical fitness needs of the individual child or class.

Special Programs for Improving Health-Related Components of Physical Fitness

The following programs are primarily designed to improve three very important health-related components of physical fitness. The first, cardiorespiratory endurance, is the ability of the heart, circulatory system, and lungs to collect, transport, and utilize oxygen during continuous movement over an extended period of time. Second, muscular endurance is the ability of muscles to repeat a strenuous movement over an extended period of time. Third, muscular strength is the ability of a group of muscles to exert a maximum amount of force. If the following principles of exercise are adhered to while participating in vigorous, physical activities, an individual will improve his muscular strength, endurance, and cardiorespiratory efficiency. Participation in these programs, particularly circuit training and general conditioning exercises, will also improve posture and many performance related components such as balance, speed, and power.

Principles of Exercise

Principle 1: Overload

The exercise activity should require an overload performance. The systems of our body constantly adapt to our daily routine. For example, if we are inactive our muscles become smaller (atrophy) and lose strength; and our breathing becomes less efficient because we do not force the expansion of the lungs, thus closing off areas of lung tissue where exchange of oxygen and carbon dioxide would otherwise take place. To become stronger or to improve cardiorespiratory efficiency, the performer must increase the intensity (how hard), duration (how long), or frequency (how much) of an activity in accordance with a target zone that sets optimum limits for each individual and for each component of physical fitness. To illustrate, if a child performs ten curl-ups (intensity) in one minute (duration) each day (frequency) without causing any "overload" effort, he will not increase his strength or endurance. He is exercising below his threshold level. At the opposite extreme, if the child shifts from ten to twenty curl-ups each day and feels extremely sore and tired, he is exercising beyond the optimum limits. Somewhere between ten and twenty is his optimum limit. This optimum limit is found by gradually increasing the number of repetitions so there can be an overload in performance without excessive soreness or fatigue.

The best method of determining whether cardiorespiratory endurance is being improved is by monitoring the person's heart rate before and after exercise. Resting heart rate for children between six and twelve years varies from eighty to ninety beats per minute.

Table 9.4 Cardiorespiratory Endurance

Heart Rate

220	**Maximum Heart Rate**
200	
190	
180	**Target Heart Rate Zone**
170	(This is between 70 and 85 percent of a child's
160	maximum heart rate.)
150	
140	
130	
120	
110	
100	
90	
80	**Resting Heart Rate Zone**
70	
60	

Maximum heart rate, obtained during very strenuous exercise, would reach about 220 (table 9.4). To improve cardiorespiratory endurance, children must increase their heart rate to about 160 to 190 beats per minute for about ten to fifteen minutes per day. This training zone heart rate is approximately 70 to 85 percent of an individual's maximum rate. It should therefore be used as a very general guideline. Hence, children who have difficulty performing an exercise, such as running or swimming, for a short period of time should adjust their training zone downward to 130 or less. The training zone can be increased to higher levels as the individual gradually improves his cardiorespiratory endurance.

Principle 2: Tolerance

The exercise or activity should be adapted to the individual's exercise tolerance. This means that the child should be able to perform an exercise or activity without undue discomfort or fatigue. Several cues help determine the child's exercise tolerance. One is to check the scores on a physical fitness test, particularly for those parts that are similar to the exercises in the physical fitness program. If a child's performance in arm and shoulder girdle strength tests was low, the teacher should expect an initial low tolerance in push-ups and pull-ups. With practice, the child's strength will improve, along with his tolerance level. Perhaps the single best means of determining a child's tolerance to an activity is the teacher's own judgment based upon such factors as the child's breathlessness, slow recuperation, and excessively sore muscles.

Principle 3: Progression

The exercise or activity should provide for progression. This principle is closely associated with the previous two. Any planned exercise program must begin where it is comfortable or within the tolerance level of the child. From there, the program should gradually overload the muscles to increase strength or to increase the demands upon the heart and lungs.

Exercise Programs

The following exercise programs adhere to the basic principles of exercise. The type of program the teacher selects depends upon the needs of her class or the individual child requiring a special posture or physical fitness program.

Jogging

Jogging is an easy or relaxed run that does not place undue fatigue upon the runner. It is one of the most effective and enjoyable means of improving muscular and cardiovascular endurance. If taught correctly, elementary children—including first graders—can participate in jogging activities in the gymnasium, on the playing field, or in a cross-country setting.

The proper form is like that of a distance runner: body erect and relaxed and arms swinging in an easy manner. The heel of the foot contacts the ground, then rocks forward to a gentle push off the front of the foot.

Before introducing jogging, it should be presented to young children as a recreational activity. Jogging should not be seen as a prerequisite to competitive cross-country running; rather, it should be seen as an activity in which the child can derive enjoyment and success as he increases the distance he can run without undue fatigue or strain. This means each child should set his own goals. And other activities should be interspersed with jogging, since young children may become bored with the same jogging pace and such tracks as "around the gymnasium" or "around the outside of the playing field."

The basic approach used to teach children to jog is to have them begin with a series of stretching exercises, then a walk. When they feel ready, they can begin to jog as far as they can without feeling overfatigued or out of breath. Once the children learn to pace themselves to a jog-walk-jog pattern, they will gradually increase the jogging distance as they decrease the walking distance.

After a few days of basic jog-walk-jog activities, introduce the "scout's pace." Have each child jog 110 yards, walk 55 yards, jog 110 yards, continuing the pattern as long as possible. The distances can be adjusted to the child's or the class's ability and condition.

As soon as the majority of the children can jog a reasonable distance, such as a mile, introduce other jogging activities into the program such as "hash running" (p. 383), orienteering (p. 257), or establishing a 100-mile club, all of which involve enjoyable recreational jogging. The 100-mile club is a program in which each child keeps his own jogging "log" or record sheet. He might receive a certificate when he reaches 100 miles; however, if the jogging program has been introduced correctly the child should find that completing 100 miles is valuable in itself and he has little need for a badge or certificate.

Circuit Training

Circuit training is repeating one or more exercises as many times as possible within a time limit. A simple circuit would be doing six push-ups, ten curl-ups, and eighteen toe touches within two minutes. The number and type of exercises are optional and the variations, unlimited.

This type of conditioning exercise program has many advantages, particularly for the self-contained classroom teacher. In the first place, circuit training allows for individual differences. The number of repetitions of each exercise is determined by each child, not by the most physically fit child in the class. And one of the most important administrative advantages is the time limit. The teacher determines how much time she wants to devote to circuit training, then proceeds to develop a tailor-made program to meet the needs of her class.

An example is provided to show how to develop a circuit for each member of your class.

Step 1: Determine How Much Time You Want to Spend on the Circuit. Time might range from six to ten minutes; our example is ten minutes.

Step 2: Select Appropriate Exercises. Let us assume the teacher has administered a physical fitness test and has noted that the majority of students show low strength and endurance in the arm and shoulder girdle (pull-ups), abdominal muscles (sit-ups), and leg muscles (600 yd. run). The circuit training program thus should contain exercises that improve these weaknesses. The five exercises listed in table 9.5 would meet these needs.

Step 3. Determine the Maximum Number of Repetitions for Each Exercise. This is the first day involving exercise. Start with the first exercise, the bicycle. All children attempt to do the exercise as many times as they can in one minute. Record the number of repetitions under the maximum number column in the sample chart. Let us assume this is the chart of a fifth-grade girl who has performed sixteen bicycle repetitions. Immediately following this test, let the children rest for one minute. Next, have them do as many push-ups as possible in one minute. Let them rest for one minute and continue the procedure to the fifth exercise.

Table 9.5 Circuit Training Program for Increasing Strength and Endurance

Exercises	Page	Maximum Number	Training Dose No. 1 (¼ dose)	Jan. 15	Jan. 16	Jan. 17	etc.
1. Bicycle (legs)	158	16	4				
2. Push-ups (arms and shoulders)	154	8	2				
3. Head raiser (trunk)	156	6	2				
4. Jumping Jack	159	20	5				
5. Elbow–knee touch (trunk)	157	11	3				

Step 4: Set the Training Dose. The training dose (see table 9.5) is the actual number of repetitions the child performs when he starts the circuit program. It might be one-quarter, one-half, or three-quarters of the maximum number. As a suggestion, start with one-quarter of the maximum number as the child's first training dose. Place these numbers in the first training dose column. Now the child is ready to perform the circuit without any rest between each exercise. In other words, he must try to complete the following three laps of exercises in ten minutes.

Lap 1	Lap 2	Lap 3
4 bicycles	4 bicycles	4 bicycles
2 push-ups	2 push-ups	2 push-ups
2 head raisers	2 head raisers	2 head raisers
5 jumping jacks	5 jumping jacks	5 jumping jacks
3 curl-ups	3 curl-ups	3 curl-ups

Step 5: Attempt to Complete the Circuit. Each child has ten minutes to complete the circuit. Let us assume this girl has completed one lap in three minutes. Now, without rest, she starts her second lap. This lap takes her three and one-half minutes, leaving three and one-half minutes to complete the third lap. She immediately starts her third lap and gets to the second exercise, the push-ups, when the whistle blows. Record her results under the appropriate date. She completed two laps and was on exercise 2 of the third lap, so "3–2" would be recorded under the date and opposite push-ups.

Step 6: Continue step number five until the child performs three laps within the time limit. Then increase each exercise by one repetition. Our girl would now do five bicycles, three push-ups, three head raisers, six jumping jacks, and four curl-ups.

The length of time devoted to a circuit training program depends foremost on the physical fitness needs of the class. If the class scored low on the physical fitness test, it would be wise to require a daily circuit for five to six weeks. The teacher might also design a ten-minute circuit for use in the classroom on those days when her class does not have access to the gymnasium. In this case, she should consider student interest and change the exercises in the circuit each month.

There is a wonderful opportunity here to help the child who scores extremely low on the physical fitness test. First, attempt to determine the reasons for the low fitness, such as obesity or chronic lack of exercise. Design a circuit for the child to do at home. This may involve drawing stick figures to explain the exercises and sending a short note to the parents or interviewing them. The results may be tremendous if the teacher shows an interest, making periodic checks with the child and the parents.

Obstacle Course

An obstacle course is an arrangement of small equipment and large apparatus designed to improve one or more of the components of physical fitness. Commercial obstacle courses normally include apparatus to climb, balance upon, vault over, and crawl through. This type of apparatus is basically for use outdoors and normally is permanently anchored to the ground. Homemade obstacle courses using the natural building materials of a region have become very popular in many elementary schools. They are generally built by parents and usually have a theme, such as a western fort or outpost, space travel, or a jungle trek.

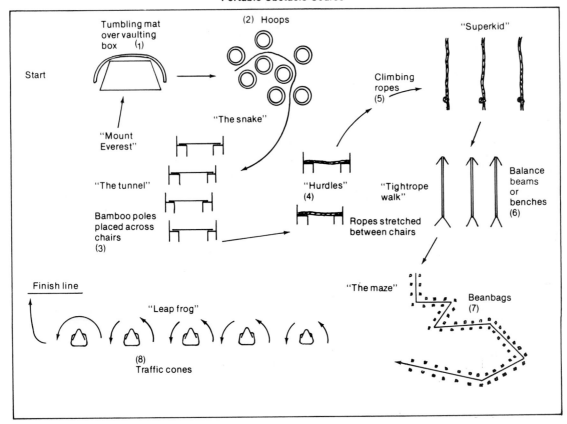

Portable obstacle courses can be made with the equipment and apparatus available in the school. These courses have several advantages: they can be arranged in different patterns and they can be located in a gymnasium or on the playground. An indoor obstacle course as illustrated above requires a minimum amount of small and large apparatus used in an imaginative and constructive way.

Each child tries to complete the course as quickly as possible. The items along this obstacle course contribute to physical fitness in the following ways:

1. *Mount Everest:* Climbing improves strength and power.
2. *The Snake:* Running through the hoops, placing alternate feet in them, improves agility.
3. *The Tunnel:* Crawling through improves strength and endurance of the arm and shoulder girdle.
4. *Hurdles:* Jumping over them improves leg power.
5. *Superkid:* Climbing the rope as high as possible improves strength of the arm and shoulder girdle.
6. *Tightrope Walk:* Walking across balance bench improves balance.

7. *The Maze:* Hopping through beanbag course improves strength and power of the legs.
8. *Leapfrog:* Straddle jumping over traffic cones (or milk cartons) improves the power of the legs.

Assign one child to start at each station in order to provide maximum participation and avoid confusion and collisions. On the signal "go" each child tackles the task at his station, then continues through the obstacle course until completing all eight tasks. If possible, duplicate stations two, seven, and eight, so that two students can begin at each of these stations.

Children thoroughly enjoy indoor and outdoor obstacle courses. Once the students understand the basic purpose of an obstacle course, they should have an opportunity to plan their own. Their designs are usually very imaginative and more demanding than the "teacher-designed course."

Rope Jumping The individual rope jumping steps described in chapter 26 can be incorporated into an excellent program for enhancing the health-related components of physical fitness. The following procedure will help develop a rope jumping program for upper primary or intermediate grades.

Figure 9.20 Rope Jumping

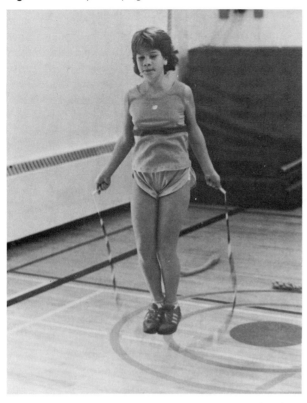

1. Set a time limit for rope jumping (duration). This program will last ten minutes.

2. Allow each child to choose three or four steps that can be performed on each turn of the rope. (Example: two foot, running, one-foot hop, or cross-arm step)

3. Set a heart rate training zone. This will be between 160 and 190 beats per minute.

4. Before starting the rope jumping session, have the class perform a series of stretching exercises.

5. For the ten minute rope jumping program, all children begin jumping rope to a cadence of eighty jumps per minute. (Use a record with a 4/4 beat and adjust the speed to eighty beats per minute.) Each child tries to jump to the pace for ten minutes. If a child stops, say at four and one-half minutes, he should immediately take his heart rate. At the ten minute mark have all remaining children take their heart rate. If half of the students' heart rates is less than 160 beats, increase the cadence to 90 beats and instruct each child to include more difficult and demanding steps (intensity).

6. On each successive day, each child tries to keep up to the cadence as long as possible. As each child improves he will continue longer and add

more demanding steps. Continue adjusting the cadence upward until all children are performing within the target zone.

Conditioning Exercises

Conditioning, or calisthenic, exercises have traditionally been used as a warm-up activity. The fundamental purposes of these exercises are to develop physical fitness and to prepare the body for the main activities of the lesson. Normally, the warm-up begins with a vigorous activity, such as running around the gymnasium, rope skipping, or playing a vigorous tag game, followed by exercises for the neck, arm and shoulder girdle, trunk, and legs. The warm-up period normally lasts about five to ten minutes; however, time allotments vary from class to class.

The following suggestions can make the conditioning exercises effective and enjoyable:

1. Demonstrate the exercise, then have the class perform it slowly so each child can learn the correct form and cadence.

2. Each exercise should be performed in a steady fashion rather than in quick or ballisticlike motions.

3. Instruct children not to hold their breath during an exercise, but to breathe normally.

4. Once the children know the exercise, let them do the repetitions at their own rates. This is particularly important when performing flexibility exercises, since children's body structures and potential ranges of movement vary.

5. Add variations to each exercise. For example, "trunk bending forward and backward" can be changed on each forward movement by such directions as "through the legs," "to the left side," or "with right foot in front."

6. Change the basic set of exercises on alternate days.

7. Perform exercises to a musical accompaniment. This becomes a "health hustle." Select music with a good 4/4 beat (see chapter 28) and adjust tempo to the class's level of physical fitness.

8. Avoid the following exercises because they may cause harmful effects or are of no value to the muscle groups involved.

    Leg Lifts: From a back lying position, raise and lower straight legs. This movement flexes the hips, placing a strain on the lower back.

    Sit-ups: From a back lying position with legs straight and on floor, raise trunk off floor. This exercise also flexes the hips, strains the lower back, and may stretch the abdominal muscles.

Hyperextension of Back: Avoid hyperextending the back and bending with the legs straight (fig. 9.21a). Bend the knees and tilt the pelvis slightly back when leaning back (fig. 9.21b).

Knee Bends: Avoid repeated and excessive knee bends (more than 90 degrees). The knee joints of young children are still maturing, hence will permit a wide range of movement. To be on the cautious side, and to develop a long-term attitude, permit half-knee bends for all children. Occasional full-knee bending activities, performed in stunts, animal walks, and some movement challenges are not considered harmful.

The exercises contained in the following pages are grouped according to general vigorous activities, neck, arm and shoulder girdle, trunk, and leg exercises. Posture exercises are also included in this section. Reference to other activities, such as gymnastic stunts, rope skipping, and rhythmic skills, are provided within each category. The stunts and movement patterns of these activities can be used as substitute movements for specific exercises.

A typical warm-up activity includes a vigorous activity followed by one or two exercises from each category. Performing the "same daily dozen" exercise routine for weeks or months leads to boredom and other class management problems. Hence, change the set of exercises every two weeks, allow children to substitute appropriate exercises from each category, or design a series of color-coated task cards containing a set of warm-up exercises that each child can select and perform according to his own level of physical fitness.

General Vigorous Activities The following general vigorous activities are used to increase cardiorespiratory circulation.

1. *Running:* Begin slowly then increase speed, exaggerate knee lift and other tasks such as, "run with hands behind neck, at sides, etc." Add additional challenges such as change direction and level, and substitute hopping, jumping, or other locomotor skills for running.

2. *Rope Jumping:* See page 439. Stress different steps performed in a stationary position as well as while traveling around the gymnasium or outdoor play area.

Figure 9.21 Hyperextension of Back

3. *Rhythmic Activities:* See page 493. In order to have children begin a vigorous rhythmic warm-up, introduce rhythmic activities in a previous lesson. Once children understand how to develop sequences or routines, the teacher need only say, "Make up a routine that has a run, hop, change of direction," then play a tape with a bouncy tune and a fast tempo.

4. *Vigorous Game:* Game or tag activities that require all children to keep moving are enjoyable and acceptable vigorous warm-up activities.

Following are some examples:

Number game: On signal all children begin to run (or any other locomotor movement called by the teacher). As they are running she calls out a number, such as three—all must immediately group into threes. The game should move very quickly to improve each child's cardiorespiratory endurance.

Simple tag, page 224.
Partner tag, page 227.
Crab tag, page 232.

Neck Exercises

Stunts

Headstand (strength), page 421.
Forward roll (flexibility), page 395.

Figure 9.22 Head Pull (strength and flexibility). Stand with feet slightly apart, back straight, chin on chest, and hands behind head. Elbows should be pointing straight ahead. Lift head up and back, and stretch elbows sideways and backward.
Variations: (1) Place hand on forehead and repeat exercise in opposite direction.

Figure 9.23 Head Circling (strength and flexibility). Begin in a sitting position with head and back erect and hands resting on floor. Rotate head and neck towards the right, touching chin to clavicle, then shoulder. Continue rotating backwards until chin touches left shoulder, left clavicle, then stop. Repeat in opposite direction.

Figure 9.24 Neck Flattener (strength and flexibility). Begin in a back-lying position, arms sideways and palms flat on floor. Push head towards floor and forcefully draw in chin.

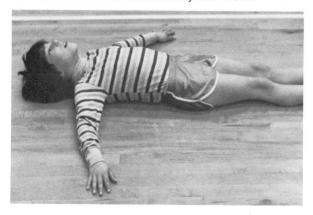

Figure 9.25 Head Lift (strength and flexibility). Lie face down with hands clasped behind head. Keep chin in good alignment (not protruding forward) and raise head upward against a firm resistance of the arms.

Arm and Shoulder Exercises

Figure 9.26 Arm Rotators (strength and endurance). Stand with feet together, back straight, and arms extended sideways. Rotate arms forward, upward, and backward in a circular movement. Gradually increase the size of the circle and change direction of arm movement after three or four rotations.
Variations: (1) From a standing position, swing each arm in the opposite direction. (2) From a standing position, bend forward and move arms in a breaststroke or crawl action. (3) From a standing position, swing both arms to the same side or cross them in front.

Figure 9.27 Push-ups (strength and endurance). Begin in a front-lying position with hands approximately shoulder-width apart, fingers pointing forward, and chin a few inches off the floor. Extend arms, keeping the back of the legs straight. Variations: (1) Instead of lowering the body straight down, lower it to one side. (2) Move hands close together, then farther apart. (3) Repeat original exercise with one leg off the floor.

Stunts

Rabbit jump (strength), page 398.
Crab walk (strength and endurance), page 393.
Measuring worm (strength and flexibility), page 399.
Seal walk (strength and endurance), page 398.
Wheelbarrow (strength and endurance), page 397.
Elephant walk (strength and endurance), page 398.
The bridge (strength and flexibility), page 417.
Pig walk (strength and endurance), page 407.
Walking down the wall (strength and flexibility), page 420.

Figure 9.28 Pull-ups (strength and endurance). One partner assumes a back-lying position with arms up. The other partner stands with feet on opposite sides of partner's shoulders and extends arms down. Both lock hands. The standing partner holds her arms straight while the lower partner pulls her body up.

Figure 9.29 Hanging (strength and endurance). Hang from a horizontal bar or from wall bars (face outward) with toes just touching or off the floor.
Variations: Perform one-half or full chin-ups.

Figure 9.30 Wall Push (strength and flexibility). Stand one to two feet from the wall with palms on the wall about shoulder high. Keeping head and trunk in good alignment, bend elbows until chest almost touches the wall, then return to starting position.
Variation: Move further away from wall, or repeat exercise standing in the corner of a room with one hand on each adjacent wall.

Figure 9.31 Head and Arm Raisers. Begin by lying face down with forehead resting on back of hands. Keeping head in line with body, raise hands, head, and elbows about two inches. Then keeping hands and head in same position, raise elbows as high as possible.
Variations: (1) Repeat to the two-inch position, then stretch one arm sideways, forward, and back to the starting position. (2) Repeat previous exercise, but raise legs and arch body.

Figure 9.33 Cat Stretcher (strength and flexibility). Begin in a partially crouched position. Stretch back upwards, hold at the highest point for a few seconds, then return to the starting position.
Variation: From original position, dip chin to floor and raise right leg upward. Repeat with left leg.

Figure 9.32 Side Stretch (strength and endurance). Lie on left hip and extend both legs. Place left hand on the floor and extend arm. Place right hand on the hip. Raise the body, keeping the left hand and foot on the floor until the legs and trunk form a straight line.
Variations: (1) When legs and trunk are straight, stretch top arm and leg forward, then backward. (2) From variation 1, raise top leg upward. (3) From variation 1, place top hand on floor, then twist body towards the ceiling and back.

Figure 9.34 Trunk Stretcher (strength and flexibility). Begin in a stride-standing position with hands at sides. Keeping knees straight, bend forward and reach towards the floor with fingertips.
Variations: (1) Repeat original exercise to opposite side. (2) Repeat original exercise and touch right hand to left toe, then repeat to opposite side. (3) Repeat original exercise and grasp left ankle and pull body downward. Repeat to opposite ankle.

Stunts

Figure 9.35 Back Arch (strength and endurance). Begin in a front lying position with hands laced behind head, and legs together. Simultaneously raise head, chest, and legs off floor. Variations: (1) Raise head and chest, and twist trunk to side. (2) Raise opposite leg and arm.

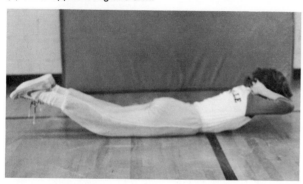

Figure 9.37 Elbow Knee Touch (abdominal strength and endurance). Lie on back with hands laced behind head, elbows forward, knees bent with feet off floor. Raise up, twist body, and touch elbow to opposite knee.
Variations: (1) Touch both elbows to opposite knees.
(2) Cross arms and repeat original exercise. (3) From original position, rotate bent legs towards the right, then left.

Figure 9.36 Curl-ups (abdominal strength and endurance). Begin by lying on back, with hands behind head and knees drawn up with feet flat on floor. Partner holds feet flat on floor. Raise trunk and touch head to knees.
Variations: (1) Sit up, turning body towards the right. Repeat towards the left. (2) Sit up and wrap arms around knees, then return to starting position. (3) Sit with arms crossed on chest.

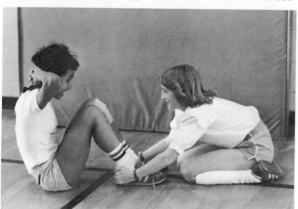

Figure 9.38 Hip Raiser (abdominal strength and endurance). Begin in a crab walk position with seat on floor. Raise trunk upward until back is parallel with floor.
Variations: (1) Raise up, lift right foot off floor, and twist body towards the left. Repeat to opposite side. (2) Raise up, lift right hand off floor, touch seat, and return to starting position.

Figure 9.39 Treadmill (strength and endurance). Lie facedown. Push off the floor with arms in an elevated push-up position. Keep one leg extended and draw the other leg forward until the knee is under the chest. Reverse leg positions in a continuous and simultaneous motion. Variations: (1) Begin with both legs together. Draw both legs forward and backward. (2) From variation 1, keep legs together and shift feet towards the right and left side.

Figure 9.40 Bicycle. Rest body weight on head, shoulders, and elbows, and place hands on hips as in a modified shoulder-stand position. Extend left leg straight up and flex right leg. Reverse leg positions with a slow cadence, gradually increasing speed.

Stunts

Kangaroo hop (strength and endurance), page 393.
Knee jump (strength and power), page 393.
Turk stand (strength and balance), page 403.
Heel click (strength and power), page 411.
Bear dance (strength and endurance), page 407.
Knee dip (strength and balance), page 403.
Leg wrestling, (strength and endurance), page 408.
Bouncing ball (strength and endurance), page 392.

Figure 9.41 Squat Jump (strength and endurance). Begin in a crouched position with arms at sides and fingers resting on the floor. Push off floor and extend body until feet are about four to six inches off the mat, with arms remaining at the sides for balance. Return to the starting position and repeat. Variations: (1) Extend arms overhead on each upward movement. (2) Change position of legs while in the air, such as extend sideways, cross, or move forward and backward.

Figure 9.42 Hurdle Stretch (strength and flexibility). Sit on floor with left leg extended forward and thigh of right leg stretched towards the side. Knee is bent and lower leg points towards the rear. Hands rest on lower leg. Slowly bend the trunk and reach towards the foot.
Variations: (1) From the starting position, alternately reach with the right then the left hand. (2) Reach back towards the rear foot (stretches the quadriceps).

Figure 9.43 Jumping Jack (strength and endurance). Stand with arms at sides. Simultaneously jump to a straddle position and repeat.
Variations: (1) Change direction of feet, such as forward and backward, or crossed in front. (2) Make a one-quarter or one-half turn on each jump. (3) Change direction of arms on each jump.

Relating Good Nutrition to Physical Fitness

Physical fitness, as defined in terms of health-related components, must include a concern for the type and amount of foot we eat. A well-planned and properly executed exercise program for young children may fail completely simply because the children lack the basic nutrients, sufficient calories, or are overweight or obese. These factors, along with high pressure advertising tactics and questionable diet programs, make it imperative that children understand what constitutes a nutritionally sound diet. The following sections explain what foods must be included in a balanced diet, how to maintain proper weight, and a few suggested activities for helping children build and maintain a nutritionally balanced diet.

Balanced Diet

The human body uses over forty different nutrients to keep its life processes operating effectively and efficiently. Within this group, ten essential nutrients must be present. These ten key nutrients (table 9.6) are found naturally in plant and animal sources and usually are accompanied by one or more of the other thirty nutrients. They provide the necessary foods for building and repairing the body tissues, supplying energy for our daily life activities, and regulating our bodily processes.

Table 9.6 Ten Essential Nutrients of a Balanced Diet

Nutrients	Function
1. *Protein* (essential amino acids)	Builds and repairs body tissues and provides energy.
2. *Carbohydrates*	Supplies energy and fiber for digestion.
3. *Fats* (essentially fatty acids)	Supplies energy.
4,5. *Minerals* (calcium, iron)	Builds and repairs body tissues and regulates essential processes.
6,7,8. *Vitamins A and B-complex* (A, niacin; B₁, thiamin; and B₂, riboflavin)	Regulates body processes.
9,10. *Vitamins C and D*	Regulates body processes.

Table 9.7 Four Basic Food Groups

Group I	Group II	Group III	Group IV
Meat	*Milk*	*Bread–Cereal*	*Fruit–Vegetable*
Meat, fish, and eggs	Milk and cheese	Grain products	
Rich in:	*Rich in:*	*Rich in:*	*Rich in:*
Protein	Calcium	Thiamin	Vitamin A
Thiamin	Protein	Niacin	Vitamin C
Niacin	Riboflavin	Riboflavin	Vitamin E
Vitamin B$_6$	Vitamin A	Iron	Floacin
Vitamin B$_{12}$	Vitamin D	Protein	Biotin
Iron	Vitamin B$_{12}$		
	Phosphorus		

Table 9.8 Minimum Daily Servings for Elementary School-age Children

Food Group	Number of Servings	Example Serving Size
Meat	2	2 ounces of lean meat
		4 tablespoons of peanut butter
Milk	3	1 cup of milk
		2 ounces of cheese
Bread and Cereal	4	½ cup of cooked pasta
		1 slice of bread
Fruit and Vegetable	4	1 orange
		1 potato

The task for parents and teachers is to translate our knowledge of the nutritional value of various food groups into a balanced daily diet for each child within our care. The U.S. Department of Agriculture has indicated that while no two foods are exactly alike in nutritional composition and value, certain foods are similar enough in nutritional content that they can be grouped into one of four basic categories. These "Basic Four Food Groups," shown in table 9.7, provide the basis for planning a balanced diet. The key to this simple grouping of foods is recognizing that each food group has a high nutritional value in only a few of the ten basic nutrients. Hence, a balanced diet includes foods from all four categories. Our task is to teach children to understand and consciously select a minimum number of servings from each food group during each day of their lives (table 9.8).

Weight Control

Diet planning based on the Four Basic Food Groups will help every person, regardless of age, receive the essential nutrients. However, the amount of food consumed within each of these food groups varies according to our age, body structure, metabolism, and daily activities. If a child's weight is within the recommended range for his age and height, his food intake (number of calories) is correct. On the other hand, if a child gains excessive weight he is consuming more calories than he needs. Consequently, his body will convert the excessive food into fat.

It is estimated that more than 10 percent of the child population and 25 percent of the adult population is overweight. The basic problems relating to overweight and obesity are appearance and low self-image, poor motor efficiency, low physical fitness levels, and a predisposition towards illness, such as high blood pressure and heart attacks.

Taking off excessive body fat and maintaining the proper weight for one's age and life-style requires a reduction in daily caloric intake and increased participation in a regular exercise program. One without the other will not lead to an effective and long-term weight control program. By reducing the amount of food one eats to a point where the body draws upon its own stored fat is the first effective part of a weight reduction program. When this program is combined with a regular and systematic exercise program, more body fat is utilized and muscle tone is improved to prevent flabbiness as weight is lost. The end result is a lower percentage of body fat, an increase in lean muscle fiber, and a general improvement in all body systems.

Teaching Suggestions

Experts in the field of nutrition have clearly indicated that optimum physical fitness and a positive life-style cannot be achieved without a balanced diet. However, what a child eats may be due to the nutritional style of his parents or friends or the availability and cost of food. We have also learned that preaching to children about what and how much they should eat is usually unproductive. Instead, a proven affective approach for leading children towards a positive nutritional life-style is the implementation of activities that allow children to investigate and relate nutritional information to their own immediate needs and life-style. The following activities and suggestions will help children begin understanding what constitutes a balanced diet and how to maintain proper weight control throughout their lives.

Bulletin Board

The bulletin board can be used to display growth charts of children, energy demands of various physical activities, or comparative nutritional values of various foods.

Measuring Body Fat

Measure each child's body fat with skinfold calipers. This test is included in the *AAHPERD Health Related Fitness Test* (AAHPERD 1980), along with norms for elementary school age children. Inexpensive skinfold calipers may be purchased through several companies listed in appendix B.

Basic Four Food Groups

Use a chart similar to the one shown in table 9.7 and have children (1) make displays, (2) workbooks, or (3) catalogues with pictures from magazines and newspapers.

Daily Food Intake

Use "Minimum Number of Daily Servings Chart" and have children keep daily records of their own food consumption. For older students, expand to include an analysis of their caloric intake and their consumption of junk foods.

Weight Control Programs

Develop a weight control program for all children in the class. Begin with each child recording his height and weight. Design daily food and exercise diaries to allow them to see how many calories were used, stored, or needed to meet their daily life activities. This type of activity can lead into effective weight reducing programs and provide information to parents and health officials concerning children who may need medical attention.

Special Diets and Food Fallacies

Numerous questions relate to food fads, diet pills, and food fallacies. The following questions may develop into interesting class discussions or lead into more extensive individual or group projects:

1. What are three popular fad diets?
2. Should we take vitamin and mineral supplements?
3. Do vegetarians eat a balanced diet?
4. Do fast-food restaurants serve nutritionally valuable foods?
5. Are there special diets for athletes?
6. What happens to our body if we fast for more than three days?

Many outstanding nutrition books and related audiovisual materials suitable for primary and intermediate children are available. Refer to appendix A for a list of these materials.

10 Mainstreaming Exceptional Children

Methods and Techniques
Individualized Teaching Strategies

Types of Exceptional Children
Perceptual-Motor Deficiencies
Physically Handicapped

Mainstreaming in the Intramural Program

Sources for Additional Ideas

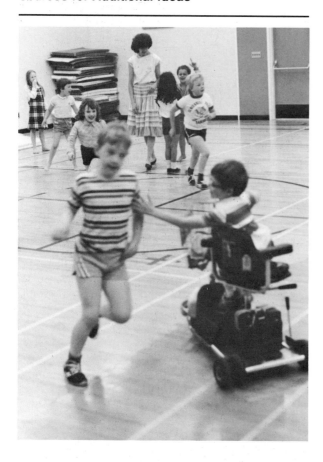

In the early 1970s, over 1.75 million children with various psychological and physical handicaps were excluded from public education because of their handicaps. Further, over one-half of the estimated 8 million handicapped children throughout the United States were not receiving appropriate educational services (Abeson and Zettel 1977). Recognizing this basic problem, the federal government passed two laws that substantially changed the education of handicapped children. Public Law 93-380 (1974) requires that, where appropriate, handicapped children be educated within regular instructional programs. It also states that special classes or other means of removing handicapped children from the regular education environment occur only when the nature and severity of the handicap cannot be handled within a regular instructional program. Public Law 94-142 (1975) stipulates that the public school system provide appropriate programs for handicapped children. Such programs must be individualized with achievable goals, specialized services, and appropriate evaluative procedures for the handicapped child.

The implication of these two laws to the elementary school physical education program is basically to integrate all children within instructional and extra-class programs and to individualize teaching strategies and activity areas to cope with the special needs of handicapped children. This chapter provides a basic description of the various types of exceptional children, teaching suggestions, and ideas illustrating how children with special needs can be integrated into the mainstream of the physical education program.

Methods and Techniques

Generally speaking, exceptional children are classified according to the nature of their physical, intellectual, or cultural handicap. While this type of classification system explains the nature of the handicap, it does not explain how to integrate and, where necessary, individualize the physical education program to meet the unique needs of exceptional children in each physical education class.

Classification System for Exceptional Children

Unrestricted: No restrictions relative to the vigor or type of activity.
Restricted: Condition is such that intensity and type of activity needs to be limited.

1. **Mild:** Ordinary physical activities need not be restricted, but unusually vigorous efforts need to be avoided.
2. **Moderate:** Ordinary physical activities need to be moderately restricted and sustained strenuous efforts need to be avoided.
3. **Limited:** Ordinary physical activities need to be markedly restricted.

A classification system based upon functional capacity has been developed by the American Heart Association and approved by the Committee on Medical Aspects of Sports of the American Medical Association (Adaptive Physical Education Guidelines, 1976).

This classification system is particularly useful to elementary school physical education teachers in the process of integrating exceptional children into the various activities of their programs. If a physical education medical referral form (see pp. 164–65 for example) is adopted by a local school district, the foundation of an effective individualized physical education program for each exceptional child has been established. This form does not require the physician to prescribe specific exercises; rather it bridges the efforts of the physician, teacher, and parent in planning an appropriate physical education program for each exceptional child.

Individualized Teaching Strategies

All teachers of elementary physical education are required to integrate exceptional children into the regular physical education program. The suggested classification system only provides the degree of participation for each handicapped child; it does not specify the method or techniques to accomplish this task. Several teaching strategies described earlier in this text are expanded in the following pages to illustrate how exceptional children can be effectively integrated into instructional and extraclass activities.

Station Work

The general organization of stations in teaching a variety of physical activities is particularly useful when attempting to individualize the instructional program (see p. 86). To illustrate this technique, presume a fourth-grade teacher is teaching a gymnastic unit. Three children in her class have moderate limitations (heart, sight, and partially spastic), hence they cannot participate in vaulting or rope climbing activities. The teacher organizes the class into six groups, with the three moderately handicapped children designated as group IV and assigned to station B along with group

Figure 10.1 Planning a physical education program to meet the unique needs of exceptional children is more readily achieved by the combined efforts of physicians, teachers, and parents.

II. All children practice the assigned skills at their stations until it is time to rotate. When the groups rotate, group II moves to the vaulting box while group IV shifts to small equipment along with group V. The teacher has demonstrated her ability to integrate the three exceptional children according to their limitations and without drastically changing the content or emphasis of her gymnastic program.

The organizational structure of station work can be effectively used to teach physical fitness activities, particularly with circuit training (see p. 148) and obstacle courses (see p. 149). This system can also be adopted when teaching a variety of game activities.

Physical Education Medical Referral Form
FORM 1
ANY CITY PUBLIC SCHOOLS
SCHOOL HEALTH DEPARTMENT
PHYSICAL EDUCATION DIVISION

Physical Education Medical Referral Form
ASAW #1313-1975

Dear Dr. _____:

(This space can be used for information about state/local physical education requirements, rationale of adapted physical education, objectives and benefits of local programs, organization and administration of local classes, purposes and uses of this form and related areas to improve understanding and communication among physicians, physical educators, parents, and others concerned with and involved in the education, health, and welfare of the student. Procedures for returning the form can be included in this section or at the end of the form.)

John J. Jones, M.D.
Director, School Health Department

George T. Smith, Supervisor
Division of Health, Physical Education and Athletics

STUDENT INFORMATION

Name _____   School _____

Home Address _____   City _____ State _____ Zip _____

Home Telephone ( ) _____   Grade & Section _____

CONDITION

Brief description of condition

Condition is   ☐ permanent   ☐ temporary

Comments _____

If Appropriate:
   Comments about student's medication and its effects on participation in physical activities

_____

Student may return to unrestricted activity _____ , 19 ___

Student should return for reexamination _____ , 19 __

FUNCTIONAL CAPACITY

☐ *Unrestricted*—no restrictions relative to vigorousness or types of activities

☐ *Restricted*—Condition is such that intensity and types of activities need to be limited (**check one category below**)

   ☐ *Mild*—ordinary physical activities need not be restricted but usually vigorous efforts need to be avoided

   ☐ *Moderate*—ordinary physical activities need to be moderately restricted and sustained strenuous efforts avoided

   ☐ *Limited*—ordinary physical activities need to be markedly restricted

Reprinted by permission of the American Alliance for Health,
Physical Education, Recreation, and Dance, 1900 Association
Drive, Reston, Va. 22091

continued . . .

FORM 1
ACTIVITY RECOMMENDATIONS

Indicate body areas in which physical activities should be minimized, eliminated, or maximized.

	Maximized	Minimized	Eliminated	Both	Left	Right	Comments Including Any Medical Contraindications to Physical Activities
Neck							
Shoulder Girdle							
Arms							
Elbows							
Hands & Wrists							
Abdomen							
Back							
Pelvic Girdle							
Legs							
Knees							
Feet & Ankles							
Toes							
Fingers							
Other (specify)							

REMEDIAL

☐ Condition is such that defects or deviations can be improved or prevented from becoming worse through use of carefully selected exercises and/or activities. The following are remedial exercises and/or activities recommended for this student. (Please be specific).

_____

_____

_____

_____

_____

Signed _____ M.D.

Address _____

_____ Zip _____

Telephone No. ( ) _____

Date _____ 19 _____

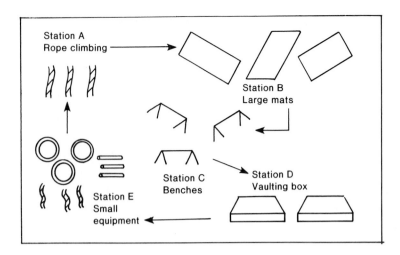

Station A
Rope climbing

Station B
Large mats

Station C
Benches

Station D
Vaulting box

Station E
Small
equipment

Task Cards

Task cards, described on page 86, are basically preset tasks that can be designed to accommodate a variety of exceptional children. Using the previous station work example, all children, with the exception of the three handicapped children, could choose cards representing three levels of required performance (level 1, 2, and 3). Special task cards for moderately blind, heart deficient, and spastic children could be designed to accommodate their expected levels of performance. Although task cards present obvious limitations when working with severely blind or mentally retarded children, numerous applications of the task card technique can accommodate exceptional children in virtually every area of the physical education program.

Movement Education

One of the most significant trends in the elementary school physical education program has undoubtedly been the widespread adoption of the movement education approach (see chapter 4). Since this approach does not include structured skills, the potential to individualize the regular instructional program is unlimited. Teachers who have adopted this approach have learned to present movement challenges that can be performed by each child in the class according to his level of maturity, ability, and interest. This approach does not exclude a child possessing a physical, perceptual-motor, or mental handicap, because a single challenge presented by the teacher can be interpreted and performed by each child in his own way.

Types of Exceptional Children

In physical education, as in all other subjects, it is first necessary to distinguish and understand the various types of exceptional children before planned exercises can be provided for them. A few of the more common handicaps will be discussed. Once they are understood, it is possible within the broad range of physical activities and individualized instructional techniques described in this text to provide for the needs of exceptional children.

Perceptual-Motor Deficiencies

In recent years there has been a growing awareness of the importance of perceptual-motor development to academic achievement, particularly in such areas as reading, writing, and drawing skills. In 1959 Delacato presented a theory known as neurologic organization, which assumes that every human being progresses sequentially through a series of motor skills. According to Delacato, children with perceptual-motor deficiencies missed specific developmental steps along this continuum.

Another theory proposed by Kephart holds that a child progresses through a sequence of learning stages (1960). His program for slow learners is based upon levels of generalization through which a child is taught. Since the ability to read is based upon previously acquired perceptual-motor skills such as directionality and laterality, emphasis is given to these skills for children possessing learning disabilities.

The general conclusion drawn from these investigators is that inadequate preschool motor development could lead to serious perceptual-motor problems. A child who does not possess these prerequisite perceptual-motor skills may in turn experience serious difficulties in learning to read, write, and perform other

Figure 10.2 A handicapped child can achieve a measure of success with guidance and encouragement.

academic skills. Although research evidence is far from conclusive, there is merit in these programs. It is therefore important that the classroom teacher know the basic perceptual-motor skills, how to detect serious deficiencies, and, finally, how to select activities that develop perceptual-motor abilities. A teacher possessing these competencies will be able to incorporate many of the perceptual-motor skills in her regular instructional program. Children with serious perceptual-motor deficiencies would then be channeled into remedial programs handled by trained specialists.

Symptoms of Perceptual-Motor Deficiencies

Perceptual-motor competency is a composite of a number of specific motor skills and movement patterns. The following characteristic symptoms are commonly observed in the primary school, particularly in kindergarten and grade one. Other characteristics such as tactile discrimination, drawing, and other fine muscle movements are not discussed in this section. Refer to the suggested references in appendix A for more detailed descriptions and classroom implications of these related perceptual-motor skills.

1. Body Image
   a. Inability to identify and locate body parts, such as the right and left hand, knee, or elbow.
   b. Inability to move parts of the body as directed by the teacher, such as raising the right arm or raising the left arm and the left foot.
   c. Inability to imitate movements performed by the teacher or another performer.

2. Balance
   a. Inability to maintain static balance, such as standing on one foot or standing with the arms folded and the eyes closed.
   b. Inability to maintain balance while moving, such as walking forward or backward in a straight line.
   c. Inability to maintain balance while in flight, such as a simple run, jump, and land, or a jump off a low box or balance bench.

3. Spatial Awareness
   a. Inability to move parts of the body in specified directions, such as crossing the right arm over the left side of the body.
   b. Inability to move the body through space, such as moving forward, backward, up, down, and around.
   c. Inability to move through space without bumping into objects or other children in the general pathway of movement.
4. Hand-eye and Foot-eye Coordination
   a. Inability to throw a ball into the air and catch it after one bounce.
   b. Inability to perform basic locomotor skills, such as running, hopping, jumping, or galloping.
   c. Inability to kick a stationary or moving ball.
   d. Inability to move to rhythm, such as performing rhythmic hand or foot tapping or walking to rhythmic accompaniment.

Assessing Perceptual-Motor Deficiencies

Several tests are widely recommended for assessing perceptual-motor abilities. Since the following tests vary in the type of components measured, as well as evidence of validity, classroom teachers should consult school district specialists in this area to determine the most suitable test.

1. *Large Muscle Screening Instrument:* H. A. Lerch et al., Perceptual-Motor Learning Theory and Practice, Palo Alto, Peek Publications, 1974, page 56. A basic screening test covering basic perceptual-motor skills. The textbook also has excellent general coverage of the subject and an extensive list of references and resources.
2. *Perceptual-Motor Rating Scale:* E. Roach and N. C. Kephart, The Perceptual-Motor Survey, Columbus, Ohio, C. E. Merrill, 1966. The test items and general information provide sufficient materials for the teacher to assess perceptual-motor abilities in a classroom setting.
3. *Six Category Gross-Motor Test:* B. Cratty and M. Martin, Perceptual-Motor Efficiency in Children, Philadelphia, Lea and Febiger, 1969, page 183. A three-level general screening test with accompanying research information. This book also includes comprehensive coverage of the subject and additional test batteries.
4. *Dayton Sensory Motor Awareness Survey for Four- and Five-year-olds:* Dayton, Ohio, Public Schools. A basic screening test for detecting children who may need further assessment and special assistance.

Guidelines for Classroom Teachers

Perceptual-motor skills and movement patterns that appear to be prerequisites to learning such academic skills as reading and drawing apply primarily to preschool and primary children. The following general guidelines will help classroom teachers incorporate and, at times, stress various types of perceptual-motor activities in the regular instructional program.

1. A child who is suspected of possessing serious perceptual-motor deficiencies should be referred to competent specialists.
2. The choice of all physical activities should be commensurate with the child's developmental level.
3. Application of individualized instructional techniques, particularly the limitation method, is imperative in coping with individual differences in levels of ability and rate of development.
4. Every movement task that is presented should allow each child to achieve a measure of success.
5. The primary physical education program should stress the following types of activities.
   a. Balance activities—floor work, with small equipment, and on large apparatus.
   b. Locomotor skills—moving in different directions, changing speed, and moving to a rhythmic accompaniment.
   c. Body awareness—activities and movement challenges stressing shapes (form) and moving different parts (unilateral and bilateral movements).
   d. Manipulative activities—stressing hand-eye and foot-eye coordination (ball-handling skills involving throwing, catching, and kicking) and a variety of manipulative skills using beanbags, hoops, and other small equipment.

Perceptual-Motor Activities

A quick reference to the numerous perceptual-motor activities contained in this book follows:

Perceptual-Motor Skills	Game Activities	Gymnastic Activities	Rhythmic Activities
Body image		ch. 25–27	ch. 28
Balance		ch. 25–27	
Spatial awareness	ch. 14–24	ch. 25–27	ch. 28–30
Hand-eye and foot-eye coordination	part 5	ch. 25–26	ch. 28–30
Locomotor movements		ch. 25–26	ch. 28–30
Rhythmic movements			ch. 28–30

Several outstanding remedial programs are in operation throughout the United States. The following sources provide general information relating to these programs.

1. Capon, J. *Motor-Perceptual Lesson Plans Level I.* Front Row Experience, Suite 217, 564 Central Ave., Alameda, California, 94501.

2. Braley et al. *Daily Sensorimotor Training Activities: A Handbook for Teachers and Parents of Pre-school and Primary Children.* Educational Activities, Inc.

3. Lerch, H. A. et al. *Perceptual-Motor Learning—Theory and Practice.* Peak Publications, Palo Alto, California, 94306.

Physically Handicapped

This broad category includes all physical handicaps, whether temporary or permanent in nature. All, however, may restrict the child to mild, moderate, or limited participation in various types of physical education activities. Some of the more common physical handicaps among elementary school children are described here.

Visual and Auditory Handicaps

It is estimated that approximately one out of every four school children has some form of visual anomaly and that about 5 percent have some form of impaired hearing. The following visual and auditory handicaps are the most common ailments of elementary children.

1. *Nearsightedness (myopia):* This condition is the result of the anterior-posterior axis of the eye being too long, resulting in the image being focused in front of the retina. Distant objects appear blurred, while nearby objects are seen clearly.

2. *Farsightedness (hyperopia):* In this ailment, the anterior-posterior axis of the eyeball is too short. This causes the image to be focused behind the retina. Distant objects are seen clearly, while nearby objects appear blurred.

3. *Astigmatism:* This condition is normally caused by an irregularity in the curve of the cornea or lens of the eye. When a child attempts to focus, the object appears blurred.

4. *Hard of hearing:* A child with this condition has a partial sense of hearing and normally functions without a hearing aid.

General Guidelines

1. Consult the school nurse and parents of children who have auditory or visual handicaps. The teacher's knowledge of each child's deficiency will provide a general guideline for the type of activity and degree of participation appropriate for the child.

2. Refer any child who chronically demonstrates one or more of the following symptoms to the school nurse for further examination.
   a. Excessive squinting.
   b. Constant leaning toward or moving close for demonstrations.
   c. Inattentiveness and a general lack of interest.
   d. Extremely low level of skill. Visually handicapped children generally show poor catching skills even with a large utility ball. Acoustically handicapped children demonstrate chronic improper responses, particularly in game situations.

Teaching Suggestions
When Instructing Deaf Children

1. If a child with a hearing loss is in your class, check with his parents on the type of oral, manual, or combined method of communication that is preferred.

2. When giving directions, face in the direction of the deaf child. This is particularly important when writing on a chalkboard. Write the directions first, then face the class and verbally clarify your directions.

3. When giving specific directions to a deaf child, position yourself so he can see you.

4. If a child is wearing a hearing aid, do not raise your voice when speaking to him.

5. When teaching outdoors, try to position yourself so the deaf child does not face the sun.

6. Always permit children with hearing losses to move freely about the instructional space in order to be within seeing or hearing range.

Teaching Suggestions
When Instructing the Blind

1. Too often, partially sighted children shy away from vigorous physical activities and thus tend to be overweight and generally uncoordinated. Whenever possible, provide a little extra encouragement and praise when these children participate in physical activities.

2. Blind children usually have extremely good memory. When teaching physical education, reinforce this strength and increase the child's self-image by asking the blind child to review instructions given in previous lessons (Sherrill 1976).

3. Partially sighted children often say they can see more than they actually do in order to act like other children. Teachers should recognize this characteristic and give subtle assistance and encouragement whenever possible.

4. Partially sighted and blind children tend to reveal less mobility and facial expressions in all forms of physical activity. Encourage these children to exhibit gestures and facial expressions in creative dance and inventive game activities.

Obesity

Obesity is a condition in which body weight exceeds the standard weight recommended for the individual on the basis of age, height, and frame size. Approximately 20 percent of elementary school children are obese. The primary causes are overeating and lack of vigorous daily activity. Dysfunction of the endocrine glands, which regulate the fat distribution in the body, accounts for a very small percentage of obese children.

General Guidelines

A child who is classified as obese usually has a very low level of physical fitness, lacks coordination and speed, and reveals emotional and social-adjustment problems. The following guidelines may help the obese child reduce his body weight and help make his participation in physical activities enjoyable and meaningful. These guidelines apply to those children whose obesity is the result of overeating.

1. Contact the school nurse and parents and attempt to establish a weight-reduction program for the obese child. Frequent counseling and encouragement by the teacher can help the child stay on a recommended diet.

2. Do not require obese children to perform balance stunts or movements they are incapable of performing.

3. Use extreme care during endurance activities. Set appropriately lower standards of distance and time for these children.

4. Because of serious social and emotional implications, attempt to guide obese children into less demanding playing positions or events.

In game activities, the goalie and defense positions are less demanding than a center or forward spot. In track and field, the shot put or tug-of-war would be more appropriate than sprints or distance running.

5. Use techniques of team or group selection that do not make the obese child the last one chosen.

6. Refer to chapter 9 for additional ideas relating to weight-control programs for the overweight child.

Cardiovascular Disorders

Cardiovascular disorders found among elementary school children include congenital heart disorders, cardiovascular diseases, and rheumatic fever. Rheumatic fever accounts for approximately two-thirds of all these disorders, hence, it should be given special consideration with respect to early diagnosis, recuperative programs, and the degree of physical activity after the child returns to the regular physical education program.

General Guidelines

1. The amount and type of physical activity for a child who has a cardiovascular disorder must be prescribed by a physician.

2. Rheumatic fever flourishes in the northern parts of the United States, particularly during winter and spring. Teachers should watch for early signs and possible suspicious factors, such as chronic colds, quick fatigue, and "serious" weight losses.

3. The vast majority of children who have had rheumatic fever can eventually participate in physical activities. Once the family doctor gives the child permission to participate in physical activities, the teacher should allow only moderate and brief participation during the first few weeks. As the child demonstrates his capacity to keep up without showing early signs of fatigue, gradually increase the amount and intensity of exercise. A simple monitoring device can be used to determine the level of exercise tolerance that is appropriate for this type of child. Take the child's pulse rate before the physical activity is started. The pulse rate should rise during exercise, then return to the resting pulse approximately three minutes after stopping the physical activity. If the pulse rate is still excessively high after three minutes, reduce the amount of exercise.

Asthma

The cause of asthma is not known; however, it is considered to be the result of an allergic condition. Basic symptoms are labored breathing and wheezing as the child exhales.

General Guidelines

1. Children with asthmatic conditions should, within the limits of their ability, attempt to increase their level of general fitness and health. Planned developmental programs can help asthmatic children reach this goal.
2. Children with asthma should avoid vigorous and sustained types of activities.
3. Any causative agent (dust on tumbling mats or pollen from flowering trees or plants) should be avoided.

Epilepsy

Epilepsy is a disease of the nervous system that is characterized by seizures or convulsions, loss of balance, and unconsciousness. The attack can last from two to approximately five minutes.

General Guidelines

The successful medical control of epilepsy now permits the majority of children suffering from the disease to attend regular school and participate in most physical activities.

1. A child who suffers from severe epileptic seizures should not be permitted on large apparatus such as climbing ropes and agility-type equipment.
2. Tolerance and understanding of an epileptic seizure is critically important to the normal growth and development of children who suffer from this disease. Each teacher should explain, within the limits of her class's understanding, the nature of the disease and what should be done when a child has a seizure. The following procedure should be carried out in a very calm, routine manner.
    a. Lay the child down, away from hard or sharp objects.
    b. Do not attempt to restrain the child's movements. The attack must be allowed to run its course.
    c. Immediately after the attack, move the child to a quiet, secluded place until he has regained consciousness. If the child falls asleep, he should be left until he wakes himself.

Orthopedic Impairments

The term *orthopedic impairment* includes any congenital or acquired impairment that has produced a motor disability. This category then includes birth defects, amputations, spina bifida, and a variety of crippling conditions caused by trauma (acid, fires, or accidents).

Each type of physical handicap within this broad orthopedic classification must be individually evaluated with respect to the nature and intensity of the activity. If the child is a member of the physical education class, however, the following general guidelines apply.

General Guidelines

1. Wherever possible, create tasks that the handicapped child is capable of performing; this leads to self-reliance and self-respect.
2. The teacher and children of any class that has a child with an orthopedic handicap should treat this child in a normal manner, helping where really necessary but never pampering him.

The Slow Learner

In the majority of cases, a slow learner is classified according to scores on one or more intelligence tests. Generally speaking, children who possess IQs between 70 and 90 are classified as slow learners. These children are usually placed in regular classes, so they become part of the normal problems encountered when planning and teaching physical education. With respect to this type of heterogenous grouping, the following suggestions presented by Ragan are as applicable to physical education as to any other subject (1961).

1. Standards of achievement for slow-learning children should be set up in terms of their ability.
2. Short, frequent drill periods are essential for slow learners.
3. Materials should be divided into short, definite learning units.
4. Opportunities to succeed in small undertakings should be provided.
5. Slow-learning children frequently need help in making adjustments to group living, as well as to school subjects.

Other types of handicaps range from the culturally deprived to restrictive allergies. The fundamental guideline to follow is to consult first with the parents and competent medical authorities to understand the nature of the disorder. The child should participate in the physical education program within the limits of his handicap.

Mainstreaming
in the Intramural Program

The intramural program provides an excellent opportunity to integrate exceptional children. Children who are physically unable to participate should be encouraged to become referees, managers, or scorekeepers, or to assist teachers or council officials in a number of positive ways.

There are a number of activities that are fun and competitive yet do not require physical skill or total body movement. Most children, for example, enjoy chess, checkers, tic-tac-toe, and many other games of this nature. Since these activities are enjoyed by all children, the handicapped child needs no special program and is treated during such events as an equal competitor who will not receive any special favors. The latter situation is a healthy example of effective integration of all children regardless of physical abilities.

Other ways of accommodating the physically handicapped child is through self-directed activities. A child paraplegic can be given a physical fitness program based upon movements he can perform and on projected levels of accomplishment. These challenges can be easily translated into points to allow the child to enhance his own image through contributing to his homeroom or house point total. Other game-type activities such as basket shooting and arm wrestling should be modified to accommodate handicapped children.

Sources for Additional Ideas

A variety of associations concerned with exceptional children will, upon request, provide resource materials to the classroom teacher. Teachers should write to the appropriate association listed below and indicate the specific type of assistance required. In addition, a number of excellent books dealing with exceptional children are in print. A few examples of the types available are listed in appendix A.

Resource Centers

Information and Research Utilization Center in Physical Education and Recreation for the Handicapped (IRUC), c/o AAHPERD, 1900 Association Drive, Reston, Va., 22091

National Center on Educational Media and Materials for the Handicapped, Ohio State University, Columbus, Ohio, 43210

The Council for Exceptional Children Information Center, 1920 Association Drive, Reston, Virginia, 22091

Note: In addition to the above, district and state departments of public instruction normally have special education divisions or departments.

Associations

American Alliance for Health, Physical Education, Recreation, and Dance, 1900 Association Drive, Reston, Va. 22091.

American Federation of the Physically Handicapped Inc., 1376 National Press Building, Washington, D.C. 20004.

American Hearing Society, 817 14th Street, N.W., Washington, D.C. 20005

American Heart Association, Inc., 1790 Broadway, N.Y., N.Y. 10019

Association for the Aid of Crippled Children, 345 East 46th Street, N.Y., N.Y. 10017

Children's Bureau, Department of Health, Education and Welfare, Washington, D.C. 20014

Muscular Dystrophy Association of America, Inc., 1790 Broadway, N.Y., N.Y. 10019

National Association for Mental Health, 10 Columbus Circle, N.Y., N.Y. 10019

National Epilepsy League, 208 North Wells Street, Chicago, Ill. 60606

United Cerebral Palsy Association, 50 West 57th Street, N.Y., N.Y. 10019

United States Office of Education, Department of Health, Education and Welfare, Washington, D.C. 20202

11 Integrating Physical Education with Other Subjects

Mathematics
Adding and Subtracting
Multiplying and Dividing
Numbers and Geometric Forms
Measuring and Graphing
Conversion to the Metric System

Language Arts

Social Studies
Home and Neighborhood
State and Nation
Other Cultures

Health and Safety

Art and Music
Art Activities
Music Activities

Science
Gravity
Levers
Motion
Force
Other Scientific Areas

One of the fundamental themes throughout this book is that physical education makes unique contributions to the general goals of elementary education. Through a broad-based program of activities and effective teaching strategies, young children progressively increase their physical attributes and learn the knowledge and skills of a variety of physical activities. And, through the medium of play, both directed and cooperative, a child also learns about self-control and cooperative behavior.

Elementary school teachers fully realize that learning in one area, such as arithmetic, can be strengthened by another area, as when adding the number of points in a game played in a physical education lesson. Research evidence provided by Humphries (1975), Krug (1973), and Cratty (1971) supports this general point of view. Their studies strongly indicate that children tend to learn certain academic concepts better through the motor activity medium than through the traditional medium. Also, teaching academic skills and concepts through a kinesthetic medium seems to be more favorable for children with average or below average intelligence.

Contemporary education uses the term *integration* to describe this mutual relationship between subject areas. Integration implies a two-way street in which each subject area has a unique place and role in the child's total education. Whenever a concept or skill in one subject area can be fortified or acquired through another subject, the relationship should be consciously planned. This chapter illustrates the potential contributions that physical education can make to other subjects in the elementary curriculum.

Mathematics

The contemporary elementary school arithmetic curriculum includes the acquisition of skills, principles, and concepts relating to whole numbers, mathematical sentences, sets, the metric system, field properties, geometry, measuring, and graphing. Classroom teachers from kindergarten to grade six have used the medium of physical activity both in the classroom and on the playing field to teach a variety of these mathematical skills and concepts. For example, a first-grade teacher has been teaching the concept of adding numbers. Of course, time has been spent in the classroom on number recognition, writing numbers, verbal counting, and manipulation of small objects into groupings. But during the physical education period a game such as "Red Light" (p. 228), involving counting, or "Squirrel in the Trees" (p. 227), involving grouping into threes, would fortify the concept of adding and sets. Numerous other mathematical skills and concepts can be taught through the games, dance, and gymnastic activities listed under the accompanying topics. Teachers should modify or add to each activity as necessary to accommodate the particular concept or skill being emphasized.

Adding and Subtracting

Activity	Concept or Skill	Page
Mousetrap	Adding	225
Beanbag Basket	Adding	225
Red Light	Adding and subtracting	228
Squirrel in Trees	Sets	227
Call Ball	Number recognition	228
Dodgeball	Subtraction	233
Loose Caboose	Sets	231
Beanbag Basket	Adding and subtracting	225
Skipping Rope Relay	Adding	243
Hopscotch	Number recognition, counting	250
Marbles	Adding and subtracting	251
Jacks	Adding and subtracting	251
Musical Chairs	One less than	265
Doubles Hopscotch	Sets	250
Juggle a Number	Adding and subtracting	262
Co-op Tag	Adding and subtracting	267
Rope Ball	Adding	270

Additional Activities

Several additional activities, such as grids, counting rhythmic beats, and keeping score, can be used to reinforce adding and subtracting skills. A few examples of each follow:

1. Grids. A rectangle, square, or patterned grid can be a very effective and enjoyable learning medium for young children. The patterns shown in figure 11.1 can be drawn on blacktop, or on plastic mats or sheets. Plastic sheets can be stored easily, and they provide a means of designing a series of learning experiences that range from simple to complex challenges. All that is required is to tape the four corners of the plastic sheet to any available surface. Adding, subtracting, and number recognition challenges can involve "hopping," "jumping," "placing parts of the body," etc. on the appropriate number.

2. Counting number of beats or steps in a dance.

3. Counting number of jumps in rope skipping.

4. Keeping team scores.

5. Number on a team or in a group.

6. Place in batting order or number assigned a player.

7. Comparing individual or team scores (example blues beat reds 10 to 5; blues won by 5 points—subtracting).

Figure 11.1 Grid Patterns

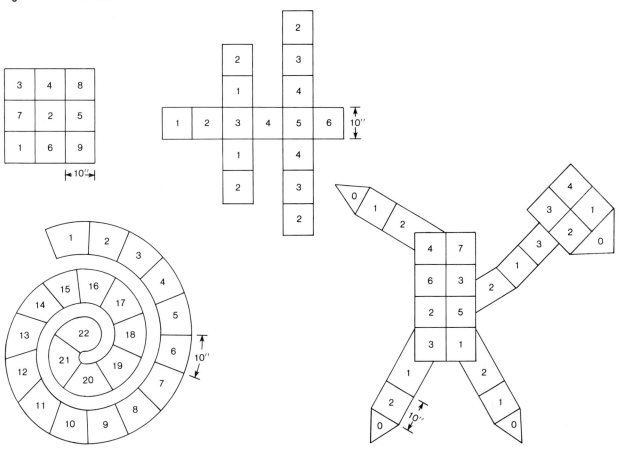

Multiplying and Dividing

Activity	Concept or Skill	Page
Call Ball	Dividing	228
Juggle a Number	Dividing	262
Cross over Blanketball	Dividing	263
Eight-legged Caterpillar	Dividing	264

Additional Activities

The accompanying activities further illustrate the tremendous contribution various physical activities can make to learning multiplying and dividing concepts and skills.

1. Grids. Another grid example is shown in figure 11.2 to demonstrate the versatility of the grid approach. Similar applications are suggested within the Language Arts section of this chapter. The grid in figure 11.2 can be used to teach the multiplication table and all forms of division. For example, a challenge such as "9 times 8 equals," requires the child to hop on *9*, then on *X*, to *8*, to the = sign, then to *7* and *2*. Partner challenges,

Figure 11.2 Grid for Teaching Multiplication and Division

using parts of the body, or combining the grid with stacks of cards with matching numbers, illustrates the various possibilities of this type of grid.

2. Dividing class into halves, quarters, thirds, etc.;
3. Dividing playing time into halves, thirds, quarters;

4. Dividing playing space into segments;
5. Moving quarter or half way up rope, along beam, or through general space;
6. Calculating batting percentages by using addition, subtraction, and multiplication.

Numbers and Geometric Forms

1. Make whole numbers with your body (fig. 11.3).
2. Make whole numbers with individual skipping ropes placed on floor. Jump over the rope according to its value.
3. Make different geometrical shapes with your body or with a partner.
4. Make different geometrical shapes with a rope, tracing out pathway of shape.
5. Throw at targets made of different geometric shapes.
6. Travel on floor or across apparatus in curved, zigzag, or straight pathways.
7. Make different angles and symmetrical or asymmetrical forms with your body, with a partner, or with a small group.

Measuring and Graphing

1. Measure length, width, height of playing field or courts.
2. Measure the number of hours and minutes spent on various physical education or other recreational activities.
3. Make drawings according to scale (e.g. $1'' = 5'$) of playing courts and field surfaces.
4. Make a circle graph showing time allotments for various physical activities in the intramural program.
5. Construct a bar graph showing changes in heart rate in relation to changes in level of physical activity.

Conversion to the Metric System

1. Measure high jump in centimeters; or convert from inches to centimeters.
2. Measure sprints and distance runs in meters; or convert from yards to meters.
3. Weigh self, teacher, balls, bats, and other equipment in kilograms; or convert from pounds to kilograms.
4. Convert school sports records to the metric scale.

Figure 11.3 Forming Numbers and Geometrical Shapes

Language Arts

Language arts in the elementary school is not a single subject. Rather, it is the basis or prerequisite for learning in all areas of education. Through language arts a child learns to communicate—to listen, speak, read, and write. While many of these skills are learned in a systematic way during the language arts period, many children learn these skills, or at least reinforce them, in other subject areas. The medium of play, whether imaginary or real, provides a rich, enjoyable, and stimulating environment in which a child can develop these communication skills.

The list of games and suggested activities on page 177 shows the types of language arts skills that can be taught through physical activities. There are numerous advantages to the physical education program when these skills are practiced or expressed through games, dance, or gymnasium activities. Rules and regulations are clarified, keener insights into movements involving game skills or dance patterns may develop, and a deeper appreciation of the art of movement may result as the child learns to integrate and communicate his ideas and feelings through speech, writing, and movement.

Additional Activities

The following activities can be used to enhance a variety of language arts concepts and skills.

1. Letter Grid. The letter grid can be used in the following ways:
   Match letters. Teacher or child calls out a letter and the performer hops, jumps, or uses parts of body to land in or touch the appropriate letter. Repeat, adding two or more letters, or spelling words.
   Vowels or Consonants. Teacher uses flash cards or calls out words with vowels. Child moves into the appropriate square.

Activity	Concept or Skill	Page
Old Mother Witch	Speaking, remembering	233
Birds and Cats	Speaking, remembering	224
Do As I Ask	Listening	225
My Ship Is Loaded	Word recognition, remembering	187
Rattlesnake and Bumblebee	Speaking	189
Puzzled Words	Spelling	190
Spell Act	Spelling	190
Charades	Spelling	190
Hopscotch	Letter recognition	249
Alphabet Game	Letter recognition, spelling	253
Modified Musical Chairs	Spelling	265

Two or three person sentences. Have the children make up a sentence with each "hopping" or using body parts to spell each word in the sequence.

2. Listen to and follow directions of a game, dance, or movement skill.

3. Listen to animal sounds made by the teacher (or a child), then do appropriate animallike movements.

4. Listen to a story or poem, then act it out.

5. Listen to music and move according to particular noises, such as loud (banging), soft (beating of triangle), or quick (fast tempo).

6. Have each child sing a nursery rhyme (chapter 26) or singing game (chapter 29) and act out or interpret the story as he sings the verses.

7. Debate value of daily physical education, Olympics, or coed physical education.

8. Make letters of the alphabet—individually, with a partner, or with three or more children.

9. Recognize and illustrate through movement, numbers, letters, shapes, or symbols printed or projected (overhead, screen).

10. Spell words with individual parts of body (finger or leg tracing letters of words), with whole body, or with a partner or small group. (In groups of three, make the letters of the words *cat, Bruce, Mississippi;* choose words according to the appropriate grade level.)

11. Write about physical education experiences such as "how I learned to swim" or "how I climbed to the top of the apple tree."

12. Read sports stories.

13. Describe a movement sequence such as a throwing skill, a gymnastic sequence, or a folk dance movement.

14. Make up new jingles and accompanying movements (in partners or groups) for contemporary popular commercials (McDonald's, Tang, etc.).

15. Write out descriptions of creative games.

Social Studies

The contemporary social studies program in the elementary school is similar to language arts in many ways. It is no longer a series of individual subjects, such as history, geography, or civics, emphasizing facts and events of past or present cultures. Rather, it is an integrated subject area that attempts to help each child, according to his ability, understand and appreciate the similarities and differences of social groups, of varying customs and morals, and of the values that are held by different people in our own or in other countries.

Physical education has been recognized as a rich environment for teaching and experiencing our own democratic ideals and other people's games, dances, and customs, and for simulating events and customs of past cultures. The following examples represent a reservoir of areas within the physical education program that can be used to help a child appreciate the importance of the interrelationship that exists among the peoples of the world.

Home and Neighborhood

1. Pantomime aspects of a child's immediate environment—items in the home (clocks, dishwasher, etc.), farm animals, and roles of people (mother, police officer, fire fighters, etc.).

2. Study groups in the immediate community with respect to your relationship to them (relatives, church, ethnic groups). Role playing to illustrate family relationships and integrating ethnic games and dances that neighbors have brought from their countries of origin are two effective areas of integrative activities.

3. Design task cards and create pantomime activities or games to orientate children to various aspects of their community. For example, task cards and games involving emergency situations such as fires or accidents, stop, go, and directional and distance signs, and helping and respecting others, such as dialing the phone for someone, showing directions, opening doors, etc.

State and Nation

1. Design maps or grids for games that involve geographical places (states, capitals), government (branches, names of leaders), or the location of historical or unique areas of our country (Washington, D.C., Grand Canyon, etc.).

2. Study native Indian or Eskimo cultures, including hunting, farming, dances, games, and other aspects that can be portrayed through physical education activities.

3. Study and participate in games and dances of early settlers, including rules, dress, or other cultural aspects of each activity (soccer, folk dances, gymnastic activities).

4. Study the history and development of games and dances created in the United States (volleyball, basketball, square dances).

5. Make up a list of games, dances, and other physical activities for special holidays. This list should include the Christmas season, Valentine's Day, Easter, St. Patrick's Day, Thanksgiving, the Fourth of July, and other special holidays that are important to the local area.

Other Cultures

1. Study and participate in singing games, folk dances, and games of other countries. This would include such factors as the historical period and the customs of the people.

2. Write about and discuss different types of physical education programs. Those of the United States, England, and the Soviet Union will illustrate many differences in the political and social environments of the countries.

3. Discuss amateurism and professionalism, particularly in light of the past two or three Olympic games. This will bring out many important questions that youngsters might understand and solve in their lifetimes.

Health and Safety

There are many close relationships between health and physical education that should be exploited by every classroom teacher. Active health programs that show children how to measure their heartbeat and breathing rates or clarify the relationship between exercise, diet, and health are examples of effective integration. The following areas illustrate how health and safety can be integrated with a variety of physical education activities.

Figure 11.4 Health can be integrated into the physical education program by showing children how to measure their heart beat and breathing rate.

1. Periodic measurement of height and weight with discussions about growth, maturation, and need for daily physical activities.

2. Discussions relating to the importance of personal cleanliness—showering, nails, hair, etc.

3. Projects that involve researching background information relating to physical fitness, personal assessment and maintenance, or remedial programs (see chapter 9).

4. Class projects that involve studying the school environment, then designing safety rules and procedures for areas and activities.

5. Learning to take pulse rate, blood pressure, and other physical assessments, then assessing the value of various types of physical activities (dance, games) with respect to increasing the efficiency of cardiorespiratory systems (see chapter 9).

6. Learning how to administer basic first aid and to design first aid materials.

7. Class projects investigating the nature and background of various physical handicaps. Project should include ways of modifying physical activities in order to mainstream children who may possess similar handicaps.

Figure 11.5 Constructing musical instruments is an art activity that can be used later in creative dance activities.

Figure 11.6 Artistic expression can be derived from physical activities.

A teacher who operates in a self-contained classroom can capitalize on the child's interests and abilities in physical activities and relate them to a variety of art forms. Drawing pictures of his gymnastic sequence or painting a picture of a sports hero can motivate the child to draw, paint, or express his ideas in some new artistic manner. Music, too, provides similar possibilities. The following examples illustrate how art, music, and physical education can be joined in mutually interesting activities.

Art Activities

1. Draw a movement sequence performed in a previous gymnastic session. A game, event, or dance skill can also be drawn.

2. Construct musical instruments that can be used in creative dance activities (see appendix B).

3. Draw symmetrical and asymmetrical shapes of the body, then include these shapes in movement sequences or creative dance activities.

4. Draw, color, or paint game, dance, or other movement activities. These activities can include sports figures or scenes, court dimensions, or dancing scenes.

5. Study sculpture, paintings, and other art forms that depict physical movements or activities. R. T. McKenzie's statues, early Greek friezes, and Egyptian paintings are rich in form and information relating to sports, dance, and gymnastic events.

6. Design bulletin boards and gymnasium murals that illustrate events, movements, or health.

7. Design adventure or creative playgrounds, which requires an understanding of the needs and interests of children, knowledge of the structure and strength of materials, and creativity to draw or illustrate ideas through a variety of materials.

8. Administration of the plumb line posture test to each other; then a discussion and creation of programs that contribute to good posture. The latter should include sitting postures when at home, when watching television, when sitting at desks, and general standing and walking postures (see chapter 9).

9. Discussion of the importance of regular physical examinations. Discussion should include what is examined, how often one should be examined, and the importance of protective or remedial measures for detected anomalies.

10. Class projects involving nutrition. These can include personal analysis of family eating patterns, types of foods eaten, calorie counting, and the relationship between dieting and exercise (see chapter 9).

11. Individual projects that investigate the health and nutritional habits of favorite movie, television, or sports personalities.

Art and Music

Art and music can be linked to physical education in a variety of ways. All three areas are used in one way or another to communicate the child's ideas and feelings about himself or objects in his immediate environment.

Figure 11.7 Music is a stimulating addition to many physical education activities.

Music Activities

1. Teach the basic elements of rhythm such as underlying beat, measures, tempo, and phrasing as it applies to rhythmic, folk, and creative dance activities (see chapter 28).
2. Use musical accompaniment for warm-up activities, rope jumping, and background music for ball bouncing and some gymnastic sequences.
3. Create songs or musical accompaniment for creative dance activities.
4. Interpret songs, sounds, and musical scores through creative movement.

Science

Within the elementary school science curriculum there are numerous scientific concepts and principles that can be illustrated and clarified through a variety of physical education activities. An understanding of gravity, force, and levers is important to understand the natural and technological environment in which we live. These scientific areas are also extremely important principles and concepts relating to human movement. The following examples provide a few illustrations of how scientific principles and concepts can be integrated with a variety of movement activities.

Gravity

1. Select a variety of gymnastic stunts such as the headstand, walking on a balance beam, or balancing on one or two feet. Show how a wide base of support and a low center of gravity provides a stable base of support. (See chapter 3 for a discussion of gravity.)
2. Set up a variety of movements where it is important to have (a) a wide base to maintain a stable resistance to an oncoming object such as catching a heavy ball and combative activities, (b) an unstable base such as a racing start or a walking movement, and (c) the center of gravity below the direction of a forceful movement such as the jump-reach.

Levers

1. Select a series of physical activities to illustrate first class levers. These could be a seesaw or rowing a boat.
2. Repeat 1 with second class levers. These could be pushing a wheelbarrow or opening a door.
3. Repeat 1 with third class levers. This is sometimes called the human lever since most physical skills involve third class levers. Examples to study are throwing a ball, lifting a weight, and kicking a ball.

Motion

1. Show how Newton's laws of motion are important in the performance of such skills as initially starting to move a ball or pushing another player and the importance of continuous force to keep the momentum, throwing two balls of different sizes, and jumping up from the floor, trampoline, or wet grass.
2. Select a series of movements to illustrate how rotary movements of the human body are transferred to linear movement of the body or objects.

Force

1. Design a series of movement challenges that illustrate the importance of applying muscular force sequentially in the direction of the movement (high jump, standing broad jump).
2. Show how the greatest force is generated through the larger muscles such as legs and hips rather than shoulder or arm muscles (bending down, keeping back straight, and lifting the legs).

3. Select a series of movements to illustrate how force should be dissipated through the widest surface and the greatest distance (landing and rolling).

Other Scientific Areas

There are numerous other scientific principles and concepts that can be illustrated through human movement activities. The following are only a few examples of integrating scientific areas of study with physical education.

1. *Matter:* Design movement challenges to illustrate movements of molecules, the solar system, and expansion and contraction of gases.
2. *Biology:* Pantomime activities to illustrate plant growth, animal movements and behavior, and human growth and development stages.
3. *Physical Science:* Design movements and challenges to explain pendulum action, wind, temperature magnetism, and sound.

These examples provide a basic idea of the tremendous potential that physical education has to offer other subject areas. See appendix A for a list of additional resource books. Integration, however, is not a one-way street. If integration is to really work, academic subject areas should also attempt, where possible, to fortify the principles, concepts, and values inherent in the content areas of physical education.

12 Adapting Physical Education Activities to the Classroom

Teaching Procedures
Participation
Safety
Noise

Classroom Games
Active Classroom Games
Quiet Classroom Games
Juggling Activities

Physical Fitness Activities
Physical Fitness Testing
Calisthenics
Isometric Exercises
Yoga Activities
Gymnastic and Movement Skills

Rhythmic and Dance Activities
Rhythmic Activities
Singing Games and Folk Dances
Creative Dance

One of the most common complaints of classroom teachers is the lack of time that can be spent in the gymnasium. In many schools, some classes are assigned only one period a week in the gymnasium. This, of course, is totally inadequate for the physical needs of young children. Inclement weather and the lack of outside playing areas may also leave the cafeteria or the classroom as the only available space for physical activity.

The information in this chapter illustrates how many of the activities described in previous chapters can be taught in the regular classroom. A few additional activities that are particularly adaptable to the classroom are also included.

Teaching Procedures

With minor adjustments and the establishment of a few basic rules and safety procedures, the classroom can be used for many physical activities. Whenever a large unobstructed space is required for a physical activity, move the desks and chairs in a safe, quiet, and efficient manner. Designating teams—by rows or any other type of classroom grouping—then creating a contest to see which group finishes first greatly speeds up this procedure.

Classrooms vary, of course, in the amount of free space available, type of furniture, and acceptable noise levels. The following suggestions, however, particularly those relating to safety and noise, should be carefully considered before introducing any physical activity to the classroom.

Participation

Provide opportunities so that every member of the class can participate in the physical activity. The game activities suggested in the next section present the greatest problem. Break the class into as many separate playing groups as possible—three groups, rather than one, playing charades—or modify the game to increase individual and total class participation.

Figure 12.1 Teaching Procedures

a. "Get ready to move your desks."

b. "Go."

c. "Good—it took just 34 seconds this time!"

Figure 12.2 "Clear your desk!"

Safety

Remove pencils and other materials from the tops of desks and keep children away from sharp corners and edges. Other safety procedures, such as permitting running only around alternate rows and only when the noise does not seriously disturb adjacent classrooms, must be translated into simple and clearly understood rules.

Noise

Although virtually every classroom differs with respect to acceptable noise levels, a few basic rules can help keep the noise problem under control. This applies to the noise within the classroom itself as well as the sound that penetrates the walls and ventilation system to other classrooms. In games and contests, modify verbal commands and require hand clapping instead of team or class yells. A lower volume may be called for in dance activities.

Classroom Games

Classroom games or what are commonly known as "rainy day activities" are simple games, relays, and contests that can be played within the classroom. These games usually require little or no adjustment of furniture or elaborate equipment. For classification purposes, these activities are generally designated as either active or quiet, although the dividing line between the two is rather vague. A very enthusiastic class can turn a quiet game into an active one and vice versa. For ease of selection, however, the more vigorous games are listed under active games and the less active under quiet games.

Figure 12.3 Classroom games can be quiet.

When to Use Classroom Games

There is no season or time of day that should be set aside for quiet or active classroom games. Their use depends upon such factors as the weather, the amount of time and space available, and, perhaps most important, the "mood" of the class. There are times during the day, for example, especially after long periods of mental concentration, when a short classroom game provides the needed relaxation for both teacher and students. The teacher should judge when and how to present a classroom game.

How to Select the Appropriate Game

When selecting classroom games, first decide on the type—active or quiet—you want to use. Second, check the righthand columns of the chart to see whether the game involves guessing, relay, imitation, tag, surprise, or small manipulation. Finally, check to see if you have the necessary equipment.

Active Classroom Games

Fox and Rabbit (K–1)

Formation   Single circle or children seated
Equipment   Two beanbags
Players   Class

One beanbag, the "rabbit," is passed around the circle. A second beanbag, the "fox," is started around the circle. When the fox catches the rabbit, the game ends. Start each game with a new player.

Teaching Suggestions
Divide class into two or three groups.

Beanbag Basket Relay (K–3)

Formation   Lines facing baskets about six to eight feet in front of first player
Equipment   Beanbags, wastepaper baskets, or hoops
Players   Class

Arrange pupils in rows facing the baskets. Draw a line across the front of the rows. On command, the first pupil attempts to throw a beanbag into the basket. One point is awarded for each basket. After shooting, each player retrieves his beanbag, gives it to the next player, and tells the teacher his score. Continue until the last player has had a turn. The team with the highest score wins.

Teaching Suggestions
Divide teams in half. Turn second half around, place baskets at back of room and play two games.

I'm Tall, I'm Small (K–1)

Formation   Single circle with one child in the center
Equipment   None
Players   Class

One child stands in the center of the circle with his eyes closed. Circle players walk slowly around, singing

I'm tall, I'm very small
I'm small, I'm very tall
Sometimes I'm tall
Sometimes I'm small
Guess what I am now.

Active Classroom Games

Name of Game	K	1	2	3	4	5	6	Page	Guessing	Relay	Imitation	Tag	Surprise	Small Manipulation
Fox and Rabbit	X	X						184					X	X
Beanbag Basket Relay	X	X	X	X				184		X				X
I'm Tall, I'm Small	X	X						184	X		X		X	X
Ringmaster	X	X	X	X				185			X			
Follow the Leader	X	X	X	X				186			X			
Go-Go Stop	X	X	X	X				186	X				X	
Circle Spot	X	X	X	X	X			186				X	X	
Beanbag Pile			X	X	X	X	X	186		X			X	
Vis-a-vis			X	X	X	X	X	186	X				X	
Simon Says		X	X	X	X	X	X	186			X		X	
Poorhouse			X	X	X	X		187					X	
Who's Leading?			X	X	X	X	X	187					X	
Balloon Hit			X	X	X	X	X	187						X

Additional Active Games
These games, found in other chapters, can be modified for use in the classroom.

Name of Game	K	1	2	3	4	5	6	Page	Guessing	Relay	Imitation	Tag	Surprise	Small Manipulation
Do as I Do	X	X						235	X		X			
Duck on the Rock	X	X						225			X			
Beanbag Basket	X	X						225			X			
Animal Walk Relay	X	X	X	X	X	X	X	243	X					
Stunt Relay	X	X	X	X	X	X	X	244	X					
Perpetual Motion Machine		X	X	X	X	X	X	261		X	X			
Recycled Snakeskins			X	X	X	X	X	262	X		X			
Twister			X	X	X	X	X	262			X			
Eight-Legged Caterpillar		X	X	X	X	X	X	264			X			
Modified Musical Chairs		X	X	X	X	X	X	265		X	X			

As the children walk and sing ''tall,'' ''very tall,'' ''small,'' or ''very small,'' they stretch up or stoop down accordingly. At the end of the singing, the teacher signals the circle players to assume a stretching or stooping position. The center player then guesses which position they have taken. If the center player guesses correctly, he remains in the center; if unsuccessful, a new player is selected.

Teaching Suggestions
Substitute other movements, such as ''wide,'' ''twisted,'' or ''narrow.''

Ringmaster (K–3)

Formation   Single circle with one child in the center
Equipment   None
Players   Class

One child selected as the ''ringmaster'' stands in the center of the circle. The ringmaster moves about the center of the circle pretending to crack his whip and calls out the names of animals. The circle players imitate the animals. If the ringmaster calls out ''All join the parade,'' the children imitate any animal they wish.

Teaching Suggestions
Call out names of mechanical objects, such as bulldozer, truck, or washing machine.

Follow the Leader (K-3)

Formation Single lines

Equipment None

Players Class

Arrange the class in two or three lines of ten to twelve players. The leader walks and begins to perform any kind of movement, such as hands on head, arms sideward, or leaping from one spot to another. All other players in the line copy the movement. Anyone who fails to perform the feat goes to the back of the line.

Teaching Suggestions

Play the game in a circle with the leader standing in the center.

Go-Go Stop (K-3)

Formation Single line with children facing forward

Equipment None

Players Class

The teacher says "Go, go, go" and all walk straight ahead. When the teacher says "Stop," all must stop. A child who fails to stop returns to the starting line and the game begins again.

Teaching Suggestions

Use other locomotor movements, such as running, skipping, sliding, or hopping. Turn your back to the students when calling "Go, go, go," then turn around and call "Stop." This increases the element of surprise.

Circle Spot (K-4)

Formation Circle with four feet between each player

Equipment Beanbags

Players Ten to twenty players

One child chosen to be "it" stands in the center of the circle. Circle players stand at least four feet apart with beanbags on the floor immediately in front of them. On signal from the teacher, everyone walks, skips, etc. around the circle of beanbags. On the second signal everyone, including "it," tries to place one foot on a beanbag. The extra child becomes "it" and stands in the center of the circle.

Teaching Suggestions

Place other parts of the body on the beanbag.

Beanbag Pile (2-6)

Formation Sitting on the floor in rows

Equipment One beanbag for each member

Players Five or six in each row

Players are seated in a single line formation with beanbags placed in a pile in front of the first player in each line. On the signal "go," the first player takes a bag and passes it to the second player. The remaining beanbags are passed back one at a time. The last player lays the first beanbag on the floor. Each succeeding bag must be placed on top of the other, with only the first beanbag touching the floor. The stack must stand without any assistance from the stacker. If the stack falls, it must be restacked. The first team to pile the bags correctly wins the relay.

Teaching Suggestions

1. Change position of players such as, kneeling, standing.
2. Require all players to run on the spot or perform other movements while passing the beanbag.

Vis-a-Vis (2-6)

Formation Scattered in partners

Equipment None

Players Class

One child is chosen to stand among the partners. When the teacher calls "back to back" or "face to face," the children do as directed. When the teacher calls "busy bee," everyone, including the extra child, must find a new partner. The child who fails to get a new partner becomes the extra player.

Teaching Suggestions

After the children have learned the game, allow the extra player to call the directions.

Simon Says (1-6)

Formation Seated in rows, with one player in front of the class

Equipment None

Players Class

One player is chosen as leader and comes to the front of the class. The other players remain at their seats. The players at their seats follow the leader's action when he prefaces his instructions with "Simon says." If he says, "Simon says hands on head place," all should follow this movement. But if the leader says, "Hands on hips place," no one should move. Any player who commits an error must make a funny face. (Do not eliminate any child from the game.)

Teaching Suggestions

Change leaders after two or three commands.

Poorhouse (3-6)

Formation   Semicircle or horseshoe formation

Equipment   None

Players   Class

Players choose partners and sit in chairs placed in a horseshoe pattern. Two chairs representing the "poorhouse" are placed at the open end of the horseshoe. Each couple has a number and must keep their hands joined throughout the game. The game begins with the couple in the poorhouse calling out two numbers. The couples whose numbers are called must change places. During the changeover, the poorhouse couple attempts to reach the chairs vacated by one of the couples.

Teaching Suggestions

Integrate math skills with this game. For example, saying "16 ÷ 4" and "8 − 6" would require number 4 and 2 to exchange positions.

Who's Leading? (2-6)

Formation   Circle formation

Equipment   None

Players   Class

One player chosen to be "it" stands outside the circle with his hands over his eyes. The teacher then selects a player in the circle to be the "leader." The leader starts any motion he chooses (blinking his eyes, waving his arms over his head, etc.). "It" opens his eyes and tries to guess who the leader is. As the game progresses, the leader slyly switches to other movements and "it" tries to find this person. Allow two or three guesses, then change the leader and "it."

Balloon Hit (2-6)

Formation   Desks and chairs moved back against the wall

Equipment   Balloons

Players   Scattered

Every player has a balloon. Each child keeps his balloon in the air by hitting it with his "best" hand. Later add "other hand," "elbows," "hit and turn around," "hit and touch the floor," etc.

Teaching Suggestions

Play a game with one half of the class against the other. Sit or kneel in a scattered formation and use five balloons. Use walls for goals and add other rules as necessary.

Quiet Classroom Games

My Ship Is Loaded (K-2)

Formation   Seated on floor

Equipment   Utility ball (nine or thirteen inches)

Players   Class divided into groups of three or four players

One child starts by rolling a ball to another and saying, "My ship is loaded with cars" (or any cargo he wishes). The player who receives the ball repeats what the first child said and adds a new item as he rolls the ball to another player. He would say, "My ship is loaded with cars and hats." Each player in turn adds a new item. When a child fails to repeat all the "cargo," the ball is given to the player on his right, who starts a new game.

Crumple and Toss (1-3)

Formation   Lines facing baskets with front player about ten feet from the basket

Equipment   Newspapers, wastebaskets, or cardboard boxes

Players   Class divided into lines of three or four players

Each player is given a piece of newspaper, which he crumples with one hand. The first player attempts to throw his crumpled paper into the wastebasket. After taking a turn, each child goes to the back of the line and the next player moves up to the line and takes a turn. The team with the most papers in the basket wins.

I Saw (1-3)

Formation   One child stands facing others seated at desks

Equipment   None

Players   Class

The child standing is "it" and says, "On my way to school I saw . . ." and pantomimes what he saw. The child who correctly guesses what "it" saw then becomes "it." If no one guesses correctly in five tries, "it" tells what he saw. If the class decides that his imitation was too poor, he must choose a new "it." If the class decides the imitation was a good one and they did not guess it within five tries, "it" continues for another time.

Name of Game	K	1	2	3	4	5	6	Page	Guessing	Relay	Imitation	Tag	Surprise	Small Manipulation
My Ship Is Loaded	X	X	X					187			X		X	
Crumple and Toss		X	X	X				187		X				X
I Saw		X	X	X				187	X		X			X
Hens and Chickens	X	X						188	X		X		X	
Ring, Bell, Ring	X	X						188	X				X	X
Who Moves?	X	X	X					188	X				X	
Hide the Thimble	X	X	X	X				189	X				X	
Crambo		X	X	X				189	X				X	
Clothespin Drop				X	X	X	X	189		X				X
Hat Race		X	X	X	X	X	X	189		X				X
Tic-Tac-Toe				X	X	X	X	189		X			X	X
Rattlesnake and Bumblebee				X	X	X	X	189	X		X		X	
Human Checkers				X	X	X		189		X			X	
Puzzled Words				X	X	X		190	X				X	X
Spell Act			X	X	X	X		190	X		X			X
Charades					X	X		190	X				X	X

Hens and Chickens (K–1)

Formation   Seated

Equipment   None

Players   Class

One child chosen to be the "hen" walks to the cloakroom or hall. While the hen is out of the room, the teacher walks around the room tapping several children, who become "chickens." All the children place their heads on their desks, hiding their faces in their arms. The hen comes in and moves about the room saying "Cluck, cluck." All the children keep their heads down and the chickens answer "Peep, peep." The hen listens and taps on the head any child she believes is a chicken. If the hen is correct, the chicken must sit up straight; if incorrect, he continues to hide his head. After the hen has selected all the chickens, she or the teacher selects a new hen.

Ring, Bell, Ring (K–1)

Formation   Seated

Equipment   Small bell

Players   Class

One child chosen to be "it" closes his eyes while another child hides the bell. The child with the bell holds it so that no sound is heard and runs to another part of the room. The teacher, after seeing that the child with the bell is located and ready, turns to "it" and tells him to call. "It," with his eyes still covered, calls "Ring, bell, ring." The child with the bell rings it a few short times. "It" must guess where the bell is. If "it" points in the right direction, he becomes the bell ringer. Change the "guesser" after each turn.

Who Moves? (K–2)

Formation   Line formation in front of class

Equipment   None

Players   Class

Five children are selected by the teacher to stand in front of the class. The children who are seated look at the line, then lay their heads on their arms. While the children have their heads down, the teacher changes the positions of two or three children in the line. On signal from the teacher, the seated children look at the line and one child is selected to arrange the line as it was originally.

Hide the Thimble (K-3)

Formation None

Equipment Small object

Players Class

The class decides on an object to be hidden, such as an eraser or small toy. The teacher chooses one player to be the "hunter" and sends him out of the room while the class hides the object. As the hunter enters the room and approaches or moves away from the object, the class hums or claps, loudly or softly, depending upon how close the hunter is to the object. When the hunter finds the object, he chooses another hunter.

Teaching Suggestions

Use various means of "hinting," such as raising or lowering the hands, hissing, and so on.

Crambo (1-3)

Formation Seated

Equipment None

Players Class

One child chosen to be "it" starts the game by saying, "I am thinking of something (inside or outside the room) that rhymes with rain." Other players ask, "Is it a train?" "Is it a drain?" and so on. The child who guesses correctly becomes "it."

Clothespin Drop (3-6)

Formation Rows

Equipment Milk bottle or container and five clothespins for each row

Players Class

Each row represents a team. Place a milk bottle in front of each row. Players take turns standing erect and above the bottle and dropping the clothespins, one at a time, into the bottle. Each clothespin counts one point.

Hat Race (1-6)

Formation Rows

Equipment Ruler and hat

Players Class

Every other row participates. All players stand in the aisles with rulers in their right hands. The first player has a hat, which he places on his ruler. On the signal "go," he passes the hat over his right shoulder to the next player who takes the hat with his ruler and passes it over his shoulder to the next player, and so on. The last player in the row walks down the empty aisle to the front of his line. If a player drops the hat, he must pick it up with the ruler; no hands are allowed.

Everyone shifts back one position and the relay continues until all players are back in their original positions.

Teaching Suggestions

Try the game sitting down.

Tic-Tac-Toe (3-6)

Formation Seated in rows

Equipment Chalk

Players Class

Number each row and draw a tic-tac-toe diagram (#) on the board between the two competing teams. Only two teams play at a time. The teacher chooses the starting team. The first player from one team makes an X in one of the spaces. The first player from the other team marks an O in one of the remaining spaces. Continue alternating until one team gets three marks in a row.

Rattlesnake and Bumblebee (3-6)

Formation Seated at desks or tables

Equipment Two small unlike objects

Players Two equal teams

One player is chosen from each team and sent out of the room. While the two players are out, team captains hide the two articles (team A hides for team B and vice versa). The two players return and begin looking for their articles. Members of either team "buzz" or "hiss" according to how close each player is to his object. Repeat with two new "finders." One point is awarded for the player, and his team, who finds the object first.

Human Checkers (4-6)

Formation Chairs in a row

Equipment Seven chairs

Players Six on each team

Place seven chairs in a row. Three girls sit on the three chairs at one end and three boys sit at the other end. The object is to move the girls to the boys' chairs and the boys to the girls' chairs in fifteen moves. Only one move can be made at a time. Moves are made by sliding into an open chair or "jumping" over one person. Players cannot move backward. For example, girl number three moves to the spare chair; on the second move, boy number four jumps girl number three, who is now in the spare position, and so on.

Puzzled Words (4–6)

Formation   Groups of five to eight players
Equipment   Pieces of paper
Players   Class

Organize the class into groups of five to eight children. The teacher gives each group a pile of letters which, after reshuffling, will form a word. On signal from the teacher, each group tries to put its word together. The first team to assemble its word wins the game.

Teaching Suggestions
After the group puts the word together, allow it to act out the word for the other children to guess.

Spell Act (3–6)

Formation   Two teams on opposite sides of the room
Equipment   None
Players   Class

Play this game as a regular spelling match. The letters *A* and *T* must not be spoken but must be indicated as follows: *A,* scratch right ear and raise left hand. *T,* scratch left ear and raise right hand.

Charades (5–6)

Formation   Small groups
Equipment   None
Players   Class divided into five or six groups

Each group is allowed sufficient time to work out a charade. A captain is elected from each group. The word or object chosen by a group should have syllables to make it easier to act out. All dramatizations must be in pantomime. One group acts out its charade in front of the class. The captain of the group asks the class to guess the syllable or complete word. If the word is not guessed within a certain time, the captain tells the class and the next group has its turn.

Teaching Suggestions
Ask the class to decide on a specific category from which all words must be chosen, such as books, cities, famous names, songs.

Juggling Activities

The basic juggling skills described in chapter 26 can be practiced in a classroom or hallway. Begin with scarves; as skill improves, gradually introduce bags or balls. If the lighting fixtures present a potential hazard, restrict juggling activities to "safe areas" within the classroom or hallway.

Physical Fitness Activities

A variety of physical fitness activities can be performed in the classroom. The following examples illustrate how physical fitness tests, circuit training, and yoga activities can be performed within the classroom with a minimum amount of furniture adjustment or noise disturbance to adjacent classrooms.

Physical Fitness Testing

Several test items within the AAHPERD's *Youth Fitness and Health Related Physical Fitness Test* can be easily administered in the classroom. These items include sit-ups, standing broad jump, fat fold and sit-and-reach. Other cardiovascular activities, such as, measuring heart rate and blood pressure, or conducting the following cardiovascular experiments are easily adapted to the classroom.

Experiment 1: Location and Size of Heart, page 136.
Experiment 2: Comparative Heart Rates, page 136.
Experiment 3: Heart Rate Recovery, page 136.
Experiment 4: Effect of Different Activities, page 136.
Experiment 5: Excitement and Fear, page 136.

Calisthenics

Simple calisthenics, with or without musical accompaniment, may be among the easiest activities to perform in the classroom. Once children appreciate the space limitations, they can do the exercises beside their desks or wherever space is available in the classroom.

Figure 12.4   Juggling skills can be practiced in the classroom.

Brief circuit-type activities, described on pages 148 to 149, also can be designed for the classroom. The advantages are that the teacher can develop a basic circuit that does not require any mats or other equipment and that all children begin and stop after a set number of minutes. In addition, where noise is a problem between adjacent classrooms, circuits can be performed in relative silence and without using a whistle or a loud voice to give or change directions.

Figure 12.5 Physical fitness testing can be a classroom activity.

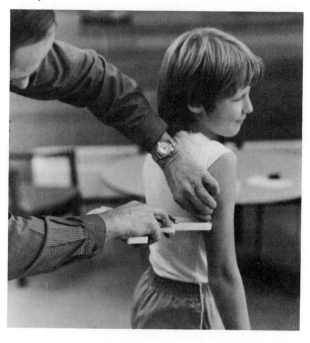

Figure 12.6 Simple Calisthenics in the Classroom

Isometric Exercises

Isometric exercises are contractions of muscles involving a push, a pull, or a twist against an object that does not move. An isometric muscular contraction, such as grasping the seat of a chair and "pulling" upward, requires a high degree of muscular tension without moving the arms or changing the joint angle. Since these exercises require maximum effort to gain strength, it is suggested that only older elementary children do them.

This type of exercise program is very adaptable to the space and equipment limitations of the regular classroom. Figures 12.7 to 12.12 illustrate the types of exercises that can be performed while seated or near the desk. Each exercise should be performed in a

Figure 12.7 Arms and Shoulders. Sit with the back straight and grasp the edge of the chair. Keep the back and arms straight and pull the trunk and shoulders upward. Maintain the same body position and push the trunk and shoulders downward.

"pushing" action (eight seconds) and a reverse "pulling" action (eight seconds) to gain maximum benefit. Also, the total series should be repeated three to four times a week.

Many other exercises involving a pushing or pulling action can be designed by the teacher or the class. In addition, individual ropes tied together, wands, or the walls of the classroom can be used to perform numerous isometric exercises.

Figure 12.8 Legs, Arms, and Abdomen. Sit with the back straight and the hands resting on top of the thighs. Keep the arms straight and push downward with the hands and upward with the legs.

Figure 12.9 Neck and Arms. Sit with the back straight and the heels of both hands resting against the forehead. Push with the hands and resist with the forehead.

Figure 12.10 Place hands behind the head and push back with the head and resist with the hands.

Figure 12.11 Arms, Shoulders, and Back. Stand with the legs apart and the body twisted towards the left. Join hands. Keeping the left arm bent and the right arm straight, pull with the right arm and resist with the left arm.

Figure 12.12 Reverse sides and repeat.

Yoga Activities

Yoga exercises are basically stretching movements, performed much slower than calisthenics. Yoga exercises improve physical and organic health and the power of concentration. They are also extremely good for developing flexibility and good postural habits.

Children from kindergarten to grade six thoroughly enjoy doing the animallike movements of the yoga program. Since the movements are performed according to each child's ability, they can be used as an alternate form of warm-up activity in the classroom or at home under a parent's guidance. The following basic program illustrates a few of the more popular movements. Additional exercises may be found in the references in appendix A.

Figure 12.13 Every yoga program should include a breathing exercise.

Basic Yoga Program

Every yoga program should begin with a warm-up activity and include a balance, a fitness, and a breathing exercise. The last exercise in the routine should be a relaxation pose. The accompanying sample program provides a guideline.

Sample Yoga Program		Page
Warm-up	Rub, rock, roll, and cross-leg stretch	
Balance	Wheel	196
Fitness	Cat Stretch	194
Fitness	Cobra	198
Fitness	Locust	197
Breathing	Breathing	198
Relaxation	Curling Leaf	199

Individualized programs can be designed to help children with recognizable muscular weaknesses or posture problems, or to "calm down" a hyperactive child. Remember, a child need only stretch as far as he can; suppleness will improve with practice.

Warm-up Activities

Warm-up movements should be quick and gentle. Begin by rubbing the body all over with the hands to increase circulation. Next, standing with knees slightly bent, hang down from the waist. Finally, rock back and forth on the back, then form a cross-legged position. Other yoga exercises are shown in figures 12.14 to 12.30. Hold each position about five seconds.

Figure 12.14 Cat-Stretch

a. Begin by kneeling on all fours.

b. Inhale, rock slightly back, and lower chest, trying to touch the throat to the floor.

c. Exhale and arch upward like an angry cat.

d. Inhale bringing the right knee toward the head.

e. Exhale as one leg is stretched backward and upward. Inhale as the leg is returned to the starting position.

Figure 12.15 Sun Salutation (fitness)

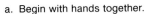

a. Begin with hands together.

b. Inhale as the arms are raised up and back.

c. Exhale and bring arms forward and down. Try to keep legs straight.

Figure 12.16 Crow (fitness and balance)

a. Squat with hands between knees about a foot apart.

b. Exhale, bend forward, press inside of knees against elbows, and lift toes off floor.

c. Variation: Begin with hands spread far apart, then shift forward into position *b.*

Adapting Physical Education Activities to the Classroom   195

Figure 12.17 Warrior (fitness and balance)

a. Begin in an upright kneeling position with knees together and feet spread apart.

b. Exhale and lower body until the back rests on the floor (use hands for support).

c. Continue to a full arch, resting palms on floor.

Figure 12.18 Wheel (balance)

a. Lie on back with knees bent and arms curved so that palms are flat on floor beside the chin, with the fingers pointing toward the shoulders.

b. Exhale, raise body, and rest head on floor. Take a few breaths.

c. Exhale and continue upward arch.

Figure 12.19   Locust (fitness)

a. Lie facedown with hands at sides.

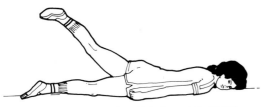

b. Inhale and raise one leg. Exhale and lower leg.

c. Advanced: Repeat, raising both legs at once as high as they will go.

Figure 12.20   Plough (fitness). Lie on back with body straight, arms at sides, and palms down.

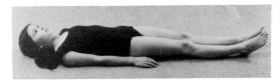

Figure 12.21   Plough (fitness). Exhale and raise legs up and over the head, stretching the toes away from the body.

Figure 12.22   Lion (fitness). Kneel with hands on thighs. Bend forward, slide fingers to floor, open eyes as wide as possible, and stick tongue out as far as possible, trying to touch the chin.

Figure 12.23 Cobra (fitness). Lie facedown with body straight and hands at sides, palms down.

Figure 12.24 Cobra (fitness). Inhale and bring head up and back. Exhale and return to starting position.

Figure 12.25 Bow (fitness). Lie facedown with hands on floor. Inhale and grasp ankles.

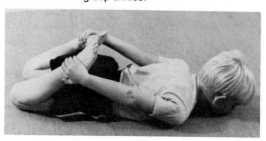

Figure 12.26 Bow (fitness). Exhale and arch upward.

Figure 12.27 Complete Breathing (breathing and relaxation). Sit on crossed legs (or in a crossed-leg position). Slowly inhale through the nose, gradually expanding the rib cage and pushing abdomen out. Take about ten seconds to fill lungs. Hold breath for a few seconds . . .

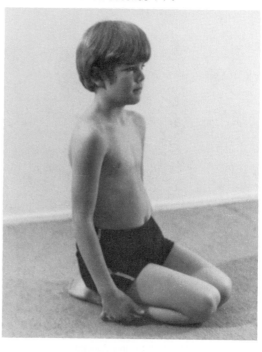

Figure 12.28 Complete Breathing (breathing and relaxation). Slowly exhale, pulling in the abdomen.

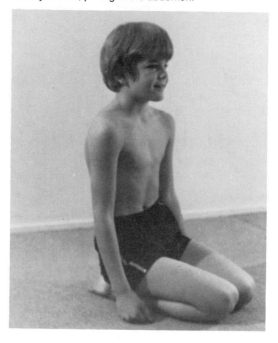

Figure 12.29 Curling leaf (relaxation). Kneel with legs together, seat on heels, and back of hands on floor.

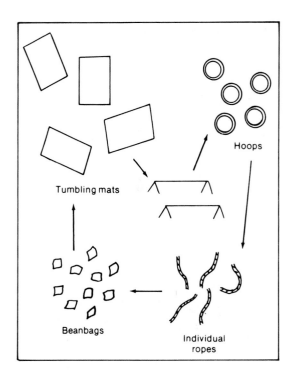

Figure 12.30 Curling leaf (relaxation). Slowly lower head and slide hands backward. Remain in this position with head resting on the floor, and chest against the knees.

Gymnastic and Movement Skills

Gymnastic movement skills include a large number of activities that can be performed in the classroom with a little planning. Activities such as individual stunts and movement skills (chapter 25), small equipment and partner activities (chapter 26), and a few large apparatus skills (chapter 27) can be adapted to the limited space of the regular classroom. The following stunts do not require a mat, hence are more appropriate for classroom use. Other individual movement skills such as shapes, weight bearing, and simple sequences could also be practiced on the available floor space.

Small Equipment

The use of small equipment such as beanbags, individual ropes, and hoops in the classroom is growing in popularity. Schools that have adopted daily physical education programs and have limited gymnasium facilities are using the classroom as an alternate exercise area. Since small equipment can be easily transported, it has many classroom applications.

The following activities can be performed in the aisles or in a cleared area at the back of the room.

Name of Stunt	Page
Beanbag Activities	439
Individual Rope Activities	439
Hoop Activities	451
Wand Activities	453
Chair Activities	459

Large Apparatus

The use of large apparatus in a typical classroom is limited by the size and weight of the apparatus. There are, however, companies producing large apparatus that is light, collapsible, and capable of numerous arrangements. The agility apparatus illustrated in figure 12.32 provides several different levels to complement the partner movement challenge. See also chapter 27.

Figure 12.31 Performing Skills with a Beanbag

Figure 12.32 Agility Apparatus

Combining Large and Small Equipment Using a Rotation System

The diagram on page 199 illustrates how station work and a rotation system give every child an opportunity to use a variety of small equipment and portable agility apparatus. Since the area is crowded with equipment, the lesson emphasizes matching balance activities. The task for every station is to develop a matching sequence with one piece of equipment. In this case, movement is limited to the space immediately around the individual piece of equipment.

Rhythmic and Dance Activities

The classroom setting has numerous advantages when teaching rhythmics, singing games, and folk-dance activities. For older children, the familiar environment of the classroom can prove to be a stepping-stone for more complex and creative movements in the gymnasium. A few examples and references to previous chapters will assist teachers in developing exciting dance and creative movement programs for both primary and intermediate grades.

Rhythmic Activities

The rhythmic activities described in chapter 28 can easily be performed in the classroom. It is suggested that the same progression—moving from individual to partner to group activities—be followed. Small equipment such as beanbags, individual ropes, and rhythm sticks can also be used in the classroom with only minor adjustments. If the noise of a record player or drum is distracting to adjacent classrooms, limit the accompaniment to light drum beats or encourage the children to move in a rhythmic pattern without musical accompaniment. In fact, the latter will produce some very interesting results.

Singing Games and Folk Dances

Young children, particularly those in kindergarten and first grade, thoroughly enjoy the singing games described in chapter 29. The classroom provides an informal atmosphere in which to learn the words of these games and to practice the basic steps and rhythm patterns. Virtually all singing games can be performed in the space available in a regular classroom.

For older children, folk dance steps, and positions, and pathways of movements can be taught in the classroom. If students have had little exposure to folk dance activities, individual and partner activities involving the basic steps and patterns can be performed in the classroom. This procedure normally breaks the ice for larger group dances that require the larger space of the gymnasium.

Figure 12.33

Figure 12.35

Figure 12.34

Figure 12.36

Creative Dance

What has been said about the value of an informal classroom atmosphere when teaching folk dance applies more so to creative dance activities. Students can begin with very simple and "directed" follow-the-leader or matching movements and then gradually be introduced to more creative tasks. In time, more creative challenges involving sound, poetry, or other forms of accompaniment can be introduced to the program. The teacher should review the ideas presented in chapter 30 to determine what other creative dance activities can be adapted to the classroom.

Comment: Although many interesting and exciting physical activities can be performed in the regular classroom, such activities are inadequate for the child's normal growth and development. It is anticipated that the reader will have the same point of view and will use the classroom to supplement rather than to replace the gymnasium.

There are times too when the mood of the class dictates a change of pace before shifting to another subject area. A five- or ten-minute break for a quick classroom game, a set of yoga exercises, or a short rhythmic routine may make the contents of this chapter worth reading and remembering.

13 Designing Extraclass Programs

Intramural Program
Time Schedules for Participation
Supervision of Program
Methods of Organizing for Competition
Types of Competition
Point and Award Systems
Officiating Intramural Activities
Types of Intramural Activities

Extramural Program
Play Days
Sports Days
Field Days

The extraclass program includes such activities as sports competition between classes, all-school track meets, and limited competition with other schools. The extraclass program should be supplemental to the instructional program. Furthermore, to be truly intramural in principle, it should be a voluntary program with a major emphasis on participation and student leadership and a minor emphasis on winning. In order to develop a comprehensive program of extraclass activities, teachers should understand the methods of organizing for competition, when to offer activities, and the types of activities that children enjoy in the intramural and extramural programs. These topics are discussed next.

Intramural Program

A contemporary intramural program for elementary school children should include competition between classes or other equal competitive groups. The intramural program should provide opportunities for every child to participate in a sport or club activity of his choice. Obviously strong, enthusiastic support and guidance by the teacher are necessary. However, once the program has been organized, the children should assume major responsibility for running virtually all aspects of it. The following information provides the basic material for developing a comprehensive intramural program (see also the film *Participation for All,* appendix A).

Time Schedules for Participation

The time scheduled for intramural activities usually depends on the nature of the school population and the available facilities. Before school can be an effective time, particularly in districts where many parents work or when children arrive early by bus. The most popular time, of course, is the noon hour; this provides an opportunity for participation by virtually all children. There is, however, a general trend to hold intramural

Figure 13.1

activities after school. In urban areas where many parents work and community recreational facilities are limited, the school playground or gymnasium is used for many after-school intramural and club activities.

Supervision of Program

The success of any intramural program depends upon the support, encouragement, and effective supervision by teachers, parents, or other adult supervisory staff. The adult's role in this program should be to help children organize themselves and their activities. Through this process, children take on more responsibility for planning and operating their program while teachers gradually shift from directing the program to a role as an interested advisor and a supervisor of facilities and student run activities.

Methods of Organizing for Competition

Since intramural activities should be voluntary, the procedure used to group children for competition is of paramount importance. Perhaps the success of these programs ultimately depends upon equal competition and adequate provision for participation by all children. This must be considered in selecting the method of organization for upper elementary grades, as well as the nature and extent of adult supervision. The following methods are currently being used in elementary schools.

Grade and Homeroom

Organizing teams by homeroom appears to be the most popular method. Sixth graders competing against sixth graders is generally fair competition; sixth graders matched against fifth graders is unfair. Therefore, in team sports such as volleyball and track use homerooms within the same grade when possible. Otherwise, competition could be unequal and the children could become disinterested.

Classification Index

By the time children reach the fifth and sixth grades, age alone is an unfair assessment of physical growth and maturation. Some other method should be used to arrange players into groups of approximate physical maturation and ability. A classification index can be used to put children into groups according to both size and age. To illustrate, let us suppose sixty fifth- and sixth-grade children registered for an after-school intramural basketball tournament. Here is how the index works.

Player No.	Score
1. 10×10 (age) $+$ 70 (weight) $=$ 170	
2. 10×11 (age) $+$ 86 (weight) $=$ 196	
3. 10×11 (age) $+$ 92 (weight) $=$ 202	
4. 10×12 (age) $+$ 123 (weight) $=$ 243	

The four examples give an idea of how to divide the sixty players into two leagues of three teams each, with ten players on a team. Assuming that about half of the children had a score of 196 or less, use this score as the dividing line between the two leagues. The actual dividing line, of course, depends upon the maturity of the children.

Teacher's Choice

Competition in team and individual sports is often more dependent upon skill and desire than upon age, height, and weight. Thus it may be desirable to organize teams and leagues according to the level of skill needed for each intramural activity. However, this method is dependent primarily upon the teacher's assessment of the child's performance.

To illustrate, let us assume that at the end of a four-week instructional unit in volleyball three sixth-grade classes wish to have a coeducational volleyball tournament after school. Ten boys and ten girls from each class register for the tournament. Since the children are not playing for their homerooms, the intramural director has asked each homeroom teacher to rate the class members as either A or B players and to divide the class into two approximately equal groups. The intramural director could then place all A players in one league and all B players in another. If only one league is desired, the director would place an equal number of A and B players on each team.

Date of Birth

If the school has an average of three classes per grade, the children's birth dates can be the most even and effective way of dividing the whole school into three or more groups. These groups can become permanent from year to year. Subgroups can be organized into leagues on the basis of ability, age, or some other criterion.

To illustrate, assume we have a school of 540 children in grades one to six, with three classes in each grade. The intramural program needs four basic groups. Divide the calendar year into four equal parts and assign the children in the following manner.

Group 1: January 1 to March 31 (approximately 135 children)

Group 2: April 1 to June 30 (approximately 135 children)

Group 3: July 1 to September 30 (approximately 135 children)

Group 4: October 1 to December 31 (approximately 135 children)

Any number of groups can be obtained by simply dividing the calendar year into the desired number of units. It is important to let each group select its own name. Themes such as Indian tribes, colors, and professional sports teams are very popular with elementary school children.

The type of administrative organization that a school decides to use depends upon its size and the interest of the students. The House System, illustrated, provides for maximum student leadership and effective communication to all children.

Children should be elected to the House Council by their own house members. All other committees can be assigned responsibilities by the House Council, and the committee members can be elected, or appointed by the House Council. The roles of the Games and Rules Committee and the Schedule Committee are obvious; the Primary Leaders Committee organizes older children who wish to help primary children. These older students can play a very important role in organizing informal and noncompetitive activities for the boys and girls in the first three grades, such as beanbag bowling, skill instruction during the noon hour, and beanbag basket shooting.

Types of Competition

There are numerous ways teams or individuals can compete. The type of tournament selected depends upon the activity, the space available, the time, and the number of competitors. An Olympic meet plan is the only feasible type of tournament for track, swimming, and gymnastic activities. Single- or double-elimination and round-robin tournaments may be used for a variety of team and individual sports. Ladder tournaments are very useful for individual activities that can be played during instruction time, the noon hour, or after school. However, careful consideration should be given to the strengths and weaknesses of each type of tournament on the basis of available time, space, and number of competitors.

Olympic Meet Plan

The Olympic meet tournament is used for contests that include a number of separate events, such as swimming, gymnastics, and track and field activites. The winners of each event are awarded points, with an aggregate individual and team champion determined on the basis of points. In keeping with the idea of wide participation, first- to sixth- or seventh-place winners are awarded points. In an all-school track meet, for instance, the first six places in a fifty-yard dash might be awarded ten, nine, eight, seven, six, and five points, respectively. To encourage participation, relay and tug-of-war contests might be awarded a higher number of points than individual events.

Single Elimination

The elimination tournament is the easiest to organize and the quickest for determining a winner. Its use, therefore, depends upon a large number of teams, limited facilities, and minimum number of days to complete the tournament. Two examples of a single elimination tournament are shown on page 205.

In the first round of tournament A, the odd-numbered teams played the even numbered, which eliminated teams 2, 3, 6, and 8 from competition. In the second round, team 4 beat team 1, and team 7 beat team 5. Teams 4 and 7 competed in the last round, and team 4 won the tournament. In tournament B three teams were given a "bye" in the first round, because there were an odd number of teams.

The single elimination tournament does not require any byes when there are an even number of teams, providing they equal any power of two (2, 4, 8, 16, etc.). With an odd number of teams, or those even-numbered teams not equaling a power of two, it is necessary to give one or more teams a bye in the first round; the number of byes required for specific numbers of teams is as follows.

Number of Teams	Number of Byes	Number of Games
3	1	2
4	0	3
5	3	4
6	2	5
7	1	6
8	0	7
9	7	8
10	6	9
11	5	10
12	4	11

In the single elimination tournament, the number of games required to complete a tournament is always one less than the number of teams.

INTRAMURAL HOUSE SYSTEM

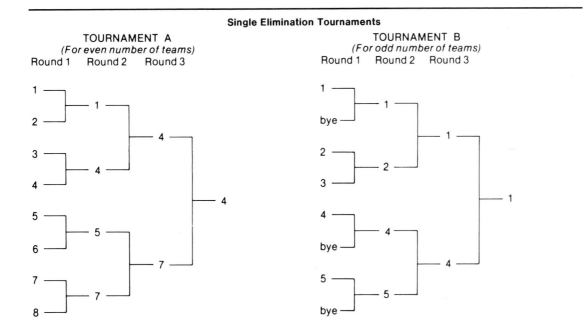

HOUSE COUNCIL
one sponsor teacher per house
one boy and one girl per house

Games and Rules Committee
2 council members
2 representatives from each house

Schedule Committee
2 council members
1 representative from each house

Primary Leaders Committee
2 council members
volunteer leader

House Captain and Assistant Captains

Referee Club

Equipment Monitors

Scorekeepers

House No. 1

House No. 2

House No. 3

House No. 4

Game Promotion
(Newspaper, decorations, notice board)

Special Events

Team Captains

Team Captains

Team Captains

Team Captains

Single Elimination Tournaments

TOURNAMENT A
(For even number of teams)
Round 1   Round 2   Round 3

TOURNAMENT B
(For odd number of teams)
Round 1   Round 2   Round 3

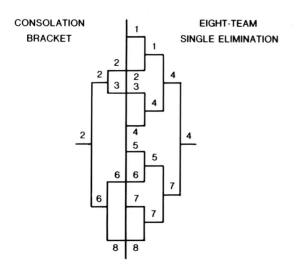

CONSOLATION BRACKET   EIGHT-TEAM SINGLE ELIMINATION

Single Elimination with Consolation Bracket

In the preceding single elimination tournament, once a team loses a game it is eliminated from all further competition. It is also quite possible for the second best team in a league to be defeated in the first round. Since the purpose of intramurals is to provide maximum activity for all competitors, a *consolation bracket* can be added to any single elimination tournament. The added bracket, as illustrated, assures each team at least two games.

Round Robin

In a round-robin tournament each team plays every other team in the league. If time and facilities permit, this is the most desirable type of competition for team and individual sports. The winner is the player or team that wins the most games. Following is the procedure for organizing a round-robin tournament.

1. Determine the number of games to be played by applying the formula $n(n-1) \div 2$ (n equals the number of teams). For example, six teams would require $6(6-1) \div 2$, or 15, games.
2. Give each team a number and arrange in two columns.
   Round 1.
   1 plays 6
   2 plays 5
   3 plays 4

3. Keep team number 1 constant and rotate all other teams one place in a counterclockwise direction until fifteen games have been scheduled.

Round 1	*Round 2*	*Round 3*	*Round 4*	*Round 5*
1 vs. 6	1 vs. 5	1 vs. 4	1 vs. 3	1 vs. 2
2 vs. 5	6 vs. 4	5 vs. 3	4 vs. 2	3 vs. 6
3 vs. 4	2 vs. 3	6 vs. 2	5 vs. 6	4 vs. 5

4. With an odd number of teams, use "bye" in place of a number and follow the same procedure. The following example is for five teams, with each bye indicating the team will not play.

1 vs. bye	1 vs. 5	1 vs. 4	1 vs. 3	1 vs. 2
2 vs. 5	bye vs. 4	5 vs. 3	4 vs. 2	3 vs. bye
3 vs. 4	2 vs. 3	bye vs. 2	5 vs. bye	4 vs. 5

Ladder Tournament

A ladder tournament is a continuous competition limited only by the space and time available. Each player or team is placed (arbitrarily, by chance, or by the results of prior competition) on a ladder, as shown in the chart below. The object is to climb to the top of the ladder and remain there until the end of the tournament. This type of competition is primarily used with individual activities during the instructional period, the noon hour, or after school. Its weakness is that only a limited number of students can participate. Its main advantage is that students, once oriented to the rules, can run their own tournaments.

The following procedure is suggested for organizing a ladder tournament.

1. Construct a ladder chart on which names can be written (in grease pencil) or placed (tagged names or cards).
2. Place all players on the ladder. The simplest procedure is to draw names from a hat and record them from the top of the ladder down.

Free Throw Tournament	
Bill	
Mary	
Jim	
Susan	
Jane	
Don	
Mike	
Jack	

3. Establish rules and post them near the tournament chart. Rules should include the following:
   a. A player may challenge only the players one rung or two above his name.
   b. The winner of a game remains on the higher rung, if originally there, or exchanges positions if originally on a lower rung.
   c. Once a challenge has been made, a deadline must be set by which the game must be played or cancelled (within two or three days).
   d. Set a completion date for the tournament.
   e. Other rules depend upon the nature of the tournament, as well as what the teacher and class would like included. Allow players to add any legitimate rule.

Pyramid Tournament

The pyramid tournament is basically a variation of the ladder tournament. The main advantage of the pyramid tournament is there are more opportunities and a greater variety for teams. The following procedures illustrates how an eight-team pyramid tournament operates.

1. Construct a pyramid and place eight (number of teams) or more circles in rows.

2. Establish a set of rules similar to the ladder tournament.

In this eight-team tournament, all teams begin by challenging any other team. To illustrate, team 7 beat team 5 hence advances to the lowest row. Similarly teams 3, 1, 4, and 8 have won their first game. A team on the lowest row may challenge any team on that row only. Winners move up to the next row. If the row immediately above is filled, winners of the lower row simply wait for a space. When all teams are on the pyramid, challenges are made to teams in the above row. The winning team takes the highest position.

Pyramid Tournament

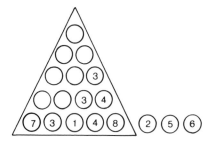

Point and Award Systems

Intramural point and award systems are designed to increase participation and to show appreciation for such things as performance, sportsmanship, and leadership. The following suggestions and guidelines will assist in developing a point and award system that will encourage informal participation as well as minimize the importance of winning.

Point Systems

Any point system that places an excessive emphasis on participation will tend to place too much pressure on team or house members to simply show up for a game or an event. Similarly, a point system that only recognizes the athletically gifted performers will disinterest virtually all other children. The following example provides a balance that reflects participation and achievement.

	Participation	Place in Tournament or Event				
		1st	2d	3d	4th	5th
Team Sports	10 points	15	10	8	7	6
Individual Sports	5 points	5	4	3	2	1
Olympic Meets						
Individual Events	1 point	5	4	3	2	1
Team Events	3 points	10	9	8	7	6

This example should be used only as a guideline. Each school should design its own point value system for the various competitive events. Whatever system is decided upon should be easy for children to tabulate. The system should also give more weight for activities involving a large number of participants and for those extending over a long period of time.

Award Systems

Ideally, participation in an intramural program should be based upon intrinsic values such as enjoyment and friendship. Hence, when presenting awards in the form of cups, ribbons, or other visual recognitions, consideration should be given to the following areas.

1. All awards should reflect the goals of the intramural program. Major awards should represent performance, sportsmanship, leadership, and participation. Special service awards to managers, particularly those who are physically handicapped, should be a priority item in any intramural program.

2. Awards should be well earned rather than a meaningless gesture.

3. Awards should be inexpensive. Exceptions should be perpetual awards, such as the aggregate trophy that is won each year by a classroom or house. The latter are initially quite expensive, however, yearly winners normally require a simple and inexpensive inscription on the base plate.

4. Intramural awards should be presented at the end of the school year during the school assembly when all other academic and achievement awards are presented to deserving students.

Officiating Intramural Activities

One of the most important factors of any intramural program is the development and performance of student officials. Whether officials are chosen by the intramural director or through the student referee's club, the following suggestions will help contribute to a successful program.

1. Encourage children who have demonstrated good leadership qualities, fair play, and an interest in officiating to join the referee's club. Although age is not a major consideration, fifth and sixth graders tend to command more respect from their fellow peers.

2. A high level of skill should not be a major requirement, hence, handicapped children, wherever possible, should be encouraged to become referees, timekeepers, or scorekeepers.

3. The intramural director or an interested staff member should provide special instructions for all officials. This should be done on a weekly basis.

4. A staff member should be present during all competitive events to provide encouragement and support to student officials. Official's decisions

Figure 13.2

should be respected by all participants and supported by the supervising teacher. If a performer or a team has a legitimate complaint, it should be directed to the referee's club or committee for resolution.

5. All officials should be given recognition for their efforts. This can be accomplished by naming the officials over the loudspeaker, awarding points to the referee's homeroom or house, or through the creation of service awards.

Types of Intramural Activities

The intramural activities that children enjoy generally are the activities they have learned in the regular instructional program. Since participation is voluntary, children should be allowed to choose their activities as well as the type and length of each tournament. The following activities have proven very popular in intramural programs for primary (K–3) and intermediate (4–6) children. Activities selected for any program should be modified or adapted to meet the uniqueness of each school.

Primary Intramural Activities

The main emphasis of primary level intramural activities should be to develop skills in an enjoyable and informal atmosphere. Through the assistance of boys and girls in the upper grades, younger children can acquire new skills as well as a positive attitude towards physical activities. The following activities should be informally organized with a major emphasis on fun and cooperative behavior.

Primary Intramural Activities

Figure 13.3 Older children assisting in primary intramural activities is an effective way for younger children to acquire new skills and a positive attitude.

Figure 13.4

Intermediate Intramural Activities

Intermediate Intramural Activities

The main emphasis of the following intramural activities for the upper elementary grades continues to be on fun, practicing skills, positive social interaction, and competition. Older children enjoy competing with their peers just as their older brothers and sisters do in high school. The task for elementary school teachers is to develop a program that has equal competition for all activities, equal playing time for all who wish to play, and, whenever possible, round-robin type tournaments to ensure maximum participation of all players and teams.

Club Activities

Club activities should be considered part of the intramural program. Teachers may find a group of children who are interested in continuing an activity learned in the instructional program but which does not lend itself to competition, such as yoga, jogging, or folk dance. Other activities that cannot be offered in the regular instructional program, such as skiing or canoeing, can also be organized as a club activity.

The basic responsibility of the teaching staff is to provide the initial organization. Obviously, if a teacher is interested in sponsoring a skiing or canoeing club,

Figure 13.5 Having fun, practicing skills, interacting socially, and competing are the primary objectives of an intermediate intramural program.

the children will gain by the teacher's efforts and talents. However, club activities can and should reach out into the community for parents and other interested citizens to assist in activities that are beyond the financial, facility, and staff limitations of the school.

Extramural Program

One of the most longlasting and controversial issues in elementary physical education is the desirability of interschool competition. Proponents of this issue can present numerous facts and opinions to qualify their argument. However, medical authorities and professional organizations have generally opposed highly organized sports for children below the ninth grade because of adverse physical and psychological effects. This point of view was formalized in the 1968 AAHPERD publication, *Desirable Athletic Competition for Children of Elementary School Age.* The majority of elementary schools have adhered to the guidelines contained in this publication.

A new set of guidelines titled *Guidelines for Children's Sports* (AAHPERD 1979) applies to children thirteen years of age and younger who wish to participate in sports. The intent of this new publication is to "encourage and promote the greatest amount of participation in sports under conditions that are safe and enjoyable for children." According to the authors of this

book, the philosophy of "child first, winning second" is easy to endorse for most adults but more difficult to practice in the heat of the game. The experts who wrote this new set of guidelines believe that in order to practice the philosophy of a child's welfare first and winning second, teachers, coaches, and parents must agree to implement the following bill of rights for young athletes (AAHPERD 1979).

Bill of Rights for Young Athletes
1. Right to participate in sports.
2. Right to participate at a level commensurate with each child's maturity and ability.
3. Right to have qualified adult leadership.
4. Right to play as a child and not as an adult.
5. Right to share in the leadership and decision making of their sport participation.
6. Right to participate in safe and healthy environments.
7. Right to proper preparation for participation in sports.
8. Right to an equal opportunity to strive for success.
9. Right to be treated with dignity.
10. Right to have fun in sports.

Many of these rights are now being realized through broad-based intramural and extramural or interschool programs. When developing an extramural program of activities the following points should be incorporated into operating policies of participating schools.

1. Interschool leagues or events should not interfere with the ongoing instructional or intramural program.
2. Boys and girls should have equal access to the interschool program.
3. Adverse parent or community pressure should not be allowed to interfere with the philosophy and general management of the interschool program.
4. All forms of competition should be minimized, with emphasis placed on participation rather than winning. Play days and sports days should be given higher priority than organized leagues between schools.
5. Adequate facilities, equipment, and supervision must be available.

6. Interschool activities should usually take place after school. Evening and weekend competition between schools should not be permitted.

7. The health, safety, and general welfare of boys and girls competing in interschool events should be stringently protected. This means medical examinations prior to competition, safe transportation to and from events, and safe facilities and equipment.

On the basis of these points, play days, sports days, and field days have become the most popular forms of extramural competition. A description of each type of competitive event follows.

Play Days

A play day involves children from two or more schools playing together on the same teams. Consider, for example, a basketball play day involving four schools. Player number 1 from each school is assigned to team A. Player number 2 from each school is assigned to team B, player number 3 to team C, and player number 4 to team D. Player 5 for each school goes to team A, and so on until all children are assigned to a team. Schools lose their identity in this type of competitive event.

Sports Days

Sports days are similar to play days except that the teams represent their own schools. Each school enters one basketball team in a round-robin tournament, with one school eventually declared the winner.

Field Days

A field day normally involves one school inviting two or more neighboring schools to participate in one activity for an afternoon. A track and field day could involve three schools on a Friday afternoon. Participants from each school participate in selected activities without keeping an aggregate school score. This type of field day emphasizes fun and meeting new friends. The cooperative activities listed in chapter 17 are particularly suited to field days of this type.

5 Game and Movement Activities

Game activities constitute a major portion of the elementary school physical education program. As children progress through the elementary grades, game activities are given more time and emphasis, and gymnastics and dance, less. Consequently, the teacher should clearly understand the organization of games so that she can select and emphasize the appropriate skills and practice activities and games without unnecessary repetition.

The next section, "Teaching Game Activities," describes how to plan instructional units and daily lesson plans for primary and intermediate grades. Suggestions relating to use of space, class management, and teaching strategies are also provided. The first three chapters of part 5 include simple team games, relays, tag activities, and individual and partner games. Chapter 17 contains modified traditional games and new cooperative games created by children in the primary and intermediate grades.

Chapters 18 through 24 are primarily designed for boys and girls in the intermediate grades. However, primary teachers should also refer to these chapters for more advanced practice activities and lead-up games that can be modified to meet the skill and ability of younger children.

Within each chapter of this section the writer has attempted to illustrate how a variety of approaches can be used to teach game activities. There are situations in every grade when skills, rules, and games should be presented in a more structured and direct way. At other times, however, application of problem-solving methods through creative or inventive games is appropriate. These chapters show how each approach can be used separately and how the structured and problem-solving methods and techniques can be blended into a single lesson or unit of instruction.

Teaching Game Activities

Teaching game-type activities to elementary school children in large instructional areas such as the gymnasium or playground can present unnecessary obstacles. The following suggestions relating to arrangement of the instructional space and class management and control will help each teacher establish an effective learning environment. The section "Developing Units and Lesson Plans" provides a format for each teacher to develop her own games program.

Arranging the Instructional Space

Most schools have one or more large playground areas that are suitable for running and simple tag games, but usually they are too large to handle a class in a normal conversational manner. To overcome this problem, assign one or two children to mark off the instructional area just before the class is taken outside; traffic cones or milk cartons are excellent markers.

Use a similar technique in a large gymnasium. Do not use equipment such as metal volleyball posts that can cause injury if knocked over.

Many of the running and simple team games described in chapter 14 require a lot of beanbags, balls, milk cartons, and other equipment. To ensure maximum use of instructional and playing time, place the equipment in cardboard boxes or nylon sacks and put them in the corners of the instructional area. Team leaders or monitors can do this job extremely well.

Classroom Management and Control

The following procedures for controlling the class can be used by teachers of any grade. Each teacher, of course, will modify the amount of freedom she allows according to her class's maturity and cooperation.

1. Divide the class into four groups. For primary children use "Sections 1, 2, 3, and 4." Intermediate children usually prefer to be called "Teams 1, 2, 3, and 4," or to be assigned the names of professional ball teams.
2. Select section leaders or team captains and rotate these positions each week to give every child a chance to be a leader.
3. Choose a place for each group to sit whenever you call "section places"—normally the middle of the instructional area. This is extremely important for good class control. Repeat the procedure until all the children move to their places quickly and efficiently.

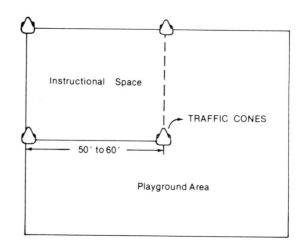

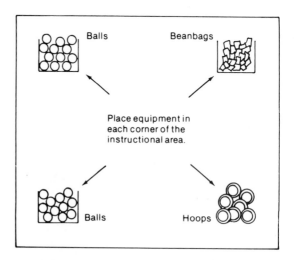

4. Follow normal and reasonable safety procedures, paying particular attention to the following:
   a. Tennis shoes should be worn during game activities, although bare feet could be allowed if the floor is free of splinters and other hazards.
   b. Goal lines should be drawn a reasonable distance from the end or side walls—three to five feet for moderately active games and six to ten feet for vigorously active games.
   c. Require that glasses, if possible, and other personal items such as chains and baggy sweaters be removed.

Developing Units and Lesson Plans

Three basic types of units can be used to organize and teach game activities (see pp. 125–27). Primary teachers normally use the alternate unit to cope with the unique characteristics of young children. Intermediate teachers tend to adapt solid or modified units when planning their games program. All teachers,

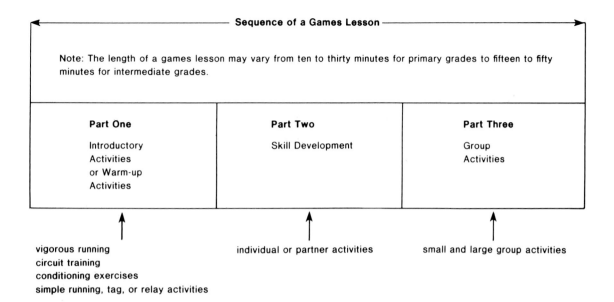

Sequence of a Games Lesson

Note: The length of a games lesson may vary from ten to thirty minutes for primary grades to fifteen to fifty minutes for intermediate grades.

Part One	Part Two	Part Three
Introductory Activities or Warm-up Activities	Skill Development	Group Activities

vigorous running
circuit training
conditioning exercises
simple running, tag, or relay activities

individual or partner activities

small and large group activities

however, should review the advantages and disadvantages of each type of unit before deciding on a particular one. Each unit may also be modified to cope with each local teaching situation.

Lesson Plans—A Flexible Design

It is impossible to recommend a standard lesson plan for every teacher to rigidly follow when teaching game activities. Each teacher must adapt to differences in the children's maturity and skill levels, the time allotment, and the supplies available. The accompanying chart provides a basic guideline for teaching individual game lessons.

All game lessons begin with some type of vigorous warm-up activity such as running, conditioning exercises, or a vigorous tag game (see chapter 14). Acquiring game skills progresses from individual to partner to group activities. This basic progression allows a child to practice a skill or movement pattern by himself during the initial phase of part two, "Skill Development." He then proceeds to partner activities which is the next step within part two of the lesson. With two performers, many more challenges and variations can be introduced and dual activities can also provide important lessons in sharing, give and take, and other forms of cooperative behavior. The third part of the lesson is devoted to group activities that stress the skills acquired earlier in the lesson.

If a first-grade teacher has only fifteen minutes to teach a games lesson, there just is not sufficient time to complete the three parts of the lesson during one class period. Hence, the first lesson starts with warm-up activities, then proceeds with individual and partner activities. Before finishing partner activities, time runs out. The next class then begins with a brief warm-up

before proceeding to partner activities and finally to a group game. A similar procedure can be followed with each succeeding lesson so long as the progression is from individual to partner to group activities for each new skill or movement pattern.

Incorporating the Inventive Games Approach

The evolution occurring within the elementary school curriculum is essentially a movement from teacher-directed activities toward a learning environment in which the teacher is a vitally important guider of children who learn by example, practice, and the joy of discovery. We have witnessed in gymnastics and dance the gradual adoption of the movement education approach, which fosters exploration, experimentation, and discovery—key elements in the creative learning process. This approach also allows the child to develop according to his own intellectual and physical ability and readiness. In essence, the style of teaching exemplified in movement education is parallel to the current practices in other areas of the elementary school curriculum.

Running, tag, and simple team games have traditionally been organized and taught on the premise that skills, rules, and strategies should be learned in an orderly and progressive manner. It would seem imperative that any new approach should still use the common terms, such as *throw, catch,* and *kick,* and that the skills and knowledge of the games should still be acquired. The approach that follows can develop these important skills and strategies while contributing to the child's needs and interests and the development of his creative

Structure of Creative Games

Primary Level Game Skills	Areas Where Limitations Can Be Imposed			
	Number of Players	Playing Space	Equipment	Skills and Rules
Locomotor and Nonlocomotor Skills	From individual activities	From limited space	From use of simple equipment	From single skills and rules
Walk				
Run				
Skip				
Slide				
Jump				
Hop				
Dodge				
Turn				
Controlling Ball with Hands	to partner activities	to use of general space		
Bounce				
Throw				
Catch				
Controlling Ball with Feet	to group activities		to use of more varied and complex equipment	to more complex skills and rules
Kick				
Pass				
Dribble				
Trap				
Projecting Ball with Hand or Equipment				
Striking ball with hand				
Hitting ball with bat, racquet, or stick				

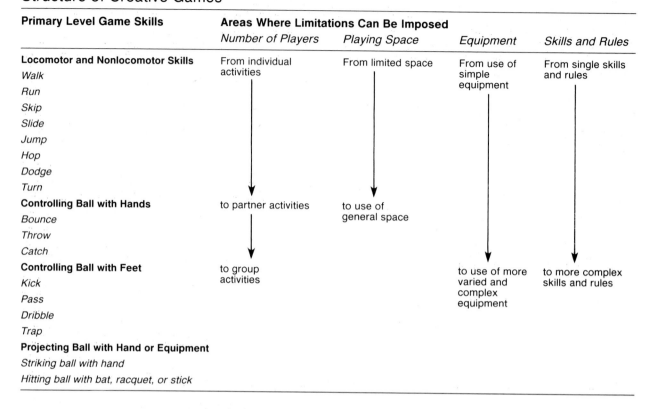

processes. This approach can be called an inventive, or creative, games approach, but it is essentially the use of the discovery method in the medium of games.

The structure within which a creative game can be played has four elements: (1) the number of players—a choice among one player, partners, or a group; (2) the area assigned or available for the game; (3) the equipment that is available or chosen by the players; and (4) the rules and skills. Within this structure, teachers and children can develop an infinite number and variety of games. Some of these games lead to the acquisition of standard sports skills, while others contribute to fun and the enhancement of creative abilities.

Games for kindergarten and grade one should be predominantly creative in nature. Beyond the first grade, however, children are exposed to more formal games. They enjoy learning the proper form of a specific sports skill and practicing drills or playing lead-up games that increase their proficiency. For these reasons, it is important that teachers not abandon specialized sports skills, drills, and lead-up games even if they are considered old-fashioned.

A structured program at any grade level can, and should, incorporate the creative games approach within a unit or a specific lesson. This blending of methods neither confuses nor restricts the learner. On the contrary, it enriches the learning environment and stimulates the creative process, and it helps the child acquire specific motor skills or more complex strategies involving perceptual, cognitive, and motor abilities.

Primary Program

There are several ways to organize and teach creative games to primary school children. The approach suggested here begins with game skills suitable for this age level, then gradually allows the children to invent or modify games within the limitations imposed by the teacher.

The procedure should be adapted to the ability, maturity, and interests of the class. And the emphasis that the teacher gives to the creative games approach obviously depends on her philosophy and the nature of the program. However, a major emphasis on creative activity is suggested for primary games programs. (See film *Teaching Games to Primary Children* listed in appendix A.)

The sample lesson that follows shows how creative games can be incorporated into more formal programs. The lesson plan for creative games is structured similar to plans for other activity areas. The format will vary, of course, according to the children's ages, interests, and prior experiences in creative-type games.

Example 1 (Grades 1–2)
Main Emphasis Bouncing a Ball

Part 1: Introductory Activity If children are used to moving around the floor freely without bumping into each other, have them begin running in different directions. Then have them change speeds, slide backwards, then to the right, then to the left. If children are used to warming up by running around the floor and then doing a series of calisthenics, it is not necessary to change the format. After finishing the warm-up, move to the second part of the lesson.

Part 2: Skill Development Each child should have a ball; any type of utility ball can be used. If the balls are different sizes, give the bigger ones to the children who are less proficient in ball-handling skills. Ask the children to take their balls and find spaces on the floor. When they are properly spaced, pose the following:

1. "Try to stay in your space and bounce the ball very low, then very high." Do not specify one or two hands—let them experiment.
2. "Can you bounce the ball with one hand?" Allow them to practice, then ask, "Can you bounce it with the other hand?"
3. Ask questions that relate to the following skills:
   a. Bounce in different directions (forward, backward, sideways).
   b. Bounce on the floor, then against the wall.
   c. Bounce around small equipment (beanbags, bowling pins, ropes).

Teaching Suggestions
1. Allow sufficient time to practice.
2. Pick out different ways of performing each task and let the other children watch.
3. Praise the children constantly while they are practicing.
4. Ask the children if they can think of another way of bouncing. A child may suggest that they try sitting down or kneeling while bouncing. Have the class try its own challenges.

Part 3: Group Activity Create a game involving the skill that has been practiced. The table on page 218 lists four areas where limitations can be imposed for the games created. As a general guideline, begin at the top and add more complex challenges as the lessons progress. In this first lesson you could challenge the children to make up a game with a partner, in their own space, using one ball, and requiring a bounce.

Teaching Suggestions
1. Give the children time to think up a game and practice it.
2. Have a few children demonstrate the games they have created.
3. If time permits, make up a new game and add beanbags, a chair, or a hoop.

Following from the first lesson, ask the children to make up a game with a partner, in their own space, using a ball, and requiring a bounce and a catch.

Other Teaching Suggestions

1. After the children have had time to create and practice their games, select a few for demonstration to the class.

2. Try other variations, such as in partners, in their own space, using two balls and a hoop, and involving a catch.

3. Allow children to make up games with their own imposed limitations.

4. Keep a creative games notebook. Children will create many exciting games that are worth remembering, so record the best ones for posterity. Next year you could use some of these games to illustrate and motivate children to develop similar ones. This project could also be incorporated into the language arts program by having each child or the whole class make up an illustrated creative games notebook.

Intermediate Program

Incorporating the creative games approach in the intermediate grades presents some problems for both the teacher and the children. (See film *Teaching Games to Intermediate Children* listed in appendix A.) Running, tag, and simple team games are normally selected from a book and taught according to specific rules and regulations. In essence, these are structured activities taught by the direct teaching method. It is possible, however, to add another dimension to these activities by injecting the creative games approach.

The four areas of limitation in the table on page 218 can be used with intermediate children with equal success. Since most children of this age range know and enjoy running, tag, and simple team games, this is the logical place to introduce creative or student designed games. The first example that follows illustrates how a teacher can begin with a familiar game and transform it into a very different and, in most cases, more enjoyable activity. The second example shows how to use the format to develop a framework for more creative student designed games.

Example 1

A fourth-grade class appears apathetic in the middle of the afternoon. The teacher decides to take the children outside for a "ten-minute game." After a brief discussion, they decide to play dodge ball using two balls. The game is played for a few minutes, then the teacher asks the class to stop and listen.

The teacher has four elements through which she can introduce a change.

1. *Number of Players:* Class divided into equal groups.
2. *Playing Space:* A large circle.
3. *Skills and Rules:* Throwing and hitting below the waist.
4. *Equipment:* Two inflated balls.

She decides to pose a challenge by varying the skills and rules. She says, "Start the game over. However, children in the middle must keep both hands on their knees at all times, and the circle players can only roll the ball." After a few minutes of play she stops the game again and poses another challange: "In the game you have just played, I changed the rules. Can you think of another rule change that you would like to try?" Several suggestions are made and the teacher chooses Mary Ann's: "Mrs. Brown, since the players inside were put out too quickly, how about all circle players rolling only with their left hand?" (Left-handed players must use their right hands.)

The process of introducing creative, or inventive, games has begun. The main tools are the four elements by which the teacher or the children can impose limitations. As the teacher learns to use the challenge method, she gives more freedom of choice to the children. And, with practice, the children appreciate the freedom to modify or create games of their own.

Example 2

Let us assume that a fifth-grade teacher has experimented with modified tag and simple team games and has noted a positive change in her class's cooperation and enthusiasm. The following suggestions could be tried as part of a regular games lesson or as a ten-minute break:

1. Arrange the class in partners (imposing a limitation on the number of players), give partners a ball and a hoop (limiting the equipment), and tell them to find their own

space in the playground area (limiting the playing space). Pose the question, "Can you make up a game with your partner that includes a bounce, a pass, and your hoop (limiting the skills and rules)?" The accompanying photograph illustrates such a game.

2. Join two sets of partners together and pose this question: "With four players, two balls, and two hoops, can you make up a new game that involves all the equipment, a bounce pass, and a dribble?"

3. Now join two groups of four and pose this challenge: "See if you can make up a game using two hoops and one ball."

These examples illustrate how the creative games approach can be used to modify existing games or provide a basis for children to invent their own. Children adapt to this method of teaching with ease and enthusiasm in a very short time. This approach will be used in later chapters, along with more structured methods and techniques, to teach individual skills, rules, and game strategies.

14 Running, Tag, and Simple Team Games

This chapter provides a culturally rich reservoir of running, tag, and simple team games. The purpose and emphasis of these activities vary from grade to grade. For primary children, particularly those from kindergarten to grade two, these games provide an important and enjoyable means of acquiring the fundamental skills and movement patterns. And if these activities are taught in a progressive manner, with a generous application of exploratory teaching methods, such characteristics as sportsmanship, leadership, and creativity can also be developed in a natural way.

The purpose of these activities remains the same as children reach the third and fourth grades. However, this is an important transitional period. These children still enjoy running and tag games, but they also are beginning to show a much keener interest in learning the more complex team games such as basketball and volleyball. And by the time children reach the fifth and sixth grades, the transition is almost complete. The major emphasis of their games program is developing knowledge and skills of the major individual and team sports. The running, tag, and simple team games provided in this chapter still have a place in the upper intermediate grades, however. They are vigorous and enjoyable activities for a classroom break, recess, or warm-up during regular instructional classes.

Games for Kindergarten to Grade Two

Since children in kindergarten and first and second grades show great differences in growth and maturity, the running, tag, and simple team games described on the following pages have been arranged according to their difficulty. The first few activities are geared to the individualistic and creative natures of five- and six-year-olds. Then, as children learn to play, share, and cooperate, they should be exposed to simple team games that involve the basic throwing, catching, and kicking skills.

Toward the end of the first grade and during the second grade, running and tag games become a little more complicated, and simple team games become more structured and require more skill and team play. Because there is such a spread of interests and abilities in each of these grades, teachers should try any game they feel is appropriate for their classes.

Running, Tag, and Simple Team Games: K–2

Name of Game	Level	Page
Tommy Tucker's Land	K	223
Brownies and Fairies	K–1	223
Old Mother Witch	K–1	223
Simple Tag	K–1	224
Automobiles	K–1	224
Birds and Cats	K–1	224
Do as I Do	K–1	225
Mousetrap	K–1	225
Eyeglasses	K–1	225
Tunnel Ball	K–1	225
Touch the Ball	K–1	225
Duck on the Rock	K–1	225
Beanbag Basket	K–1	226
Roll Ball	K–1	226
Wild Horse Roundup	1	226
North Winds and South Winds	1–2	226
Animal Tag	1–2	227
Uncle Sam	1–2	227
Midnight	1–2	227
Partner Posture Tag	1–2	227
Squirrel in the Tree	1–2	227
Jet Pilot	1–2	228
Red Light	1–2	228
Fire Engine	1–2	228
Queen Bee	1–2	228
Call Ball	1–2	228
Hot Ball	1–2	229
Ball Stand	1–2	229
Cat and Mouse	2	229
Crows and Cranes	2	229
Two Square	2	229
Simple Dodge Ball	2	230
Boundary Ball	2	230
Three Down	2	230
Snowball	2	230

Tommy Tucker's Land (K)

Skills Running, dodging, and tagging

Playing area Playground, gymnasium, or classroom

Equipment Eight or ten beanbags for each game

Players Six to ten

Formation Ten to fifteen-foot square with beanbags scattered inside the square

One child chosen to be "Tommy Tucker" stands in the center of the square. As Tommy Tucker guards his treasures, the other players sing

"I'm on Tommy Tucker's land,
Picking up gold and silver."

As they sing, they try to pick up as many beanbags as they can without being tagged by Tommy. If a child is tagged, he drops his treasures, goes outside the square, then starts again. The game is completed when all the beanbags have been taken or when only one player is left.

Suggestions and Variations
If the game is too slow, add another Tommy Tucker.

Brownies and Fairies (K–1)

Skills Running, dodging, and tagging

Playing area Playground, gymnasium, or classroom

Equipment None

Players Class divided into two groups

Formation Two lines drawn about thirty feet apart with teams lined up along each line

Divide the class into two groups, "brownies" and "fairies." The fairies turn their backs to the brownies. The brownies creep up to the fairies as quietly as possible. When they get close, the teacher calls out, "Brownies are here!" The fairies then try to tag the brownies before they can run back over their own line.

Suggestions and Variations
1. Change method of moving after each game.
2. Change names to animals or to complement word development in language arts.

Old Mother Witch (K–1)

Skills Locomotor skills, dodging, and tagging

Playing area Playground or gymnasium

Equipment None

Players Class

Formation Scattered around a small circle

One player selected to be the "old witch" stands in the middle of a circle drawn near one end of the playing area. A line is drawn across the other end; this is the "safe line." Children approach the circle and begin to tease the Old Witch by chanting

"Old mother witch
Fell in a ditch,
Picked up a penny,
And thought she was rich."

At the end of the verse the witch asks, "Whose children are you?" and the children answer with any name they wish. When a child says, "Yours," the witch begins chasing the players and tries to tag one before he crosses the "safe line." If the child is tagged, he becomes the "old witch."

Suggestions and Variations
1. Add one or more witch's helpers.
2. Change method of moving after each game.

Simple Tag (K-1)

Skills Locomotor skills, dodging, and tagging

Playing area Playground or gymnasium

Equipment None

Players Class

Formation Scattered

One child is chosen to be "it." All players are scattered within a designated playing area. "It" tries to tag another player. When a player is tagged, he must call out, "I'm it," and the game continues.

Suggestions and Variations
1. Vary the locomotor skill, such as requiring all to hop or skip, or require animal walking movements, such as "crab walk," "bear walk," and so on.
2. "It" tags a particular part of the body, such as the side, back, or leg.
3. Any player is safe when he assumes a particular position such as balancing on one foot, crouching, or standing back to back with another child.
4. Add one or more taggers.

Automobiles (K-1)

Skills Running and tagging

Playing area Playground or gymnasium

Equipment None

Players Class

Formation Circle

The teacher stands in the middle of the circle. On "go," the children run around the circle pretending to be automobiles. A child may move out to "pass" another but must then move back into the circle. No one may reverse directions. When the teacher calls "stop" or blows a whistle, everyone must come to a full stop. A player who fails to stop or who bumps into another player must run and touch the teacher, then return to his place in the circle.

Suggestions and Variations
1. Play same game moving in a reverse direction.
2. Substitute hand signals or flash cards for "go" and "stop."
3. Change game to "animal pass." Children move like crabs, monkeys, and so on, and follow same rules as automobiles.

Birds and Cats (K-1)

Skills Running and tagging

Playing area Playground, gymnasium, or classroom

Equipment None

Players Class

Formation Circle

One child chosen to be the "cat" stands in the center of the circle. Circle players are "birds." Circle players hold hands and walk in the circle singing

"Little birds are we,
We live up in the tree,
The old grey cat is coming
But can't catch ME."

As they sing "me," the "birds" stoop. The cat tries to tag any "bird" before he has stooped. The "bird" who is caught becomes the cat and the old cat takes his place in the circle.

Suggestions and Variations
1. Change locomotor skill after each game.
2. On "me" allow children to scatter, with the first one caught becoming the "cat."

Do as I Do (K-1)

Skills Locomotor or other "inventive movements"

Playing area Playground, gymnasium, or classroom

Equipment None

Players Class

Formation Line or circle

One child is chosen to start the game. When he says, "Do as I do," he makes a movement, such as hopping, running, or an animal walk, and all must follow his movement. After each child has had one or two turns, choose a new leader and repeat the game.

Suggestions and Variations
1. Repeat same game but with no talking. As soon as children copy a movement, they continue moving until the leader changes the movement.
2. Limit game to animal or mechanical movements.

Mousetrap (K–1)

Skills Running and dodging

Playing area Playground or gymnasium

Equipment None

Players Class

Formation Circle

Five children are chosen to be "mice," while the remaining children form a large circle called the "trap." The teacher starts the game with the mice outside the circle and the circle players holding hands. When she says, "Open trap," the circle players raise their hands as high as their heads and hold them in this position. The teacher then calls, "Run, little mice, run!" and the mice run freely in and out of the circle. When she says, "Snap," the circle players lower their joined hands. Any mice caught inside the circle must join the circle players. Continue until all mice are caught. Choose new mice and repeat the game.

Suggestions and Variations
1. Always have five "mice" playing; if two are caught, immediately replace with two new "mice" before the next "call."
2. Change name to other animals and move in that fashion (crab trap with a crab walk).

Eyeglasses (K–1; from Korea)

Skills Running, jumping, and tagging

Playing area Playground or gymnasium

Equipment None

Players Class

Formation Draw a pattern in the shape of eyeglasses and allow players to stand anywhere inside the area

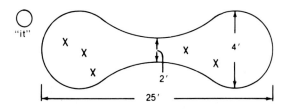

One child chosen to be "it" stands outside the "glasses." Other children scatter inside the area. "It" tries to tag any player inside the area or to get him to step over the line. The tagger may jump across the playing area but may not step inside. Players may move anywhere within the boundaries of the "glasses." If a player is tagged or steps on or over the line, he becomes "it." If one of the circles becomes empty, the tagger can jump into and conquer it. When this occurs, the teacher chooses another "it."

Suggestions and Variations
1. Design new patterns such as letters or numbers.
2. Require that every child always be moving.
3. Change method of moving.

Tunnel Ball (K–1)

Skills Rolling and catching

Playing area Playground or gymnasium

Equipment Utility ball (nine or thirteen inches)

Players Five to six

Formation Circle with children facing the center and one player standing in the middle

Children form a circle with each player in a "stride" position (legs apart). One child chosen to be "it" stands in the center of the circle with the ball. He attempts to roll the ball between the legs of any circle player or between any two players. Circle players may use their hands to stop the ball; however, they cannot move their feet. If a circle player allows the ball to roll out of the circle, he becomes "it."

Suggestions and Variations
For an element of surprise, have all circle players face outside the circle. The ball must be rolled through the legs.

Touch the Ball (K–1)

Skills Throwing and catching

Playing area Playground, gymnasium, or classroom

Equipment Large rubber ball

Players Five to six

Formation Circle

Children form a circle, with the person chosen to be "it" in the center. Circle players throw the ball to other players and "it" tries to tag the ball. If he touches the ball, the player who threw it becomes "it."

Suggestions and Variations
1. Change the type of throw (one hand, from the side).
2. Increase the distance between players.

Duck on the Rock (K–1)

Skills Throwing

Playing area Playground or gymnasium

Equipment One milk carton for each game and one beanbag for each player

Players Two for each game

Formation Arrange throwers in a line ten feet from the milk cartons

Place a beanbag ("duck") on top of a milk carton ("rock"). One player, the "guard," stands three feet to one side of the duck. The guard cannot stand in front of the duck. The first player throws his beanbag and tries to knock the duck off the rock. If he succeeds (including knocking the rock over), he runs to retrieve his beanbag and returns to his place behind the line.

The guard tries to stand the rock up, place the duck on top, and tag the thrower before the thrower retrieves his beanbag and runs back. If tagged, the thrower and guard exchange positions. If the thrower is unsuccessful in knocking the duck off, he changes places with the guard.

Suggestions and Variations
1. If the guard is too successful, move him four or five feet away from the rock.
2. Have throwers bowl their beanbag.

Beanbag Basket (K–1)

Skills Throwing

Playing area Playground, gymnasium, or classroom

Equipment Three beanbags and one wastebasket or box for each team

Players Three on each team

Formation File formation behind a starting line, with about five-to-six feet between each team and a wastebasket five feet in front of each team

Each child is given three consecutive throws at the basket. After each player completes his third throw, he collects the bags and gives them to the next player and then goes to the rear of the line.

Suggestions and Variations
1. As skill improves, use smaller baskets or increase the throwing distance.
2. Use nerf or other soft balls.
3. Change target; for example, to line on floor or square on wall.

Roll Ball (K–1)

Skills Rolling and catching

Playing area Playground or gymnasium

Equipment One utility ball and three milk cartons or bowling pins for each group

Players Two per group

Formation Milk cartons arranged in a row about ten feet away

Player 1 stands behind the starting line with three balls. Player 2 stands behind milk cartons. Player 1 bowls the first ball. Player 2 returns ball and resets cartons. Change places after the third ball is bowled.

Suggestions and Variations
1. Change pattern of cartons.
2. Use different type and size of ball.

Wild Horse Roundup (1)

Skills Running and tagging

Playing area Playground or gymnasium

Equipment None

Players Class

Formation Large circle or square called the "range" and a small circle beside the range called the "corral"

Four children chosen to be the "cowboys" start inside the "range." All other players are the "wild horses" and scatter outside the range. When the teacher calls, "Wild horses!" the horses must enter and stay in the range and avoid being caught by the cowboys. When a horse is tagged, he is taken to the corral. The last horse caught becomes the new "foreman" and chooses three new cowboys to begin the game again.

Suggestions and Variations
Play the same game in partners.

North Winds and South Winds (1–2; from Sweden)

Skills Running and tagging

Playing area Playground or gymnasium

Equipment Two blue ribbons and one yellow ribbon (colors are optional)

Players Class

Formation Large rectangular area and scattered formation

This is essentially a "tag" game with the delightful addition of a player who can *free* any tagged player. Two players chosen to represent the "north wind" are marked with blue ribbons. One child chosen to represent the "south wind" is marked with a yellow ribbon. All other children are scattered in the rectangular playing area. The two north wind players, representing "cold" and "danger," tag as many players as possible. When a player is tagged by a north wind player, he squats down on all fours and becomes stiff and motionless. The south wind player tries to free as many tagged players as possible by touching them and shouting, "Free!" As soon as a player is touched, he is free and continues to take part in the game. The teacher sets a time limit and the number of unfreed players that determines who wins. For example, the games might last two minutes, and if there are fewer than three tagged players, the south wind wins. But if more than three tagged players remain, the north wind wins.

Suggestions and Variations
When a player is tagged he must shake all over until he is "freed."

Animal Tag (1-2)

Skills Locomotor skills, animal movements, and tagging

Playing area Playground or gymnasium

Equipment None

Players Class

Formation Two parallel lines about thirty to forty feet apart

Place half the class behind each line. Players behind one line choose an animal they wish to imitate. They tell the teacher the name of the animal. They then move to within five or six feet of the opposing line and begin to imitate the animal. The opposing team members try to guess the name of the animal, raising their hands. When the teacher hears the correct name, she calls, "Chase," and the animals try to run back across their own line before being tagged. Change sides and the type of animals after each game.

Suggestions and Variations

Play same game imitating mechanical object or things of nature (wind, clouds, etc.).

Uncle Sam (1-2)

Skills Running and tagging

Playing area Playground or gymnasium

Equipment None

Players Class

Formation Two lines drawn thirty to forty feet apart, with the children placed along one line and the other line called the "river"

One player chosen to be "Uncle Sam" stands in the center of the play area. Other players stand behind the line and call, "Uncle Sam, may we cross your river?" Uncle Sam says, "Yes, if you have on—blue" (or whatever color). All children wearing blue run to the opposite side. Uncle Sam tries to tag as many as he can before they cross the opposite line. Those caught must help Uncle Sam. The last person caught wins the game.

Suggestions and Variations

1. Use two or three "Uncle Sams" to begin the game.
2. Change method of moving after each game.

Midnight (1-2)

Skills Running and tagging

Playing area Playground or gymnasium

Equipment None

Players Class

Formation Draw two lines twenty-five to thirty feet apart, with the class placed behind one, called the "home" line. In the middle of the other line draw a five-foot square; this is the "fox's den."

One player chosen to be the "fox" stands in his den. The "chickens" approach the fox's den and ask, "What time is it?" The fox can give any time for an answer. When the fox answers, "Midnight," he tries to tag as many chickens as he can before they cross the home line. Any chicken tagged must go to the fox's den and help him catch the remaining chickens.

Suggestions and Variations

Change the method of moving after each game.

Partner Posture Tag (1-2)

Skills Running, balancing, and tagging

Playing area Playground or gymnasium

Equipment Class set of beanbags

Players Class

Formation Scattered

One player is chosen to be "it" and another to be the runner. The runner and "it" have beanbags on their heads and cannot hold them on. "It" chases the runner and tries to tag him. When caught, they exchange positions.

Suggestions and Variations

1. Change positions after three tries.
2. Place beanbag on different parts of the body.
3. Play same game with one-third of class without beanbags, and standing still. A player being chased may transfer his beanbag to any standing player's head.

Squirrel in the Tree (1-2)

Skills Running

Playing area Playground or gymnasium

Equipment None

Players Class

Formation Scattered in groups of three

Arrange class in groups of three, scattered about the play area. Two join hands to form a "hollow tree" and the third player, the "squirrel," stands in the middle. Two or three extra squirrels should be placed randomly throughout the play area. On signal from the teacher, all the squirrels try to find new trees.

Suggestions and Variations

1. After three turns, have players return to their original positions. Rotate players and continue game.
2. Change method of moving.

Jet Pilot (1–2)

Skills Running and turning

Playing area Playground or gymnasium

Equipment None

Players Class

Formation Two lines drawn across the ends of the playing area, with one line the "takeoff" line and the other the "turning" line

All players line up behind the takeoff line. One child chosen to be the "captain" calls out, "Pilots, take off!" All pilots run to the turning line, then back across the takeoff line. The first pilot back across the takeoff line becomes the new captain and the game continues.

Suggestions and Variations
1. Change method of moving.
2. Add "force landing." As children are running, call "force landing," which means, go back to the starting line; do a trick or some other movement.

Red Light (1–2)

Skills Running and stopping

Playing area Playground or gymnasium

Equipment None

Players Class

Formation Two lines drawn across the ends of the playing area

One player chosen to be "it" stands on one line with his back to the opposite line. All other players stand on the opposite line. As "it" begins to count to ten, all players begin running toward his line. At any time before reaching ten, "it" may call out, "Red light," and turn around. If "it" sees anyone moving, he sends him back to the opposite line. The game continues until a player crosses the line. That player becomes "it" and the game starts over.

Suggestions and Variations
1. Use a variety of locomotor movements.
2. Use letters or children's names instead of numbers.

Fire Engine (1–2)

Skills Running, dodging, and tagging

Playing area Playground or gymnasium

Equipment None

Players Class

Formation Two lines drawn across the ends of the playing area and one across the center

One child chosen to be the "fire chief" stands on the centerline. All others stand on one of the end lines and

are given a number between one and five, which represents the "alarm number." The fire chief begins to call out the numbers and after any of them may yell, "Fire!" All the children with this number must run to the opposite line before being tagged. The first to cross the opposite line becomes the new fire chief.

Suggestions and Variations
1. Call "General alarm!" which signals that all must run.
2. Clap hands instead of calling a number.

Queen Bee (1–2)

Skills Locomotor skills

Playing area Playground or gymnasium

Equipment Beanbags (or colored paper squares) for each child

Players Class

Formation Scattered

Choose three children to be "queen bees." All other children place a beanbag (a "flower") on the floor and stand beside it. Have them scatter the beanbags evenly throughout the playing area. On signal from the teacher, the queen bees "fly" around the "garden," tapping "bees" on the shoulder. The tapped bees follow the queen bees. When the teacher says, "Fly home," all the "bees" and the three "queen bees" run to any available "flower." The three remaining players become the new queen bees.

Suggestions and Variations
1. Change to a new locomotor skill after each call "Fly home."
2. "Bee sting." Keep three queen bees and, when you call "Fly home," queen bees try to "sting" (touch) as many bees before they reach a beanbag.

Call Ball (1–2)

Skills Throwing and catching

Playing area Playground or gymnasium

Equipment One ball for every five or six players

Players Five to six

Formation Circle, with one player standing in the center

The center player tosses the ball into the air and calls out the name of a circle player who must catch the ball before it bounces. If the circle player is successful, he becomes the next thrower.

Suggestions and Variations
1. If skill level is very low, allow one bounce before attempting to catch the ball.
2. Use different types and sizes of balls.

Hot Ball (1–2)

Skills Kicking

Playing area Playground or gymnasium

Equipment One ball for every six to eight children

Players Six to eight

Formation Circle

One child chosen to start the game pretends to set a fire under the ball. He then kicks it and says, "The ball's hot." Circle players try to kick the ball away from them to keep from getting "burned." If the ball goes out of the circle, the person who last touched it becomes "it" and pretends to set the ball on fire again.

Suggestions and Variations
1. Play the same game using hands.
2. Allow circle players to use only the left or right foot to kick the ball.

Ball Stand (1–2)

Skills Running, stopping, and throwing

Playing area Playground or gymnasium

Equipment Utility or nerf ball

Players Class

Formation Circle, with one player standing in the center holding the ball

The center player places the ball on the ground and calls a circle player's name. This player runs to the ball while all the other players run as far away from the ball as possible. When the player picks up the ball, he calls, "Stand," and all players must stop immediately. The player now tries to throw the ball and hit a player. Players must keep their feet on the ground, although they are allowed to bend, twist, or duck to avoid being hit. If a player is hit, he becomes the center player and the game is repeated.

Suggestions and Variations
1. When a player throws the ball, all other players remain with both feet on the ground and try to catch the ball. The player who catches the ball becomes the thrower.
2. Play same game, but hit the ball with the hand or arm, or kick it.

Cat and Mouse (2)

Skills Running, dodging, and tagging

Playing area Playground or gymnasium

Equipment None

Players Class

Formation Circle

One child chosen to be the "cat" stands in the center of the circle. Another child chosen to be the mouse stands outside the circle. Circle players hold hands and try to prevent the cat from tagging the mouse by moving their arms up and down. Both the cat and mouse may move in and out of the circle. When the mouse is caught, the game is repeated with a new cat and mouse.

Suggestions and Variations
Circle players hold hands about knee-high. Cat and mouse pass under arms.

Crows and Cranes (2)

Skills Running, dodging, and tagging

Playing area Playground or gymnasium

Equipment None

Players Class

Formation One line drawn at each end of the playing area and two lines drawn about three feet apart in the center

Divide class in half and call one group "crows," and the other "cranes." Each team lines up on its centerline, facing the other. When the teacher calls "Crrr—ows," the crows turn and run toward their goal line and the cranes try to tag them before they cross it. If a player is tagged, he joins the opposite team. The game continues until the last player is caught.

Suggestions and Variations
1. Draw out the beginning of both words to keep the children in suspense as long as possible.
2. Use other words from the language arts program.
3. Add a third "neutral" word such as "Creep." If players move when a neutral word is called they make a funny face or perform a special trick.

Two Square (2)

Skills Bouncing and hitting

Playing area Playground or gymnasium

Equipment Utility ball (nine or thirteen inches)

Players Two to four

Formation Two five-foot squares drawn side by side, with one player in each

One player stands in each square while the remaining players stand just outside the squares. Player in one square bounce-serves the ball into the other square. (It may be wise to let players throw the ball at first instead of bounce-serving it. As skill increases, require a bounce-serve.) After the ball bounces in the opposing player's square, that player returns it into the server's square by batting it upward with one or both hands. Continue play until one of the following violations occurs:

1. The ball lands out of the square (liners are good).
2. The ball is hit with the fist.
3. The player holds the ball (catches it).
4. The ball is hit downward.

A player committing a violation leaves the game and the next waiting player takes his place.

1. Play same game with different types and sizes of balls (nerf, tennis, etc.)
2. Add a trick, such as a bounce hit, then turn around or jump in the air and clap hands.

Simple Dodge Ball (2)

Skills   Throwing and retrieving

Playing area   Playground or gymnasium

Equipment   Volleyball or utility ball

Players   Class

Formation   Circle

Divide players into two teams; one team remains in circle formation, while the other stands in the center. On signal, players in the outside circle try to hit inside players below the waist with the ball. To avoid being hit, the inside players move anywhere within the circle. Outside players may enter the circle to retrieve the ball; however, they may not throw at an opponent while inside the circle. Any player hit below the waist joins the outside circle. The last person remaining in the circle is the winner.

Suggestions and Variations
1. Once children understand the game, play two games by dividing the class into four teams.
2. Avoid using two or more balls because children in the middle cannot dodge more than one ball.
3. Require all players to be constantly on the move.

Boundary Ball (2)

Skills   Kicking and trapping

Playing area   Playground or gymnasium

Equipment   Two soccer balls

Players   Ten to fifteen on each team

Formation   Three parallel lines drawn twenty to thirty feet apart, and each team scattered on each side of the centerline.

Each team has a ball which it kicks toward the opponent's goal line. Players on both teams move about freely in their own half of the playing area, trying to prevent the opponents' ball from crossing the goal line. Players cannot touch the ball with their hands. One point is scored each time the ball crosses the opponents' goal line.

Suggestions and Variations
1. Once children understand the game, play two games by dividing class into four teams.
2. Change to a throwing game.

Three Down (2)

Skills   Rolling a ball

Playing area   Playground or gymnasium

Equipment   Two balls and four clubs or milk cartons per group

Players   Six to eight per game

Formation   Circle

Four clubs are arranged in a square about three feet apart in the middle of the circle. Two players are pinsetters. Circle players roll the two balls at the clubs, attempting to knock them down, while the pinsetters keep setting up the clubs. When three clubs are down, the circle players call, "three down." The pinsetters then choose two new pinsetters and the game continues.

Suggestions and Variations
1. If pinsetters are too good, reduce to only one pinsetter.
2. Throw or kick the ball.

Snowball (2)

Skills   Running, throwing, and dodging

Playing area   Playground or gymnasium

Equipment   Ten to twelve yarn, fleece, or nerf balls

Players   Class

Formation   Two end lines and one centerline, with each team scattered along its side of the centerline

Divide the class into two equal teams and give each team an equal number of balls (about five or six each). On signal, players attempt to hit opposing players with the balls. Any player who is hit must move to the sideline. Sideline players may retrieve balls and throw them to teammates, but they may not throw them at opponents. The game ends when one player remains.

Suggestions and Variations
Play same game with both teams grouped in "twos" or "threes."

Games for Grades Three and Four

Children in grades three and four are at a transitional stage with regard to game activities. They still thoroughly enjoy running, tag, and simple team games, particularly if these games are rough and involve team spirit and competition. Children in these grades also are becoming interested in team games. If skill level and student interest are extremely high, do not hesitate to draw from the lead-up games in chapters 17 through 24. Page references to various games follow.

Running, Tag, and Simple Team Games: 3–4

Partner Tag (3)

Skills Running and tagging

Playing area Playground or gymnasium

Equipment None

Players Class

Formation Partners scattered around the play area

One child is chosen to be "it" and another to be the "chaser." The other children link elbows with partners they select. The chaser tries to tag "it," who may run anywhere in the play area. Whenever "it" links elbows with a player, he is safe, but the partner of the player "it" links onto becomes the new "it." If the chaser tags "it," they change positions and the game continues.

Suggestions and Variations
1. Vary partner positions, such as follow-the-leader, or face partner with both hands joined.
2. Have all players hop or jump.

Fly Trap (3)

Skills Running, stretching, and stopping

Playing area Playground or gymnasium

Equipment None

Players Class

Formation Scattered

Have half the class sit cross-legged in a scattered formation. These children are the "trappers." The other half are the "flies." On signal, the flies run in any direction within the playing area. When the teacher calls, "freeze," the flies come to an immediate stop. The trappers, still seated, try to touch the flies. Any trapper who can touch a fly changes places with the fly and the game continues.

Suggestions and Variations
1. If there is sufficient room, require the trappers to keep only one foot on the floor as they stretch toward the fly.
2. Change locomotor skill.

Loose Caboose (3–4)

Skills Running, dodging, and tagging

Playing area Playground or gymnasium

Equipment None

Players Class divided into groups of three

Formation Scattered

Each group of three forms a line with each member holding onto the waist of the player in front. The first player is the "engine," the second the "baggage car," and the last the "caboose." Choose two players to be "loose cabooses." On signal, each train tries to prevent a loose caboose from attaching onto its own caboose. When this occurs, the engine becomes a new loose caboose, and each player moves up one place on the train. If a train pulls apart trying to avoid a loose caboose, this constitutes being caught.

Suggestions and Variations
Have players hop or jump or move backwards.

Crab Tag (3–4)

Skills Running and tagging
Playing area Playground or gymnasium
Equipment None
Players Class
Formation Scattered

This game is played the same way as simple tag, except that a player in a crab walk position is safe.

Suggestions and Variations
Change the "safe" position to a seal walk or an elephant walk or to a continuous exercise movement such as push-ups. This could become a "fun" approach to the warm-up period.

Dumbbell Tag (3–4)

Skills Running and tagging
Playing area Playground or gymnasium
Equipment "Dumbbell" (beanbag or towel)
Players Class
Formation Scattered

One player selected to be the runner is given the "dumbbell." Another player selected to be "it" starts the game by chasing the runner with the dumbbell. The runner may give the dumbbell to any player at any time, and that player must take it. If "it" tags the player who has the dumbbell, that player becomes "it." The new "it" must count to three before chasing anyone; during this time, the "old it" gives the dumbbell to another class member, who then becomes the new runner.

Suggestions and Variations
1. Change method of moving.
2. Give everyone a ball, including the player with the dumbbell. Same game, only everyone must keep bouncing their ball.

Stealing Sticks (3–4)

Skills Running, dodging, and tagging
Playing area Adjust playing area to meet available space
Equipment Eight to twelve beanbags, quoits, or balls
Players Class divided into two teams
Formation Scattered

Each team is positioned on opposite sides of the centerline (diagram below). Four to six beanbags are placed in each "stick" area. Players from each team attempt to cross into their opponent's half and steal a "stick" (only one at a time) without being tagged. A player can only be tagged while in his opponent's half of the field. Once a player steals a stick, he holds it above his head, returns to his own side without being tagged, and places the "stick" in his own "stick" area. If a player is tagged, he goes to the opponent's prison.

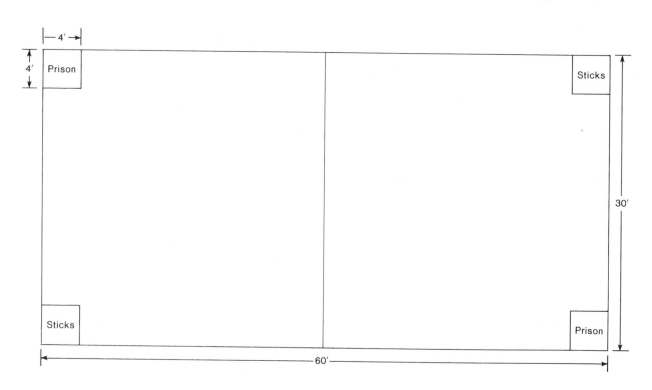

No sticks may be stolen from the opponent if there are prisoners in the opponent's prison. If a teammate touches a prisoner (only one) without being tagged, both prisoner and player hold both hands together above their heads to signify they have safe passage back to their own half of the playing area. The team with the most sticks wins the game.

Suggestions and Variations
1. Place a hoop in the middle of each half. The hoop is a ''safe house'' for opponents.
2. Place obstacles throughout the playing area to encourage climbing and dodging.

Up the Field (3–4)

Skills Throwing and catching

Playing area Playground

Equipment Utility ball

Players Class divided into two teams

Formation Large rectangle (100 by 50 feet), with line drawn across the center and the end lines as goal lines

Arrange each team in a scattered formation on its own half of the playing area. Players must stay on their own side of the field. The ball is given to a player who is standing on his own goal line. The object is to throw the ball over the opponent's goal line. Three passes are allowed before the ball crosses the centerline. To score, the ball must be in the air as it crosses the opponent's goal line and it cannot have been touched by any defending player.

Suggestions and Variations
1. Use two balls.
2. Alternate throwing from boy to girl.
3. Change the type of throwing skill.

Jump the Shot (3–4)

Skills Jumping

Playing area Playground or gymnasium

Equipment Rope

Players Eight to ten per game

Formation Circle with one player in the center

Center player holds the rope by one end and swings it in a circle, keeping it about one foot off the ground. Circle players try to jump the rope as it approaches. If hit, they are charged with one shot. The game continues for a designated period. The winner, who is the player with the least number of shots charged against him, becomes the ''turner'' in the next game.

Suggestions and Variations
1. Vary the length and speed of the rope according to level of skill.
2. Have circle players join hands with a partner.
3. Have circle players bounce a ball as the rope is turned; start with a two-hand bounce.

Keep Away (3–4)

Skills Passing, catching, and guarding

Playing area Playground or gymnasium

Equipment One utility ball or basketball

Players Eight to ten on each of two teams

Formation Scattered formation within a designated playing area

The teacher gives the ball to a player on one team, who then passes it to a teammate. The opposing players attempt to intercept the ball or break up the pass. If successful, they pass the ball to each other. Fouls are called whenever a defensive player grabs or holds onto an offensive player.

Suggestions and Variations
1. Do not let players run with the ball.
2. If adequate space is available, play two games by dividing the class into four teams.
3. If the teams are large and the playing area is limited, rotate in fours or fives every few minutes.

Progressive Dodge Ball (3–4)

Skills Throwing and dodging

Playing area Playground

Equipment Ball

Players Class

Formation Three parallel twenty-foot squares designated as A, B, and C

This game is played in three periods of three to five minutes each. Teams rotate playing areas (A, B, and C) after each period. On signal, a player in one square tries to hit players with the ball (below the waist) in either of the other two squares. No player is eliminated, so a player who is hit should try to get the ball and throw it at an opponent as soon as he is hit. Scores are made by hitting players on another team. The teacher or leader keeps the score for each team, and the team with highest score after three periods wins. Players may not cross boundary lines.

Suggestions and Variations
Require every player to be constantly on the move.

Place Kickball (3–4)

Skills Running, kicking, and catching

Playing area Playground

Equipment Utility or soccer ball

Players Six to eight on each team

Formation Softball diamond with thirty feet between bases; one team in the field and one in a line formation behind home plate

Place the fielding team in the playing area outside the baselines. Each player on the kicking team is given one stationary kick from home plate. If the kick is fair (inside the boundary lines), the kicker tries to run around the bases before a member of the fielding team can get the ball and beat him to home plate. The kicker is out if a fly ball is caught.

Suggestions and Variations

1. After the stationary kick is learned, introduce a "dribble and kick." Draw a line ten to fifteen feet behind home plate and require the kicker to dribble to the plate and then kick the ball.
2. Require that the kick be made with the opposite foot the second time "up to bat."
3. If only a few players make it around the bases, have players run to first base and back.

Battle Ball (3–4)

Skills Kicking and trapping

Playing area Playground

Equipment A slightly deflated soccer ball

Players Ten to twelve on each team

Formation Two parallel lines twenty feet apart, with one team on each line and the players holding hands

Side A tries to kick the soccer ball over side B's goal line. Side B tries to stop the ball and kick it back over side A's line, and so on. The team that kicks the ball over the opponent's line receives two points. The first side to reach a score decided by the teacher wins the game. A team loses a point if one of its players touches the ball with his hands, or if the ball is kicked too high—over the heads of the other team.

Suggestions and Variations

1. Have players pass the ball from teammate to teammate before kicking it toward the opponent's line.
2. Allow children to use their hands to prevent the ball from hitting their faces.

Crab Soccer (3–4)

Skills Kicking

Playing area Playground or gymnasium

Equipment Utility or soccer ball

Players Six to eight on each team

Formation Playing area divided into two equal sections, with goals placed on end lines

Players from both teams start in a crab walk position and move anywhere in the court area. All players except one goalie for each team remain in a crab walk position. The goalies may use their hands; however, all other players must move the ball with their feet. A foul occurs when a player catches the ball or strikes it with his hands. The teacher should stop the game when a foul occurs and give the ball to the nearest opponent. Award one point for each goal scored.

Suggestions and Variations

1. Practice the crab walk first.
2. After the game is well understood, require striking with hands only or allow a combination of hands and feet.

Bat Ball (3–4)

Skills Batting, running, and throwing

Playing area Playground

Equipment Softball, bat or batting tee, and two bases

Players Nine on each team

Formation Softball diamond with thirty to thirty-five feet between each base, one team in the field and the other in a file formation behind a restraining line drawn ten feet back and to the right of home plate

One team is in the field and the other is at bat. Players at bat try to hit the ball into the field and run to first base and back home in one complete trip. The batter may not stop on base. A player who makes a complete trip without being put out scores one run. The batter is out if (1) a fielder catches a fly ball or (2) a fielder touches the runner with the ball before he reaches home. When the team at bat has three outs, it goes into the field and the team in the field comes to bat. The team with the most points at the end of the playing period is the winner. (Teams must have the same number of times at bat.)

Suggestions and Variations

1. Alternate pitchers and catchers.
2. Alternate boy and girl in the batting order.
3. Try two outs if one team stays up too long.
4. Vary the distance between bases according to the level of skill.
5. Use a batting tee if the skill level is too low.

Guard Ball (3–4)

Skills Throwing, catching, and guarding

Playing area Playground or gymnasium

Equipment Utility ball (8½ inches)

Players Class divided into two teams

Formation A large rectangle (thirty by ninety feet) divided into three equal sections, A, B, and C, with team 1 scattered in section B and team 2 scattered equally in sections A and C.

Players on team 2, using a roll or a bounce pass, try to pass the ball to teammates in the opposite section. The ball must be passed below head level. Players on team 1 attempt to block the passes with their hands. Award one point for each successful pass. Rotate teams every two or three minutes.

Suggestions and Variations

Vary the type of pass.

Long Ball (4)

Skills Running, pitching, catching, and batting

Playing area Playground

Equipment Softball, bat, and two bases

Players Nine on each team

Formation Softball diamond with thirty to thirty-five feet between each base, one team in the field and the other in a file formation behind a restraining line drawn ten feet back and to the right of home plate

Divide players into two teams and number each player. Each team selects a pitcher and a catcher; other players are fielders or batters. When a ball is hit, the batter runs to first base and, if possible, returns home. The runner may stop on first base, and any number of runners may be on base at the same time. Runners may not steal home. Any hit is good; there are no fouls in this game. Batter is out when he strikes out, is touched with the ball off base, steals home, throws the bat, or a fly ball is caught. One point is awarded for each run to the base and back.

Suggestions and Variations
1. Alternate pitchers and catchers.
2. Move pitcher closer as skill indicates.
3. Use a batting tee if skill level is too low.
4. Use a nerf ball and hit ball with arm.
5. Shorten bases if necessary.

High Ball (4)

Skills Throwing, catching, and volleying

Playing area Playground

Equipment Volleyball, net, and court

Players Six to eight on each team

Formation Drop the volleyball net down to about six feet or string a rope between two standards. Place one team on each side of the net in a scattered formation.

A player on one team throws the ball over the net. Any player on the other team must catch it before it hits the ground and return it over the net. When a player drops the ball, the other team gets a point.

Suggestions and Variations
1. Add the following rule: As soon as a player catches the ball, he must throw it to one of his teammates, who, in turn, must hit it over the net.
2. Keep children in their assigned areas; allow no wandering.

Bounce Net Ball (4)

Skills Volleying

Playing area Playground or gymnasium

Equipment Volleyball, net, and court

Players Six to nine on each team

Formation Drop the volleyball net to about six feet or string a rope between two standards. Place one team on each side of the net in rows or in scattered formation.

Play is started by one player hitting the ball over the net. The ball must bounce before being returned. Any number of players can hit the ball any number of times; however, the ball must bounce once between each player. The team that loses the point starts the ball the next time. Fouls occur when the ball is (1) thrown, (2) caught and held, (3) allowed to bounce more than once, or (4) hit out of bounds. When a team commits a foul, the opposite team gets one point.

Suggestions and Variations
1. Instead of requiring one bounce between players, make them hit the ball directly from a volley pass.
2. Change the type of ball; try beach or nerf balls.

Bombardment (4)

Skills Running, throwing, catching, and guarding

Playing area Playground or gymnasium

Equipment Twelve to twenty milk cartons or Indian clubs, ten balls

Players Class divided into two teams

Formation Players scattered in playing area divided in half with a four-foot restraining line next to each team's end line.

Place equal numbers of milk cartons or Indian clubs in these four-foot sections. Each team starts with five balls and tries to knock down the cartons or clubs in the opponent's goal area. Players may use their hands or legs to prevent the cartons or clubs from being knocked over. All players must stay in their own half of the playing area. Defending players must also stay in front of the four-foot restraining line. The team that first knocks down all of its opponent's milk cartons or Indian clubs wins. If the game is played in time periods, the team knocking down the most pins wins.

Suggestions and Variations
1. Require one or two passes before attempting to score a goal.
2. Use different types of balls.

Games for Grades Five and Six

Running, tag, and simple team games become less important as children reach grades five and six. Their dominant interest, of course, is team games. However, boys and girls of this age occasionally enjoy a vigorous running game or a simple team game such as California kickball or ricochet. Teachers should also review the games listed in the previous pages as possible additions to their programs.

Running, Tag, and Simple Team Games: 5–6

Name of Game	Level	Page
Circle Tug-of-War	5–6	236
Borden Ball	5–6	236
Goodminton	5–6	236
California Kickball	5–6	237
Long Ball (Danish)	5–6	237
Ricochet	5–6	238
Quadrant Dodge Ball	5–6	238
European Handball	5–6	239

Additional Team Games

Numerous lead-up games included in chapters 18 to 23 may be used as simple team games to enrich this area.

Circle Tug-of-War (5–6)

Skills Pulling and pushing

Playing area Playground or gymnasium

Equipment Six to eight Indian clubs or milk cartons

Players Ten to twelve

Formation Circle

Scatter the Indian clubs inside the circle reasonably close together. All players join hands. On signal, each player pushes or pulls and tries to make other players knock down the clubs. Any player who knocks down a club receives one point. When two circle players break or lose their grip, each player receives a point. The player with the least number of points wins the game.

Suggestions and Variations

1. Alternate boys and girls in the circle.
2. Have each player hold a utility ball between his knees when playing. Losing the ball counts as one point.

Borden Ball (5–6)

Skills Throwing and catching

Playing area Playground or gymnasium

Equipment Football and two posts or traffic cones

Players Class divided into two teams

Formation Playing areas divided into two equal sections, with each team scattered in each section

Place one goalie from each team in an eight-foot goal area in the center of each end line (use two posts or traffic cones as goalposts). The object is to throw the ball through the opponent's goal. The game begins with a jump ball between two opposing players at the centerline. The ball may be thrown in any direction, but it may not be hit or kicked. A player may take a maximum of three steps while holding the ball no longer than three seconds. On penalties the ball is given to the nearest opponent. Members of the team that do not have possession of the ball may check the player with the ball, but they may not touch, hold, or push him. One point is awarded for each goal. After a point is scored, at halftime, or at any official stopping of play, restart play with a jump ball at the center. If the ball goes over the sidelines, a player on the opposing team throws it into the field of play.

Suggestions and Variations

1. Use different types and sizes of balls.
2. Change the three-second rule or number of steps to meet skill level of the class.

Goodminton (5–6)

Skills Batting

Playing area Playground or gymnasium

Equipment Volleyball net (or rope), bats (see diagram in appendix B), badminton bird (used ones are quite suitable) or yarn ball (covered with tape or cloth)

Players Six or less on each team

Formation Playing area divided into two equal sections by a net or rope.

This game is played like volleyball with the following basic rules: The server has only one serve to get the bird over the net, and the bird must clear the net on each serve. The server continues to serve so long as his team wins points. After the first serve has been taken by each team, and after each succeeding "side out," the team receiving the serve rotates one position clockwise. (The front row players move to the right, the back row players to the left, and the left back moves to the left forward position.) Teams change sides after each game.

The bird may be batted in any direction, but scooping, lifting, and any form of holding are not permitted. The bird, except on service, may be recovered from the net, provided the player avoids touching the net. The bird may be batted only three times by one team before being returned over the net. A player may not hit the bird twice in succession, but he may give it the first and third hits.

If any player on the serving team commits any of the following acts, it shall be "side out." If any player on the receiving team commits any of the acts, the serving team is awarded a point. The illegal acts are: serving illegally; catching or holding the bird; touching the net with any part of the body or bat (if two opponents touch the net simultaneously, the bird shall be reserved); reaching over the net; playing out of

Figure 14.1 Goodminton

Figure 14.2 California Kickball

position; touching the floor on the opposite side of the centerline; allowing hands or bats over the centerline; "spiking" or "killing" the bird when playing a back position.

Suggestions and Variations
1. Play the same game with a nerf ball. Try eliminating the bat and use the flat of the hand.
2. Limit game to nondominant hand.

California Kickball (5–6)

Skills   Running, throwing, catching, and kicking

Playing area   Playground or gymnasium

Equipment   Utility ball or old volleyball

Players   Nine per team

Formation   Arrange the playing area the same as in a softball game. Modify the length of bases and other rules according to space and other conditions.

The game is played like softball with the following modifications: (a) Use a utility ball or old volleyball; (b) the pitcher rolls the ball and the "batter" kicks it; (c) the batter runs whether the ball is kicked fair or foul; (d) first base is the only base that the fielding team can touch to get a batter out—on all other bases the fielder must tag the runner or throw the ball and hit him to get him out; (e) any number on the batting team may get on a base and stay, running when they think it is safe to try for another base; (f) on any hit balls, if the fielding team throws the ball to the pitcher, any runner who is between bases must go back to the previous base; (g) any runner caught between bases on a caught fly ball is automatically out; (h) change teams after three to six outs, or when everyone on the batting team has had a turn at bat.

Suggestions and Variations
Use a nerf ball and bat the ball with the arm.

Long Ball (5–6; from Denmark)

Skills   Hitting, catching, running, and rolling

Playing area   Gymnasium or playground

Equipment   One ball

Players   Class

Formation   As in the diagram

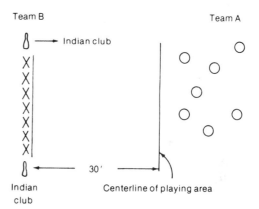

Players on team A scatter behind the centerline. Players on team B stand along the end line between two Indian clubs. The first player on team B hits a volleyball over the centerline. When a player on team A catches the ball, all his teammates line up behind him. The ball is then rolled back between the legs of all the players. The last player in the line picks up the ball and runs to the front of the line and holds the ball over his head. Meanwhile, after the first player on team B serves the ball, he runs around the Indian clubs. A run is scored when the player runs around both clubs before the team A player reaches the front of his line and has the ball held overhead. Continue until every player on team B has had a turn. Teams change positions and repeat game. The team with the highest score wins the game.

Suggestions and Variations

1. Allow players on team B to throw the ball.
2. Ask each team to design a new set of rules for both teams.

Ricochet (5–6)

Skills Throwing

Playing area Gymnasium

Equipment One large utility ball (twenty-four inches) and approximately twenty small play balls (six inches)

Players Class

Formation Two end lines approximately three feet from each wall and a line drawn across the center of the playing area

Divide the class in half and arrange students along the end lines, facing each other. Give ten play balls to each team and place the large utility ball in the center of the playing area. On signal, both teams begin throwing the small balls at the large utility ball, attempting to force it over the opponent's goal line. Players may retrieve the play balls from their own half of the playing area, however, they must go back over their own end line before they attempt another throw. The team that forces the ball over its opponent's goal line wins the game.

Suggestions and Variations

1. Have players use different types of throws.
2. Introduce two to four large "throwing" balls.

Quadrant Dodge Ball (5–6)

Skills Throwing, dodging, and catching

Playing area Gymnasium

Equipment Two utility balls (8½ inches) or volleyballs

Players Class

Formation Square divided into four quadrants, as shown in the diagram

Divide class into two equal teams and put half of each team in diagonally opposite quadrants. Give each team a ball. Any player may move freely from his quadrant into his team's other quadrant. On signal, each team tries to hit members of the opposing team below the waist. Only direct hits count. Play continues for a set period of time, and the team with the most hits wins.

Suggestions and Variations

1. Players hit must join the opposing team.
2. Introduce another ball.

European Handball (5–6)

Skills Throwing, running, catching, and checking

Playing area See diagram

Equipment Four goalposts or four upright markers (six feet), utility ball or volleyball

Players Six on each team

Formation As shown in diagram

The object of the game is to throw the ball through the goalposts. The game begins with a jump ball between two opposing forward players. Once the ball is tapped out of the center circle, any player may attempt to retrieve it. A player who has possession of the ball may take one to three steps, bounce it, take three more steps, etc., or attempt to throw it through the goalposts. A player has three seconds to get rid of the ball. A player may check an opponent in the same way as in basketball. If a defensive player fouls his opponent, the opponent is given a free throw at the point of infraction. All defensive players must stay ten yards away until the throw is made. If the ball goes over the sidelines or end lines, the nonoffending team throws the ball back into play (one- or two-hand throw, according to age and ability). The goalie must stay within the crease (the semicircle around the goalposts); however, no other player may enter this area. One point is awarded for each goal scored from outside the crease area.

Suggestions and Variations
1. Play the game without allowing a bounce.
2. Add "nonscoring" sideline player similar to sideline soccer.
3. Play same game with a nerf ball but allow no dribbling or holding.

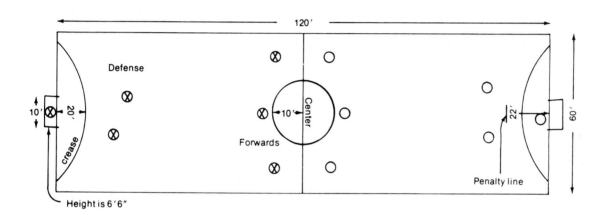

15 *Relay Activities*

General Considerations

Relay Formations
Line Formation
File Formation
Shuttle Formation
Circle Formation

Applying the Inventive Games Approach

Relay Activities
Partner Relays
Group Relays
Sports Skill Relays

Relay activities can be played in the gymnasium or on the playground. They require a minimum of class organization, skill development, and playing facilities. Generally speaking, relays develop such skills as running, jumping, dodging, and stopping. And indirectly they help develop more advanced skills, such as throwing and kicking, and improve speed, reaction time, and coordination.

However, teachers should carefully consider their use of relays. They can be overused. Another negative aspect of relays is the general lack of activity by the majority of children. Both of these criticisms can be met by careful planning and the use of more exploratory teaching techniques.

General Considerations

The teacher should establish a procedure for presenting relay activities applicable to the grade level and facilities available. The following suggestions should help:

1. Divide the class into as many equal teams as space and equipment permit.
2. Appoint team leaders and give them specific responsibilities.
3. Arrange teams in the correct formation before explaining the rules.
4. Tell the children the name of the relay.
5. Explain the basic rules and have several pupils demonstrate the relay.
6. Start the relay with a definite signal, such as a whistle, verbal command, or loud drum beat.
7. Always pick a certain number of winners and give them credit for their success.
8. Encourage student participation in rule changes and modifications of the relay.

9. Establish a few basic safety rules. These should include the following:
   a. Put the turning line a minimum of eight feet from any wall or obstruction.
   b. Traffic patterns should be clearly understood and followed by every player. For example, have the children run forward, turn around with the right side toward the turning post, then run back around the right side of the team.
   c. Allow adequate space between each competing team.
10. Have the students help judge turning points and winners, particularly when you cannot watch every line.
11. Whenever possible, place the slower and less skilled players in the middle of the team. If given the opportunity, children usually place their slowest runners at the beginning, hoping to make up for lost time with faster runners at the end. This places a lot of pressure on the slower players, causing unnecessary anguish.

Relay Formations

Four basic formations are used to organize players for relays. Although the file formation is most often used in elementary schools, line, circle, and shuttle relays are also appropriate. The formation a teacher selects depends on the type of relay, the space available, and the skill required of the children.

Line Formation

A number of teams are selected and players are arranged one behind the other as shown in the diagram. Each player runs to the turning line and back.

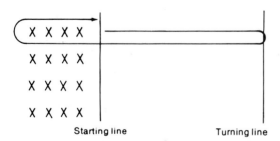

Starting line   Turning line

Variations

1. Running through obstacles (chairs or beanbags) to the turning line.
2. Running around an obstacle at the turning line.
3. Running to the turning line and stopping, usually to throw something back to the next player.

To prevent cheating, require the returning player to run around his team and back to the front of the line.

File Formation

This formation is quite similar to the line formation except that players face one or more players positioned in front.

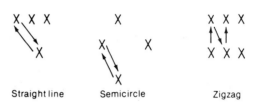

Straight line   Semicircle   Zigzag

Shuttle Formation

The shuttle formation is basically a line formation with half of each team placed behind an opposite line. As soon as player 1 reaches player 2, player 2 moves forward and player 1 walks back to the end of this line. Each player then moves forward one place.

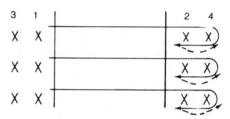

Circle Formation

Players are placed equidistant apart on a circle.

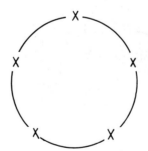

Teaching Suggestions

1. Use available painted circles or draw them with chalk inside or with a stick on the ground outside. Tie the chalk or stick on the end of string to make circles.
2. Provide adequate space between each circle.

Applying the Inventive Games Approach

In the previous chapter the inventive games approach was described as the application of the problem-solving method in order to change a game or create a new one. This approach can also be quite effective with relay activities. When children are permitted to inject their own ideas, they usually show increased enthusiasm, cooperation, and team loyalty. Improved skill development and cardiorespiratory fitness often accompany this type of program.

The following examples illustrate how to apply this process to structured relays and how to develop new types of relays. Refer to the four areas where limitations can be applied (p. 218) when changing the structure of a relay. These areas are the number of players, the playing space, the amount and type of equipment, and the skills and rules.

Let us use the circle post relay to illustrate the use of the inventive games approach. The teacher begins the process after the class has completed one relay. In the next race, the teacher imposes any of the following limitations:

1. Join with a partner and repeat the relay (changing the number of players).
2. Join with a partner in piggyback position and repeat the relay (changing skills and rules).
3. Add two or more posts spaced five feet apart and behind the first turning post. Players must circle all posts (changing skills, rules, playing space, and equipment).

If the class has had previous experience with this approach, try one of the following ideas:

1. Repeat the original relay, but add these directions: "You must now move on three parts of your body." This allows each child or team to choose a way of traveling.
2. Give each team two hoops and ask them to think up a way to use the hoops in the relay. Let each team demonstrate and, if time permits, try all the ideas.

Relay Activities

It is very difficult to arrange relay activities according to grade level. Most of the relays that follow can be enjoyed by children in grades one through six. Teachers should vary the running distance or limit the number and type of obstacles to meet the abilities of their classes. Most are running-type relays.

Locomotor Skill Relay

Formation Line

Equipment None

Players Three to four on each team

Draw a turning line twenty to forty feet away from the starting line; adjust the distance to the age and ability of the children. Each player performs any specified locomotor movement—run, walk, hop, leap, slide, or gallop—to the turning line and back.

Leapfrog Relay

Formation Line

Equipment None

Players Four to five on each team

Place teams in a line formation with enough space between players so that each player can reach the player's hips in front of him. Player 1 bends over, places his hands on his knees, and tucks his head. Player 2 places his hands on 1's hips, jumps over him, and assumes the same position as 1. Each succeeding player moves forward and continues action until the last player reaches the front of the line.

Teaching Suggestions

Make sure all keep their heads tucked until players have leaped over them. Vary relay by having players crawl under each other's legs.

Rescue Relay

Formation Line

Equipment None

Players Four to five on each team

Each team stands in a line formation behind the starting line. The captain stands behind a second line drawn twenty feet in front of the starting line. On signal, the captain runs to the first member of his team, grasps his hand, and runs back with the player to his turning line. The player whom the captain brought over returns to the starting line and brings the next player back. Continue the relay until the last child has been brought over the captain's line.

Teaching Suggestions

Vary the way players are brought back, such as holding both hands, locking elbows, back to back, and piggyback.

Shuttle Relay

Formation   Half of each team behind each of two restraining lines, spaced approximately twenty feet apart

Equipment   None

Players   Four to five on each team

Place half of each team behind each of the two restraining lines. Put players 1, 3, and 5 on one side, and players 2 and 4 on the other side. Player 1 runs across around the left side of his team and tags number 2. Player 2 runs back around opposite side and tags 3, and so on, until all have had a turn.

Zigzag Relay

Formation   Line formation with players six to eight feet apart

Equipment   None

Players   Four to five on each team

Player 1 runs in and out of his teammates in a zigzag pattern to the last player on the team, circles him, then repeats the movement back to his original position. Player 2 starts zigzagging backward around player 1 and continues the zigzag pattern up the line, then back to his original position. The first team back in the original position wins the relay.

Animal Walk Relay

Formation   Line

Equipment   None

Players   Three to four on each team

This is a basic line relay, but the movement is an imitation of a specific animal walk. Some of the most enjoyable animal walks for relays are described on the following pages:

Crab walk, page 393

Lame puppy walk, page 392

Seal walk, page 398

Rabbit jump, page 398

Kangaroo hop, page 393

Wicket walk, page 392

Stunt Relay

Formation   Line

Equipment   None

Players   Three to four on each team

Teams stand behind the starting line. A turning line is drawn about thirty to forty feet away. On signal, the first player runs to the turning line and performs a stunt on his way back. Some of the most popular stunts are:

1. Turning around four or more times.
2. Picking up a ball and bouncing it a number of times.
3. Performing a balance stunt.

Teaching Suggestions

The teacher may require the stunt to be performed from different positions—a front lying or a sitting position.

Skipping Rope Relay

Formation   Line

Equipment   One skipping rope for each team

Players   Three to four on each team

Teams line up behind the starting line with the first player holding a skipping rope. Draw a turning line about twenty feet away. On signal, the first player skips to the turning line and back. Continue until every player has had a turn.

Teaching suggestions

Skip backwards. Or have each player stop on the turning line and do ten, fifteen, or twenty stationary skips before returning to the starting line.

Circle Post Relay

Formation   Line

Equipment   Posts, pins, or chairs

Players   Three to four on each team

Arrange each team behind the starting line and draw a turning line twenty feet in front of the starting line. Place a chair or pin on the turning line directly in front of each team. Player 1 runs forward, makes a full circle around the post, moving left, then runs back around his own team and tags player 2. Continue until each player has circled the post.

Stick and Ball Relay

Formation   Line

Equipment   One stick and one ball for each team

Players   Three to four on each team

Draw a turning line about twenty to fifty feet in front of the starting line. The first player holds the stick in contact with the ball and guides it while running to the turning line and back. Continue until every player has had a turn.

Obstacle Relay

Formation Line
Equipment Chairs
Players Three to four on each team

Place chairs (or Indian clubs) six to ten feet apart and directly in front of each team. The first player runs "in and out" around the chairs and back around his team to the starting position. Continue until every player has had a turn.

Teaching Suggestions
If sufficient chairs, clubs, beanbags, or wands are available, create a variety of obstacles to go around, under, or through.

Scooter Relay

Formation Line
Equipment Twelve to twenty-four scooters
Players Variable

Scooters provide an additional reservoir of file relays. Since this may be a new activity to many teachers, possible relay positions are listed.

Two-hand relay (hands on scooter)
One-hand relay (one hand on scooter)
One-hand, one-foot relay
Two-hand, one-foot relay
Sitting relay using feet to propel
Kneeling relay using hands to propel
Lying relay using hands to propel
Two-feet relay propelling with hands
Seat and feet relay propelling with hands

Figure 15.1   Kneeling Relay on a Scooter

Partner Relays

Partner relays are the same as previous relays except that they are performed with partners. It is important to match partners according to size. Partners should exchange positions after each turn.

Wheelbarrow Relay

Formation Partners in line formation
Equipment None
Players Six to eight on each team

Divide each team into pairs of equal height and weight. On signal, one partner places his hands on the floor and raises his legs to other partner's hips. The standing partner holds his partner's feet close to his sides and they walk to the turning line twenty to twenty-five feet away. When both have crossed the turning line, they exchange positions and return to the starting line.

Teaching suggestions
Instruct the standing partner not to push the "walking" partner but only to hold his feet and walk. Increase distance as strength increases.

Two-Legged Relay

Formation Partners in a line formation
Equipment None
Players Six to eight on each team

Each team lines up in pairs. Partners grasp each other around the waist with their inside arms and raise their inside legs off the floor. On signal, each pair hops to the turning line twenty to thirty feet away. Once behind the line, they change positions and hop on the other foot. As soon as they are ready, they return to the starting line and the next pair repeats the action.

Back-to-Back Relay

Formation Partners in a line formation
Equipment None
Players Six to eight on each team

Each team lines up in pairs. The first pair stands back to back and links elbows. Partner 1 faces the turning line, and partner 2 faces his team. Partner 1 is the carrier and his elbows are inside his partner's. On signal, partner 1 leans forward and lifts his partner off the ground and carries him to the turning line about twenty to thirty feet away. Once they cross the turning line, they change positions and return to the starting line. The relay continues until the last pair has crossed the finish line.

Siamese Twins

Formation Partners in line formation
Equipment One four-foot stick for each team
Players Six to eight on each team

Each team lines up in pairs. The first two players stand back to back and straddle the stick, grasping it between their legs with both hands in front. Partner 1 faces the turning line about twenty to thirty feet away, and partner 2 faces his team. On signal, the partners run to the turning line, partner 1 running forward and partner 2 running backward. Once they cross the line, they reverse positions and return to the starting line. The relay continues until the last couple has crossed the finish line.

Piggyback Relay

Formation Line formation
Equipment None
Players Four to six on each team

Player 1 piggybacks player 2 to the turning line about twenty to thirty feet away. Player 2 runs back to the starting line and piggybacks player 3 to the turning line. The relay continues until all players have crossed the turning line.

Paul Revere

Formation Shuttle
Equipment None
Players Four to six on each team

Draw two parallel lines about thirty to forty feet apart. Each team chooses one ''rider'' and the remaining players count off. The even-numbered players line up behind one line and the odd-numbered players line up behind the other line, directly opposite their teammates. On signal, the rider mounts the back of player number 1, who carries him to the other line. The rider must change mounts to player 2 without touching the ground. Player 2 carries the rider back to player 3, and so on until all mounts have carried the rider. If the rider falls off, he must mount at the point where he fell off. If he falls while changing mounts, he must get back on his original mount before changing to his new one.

Group Relays

Group relays are thoroughly enjoyed by upper elementary children. They require a lot more teamwork, strength, and timing than individual and partner relays. Allow the children to practice the skill or movement pattern involved in the relay, then make a practice run before the competition begins.

Skin-the-Snake Relay

Formation Line formation
Equipment None
Players Four to six on each team

Each player extends his left hand back between his legs and grasps the right hand of the player behind him. On signal, every member of the file except the last player starts moving backward. The last player lies down on his back, still holding onto the player in front. The second rear player, after passing over the last player, lies down, still maintaining his grasp with both hands. Pattern continues until everyone is lying down. As soon as all are lying on their backs, the one at the rear stands and moves forward, pulling the second player to his feet. Continue this until everyone is standing up. The first team up wins.

Caterpillar Race

Formation Line
Equipment None
Players Five to six on each team

Each player bends forward and grasps the ankles of the player in front. On signal, the team moves forward toward the turning line about twenty to thirty feet away. The lead player may use his hands in any manner, but all other players must keep their hands on the ankles of the player in front. If a player releases his grip, he must regrasp the player's ankles before his team can continue. The first team crossing the turning line wins.

Chariot Race

Formation Line
Equipment None
Players Nine to twelve on each team

Players on each team run in groups of three. Player 1 stands erect, player 2 bends forward and holds player 1's hips, and player 3 rides on player 2's back. On signal, the three players on each team run to the turning line about twenty feet away and back to the starting line. If a rider falls off or if player 2 releases his grip, the group stops and reforms before continuing the race. As soon as each chariot has crossed the starting line, the next chariot starts. The relay continues until everyone has had a turn.

Row-a-Boat Relay

Formation Shuttle
Equipment None
Players Four to six on each team

Each team lines up behind the starting line and counts off. Even-numbered players face odd-numbered players. Player 1 sits down and places his feet on the starting line. Player 2 sits down facing player 1, and they join hands. Player 3 sits down behind player 1 and puts his arms around 1's waist and his feet on either side of player 1. Player 4 does the same with player 2, and so on until all players are seated. On signal, each team tries to row to the turning line without loosing their grips. The first team to completely cross the turning line, about fifteen to twenty feet away, wins the relay.

Sports Skill Relays

In most intermediate physical education programs, sports skill relays are taught as part of a team sport, such as soccer, volleyball, or basketball. However, primary children, particularly second and third graders, should also participate in sport skill relays to develop the basic skills of team and individual sports. Primary teachers should modify the following relays to meet their classes' level of skill.

Sports Skills	Name of Relay	Page
Soccer Skills	Shuttle Dribbling	286
Volleyball Skills	Shuttle Volleying	224
	Zigzag Volleying	224
Basketball Skills	Circle Passing	341
	Line Dribble	342
	Wall Passing	341
Softball Skills	Softball Throw Relay	361
Track & Field Skills	Call Race	382

16 Individual and Partner Games

Teaching Individual and Partner Games

Applying the Inventive Games Approach

Individual and Partner Games

Several games for elementary school children can be played by one, two (singles), three, or four (doubles) players. These games have usually been played before school, during recess, and after school. However, the trend toward more individualized teaching has increased the popularity of individual and partner games during the regular instructional period. When taught during the regular class period, all children have an opportunity to learn the basic skills and rules of these activities. In addition, the basic fundamentals of the more advanced games, such as handball and paddle tennis, can be introduced systematically. Finally, the inventive games approach can be easily applied to these activities.

Teaching Individual and Partner Games

Although many of the games listed on the following pages are very familiar to elementary school children, others may be new. If adequate space, equipment, and supplies are available, a game can be explained and demonstrated, and then the entire class can play it. In most instances, however, teachers do not have enough equipment for this type of lesson format. The following organization and method of instruction deal with this problem. (See films *Teaching Games to Primary Children* and *Teaching Games to Intermediate Children* listed in appendix A.)

Station Work

To illustrate the station work technique, let us assume that a third-grade class knows how to play chair bowling and four square. The teacher wishes to introduce beanbag horseshoes and barnyard golf in the next lesson. During the first few minutes of this lesson the teacher assigns each team to a station, as illustrated on page 248. Brief demonstrations of beanbag horseshoes and barnyard golf are given before each team is allowed to play its assigned game. Each game is played for a few minutes. The teacher then asks the class to stop, return the equipment to its original position, and

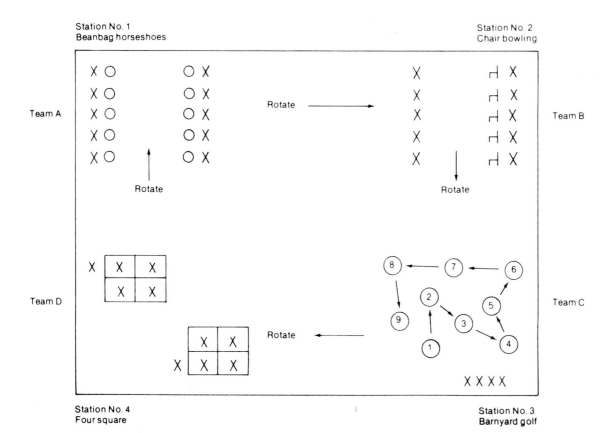

Station No. 1
Beanbag horseshoes

Station No. 2
Chair bowling

Team A

Rotate →

Team B

Rotate ↑

Rotate ↓

Team D

Team C

Rotate ←

Station No. 4
Four square

Station No. 3
Barnyard golf

Figure 16.1

rotate to the next station. This procedure continues until all the teams have played the four games. If time does not permit the class to complete the rotation, pick it up in the next lesson.

Applying the Inventive Games Approach

The problem-solving method described in chapters 14 and 15 can be applied to individual and partner games. If children are familiar with this approach, a question such as, "With your partner can you make up a new hopscotch game?" or "Can you change the alphabet game (p. 253) to a game that includes numbers?" should be sufficient direction for the children to undertake the challenge.

Individual and Partner Games

Individual and partner games are so enjoyable that they belong to virtually every grade level. The difference is the children's skill and finesse as they mature and develop more speed and coordination. The following games have been organized according to grade levels, but the children's interest and, to a much lesser degree, the relative order of difficulty also have been considered.

Name of Game	Grade Level	Skills	Page
American Hopscotch	1–4	Throwing, hopping	249
Chair Bowling	1–6	Rolling	250
Marbles	1–6	Shooting	251
Jacks	1–4	Throwing, catching, balancing	251
Beanbag Horseshoes	2–6	Throwing	251
Softball Croquet	2–6	Hitting	252
Tetherball	2–6	Hitting	253
Barnyard Golf	2–6	Throwing	253
Alphabet Game	3–6	Vaulting	253
Four Square	3–6	Bouncing and catching	254
Paddleball	3–6	Serving, running, hitting	254
Deck Tennis	3–6	Running, throwing, catching	255
Sidewalk Tennis	3–6	Serving, running, hitting	256
Shuffleboard	4–6	Shooting	256
Shufflecurl	4–6	Shooting	256
Orienteering	4–6	Running	257
Frisbee	3–6	Throwing and catching	259

American Hopscotch (1–4)

Formation   Pattern as shown in diagram on page 250

Equipment   Beanbags, buttons, beads, or other small objects

Players   Two to four

The first player stands on her right foot, (this is her declared "hopping" foot and must be used throughout her turn) outside area 1, holding the "puck" (beanbag, button, etc.) in her hand. She tosses the puck into area 1, hops into this area, picks up the puck while balancing on her right leg, then hops out. She next throws the puck into area 2. She then hops into area 1, straddles ("spread eagle") areas 2 and 3, picks up the puck, hops back into area 2, then out. She continues this pattern, hopping and landing with one foot in single spaces and with both feet in adjacent areas. Two hops are permitted in area 10 in order to turn around. A player is out if she steps on a line, tosses the puck onto a line or into the wrong area, changes feet on single hops, or touches her hand or other foot during any hopping or retrieving movement. When a child commits an error, she goes to the back of the line.

Figure 16.2   American Hopscotch

Variations

1. French Hopscotch. The game follows the basic rules of American hopscotch with the player hopping on one foot in single squares and landing with both feet in adjacent squares. However, when a player lands with one foot in area 7 and the other in area 8, he must jump up, turn around in the air, and land in the same areas.

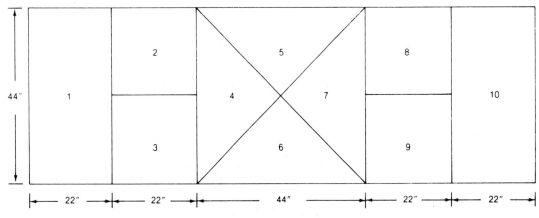

American Hopscotch

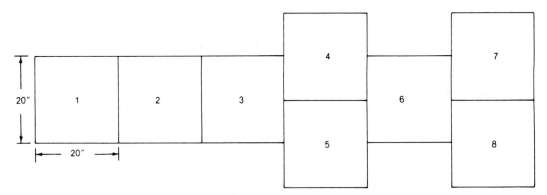

French Hopscotch

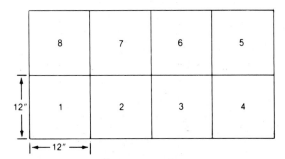

Italian Hopscotch

2. Italian Hopscotch. The first player stands on one foot outside square 1, holding a "puck" (beanbag, etc.) in his hand. He throws the puck into square 1 and then hops into this area. Still standing on one foot, he kicks the puck into square 2, then hops into that square. He continues this pattern to square 8. When he reaches square 8, he places both feet on the ground, picks up the puck, and hops backwards through all squares to the starting position. A player is out if he steps on a line, if his puck stops on a line, if he puts both feet down in any square except 8, or if he changes feet. When a child commits an error, he goes to the back of the line.

3. Ask children to design their own pattern (zig-zag, circle, etc.) and also make up their own rules.

Chair Bowling (1–6)

Formation Two parallel lines drawn approximately fifteen to thirty feet apart, depending on the level of skill, with a chair placed on one line

Equipment One chair, one ball (sponge ball, tennis ball, or softball), pencil, and score sheet for each couple

Players Two per game

Partner 1 stands behind one line with a ball and partner 2 stands directly opposite, behind the chair. The chair's backrest faces partner 2. The score sheet and pencil are placed on the seat of the chair. Partner 1 rolls three balls, then changes places with his partner. Award five points for each ball that rolls through the legs of the chair. The game may be played to any score, selected on the basis of skill and available time.

Variations
1. Hit a milk carton or draw a target on the wall at floor level, rather than using a chair.
2. Substitute beanbags for balls.
3. Bowl backwards through outstretched legs.

Figure 16.3 Playing Marbles

Marbles (1–6)

Formation   Circle five to six feet in diameter

Equipment   Marbles of various sizes

Players   Two to four

Each player places one or two marbles in the center of the circle. The playing order is determined by each player throwing his shooting marble (called the taw) toward a line six to ten feet away. The player whose marble is closest to the line shoots first; the player whose marble is next closest shoots second, and so on. A player may shoot from anywhere outside the circle, trying to knock the marbles out of the circle. His taw must remain inside the circle. If successful, he continues from where his taw has stopped. After all players have had a turn, they remove their taws from the circle. At the end of the game all marbles should be returned to their owners; however, the author remembers his boyhood days when he would go home with more, or less, marbles than he started with.

Variations

1. Play doubles. Player 1 of team A shoots until he misses. Player 2 of team A shoots next, followed by player 1 of team B.
2. Exchange taws. Same as marbles except opponents exchange taws.
3. Marble Golf. Sink five or six small cans in a golf course pattern. Use same rules as for barnyard golf, page 253.

Jacks (1–4)

Formation   Circle on a hard surface

Equipment   Six jacks and a small rubber ball

Players   Two to four

The first player tosses the jacks on the ground. He then throws the ball into the air. With the same hand, he picks up one jack and tries to catch the ball before it lands. If successful, he places the jack in his other hand and continues playing until he picks up all the jacks. If unsuccessful, the next player takes a turn. If a player picks up all the jacks, one at a time, he repeats the game, picking up two at a time. Continue with three at a time, and so on.

Variations

1. Pigs in the Pen. Jacks are brushed into the other hand which is held in a cupped position.
2. Eggs in the Basket. Jacks are picked up and transferred to the opposite hand before the ball is caught.
3. Lazy Susan. The ball is allowed to bounce twice before the jacks are picked up.

Beanbag Horseshoes (2–6)

Formation   Two hoops or old bicycle tires placed about twenty to thirty feet apart, depending upon the level of skill

Equipment   Three beanbags and two hoops per game

Players   Two or four

Player 1 stands behind his hoop and attempts to throw each beanbag into the middle of player 2's hoop. Five points are awarded if the beanbag lands inside the hoop, and three points if it lands on the rim. Player 2 then takes his turn. The first player to score fifteen points wins.

Variations

1. Use quoits instead of beanbags.
2. Use different targets such as wastepaper baskets, seat of chairs, or small mats.
3. Quoit horseshoes. Play the same game, substituting quoits for beanbags and a broomstick on a board for the target. Five points are awarded for a ringer, three for a quoit that touches the peg, and one for any quoit that touches the base.

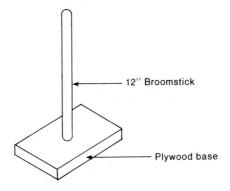

12″ Broomstick

Plywood base

Softball Croquet (2–6)

Formation Place arches as shown in diagram below with distances adjusted according to level of skill and available space

Equipment Two mallets (see diagram at right for constructing), two softballs, nine coat hangers (cut near neck and straighten)

Players Two per game

Player A hits the ball from behind the starting line. If the ball goes through both arches, A is given another hit. Player B hits the ball. Players alternate hitting throughout the game. Whenever a player hits the ball through an arch, he is given another hit. If a player's ball travels and hits his opponent's ball, no infraction occurs. The first person to hit his ball across the starting line wins the game.

Variations

1. Change the pattern of the arches.
2. Play "doubles" croquet and make up your own rotation rules.
3. Play the same game with different size balls such as field hockey, tennis, or nerf balls.

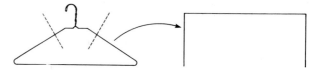

2½' Broomstick

4" × 4" Block

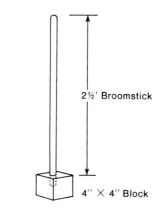

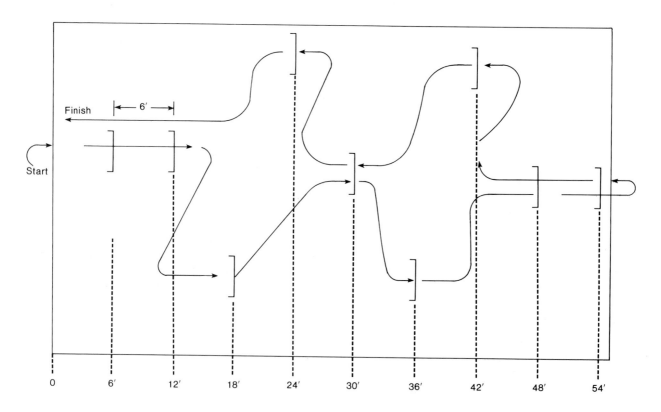

Tetherball (2-6)

Formation Court area as shown in diagram

Equipment Tetherball, pole, and rope

Players Two per game

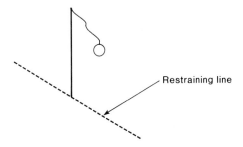

Restraining line

Players stand on opposite sides of the restraining line. One player starts the game by throwing the ball into the air and hitting it in any direction with his hand or fist. The opposing player strikes the ball in the opposite direction only after the ball passes him on the second swing around the pole. The player who winds the ball around the pole first is the winner.

A foul occurs when a player,

1. Hits the ball with any part of his body other than his hands.
2. Touches the rope or pole.
3. Catches the ball.
4. Throws the ball.

The penalty for a foul is to forfeit the game to the opponent.

Variations
1. Play "doubles." Players of each team alternate hitting the ball.
2. Play same game using a paddle.

Barnyard Golf (2-6)

Formation Nine hoops or old bicycle tires (or circles drawn on blacktop) scattered and numbered as "holes"

Equipment One beanbag for each player, nine hoops

Players Four on each game

Allow each group of four to arrange its own "golf course," scattering the hoops in the space allocated. Player 1 begins from behind the starting line and attempts to throw his beanbag into the first hoop. If it lands inside or on the rim, he is awarded one point. He then picks up his beanbag and moves to the side of the first hoop and throws his beanbag into the second hoop. As soon as player 1 starts his second throw, player 2 begins his first throw. The game continues until every player has completed the course. The player with the most points wins the game.

Variations
1. This version is more similar to golf. Each player attempts to throw his beanbag into the first hoop. If he fails, he fetches it and tries again. No player can advance to the next "hole" until his beanbag lands in the hoop. This pattern continues around the course. The winner is the player with the lowest score.
2. Tin Can Golf. Sink tin cans into the ground and use old tennis balls and hockey sticks. Play according to the rules of variation 1.

Alphabet Game (3-6)

Formation Pattern drawn as in diagram on dirt, gravel, or blacktop surface, with the size of the squares adjusted according to level of ability

Equipment One wand for each game

Players Two per game

Z			
Y	P	G	O
F	X	R	C
L	J	T	N
S	Q	B	H
W	E	M	D
K	I	V	U
		A	

Player 1 begins in square A. With the aid of his wand, he attempts to move from square A to Z, in alphabetical order, without touching any lines. As soon as player 1 touches a line, he is out and player 2 begins. The winner is the player who progresses to the highest letter in the alphabet.

Variations
1. Have each child "touch" a four-letter word (or a longer word) before touching Z.
2. Change letters to numbers, then make up challenges involving adding, subtracting, multiplying, and dividing. (See chapter 11 for additional ideas).

Four Square (3–6)

Formation Sixteen-foot square divided into four, four-foot squares designated as squares A, B, C, and D

Equipment Large utility ball

Players Five to six per group

One player stands in each square. The player in square D starts the game by bouncing the ball, then hitting it with one or both hands so that it bounces into one of the other squares. The player receiving the ball hits it after one bounce to any of the other squares. The game proceeds until a player fails to return the ball properly or commits a foul. When this happens, the offending player goes to the end of the waiting line. All players move one square toward D and the waiting player moves to square A.

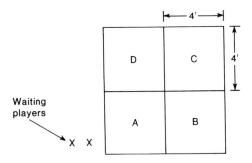

Basic Rules

1. The ball must arc before landing; it cannot be struck downward.
2. Service always begins from square D.
3. A player may go anywhere to return a fair ball, even out of his own square.
4. The ball may not be held.

Fouls occur when—

1. A ball hits any line.
2. A ball is struck with closed fists.
3. A ball hits a player who is standing in his own square.

Variations

1. Two Square. Play same game with two squares, and three or four players.
2. Team Two Square. Same as variation 1, except teammates take alternate turns.

Paddleball (3–6)

Formation Court drawn as in diagram at the top of page 255 using any available wall and floor space. Use chalk or plastic tape to mark court dimensions.

Equipment Bats and tennis or sponge ball

Players Singles (two players), doubles (four players), and triples (three players)

Singles

The server, standing anywhere between the wall and the serving line, bounces the ball and hits it toward the front wall. The ball must hit the wall above the two-foot line and land behind the serving line inside the court. If it does not, the next player serves. After the ball has bounced once, the receiver hits it back to the wall. All returned balls by either player must hit above the two-foot line, but they may land anywhere inside the full court area (sixteen by twenty-six feet). The players alternate hitting the ball. If the server hits the ball above the line and back over the serving line, and the receiver fails to return the ball, the server receives one point. One player continues serving until he faults or misses the ball. Any player may go outside the court to return a ball. Game may be played to eleven, fifteen, or twenty-one points.

Doubles

The game is played according to singles rules with a few modifications. On the serve, the server's teammate stands outside the court to prevent any hindrance to the opponents who are trying to return the service. When the server loses his serve, his teammate takes a turn. Each team, therefore, has two serves in succession. On the serve, either opponent may return the ball. Thereafter, players on each team alternate hitting the ball.

Triples

This game is played according to singles rules with the following modifications. The server represents one team and, therefore, is playing against the other two players as a team. When the server loses his service, he moves to the right back court. The right back court player shifts to the left, and the left back court player becomes the new server. After the serve, the server hits every other ball. For example, the server hits, then player A of the opposing team, then the server, then player B. Each player keeps his own score.

Variations

1. Handball. Game is played the same as paddleball except the ball is hit with the hand. Use tennis, sponge, or nerf balls.
2. Allow two bounces for either paddleball or handball.
3. Adjust serving and restraining line to meet level of ability.

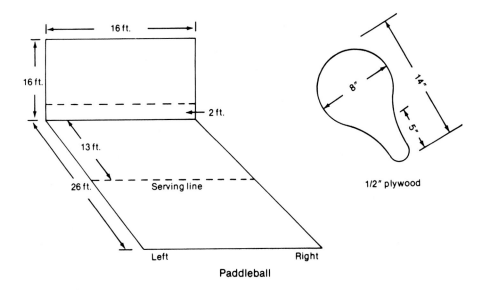

Paddleball

1/2″ plywood

Deck Tennis (3–6)

Formation Court drawn as in diagram below, or use any existing volleyball or badminton court

Equipment Deck tennis ring made of rope or plastic tubing, which can be purchased through local sports stores

Players Singles (two players) or doubles (four players)

Singles

The server, standing outside the baseline and on the right half of the court, delivers the ring in a forehand fashion. The ring must rise to an arc before it begins to descend into the opponent's right court outside the neutral area. After the serve, the ring may land anywhere in the court. The server must serve into alternate courts each time. The receiver must catch the ring with one hand and immediately return it. The server scores a point if the receiver fails to return the ring or commits one of the following fouls:

1. Catching the ring with both hands.
2. Changing the ring to his other hand before returning it.
3. Holding the ring too long before returning it (count three seconds).

4. Stepping over the net line.
5. Failing to make the ring arc before it begins to descend into the opponent's court.

If the server faults or misses the return throw, his opponent then serves. However, no point is scored by the opponent. Game may be played to eleven, fifteen, or twenty-one points.

Doubles

The game is played according to singles rules with some modifications. Each team has two serves in succession. After the receiver has returned the server's toss, any player may return a toss. For example, player A from team one serves, and player C of team two catches the ring and returns it to player A. It is legal for player A to catch the ring and return it.

Variations

1. Nerfball Deck Tennis. Play the same game with a nerf ball. Allow one bounce, and hit with an open palm.
2. Paddle Tennis. Play variation 1 with a paddle.

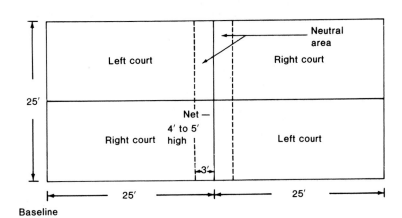

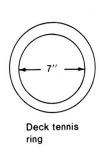

Deck tennis ring

Sidewalk Tennis (3–6)

Formation   Court drawn as in diagram. A regular sidewalk can be used for this game, with four squares making a court

Equipment   Tennis ball, sponge ball, or other small rubber ball

Players   Singles (two players) or doubles (four players)

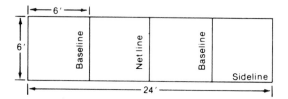

The server, standing behind the baseline, bounces the ball and then hits it with an underhand hit over the net line. The ball must land in the opponent's court. The receiver hits the ball with an open palm after it has bounced once. The ball must then pass over the net line. After the receiver has returned the first serve, players may return the ball while it is in the air ("on the volley") or on the first bounce. The server scores one point if the receiver fails to return the ball or commits one of the following fouls:

1. Hitting the ball with any part of the body other than the open palm.
2. When returning a serve, hitting the ball before it bounces once.

If the server commits any of the following fouls, there is a change in servers:

1. Stepping over the baseline when serving.
2. Serving the ball with a side or overhand serve.

Games may be played to eleven, fifteen, or twenty-one points. If the score is tied at ten, fourteen, or twenty, a player must make two consecutive points to win the game.

Variations

1. Doubles. The same rules apply, with partners alternating on serves and returns. When a teammate loses his serve, it goes to an opponent.
2. Place a rope or net across the net line.
3. Hit the ball with a paddle.
4. Use a large utility ball. If this is too difficult, increase the size of the court.

Shuffleboard (4–6)

Formation   Court drawn as in diagram on page 257. Shuffleboard must be played on a smooth, flat surface; a gymnasium floor is ideal, but blacktop or a cement surface is adequate

Equipment   Two or four cues (forked sticks) and eight disks

Players   Singles (two players) or doubles (four players)

Singles

Each player is given four disks (player A's are red; B's are black). Player A begins the game by pushing one of his disks with his cue from the righthand side of the ten off area, trying to get his disk into scoring position at the opposite end of the court. Player B then pushes one of his disks, trying either to get it into scoring position or to knock player A's disk out of scoring position. Both players shoot from the same ten off area. The players take turns hitting their remaining disks until all eight have been played. Disks that land between the dead lines are taken off the playing surface.

After the last disk is played, the players walk to the opposite end and count their scores. If a disk lands in the ten off zone, ten points are deducted from the player's score. Any disk that touches a line is not counted. Player B starts the second round at the opposite end of the court and the process is repeated. Games may be played to 50, 75, or 100 points.

Doubles

Two opponents play from each end and remain there throughout the game. The red player plays first at each end. At the beginning of the second round, the black player plays first at each end. Continue the rotation.

Variations

1. Play the same game using beanbags.
2. If outdoors, double the size of the target areas and roll softballs instead of pushing disks.

Shufflecurl (4–6)

Formation   Court drawn as in diagram on page 257. Chalk lines are adequate.

Equipment   Shuffleboard cues and disks

Players   Singles (two players) or doubles (four players)

The rules are the same as in shuffleboard, but the object is to slide the disks as close to the center of the circle as possible. Players in this game also try to knock the opponent's disks out of scoring position. When each player has used his four disks by sliding them to the opposite circle one "end" has been completed. Two "ends" make one round, and a game may be five, ten, or any other number of rounds. To score, award one point for each disk that a player has placed closer to the center of the circle than the closest disk of his opponent. (In the diagram, the player with the black disks would score three points.)

Variations

1. Indoors. Play same game using beanbags.
2. Outdoors. Play same game using softballs or partially deflated utility balls.

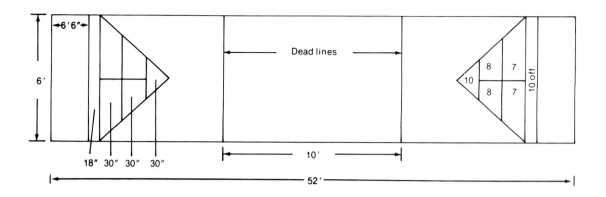

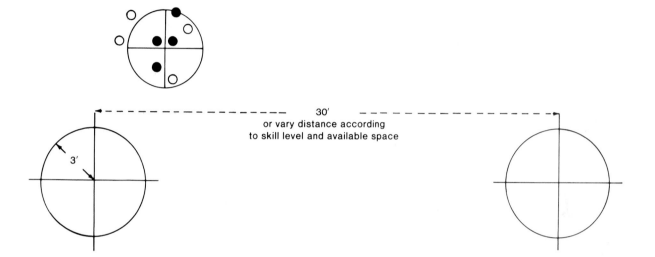

Orienteering (4–6)

True, or official, orienteering is a competitive way of navigating across country on foot, using a map and a compass (Schaanning 1965). Both Norway and Sweden claim to have originated this sport, and its beginnings can be traced to World War II, when many Scandinavians were initiated to orienteering through the Resistance movement. Accurate navigation often meant the difference between life or death, since a compass was needed to find supplies, avoid enemy camps, and seek out hidden installations.

Today orienteering is a wholesome outdoor activity and a lifesaving skill for the everincreasing number of people who are taking up camping and other outdoor recreational activities. Orienteering is taught in many Scandinavian schools, and the writer believes this sport has a place in many elementary and secondary schools in North America. Several schools in Canada and the United States already have incorporated orienteering in their programs.

Since authentic maps and compasses are expensive, another type of orienteering—called score orienteering—is described for use in elementary school programs. It is extremely popular with boys and girls in the intermediate grades as well.

Figure 16.4 Plotting a Route

Score Orienteering

Each player is given a hand-drawn map of the area, including all necessary landmarks—buildings, statues, trees, paths, and so on. The diagram below shows a school and the immediate major landmarks. Each player is also given a "word description chart." Note in Table 16.1 that each description is simple, and that the farthest sites are awarded the highest points. Players leave the starting point at a designated time and, with the aid of their maps and charts, try to find the various landmarks or checkpoints.

General Procedure and Instructions

Each student writes his name on his chart and leaves everything else blank. Four or five runners leave the starting point at the same time; to avoid congestion, allow thirty seconds between groups. The teacher marks the starting time on each chart, and the runners have ten minutes (or whatever time the teacher sets) to go to as many check points as possible before returning to the recorder's desk. The teacher has placed a code letter on each landmark, or checkpoint, before the orienteering lesson, and when a runner arrives at the checkpoint, he places that code letter in the appropriate space on the recording sheet. Runners may choose their own order of reaching checkpoints. A runner is penalized five points for each minute he exceeds the ten-minute time limit.

Figure 16.5

Teaching Suggestions

Competitions can be developed on the basis of one type of landmark, such as trees, flowers, or buildings. If a school is near a park or wilderness area, the possibilities are almost unlimited. Also, the addition of compasses and authentic maps of the area open the door to an enjoyable and constructive recreational pursuit. Finally, if a teacher is not skillful at reading a compass or a geographical map, she can find many people in the community, such as scout leaders and surveyors, more than willing to donate their services.

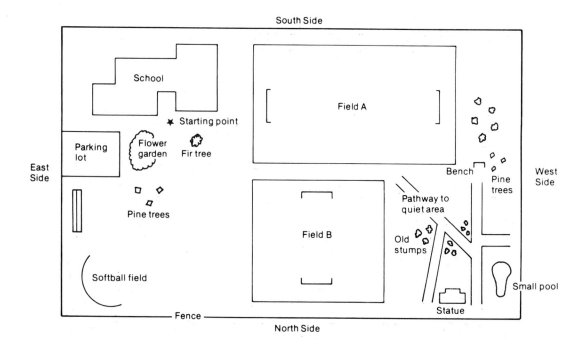

Table 16.1 Word Description Chart

Name: John Smith

Time Allowed: 10 minues
Start Time:
Finish Time:
Penalty Points: (at 5 points a minute)

No.	Description of Landmark (Checkpoint)	Value	Insert Code Letter
1.	On the east end of softball backstop	15	T
2.	On the north side of flower garden	10	B
3.	On the south goalpost of field B	5	C
4.	On the northwest side of an old stump	10	F
5.	On the northeast end of the softball stands	15	R
6.	On the bench near three pine trees	15	U
7.	On the southwest side of field A	10	A
8.	On the west corner of statue	25	Y

Total points _____
Penalty points _____
Final Score _____

Frisbee (3–6)

Frisbee activities, whether throwing the disc for distance, catching it in a variety of unusual ways, or playing new types of Frisbee games, have become very popular with elementary school children. It involves a new way of throwing an object and a flight pattern different from that of a thrown or hit ball. More important, Frisbee activities provide a reservoir within which children can invent unlimited numbers of creative and cooperative game activities.

The backhand throw is the easiest and most popular way of throwing the Frisbee. Stand with feet about shoulder-width apart and weight evenly distributed over both feet. The right foot points towards the target. The disc is held with the thumb on top, index finger on the rim, and the remaining fingers curved under the rim of the disc (fig. 16.6a). Shift the weight to the rear foot, then simultaneously twist the trunk towards the target and pull the right arm forward (fig. 16.6b). Continue forward and release the disc with a snap of the wrist when the disc is parallel to the ground (fig. 16.6c).

Variations

The following activities are simple modifications of partner or team games. Teachers and children are encouraged to invent other variations as well as entirely new Frisbee games.

1. Throw and Catch with Partner. Throw and catch at different levels using a variety of catches. Other variations such as increasing the distance, using either hand, or performing a trick when catching the Frisbee, can be added to partner activities.

2. Frisbee Horseshoes. Play the same game as beanbag horseshoes (p. 251) except expand the distance between the pegs or substitute a batting tee for the smaller peg.
3. Frisbee Golf. Play the same game as barnyard golf (p. 253) except expand the distance between "holes."
4. Frisbee Tennis. Play the same game as deck tennis (p. 255) and add or modify any rule to accommodate levels of skill and interest.

Figure 16.6 Throwing a Frisbee

a

b

c

17 *Cooperative Games*

Elements of a Cooperative Game

Cooperative Games

Creative Cooperative Games

Since the publication of Terry Orlick's *Cooperative Sports and Games Book* and Andrew Fluegelman's *The New Games Book,* many children have been introduced to a delightful cooperative and nonthreatening games program. Cooperative games may be new, borrowed from other cultures, or modified versions of team games that children have played for generations.

The first part of this chapter describes the basic elements of a cooperative game. The next section includes examples of several cooperative games that have become very popular with elementary school-age children. The last section describes how teachers can guide children toward creating their own cooperative games.

Elements of a Cooperative Game

Webster's Dictionary defines *cooperation* as "association of persons for common benefit."* On the basis of this definition, any competitive game, such as volleyball, basketball, or dodgeball would meet this criteria since a measure of cooperation is required if the team is to win the contest. The contemporary meaning of "cooperative games" however, goes beyond Webster's definition. These new cooperative games, described in the next two sections, are essentially noncompetitive activities that emphasize the interaction of people rather than the game or the final score. And, they normally possess one or more of the following distinguishing characteristics or elements of cooperative behavior.

1. *Equality:* Everyone has an equal role in the game; that is, each player "hits the ball" roughly the same number of times as any other player, "rotates" to every other position and, if part of the game, assumes the leadership role on a rotational basis.

2. *Participation:* Everyone is actively involved in the game. The rules of the game cannot eliminate any player from playing. If a player is "hit," "touched," or misses a "catch," he, in some marvelous way, continues to play.

*By permission. From Webster's Ninth New Collegiate Dictionary © 1984 by Merriam-Webster Inc., publisher of the Merriam-Webster® Dictionaries.

3. *Success:* Everyone experiences success. Cooperative games have no losers! Success must also be personally defined rather than determined by a group standard.

4. *Trust:* Everyone must be able to place a measure of trust in other players. This means that situations within the game require a player to rely on another player to "miss him," "hold him," "balance him," or perform a movement that considers his safety and well-being.

Cooperative Games

All games described in this section are cooperative in nature. Some of these games, such as doubles hopscotch and modified musical chairs are modified versions of competitive games children have played for years. These modified versions, however, stress the elements of equality, participation, success, and trust, rather than "winners and losers."

Cooperative Games

Name of Games	Players	Level	Page
Doubles Hopscotch	2	1–3	261
Perpetual Motion Machine	3 to 4	1–6	261
Recycled Snake Skins	4	2–6	262
Airplanes	5	4–6	262
Juggle a Number	5	3–6	262
Twister	5 to 6	2–6	263
Cross-over Blanket Volleyball	6 to 7	4–6	263
Merry-Go-Round	8	2–6	264
Nine-Person Skip	11	4–6	264
Eight-Legged Caterpillar	Class	1–6	264
Modified Musical Chairs	Class	1–6	265
One-Hole Parachute Golf	Class	2–6	266
Pass a Person	Class	3–6	266
Tug-O-Peace	Class	3–6	266
Co-Op Tag	Class	1–6	267

Doubles Hopscotch (1–3)

Partners hold inside hands. Follow the rules of hopscotch (page 249) except hop on inside feet in squares 1, 4, 7, and 10, and on outside feet in the other squares. Use one puck between partners and modify any other rule to accommodate doubles hopscotch.

Figure 17.1 Noncompetitive activities emphasize the interaction of people.

Suggestions and Variations
1. Change methods of holding, moving, and throwing the puck.
2. Adapt "doubles hopscotch" to other games such as marbles, jacks, and beanbag horseshoes.
3. Change partners after every game.

Perpetual Motion Machine (1–6)

This game should start with about three or four players. Add more players as their timing and cooperative behavior improves. To begin, the first player starts to move in any way and in any direction that she chooses. The second player joins on behind and copies the exact motions of the first player. Repeat with each remaining player.

Suggestions and Variations
1. As soon as the class understands the nature of the game, add the following variation. The first player starts as usual; the second player attaches, copying the movements of the first player, and adds a new movement of his own. Continue with each player adding a new movement.
2. Repeat variation 1, keeping in time to a musical accompaniment.

Figure 17.2 Perpetual Motion Machine

Figure 17.3 Airplanes

3. Change the leader after each game.
4. Repeat game with a beanbag on each person's head. If any player drops the beanbag, the game starts over.
5. Add small equipment such as hoops, balls, or wands to the game.

Recycled Snake Skins (2–6)

This modified version of "Skin the Snake" is played with the following variations. Four players per team stand and scatter in the playing area. As soon as all players on a team are lying down, the player at the front of the team releases his grip and runs to find a new group of "threes." Taking the front position, he signals the rear player to stand and move forward. The game continues until there is a complete change or "a new skin."

Suggestions and Variations
1. Repeat the game, but with the new snakes alternating boy, girl, boy, girl.
2. Repeat game but reverse directions.

Airplanes (4–6)

Arrange groups of five players behind a starting line. One player in each group lies face down with arms and legs stretched sideways. The four carriers grasp the "airplane's" elbows and ankles and carry her to a turning line then back to the starting line. Repeat for each player on the team.

Suggestions and Variations
1. Since this is not a relay race, team members carry their airplane back and forth at their own speed.
2. Do not play this game on rough gravel or other dangerous surfaces.
3. For safety, have the airplane land first with feet, then hands.

Juggle a Number (3–6)

Begin with five players in a circle formation. Number each player in a random fashion rather than sequentially around the circle. Place five balls behind player 1. Player 1 throws a ball to 2, 2 to 3 and so forth until the ball is returned to player 1. Repeat two or three times, or until all players know the rotation pattern. Members of each group decide how many balls they can keep moving, then player 1 starts throwing the first ball to player 2, and then picks up a second ball and repeats until the selected number of balls are all moving from player to player. If a ball drops, any player may pick it up and try to get it back into the throwing sequence.

Suggestions and Variations
1. Have each group try to keep all five balls moving.
2. Play same game, but with players using one hand.
3. Play the game with a balloon instead of a ball and have each player keep a beanbag on his head, elbow or lower back.

Figure 17.4 Juggle a Number

Figure 17.5 Twister

a

Twister (2–6)

Begin with five or six players in a circle formation. Each player joins each hand with a different person. When all hands are joined, the group tries to untwist itself without letting go of any handgrip.

Suggestions and Variations
1. Start with three players, then gradually increase the number.
2. Play same game but with each player balancing a beanbag on his head.

Cross-over Blanket Volleyball (4–6)

Arrange two teams of six or seven players on each side of a volleyball net (rope will do). Each team holds a blanket, keeping the net side open. One team starts with the ball on the blanket and tries to flip it over the net to the other team. As soon as the ball leaves the blanket, one player from the "sending team" crosses under the net and joins the other team. Receiving team tries to catch the ball in the blanket and return it back to the other team. Each time the ball is returned, a player crosses under the net. One "collective" point is awarded to the group each time the ball crosses over the net and is successfully caught.

Suggestions and Variations
1. Try same game with two or three players crossing under the net after each toss.
2. Play same game with different types and sizes of balls.
3. Play same game with two or more balls—all balls must be tossed together.

b

Figure 17.6 Merry-Go-Round

a

b

c

Figure 17.7 Nine-Person Skip

Merry-Go-Round (2–6)

Four players lie on the floor and each player crosses his right foot over the top of the adjacent player's left ankle (fig. 17.6a). Next, four standing players grasp the wrists of the players lying on the floor (fig. 17.6b). On signal, standing players begin to move in a clockwise direction (fig. 17.6c).

Suggestions and Variations
1. Begin clockwise motion with a slow walk, then gradually increase speed.
2. Change run to a gallop or slide.

Nine-Person Skip (4–6)

Three to nine players stand next to a rope. On signal, outside players turn the rope and all players jump rope (fig. 17.7).

Suggestions and Variations
1. Start game with three or four players, then gradually increase the number.
2. Have each jumper enter one by one.
3. Have jumpers hold or bounce a ball.

Eight-Legged Caterpillar (1–6)

This game illustrates how a competitive relay (caterpillar race) can be changed into a cooperative activity. Arrange class into partners. One player stands behind the other, bends forward, and grasps the ankles of his partner. On signal (voice or musical), all partners move in a caterpillarlike fashion. When the teacher calls "fours," two partners join up and keep moving like a caterpillar. Continue to "eight" or "ten," then start over.

Suggestions and Variations
1. Play same game in wicket or crab walk positions.
2. Start with partners of the same sex. When you call 4s, 6s, etc., each new set added must be of the opposite sex.

Figure 17.8   Eight-Legged Caterpillar

Figure 17.9   Aerial Musical Hoops

Modified Musical Chairs (1–6)

This game is played like musical chairs, except no one is eliminated. Start with the whole class and fifteen chairs. When the music stops, players rush to sit down. Now, instead of eliminating the remaining players, they sit on the knees of seated players, placing their own knees together so that the next players can sit down. Start music again, remove one or more chairs, and continue playing until one chair remains. Allow children to use their hands to help balance other players.

Figure 17.10   Floor Musical Hoops

Suggestions and Variations
1. Aerial Musical Hoops. Start with every player in a "hula-hoop" position. Say "go" and everyone runs. When you call "2s," players join up in twos and keep moving. When you call "4s," all join up in fours and continue moving. Continue to eight then start game over (fig. 17.9).
2. Floor Musical Hoops. Similar to variation 1 except everyone places his hoop on the floor. Start music, all run, remove three hoops, and stop music. Everyone runs and stands inside a hoop. Instead of eliminating players, any number of players may stand inside a hoop. Continue playing music and removing hoops. Game gets very exciting and fun when only two or three hoops remain (fig. 17.10).

One-Hole Parachute Golf (2–6)

The game starts with children holding the parachute in the fruit-basket position (page 457). Place two different colored balls on the chute. The object is for the group to drop the ''red'' ball through the hole followed by the ''blue'' ball. As soon as the class has had a few successful games with two balls, add another ''red'' and ''blue'' ball, alternating a different color as each ball drops through the hole. Continue same game progressively adding two more balls as success is attained.

Suggestions and Variations
1. Start with one ball and see if class can move the ball in a clockwise direction around the chute. Reverse directions. Use one hand, kneel, or add other features to the game.
2. Virtually all parachute exercises, games and rhythmic activities are cooperative activities. Modify the rules of these activities to minimize their competition and maximize their cooperative nature.

Pass-A-Person (3–6)

Divide class into two groups. Two groups lie on their backs with heads touching and arms extending upwards. One player starts from one end and is moved to opposite end of line. The next player stands up and repeats action. As each player finishes, she joins the end of the line.

Suggestions and Variations
1. Roll a person. All class members lie side by side facing downwards. One player lies across the backs of players then all players begin to roll towards the opposite end. As each player is rolled ''off,'' he joins the end of the ''rolling line.''

Tug-O-Peace (3–6)

Begin with class standing equal distance apart along the side of a rope. Class members count off in ''twos'' then turn and face each other (fig. 17.12). On signal ''pull,'' 1s pull against 2s—usually with no winner but a lot of fun (fig. 17.12).

Suggestions and Variations
1. Arrange class in the same fashion as the first game except have an extra 1 and 2 player stand next to their own teammates. On signal, extra players tickle the opposing player who is attempting to pull. The end result is shown in figure 17.13.
2. ''Ones'' face ''twos'' and sit as shown in figure 17.14. On signal ''pull,'' each pulls and stands up.

Figure 17.11 Pass-A-Person

Figure 17.12 Tug-O-Peace

Figure 17.13 Tug-O-Peace Variation

Figure 17.14 Tug-O-Peace Variation

Co-Op Tag (1–6)

The following co-op tag games are similar to other tag activities, except a player is safe when involved in a designated type of cooperative behavior.

1. Back-to-Back Tag. One person designated as "it" tries to tag the other players who run to avoid him. A player is safe when in a back-to-back position with another player. Back-to-back players keep moving and then separate after five seconds.
2. Elbow-Linked Tag. Same as variation 1, except players are safe when they link elbows.
3. Hug Tag. Same as variation 1, except players are safe when they are hugging. Set special rules, such as "partners may hug for a maximum of five seconds," "fours for seven seconds," "sixes for eight seconds," and so forth. Let players keep their own count!
4. Ball Balance Tag. Arrange class into partners. Partners hold a ball (utility or nerf) between their heads, sides, backs, or any other specified part of their bodies. Designate one set of partners to be "it." All, including "it" partners, move in the designated contact position.

Other Cooperative Activities

Numerous cooperative activities are included in the gymnastic and dance sections of this book. The following activities include cooperative movements between partners, small groups, or the whole class. Many of these activities can be incorporated into a variety of cooperative games.

Name of Games	Page
Partner Rope Skipping	447
Partner Balance Stunts	406
Leap Frog	397
Wheelbarrow	397
Elephant Walk	398
Chinese Get-Up	400
Bearhug Walk	400
Twister	401
Pig Walk	407
Partner and Group Pyramid	423
Wand Activities	457
Juggling Activities	463
Scooter Activities	244
Rhythmic Activities	493
Creative Folk Dance Activities	537

Table 17.1 Elements of a Cooperative Game

Game Elements				Cooperative Elements
Players	*Space*	*Equipment*	*Skills and Rules*	
From two to all class members	From limited to all available space	From no equipment to many types and pieces of equipment	From no required skills and rules to many skills and specified rules	Includes equality, participation, success, and trust

Creative Cooperative Games

The process used in guiding children to create their own cooperative games is a simple extension of the approach used when teaching creative games. To illustrate, the first four columns of table 17.1 are used to set limitations for children to create their own games. Hence, if we pose a challenge such as, "make up a game with your partner, in your own space, using one ball and two hoops and a dribble," children may or may not create a cooperative game. Their game might become a dribbling contest around the hoops or a cooperative game, such as dribbling and passing as they each dribble around their own hoop. By adding the fifth column, "cooperative elements," we lead children to develop a creative game that possesses one or more of the elements of *equality, participation, success,* and *trust.*

It is extremely important that children first understand the meaning of *cooperation, equality, participation, success,* and *trust* before incorporating these elements into a cooperative game challenge. Discuss these concepts in class or illustrate them by playing several cooperative games described in the previous section. When the children understand these terms, pose a cooperative game challenge that stresses one or two of the cooperative elements listed in the last column. The following eight examples are cooperative games that children from grades two to six created after the challenge described under each game was presented to them. It should be noted that each game usually stressed all the elements of a cooperative game. The important aspect of a challenge is to get children to consciously think about one or two key cooperative elements, then stress them in their game.

Creative Cooperative Games

Name of Game	Number of Players	Age of Children Who Designed Game	Page
Hoopscotch	2	10 and 11	268
Cross the City Bridge	2	11 and 12	268
Copy Cat	2	9 and 10	269
Four-Legged Obstacle	3	11 and 12	269
Blind Chariot Race	3	11 and 12	270
Hula Pass	4	10 and 11	270
Rope Ball	5	10 and 11	270
Piggyback Earthball	Class	7 and 8	271

Example 1: Hoopscotch

Grade Level   Five

Challenge   Make up a game with your partner in your own space and use one or more pieces of small equipment. Your game must stress *equality* and *participation.*

Hoops are arranged and each is given a number as shown in figure 17.15. Players start one behind the other facing hoops 1 and 2. They jump together landing with one foot in each hoop. Players jump again placing both feet in hoop 3. Next, they jump and place their feet in hoop 4 and 6 and their hands in hoop 5. After another jump, they land with one foot in hoop 7 and one in 8. They jump again, both landing in hoop 9. They then return backwards repeating the same foot and hand movements.

Example 2: Cross the City Bridge

Grade   Six

Challenge   Can you design a cooperative game with your partner using any available equipment and apparatus? Your game must stress *equality* and *trust.*

Start from opposite ends of the balance bench, walk to the center, and pass each other while abiding by the following rules:

1. Touch the hoop only with your hands (fig. 17.16).
2. Do not touch the other player with any part of your body.
3. If any part of either player's body touches the floor, both must start again from the ends of the bench.

Figure 17.15   Hoopscotch

Figure 17.16   Cross the City Bridge

Figure 17.17   Copycat

Example 3: Copycat

Grade   Four

Challenge   Can you invent a game with your partner using all available space, two beanbags and two or more locomotor steps? Your game must stress *participation* and *success.*

Players start by facing each other with a beanbag on their heads (fig. 17.17). First, zig-zag with a shuffle movement of feet. Next, jump and make a one-half turn, hook elbows, and walk in a circle. Perform another one-half turn, join hands and jump side to side and release hands. Repeat the routine until a beanbag falls off someone's head.

Example 4: Four-Legged Obstacle

Grade   Six

Challenge   Make up a game with three players, three balls, and any other equipment you can find. Your game must stress *equality, participation,* and *success.*

Three girls stagger four traffic cones approximately twenty feet apart. They tie their inside ankles together and hold each others inside hands or wrists (fig. 17.18). Their task is to stay together while each player moves her ball around each traffic cone and back to the starting position (fig. 17.19).

Figure 17.18 Four-Legged Obstacle

Figure 17.19 Four-Legged Obstacle

Figure 17.20 Blind Chariot Race

Example 5: Blind Chariot Race

Grade Six

Challenge Create a game with three players and stress *trust*. Use any available equipment.

Two blindfolded girls assume a crouched position (fig. 17.20). The other girl loops a rope around the blindfolded players and sits on their backs. The top player uses the rope to guide her "horses" around a series of obstacles. Players rotate positions after completing the series of obstacles.

Example 6: Hula Pass

Grade Four

Challenge See if your group of four can make up a game with four Hula-Hoops, four balls, and a throw and catch. Your game must emphasize *equality*, *participation*, and *success*.

Four players hula-hoop and pass the ball to another player (fig. 17.21). If a player drops the hoop or ball, everyone stops, then starts together.

Example 7: Rope Ball

Grade Four

Challenge Can you make up a game with a long rope, six players, and one ball? Your game must stress *participation* and *trust*.

Two people turn the rope. The remaining four players begin jumping the rope with the front player holding a ball. As everyone jumps the rope, the ball is passed back to the end player, then forward to the first player. If the jumpers stop or the ball is dropped, the game starts over. Players rotate positions after every successful game.

Figure 17.21 Hula Pass

Figure 17.22 Rope Ball

Figure 17.23 Piggyback Earthball

Example 8: Piggyback Earthball

Grade Two

Challenge See if you can make up a game for the whole class using all of the playground and an earthball. Your game must stress *participation* and *trust.*

They get into a piggyback position and try to keep the earthball off the ground. The game has become a favorite and allows the teacher to play.

The process of teaching creative cooperative games as outlined in this chapter should be considered a flexible guideline. This approach is successful when challenges begin with two or three players and involve one or two cooperative elements. Gradually increase the size of the group and add more elements as children demonstrate an understanding and acceptance of these elements of cooperative behavior. Finally, the four elements stressed in the eight example games are important but not all-inclusive. Other elements, such as, *communication, loyalty,* and *sportsmanship* could be added to column five according to the interests and maturity of each class.

18 *Soccer Activities*

Emphasis and Skill Presentation

Teaching Procedures
Developing a Soccer Unit
Structure of a Lesson

Description of Skills
Kicking
Punting
Trapping
Dribbling
Heading
Throw-in
Tackling

Practice Activities
Kicking and Trapping
Dribbling
Heading and Throw-in
Tackling

Lead-up Games

Soccer: Rules and Regulations

Evaluative Techniques
Test 1: Kick and Trap
Test 2: Dribbling
Test 3: Shooting
Test 4: Subjective Evaluation

Of all the major sports played in the United States and Canada, soccer has shown the most rapid increase in participation in recent years. It requires a great deal of skill in kicking, running, and dribbling. However, it is an inexpensive sport—only requiring a ball and two goalposts—and involves total body movement, making it an excellent activity for upper elementary children. Furthermore, only a few basic skills and rules need to be learned to enjoy the game.

This chapter provides sufficient information to develop a major soccer unit. The central purpose is to give the children an opportunity to acquire the basic soccer skills, rules, and playing strategies through as many enjoyable gamelike situations as possible. Modification of practice activities and lead-up games, coupled with the application of the inventive games approach, should be the rule rather than the exception when teaching soccer.

Emphasis and Skill Presentation

Children have usually learned to kick a stationary or moving ball by the end of third grade. Their ability to stop the ball is normally limited to a very basic foot or shin trap. They understand dribbling but are not very proficient at it as they tend to use their toes and to "kick and chase."

As outlined in table 18.1, a systematic presentation of the basic soccer skills and rules should begin in fourth grade. These children should learn to kick and pass with either foot, to trap with the side of the foot, and to increase their control while dribbling. A few of the basic rules relating to kicking, handling the ball, and checking should also be introduced in this grade. Lead-up games such as circle soccer and soccer dodgeball should be emphasized, rather than playing the official game or a modified version.

Throughout fifth grade improved passing, trapping, and dribbling skills should be emphasized. After these basic skills are acquired, the children should be introduced to a few of the more specialized kicking skills, the side-of-leg trap, and heading the ball. More advanced lead-up games such as forwards and backs and seven-man soccer with more specific rules and playing positions are also indicated.

Previously learned skills should be refined and a few of the more advanced skills and rules of the official game should be learned in sixth grade. Although sixth graders should play seven- and eleven-person soccer, their skill level still calls for a lot of individual and small group practice and lead-up activities. Therefore, balancing the time spent on these two types of activities with the regulation soccer game is very important. Seven-man soccer, which uses half the field, is also more desirable for the intramural program than the official eleven-person game because it allows more children to participate.

Teaching Procedures

The general instructional procedures discussed in previous chapters also apply to teaching soccer activities. Of particular importance are the development of a unit of instruction discussed on pages 125–27 and the illustrated lessons on pages 128–30. In addition, the inventive games approach (p. 217) can be applied successfully when teaching soccer and all other team game activities.

Developing a Soccer Unit

Since each teaching situation varies according to the length of the unit and lesson and the available facilities and equipment, the following approach should be considered as only a basic guideline. Soccer is a relatively new sport to many teachers and children, so this outline should be modified to meet each situation.

Step One: Determine the length of the unit. Since a class may have from one to five physical education lessons a week, the units should be expressed in terms of the number of lessons.

Step Two: Assess the class's level of ability. The evaluative techniques at the end of this chapter can be used. Having the class play one or two lead-up games also provides an overview of its ability.

Step Three: List sequentially the skills, rules, and playing strategies that will be emphasized (p. 274).

Step Four: Choose the appropriate practice activities and lead-up games. The practice activities (p. 283), listed by skill, are organized into individual, partner, and group activities. The lead-up games (p. 288) are arranged in order of difficulty.

Structure of a Lesson

The following approach is a basic guideline for planning and teaching a lesson. Each lesson should include a vigorous introductory activity that has some relationship to the general theme of the lesson. The second part of the lesson should be devoted to acquiring and practicing one or more skills. And finally, the third part should stress a group activity that applies the skills and knowledge learned.

INTRODUCTORY ACTIVITIES	SKILL DEVELOPMENT	GROUP ACTIVITIES
Vigorous running, dodging, and conditioning exercises	Demonstrations Individual practice Partner and practice activities Exploratory activities	Lead-up games Inventive games Modified or official game of soccer

Table 18.1 Suggested Sequence of Presenting Soccer Skills and Rules

Skills and Rules	Grade Level			
	Grade 3	Grade 4	Grade 5	Grade 6
Kicking				
Instep Kick	Acquired or introduce	Pass with either foot	Increase distance and accuracy	Increase distance and accuracy
Inside-of-Foot Kick	Introduce	Pass with either foot	Increase distance and accuracy	Increase distance and accuracy
Outside-of-Foot Kick		Introduce	Increase distance and accuracy	Increase distance and accuracy
Punting			Introduce	Increase distance and accuracy
Volley Kick				Introduce
Rules: Kickoff		Introduce		
Free Kick			Introduce	
Corner Kick		Introduce		
Goal Kick		Introduce		
Penalty Kick			Introduce	
Trapping				
Foot Trap	Acquired or introduce	Refinement	Refinement	Refinement
Side-of-Foot Trap		Introduce	Refinement	Refinement
Shin Trap	Acquired or introduce	Refinement	Refinement	Refinement
Leg Trap			Introduce	Refinement
Body Trap				Introduce
Rules: Handling the Ball		Introduce		
Dribbling				
Inside of Feet	Acquired or introduce	Increase accuracy and speed	Increase accuracy and speed	Increase accuracy and speed
Outside of Feet		Introduce	Increase accuracy and speed	Increase accuracy and speed
Heading				
Stationary Heading			Introduce	Refinement
With Feet Off Ground				Introduce
Throw-in				
From Behind Head		Introduce	Increase distance and accuracy	Increase distance and accuracy
Rules: Throw-in		Introduce		
Tackling				
With Feet and Shoulders		Introduce	Refinement	Refinement
Rules: Charging		Introduce		
Other Rules				
Team Positions		Introduce		
Goalkeeper Privileges			Introduce	
Rules: Offside			Introduce	

Each soccer lesson should begin with running, dodging, and general conditioning activities to increase the children's cardiorespiratory endurance and to prepare them for the next part of the lesson.

During the first few lessons, the second part should be given a considerable amount of time in order to introduce and practice skills and playing strategies. After a skill is explained and demonstrated, each child should have an opportunity to practice it without excessive pressure and to test and explore other ways of performing a movement pattern. Once the children understand the skill and can perform it, they should practice with partners. Since most classes are coeducational, partner activities are an excellent way to cope with varying levels of ability and to mix boys and girls subtly.

Partner activities also provide a springboard for introducing inventive games. For example, in lessons emphasizing passing and trapping, partners can be challenged to "make up a game with your partner that involves a pass and a trap . . . and a hoop" (or any other piece of small equipment). Refer to chapter 26 for more ideas. The more structured practice activities that are used in this part of the lesson can be presented initially in a more formal or direct manner. After the class has practiced the activity, the teacher can introduce variations by presenting simple challenges to each group. For example, if the class is practicing the game Keep Away, a challenge such as "See if you can play the same game but add a hoop" (or three beanbags) gives each group a chance to create a new version of the game.

During the third part of the lesson, lead-up games provide a low-key means of practicing skills in a game-like situation. Playing space should be used to maximum capacity. Divide the playing field into halves or quarters so that two or four games can be played. The inventive games approach also works extremely well with lead-up games. Limit these games in some small way at first; later, challenge each group to design its own game or to choose any equipment it wants. This will open the door to many new and exciting soccer-type games.

As the soccer unit progresses, more time should be devoted to the third part of the lesson and less to the second part. Group activities should include a wide variety of lead-up games, inventive games, and, to a lesser degree, modified or official soccer. The more competitive aspects of soccer and other team games should be reserved for the junior and senior high school physical education program.

The following suggestions can also help in developing a safe and effective program of activities.

1. Limit the playing field to a small, manageable instructional area. Mark off a 100-foot-square section of the field with traffic cones or milk cartons (p. 216) for demonstrations and practice activities. Enlarge the area as needed.

2. Soccer requires a great deal of endurance, particularly of the heart and lungs and the leg muscles. Increase running and other endurance activities gradually and systematically. Watch for overfatigued children and switch them to less demanding positions.

3. Although soccer rules do not allow any players except the goalie to use their hands, adjustments should be made for the children's safety. They should be taught to protect their faces against oncoming balls, and, in addition, girls should be instructed to fold their arms across their chests to prevent injury.

4. One of the cardinal principles of good teaching is total participation by all children. Whenever possible, keep each team small and divide up the playing area so two or more games can be played.

Description of Skills

Soccer is basically a kicking and running game; however, when played correctly, skills such as dribbling, trapping, heading, and throwing are also necessary for maximum success and enjoyment. Each of these skills is described along with the more common faults to observe and correct.

Kicking

In soccer, the ball may be kicked with either foot from a stationary, running, or volley (while in the air) position. Certain fundamentals should be stressed in every practice and game situation. First, the player should keep his eye on the ball as it approaches him or as he approaches the ball. Second, the player should kick the ball with his instep (top side of the foot)—never with his toes. Finally, after the ball has been kicked, the player should follow through with his kicking foot for a short distance in the direction of the kick. Each of these fundamentals applies to the following five basic kicking skills.

Figure 18.1 Instep Kick

a   b   c

Instep Kick

The instep kick (fig. 18.1), used for passing and for shooting at the goal, is the most common skill in soccer. Just before the ball is kicked, the nonkicking foot is slightly flexed and even with the ball. The head and trunk lean slightly forward with the arms extended sideways, and the kicking leg is well back with the knee slightly bent (fig. 18.1a). As the kicking leg moves downward and forward, the knee moves forward and over the ball. The ankle extends downward to allow the top of the instep to contact the ball (fig. 18.1b). Follow through by continuing the forward movement of the kicking leg (fig. 18.1c).

Common Faults

1. Contacting the ball too high above its center; the ball will not rise or gain much speed
2. Contacting the ball too far below its center; the ball will rise too high
3. Failing to follow-through

Inside-of-Foot Kick

This (fig. 18.2) is a variation of the instep kick and is used for short, accurate passes or for shooting at the goal. The body is bent slightly forward, with the weight evenly distributed on both feet. The front of the ball should be even with the toes about six inches to the side of the kicking foot. Shift weight to the nonkicking foot and swing the kicking foot outward, with knee slightly bent (fig. 18.2a). Swing the foot down and toward the ball, contacting it with the inside of the foot (fig. 18.2b). Follow through with the kicking foot crossing in front of the opposite leg (fig. 18.2c).

Common Faults

1. Failing to turn the kicking foot outward
2. Kicking with the toes
3. Contacting the ball too low
4. Failing to follow through after contacting the ball

Outside-of-Foot Kick

This kick requires a pushing or jabbing action with the outer part of the foot. It is used for short passes or dribbling without breaking the running movement. The player stands slightly to the side of the ball. Bend the nonkicking leg and shift weight onto it (fig.18.3a). Bend knee of kicking leg with toe pointing down, then swing leg towards the ball (fig. 18.3b). Contact the ball with the outer edge of the foot and follow through in the direction of the kick (fig. 18.3c).

Common Faults

1. Too much backward lean prior to kicking the ball
2. Contacting the ball too soon or too late
3. Failing to follow through

Volley Kick

The volley is performed when the ball is in flight. This is a difficult kick, so elementary school children should not be expected to do it with a high degree of accuracy. However, because this kick is a time-saver and because it generates much force, children will attempt to perform it. The player stands with his nonkicking foot in front and his weight evenly distributed on both feet. His head and body face the ball and his body tilts forward slightly (fig. 18.4a). As the ball approaches, the

Figure 18.2 Kicking with Inside of Foot

a   b   c

Figure 18.3 Kicking with Outside of Foot

a   b   c

Figure 18.4 Volley Kick

a   b   c

Figure 18.5 Punting

a. Hold ball chest high   b. Swing kicking leg forward   c. Contact ball with top of foot   d. Follow through to an extended leg position

player shifts his weight to his nonkicking foot and raises his kicking leg, with the knee slightly bent and the toes pointing down (fig. 18.4b). He contacts the ball with the top of the instep and follows through in a forward and upward direction (fig. 18.4c).

Common Faults
1. Contacting the ball too late
2. Failing to follow through

Punting

The goalkeeper is the only player allowed to punt. The ball is held about chest high (fig. 18.5a). The kicking leg swings forward and upward as the ball is dropped (fig. 18.5b). As the leg moves in a forward and upward direction the ball contacts the instep (fig. 18.5c). Follow through into an extended leg position (fig. 18.5d).

Common Faults
1. Throwing the ball downward rather than dropping it
2. Contacting the ball too late, causing a high upward lift

Trapping

Trapping is stopping the ball while it is moving through the air or on the ground. Any part of the body except the hands and arms may be used. The type of trap a player uses depends upon the flight of the ball, the position of opponents, and the amount of time the trapper has. Upper elementary school children should be able to perform the following five trapping skills.

Front Foot Trap

The front foot trap is used to trap a rolling or bouncing ball. As the ball approaches, the player raises her foot about six inches off the ground with her toes up forming a **V** between the ground and the sole of the foot (fig. 18.6a). When the ball contacts the sole, the foot relaxes to let the ball lose its recoil action and remain beneath the foot (fig. 18.6b).

Side-of-Foot Trap

The side-of-foot trap is used in the same manner as the front foot trap; the main difference is the direction from which the ball approaches. The player raises her trapping leg four to five inches off the ground, with the inside of the foot toward the ball. As the ball strikes, the foot relaxes to absorb the force of the ball, allowing it to drop rather than to recoil forward (fig. 18.7).

Shin Trap

The shin trap is one of the easiest trapping skills and is used in much the same way as the foot trap. As the ball rolls toward the player, she flexes both knees, bends her trunk forward slightly, and extends her arms to the side. At the moment of contact, her legs extend slightly and her weight shifts to her nonkicking foot in preparation for the next move (fig. 18.8).

Figure 18.6 Front Foot Trap

a

b

Figure 18.7 Side-of-Foot Trap. The foot gives slightly.

Figure 18.8 Shin Trap. Legs extend slightly at contact.

Figure 18.9 Leg Trap. The leg gives slightly when the ball makes contact.

Leg Trap

The leg trap is used when the ball is approaching from a high volley or a low bounce. As the ball approaches, the player shifts her weight to the foot nearest the oncoming ball. Her trapping leg bends at almost a right angle and her foot is well off the ground. When the ball makes contact, the leg gives a little to prevent the ball from rebounding too far forward (fig. 18.9).

Figure 18.10 Body Trap. Arm position creates a hollow chest or pocket.

Figure 18.11 Chest Protected Body Trap.

Body Trap

The body trap is used when the ball is descending from a high volley or when a player wants to prevent a high-rising ball from getting past him. To perform this type of trap, the player brings extended arms forward but does not touch the ball with his hands or arms. The arm position helps to create a "hollow" chest or pocket for the ball (fig. 18.10). However, the player's chest is held in a normal position up to the moment the ball makes contact. Upon contact, the player relaxes his chest muscles, which creates a pocket for stopping the ball and thus drop directly below. Girls should fold their arms across their chests and press elbows snugly against the body when attempting this trapping skill (fig. 18.11).

Common Faults
1. Failing to keep the eyes on the oncoming ball
2. Failing to move into position to trap the oncoming ball
3. Failing to give as the ball makes contact with the body

Dribbling

Dribbling in soccer is moving the ball with short pushes by the inside or outside of either foot. These pushes permit the player to control the ball whether she is dribbling forward or sideward. While dribbling with the inside of the foot is quite easy, good ball control requires use of the outside of either foot. Dribbling backwards is bad practice as it only helps the opponent.

The body should be bent forward slightly, with the head over the ball. Gently push or "persuade" the ball, keeping the head up high enough to make an offensive move and to watch oncoming opponents (fig. 18.12).

Common Faults
1. Holding the body too erect or leaning too far back while dribbling
2. Kicking rather than pushing the ball
3. Using the toes rather than the instep or the outside of the feet
4. Keeping the head down and not watching opponents while dribbling

Heading

Heading is actually hitting or bunting the soccer ball with the front or side of the forehead. The player drops her head back as the ball approaches, raises her arms, and shifts her weight to her back foot (fig. 18.14a). She then shifts her body weight forward and upward and brings her head forward to meet the ball (fig. 18.14b). The ball must be contacted with the front or side of the forehead with a continuous forward movement of the body in the direction of the intended flight of the ball (fig. 18.14c). The key to good heading lies in correctly judging the speed and the height of the oncoming ball.

Figure 18.12 Dribbling. Push or "persuade" the ball.

a
b
c

Figure 18.13 Heading

Common Faults
1. Closing the eyes before the ball contacts the head
2. Failing to drop the head back in preparation for the forward thrust of the head and neck
3. Contacting the ball on the top of the head
4. Trying to hit the ball solely by moving the head, rather than using the whole body with the head as the point of contact

Figure 18.14 Heading

a. Head drops back in preparation.   b. Contact with forehead.

c. Continuous forward movement.

Figure 18.15   Throw-in

a. One foot in front of the other.

b. Ball starts from behind head.

c. Release and drag back foot.

Throw-in

Whenever the ball goes over the sidelines, it is put back into play by a throw-in. The ball is thrown from behind the head with both hands. Part of both feet remain on the ground until the ball leaves the player's hands, although any position of the feet is permissible. Begin with one foot in front of the other or with the feet parallel (fig. 18.15a). Bring the ball back to the top of the shoulders and arch the back (18.15b). Shift the body weight forward and upward and bring the ball over the head, extending the arms toward the direction of the throw. Release the ball and follow through with hands and arms (fig. 18.15c).

Common Faults
1. Failing to bring the ball back far enough
2. Throwing the ball with one hand like a baseball pass
3. Taking both feet off the ground before the ball is released

Tackling

In soccer, players of the team in possession of the ball are known as the *offensive,* or *attacking,* team. Any defensive player may legally tackle a player who has possession of the ball, but only from the front or side with the feet or shoulders. Using the hands or tackling from behind is clearly against the rules. When tackling, the defensive player watches the ball and her opponent's feet for clues to the direction she may take (fig. 18.16a). The body weight should also be evenly distributed on both feet in order to shift right or left. The tackle should be made when the opponent is slightly off balance, which is just before she begins to dribble or pass the ball (fig. 18.16b).

Important points to remember in tackling an opponent are—

1. Be quick and decisive when approaching an opponent who has possession of the ball.
2. Tackle the opponent when she is in control of the ball but is slightly off balance, usually when she pushes the ball forward a little.
3. Be ready to pass the ball as soon as you gain possession.

Figure 18.16   Tackling

a. Watch feet for clues.

b. Tackle when opponent is off balance.

Practice Activities

The following practice activities are organized by skill. Where possible, the activities progress from individual movements, to partner activities, and then to group drills.

Kicking and Trapping

The majority of practice activities relating to kicking and trapping skills involves two or more players. However, the few individual activities that follow give each child opportunities to get used to the bounce of the ball and control the ball with his feet. Partner and small group activities provide more realistic ball-handling situations including one or more skills.

Individual Activities

Throw, Bounce, and Trap

Each child has a ball (any inflated ball can be used) and finds his own space in the playing area. Have the child throw his ball into the air, allow it to bounce once, and then try to trap it with one foot. Add other limitations, such as trapping with the left foot, the side of the leg, or the shins.

Wall Kicking

Arrange children in a line formation along available wall surface. Each player stands about six feet from the wall, kicks the ball to the wall, and retrieves his own rebound with a foot or shin trap.

Variations
1. Allow each child to kick the ball as it rebounds (no trap required).
2. Start several yards back from the ball, run up and kick it, and trap the rebound.
3. Start several yards back, dribble to a line, kick the ball to the wall, and trap the rebound.
4. Place a target on the wall (a circle or square) and repeat previous activities.
5. Repeat previous activities with the opposite foot.

Partner Activities

Passing and Trapping

Partners sharing one ball find a space in the playing area. They stand about ten to fifteen feet apart. One player passes to the other, who traps the ball and returns the pass.

Variations
1. Change the type of pass and trap.
2. Repeat above with one player stationary and the receiving player on the move.
3. Repeat above with both players on the move.
4. One player tries to kick the ball through the outstretched legs of his partner.

Wall Passing and Trapping

This drill is essentially the same as wall kicking listed under individual activities. One player kicks the ball to the wall and his partner traps it and returns the kick. All other variations can be adapted to partner activities.

Target Shooting

Partners share one ball and two traffic cones (or milk cartons). Arrange partners and equipment as shown. One partner kicks the ball through the goals (cones) and the other partner traps the ball and repeats the kicking skill.

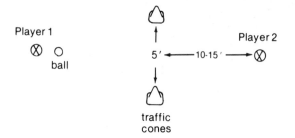

Player 1
⊗ ○
ball

5' ←—10-15'—→ ⊗ Player 2

traffic
cones

Variations
1. Change the type of kicking and trapping skills.
2. Change the angle of shooting.
3. Change the distance between goals.
4. Change the distance from the goals.

Circle Passing

One player runs around a stationary partner. Stationary partner passes and traps the ball while circling player dribbles and passes.

Variations
1. Change the type of pass and trap.
2. Reverse directions.
3. Repeat activity without involving a trap.

Teaching Suggestions

This is an opportune time to introduce the problem-solving method. For example, after practicing several variations of the previous activity, pose a question such as ''Can you change the position of your traffic cones and make up a drill that involves an inside-of-foot pass and a shin trap?'' If children have experienced the inventive games approach, a challenge such as ''Using two cones and a ball, create your own passing and trapping drill'' will produce a wide variety of responses.

Group Activities

Several simple games and relay activities described in previous chapters may be adapted for practicing soccer skills. They include keep away (p. 233) and crab soccer (p. 234).

Zigzag Kicking

Divide the class into squads of four players. Arrange the squads in two lines about fifteen feet apart, with partners facing. Player A kicks the ball to B. Player B uses his hands or feet, depending on the level of trapping skill, to stop the ball and then places the ball on the ground and kicks it to C. Continue pattern to D and back to A.

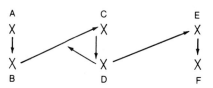

Variations
1. Player A rolls the ball to B, who kicks it to C, who kicks it to D, who kicks it to A. Continue pattern.
2. Player A bounces the ball to B, who kicks it to C who stops the ball, picks it up, and bounces it to D. Continue pattern.
3. Repeat number 2 with the opposite foot.

Circle Kicking

Divide the class into three squads of five to six players. Arrange each squad in a large circle with at least fifteen feet between players. Player A turns, faces B, and kicks the ball to him. Player B traps the ball (or stops it with his hands), turns, and kicks the ball to C. Continue pattern until A receives the ball.

Variations
1. All children remain facing the center of the circle. Player A kicks to B with the inside of the left foot. Player B traps the ball with his right foot, then kicks it to C with his left foot.
2. Repeat variation 1 in the opposite direction, trapping with the left foot and kicking with the right.
3. Place one child in the center. Center player kicks to A who traps the ball and kicks it back to the center player, who traps it and kicks to B. Continue pattern.

Give and Go

Divide class into groups of three. Player A is in the goal (use traffic cones or milk cartons). Player B has the ball and stands about forty feet from the goal. Player C stands about twenty feet from the goal.

Player B passes to C, then runs forward. Player C traps the ball, then passes it to oncoming B, who attempts to shoot the ball through the goal. Rotate players after three or four kicks.

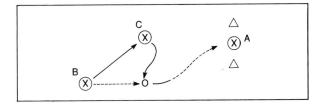

Variations

1. Change positions of B and C.
2. Add a defensive player to check C.

Kicking for Distance

Divide the class into squads of four or five players. One squad lines up to kick, while the other scatters in the field to retrieve the ball. The field can be marked with lines every five yards or the retrievers can simply mark the kick. Each child on the kicking squad kicks the ball three or four times, depending upon the number of balls available. Mark where the ball lands, not where it rolls. After each player on the kicking squad has had a turn, change squad positions.

Variations

The kicking squad may vary the type of kick—a stationary kick, a punt, or a kick while the ball is rolling forward.

Goal Kicking

Divide the class into squads of four to six players and arrange them in semicircles on each side of the goalposts (traffic cones or milk cartons). Player on team A kicks the ball through the goal, and any player on the opposite team traps the ball and returns the kick. If the ball goes through the retrieving team, allow the player who was closest to the ball as it passed by to retrieve it.

Variations

1. Vary the type of kick—a stationary kick, kicking a moving ball, using the inside and outside of the instep. (Move closer to the goal when practicing this type of kick.)
2. Place a player in the center of the goalpost to practice goaltending (guarding the goal).
3. Practice volley kicking. Players on team A must throw the ball over the goalposts. Any player on team B may attempt to kick the ball through the goalposts before it lands.

Dribbling

The procedure used to teach passing and trapping can be followed when teaching dribbling skills. Begin with individual activities, add small equipment, then move on to partner activities, and finally to group activities.

Figure 18.17 Dribble and Stop

Individual Activities

Individual Dribbling

Each child has a ball (any inflated ball) and finds his own space in the playing area. Allow children to dribble anywhere within the playing area so long as they do not bump into other players.

Variations

1. Dribble and stop on whistle or voice command (fig. 18.17).
2. Dribble in different directions on voice command (right, forward, left, right).
3. Dribble with the outside of the foot.
4. Give each player two or more pieces of small equipment (beanbags, hoops) and have him dribble around them.
5. Add other skills, such as dribbling, stopping, trapping, and then shooting at the wall.

Figure 18.18 Follow the Leader

Partner Activities

Follow the Leader

This is an excellent activity to teach ball control and keeping an eye on another player. Each player has a ball. One partner dribbles in any direction and her partner follows.

Variations
1. Partners dribble side by side.
2. Add one or more obstacles to dribble around.

Dribble and Pass

Partners dribble and pass a ball back and forth.

Variations
1. Add two or more obstacles to dribble around.
2. Repeat earlier drills with outside of feet.
3. Add other skills such as dribble, pass, and trap.

Group Activities

Shuttle Dribbling

Divide the class into squads of four to six players. Half of each team stands behind one line and the other half stands behind a second line thirty feet away. Player A dribbles the ball to the second line and stops it in front of B. Player B repeats to C, while A moves to the back of B's line. Continue pattern.

Variations
1. Player A must go around B's team, then back to B.
2. Dribble to a centerline, stop the ball, and then pass to the next player.
3. Place obstacles between lines and have players dribble around each obstacle.

Heading and Throw-in

Heading and throw-in skills are normally practiced together in partner or group activities. However, if a wall is available, individual activities can be practiced.

Individual Activities

Throw and Head

Each player has a ball and stands about five or six feet from the wall. Practice the throw-in, then do a throw-in and head the rebound back to the wall. Repeat the throw-in, then turn sideways and attempt to head the ball back to the wall.

Partner Activities

Throw and Head

Partners stand about eight to twelve feet apart facing each other. One partner, using a throw-in pass, throws the ball high into the air so that it descends just in front of his partner. That partner attempts to head the ball forward and downward toward the first partner's feet. Repeat several times, then change positions.

Variations
1. Tie a rope between two posts; the height may vary from four to six feet. Repeat the original activity, but with the throw-in going over the rope and the headed ball returning under the rope.
2. Place a hoop on the floor between the players. Repeat the original drill, requiring the headed ball to hit the center of the hoop.

Group Activities

Around the Square

Divide the class into squads of four players. Arrange the squads into squares with ten feet between players. Letter each player A, B, C, and D around the square. Player A, using a regulation throw-in, throws the ball to B, who attempts to head the ball to C. Player C catches it and throws to D, who heads it to A. Continue pattern.

Variations

Player A throws to B, who heads it to C. Player C attempts to head the ball to D, who heads it to A. Continue pattern.

Figure 18.19 Throw and Head with Partners

Goal Heading

Divide the class into as many squads as you have goals. (Wire backstops or any substitute goal area will work for this drill.) Arrange squads in a line ten feet in front of and parallel to the goal. Player A in each squad moves fifteen feet in front of his team beyond the goal, turns, and faces the second player in the line. Player A throws to B, who attempts to head the ball through the goal. Player B chases his own ball, throws it to A, and then returns to the end of the line.

Variations

Make two lines facing the goal, with A standing on the goal line and the front players of the two lines standing ten feet away. A throws the ball up between the first two players. Both attempt to head the ball back to A.

Tackling

Tackling is normally practiced in combination with another skill, and two or more players are involved.

Partner Activities

Partner Keep Away

One player is given a ball and tries to keep it by dribbling, dodging, stopping, and pivoting away from his partner. As soon as the defensive partner touches the ball, players exchange positions and repeat the drill.

Variations

Partners stand about twenty feet apart facing each other. On signal, each approaches the other. The player with the ball tries to dribble past his opponent, while the defensive player attempts to gain possession of the ball.

Group Activities

Shuttle Dribble and Tackle

This is a basic shuttle relay formation, with the following modifications. Player 1 dribbles the ball toward the other line while player 2 moves out to tackle player 1. Player 1 tries to reach the opposite line without being tackled, and player 2 attempts to touch the ball. Allow about twenty seconds of play, then blow the whistle and start the next two players.

```
3    1                           2    4
X    X  ◄─────── 30' ───────►    X    X
```

One Versus Two Players

Two players attempt to keep the ball away from the third player. If player 3 touches the ball, the opposing player who last touched it changes position with him.

Variations

1. Add a goal behind the defensive player and require the two offensive players to move in and attempt to score.
2. Repeat the previous activities and change the combination to one of the following:
   a. One defensive player versus three offensive players
   b. Two defensive players versus two offensive players
   c. Two defensive players versus three offensive players

Lead-up Games

The lead-up games described in this section are arranged according to level of difficulty. Slight modifications can make any of them suitable for any upper elementary school grade, however.

Several games described in other chapters can be adapted to a soccer-type activity. See California kickball (p. 237) and keep away (p. 233).

Circle Soccer (4)

Formation   A large circle, with two feet between each player, divided into two semicircles, thus creating two teams.

Equipment   One soccer ball

Players   Four to five on each team

Skills   Kicking and trapping

The captain of one team begins play by kicking the ball toward the opponents. The players on each team attempt to kick the ball past the opposing players, below their waists. They also must try to prevent the ball from going out of the circle on their own side. Every player remains at his place in the circle while the ball is in play. One point is awarded each time the ball is kicked out of the circle.

Variations
1. Introduce a second ball to the game.
2. Restrict kicking to the right foot, then to the left foot.
3. Expand the size of the circle.

Soccer Dodge Ball (4–5)

Formation   A large circle formed by half the players, with the other half scattered inside.

Equipment   One soccer ball

Players   Half of the class on each team

Skills   Kicking and trapping

The circle players attempt to hit the players inside by kicking the ball at them. Inside players cannot use their hands to stop the ball, except for a pass that may strike the face. When a player is hit below the waist, he joins the circle. The winners are the last three players remaining inside the circle.

Variations
1. Introduce a second ball to the game.
2. Add a new rule, such as every player must be constantly moving, or inside players must hop while circle players use only a side-of-foot kick.
3. Ask each team to make up a new rule for the opposing side.

Boundary Ball (4–5)

Formation   Playing area divided by a centerline, with players scattered on their own side of the centerline

Equipment   Two soccer balls

Players   Ten to fifteen players on each team

Skills   Kicking and trapping

Each team has a ball, which it kicks toward the opponent's goal line. Players may move about freely in their own half of the field to prevent the opponent's ball from crossing the goal. However, they cannot touch the ball with their hands. One point is scored each time a ball crosses a goal line.

Variations
1. Restrict players to one type of kick and one type of trapping skill.
2. Give each team an additional ball.
3. Ask children to suggest a new rule.

Circle Soccer Tag (4–5)

Formation   Large circle with approximately two feet between players and one child in the center

Equipment   One soccer ball

Players   Ten or fewer

Skills   Kicking, passing, trapping, and heading

Circle players try to keep the center player ("it") from touching the ball (keep away). If the ball goes outside the circle, the person who missed the ball becomes "it." If "it" touches the ball, he is replaced by the last person to kick the ball. A player who misses the ball must retrieve it, return to his position, and proceed to pass the ball. Stress accurate passing and trapping.

Variations

1. Add a second "it."
2. Restrict players to one type of pass or trap.
3. Substitute a throw-in skill for a pass.

Sideline Soccer (4–5)

Formation Playing area and teams arranged as in diagram

Equipment Soccer ball, four markers, and four goalposts (traffic cones or milk cartons)

Players Ten to fifteen on each team

Skills Passing, trapping, heading, and tackling

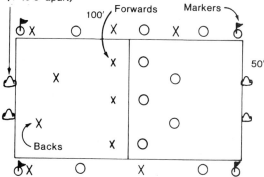

Five players from each team line up inside the playing area as shown. The remaining players line up outside the court. A kickoff by the center player starts the game and restarts it after each point is scored. Once the game is started, inside players move anywhere within the court. Sideline players stay behind the line but may shift sideward to the next player. Sideline players can trap and pass to court players, but only court players may score. If a ball goes over the side lines or end lines, the ball is given to the nearest sideline opponent of the team last touching the ball. The same procedure is followed for any other violation, such as touching the ball with hands or sideline players entering the court area. One point is awarded for each goal. Rotate sideline and field players every two minutes.

Variations

1. Allow only forwards to cross over the centerline.
2. Add a second ball.
3. Limit sideline players to trapping the ball, then using a throw-in to return ball into court area.
4. Sideline players receive the ball on every third pass.

Pin Soccer (5–6)

Formation Playing area and teams arranged as in diagram

Equipment Five or six Indian clubs (or milk cartons), two soccer balls

Players Six to eight on each team

Skills Kicking and trapping

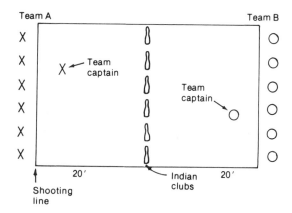

A captain is chosen for each team. He remains in his own half of the playing area. One ball is given to a player on each team, who kicks the ball from behind the shooting line and tries to knock over one or more Indian clubs. One point is awarded for every Indian club knocked over. The team captain retrieves all balls and resets any clubs knocked over by his teammates.

Variations

1. Increase the number of balls.
2. After a player has scored, make him the team captain.
3. Increase the distance between end lines as skill increases.
4. Vary the type of kick and trap.

Forwards and Backs (5–6)

Formation Playing area and teams arranged as in diagram

Equipment One ball

Players Ten to twelve on each team

Skills Passing, dribbling, and trapping

The center forward of team A starts the game with a kickoff. Team A forwards try to kick the ball over the opponent's goal line. Players on team B try to gain possession of the ball and kick it over their opponent's goal line. Forwards may not cross back over their own center zone line, and backs may not cross the center zone line. Only forwards can score a goal. Each goal counts one point. If the ball goes over the end line or side line, it is thrown in by the nearest player on the opposite team.

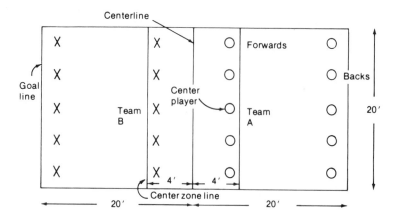

Variations

1. Change forwards and backs every few minutes.
2. Add sideline players with rules similar to Sideline Soccer.
3. Vary the type of kick and trap.

Alley Soccer (5–6)

Formation   Playing area and teams arranged as in diagram

Equipment   Soccer ball

Players   Ten to twelve on each team

Skills   Passing, trapping, kicking

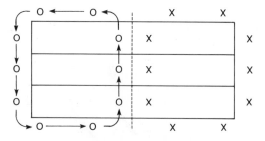

Each team has three forwards who may move anywhere within their own alley. All remaining players on each team remain on the side line and goal line of their own half of the field. No player may touch the ball with his hands. The player in the middle alley starts the game by passing the ball to another forward player. Forwards pass the ball back and forth to other forwards or to sideline players as they attempt to move it forward and kick it over the opponent's goal line below the waist of the opposing players. One point is awarded for each goal. If the ball goes over the side line, it is thrown in by the nearest player on the team that did not allow it to go over the line. Only forwards may score a goal. Rotate players after a set time and according to the rotation pattern shown in the diagram.

Variations

1. Add one free forward who may roam anywhere.
2. Limit skills to one type of pass and one type of trap.
3. Allow sideline players to score a goal.

Punt Back (5–6)

Formation   Players on each team scattered on their own half of the field

Equipment   One soccer ball

Players   Four to twenty

Skills   Trapping and kicking

A captain is chosen for each team. The ball is placed in the middle of the field and the captain of the kicking team kicks the ball to start the game. Once the game has started, opposing teams stay at least fifteen feet apart. Any member of the receiving team may trap the ball. The player who traps the ball kicks it toward the opponent's goal. If a player kicks the ball over the opponent's goal, his team receives one point. The team that did not score starts the ball from the center of the field. Any player who contacts another player who is attempting to kick the ball commits a foul. A free kick is then awarded to the other team.

Variations

1. Add two or more balls.
2. Limit kicks to either an instep, side-of-foot or punt kick.
3. Ask each team to suggest a new rule.

Seven-Man Soccer (5–6)

Formation   Playing area and teams arranged as in diagram

Equipment   Soccer ball and colored arm bands or pinnies to identify teams

Players   Seven on each team

Skills   All soccer skills, as this is essentially a miniature version of soccer

See the official rules of soccer in the following section. Since there are seven players on each team, this is an ideal game to accommodate an average-sized physical education class. The playing field is normally divided in half to allow two games to be played at the same time. Modify any rule to cope with local conditions.

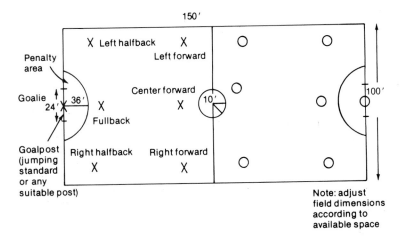

150'

X Left halfback X
Left forward

Penalty
area

Center forward

Goalie
36'
X 24' X

Fullback

Goalpost
(jumping
standard
or any
suitable post)

Right halfback Right forward
X X

100'

10'

Note: adjust
field dimensions
according to
available space

Variations

Young players tend to "follow the ball" rather than
play their positions. Too often the fullback and
halfbacks are "caught" too far in front of their
forwards. To prevent this, play seven-man soccer but
after the kickoff require—

1. forwards to remain in their opponent's half of the
   field; and
2. backs to remain in their own half of the playing
   field.

Soccer: Rules and Regulations

By the time children reach fifth grade they should have
learned the majority of skills necessary to play soccer.
This does not imply, however, that time should not be
devoted to practice activities and lead-up games. With
some basic modifications, the game of soccer should be
played in its entirety periodically during an instructional unit. This will help children understand that
practice sessions and lead-up activities are designed to
improve the speed and accuracy of the required skills.

I. Field of play:
   Length of field—not more than 120 yards and
   not less than 110 yards
   Width of field—not more than 75 yards and
   not less than 65 yards
II. Names of players and line-up positions
   (positions of players at the start of the game,
   after a goal is scored, and after halftime):
   A. Left wing (outside left)
   B. Inside left
   C. Center forward
   D. Inside right
   E. Right wing (outside right)
   F. Left halfback
   G. Center halfback
   H. Right halfback
   I. Left fullback
   J. Right fullback
   K. Goalie

III. Penalty kick: If a defensive player other than
   the goalie touches the ball in the eighteen-by-
   forty-four-yard penalty area, a penalty kick is
   awarded to the offensive team. This kick is
   made from the twelve-yard penalty mark by
   any member of the offensive team. The goalie
   stands on the line between the goalposts, and
   all other players stand outside the penalty area
   until the ball is kicked. After the ball is
   kicked, any player from either team may enter
   the penalty area.
IV. Free kicks: The direct free kick and the
   indirect free kick.
   A. Direct free kick: This is a kick from which
      a goal may be scored directly. In other
      words, the ball can be kicked from where
      an infraction occurred and travel directly
      through the goal. This kick is awarded to a
      team when any opposing player commits
      any of the following infractions outside the
      penalty area (a kick inside the penalty
      area is a penalty kick, taken from the
      penalty mark).
      1. Kicking an opponent
      2. Charging in a violent and dangerous
         manner
      3. Tripping an opponent

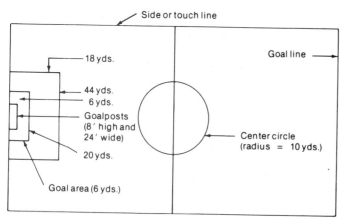

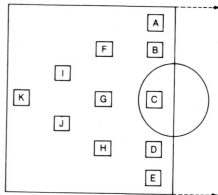

4. Handling the ball (The goalkeeper may handle the ball only when he is inside the penalty area. If he handles the ball when he is outside the penalty area, a direct free kick is awarded to the opposing team.)

5. Pushing with the hands or arms. The ball is placed on the spot where the infraction happened. Any player on the team awarded the kick lines up three or four yards behind the ball and players from both teams stand anywhere in front of him, providing they are at least ten yards away. The whistle sounds, the ball is kicked, and play resumes.

B. Indirect free kick: This is a kick from which a goal cannot be scored, unless the ball is touched by another player before it enters the goal. (The goalie does not count as another player.) This kick is awarded to a team when any opposing player commits any of the following infractions.

1. A player kicks the ball a second consecutive time after a kickoff, a free kick, a goal kick, or a corner kick.

2. A ball is not kicked forward from a penalty kick.

3. The goalie carries the ball more than four steps. He must bounce the ball on the ground before he takes one or more steps.

4. Ungentlemanly conduct—improper language, unnecessary arguing, and so on.

5. Offside.

6. Obstruction other than holding.

V. Throw-in: When the ball is pitched, headed, or legally forced over the sideline by a player, the opposing team is awarded a throw-in. The ball is put back into play from behind the sideline at the point where the ball went out. The player who makes the throw-in must have both hands on the ball and throw it from behind his head. He must also have part of both feet in contact with the ground until the ball is released. If the ball is not thrown in properly, the opposing team is awarded the second throw-in.

VI. Corner kick: When the ball is kicked, headed, or legally forced over the goal line by a defensive player, the opposing team is awarded a corner kick. The ball is placed on the corner of the field (where the side line meets the goal line) on the side the ball went out. Usually a wing player kicks the ball into play. All other players stand anywhere on the field, providing they are at least ten yards from the ball.

VII. Goal kick: When the ball is kicked, headed, or legally forced over the goal line by a player on the attacking team, a goal kick is awarded to the defensive team. The ball is placed in the goal area on the side nearest to where the ball crossed the line. Any defensive player may kick the ball back into play; however, it must cross the penalty line to be in play. If it does not, the kick is repeated. The offensive team remains outside the penalty area until the ball crosses the penalty line.

VIII. Offside: A player is offside if he is nearer his opponent's goal line than he is to the ball at the moment the ball is played. He is not offside, however, if (1) he is in his own half of the field; (2) two opponents are nearer their goal than he is at the moment the ball is played; or (3) he received a ball directly from a corner kick, a throw-in, or a goal kick.

A. Example of offside: The right winger is offside because he did not have two defensive players in front of him at the moment the ball was kicked.

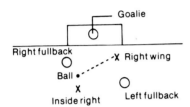

B. Not offside: In this case, "at the moment" the inside right kicked the ball, the right winger had two defensive players in front of him. Now the right winger may dribble in and attempt a shot at the goal.

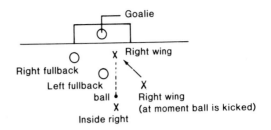

IX. Scoring: One point is awarded to the attacking team if any player kicks, heads, or legally causes the ball to cross over the goal line between the goalposts and under the crossbar. A ball accidentally kicked through the goal by a defensive player, therefore, would count for the attacking team.

Evaluative Techniques

Although a number of standardized tests measure soccer skills, they generally are designed for secondary and college level students. These tests, however, can be modified to meet the ability of upper elementary children. The following test battery is an example of a "teacher-made" test that can be administered without elaborate equipment and in a short period of time. Keep scores from year to year in order to develop appropriate norms for your school.

Test 1: Kick and Trap

Draw a line five feet from the wall. The ball is placed on the line. Each player attempts to kick the ball and hit the front wall as many times as possible within thirty seconds. All kicks must be taken from behind the five-foot line. If a player loses control of the ball, he may retrieve it with his feet and continue kicking. Award one point for each successful hit. Allow two trials and record the highest score.

Soccer Skill Test

Name	Kick and Trap (total pts.)	Dribbling	Shooting	Subjective Evaluation	Total Score	Grade
1 2 3 4 5		Rank total scores for the class, then convert to letter grades or ratings (superior, good, etc.).				

Test 2: Dribbling

Arrange four chairs as shown in the diagram. Place a ball on the starting line. Each player starts behind the starting line with both hands resting on his knees. On the signal "go," he dribbles the ball around the chairs in a zigzag pattern. One point is awarded for each time he passes a chair as he moves forward and as he returns to the starting line. Allow thirty seconds for the test. Allow two trials and record the highest score.

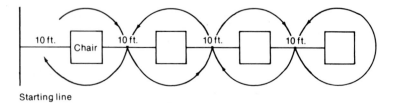

Starting line

Test 3: Shooting

Arrange the field markings in front of the goalposts as shown. A player may use the right or left approach. The player starts dribbling the ball in the approach area and continues moving into the shooting zone. While in the shooting zone, the player attempts to kick the ball through the goalposts. Ten trials are given, with five points awarded for each successful goal.

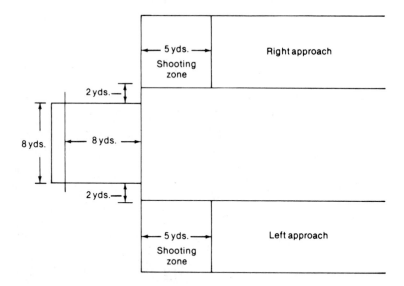

Test 4: Subjective Evaluation

Establish criteria that represent the skills and playing ability required in soccer. For example, using such skills as passing, dribbling, team play, and defensive ability, the teacher awards each player a total score from zero to fifty points. Three players can be used as judges, with the average score recorded.

19 *Hockey Activities*

Emphasis and Skill Presentation

Teaching Procedures

Description of Skills
Grip
Dribbling and Stopping
Driving
Scoop Shot
Fielding
Tackling
Dodging
Face-off (Bully)

Practice Activities
Dribbling
Passing and Fielding
Dodging and Tackling

Lead-up Games

Field Hockey: Rules and Regulations

Evaluative Techniques

Field hockey is a relatively new game to many North Americans. Its origins, however, date back over two thousand years to ancient Greece and Egypt. During the Middle Ages, field hockey was known as "hurling" in Ireland; as "shinty" in Scotland; and as "hoquet" in France. The modern version of hockey started in England around the middle of the nineteenth century. Today, the game is played in over a hundred countries and is enjoyed equally by men and women.

Field hockey has also become very popular with elementary school-age children. Because it is relatively new, it provides an enjoyable medium for boys and girls to learn to play together on an "even skill" basis. Improvised equipment, along with numerous modified lead-up hockey-type games has made field hockey one of the fastest growing activities in the elementary school physical education program.

Emphasis and Skill Presentation

Many of the basic skills and simple playing strategies of hockey are introduced in grades three and four through street hockey and organized floor hockey during school hours. Although field hockey is similar to these games, it has several unique skills and rules that should be learned correctly and in an organized manner in grades four, five, and six.

During the fourth grade, the main emphasis should be on learning the correct way to dribble, pass, and shoot a ball. Fourth graders should also learn how to stop a ball and a few basic rules of the game. The major portion of any unit of instruction should be devoted to practice activities and lead-up games.

The basic dribbling, passing, and shooting skills should still be emphasized through grades five and six. Teachers should expect a general increase in the accuracy, speed, and control of these skills. New skills such as the scoop shot, tackling, and dodging should be introduced in fifth or sixth grade. More time should also be devoted to seven-person hockey, and sufficient time should be allowed for playing eleven-person field hockey. The latter is important in order to give each child an opportunity to understand and appreciate the importance of good ball control and positional play.

Table 19.1 Suggested Sequence of Presenting Hockey Skills and Rules

Skills and Rules	Grade Level		
	Grade 4	Grade 5	Grade 6
Dribbling	Introduce		
Rules		Increase speed and accuracy	Increase speed and accuracy
Dribbling with Face of Blade	Introduce	Refinement	Refinement
Driving	Introduce		
Left Drive		Increase distance and accuracy	Increase distance and accuracy
Scoop Shot		Introduce	Increase accuracy
Rules: Hit with Face of Blade		Introduce	
Fielding	Introduce		
Rules		Increase accuracy	Increase accuracy
Tackling		Introduce	Increase accuracy
Rules			
Fouls		Introduce	
Dodging		Introduce	Increase accuracy
Rules			
Offside		Introduce	
Face-off	Introduce	Increase accuracy	Increase accuracy
Rules			
Player Positions and Three Hits		Introduce	

Teaching Procedures

Throughout this chapter numerous references are made to various sections in chapter 18, "Soccer Activities." The reason for this is that both soccer and field hockey may be relatively new to many elementary school children and the same approach can be used to teach both activities. In addition, many practice activites and lead-up games described in chapter 18 can be easily adapted to field hockey skills. Teachers should also adapt the information on page 273 when organizing and planning a hockey unit.

The following suggestions will assist teachers in coping with several problems that are unique to hockey.

1. Hockey can be a dangerous sport if children are not taught proper stick handling and legal checking methods. Since boys and girls may play this activity together, it is especially important that the proper skills be taught and enforced.

2. Since sticks may be unavailable for every member of the class, station work (p. 86) and a rotation system should be used.

3. Hockey, like soccer, requires a high level of strength and endurance. Teachers should plan practice activities and lead-up games so the children gradually build up their cardiorespiratory endurance. Station work can be used for alternating vigorous running drills with less tiring shooting activities.

Description of Skills

Field hockey skills are classified as dribbling, passing or driving, and fielding skills. The following skills should be taught to elementary school children in a systematic and progressive way. Special attention must be given to proper stick handling, reinforcing it throughout every lesson.

Grip

The basic hockey grip is fundamental to all shooting, dribbling, and fielding skills. The left hand stays at the top of the stick while the right hand slides up or down the stick according to how the ball should be moved. To begin, grasp the stick in the middle with the right hand and hold it parallel to the ground. The toe of the blade should be sticking up with the side of the blade facing left. Grasp the top of the stick with the left hand, with the thumb pointing down toward the blade. Lower the stick to the ground and turn the blade so that it faces outward. Keeping the same grip with the left hand, reposition the right hand six to twelve inches below the left hand. The result is that the hands grip the handle from opposite sides (fig. 19.1). The player will want to experiment to find the most suitable distance between his hands.

The player should carry his stick ahead and to the right of his feet, with his body leaning forward slightly and his head over the ball.

Common Faults
1. Holding the left hand too loose while contacting the ball
2. Holding the right hand near the top of the stick

Figure 19.1   Grip

Figure 19.2   Dribbling and Stopping

a   b

Figure 19.3   Controlled Dribbling

a   b   c

Dribbling and Stopping

Dribbling in hockey is a controlled means of propelling the ball along the ground with the hockey stick. The ball is dribbled in the front and slightly to the right of the feet by making short taps with the flat side of the blade (fig. 19.2a). The movement is from the shoulder rather than from the wrists. In open field play and when the opponent is not near, the ball may be tapped ten to fifteen feet ahead, followed by short running steps, then another tap of the ball. The flat side of the blade should always be to the ball, and the blade should be close to the ground. To stop the ball, rotate the wrist to bring the flat side of the stick over the ball (fig. 19.2b).

For more controlled dribbling, spread the hands further apart (fig. 19.3a). To push the ball right, rotate the stick with the left wrist so that the flat side of the stick taps the left side of the ball (fig. 19.3b). Keep the ball and stick in front of the body, then rotate the stick back to the right side of the ball (fig. 19.3c).

Common Faults
1. Holding the arms too close to the body and using wrist action when hitting the ball
2. Failing to look up and around while dribbling
3. Failing to keep the ball in front of the body

Figure 19.4   Driving

a. Stick below shoulder height.

b. Swing through the ball.

Driving

Driving is forcefully hitting the ball along the ground. The left drive is the most common driving stroke, used for long and medium passes, shots on goal, and free and corner hits. When moving into position to hit the ball, the left shoulder points into the direction of the drive, and the head is over the ball. Swing arms back, keeping the stick below shoulder level (fig. 19.4a). Then bring arms forward and downward and contact the ball just off the left foot (fig. 19.4b). Follow through low and in the direction of the hit.

Common Faults
1. Holding the stick with a loose grip
2. Holding the hands too far apart
3. Failing to point the left shoulder in the direction of the hit
4. Hitting the ball too soon or too late

Scoop Shot

The scoop shot is used to lift the ball slightly off the ground in order to dodge an opponent, to pass, or to shoot the ball into the corner of the goal. Contact the ball in front with the stick tilted back as it is placed under the ball (fig. 19.5a). Then make a strong lifting and shovellike action with the right arm, but using no follow-through (fig. 19.5b).

Common Faults
1. Hitting the ball rather than lifting it (no sound on contact)
2. Too much follow-through, leading to "high sticking"

Figure 19.5   Scoop Shot

a

b

Figure 19.6　Fielding

Fielding

Fielding a hockey ball or puck (figs. 19.6 and 19.7) is very similar to fielding a grounder in softball. The face of the stick is at a right angle to the direction of the oncoming ball. As the ball contacts the stick, loosen the grip slightly to absorb the impact of the ball. Contact the ball as far away from the body as possible to allow the force to be absorbed over the greatest distance.

Common Faults

1. Failing to get in line with the ball
2. Tilting the stick backward, causing the ball to bounce over the stick
3. Failing to relax the grip as the ball makes contact with the face of the stick

Tackling

A tackle is a legal means of taking the ball away from an opponent. Move in toward the opponent with eyes on the ball, body well forward with weight evenly distributed over both feet. Hold the blade of the stick close to the ground (fig. 19.8a). Make the tackle when the ball is farthest from the opponent's stick. At that moment, place the face of the blade on the ball perpendicular to the ground (fig. 19.8b). As soon as you have possession of the ball, immediately pass it to another player or quickly dribble it away from the opponent.

Common Faults

1. Taking one's eyes off the ball as the opponent approaches
2. Swinging the stick forward
3. Failing to pass or dribble when possession of the ball is gained

Dodging

A dodge is an evasive movement that an offensive player uses to move the ball past an opponent. It is essentially a controlled pass to oneself. In the diagram, the dribbler pushes the ball to the right, then runs around the other side to pick up his own pass. Timing is the most important part of this movement. The ball must be pushed late enough to prevent the opponent from backing up to gain possession of the ball.

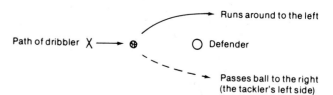

Common Faults

1. Slowing down just before making a move and a pass
2. Keeping the ball too far in front, thus allowing the defensive player to tackle and gain possession of the ball

Face-off (Bully)

The face-off, or "bully," is used to start the game, after a goal is scored, and when the ball is prevented from further play by two opposing players. The face-off is taken between two opposing players, who stand on either side of the ball with their left sides facing their opponent's goal line. Both players start with the blades of their sticks on the ground and on their own side of the ball (fig. 19.9). Both players then lift and touch their sticks over the ball, then touch the ground. They do this three times, then each tries to gain possession of the ball.

Figure 19.8 Tackling

a. Approach with blade close to the ground.

b. Blade is on the ball and perpendicular to the ground.

Figure 19.9 Face-off (bully). Stick is on player's own side of the ball.

Practice Activities

The following practice activities are, in many respects, modifications of soccer drills and relay activities. A few hockey-type activities are also included in this section. Since field hockey may be a completely new game to many children, these practice activities are extremely important in developing basic skills.

Dribbling

One of the most important skills to learn is dribbling the ball using the flat surface of the blade. The following activities should help children learn to move the ball in a variety of directions by shifting their bodies and the blade surface in the direction they want the ball to go.

Individual Activities

Free Dribbling

Give the children an opportunity to see how well they can move the ball anywhere in the field. Begin with a walking speed, then increase to a jog, and finally go to a run. After several minutes of practice have each child attempt one of the following.

1. Dribble forward, shift left, shift right, and repeat.
2. Repeat above, but stop and control ball before shifting to a new direction.

Dribble around Obstacles

Set up one obstacle (milk carton, tin can, or traffic cone) and dribble around it. Dribble around the right side, then the left side. Dribble around either side, stop the ball, turn around, and return around the opposite side. Add two or more obstacles and repeat.

Partner Activities

The partner activities suggested for soccer (pp. 283–84) can be modified for dribbling with a stick.

Group Activities

The group activities suggested for soccer (pp. 284–85) can be modified for dribbling with a stick.

Passing and Fielding

The partner activities suggested for soccer (pp. 283–84) can be used when partners practice passing and fielding a hockey ball. Teachers should also note the suggestions on page 284 about applying the problem-solving method. This approach can work extremely well with passing and fielding activities.

Group Activities

The following group relays can be adapted to passing and fielding a hockey ball.

1. Zigzag passing, page 284
2. Circle passing, page 284
3. Goal shooting, page 285

Push Pass

Arrange three players as in diagram. Player 1 passes to player 2. Player 2 returns to player 1, who then passes to player 3. Player 3 returns the ball to 1 and the sequence begins again.

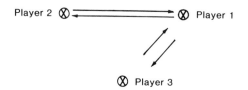

Variations

1. Pass from player 1 to 2 to 3 to 1 and continue in the same pattern.
2. Repeat above with every player moving one position to the left. Player 1 dribbles to 2's position and passes to 2, who has shifted to 3's position.

Dodging and Tackling

The partner and group activities suggested for soccer can be adapted to practicing dodging and tackling skills used in hockey activities (see p. 287).

Lead-up Games

The lead-up games described in this section are arranged according to their level of difficulty. Modify the rules to meet the class's general level of ability. Also modify any game to accommodate play on indoor or outdoor surfaces.

Lead-up Game	Grade	Page
Zone Field Hockey	4–6	303
Line Field Hockey	4–6	303
Alley Hockey	4–6	290
Sidelines Hockey	4–5	289
Pin Hockey	5–6	289
Seven-Man Hockey	5–6	291

Note: Substitute field hockey ball and sticks in the games described in previous chapters.

Zone Field Hockey (4–6)

Formation   Playing area arranged as in diagram

Equipment   One stick for each player and one ball for each game

Players   Ten to twelve on each team

Skills   All hockey skills

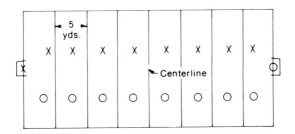

The game starts with a face-off between two opposing players at the center of the field. All players must remain in their own five-yard zone. The game is played like regular field hockey. After each goal is scored, the player in the zone closest to the centerline becomes the new goalie, and all other players move forward into the next zone.

Line Field Hockey (4–6)

Formation   Arrange playing area as shown in diagram. Players are numbered from one to the last player.

Equipment   One stick for each player and one ball for each game

Players   Six to eight on each team

Skills   Shooting, passing, and stopping

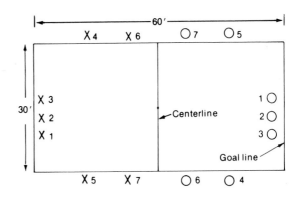

The ball is placed in the middle of the field. On signal, player 1 from each team runs out and tries to gain possession of the ball. Once the ball is in possession, a player may pass to any side player or try to shoot the ball over his opponent's goal line. No other player on his team may enter the field of play or score a goal. After each goal, rotate players and start the game again.

Variations

1. Allow two players to come out each time.
2. Shorten the distance between goals as skill improves.

Field Hockey: Rules and Regulations

The following basic rules of field hockey are essentially a modification of regulation field hockey. By dividing a playing field in half, two games with seven players on a team can be played (one goalie, one fullback, two halfbacks, and three forwards). Since the game is similar to soccer, it is wise to introduce it after the class has been exposed to a unit of soccer.

Note: The playing positions for field hockey are the same as for soccer (p. 292). Also, the same field dimensions can be used for both games. Inclusion of the semicircle (or penalty area) is the only difference in the general layout of the field.

I. Field of play and players: Field is 60 by 100 yards. Adjust to available space.

II. Time: Two periods of thirty minutes (divide your available time in two). Teams change ends at halftime.

III. Face-off (or "bully"): This is taken at the center of the field at the start of the game, after each goal, and after halftime. After the third hit of the sticks, one of the two players hits the ball, putting it into play. During the face-off, all other players stand on their own side of the face-off line until the ball is played.

IV. Ball rolls over side line: When a ball is forced over a side line, a push-in is awarded to the opposing team. A push-in must be performed with the stick in contact with the ball throughout the stroke. All other players must be five yards away.

V. Ball sent over end line:
A. If by the attacking team, the defending team is awarded a free hit sixteen yards from the end line opposite the spot where the ball crossed.

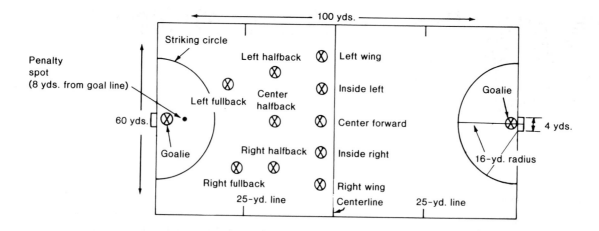

B. If by the defending team, the attacking team is awarded a corner hit. The hit must be taken from a point on the end line within five yards from the corner of the field.

VI. Fouls committed outside the penalty area (the semicircles in front of goals): A free hit is awarded to the opposing team. All players must be five yards away from the player taking the hit. Fouls are—
A. using any part of the stick except the *flat surface of the blade;*
B. raising the stick above the shoulder;
C. using any part of body to propel the ball, although the hand may be used to stop the ball;

D. hitting another player, or hooking, slashing, or interfering with opponent's stick;
E. being offside, which means that an offensive player who is in his opponent's half of the field and does not have possession of the ball must have three opponents between him and the goal line.

VII. Fouls committed inside the penalty area:
A. If by the attacking team, the defending team is awarded a free hit from anywhere inside the semicircle.
B. If by the defending team, any player on the attacking team is given a free hit on a spot five yards in front of the center of the goal. All other players, except the goalie, must remain behind the 25-yard line until the penalty hit is taken.

Evaluative Techniques

Very few standardized hockey tests are available for elementary school children, so the teacher must develop her own. Since hockey is a relatively new activity, several of the basic skills can be easily developed into objective test items. And most classroom teachers can also make reasonably accurate subjective ratings of the child's general playing ability.

If a teacher wishes to develop a simple test battery, tests 2, 3, and 4 from the previous chapter on soccer activities can be modified for hockey. Other items should be added according to the teacher's discretion.

20 Flag or Touch Football Activities

Emphasis and Skill Presentation

Teaching Procedures
Station Work
Inventive Games Approach

Description of Skills
Passing
Catching
Stance
Punting
Blocking

Practice Activities

Lead-up Games

Touch Football: Rules and Regulations

Evaluative Techniques
Test 1: Accuracy Pass
Test 2: Punting
Test 3: Ball Carrying
Test 4: Subjective Evaluation

When football is suggested as an activity for elementary school children, parents and teachers usually think of it in terms of the competitive game involving expensive equipment, elaborate coaching, and the problems associated with a contact sport. These are valid points that should be taken into consideration. However, this does not mean that modified games involving many of the skills of football should not be taught to children in the upper intermediate grades. Appropriate football skills and rules can be taught through modified games such as field ball, flag football, and touch football. None of the practice activities or lead-up games suggested in this chapter involves tackling or any other form of body contact. Thus, the nature of these activities, coupled with such instructional techniques as station work and inventive games, provides an opportunity for boys and girls to participate in a cooperative and enjoyable way.

This chapter has been arranged to help teachers develop an instructional unit that takes into consideration such factors as coeducational classes, variable levels of instruction, and available equipment. It is strongly suggested that flag rather than touch football be emphasized in the regular instructional period. Flag football is the same as touch football, except two flags located on the seat of each player are removed. Pulling off these flags avoids disputes over whether a player was actually touched with two hands, and it is a safer game.

Emphasis and Skill Presentation

The problems of teaching football skills are very similar to those found in teaching basketball and softball. Many boys, even ten- and eleven-year-olds, can throw a spiral pass, punt a ball, and elucidate the advantages of a single- or double-wing formation. Other children may not have even thrown or kicked a football. While girls enjoy throwing and catching a football and playing many of the lead-up games described in this chapter, cultural patterns have generally denied them equal opportunity to play football. Consequently, their understanding and skill are much less developed than that of boys.

Although major differences in the level of skill appear within each grade, the following suggested sequence of presenting skills provides a basic guideline for most elementary school situations.

Basic throwing and catching skills have normally been learned in the primary grades, so the main task for fourth graders is to learn to throw and catch an oblong-type ball. They should also be introduced to punting.

The major skills and playing strategies should be taught in the fifth and sixth grades. Children in these grades should learn the various stances and how to throw a ball to a moving receiver. They should also learn other ways of passing the ball and a few simple play patterns.

Table 20.1 Suggested Sequence of Presenting Football Skills and Rules

Skills and Rules	Grade Level		
	Grade 4	Grade 5	Grade 6
Passing			
Forward Pass	Introduce	Increase accuracy and distance	Increase accuracy and distance
Lateral Pass		Introduce	Increase accuracy
Centering	Introduce	Increase accuracy	Increase accuracy
Rules: Passing and Receiving	Introduce		
Scoring	Introduce		
Catching			
Pass Receiving	Introduce	Refinement	Refinement
Receiving a Kicked Ball	Introduce	Refinement	Refinement
Stance			
Three-Point Stance		Introduce	Refinement
Four-Point Stance		Introduce	Refinement
Rules: Line of Scrimmage		Introduce	
Punting		Introduce	Refinement
Rules: Kickoff	Introduce		
Safety		Introduce	
Blocking		Introduce	Refinement
Rules: Use of Hands and Shoulders		Introduce	
Other Rules			
Downs		Introduce	
Position and Plays		Introduce	

Teaching Procedures

Teaching flag or touch football activities presents a few major problems for most upper elementary school classes. As stated earlier, football has been mainly a boy's activity. Even with coeducational classes, girls were usually given other games to play while the boys enjoyed touch or flag football. But most girls enjoy football activities and, therefore, should participate in many practice activities and lead-up games, with a few modifications to cope with differences in skill levels and previous football experience.

An inadequate number of footballs is also often a major problem for teachers planning partner and small group practice activities.

The following suggestions are intended to assist the teacher in developing an integrated and meaningful football unit.

Station Work

Station work is basically organizing the field into stations where specific skills are practiced by small groups. Each group practices the skill assigned to a station for several minutes, then rotates to the next station. In the diagram below, boys and girls may be mixed at each station, or they may be separated if their level of skill varies widely or they definitely prefer to work with their own sex. If only a few footballs are available, use them at stations 3 and 5 and use a soccer, nerf, or utility ball for the other stations.

In addition, the following considerations and safety procedures should be included in a football instruction unit.

1. Use junior-size footballs.
2. Play flag rather than touch football. If commercial flags are not available, strips of plastic or cloth may be used.
3. All positions should be rotated frequently to permit each player to experience and enjoy the skills required for each position.
4. If there is a marked difference in the skill level between boys and girls, separate games may be warranted.

Inventive Games Approach

It has been stated in previous chapters that the inventive games approach can be used to teach skills as well as to nurture children's creative abilities. This approach can be applied to football, too. If two boys and two girls are assigned a drill such as "center, throw, and catch," the boys will normally show more skill and thus will dominate the practice session. However, a challenge such as, "In groups of four, make up a drill in which the ball must be alternately passed from a boy to a girl," encourages cooperative planning and copes with the problem of one sex dominating.

Adding small equipment such as milk cartons or traffic cones can also break down the rigidity of many football drills and make the practice activity less competitive and more enjoyable. The teacher could add, "In some way use four milk cartons in your drill," to the earlier challenge. Passing is still emphasized in the drill, but the additional equipment adds to the challenge and encourages everyone in the group to suggest ways of incorporating it.

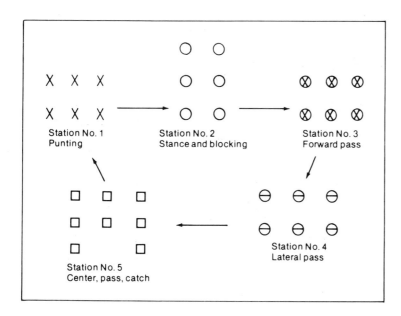

Description of Skills

Touch or flag football requires the same skills as the competitive game, with the exception of tackling and blocking. For elementary school children the emphasis should be on passing, catching, and kicking skills, team positions, and simple play formations.

Passing

Three types of passing are used in touch football. The forward pass is similar to the baseball throw; however, it requires a different hand grip and release so that the ball spirals. Lateral passing is a sideward throw of the ball and is an effective technique virtually anywhere in the field of play. Hiking or centering the ball is a throw used solely by the center to start each play from the line of scrimmage.

Forward Pass

When executing a forward pass, the player stands with the opposite foot to his throwing arm forward and pointing in the direction of the throw. His weight is evenly distributed on both feet, and he holds the ball with both hands. The fingers of his throwing hand grip the lace behind the center of the ball, and the other hand holds the front and side of the ball. The ball is shifted back past the ear and the body is rotated away from the throw. The elbow of the throwing arm should be kept high (fig. 20.1a). Young children with proportionately smaller hands find this difficult and tend to drop the elbow in order to hold the ball in this position. The ball is then rotated toward the target, the forearm and wrist are thrust forward, and the wrist is dropped to allow the ball to roll off the fingers (figs. 20.1b and c). This "roll-off" gives the ball the spiral action.

Common Faults

1. Holding the ball too close to the palm of the hand
2. Releasing the ball too soon
3. Failing to snap the wrist just before the ball is released off the fingertips

Lateral Pass

The lateral pass is basically a sideways throw of the ball. The ball is shifted from a one-arm carry to two hands. Once the ball is firmly held in both hands, shift it to the opposite side of the intended throw (fig. 20.2a). Then bring the ball across the body and release it about waist high (fig. 20.2b).

Common Faults

1. Releasing the ball too soon
2. Releasing the ball with too much force, causing it to rebound out of the receiver's hands

Centering or Hiking the Ball

Once the ball is placed into position for the next play, it cannot be removed from the ground until a pass, or hike, is made by the center player. The center player positions his body in a wide stride position, with his knees bent and his body weight well forward over his shoulders and arms. He then grasps the ball with the fingers of his right hand spread over the lace, and the left hand on the side and near the back of the ball. On signal from the quarterback, the center extends his arms and hands backward through his legs and releases the ball off his fingertips (fig. 20.3).

Figure 20.1 Forward Pass

a   b   c

Figure 20.2 Lateral Pass

a. Shift ball to opposite side.

b. Release ball about waist high.

Figure 20.3 Hiking or Centering the Ball

Common Faults
1. Lifting the ball off the ground before the quarterback has called the signal
2. Passing the ball backward too low or too high for the receiver

Catching

A ball thrown from a hike or a lateral pass is normally caught with an underhand catch. But a forward pass is usually caught while on the run, requiring balance, timing, and a cradling action of the hands. This skill requires an accurate pass and lots of practice on the part of the receiver.

At the moment the receiver is ready to catch the ball, he turns slightly toward the passer, with his hands held forward and upward (fig. 20.4a). His elbows are slightly flexed and his fingers spread. He reaches for the ball (fig. 20.4b) and immediately pulls it toward his body (fig. 20.4c), then shifts it to a carrying position. The ball is carried with one hand under and around the front end of the ball. The other end of the ball is held close to the body by the inside of the forearm and elbow.

Common Faults
1. Failing to judge and reach the position to catch the ball
2. Failing to reach for the ball
3. Holding the ball too far from the body while running with it

Stance

The type of starting position a player takes depends upon whether he is in an offensive or defensive situation and whether he is playing on the line or in the backfield. The following stances are typical positions for defensive or offensive playing situations.

Three-Point Stance

Assume a wide crouched and stride position with the knees slightly bent, the seat down, the left arm forward, and the knuckles of the hand touching the ground (fig. 20.5). The body weight should be well forward, and the head should be up and the eyes focused straight ahead.

Figure 20.4 Catching

a. Elbows flexed
   and fingers spread

b,c. Cradling action of hands

Figure 20.5 Offensive Position: Three-Point Stance

Figure 20.6 Defensive Position: Four-Point Stance

Four-Point Stance

Assume a wide crouched and stride position with the knees slightly bent, the seat down, both arms forward, and the hands touching the ground (fig. 20.6). The body weight should be well forward.

Common Faults
1. Failing to lean forward over the hands
2. Looking or pointing in the direction of the move

Figure 20.7 Punting

a. Hold ball in front.   b. Drop ball.   c. Contact ball on top and outer side of foot.   d. Follow through.

Punting

In touch football, the ball may be punted or kicked from a stationary, or "placekick," position. Punting a football is very similar to punting a soccer ball, with the football contacted on the top side of the instep and with a more pronounced follow-through of the kicking leg. Since tennis shoes are usually worn in physical education class, the placekick should be performed with the top of the foot and not the toe. This means the ball should slant toward the kicker.

The player stands with his right foot slightly forward and his weight evenly distributed over both feet. He holds the ball with his right hand on the right side near the front of the ball. His left hand holds the left side of the ball (fig. 20.7a). He steps right, then left, and simultaneously drops the ball as he brings his kicking leg forward (fig. 20.7b). The ball should be contacted with the top and slightly outer side of the foot (fig. 20.7c). He then continues the forward and upward movement of his kicking leg (fig. 20.7d). His arms should extend sideways to assist balance.

Common Faults

1. Throwing rather than dropping the ball from the hands
2. Kicking the ball with the toe
3. Failing to keep eyes on the ball until it is kicked
4. Failing to straighten the leg and follow through sufficiently

Blocking

A player in flag or touch football may block by simply placing his body in the way of an opponent. When an offensive player blocks, he must have both feet on the ground and his forearms must be held against his chest

Figure 20.8 Act as an obstruction.

when he contacts the defensive player. The defensive player may use his hands to protect himself but is limited to touching the shoulders and body of the blocker (fig. 20.8).

Common Faults

1. Using fists and shoulders to stop an opponent
2. Failing to move into an effective blocking position

Practice Activities

Football normally requires two or more players in practice situations. Begin with partner activities; if there is a limited supply of footballs, use soccer or utility balls.

Partner Activities

Normally two or more football skills are practiced in the same drill. The following partner activities can be adapted to each grade level.

1. Partners pass and catch.
2. One partner runs and tries to catch the other's pass.
3. One partner centers, then runs forward to catch the other's pass.
4. Both run and pass back and forth, using a lateral pass.
5. Inventive drills. Make up drills involving passing and catching. Later, add small equipment.
6. Partners punt and catch.
7. One partner runs with (or without) the ball and the other partner tries to block, as in basketball.
8. Repeat above with one partner trying to tag the other.

Group Activities

Several relays described in other chapters can be used to practice football skills. Refer to the following.

Activity	Page	Used for	Change to Football
Zigzag Relay	284	Volleyball	Substitute a football
Shuttle Volleying	286	Volleyball	Substitute a football

Blocking Practice

Arrange the field and players as shown in diagram. One player is designated as the offense, the other as defense. Both assume a football stance position. On signal "hike," the offensive player attempts to get past the defensive player. The offensive player must stay within the eight-foot line and may feint, dodge, or do any movement to get around the defensive player.

```
X        X  Offense  X       X           X
|← 8 ft. →|  _____  _____  _____  _____

O        O  Defense  O       O           O
```

Variations
Repeat the drill with a ball.

Pass and Defend

Arrange field and players as shown in diagram. The center snaps the ball to the passer. As soon as the passer has the ball, the receiver runs forward and tries to catch the pass. The defender moves at the same time and tries to prevent the receiver from catching the pass or tries to intercept it. If the skill level is high enough, allow the receiver and defender to move at the moment the snap is made.

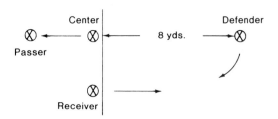

Lead-up Games

The lead-up games described in this section may be played by boys and girls together or separately, depending upon the children's ability. If their skill and experience vary widely, girls and boys will normally be much happier playing separate games. This is particularly true with fifth and sixth grade children.

Lead-up Game	Grade	Page
One-Down Football	4–6	313
Punt and Catch	4–6	313
Punt Back	4–6	313

The following games described in other chapters can also be adapted to touch football activities.

Activity	Page
Soccer Dodge Ball	288
Boundary Ball	288
Sideline Soccer	289
California Kickball	237
European Handball	238
Borden Ball	236

One-Down Football (4–6)

Formation   Field and team positions arranged as in diagram

Equipment   One football

Players   Eight on each team

Skills   Throwing, catching, and tagging

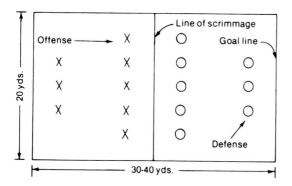

To start the game, both teams line up on opposite sides of the centerline. One team is designated as the offense and is given one down to score a touchdown. After the hike, the ball may be run or passed any number of times in any direction from any position on the field. The defensive team attempts to tag the ball carrier below the waist with two hands. If a player is tagged before he reaches the opponent's goal line, the ball is downed and the other team takes its down at this point. If a ball is intercepted, the game continues with the defensive team becoming the offensive team.

Variations
1. When introducing this game, have all players play "man-to-man," that is, linemen checking linemen and backs checking backs. Later, variations can be made to meet the wishes of the defensive team.
2. Play same game using only the lateral pass.

Punt and Catch (4–6)

Formation   Field and team positions arranged as shown in diagram.

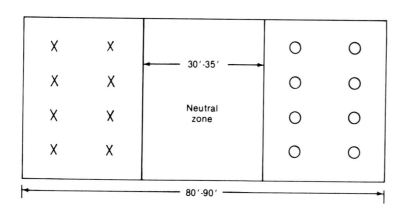

Equipment   One football

Players   Six or eight on each team

Skills   Punting and catching

A player from one team punts the ball over the neutral zone into the opponent's area. The opponent closest to the ball tries to catch it. If successful, he punts the ball back and the game continues. If an opponent misses a catch (it must be in the air), the kicking side is awarded one point. If the ball does not pass out of the neutral zone, the captain of the opposite team may enter the zone to retrieve it. No score is awarded if the ball lands outside the playing area.

Variations
1. Rotate the lines on each team after a number of points have been scored or at set intervals.
2. Play the same game using a forward pass.

Punt Back (4–6)

Formation   Half of a regular playing field, with each team scattered on its own side of the field

Equipment   One football for each game

Players   Five or six on each team

Skills   Punting and catching

The object of this game is to punt the ball over the opponent's goal line. One player begins the game by punting the ball from his own twenty-five-yard line. Once the game is started, opposing players must stay at least ten yards apart. If the ball is caught by a player on the opposite team and he calls "mark" and remains motionless for two seconds, he then has two options: (1) he may take five steps and then punt the ball, or (2) he may pass it to any teammate. All players on his team, however, may be checked (as in basketball) as they try to catch the pass. If a player catches the ball, he must kick it from the point of the catch. If the catcher moves his feet while he is catching the ball or fails to call "mark," he is allowed only three steps before kicking the ball. If the ball is not caught, the player who secures the ball must punt it from the point where it was stopped.

A ball that goes over the sideline is punted back from the point where it went over the line. A ball that is caught in the air behind the goal line does not count as a point; it is put back into play by a punt from the goal line. One point is awarded for a successful punt over the goal line provided it is not caught. The ball is put into play again at the twenty-five-yard line.

Variations
Use a placekick or a forward pass instead of a punt.

Touch Football: Rules and Regulations

It is recommended that upper elementary school children play seven-person touch or flag football. Commercial flags may be purchased from local sports stores, or you may improvise your own. (Flags are sometimes called tags.)

I. Field layout and lineups: See diagram.
II. Start of game: The game is started with a kickoff (punt or placekick) from the goal line. The ball must be kicked past the centerline and must land within the field of play. If the first ball is kicked out-of-bounds, it is kicked again. If the second kick goes out-of-bounds, the other team starts play at its twenty-yard line. The kickoff team may recover the ball only after the other team touches and fumbles it.

III. Offensive play:
A. Once a player who is returning the kickoff is touched, the ball is placed on the spot where he was tagged. The line drawn through this spot is known as the *scrimmage line*. In all cases the ball must be placed five paces in from the sideline.
B. The offensive team has four downs to move the ball into the next twenty-yard zone or to score a touchdown. Always start a new series of downs whenever a team crosses a zone line.
C. The offensive team must have at least three players on the scrimmage line when a play begins. The center player must pass the ball backward through his legs. A backfield player who receives the ball may

Field layout:

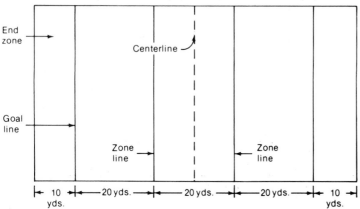

Offensive and defensive lineup positions:

run with it, hand off, or throw a lateral or forward pass from behind the line of scrimmage. Any player except the center may receive the forward pass. The offensive team may punt on any down, providing it calls for a punt formation. When this occurs, neither team may cross the scrimmage line until the punt receiver has caught the ball.

IV. Defensive play:
  A. The defending team must remain behind the scrimmage line until the ball has left the opposing center's hands. A special rule applies to a punt, as previously described.
  B. A defensive player may stop the ball carrier if he places two hands on or below his opponent's waist.

V. Blocking: A player may block only by placing his body in the way of an opponent. See description of blocking on page 311.

VI. Scoring: Points are awarded for the following:
  A. Touchdown: Six points. Following the touchdown, one play or down is given to the scoring team from the three-yard line,

and one more point is awarded if the team crosses the goal line.
  B. Safety: Two points. The defensive team is awarded two points if the team in possession of the ball is tagged behind its own goal line. Immediately following the safety the ball is put into play by the team scored against by a kickoff from behind the goal line.

VII. Touchback: A touchback occurs when a defensive player intercepts a ball behind his own goal line and does not run it out or when the ball is kicked over the goal line by the offensive team. The ball is taken to the twenty-yard line and given to the defending team.

VIII. Penalties: Award five yards to the nonoffending team for the following infractions:
  A. Pushing, holding, or tripping
  B. Unsportsmanlike conduct
  C. Interfering with the pass receiver
  D. Offside

IX. Length of game: Two eight-minute periods

Evaluative Techniques

A few standardized tests are designed to measure the basic football skills. The majority of these tests, however, are designed for high school or college level players, so they must be modified for elementary school-age players. The "teacher-made" test battery below can be administered without elaborate equipment and in a short period of time. Use students to assist in testing, and keep scores from year to year in order to develop appropriate norms for your school.

Test 1: Accuracy Pass

Place a target on the wall as shown in the diagram. Each player is given ten consecutive throws from behind the starting line. He must use a forward pass. Score six, four, and two points for hits within each respective circle. If the ball hits a line, award the higher score. Record the total score.

Touch Football Skill Test

Name	Accuracy Pass (total pts.)	Punting (total pts.)	Ball Carrying (total pts.)	Subjective Evaluation (50 pts.)	Total Score	Grade
1						
2		Rank total scores for the class, then				
3		convert to letter grades or ratings				
4		(superior, good, etc.).				
5						

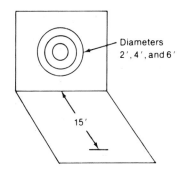

Diameters 2', 4', and 6'

15'

Test 2: Punting

Place lines on the field as shown in the diagram. Stakes can be used as a substitute for gypsum lines. Each player must punt a regulation-size football from behind the starting line. Mark where the ball lands with a stick or small object. Allow a total of three kicks and record the highest score. Yards are equivalent to points.

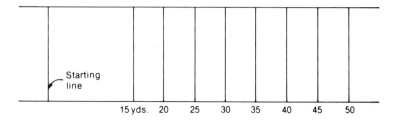

Test 3: Ball Carrying

Arrange four chairs as shown in the diagram. Place a ball on the starting line. Each player stands behind the starting line with both hands resting on his knees. On signal, he picks up the football, places it in his left hand, and runs around the left side of the first chair. He continues the zigzag running pattern, changing the ball to his opposite hand as he passes each chair. Allow thirty seconds for the test. One point is awarded for each chair he passes correctly. Two trials are allowed, with the highest score recorded.

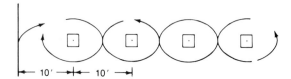

Test 4: Subjective Evaluation

Establish criteria that represent the skills and playing ability required in touch football, such as passing, feinting, kicking, and defensive ability. The teacher or a group of three players awards each player a total score ranging from zero to fifty points. When three players are judging, take an average of their scores.

21 *Volleyball Activities*

Emphasis and Skill Presentation

Teaching Procedures

Description of Skills
Passing or Volleying
Serving
The Set
Net Recovery

Practice Activities
Passing
Serving
Setting Up

Lead-up Games

Volleyball: Rules and Regulations

Evaluative Techniques
Test 1: Wall Volley
Test 2: Serving over the Net
Test 3: Subjective Evaluation of Playing Ability

Volleyball was originated by William G. Morgan in 1895 while he was teaching at the YMCA in Holyoke, Massachusetts. Although the rules, number of players, and size of the ball have changed since that first game, volleyball can be classified as an American contribution to the world of sports. Today, it is played by millions of people in more than sixty countries each year. This phenomenal growth in such a short time is probably due to the game's simplicity, enjoyment, and contributions to physical fitness.

Because volleyball can be adapted to the available facilities and varying levels of proficiency, it is a particularly good activity for the upper elementary school physical education program.

Emphasis and Skill Presentation

One of the most difficult tasks in teaching physical education is determining whether the children are familiar with the activity you wish to teach and whether they have the potential to develop the required skills. Volleyball is no exception. Some children already understand the rules of the game and have acquired a few of the basic skills. Others may not have seen a volleyball game or even have hit the ball correctly. With these factors in mind, the following suggested sequence for presenting skills and rules should be considered as a basic guideline.

Prior to grade four most children have learned to hit a utility ball from a bounce (two square and four square) or to hit a balloon or beachball with a two-hand overhand hit. The main skills of volleyball, however, are normally taught in grades four through six. In grade four, as indicated in the table below, the overhand pass and underhand serve should be introduced with a utility ball or beachball. Once the skill level is high enough, a regulation volleyball should be used. Serving distances, as well as the height of the net, should also be adjusted to each class's ability.

The major emphasis throughout grade five should be on developing the accuracy and power of the pass and the serve. These children are also ready to learn the forearm or bump pass and how to set up the ball to their teammates. Although children in this grade enjoy playing regulation volleyball, it should be played on a limited basis. Such games as modified volleyball and sideline volleyball are more appropriate, as they contribute to skill development yet allow for greater participation and success by every player.

Sixth-grade children still need a lot of practice in the underhand serve and in volleying with both the overhand and underhand pass. The lead-up games in this chapter provide this opportunity and should be extensively used in any unit of instruction. These children should have an opportunity, however, to learn and practice the overhand serve and net recovery skills and to apply them in a regulation game. Spiking and blocking skills are too difficult for this age level, hence should be left for the junior and senior high school programs.

Table 21.1 Suggested Sequence of Presenting Volleyball Skills and Rules

Skills and Rules	Grade Level		
	Grade 4	Grade 5	Grade 6
Volleying			
Overhand Pass	Introduce	Refinement	Refinement
Forearm Pass (bumping)		Introduce	Introduce
Rules: Number of Hits	Introduce		
Rotation	Introduce		
Line Violations	Introduce		
Personal Fouls		Introduce	
Serving			
Underhand Serve	Introduce	Refinement	Refinement
Overhand Serve			Introduce
Rules: Serving Positions		Introduce	
Side Out and Points		Introduce	
Setup		Introduce	Refinement
Recovery from Net			Introduce
All Other Official Rules			Introduce

Teaching Procedures

A general format for planning a unit of instruction has been discussed extensively in previous chapters. Teachers should review page 125 prior to developing a volleyball unit. In addition, the sample lesson plans described on page 220 and the suggestions about incorporating the creative games approach can be applied to volleyball activities.

The following suggestions may help the teacher with some of the problems that are unique to teaching volleyball activities.

1. When there is only one instructional area, such as a gymnasium, choose or modify activities to be played on smaller courts (divide the volleyball court in half) and require fewer players (six or less) on a team.

2. During the initial stages of a volleyball unit, use lightweight utility balls (8½ inches) or heavy balloons. Young children, particularly fourth graders, normally lack sufficient arm and wrist strength to hit a heavy ball. Lighter balls are also slower, allowing children more time to get into position.

3. Adjust the height of the net to the ability of the class. As a general guideline, the net should be six feet high for fourth graders and seven feet high for fifth and sixth graders. Ropes with a few ribbons spaced every few feet can be substituted as a net.

4. Require the ball to be rolled to the server in all lead-up games or any type of modified volleyball activity that involves two teams on opposite sides of the net. Experienced teachers can verify the amount of time this simple procedure will save.

Description of Skills

There are two basic skills in volleyball, serving and passing, or volleying, a ball. Each of these skills, however, can be modified, such as the two-hand underhand volley requiring use of the forearms. Basic skills for intermediate grades are described and illustrated in this section.

Passing or Volleying

The ball may be passed or volleyed to another player or over the net by an underhand or overhand hit. Both hands must be used in the overhand pass, while the forearms are normally used in the underhand pass. Children should be taught to watch the ball, not their hands or opponents. The body weight should be evenly distributed on both feet before the ball reaches the player. Finally, stress follow-through with the hands and arms after the ball has been hit.

Two-Hand Overhand Pass (Face Pass)

The two-hand overhand pass is the most important volleyball skill for elementary school children to learn. It is virtually the prerequisite to playing volleyball; therefore, it requires a great deal of practice and constant correction by the teacher. The feet are in a forward stride position, with knees bent, back straight, and weight evenly distributed over both feet. Arms are extended upward and forward with elbows rotated outward. The wrists are hyperextended, thumbs pointing towards each other, fingers relaxed and pointing diagonally upwards (fig. 21.1a). As the ball approaches, the player should be able to see through the window created by his thumbs and fingers. As the ball drops, the player extends body upward and slightly forward, flexing the wrist and fingers, and contacts the ball on the fingertips (fig. 21.1b). After the ball is hit, follow-through is in the direction of the ball (fig. 21.1c).

Common Faults

1. Failing to get into correct position prior to executing the pass
2. Contacting the ball with the body erect
3. Contacting the ball below the shoulders, usually with the palms
4. Hitting the ball forward rather than upward and slightly forward
5. Relaxing the fingers, wrist, and arms as the ball is hit

Figure 21.1 Two-hand Overhand Pass

a   b   c

Figure 21.2 Forearm Pass

a   b   c

Forearm Pass

The forearm pass, also known as a "bump" or "bounce" pass, is used to receive a serve and to handle a ball that is too low or too far from the midline of the body to use an overhand pass.

As the ball approaches, the player moves into a position in which the midline of the body is in line with the ball. In the ready position (fig. 21.2a), feet are in a forward stride position, with the back straight, seat down, knees bent, and weight evenly distributed over both feet. The arms are held at a 45 degree angle forward and away from the body, with elbows straight, palms up, and fingers together. Simultaneously, one hand is placed diagonally onto the fingers of the other hand, and legs are extended to lift body and arms upward. As the ball is contacted just above the waist, the arms are straight and the thumbs are pointing downward (fig. 21.2b). Follow-through is a continuation of the upward extension of the legs and a very slight upward movement of the arms (fig. 21.2c).

Figure 21.3 Serving

a   b   c

Common Faults
1. Failing to get into correct position prior to executing the pass
2. Failing to bend the knees prior to contacting the ball
3. Swinging at the ball
4. Hitting the ball off one arm
5. Hitting the ball with the arms directed upward

Serving

It is permissible to serve the ball from either an underhand or overhand position. The hand may be open or closed. Boys and girls in the intermediate grades are capable of developing a high level of skill in both serves. Begin with the underhand serve and, after sufficient skill has been developed, introduce the overhand "float" serve.

Underhand Serve

The underhand serve is performed with the left foot (right foot for left-handed players) slightly in front of the right foot. The weight is on the rear foot and the body is bent forward slightly (fig. 21.3a). The ball is held with the palm of the left hand in a "ready" position in front of the right knee. The right arm is extended backward and upward. As the right arm swings down and forward, the weight shifts to the front foot. The ball is hit with the heel of the right hand (fig. 21.3b) or the side of the fist. Immediately before the hand contacts the ball, the ball is released out of the left hand. Continue the follow-through action of the right arm (fig. 21.3c).

Common Faults
1. Holding the ball too far to the left, causing the right arm to swing across the body forcing the ball to move sideways
2. Contacting the ball with the fingertips
3. Contacting the underside of the ball, causing it to rise straight up rather than over the net
4. Failing to follow through

Overhand Serve

The overhand serve should be learned only after a player has mastered the underhand serve. The advantages of the overhand, or "float," serve are that it can place the ball accurately and it has an element of deception caused by its floating, wobbling action.

The server stands with hips and shoulders square to the net, ball held chest high and in line with the right shoulder. Feet are in a stride position with the left foot pointing towards the net and the right foot pointing diagonally towards the right. Weight is evenly distributed over both feet. The server's right hand is held in a ready position just above the right foot. The ball is tossed up with the left hand two or three feet above the right shoulder (fig. 21.4a). As the toss is made, the weight shifts to the back foot. As the ball begins to descend, the weight is shifted to the front foot and the striking arm snaps forward (fig. 21.4b). Contact is made near the center of the ball with the fingertips or a clenched fist. The wrist remains rigid as contact is made (fig. 21.4c). Follow-through continues in the direction of the ball.

Figure 21.4   Overhand Serve

a   b   c

Common Faults

1. Contacting the ball with the forearm, wrist, and fingers too relaxed
2. Contacting the ball as it descends below shoulder height
3. Contacting the ball too far to the left of the body
4. Contacting the ball too far forward or too far back.

The Set

The setup is a two-hand overhand hit, normally the second hit in the series of three that is allowed each team. This overhand hit is used to pass the ball about fifteen feet above the receiver and approximately one foot away from the net. Since the ball moves in the direction the body is facing, it is extremely important for the setter to get into position under the ball and facing the intended receiver just before the pass is made.

Common Faults

1. Failing to get into proper position prior to passing the ball
2. Failing to raise the ball high enough so that it drops or floats down to the spiker

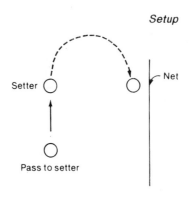

Setup

Net Recovery

The one- or two-hand forearm pass is used to recover a mispassed ball from the net. The player stands with his side to the net in order to move quickly towards or away from the net, or to pass in any direction. Whenever possible, use a two-hand forearm pass (fig. 21.5) and contact the ball as low as possible. Normally, the lower the ball, the farther it is away from the net, hence the easier it is to pass to another player or directly over the net. The one-hand forearm pass (dig) should only be used when poor position or lack of time prevents application of the two-hand pass (fig. 21.6).

Common Faults

1. Failing to move quickly into correct ready position
2. Hitting the ball back into the net
3. Hitting the ball too soon

Figure 21.5 Two-hand Forearm Pass

Figure 21.6 One-hand Forearm Pass

Practice Activities

The following activities are designed to allow students to practice one or more volleyball skills in an enjoyable, gamelike situation. Each skill should begin with individual activities so that the child develops a basic understanding of the skill and can explore the limits of his ability. Partner activities should follow, stressing ball control and positional play. Finally, group activities involving three or more players provide a gamelike experience while concentrating on one or two basic skills. There is ample opportunity in each type of activity for teachers to inject the inventive games approach by modifying existing drills or creating student-designed practice activities.

Passing

The most important contribution of passing, or volleying, activities is to teach the young performer the importance of getting into the proper position to pass or receive a hit and executing the skill with reasonable accuracy and control. Simple practice activities that allow children to hit the ball repetitively from any position and in any manner simply to keep the ball moving will not develop good volleyball skills. There should always be a conscious concern on the part of the teacher and performer to execute each skill correctly and with the highest level of performance.

Individual Activities

Individual Volleying

Arrange players in a scattered formation. This drill requires one ball for each child; however, any type of inflated ball can be used. Begin with each player throwing the ball into the air and catching it close to his forehead after one bounce. He should be in a semicrouched position. Gradually introduce the following individual variations.

1. Throw the ball up, perform an overhand volley on the returning ball, then catch it.
2. Throw . . . set . . . set . . . catch.
3. Throw . . . set . . . set . . . continue.
4. Throw . . . set . . . allow one bounce . . . set . . . catch.
5. Throw . . . kneel and set . . . stand and set . . . catch.
6. Repeat variations 1 to 3 while sitting.
7. Arrange the class in a line formation around the gymnasium approximately six feet from the wall. Have the children—
   a. throw the ball against the wall, set, and catch;
   b. throw against the wall, set, set, and catch;
   c. throw against the wall and continuously set the ball back to the wall;
   d. throw against the wall, allow one bounce, set, and catch.

Partner Activities

Partners standing about ten feet apart are arranged in a scattered formation.

1. One partner throws a high pass and the other catches it. Stress moving into position to receive the ball.
2. Player 1 throws to player 2. Player 2 sets back to 1, who catches the ball.
3. Player 1 throws to 2. They continue to set to each other.
4. Player 1 throws to 2. As soon as player 1 has thrown, he moves to a new position. Player 2 then sets to 1, then moves to his new position. Continue pattern.

Partners are arranged around the gymnasium about ten feet from the wall.

1. Player 1 throws against the wall and player 2 sets the ball above player 1. Player 1 catches. Partners change positions and repeat.
2. Player 1 throws against the wall, player 2 sets back to wall. Continue drill, alternating sets.
3. Repeat above variation, but require a bounce before the return set is attempted.

Arrange partners on opposite sides of a net or rope.

1. Player 1 throws over the net and player 2 sets back over the net to 1, who catches the ball.
2. Repeat above variation, but continue setting back and forth.

Group Activities

The following basic relay formations have been adapted to volleyball activities. Adjust distances to meet the class's ability. After the children are familiar with each activity, ask them to add new ideas or rules to improve the activity or to make it more exciting.

Shuttle Volleyball

Divide class into squads of three or four players. Arrange squads in a shuttle formation with about six feet between players.

Player 1 throws the ball to player 2. Player 2 volleys it to player 3, who has taken player 1's position. Each player goes to the end of the line after volleying the ball. Reverse the direction of the throw after everyone has had a turn.

Variations
1. Same formation with net between lines.
2. Volley with one or two hands.
3. As proficiency develops, increase the distance between the lines.

Circle Volleying

Divide class into squads of five or six players. Arrange each squad in a circle formation with about five feet between each player.

Player 1 throws the ball up and toward player 2, who volleys it to player 1. Player 1 then throws to player 3 and so on until every circle player has volleyed the ball back to player 1.

Variations
1. As proficiency increases, have player 1 throw to player 2, who volleys to player 3. Player 3 volleys to player 4, and so on around the circle.
2. Keep it up. After the first player has started the drill, allow anyone to hit the ball and see how long the squad can keep it up.

Zigzag Volleying

Divide the class into squads of four to six players. Arrange squads in a zigzag formation with about ten feet between each line.

Player 1 throws the ball across to player 2, who volleys the ball to player 3. Continue the zigzag volleying pattern.

Circuit Volleyball

Divide the class into five teams and arrange as in the diagram below.

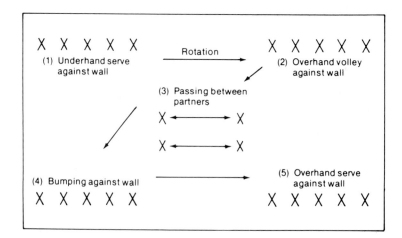

On "go," each team practices its respective skill for a set period of time (ranging from one to several minutes). At the end of each practice period, each team places the ball on the floor and rotates to the next station. Continue rotation.

Serving

Children in the intermediate grades should be able to perform a reasonably accurate underhand serve from the end line over the net before moving on to an overhand serve. Fourth and fifth graders should spend a major portion of their practice time on the underhand serve. Introduce the overhand serve late in fifth grade and allow proportionately more time for this skill during the sixth grade.

Individual Activities

Arrange the class in a line formation around the gymnasium about ten feet from the wall.

1. Serve to the wall and catch the rebound.
2. Combine serve and set. Serve to the wall, set the rebound back to the wall, catch, and repeat.

Partner Activities

Arrange partners on opposite sides of the net. Adjust the distance to the class's level of ability.

1. Have partners free serve back and forth.
2. Move partners closer together. Player 1 serves to player 2, who sets the ball back to player 1. Change positions and repeat.
3. One partner serves to the wall, the other catches the ball and repeats the serve.
4. One partner serves and the other sets back to the wall. Continue setting until one partner misses a return.

Group Activities

If enough space is available, shuttle and zigzag formations can be used equally as well with the following activities to practice serving skills.

Baseline Serving

Divide class into two squads, with each evenly distributed along its baseline. One player from each team is assigned to the retriever position. Use as many balls as you have available.

Any child on the baseline may begin by serving the ball over the net. The ball is then served back by the child who retrieves it. No serving order need be kept. The retriever's job is to catch and pass the ball back to anyone on his team.

Variations

1. Raise or lower height of net according to skill level of class.
2. Place one or more large mats on each side of net and near the middle of the court. Direct players to try and hit the mat.

Alley Serving

Divide the class into four squads, with the first player on each team behind the baseline. Create two playing areas. Divide the playing area on both sides of the net into three equal sections and place one retriever in each section as in the diagram. The retrievers return balls to the appropriate lines. Retrievers rotate after everyone has served.

Each player has three serves. He attempts to serve one ball into each of the three areas.

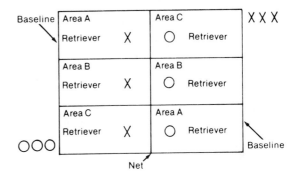

Variations

1. Have players serve into one area only.
2. Adjust the serving line to meet the skill of the students.
3. Substitute a utility ball for younger players.

Setting up

Adjust the height of the net according to the class's ability.

Hit the Square

Arrange the practice area as in diagram.

The leader tosses the ball to the first player, who tries to return a high arc set into the square. Each player is given three turns before going to the back of the line. The leader rotates after every player has had a turn.

Variations

The leader throws, the first player returns a set and then goes to the back of the line, and the leader returns a set to the second player in the line.

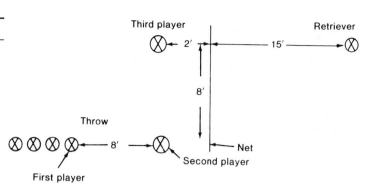

Set Up the Ball

Arrange the practice area as in the diagram at right.

Player 1 throws a high arc pass to player 2, who sets up the ball for player 3. Player 3 attempts to pass the ball over the net to the retriever. After each play, the retriever goes to the back of the line and all other players move up one position.

Variations

1. Player 1 throws the ball up to himself, then volleys it to player 2. The drill continues as previously described.
2. Repeat original drill with retriever attempting to pass the ball to the next thrower.

Lead-up Games

The lead-up games described in this section are very popular with upper elementary school children. Grade four requires the greatest number of modifications to the rules and court dimensions in order to provide a game that is within this age group's general level of ability. The following lead-up games described in previous chapters can be adapted to volleyball with minor changes in the rules and playing strategies. They are high ball, page 235; and the bounce net ball, page 235.

Lead-up Game	Grade	Page
Nebraska Roll	4–5	326
Bound Ball	4–5	326
Mass Volleyball	4–5	327
Newcomb	4–5	327
Keep It Up	5–6	327
Modified Volleyball	5–6	327
Volleyball Keep Away	5–6	328
Four-Way Volleyball	5–6	328
Sideline Volleyball	5–6	328

Nebraska Roll (4–5)

Formation Players arranged in a scattered formation on each side of the net (or rope)

Equipment Volleyball court, net or rope, beach ball or large utility ball

Players Four or five on each team

Skills Serving and passing

Establish a serving line approximately ten to fifteen feet from the net. One player serves the ball over the net. Any number of players may hit the ball before it returns over the net. A point is scored when the ball hits the floor. Start play on the side where the ball hits the floor.

Variations

1. Lengthen the distance of the serving line.
2. Limit the number of passes to five, four, then three.
3. Limit passing to forearm passes.

Bound Ball (4–5)

Formation Players on each team lined up in two rows on either side of a volleyball court divided by a line rather than a net

Equipment Beachball or volleyball

Players Six on each team

Skills Serving and volleying

The server standing anywhere behind the end line bounces the ball once and then hits it over the centerline. The ball must bounce once before an opposing player is allowed to return it over the line. Each team is allowed three hits; however, the ball must bounce between each hit. No player is allowed to hit the ball twice in succession. If the ball hits the centerline, it is considered dead and the play is retaken. Balls hitting boundary lines are still in play. If the nonserving team fails to return the ball within three bounces, the serving team is awarded one point. If the serving team fails to get the serve over the centerline or fails to return a played ball, no point is scored and the ball is given to the other team. Game continues to fifteen points.

Variations

1. Have server begin from behind a fifteen-foot serving line.
2. Add a net or rope and require players to pass the ball over it.

Mass Volleyball (4–5)

Formation Players of each team arranged in equal rows on each side of the net

Equipment Volleyball court, net, volleyball, or large utility ball

Players Six to nine on each team

Skills Serving and volleying

Any player may serve the ball from anywhere in his court. Teams volley the ball back and forth across the net. Anyone may hit the ball as many times as he wishes; however, only three players may touch the ball before returning it over the net. Change the serve after a team fails to return the ball. The serving team scores one point whenever the opposing team commits one of the following fouls: (1) failing to return the ball; (2) catching the ball; (3) knocking the ball out-of-bounds; (4) allowing the ball to touch the floor; or (5) touching the net. A game may be played to any number of points (eleven or fifteen is desirable).

Variations

1. Have players serve from behind a serving line.
2. Allow any number of players to hit the ball as many times as they wish before returning it over the net.
3. Limit passing to either overhand or forearm passes.

Newcomb (4–5)

Formation Volleyball court with teams arranged in equal rows on each side of net

Equipment Volleyball court, net, volleyball or large utility ball

Players Six on each team

Skills Serving and volleying

Server serves the ball over the net. The other team tries to return the ball after the serve, with any number of players allowed to hit the ball. The server continues until his team loses the ball. Only the serving team scores. A predetermined time limit or score is set.

Fouls are (1) hitting the ball out-of-bounds; (2) holding the ball; (3) touching the net; (4) walking with the ball; (5) throwing the ball out-of-bounds; or (6) letting the ball hit the floor.

Variations

If skill level is too low, allow the ball to bounce once before it is hit. Also, adjust the position of the serving line to the level of skill.

Keep It Up (5–6)

Formation Squads arranged in circle formation with or without a player in the middle

Equipment One volleyball for each circle

Players Six to eight on each team

Skills Volleying

Each circle tries to keep its ball up in the air by volleying it from player to player. The ball may be hit to any player in the circle. The team that keeps the ball up the longest wins.

Variations

1. Simplify the game by allowing one bounce between each hit.
2. Place a player in the middle of the circle.
3. As skill improves, allow only one type of pass.

Modified Volleyball (5–6)

Formation Teams arranged as in the diagram below

Equipment One volleyball per game

Players Six to nine on each team

Skills Serving, volleying, and rotating

The server stands behind the end line and serves the ball over the net. If the level of skill is too low, allow any player in the front line to assist the ball over the net. The opposing team attempts to get the ball back over the net before it touches the ground. The ball can be volleyed by as many players on either team as is necessary to return the ball over the net. All other volleyball rules and scoring apply to this game.

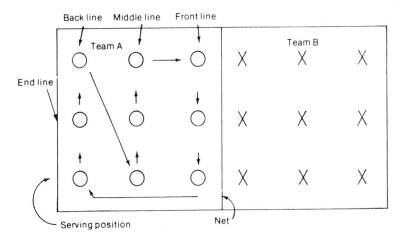

Variations

1. Allow the server two tries to get the ball over the net.
2. Use only one type of pass.

Volleyball Keep Away (5–6)

Formation Teams arranged in a scattered formation within a designated play area

Equipment Volleyball or large utility ball

Players Any number on each team

Skills Volleying

By volleying the ball from one team member to another, the team with the ball tries to keep the ball away from the other team. Members of the other team try to intercept the ball. It can be intercepted only when it is dropping (on the downward arc). After the ball has been intercepted, the team in possession volleys the ball. The team volleying the ball the highest number of times wins. A time limit also may be used.

Variations

1. Limit playing area to enhance ball control.
2. Limit game to one type of pass.

Four-Way Volleyball (5–6)

Formation Volleyball court and teams arranged as in the diagram below

Equipment Two nets (or ropes) and one volleyball

Players Four to six on each of four teams

Skills Serving, volleying, blocking, and rotating

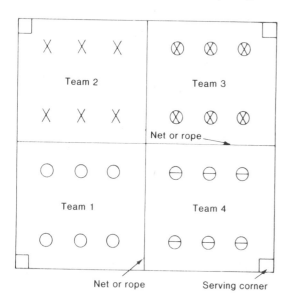

There are four separate teams in this game. Players in courts 1 and 2 may serve only into courts 3 and 4. Similarly, players in courts 3 and 4 may serve only into courts 1 and 2. However, after the serve a team may hit the ball into any of the other three courts. When a fair serve is made and the ball touches the floor or fails to get out of the receiver's court within the allotted three hits, the serving team scores one point and continues serving as in regular volleyball. However, when a receiving team hits the ball into another court fairly, this team becomes the serving team the moment the ball leaves its court. If the new receiving team fails to pass the ball out of its court, the new serving team is awarded one point. All other regular volleyball rules apply.

Variation

Limit any receiving team to only one pass.

Sideline Volleyball (5–6)

Formation Volleyball court and teams arranged as in the diagram below

Equipment One volleyball or utility ball for each game

Players Eight to ten on each team

Skills Serving, volleying, and rotating

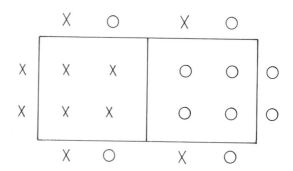

This game is played like regular volleyball with the addition of active sideline players. Sideline players stay in their assigned positions; they cannot enter the court area, but they are permitted to pass any loose balls from either team, providing the balls have not touched the ground. Sideline players cannot pass to each other. A hit made by a sideline player is a free hit for his team and does not count as one of the team's hits. Rotate the court and sideline players after six points are scored and continue the game to fifteen points.

Variations

1. Count sideline hits.
2. Restrict sideline hits to one type of volley.

Volleyball: Rules and Regulations

Although there are fewer skills to learn in volleyball than the other major sports, it is one of the more difficult games for boys and girls in grades four through six. The difficulty, in most cases, is the result of inadequate arm and shoulder girdle strength and inaccuracy in serving and volleying. Nevertheless, fifth and sixth graders should be exposed to the complete game of volleyball early in the instructional unit. Modify the rules to meet the level of skill, available facilities, and number of children. Consider modifying the length of the game, the number of players, the height of the net, and the size of the playing court.

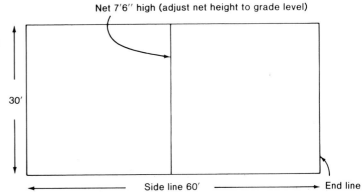

I. Field of play: See the diagram at right.
II. Recommended net heights:
   Grade four—six feet
   Grade five—seven feet
   Grade six—seven feet
III. Positions and Rotation Pattern (after opponents lose their serve): See the diagram below.

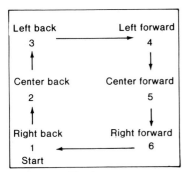

Six players

IV. To start the game: The right back player starts the game by serving the ball from behind the end line. He is allowed only one serve.
V. To return the ball: After the ball has been served, players on both sides must abide by the following rules.
   A. Any player who receives the ball is allowed one volley (hit) over the net or to another teammate.
   B. The ball may not be volleyed (hit) more than three times by a team before it is sent over the net.
   C. A ball that hits the net on the return volley and falls into the opponent's court is a fair ball.
   D. A ball that hits the net on the return volley and falls back into the court from which it was sent may be played before it hits the ground, provided (1) it is not volleyed by the player who hit it into the net and (2) it was not volleyed by more than two players before it hit the net.

VI. To play: The server hits the ball over the net. If the opposing team fails to return it over the net, one point is awarded to the serving team. However, if the ball is returned to the serving team and it fails to return again, the serving team loses the serve. No point is awarded on the loss of serve. Player rotation should be made only by the team receiving the serve.
VII. Violations: If any of the following violations is committed by the serving team, the serve is lost. This is called *side out.* If one is committed by the receiving team, the serving team is awarded one point.
   A. Failing to make a fair or legal serve.
   B. Returning the ball in any way other than by hitting it. Balls may not be caught and thrown over the net.
   C. Volleying the ball more than three times before it goes over the net.
   D. Letting the ball touch the floor outside the court lines. Note: A ball may be played from outside the court area if it has not touched the ground.
   E. Failing to return the ball over the net.
   F. Failing to rotate in the proper order.
VIII. Scoring:
   A. Only the serving team can score.
   B. Eleven, fifteen, or twenty-one points constitutes a game. A team must win by two points; thus, if the score is ten-all in an eleven-point game, one team must score two successive points to win.

Evaluative Techniques

There are numerous methods of measuring volleyball skills and knowledge. The majority of tests used by classroom teachers are of an objective nature and usually are modifications of existing standardized test batteries. Teachers should be encouraged to develop their own test batteries and keep scores of each test in order to develop appropriate norms for their teaching situations.

The following test battery is an example of a "teacher-made" test that can be administered to the children in a short period of time.

Test 1: Wall Volley

Draw one line on the wall six feet up from the floor and a second line on the floor three feet from the wall. The player must stand behind this line, toss the ball in the air, and volley it against the wall above the six-foot line. One point is awarded for each hit above the line. Score the number of hits made in twenty seconds. A player who drops the ball within this period may pick it up and continue volleying. Allow two trials and record the highest score.

Test 2: Serving over the Net

Each player is given ten consecutive serves, with each successful serve awarded five points. This test can be modified by dividing the opposite court into zones, with each given a different point value. For example, make three equal zones running perpendicular to the net; the zone farthest from the server would equal five points; the next one, three points; and the nearest zone, one point.

Test 3: Subjective Evaluation of Playing Ability

Establish criteria that represent the skills and playing ability required in volleyball. For example, using such factors as positional play, alertness, volleying ability, and team play, the teacher awards each player a score from zero to fifty points. Three players can be used as judges, with the average score recorded.

Volleyball Skill Test

Name	Wall Volley (total pts.)	Service Over Net (20 pts.)	Subjective Evaluation (50 pts.)	Total Score	Grade	
1						
2		Rank all total scores for the class, then				
3		convert to letter grades or ratings				
4		(superior, good, etc.).				

22 *Basketball Activities*

Emphasis and Skill Presentation

Teaching Procedures
Developing a Basketball Unit
Structure of a Lesson

Description of Skills
Passing
Catching
Dribbling
Shooting
Pivoting
Defensive Skills

Practice Activities
Passing and Catching
Dribbling
Shooting
Offensive and Defensive

Lead-up Games

Basketball: Rules and Regulations

Evaluative Techniques
Test 1: Passing
Test 2: Dribbling
Test 3: Shooting
Test 4: Subjective Evaluation

Basketball, like volleyball, originated in the United States and has since become a sport that is played in nearly every country in the world. There is no single reason for its popularity as both a participant and spectator sport. Children, youth, and adults enjoy the game because it is fun, challenging, and contributes to many important components of physical fitness. Since the game can be modified to meet court size limitations and varying levels of skill, it should be considered as a basic activity for the upper elementary school physical education program. This chapter has been organized to provide a format for teaching basketball skills and knowledge to these children.

Emphasis and Skill Presentation

Many basketball skills have been learned in earlier grades or out of school. The many backyard basketball courts not only attest to the popularity of the sport, but they also provide the opportunity for elementary school children to learn basketball skills from their older brothers and sisters and parents. Consequently, there is a wide variation in the level of basketball skill in virtually every intermediate grade in the elementary school. With these considerations in mind, the suggested sequence of presenting skills and rules in table 22.1 is provided as a basic guide.

Table 22.1 Suggested Sequence of Presenting Basketball Skills and Rules

Skills and Rules	Grade Level			
	Grade 3	*Grade 4*	*Grade 5*	*Grade 6*
Passing				
Chest Pass	Acquired or introduce	Increase distance and accuracy	Increase distance and accuracy	Increase distance and accuracy
Bounce Pass	Acquired or introduce	With one hand	To a moving target	Refinement
Baseball Pass	Acquired or introduce	Increase distance and accuracy	Increase distance and accuracy	Increase distance and accuracy
Overhead Pass			Introduce	Refinement
Rule: Held Ball			Introduce	
Catching				
From below the Waist	Acquired or introduce	Increase distance and proficiency	Catching while moving	Refinement
From above the Waist	Acquired or introduce	Increase distance and proficiency	Catching while moving	Refinement
Rules: Line Violations		Introduce		
Out-of-bounds		Introduce		
Dribbling				
While Standing and Moving	Acquired or introduce	Forward and backward	Dribble and weave	Dribble and change pace
		With either hand	Dribble and pivot	Refinement
Rule: Traveling		Introduce		
Shooting				
Two-Hand Chest	Acquired or introduce	Increase distance and accuracy	Increase distance and accuracy	Increase distance and accuracy
One-Hand Push		Introduce	Increase distance and accuracy	Increase distance and accuracy
Lay-up		Introduce	With either hand	Refinement
Free Throw			Introduce	Refinement
Rules: Scoring		Introduce		
Key Positions			Introduce	
Related Skills				
Pivoting		Introduce	Refinement	Refinement
Feinting			Introduce	Refinement
Guarding		Introduce	Refinement	Refinement
Rebounding				Introduce
Rules: Personal Fouls			Introduce	

By the time children have reached fourth grade, most of them have learned several of the basic skills involved in passing, catching, dribbling, and shooting. However, the acquisition of these skills prior to grade four should not result in a conscious extension of the basketball program down to the primary grades. Rather, the primary grades should continue to emphasize low-organization games, with some of the specialized skills of basketball and other sports being acquired in the process.

Children in fourth grade should continue practicing the basic passing, catching, dribbling, and shooting skills to improve their accuracy and proficiency. They should also be introduced to a few new shooting skills and several main rules of basketball.

The fifth and sixth grade program places more emphasis on using both hands, pivoting and weaving, and general playing ability. It is a period of refining playing skills and team strategies.

Teaching Procedures

Teaching the skills and team strategies of basketball to upper elementary children presents several problems. A main one, as stated earlier, is that the skill level and playing ability of these children vary widely. Some children have played on out-of-school teams or have their own backyard hoops, while others have not had any experience with the game. The challenge to the teacher is to cope with these major differences in the design and presentation of an instructional unit.

Developing a Basketball Unit

The general instructional procedures discussed in previous chapters also apply to basketball activities. Of particular importance is the process of developing units of instruction on pages 125–27 and the illustrated lessons on page 130. In addition, the inventive games approach described on page 217 can be applied to the teaching of basketball activities.

Since the length of the unit and the lesson, as well as the facilities and equipment available, will vary in each teaching situation, the following suggested approach should be considered as a basic guideline. Modify it to cope with your individual situation.

Step One: Determine the length of your basketball unit. Express this in number of lessons rather than weeks.

Step Two: Assess the general level of ability of your class (see evaluative techniques on p. 349).

Step Three: Select the skills and rules you wish to emphasize in your unit (see the suggested sequence of presenting skills and rules on page 332).

Step Four: Choose the appropriate practice activities (p. 341) and lead-up games (p. 344).

Structure of a Lesson

The detailed explanation of how to plan a lesson described in chapter 18, "Soccer Activities," should be followed when preparing and presenting basketball activities. The suggested procedure of moving from individual to partner to group activities can be adapted successfully to each basketball lesson.

Description of Skills

Basketball skills can be broadly classified as passing, catching, dribbling, shooting, guarding, and feinting. Each skill, in turn, can be subdivided, such as the chest pass, two-hand overhead pass, and the baseball pass. Each of these skills is described in this section, accompanied by a list of the more common faults.

Passing

Passing is transferring the ball from one player to another from a stationary position or while in motion. A player may pass the ball with one or both hands and from a variety of positions. The basic fundamentals of all passes are (1) accuracy—avoiding "wild throws"; (2) following through with every pass; and (3) shifting the ball as quickly as possible from a receiving position to a passing position.

Figure 22.1 Two-Hand Chest Pass

a   b   c

Two-Hand Chest Pass

The two-hand chest pass, or push, is one of the most useful and effective passes in basketball. Since its main advantage is ease and speed of delivery, it is the most often used pass, particularly for short distances.

Assume a forward-stride position with weight evenly distributed over both feet. Grip the ball with both hands, fingers spread around sides of ball with thumbs behind and close together (fig. 22.1a). Simultaneously shift weight to rear foot and the ball towards chest, keeping elbows comfortably at the side of the body waist high (fig. 22.1b). Step forward, extend arms, and turn thumbs downward. Release the ball with a quick wrist snap downward and outward, giving the ball a slight backspin (fig. 22.1c).

Common Faults

1. Holding the ball with the palms touching its surface
2. Holding the elbows too far from the body
3. Pushing more with one hand than the other
4. Failing to release the ball with a quick wrist snap in a downward and outward direction

Baseball Pass

The baseball pass is used when a player wishes to throw the ball a long distance. Care must be exercised in using this pass, particularly with beginners, as it may lead to inaccurate passing. Begin the pass with one foot slightly forward and weight evenly distributed over both feet. Hold the ball in front of the body, with elbows bent and fingers spread around the sides of the ball. Bring arms back and transfer the ball to the right hand when it is above the shoulder and behind the ear (fig. 22.2a). Shift body weight to the right foot as the hands shift backward. Extend right arm forward, rotate body toward the left, and shift weight to forward foot (fig. 22.2b). Release the ball with a final snap of the wrists and fingers (fig. 22.2c).

Common Faults

1. Throwing the ball with a side arm action, causing a sideward spin of the ball
2. Failing to finish with a final wrist and finger snap
3. Releasing the ball too late, causing the ball to hit the floor in front of the receiver

Overhead Pass

The two-hand overhead pass is extremely effective when a player wishes to throw the ball to a teammate above the reach of an opponent. In addition, when the ball is held overhead, it is very easy to "fake" or pretend to pass, thus putting the opponent off guard before the ball actually is released.

Start the pass with weight evenly distributed over both feet. Hold the ball above the head with the hands on the side of the ball and wrists extended (fig. 22.3a). Shift the arms forward and release the ball with a wrist and finger snap (fig. 22.3b).

Common Faults

1. Using only arm action
2. Holding the ball too far back or too far in front of the body, which gives the defensive player a better chance to get the ball

Figure 22.2 Baseball Pass

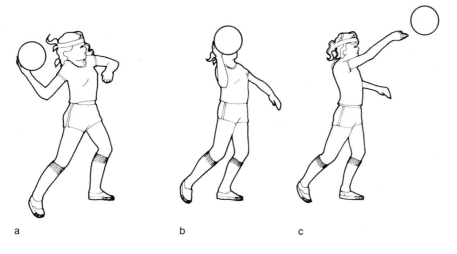

a   b   c

Figure 22.3 Overhead Pass

a   b

Figure 22.4 Two-Hand Bounce Pass

Bounce Pass

The bounce pass can be any one of the three previously described passes but it is performed with a bounce on the floor before it rebounds to the receiver. This type of pass provides a deceptive action to get the ball past an opponent to another teammate. In order for a teammate to receive the ball about waist high, the ball should strike the floor about one-half to three-quarters distance between the passer and the receiver (fig. 22.4).

Common Faults

1. Striking the floor too soon, resulting in too low a rebound
2. Lack of deceptive action, resulting in opponent intercepting the pass

Figure 22.5 Catching

Catching

Basic catching skills have been described in an earlier section of this book (p. 65). In basketball, the overhand catch (fig. 22.5a) is used when the ball is caught above the waist. The fingers point up for this catch. The underhand catch (fig. 22.5b) is used to catch a ball below the waist. The fingers point down. In both types of catches the receiver reaches out and catches the ball on his fingertips, then gradually relaxes his arms to reduce the speed of the oncoming ball. However, because young children often do not have adequate strength to catch the basketball in this manner, allow them to catch the ball with their palms, then quickly shift to a fingertip grip.

Common Faults
1. Standing and waiting for a pass rather than shifting to meet the ball
2. Failing to relax the arms to provide "give" as a fast-moving ball is caught

Dribbling

Dribbling is controlled bouncing in any direction and at varying speeds. The basic fundamentals to stress in teaching this skill are: (1) do not slap the ball downward—push it toward the floor; (2) learn to dribble with either hand; and (3) when not being guarded, bring the ball in front of the body and raise the height of the dribble to increase running speed.

The dribbler's body leans forward slightly, with knees partially flexed, and head up. The wrist of the dribbling hand is relaxed, with fingers cupped and spaced apart (fig. 22.6a). "Push" the ball toward the floor off the fingertips (fig. 22.6b). As the ball rebounds, fingers, wrist, and arm "ride" back with the ball (fig. 22.6c).

When being checked, place the body between the opponent and the ball. When dribbling, keep an eye on the opponent to watch for sudden moves and to shift the ball to a more advantageous position. Also, when being guarded, keep the ball close to the body and lower the bounce to between the waist and the knees.

Common Faults
1. Slapping the ball with the palm of the hand
2. Watching the ball while dribbling
3. Dribbling the ball on the same side as the approaching opponent

Shooting

While all the skills of basketball are important, none is as important as shooting. When teaching the following basic shooting skills, stress two fundamental principles: (1) Watch the target instead of the ball and (2) follow through after every shot.

If elementary school-age children are to learn shooting skills correctly and efficiently, the height of the basket rim should be lowered from the official ten feet to a height that allows the children to shoot without undue strain. The appropriate height for upper elementary school children should be between eight and nine feet, depending upon the children's age and ability.

Two-Hand Set Shot (Push Shot)

The two-hand set shot is the same as the one-hand set shot (description follows), except that two hands are used. Begin the shot with one foot slightly in front of the other and the weight evenly distributed over both feet. Hold the ball between spread fingers in front of the chest, with the elbows close to the sides (fig. 22.7a). Bend the knees slightly to aid in the upward motion, then simultaneously straighten the knees and extend the body forward and upward, pushing the ball toward

Figure 22.6 Dribbling

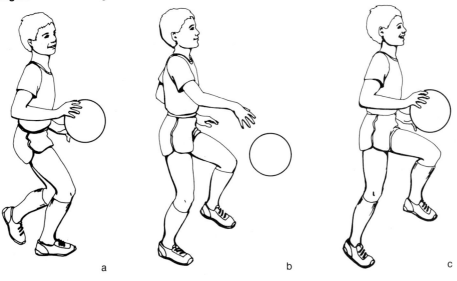

a   b   c

Figure 22.7 Two-Hand Set Shot

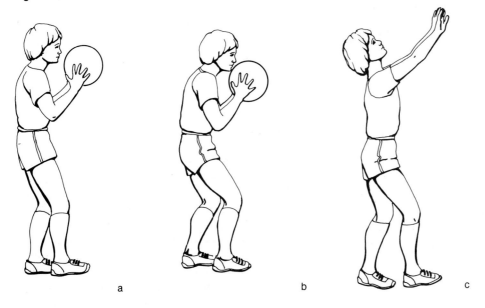

a   b   c

the basket (fig. 22.7b). Release the ball with a slight snap of the wrists and fingers. Continue the follow-through with the arms and palms extended toward the basket (fig. 22.7c).

Common Faults
1. Lowering the arms in a "preparatory" move, then raising them to shoot. Lowering the ball gives the opponent an opportunity to get the ball or stop the shot
2. Pushing more with one hand than the other
3. Failing to follow through after releasing the ball

Figure 22.8   One-Hand Set Shot

a   b   c

One-Hand Set Shot (Push Shot)

The one-hand set shot is performed by placing the same foot as the shooting hand slightly in front of the body. The ball is held with both hands opposite the chin and above the lead foot (fig. 22.8a). The back is straight with knees partially bent. In a simultaneous action, straighten the knees, release the nonshooting hand, extend the shooting arm forward and upward, and push the ball toward the basket (fig. 22.8b). Release the ball with a slight snap of the wrist and fingers (fig. 22.8c).

Common Faults
1. Placing opposite foot forward
2. Failing to extend the wrist and fingers

Lay-up Shot

The lay-up, which involves dribbling, leaping, and the ability to judge distance, can be learned by boys and girls in the intermediate grades. In fact, most children are more successful at this skill than other shooting skills, such as the one- or two-hand set shot. The reason is the short distance between the hand and the rim of the basket when the ball is released.

Approach the basket at a forty-five degree angle (fig. 22.9a). Just prior to shooting, shift the weight to the foot opposite the shooting hand, and raise the ball as far as possible with both hands. Release the non-shooting hand as the shooting arm carries the ball up

(fig. 22.9b). Then release it off the fingertips (fig. 22.9c). The ball should bounce against the backboard about eighteen inches above the hoop, then drop into the hoop.

Common Faults
1. Dribbling, then stopping before executing the upward phase of the skill
2. Taking off too soon and from the wrong foot
3. Throwing the ball rather than extending the arm and "pushing" the ball against the backboard

Free Throw (Two-Hand Underhand)

Although any shot may be taken from the free throw line, the two-hand underhand shot is normally the easiest to perform. Since this is an "unguarded" shot, it is recommended only for the free throw.

Stand with the back straight, knees slightly bent, arms straight, and weight equally distributed over both feet. Hold the ball with the fingertips of both hands slightly under the ball (fig. 22.10a). In a simultaneous action, swing arms forward and upward and straighten the knees (fig. 22.10b). It is important to keep the back straight throughout this movement and to release the ball off the tips of the fingers.

Common Faults
1. Bending too far forward and not keeping the back straight
2. Releasing the ball too soon, causing a low arc as the ball moves toward the basket

Figure 22.9 Lay-Up Shot

a   b   c

Figure 22.10 Free Throw

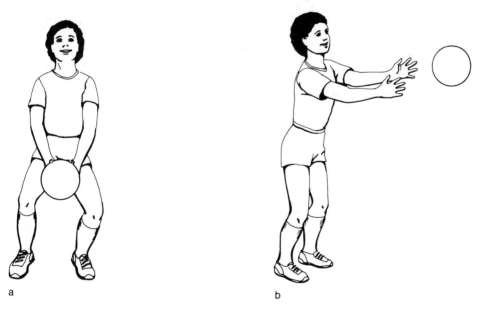

a   b

Pivoting

Footwork in basketball involves stopping, starting, pivoting, and turning in all directions and at varying speeds. When teaching the pivot and turn, stress the importance of gaining body control before attempting the pivot or turn. Also, teach pupils not to change the

pivot foot once it is declared; otherwise, traveling will be charged. Finally, emphasize the need to maintain fingertip control of the ball for quick release after the pivot is made.

Figure 22.11 Pivoting

a   b   c

Prior to performing a pivot, make sure the weight is evenly distributed on both feet (fig. 22.11a). Hold the ball firmly with the fingertips of both hands and keep the elbows out to protect the ball. As soon as one foot becomes the pivot foot, it must remain on the floor. The player may turn in any direction on his pivot foot (figs. 22.11b and c); however, he may not drag it away from the original pivot spot. The opposite foot is permitted to step in any direction.

Common Faults
1. Changing pivot foot after it has been declared
2. Not extending elbows out to protect the ball
3. Dragging the declared pivot foot

Defensive Skills

It is essential that elementary children first learn to move the ball by dribbling and passing, and then learn the basic skills of defense. It is important to stress the fact that legally stopping an opponent from scoring is just as important as scoring itself. The following basic defense techniques should be emphasized, particularly in the fifth and sixth grades.

1. Never cross the feet when guarding an opponent—use a sliding step.
2. Keep the buttocks low and the back upright.
3. When checking, keep one hand up at all times.
4. Do not reach across for a ball; move the body to a position in front of the offensive player and then attempt to take the ball.
5. Always try to get the body in front of the offensive player.
6. Guard with one hand toward the ball and the other hand toward the opponent.

Figure 22.12 Defense Techniques

Practice Activities

The following practice activities will assist in developing passing, shooting, dribbling, and pivoting skills. Modify any of them to meet limitations of the playing area and variations in the children's level of skill and interest.

All activities described in this section are designed to give each student the maximum amount of practice. If there are not enough basketballs, use soccer balls, volleyballs, or utility balls. Also, it is important for the teacher to circulate among the students during practice activities in order to correct errors or to provide encouragement and praise where needed.

Many of the low-organization games and relays described in chapters 14 and 15 can be modified and used as passing, catching, and other basketball skills.

Passing and Catching

Passing and catching activities are normally practiced together.

Partner Passing

Partners scattered around playing area stand about ten to fifteen feet apart, depending on skill.

Each player remains in a stationary position. After a few minutes of practice, have one player remain stationary and the other move around him. After a few more minutes of practice, have both players move, pass, and catch.

Wall Passing

Line formation around available wall surface. Players should stand approximately five feet from the wall and gradually move back as their skill increases. This wall drill can be used to practice all types of passing and catching skills.

Variations
1. Put lines or targets on the wall to increase accuracy.
2. Add timing contests—for example, the number of hits in ten seconds.

Pig in the Middle

Arrange three players in a line with approximately six feet between each. The two outside players are the end players, while the middle player is designated as the "pig."

Allow the end players to move to the right. They attempt to pass the ball to each other without the middle player (the pig) touching the ball. If the pig touches the ball, he replaces the person who threw it. The ball may not be thrown above the reach of the middle player and he must always advance toward the ball.

Circle Passing

Divide the class into squads of five or six players. Arrange the children in circles with approximately six feet between them.

Player 1 turns toward player 2 and passes the ball to him; player 2 catches the ball, turns toward player 3 and passes to him, and so on. If the ball is dropped, it is retrieved by the receiver, who returns to his place in the circle and continues the drill.

Variations
1. Five against one: One player goes to the center of the circle. The five outside players pass the ball to each other, always skipping a person, while the center player tries to intercept the pass. When the center player intercepts a pass, he switches positions with the player who threw the ball.
2. One player goes to the center of the circle with the ball and passes to each player in the circle.
3. Double passing: This is similar to variation 2, with the addition of one more ball. Require the center player to make a bounce pass, while the circle players make direct passes.

Dribbling

Dribbling activities normally begin with each player practicing the skill alone, then shift to partner activities, and finally to group activities.

One-Knee Dribble

All players are scattered. They kneel on one knee and begin bouncing the ball with the same hand as the kneeling knee. This drill eliminates unnecessary arm action. Players should keep their eyes on the teacher and "feel" for the ball.

Figure 22.13 One-Knee Dribble Activity

Figure 22.14 Move the ball under the leg to the other hand.

Variations
1. Dribble the ball, with the elbow of the opposite arm at the side.
2. Move the ball backward and forward.
3. Move the ball around the front of the opposite leg and change hands.
4. Move the ball under the leg to the other hand (fig. 22.14).
5. Bounce the ball in rhythm set by the teacher.
6. Play follow the leader while kneeling. This makes everyone look at the leader and not the ball.
7. Repeat above drills while standing.

Figure 22.15 Movement Drill

Movement Drill

The teacher or a leader stands in front of the group, then dribbles to the right, left, forward, or any other direction. All players move in the same direction as the leader, but with a mirror image, bouncing the ball with the appropriate hand.

Variation
The leader may use hand directions instead of actually shifting positions.

Line Dribble

Divide class into squads of about three or four players. Arrange each squad in a line formation and place one pin (or chair) twenty feet in front of each line.

Player 1 dribbles around the pin and back around his squad and passes the ball to player 2. Player 1 goes to the end of the line and player 2 continues the relay.

Weave Dribble

Divide the class into squads of about four or five players. Arrange each squad in a straight line formation with about ten feet between each player.

Player 1 dribbles around player 2, back and around the opposite side of each successive player until he is back in his original position. Everyone moves up one position and player 1 goes to the rear of the line.

Variation
Use chairs or pins instead of players for obstacles.

Whistle Dribble

Divide class into squads of about three or four players. Line the squads up at one end of the floor. The teacher stands in the center of the playing area.

When you blow the whistle, the first player from each squad dribbles forward. When you blow the whistle again, all players stop immediately and hold the ball ready for the next move. As soon as any player reaches a line parallel to you, he turns and dribbles back to his team.

Variations

1. Use hand signals rather than the whistle for stopping and starting; this encourages the ''head-up'' dribble. A hand over the head means dribble; a hand straight down means stop.
2. Extend arms sideward (right or left) as a signal to pivot right or left. The signals then would be hand over head (dribble forward), hand down (stop), arm out to right (pivot right, then back and ready for the next command).

Shooting

A variety of shooting skills can be used in the following activities. Other skills, such as passing, dribbling, and guarding, can be added to most of these simple practice activities.

Basket Shooting

Divide the class into as many squads as you have baskets. Arrange each squad in a file formation behind the free throw line. One player remains on the end line behind the basket.

The first player dribbles forward, and the player on the end line comes forward to guard the basket. The player with the ball attempts a shot, and then both players try to recover the rebound. Whoever retrieves it passes it on to the next player. The two rebound players exchange positions, that is, the player who took the shot moves behind the end line and the guarding player goes to the end of the line behind the free throw line.

Variations

1. Have two offensive players team up and try to get by the guard and shoot.
2. Do the same with two guards and two offensive players.
3. Repeat with two guards and three offensive players.

Dribble and Shoot

This drill follows three stages, with the last stage arranged as shown in the diagram below.

1. Each player stands three to four feet away from the basket, takes one step with the left foot (if shooting with the right hand) and shoots.
2. Same as stage 1, but begin with the right foot.
3. Place chairs in a line at approximately a forty-five degree angle. Chairs should be about three to four feet apart. Players dribble around the chairs and shoot.

Set Shot Shooting

Arrange six to eight players in a semicircle near a basket. One player, the leader, is stationed under the basket with a ball.

The leader passes the ball to the first player in the semicircle, who attempts a set shot. The leader recovers each ball and passes it to each player in sequence. Adjust the distance from the basket according to the group's level of skill.

Variations

Use two or more balls and have the leader return the balls to any player.

Lay-up Shooting

Arrange two lines of players at a forty-five degree angle to the basket. The first player in each line should be about twenty feet from the basket.

The first player in the shooting line dribbles toward the basket and attempts a lay-up shot, then goes to the end of the retrieving line. The first player in the retrieving line leaves his line at the same time as the shooting player to retrieve the ball and pass it to the next player in the shooting line. The retriever then goes to the end of the shooting line. Continue the drill to the last shooting player; then reverse lines and repeat drill.

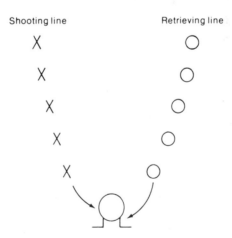

Shooting line   Retrieving line

Offensive and Defensive Activities

One on One

Partners, facing each other, are scattered around the gymnasium.

Without a ball, one player attempts to run past the other. The defensive player moves his body into position to stop the offensive player. He may not use his arms and feet to stop the player or lean into him. Players are not allowed to touch each other.

Variations
1. Repeat drill with a ball.
2. Repeat variation 1 and dribble toward a basket.
3. The following combinations can be used in a variety of ways. Begin each with passing only, then add dribbling, and finally add a target. (Improvise according to available backboards.)
   Two on one
   Two on two
   Two on three
   Three on one
   Three on three

Pivot and Pass

Circle formation with six to eight players standing about ten feet apart.

Each player faces the center of the circle. A player on each side of the circle is given a ball. On signal, each player with a ball keeps his left foot on the ground and pivots a quarter-turn away from the center of the circle, then steps forward on his right foot and passes to the next player. Continue the drill around the circle, then repeat reversing directions.

Pass, Post, and Shoot

Arrange players as shown in diagram.

The post player remains stationary throughout the drill. The ball is given to the offensive player, who tries to maneuver past the defensive player and take a shot at the basket. The ball may be passed back and forth between the offensive player and the post player until the offensive player is ready to move toward the basket and attempt a shot. Allow about thirty seconds to complete the drill, then blow the whistle and rotate players to the next position.

X Defensive player

 Post player

◯ Offensive player

Teaching Suggestions

Set up two drills on each side of the key. If facilities and equipment are limited, draw circles on the wall and place traffic cones or other markers on the floor and restrict players to their assigned areas.

Lead-up Games

The lead-up games described in this section are designed to give children practice in playing games that require one or more basketball skills. Each game can be modified to meet the class's ability and the available facilities and equipment. Whenever possible, divide the playing area into two, three, or four sections to allow two or more games to be played at the same time.

Lead-up Game	Grade	Page
Bucket Ball	4–6	345
Guard Ball	4–6	345
Keep Away	4–6	345
Basketball Touch	4–6	345
Sideline Basketball	4–6	345
Five Passes	4–6	346
Twenty-One	4–6	346
Basketball Snatch Ball	5–6	346
In-and-Out Basketball	5–6	346
Captain Ball	5–6	347

Bucket Ball (4–6)

Formation   A rectangle drawn approximately thirty by forty feet or the gymnasium divided into two playing courts

Equipment   Two wastepaper baskets and one ball for each game

Players   Five or six on each team

Skills   Passing, catching, dribbling, shooting, and guarding

Place wastepaper baskets on the floor at the center of the end lines. If desired, a player may stand on a chair and hold the basket. Players on team A pair off with players on team B, and each checks the other. The game begins with a jump ball between two opposing players. The game continues until one team makes a basket. The general rules of basketball are followed; however, modify any rule as desired.

Variations
1. Play the same game, but use two hoops suspended from the ceiling or walls as goals.
2. Play the same game, but require one type of locomotor movement such as jumping, hopping, or sliding.

Guard Ball (4–6)

Formation   Two lines drawn approximately ten to fifteen feet apart, with teams arranged as shown in diagram

Equipment   Three or four balls

Players   Three or four on each team

Skills   Passing, catching, and guarding

Players on teams A and B must stay behind their own lines, and players on team C must stay between the lines. On signal, players on teams A and B try to pass the balls back and forth to each other. All passes must be below head height of the opposing player. Players on team C attempt to intercept the passes. If a pass is intercepted, player C returns the ball to the passer and stays in position while the game continues. Play the game for one minute and count the number of successful passes. Rotate teams after each game.

Variations
1. Play same game but require only one type of pass.
2. Play same game and require everyone to be constantly moving.

Keep Away (4–6)

Formation   Two teams arranged in a scattered formation within a designated play area

Equipment   One basketball

Players   Three or four on each team

Skills   Passing, catching, pivoting, and dribbling

On signal, the teacher gives the ball to one team, which passes it among themselves, trying to keep it away from the other team. Players on the opposing team check as in regular basketball. If teams are large and space is limited, rotate in fours or fives every few minutes.

Variations
1. Limit person in possession of the ball to three steps before passing the ball.
2. Require every player to pivot before passing the ball.

Basketball Touch (4–6)

Formation   Two teams arranged in a scattered formation within a designated playing area with one goalie standing on the baseline

Equipment   One basketball for each game

Players   Four or five on each team

Skills   Passing, catching, and guarding

Arrange two teams in scattered positions within the court area. Goalies stand on opposite lines and may move up and down their own line. Court players are allowed to pass the ball any number of times as they try to pass it to their goalie. Players may check but are not allowed to dribble the ball. Start game with one player throwing in the ball from the middle of the side line.

Variations

Add limitations, such as only use an overhand pass or every player must dribble three steps, pivot, then pass the ball.

Sideline Basketball (4–6)

Formation   Five players from each team play in the court area, while the remaining players from both teams are placed alternately along the side lines and end lines. Leave equal spaces between line players.

Equipment   One basketball for each game

Players   Ten to twelve per team

Skills   Catching, passing, shooting, dribbling, and pivoting

Basketball rules are followed, except the ball may be passed to a sideline player. Sideline players cannot enter the court, dribble, or pass to another sideline player. Start the game with a jump ball in the center of the playing area. The team that gains possession is designated as the offensive team. If the defensive team intercepts the ball, it must pass to one of its sideline players before it becomes the offensive team.

Stepping over the side line gives the ball to opponents on their side line. Players on the side lines rotate with players on the floor. Field goals score two points and free throws one point.

Variations

1. Require every third pass to go to a sideline player.
2. Limit number of steps court players may travel before passing or shooting the ball.
3. Ask each team to suggest a new rule.

Five Passes (4–6)

Formation   Two teams arranged in a scattered formation on one side of the playing court or within a designated playing area

Equipment   One basketball

Players   Four or five on each team

Skills   Passing and catching

Play is started with a jump ball between any two opposing players. Basketball rules are followed with respect to traveling, fouling, and ball handling. Passes must be counted out loud by the passer. One point is awarded whenever a team completes five passes in a row. The ball cannot be passed directly back to the person from whom it was received, and no dribbling is allowed. Whenever a series of passes is interrupted by an interception or a fumble, a new count is started by the team that gains possession of the ball. A free pass from one teammate to another is awarded to the team that did not commit the foul.

Variations

1. Limit game to one type of pass.
2. Require a pivot before each pass.

Twenty-One (4–6)

Formation   Players of each group arranged in a scattered formation around one basket

Equipment   One basket and one ball for each group

Players   Three or four players in each group

Skills   Shooting and catching

The object of this game is for any player to score twenty-one points by a combination of field shots and free throws. Player 1 shoots from the free throw line, while the other players stand wherever they wish in the playing area. Player 1 continues shooting from the free throw line until he misses, with each successful basket counting one point. When he misses, any player who can get possession of the ball may try for a field goal; if successful, it counts two points. If the try for a field goal fails, any player who can get the ball may try for a field goal. This procedure continues until a field goal is made. After a field goal is made, the ball is given to player 2, who takes his turn at the free throw line. Continue until one player has twenty-one points.

Variations

1. Reduce game point to nine or eleven.
2. Restrict field goals to one- or two-hand set shots.
3. Allow field goal attempts to be a lay-up shot from the closest side to the basket.

Basketball Snatch Ball (5–6)

Formation   Divide class into two equal groups. Arrange each game as follows. Each team on opposite lines. Place two basketballs on a line midway between two opposing teams.

Equipment   Two basketballs

Players   Five or six per team

Skills   Catching, shooting, and dribbling

Players are numbered consecutively and must stand in this order on the side line of the playing area. When the teacher or leader calls a number, that player from each team runs to one of the balls, picks it up, dribbles it to the basket, and shoots until he makes a basket. When he succeeds, he dribbles back and replaces the ball. The first player to make a basket and return the ball scores one point for his team.

Variations

1. Players may run by pairs, with two players from each team having the same number. In this case, the ball must be passed between the players three times before and after the shot is made.
2. Require specific types of shooting skills.
3. Add a math challenge for fun, such as "8–5" or "1/4 of 12," instead of the simple number.

In-and-Out Basketball (5–6)

Formation   Two teams playing in half of the basketball court, and a third "waiting" team on the side line

Equipment   Two basketballs

Players   Six teams of five players each

Skills   Shooting, catching, dribbling, and pivoting

Regular basketball rules apply with the following modifications: (1) Three teams play in half the court; (2) two teams play, while the third team remains on the side line; (3) when a field goal or free throw is made, the third team takes the loser's place; and (4) each player is allowed only two dribbles.

Variations

1. If goals are not being scored, use a time limit instead.
2. Have waiting team practice passing or dribbling skills while they are waiting.

Captain Ball (5–6)

Formation   Playing area arranged as in diagram. Note: Two games can be played in each half of a typical elementary school gymnasium.

Equipment   Two basketballs, 8 hoops

Players   Eight on each team

Skills   Dribbling, passing, catching, and guarding

The captain and three forward players of team A must keep one foot inside their hoops. Four guards from team A may roam anywhere in team B's side of the playing area; however, they cannot enter the hoop of any opposing player. The object of this game is for the guards to get the ball to any of their forward players. The forward players, in turn, try to get the ball to their captain. Start the game with a jump ball between two opposing guards. Award two points each time the captain receives the ball from one of his forwards.

Fouls occur when—

1. A guard steps into an opposing player's hoop, steps over the centerline or boundary line, or throws the ball directly to the captain (ball is given to the nearest forward player on opposing team);

2. A forward steps out of his circle, holds the ball longer than five seconds, or commits unnecessary rough play (ball is given to the nearest guard on the opposing team).

Variations

1. Add more circle or guard players. Even numbers make the game more difficult.
2. Require only one type of pass.
3. Add any rule or modification as desired.

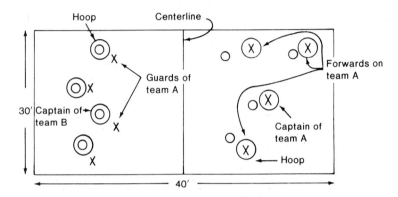

Basketball: Rules and Regulations

Basketball is probably the most popular team sport in the upper elementary grades, particularly with boys. Although skill development, especially ball handling and shooting skills, necessitates that the majority of the time be spent on drills and lead-up games, the full game should be played several times during a unit of instruction. Modify the rules, such as lowering the height of the basket and limiting the number of dribbles, to encourage the development of specific skills. Care should be taken, however, not to play the full game too often, perhaps neglecting needed skill development.

I. Field of play: Adjust court and key dimensions to available space.

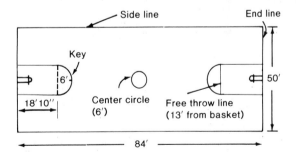

II. Positions:

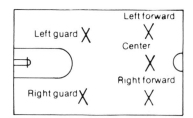

III. To start game: The game is started at the center circle. The referee tosses the ball in the air between the two opposing centers, who attempt to tap it to one of their teammates. This jump ball is also used when the ball goes out of bounds and the referee is uncertain which team caused it to go out, and to start the second half of the game.

IV. After a successful free throw: The ball is put into play at the end of the court by the defending team.

V. After a ball goes out of bounds: The ball is put into play from behind the line and immediately in front of the place where it went out. Any player from the team that did not cause it to go out may put it into play.

VI. Game time: The game is divided into four quarters of six minutes each.

VII. Points: Two points are awarded for every field goal, and one point for every successful free throw.

VIII. Substitution: One or all substitutes may enter the game whenever the ball is not in play (out of bounds, before a jump ball, etc.).

IX. Violations: A violation is charged against a player if he
  A. travels—takes more than one step with the ball without dribbling
  B. double dribbles—dribbles the ball, stops, then dribbles again without another player handling the ball, or palms the ball, that is, does not clearly dribble, or dribbles with two hands
  C. steps on or over a boundary line while in possession of the ball
  D. kicks the ball
  E. stays longer than three seconds in the key area under the offensive basket, in which case play is stopped and the referee awards a throw from the side line to the other team near the point where the infraction occurred

X. Fouls: A foul is charged against a player if he
  A. kicks, trips, or pushes another player
  B. holds or charges another player
  C. commits unsportsmanlike conduct

XI. The penalty: Play is stopped and the referee awards one or two free throws to the nonoffending team from the free throw line. The number of free throws awarded is based upon the following:
  A. One free throw is awarded to a player who is fouled while participating in an activity other than shooting. If the free throw is successful, the defending team puts the ball into play from behind the end line. If the free throw is unsuccessful, the ball continues in play.
  B. Two free throws are awarded to a player who is fouled when he is shooting. If the second free throw is successful, the defending team puts the ball into play from behind the end line. If the second free throw is unsuccessful, the ball continues in play.

Evaluative Techniques

Several tests can be used to measure the basic passing, dribbling, and shooting skills. The following test items are reliable and quite easy to administer. Modify any of them to meet your own teaching situation and add additional ones if desired. Also keep scores from each year in order to build appropriate norms for your school.

Basketball Skill Test

Name	Passing (total pts.)	Dribbling (total pts.)	Shooting (50 pts.)	Subjective Evaluation (50 pts.)	Total Score	Grade
1 2 3		Rank total scores for the class, then convert to letter grades or ratings (superior, good, etc.).				

Test 1: Passing

Place a target on the wall as shown in the diagram. The player must stand and pass from behind the ten-foot line. He has thirty seconds to hit the target as many times as possible. If a player drops the ball within the time period, he may pick it up, return to the ten-foot line, and continue adding to his cumulative score. One point is scored for each pass that lands on the target area. Allow two trials and record the highest score.

Test 2: Dribbling

Arrange four chairs as shown in the diagram. A ball is placed on the starting line. Each player stands behind the starting line, with both hands resting on his knees. On signal "go," he picks up the ball and dribbles around the chairs in a zigzag pattern. One point is awarded each time he passes a chair. Allow twenty seconds for the test. Two trials are allowed with the highest score recorded.

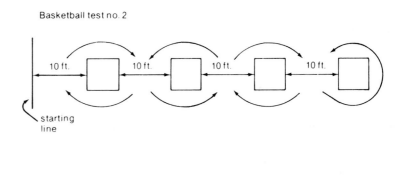
Basketball test no. 2

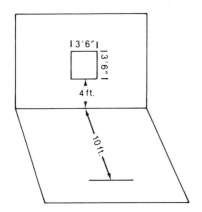

Test 3: Shooting

Draw a line at a forty-five degree angle thirty feet from the basket. Each student attempts ten lay-up shots. He must begin dribbling from the thirty-foot line and attempt a shot when he reaches the basket. Award five points for each successful basket. Other shooting tests, such as free throws or one- or two-hand sets, may be substituted for the lay-up test.

Test 4: Subjective Evaluation

Establish criteria that represent the skills and playing ability required in basketball. Using shooting ability, dribbling, defensive skill, and passing, the teacher can award each player a total score from zero to fifty points. Three players can be used as judges, with the average score recorded.

23 *Softball Activities*

Emphasis and Skill Presentation

Teaching Procedures

Description of Skills
Throwing
Catching and Fielding
Hitting the Ball
Base Running

Practice Activities
Throwing and Catching
Batting

Lead-up Games

Softball: Rules and Regulations

Evaluative Techniques
Test 1: Accuracy Throw
Test 2: Distance Throw
Test 3: Fielding
Test 4: Subjective Evaluation

Softball is an extremely popular recreational activity throughout Canada and the United States and in many other countries. Its popularity is probably due in part to the game's relative ease and safety. In addition, softball requires only a minimum amount of protective equipment and a smaller playing field than is required for baseball.

If softball is to be played as a competitive recreational game, every participant must know the rules and be reasonably proficient in the basic throwing, catching, and batting skills. Furthermore, each child should be given an opportunity to play every position. Assigning only the more proficient players to the catcher, pitcher, and first-base positions is educationally unsound.

This chapter has been organized to provide a basic approach to teaching softball to upper elementary school children. Although lead-up games should be emphasized more than regulation softball during the instructional period, the official game or a modified version should be played occasionally to provide an opportunity for the class to understand the skills and playing strategies and, of course, for the teacher to test the children's abilities as batters and fielders.

Emphasis and Skill Presentation

The problems of selecting and teaching softball skills and rules are very similar to those found in teaching basketball activities. Through television, organized leagues, and "sandlot" games, most children of this age level are already acquainted with many of the skills and rules of softball. Thus, there will be a very wide variation in the development of softball skills in virtually every grade and within each class. The suggested sequence of presenting skills and rules in table 23.1, therefore, should be used as a basic guideline.

Table 23.1 Suggested Sequence of Presenting Softball Skills and Rules

| Skills and Rules | Grade Level | | | |
	Grade 3	Grade 4	Grade 5	Grade 6
Throwing				
Overhand Throw	Acquired or introduce	Increase distance and accuracy	Increase distance and accuracy	Increase distance and accuracy
Underhand Throw	Acquired or introduce	Increase speed and accuracy	Increase speed and accuracy	Increase speed and accuracy
Pitching	Acquired or introduce	Increase speed and accuracy	Increase speed and accuracy	Increase speed and accuracy
Sidearm Throw			Introduce	Increase speed and accuracy
Rules: Safe and Out	Acquired or introduce			
Fair and Foul Ball	Acquired or introduce			
Strike Zone	Acquired or introduce			
Pitching Rule		Introduce		
Catching and Fielding				
Catching Low and High Throws	Acquired or introduce	Refinement	Refinement	Refinement
Catching Fly Balls	Acquired or introduce	Refinement	Refinement	Refinement
Fielding Grounders	Acquired or introduce	Refinement	Refinement	Refinement
Rules: Fielding Positions	Acquired or introduce			
Foul Tip		Introduce		
Bunt Rule				Introduce
Batting				
Batting	Acquired or introduce	Increase distance and accuracy	Increase distance and accuracy	Increase distance and accuracy
Fungo Hitting			Introduce	Increase distance and accuracy
Bunting				Introduce
Rules: Balls and Strikes	Acquired or introduce			
Base Running				
To First Base	Acquired or introduce	Increase speed	Increase speed	Increase speed
Around Bases		Introduce	Increase speed	Increase speed
Rules: Touching Base	Acquired or introduce			
Off Base on Caught Fly		Introduce		
Related Skills				
Positional Play			Introduce	Refinement
Stealing Bases			Introduce	Refinement
Double Play				Introduce
Sacrifice				Introduce

This table indicates that children normally have been introduced to most throwing, catching, and batting skills by the third grade. The emphasis prior to grade four, however, has been on acquiring these skills through enjoyable lead-up games rather than regulation softball.

Several changes should occur in the fourth grade. More care and attention should be given to increasing the distance and accuracy of throwing skills. The pitching rule should be introduced, and all boys and girls in this grade should have an opportunity to play this position. More consistency in batting should also be expected

The fifth- and sixth-grade programs should be seen as continuous periods of refining the basic softball skills. More experienced players will also develop a reasonable level of skill in the sidearm throw and bunting. Major improvement in general positional play should also be shown by most of these children. And it is not uncommon for sixth graders to be able to steal a base, sacrifice, or make a double play.

Teaching Procedures

There is a very close similarity between the approaches used to teach softball and basketball. Many elementary school children have played modified versions of softball such as scrub and two-man softball; their skill and general understanding of the game are well beyond the beginner stage. But children who have not had this advantage are far behind in skill development and general playing ability. Since the teaching approach suggested for soccer can apply equally to softball, review page 273 to see how a unit of instruction and individual lessons can be developed.

The inventive games approach suggested in previous chapters can also be applied with equal success to softball activities. Presenting challenges such as "Make up a four-person drill emphasizing grounding and a sidearm throw" provides freedom for a group to develop an activity that is challenging and enjoyable yet concentrates on one or two important skills. You can also cope with problems associated with sex and peer performances through this problem-solving approach.

The following suggestions apply more specifically to problems associated with teaching softball activities.

1. Softball is too inactive for most of the players. To help overcome this problem
   a. Rotate positions as often as possible.
   b. Use a batting tee if pitching and batting abilities are generally low.
   c. Select lead-up games that require smaller playing areas and fewer players.
   d. Modify the official game, such as two outs before changing positions or all players hitting before changing sides, or shorten the distance between bases.

2. Several safety precautions should be considered during every instructional and recreational period involving softball activities.
   a. All waiting batters should stay behind a designated safety line located to the rear and on the first base side of the catcher.
   b. Every player should be taught how to release the bat after hitting the ball. Stringent enforcement of this rule is extremely important for everyone's safety.
   c. Proper-fitting face masks should be provided for the catcher.
   d. Sliding should be prohibited since it can cause unnecessary injury and tear street clothes.
   e. All bases should be made of soft material.

3. An umpire should be used in the more complex lead-up games and in every modified or regulation softball game. Establish a procedure for rotating the umpire as the teams change positions.

4. Modify every game to cope with the class's general level of ability and interest.

Description of Skills

Softball skills for elementary school children can be classified as hitting and fielding skills. All throwing and catching skills are appropriate for this age range. As for batting skills, most children have little difficulty learning to hit a ball with a full swing, although bunting and fungo batting present some problems.

Throwing

The major part of all fielding and defensive play depends upon how fast and how accurately a player can throw the ball. Although the skill and style of performance varies from child to child, each is capable of throwing an overhand, sidearm, and underhand toss or pitch with relative ease and accuracy.

Gripping the Ball

The softball can be gripped in two basic ways. If the hand is large enough, the ball can be held between the thumb and first two fingers, with the third and fourth fingers just resting against the side of the ball. Elementary school children's smaller hands make it necessary for them to grip the ball with the thumb, and all four fingers spread around the side and bottom of the ball (fig. 23.1a). However, only the top surface of the fingers should touch the ball. The grip is correct if the young thrower can see daylight between the ball and his hands (fig. 23.1b).

Overhand Throw

This is the basic throw for all players except the pitcher. The upper arm of the throwing arm is raised shoulder-high, then the forearm is lifted above the head and the wrist flexed so the hand points backward (fig. 23.2a). At that point, the left side faces the direction of the throw and the left arm extends forward. The weight is on the rear foot. In a simultaneous movement, the upper right arm is lifted upward and forward and the left arm moves down and back as the weight shifts to the front foot (fig. 23.2b). The ball is released off the fingertips

Figure 23.1 Gripping the Ball

a. Thumb and four-finger grip   b. See daylight

Figure 23.2 Overhand Throw

a. Forearm above the shoulder   b. Arm raised upward and forward   c. Follow-through

Figure 23.3 Sidearm Throw

a   b   c

when the arm is about shoulder-high. Follow-through should be in a downward direction, ending with the palm of the throwing hand facing the ground (fig. 23.2c).

Common Faults
1. Holding the ball too close to the palm of the hand
2. Failing to lead the throw with the elbow
3. Keeping the upper arm too close to the body
4. Failing to follow through in a downward direction

Sidearm Throw

The sidearm throw is used when the ball must be thrown a short distance and in a hurry; thus it is the most effective throw for infielders. The general body action of this throw is similar to the overhand throw, except the upper throwing arm is extended diagonally out and down from the shoulder and the forearm is extended straight up from the elbow (fig. 23.3a). As the arm swings forward, the forearm drops down and swings parallel to the ground (figs. 23.3b and c). As the ball is released, the arm continues across and around the body.

Common Faults
1. Failing to extend the upper arm diagonally out
2. Swinging the throwing arm forward and downward
3. Failing to follow through across the body

Figure 23.4 Forward Pendulum Action of the Arm

Underhand Toss

The underhand toss is used for short, quick throws, most often around the infield area. The player extends his upper arm and forearm backward as his weight shifts to his rear foot. On the forward movement, his arm swings down and forward and his weight is shifted to the front foot (fig. 23.4). As the ball is released, the player follows through with his upper arm and hand in the direction of the throw.

Figure 23.5   Pitching

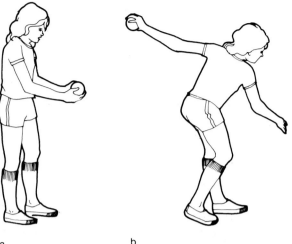

a   b   c

Common Faults

1. Failing to shift the weight to the back foot
2. Releasing the ball too soon or too late
3. Failing to follow through in the direction of the throw

Pitching

The pitcher stands with feet parallel, holding the ball in front with both hands and facing the batter. She moves both hands forward until her arms are extended to about waist-high (fig. 23.5a). She then releases her right hand from the ball as she brings her throwing arm down and back. At the top of the backswing, her body twists slightly toward her pitching arm and her weight is on her foot (fig. 23.5b). In a simultaneous action, she swings her left arm forward close to the body, rotates her shoulders toward the right, and steps forward on her left foot (fig. 23.5c). As the ball is released off the fingertips, she follows through with the pitching arm.

Common Faults

1. Failing to extend the throwing arm back and up prior to pitching
2. Failing to rotate the shoulders toward the left on the forward swing of the throwing arm
3. Releasing the ball too soon or too late

Figure 23.6   Fielding

Catching and Fielding

Good fielding ability requires the player to be able to catch a high fly ball and a variety of throws and to stop a ball hit along the ground. In all types of fielding it is important to be in a ready position, with the feet spread apart comfortably and the weight on both feet. The trunk leans forward slightly and the knees are flexed. The hands are in front of the body about knee-high. The eyes are on the ball (fig. 23.6).

Catching

If the ball approaches below the waist, the fingers point with the little fingers together (fig. 23.7a). When the ball approaches above the waist, the thumbs are together and the fingers point upward (fig. 23.7b). As the ball is caught, the hands recoil toward the body to deaden or soften the force of the oncoming ball.

Common Faults

1. Failing to get in line with the ball
2. Failing to reach out to catch the ball
3. Failing to "give" or recoil with the ball

Figure 23.7 Catching in the Field

a. Catching below the waist   b. Catching above the waist

Fielding Grounders

The first important move in grounding a ball is to shift the body toward the direction of the oncoming ball. As the fielder moves toward the ball, she shifts her weight forward, holding her arms low and in front of her body (fig. 23.8a). Just before grounding the ball, she stops, with her right foot slightly in front of her left foot, her knees bent, and her trunk well forward (fig. 23.8b). She contacts the ball just inside her front foot with her left hand, then covers or traps it with her throwing hand (fig. 23.8c). The eyes should be kept on the ball until it is firmly held. Once the ball is caught, the fielder begins to straighten up and takes a step in the direction of the throw.

Fielding a ground ball requires good fielding position and split-second timing to catch the ball on a good bounce. Because of these factors, plus the use of poor and uneven playing fields, the "sure-stop" grounding skill should be used, particularly by outfielders. This is similar to the regular grounding skill, except that the fielder turns toward the right and lowers one knee to the ground. The thigh and lower leg provide a good rebound surface for a ball that is missed (fig. 23.9).

Common Faults

1. Failing to keep the eyes on the ball until it is caught
2. Failing to get in line with the ball
3. Failing to "give" with the fingers, hands, and arm as the ball is caught

Figure 23.8 Fielding Grounders

a   b   c

Figure 23.9 "Sure-Stop" Grounding

Hitting the Ball

A softball can be hit in three basic ways. The first, and most important, is hitting a pitched ball with maximum force and follow-through. *Bunting* is a form of hitting a pitched ball; however, it requires basic differences in grip, force, and follow-through. *Fungo batting* is simply throwing the ball up with one hand, regrasping the bat, and hitting the ball before it hits the ground.

The bat may be gripped in one of three positions, depending upon the batter's strength and the type of hit he wishes to make. In the long grip (fig. 23.10a), the hands are placed close to the bottom of the bat. For the medium grip (fig. 23.10b), the hands are moved up about one to two inches. And, for the choke grip (fig. 23.10c), the hands are about three to four inches from the knob of the bat. In each grip, the bat is held with the hands together and the fingers and thumbs wrapped around the handle. For right-handed batters, the right hand grips the handle above the left hand.

Figure 23.10 Gripping the Bat

a. Long grip

b. Medium grip

c. Choke grip

Figure 23.11 Batting

a   b   c

Batting

The batter stands with his feet parallel about shoulder-width apart. The left side of the body faces the pitcher. The bat is held at the back of the head about shoulder-high. The arms are bent at the elbows and held away from the body (fig. 23.11a). As the ball leaves the pitcher's hand, the batter shifts his weight to the rear foot (fig. 23.11b). He then swings the bat forward as his weight shifts to the lead foot (fig. 23.11c). After the ball is contacted, the batter continues to swing the bat around in a wide arc, ending over the left shoulder.

Common Faults
1. Holding the bat on the shoulder and keeping the elbows too close to the sides
2. Swinging the bat up and under the ball
3. Contacting the ball with a relaxed grip

Bunting

In bunting, the bat is placed in the way of the on-coming pitch, then allowed to "give" as the ball contacts the bat. Begin in a normal batting position (fig. 23.11). As the ball moves toward the strike zone, the batter draws his rear foot forward and squares his body to the pitcher. At the same time, he slides his top hand up the bat, keeping the hand cupped and the fingers resting just behind the hitting surface (fig. 23.12). When the ball is hit, the bat is angled in the direction of the intended bunt.

Figure 23.12 Bunting

Common Faults
1. Moving into the bunting stance too soon
2. Failing to "give" as the ball contacts the bat
3. Failing to direct the ball to the right field position

Figure 23.13 Fungo Batting

a   b   c

Fungo Batting

Fungo batting is useful for hitting the ball during fielding practice and in many lead-up games. Start with the feet parallel and comfortably spread apart, with the weight evenly distributed on both feet. Suspend the bat over the right shoulder while holding the ball in the left hand (fig. 23.13a). Simultaneously toss the ball up and swing the bat down and forward, grasping it with both hands (fig. 23.13b). Continue forward, transferring the weight to the front foot and twisting the body toward the left. Hit the ball approximately in front of the left foot (fig. 23.13c) and follow through with a swing around the left shoulder.

Common Faults
1. Throwing the ball too far in front of the body
2. Hitting the ball too far in front of the body

Base Running

As soon as a ball is hit, the batter drops his bat and runs as fast as possible to and through first base. The base runner touches the foul line side of the bag with either foot. If he decides to try to run to second base, he begins curving to the right a few feet before reaching first base, touches the inside corner of the bag and continues running to second base.

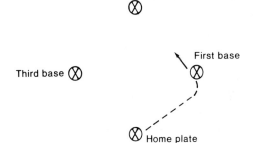

Common Faults
1. Failing to run on every hit
2. Failing to run "through" first base
3. Failing to touch the base

Practice Activities

One of the most common complaints by elementary school teachers is the insufficient number of balls and bats for practice activities. This can be overcome by using a station system and rotating groups. The accompanying illustration shows several partner and group activities involving a variety of skills going on simultaneously. Each group rotates to the next station after a set period of time. If the groups do not have time to rotate through all the stations in one lesson, simply continue in the next lesson.

Most practice activities for softball involve partners or small groups. Each of the following drills and practice activities should be modified to cope with the available space, time, and equipment.

Throwing and Catching

Perhaps the most common type of softball practice activity involves two players. Some of the most useful partner activities are described.

Partner Activities

1. Have the partners throw and catch. Have both partners remain stationary, varying the distances; then have one remain stationary while the other moves, practicing grounders.

2. Have the pitcher and catcher alternate positions.
3. Practice hitting a target. Set up a target on a wall or the ground for pitching or accurate throwing practice.

The inventive games approach can be used quite effectively in partner activities to increase skill and to provide an avenue for unique and enjoyable practice activities. The following example should provide a general idea:

Situation: Divide the class into partners. Give the partners a ball and one piece of small equipment (bat, hoop, traffic cone).
Challenge: "Can you make up a game (or drill) with your partner that includes a sidearm throw, a grounder, and one piece of small equipment?" Allow the class several minutes to make up their games, then select one or two partner groups and have them demonstrate their games.

Group Activities

Several relays described in previous chapters can be adapted for practicing softball skills. See Zig-Zag Volleyball, page 284, and Shuttle Volleyball, page 286.

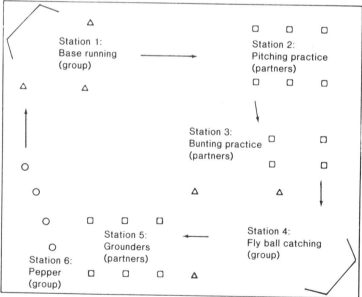

Station System for Softball

Station 1: Base running (group)

Station 2: Pitching practice (partners)

Station 3: Bunting practice (partners)

Station 5: Grounders (partners)

Station 4: Fly ball catching (group)

Station 6: Pepper (group)

Available field space

Overtake the Base

Divide the class into squads of eight to ten players. Arrange the squads around the bases, with player A at the pitcher's line, B on home plate, C on first base, D on second, and E on third. The remaining players form a line near home plate.

When the whistle blows, player A throws to B, B throws to C, and so on around the diamond to home plate. At the same time A throws the ball, F takes off for first base and continues around the bases, attempting to reach home plate before the ball. Two rules apply: (1) The base runner must touch all bases and (2) the players rotate after each run. A takes B's position, B goes to C, F takes A's. Everyone shifts one place to the right, with the player E on third going to the back of the line.

Variations

1. Make two diamonds, with the smaller one for runners and the larger one for throwers.
2. Add one or more fielders.

Fly Ball Catching

Place one batter at home plate and scatter the remaining players in the field.

The batter, using fungo batting, hits fly balls into the field. When a fielder catches a fly ball, he becomes the batter.

Variations

1. Place all fielders in a large semicircle and require the batter to hit two balls to each player in turn. Rotate after the last player has received his second fly.
2. Add a pitcher and a catcher.

Throw for Distance

Arrange field as in diagram.

The throw must be made from within two restraining lines. After a reasonable warm-up, the player throws the ball as far as possible from behind the restraining line. He may take one or more steps, providing he remains within the lines. The player with the longest throw or the team with the most total yardage wins. Rotate retrievers after each throw.

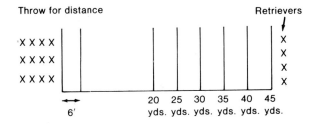

Variations

1. Vary the type of throw, such as underhand, sidearm, or overhand.
2. Throw for distance and accuracy. Select a zone between 30 and 35 yards and award 10 points if a player hits within this zone, and 5 or 2 points, respectively, for adjacent zones.

Softball Throw Relay

Arrange teams in equal lines behind a starting line, with approximately six feet between each team. Draw a throwing line ten feet in front of the starting line. Place a catcher for each team on a third line twenty-five feet in front of the throwing line.

A player on each team runs to the throwing line to receive the ball thrown by the catcher, then throws it back to the catcher. The thrower returns to the starting line and tags the next player, who continues the relay.

Variations

1. Have the children use various throwing skills—underhand, overhand, left-handed, and right-handed.
2. Alternate catchers each time a team wins; the first person in line becomes the catcher.

Batting

The success of any softball game centers on each player's ability to hit the ball. Too often, however, batting practice is one player hitting the ball to ten or more very inactive fielders. The following partner activities are very effective in developing batting skills.

1. One player hits the ball off a tee to his partner. Use a traffic cone mounted on a cardboard box as a substitute tee.
2. One player fungo hits to his partner.
3. Add a third player. One player pitches, another bats, and the third player fields the ball. Rotate after three hits.
4. Practice close-range bunting. One player pitches, while the batter attempts to bunt the ball back.

Group Activities

The following group activities should be modified to meet the class's level of ability.

Swing at Four

Divide the class into two or three squads of ten to twelve players. Arrange squads in infield positions, with spare players in a line behind home plate.

The pitcher throws four balls to each batter, who attempts to hit them into the infield. Infield players retrieve the ball and throw it to first base. The first baseman returns the ball to the pitcher. Rotate players after each player has had four hits. The batter takes the third baseman's position and everyone shifts one place to the left. The catcher goes to the back of the "waiting" line, and the pitcher becomes the catcher.

Variations

Add outfielders and allow batters to hit anywhere.

Pepper

Divide the class into groups of five or six. Place five players in a line, with about ten feet between each player. One player, the "leader," stands about twenty feet in front of the line with his bat.

The first player in the line pitches the ball to the leader, who hits it to the next player in line. The second player fields the ball and pitches it back to the leader. Continue the drill to the last player, then rotate the leader.

Variations

If a line player misses the ball, he goes to the end of the line. If a batter misses a fair pitch, he changes places with the player at the end of the line.

Lead-up Games

The following lead-up games are designed to provide maximum participation and practice in one or more softball skills. As a general guideline, use these games extensively in grades four and five and proportionately less in sixth grade. Playing the official game of softball can be a challenging and enjoyable experience for upper elementary school children, but only when the majority of players have developed adequate throwing, catching, and batting skills. These lead-up games can be played in smaller areas and require fewer players than the regulation game.

Six-Player Softball (4–5)

Formation   Playing field and players arranged as in diagram

Equipment   Three bases, one bat, and one softball

Players   Six on each team

Skills   Throwing, catching, and hitting

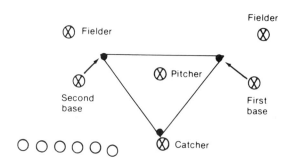

This game is similar to softball with the following modifications: (1) A game has six complete innings; (2) there are four outs in each inning; (3) a batter is out after two strikes; (4) a foul ball counts half a strike; and (5) a base-on ball is given after three balls rather than four. All players rotate one field position after each inning.

Variations

1. Use a batting tee if skill level is too low.
2. Use an 8½ inch utility ball, and bat with a stiff arm.

Danish Rounders (4–5)

Formation Playing field and players arranged as in diagram

Equipment Tennis ball or five-inch utility ball

Players Ten on each team

Skills Throwing, catching, and base running

The pitcher throws an underhand pitch slightly above the batter's head, and the batter tries to hit the ball with his hand. Whether he hits the ball or not, he must run to first base, and farther, if possible. The fielding team tries to return the ball to the pitcher, who tries to touch his base with it before the batter reaches first base. If the ball touches the pitcher's base before the runner reaches first base, he is out. Any number of batting players may be on any base at the same time, and on any strike or hit they may remain on base or run to the next one. But when the pitcher downs the ball, any base runner who is off base is out. Also, a caught fly automatically puts out the batter and any player who is running between bases. Play continues until every member of the batting team has had a turn at bat; then the teams change positions. A point is scored when a player makes it to home plate.

Variations
1. Specify one type of throw.
2. Have fielding team return ball to first, second, or third base, rather than to the pitcher.

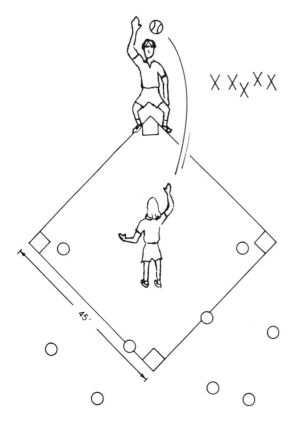

Flies and Grounders (4–6)

Formation One batter and five other players scattered in the playing area

Equipment One bat and ball for each group

Players Six in each group

Skills Throwing, batting, and fielding

The batter hits the ball into the field off the tee or fungo-style. The player in a position to catch the ball calls ''Mine'' and attempts to catch it. A player receives five points for catching a fly ball, three points for a ball caught after one bounce, and one point for a grounder. The first player to reach fifteen points becomes the new batter.

Variations
1. Substitute a pitcher for fungo hitting.
2. Require only one type of throw.

One Old Cat (4–6)

Formation Players divided into two teams of nine each, with one team in the field and one at bat

Equipment Softball and bat, two bases (first and home)

Players Nine on each team

Skills Throwing, catching, and batting

The first player on the batting team hits the ball into the field and tries to run to first base and home in one complete trip. He may not stop on the base. If he makes a complete trip without being put out, he scores one run for his team. The runner is out if (a) a fielder catches a fly ball, or (b) a fielder touches the runner with the ball before he reaches home. When the team at bat makes three outs, it goes into the field and the team in the field comes to bat. The team with the highest score at the end of the playing period wins. (Teams must have the same number of times at bat.)

Variations
1. Alternate pitchers and catchers. Alternate boy and girl in batting order.
2. Try two outs if one team stays up too long.
3. Vary the distance to base according to the level of skill.
4. Use batting tee if skill level is too low.

Long Ball (4–6)

Formation Class divided into two equal teams. The fielding team consists of a pitcher and a catcher, with the remaining players scattered in the field.

Equipment Softball, bat, and two bases (home and first)

Players Nine on each team

Skills Throwing, catching, and hitting

Each team selects a pitcher and a catcher. Other players are fielders or batters. When a batter hits the ball, he runs to the base, and, if possible, returns home to score a point. Any hit is good and there are no fouls. The base runner may stop on first base, and any number of runners may be on base at the same time. Runners may not steal home. The batter is out when he strikes out, is touched off base, steals a base, throws the bat, or hits a fly ball that is caught. One point is awarded for each run.

Variations

1. Substitute a batting tee if skill level is too low.
2. Change any rule or add new ones as need or interest dictates.

Tee Ball (4–6)

Formation Regulation softball

Equipment Softball, bases, and tee (commercial tee or traffic cone mounted on a cardboard box)

Players Nine on each team

Skills All softball skills except pitching and stealing bases

This game is played in the same way as softball, with the following modifications.

1. The batter is allowed one hit off the tee.
2. Since there is no pitcher, no one is permitted to steal a base. A runner must stay on base until the ball is hit by a teammate.

Cricket Softball (4–6)

Formation Playing field arranged as in diagram

Equipment One softball, two bats, four Indian clubs, and two bases

Players Ten arranged in partners

Skills Batting, throwing, catching, and fielding

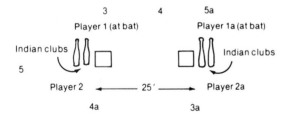

The object of this game is for each set of partners to score runs by hitting the ball and running to opposite bases before the Indian clubs (or milk cartons) are knocked down by any fielder. The game begins with players 1 and 1a at bat. Players 2 and 2a are pitchers and stand beside each base. All other players are fielders. There are no boundaries. The batter must begin with the butt end of the bat touching the base.

Player 2 throws the ball at the Indian clubs and the batter protects them by hitting the ball. If the pitcher knocks over a club, an out is called. When this occurs, players 1 and 1a become fielders and players 2 and 2a become the new batters. If 1a hits the ball, he exchanges positions with his partner. The fielders try to recover the ball and knock over the Indian clubs by rolling or throwing the ball at them before the runners can change places. A run is scored if the fielders cannot knock down the Indian clubs before the runners exchange positions. As long as the clubs remain standing, the batters may exchange bases any number of times, scoring a run for each exchange. Pitchers must alternate throwing after each successful run. A caught fly is an out for the batting team. After an out players 2 and 2a become the new batters and players 3 and 3a become the new pitchers.

Twenty-one Softball (4–6)

Formation Arrange teams as in regular softball

Equipment One bat, one ball, and four bases

Players Nine to ten on each team

Skills Throwing, catching, and hitting

Play according to regular softball rules, with the following exceptions: The batter gets three swings to hit the ball. When he hits the ball, he runs the bases in order until he is put out. A runner safe at first scores one point; at second, two points; at third, three points; and at home, four points. Teams exchange places after three outs. The first team to score twenty-one points wins.

Variations

1. Change pitcher and catcher each time the teams change positions.
2. Use fungo or hit off a tee.
3. Change scoring to eleven or fifteen points rather than twenty-one.

Overtake the Ball (4–6)

Formation Class arranged in a large circle with ten to twenty feet between each player

Equipment One softball per team

Players Five to seven per team

Skills Throwing and catching

The players stand in a circle and count off by twos. The ones are members of one team and the twos, the other. Each team selects a captain, who stands in the center of the circle. Both captains have a ball. On signal, each captain tosses his ball to any team member, who tosses it back to the captain. The captain tosses it to the next team member (in a clockwise direction), who also tosses it back to the captain. The ball is tossed in this manner clockwise around the circle by both teams until each ball has been thrown to all members of the team and is back in the captain's hands. One team "overtakes" the other when its ball passes that of the other team as the balls are tossed around the circle. The team that tosses the ball completely around the circle first scores one point. When a team overtakes and finishes first, it scores two points. The first team to score five points wins the game.

Variations
1. Play the game with various kinds of balls and different throws and passes.
2. Vary the distance according to the level of skill.

Roll at the Bat (4–6)

Formation Outdoor playing area with fielders in a scattered formation facing the batter

Equipment One bat and one softball

Players Four to five for each game

Skills Fungo or tee hitting, catching, and throwing

One player chosen to be the first batter hits the ball anywhere into the field of play. If a player catches a fly ball, he rolls it back and tries to hit the bat, which has been placed on the ground. The length of the bat must face each "roller." If the ball is not caught, it is thrown back to the batter again. A fielder becomes the new batter when (a) he successfully rolls a ball back and hits the bat, (b) he catches two fly balls, or (c) he successfully retrieves three grounders. All players start at zero when a new batter takes a turn.

Beatball Softball (5–6)

Formation Teams arranged as in regular softball

Equipment Bat, softball, and four bases

Players Nine on each team

Skills Throwing, catching, and hitting

Play according to regular softball rules, with the following exceptions: Any fielder who gets the ball must throw it to the first baseman, who must touch the base with the ball in his hand, then throw from first to second, second to third, and third to home. If the ball gets home ahead of the runner, he is out. If the runner beats the ball home, he scores a run for his team. After three outs the teams exchange places.

Variations
1. Use fungo or tee hitting.
2. Move the bases closer together.
3. Require one type of throw such as a sidearm or underhand toss.

Scrub (5–6)

Formation Playing field with a home base, pitcher, and first base

Equipment One ball, one bat, and three bases—home, first, and pitching

Players Seven to nine for each game

Skills All softball skills

One player (the "scrub") stands at bat. All other players are numbered; the catcher is one; pitcher, two; first baseman, three; and fielders, four and up. The batter hits a pitched ball and must run to first base and back. He is out if he is tagged at first or home, strikes out, slings his bat, or hits a fly ball that is caught. If he gets home, he bats again. The batter is allowed only three times at bat; then he becomes the last fielder. If the batter is put out, every player moves up one position.

Variations
1. If a player catches a fly ball, he exchanges positions with the batter.
2. Two players may be up at the same time. In this situation, the first batter is permitted to stop on first base and be hit home by the other batter.
3. Use tee or fungo hitting.

Five Hundred (5–6)

Formation Outdoor playing area with fielders in a scattered formation facing the batter

Equipment One softball and one bat

Players Four to six players for each game

Skills Fungo batting, throwing, catching, and fielding

One player is chosen to be the first batter. The object of the game is for each fielder to try to be the first to reach 500 points. Points are scored as follows: 100 for catching a ball on the fly; 75 for a ball caught on the first bounce; and 50 for fielding a grounder. The same number of points is deducted from a player's score if he commits an error. As soon as a player has reached 500 or more points, he exchanges positions with the batter.

Variations
1. Use a pitcher.
2. Require only one type of throw.
3. Add a roll at the bat and award another 100 points for hitting it.

Softball: Rules and Regulations

Although skill development varies for each grade and class, the complete game of softball should be played periodically throughout a softball unit. By playing the game according to the basic rules, children learn to appreciate the value of practice and team play. Modifications might include shortening the length between bases and substituting a batting tee for a pitcher. While children are playing the full game, the teacher should note their major weaknesses so she can select appropriate drills and lead-up games that can be used to improve these deficiencies.

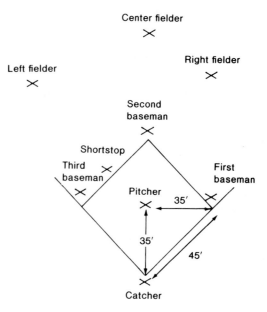

I. Field of play and positions: See illustration.

II. Batting order: Players are permitted to hit in any order; however, it is wise to have players bat according to their positions. Once an order is established, it cannot be changed, even if players change their positions.

III. The batter advances to first base when he
   A. hits a fair ball and reaches base before the ball does;
   B. is walked (receives four called balls);
   C. is hit by a pitched ball;
   D. is interfered with by the catcher when batting.

IV. The batter is out when he
   A. has three strikes;
   B. is thrown out at first;
   C. is tagged before reaching first base;
   D. hits a fair or foul ball that is caught on the fly;
   E. hits the third strike and the ball is caught by the catcher;
   F. bunts a foul on the third strike;
   G. throws the bat more than ten feet;
   H. steps on home plate when batting;
   I. interferes with the catcher when he is catching a fly or putting out a runner coming home;
   J. fouls any ball to the catcher that rises above the batter's head and is caught.

V. When traveling the bases the base runner
   A. may advance to the next base after a fly is caught;
   B. must advance to the next base when forced to do so by another base runner;
   C. may advance one base on an overthrow at first or third base;

D. may advance two bases when overthrows are in the field of play;
   E. may attempt to steal a base as soon as the ball leaves the pitcher's hand;
   F. may advance to the next base on a fair hit that is not caught on the fly.

VI. The base runner is out when he
   A. leaves the base before the ball leaves the pitcher's hand;
   B. is forced to run to the next base and does not arrive before the fielder touches the base with the ball in his possession;
   C. leaves the base before a fly ball is caught and a fielder tags him or that base before he returns;
   D. is hit by a batted ball when off base;
   E. intentionally interferes with a member of the fielding team;
   F. is tagged when off base;
   G. fails to touch a base and the fielder tags him or the base before he returns;
   H. passes another base runner;
   I. touches a base that is occupied by another base runner.

VII. The pitcher
   A. must stand with both feet on the rubber, face the batter, and hold the ball in front with both hands;
   B. is allowed one step forward and must deliver the ball while taking that step;

366   *Chapter 23*

C. must deliver the ball with an underhand throw;

D. cannot fake or make any motion toward the plate without delivering the ball;

E. cannot deliberately roll or bounce the ball;

F. cannot deliver the ball until the batter is ready.

VIII. If there is an illegal pitch, the batter is entitled to take a base.

IX. The game is five to seven innings, as agreed by both teams. When there is not sufficient time to complete the game, the score reverts to the even innings score (the score after both squads have been up to bat the same number of times).

X. One point is scored each time a batter touches home base after touching each base sequentially.

Evaluative Techniques

Several tests can be used to measure the basic softball skills. The following tests are quite reliable and can be administered with student help in a short period of time. Modify any test item to meet your own teaching situation and add items if desired. Also, keep scores from year to year in order to build appropriate norms for your school.

Softball Skill Test

Name	Accuracy Throw (total pts.)	Distance Throw (total pts.)	Fielding (total pts.)	Subjective Evaluation (50 pts.)	Total Score	Grade
1 2 3 4		Rank total scores for the class, then convert to letter grades or ratings (superior, good, etc.).				

Test 1: Accuracy Throw

Place a target on the wall as shown in the diagram. Use a regulation softball. A player is given ten consecutive throws from behind the throwing line. He must use the overhand throw. Score six, four, and two for hits within each respective circle. If a ball hits a line, award the higher value. Allow only one trial and record the total score.

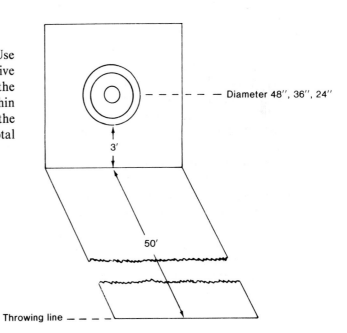

Diameter 48″, 36″, 24″

3′

50′

Throwing line

Test 2: Distance Throw

Place lines on the field as shown. Stakes can be used as a substitute for white gypsum lines. Use a regulation softball. Award points according to where the ball lands.

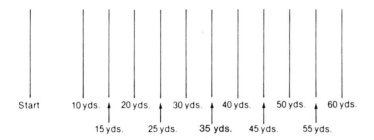

Test 3: Fielding

Place lines on a field as shown. Stakes or other "corner" markers can be substituted for lines. The teacher (or a student who is proficient at fungo batting) bats a grounder into the field area. As soon as the ball is batted, the player runs from the starting line, picks up the ball inside the field area, and throws it to the catcher. Ten trials are given, with five points awarded for each successfully fielded ball. Since it is difficult to hit grounders with reasonable consistency, use your discretion to allow retrials on any ball you feel was unfair to the contestant. Also, if batting skill is too poor, substitute a throw for the fungo batting.

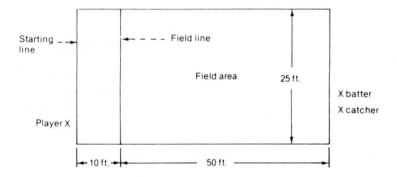

Test 4: Subjective Evaluation

Establish criteria that represent the skills and playing ability required in softball. Since it is difficult to construct a fair and reliable test for batting, include this skill as part of your subjective evaluation. Consider other skills such as base running, catching, and team play. Award a total point score (zero to fifty points) and use three players as judges. Take an average of the three ratings.

24 Track and Field Activities

Emphasis and Skill Presentation

Expected Proficiencies

Teaching Procedures

Description of Skills
Starting
Running
Standing Long Jump
Long Jump
Hurdles
High Jump
Triple Jump: Hop, Step, and Jump
Shot Put

Practice Activities

Track and Field Meet: Rules and Regulations

Evaluative Techniques

Upper elementary school children have a keen interest in track and field activities. They can participate in these events according to their ability and motivation. Furthermore, track and field activities are relatively easy to teach, require little expense, and provide vigorous competitive experience for all children. The inherent values of this activity, coupled with the feasibility of modifying facilities, make it one that should be considered a basic requirement in the elementary school physical education program.

This chapter describes the basic track and field events and presents methods of organizing and teaching these activities. Special attention has been given to developing improvised equipment and planning track meets.

Emphasis and Skill Presentation

Skill development in any of the official track and field events is dependent upon the performer's potential or inherent ability and the amount and type of previous training. Taking these factors into consideration, the suggested sequence of skills shown in table 24.1 is provided as a rough guideline. In this type of activity, the improvement in individual events is not simply the accumulation of new skills; it is the sequential addition of skills plus improvement in form and general conditioning.

The fourth grade is an important starting point for many track and field skills. Correct starting positions, sprints, and distance running should be introduced to children in this grade. They also should develop reasonable skill in the standing and running long jump, as well as the high jump using the scissors method.

Most of the remaining track and field skills are introduced in grade five. These youngsters are interested in and capable of learning baton passing, hurdling, high jumping using the straddle method, and putting the shot. They display a major increase in skill and performance levels in both track and field events. Children in grade six learn the triple jump and continue to improve their form and performance in other events.

Table 24.1 Suggested Sequence of Presenting Track and Field Skills and Rules

Skills and Rules	Grade Level			
	Grade 3	Grade 4	Grade 5	Grade 6
Starting				
For Distance Runs		Introduce	Refinement	Refinement
For Sprints		Introduce	Refinement	Refinement
Rules: False Start		Introduce		
Running				
Sprints	30- to 40-yd. dashes	40- to 60-yd. dashes	50- to 80-yd. dashes	50- to 100-yd. dashes
Relay Running			Introduce	Refinement
Hurdling			Introduce	Refinement
Distance Running		500- to 600-yd. run	Increase distance and speed	Increase distance and speed
Jogging		1 to 2 miles	2 to 3 miles	3 to 4 miles
Rules: Lane Position			Introduce	
Passing Rule			Introduce	
High Jumping				
Scissors Method	Introduce	Increase height and form	Increase height and form	Increase height and form
Straddle Method			Introduce	Increase height and form
Rules: Number of Jumps		Introduce		
Broad Jump				
Standing Long Jump	Introduce	Increase distance and form	Increase distance and form	Increase distance and form
Long Jump		Introduce	Increase distance and form	Increase distance and form
Rules: Foot Fault		Introduce		
Triple Jump				
Rules: Foot Fault				Introduce
Shot Put				
Rules: Foot Fault			Introduce	Increase distance and form
Other Rules				
General Track Meet Rules		Introduce		

Expected Proficiencies

Since proficiency in track and field events is measured in time or distance, table 24.2 provides a rough estimate of what can be expected of elementary school children. If teachers are introducing track and field activities similar to those listed, it is wise to establish school records. Use the suggested high and low records as a guide in establishing "expected" records within your school.

Table 24.2 Proficiency Levels for Track and Field

| Events | Minimum to Optimum Records | | | | | | | |
| | Grade 4 | | Grade 5 | | Grade 6 | | Grade 7 | |
	Low	High	Low	High	Low	High	Low	High
50–yd. Dash (seconds)	10.0	6.0	9.5	6.0	9.0	6.0	8.9	5.8
220–yd. Run (seconds)	42.0	31.0	40.0	32.5	38.0	30.5	37.0	30.0
150–yd. Run (seconds)	27.0	22.0	25.0	19.1	23.0	18.2	22.5	18.0
High Jump	2'11''	3'4''	3'0''	3'10''	3'6''	4'2''	3'8''	4'6''
Standing Long Jump	4'0''	6'4''	4'8''	6'8''	4'10''	6'11''	4'5''	8'9''
Running Long Jump	11'0''	12'2''	12'0''	13'2''	13'0''	14'2''	13'6''	15'0''
Triple Jump	12'	15'	13'	16'	14'	17'	16'6''	21'6''
Softball Throw	35'	175'	70'	205'	76'	207'	88'	245'
Shot Put	9'	15'	10'	16'	12'	17'	15'	21'

Teaching Procedures

Several important factors must be considered when planning a track and field unit. Although it is important for all children to experience the enjoyment and challenge of all the events, they should be allowed to concentrate on a few events that they enjoy and do well. This means the teacher should introduce the children early to as many track and field events as possible. Each child can then select a certain number of events for more extensive practice.

A second major consideration is how to cope with available space and equipment. Since there is never enough equipment for all children to practice the same event at the same time, station work should be used. The track and field circuit on page 372 provides a basic guideline.

It is important to put each event in a relatively permanent place on the field. Jumping pits are normally located in the corners of the field. A temporary track can be made by placing traffic cones or milk cartons filled with sand or earth in an oval pattern. Placing the shot put circles inside the oval provides a safe, restrictive area for this event. Sprints and hurdles can be located near each other for dual instruction purposes.

Once the general layout is established, the teacher can divide her class into squads and assign each to a station. Give brief demonstrations at each station, then allow time for practice before the squads are rotated to the next station. Rotation should be from a track event to a field event.

The following general considerations and safety procedures should be included in every track and field unit of instruction.

1. All facilities and equipment should be checked before the class begins. In particular, look for broken glass or other hazardous materials in jumping pits and field areas.
2. Each lesson should begin with a comprehensive warm-up or conditioning period involving running, jogging, and conditioning exercises designed to increase strength, endurance, and flexibility.
3. Whenever possible, provide instruction to mixed groups rather than separating boys and girls. The difference in performance levels of boys and girls at this age is more often due to motivation and prior experience than to inherent physiological differences.

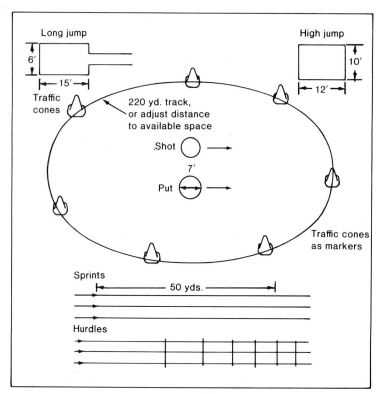

Track and Field Circuit

Description of Skills

There are two basic types of events in track and field: (1) running events, which include sprints, hurdles, and longer endurance runs and (2) field events which include the high jump, the long jump, the triple jump and the shot put. These skills should be taught to all students, regardless of their inherent ability. Once the children have been exposed to these skills, allow them to select and concentrate on those events that are best suited to their potential capabilities.

Starting

The starting position for running events is determined by the length of the race. For short races, such as twenty- and thirty-yard dashes, the "kneeling start" or "sprint start" is best. For longer races, the "standing start" is more acceptable.

Standing Start

In the standing start (fig. 24.1), one foot is close to the starting line and the other foot is slightly to the rear. The head is up, the trunk is bent forward, the knees are slightly flexed, and the weight is on the front foot. The opposite arm to the lead foot is held forward with the elbow flexed, while the other arm is down and slightly back.

Figure 24.1 Standing Start. Body leans forward slightly

Sprint Start

The sprint start is important to the success of any beginning sprinter. The form and techniques of this skill are quite easy to master, even for fourth graders.

On the "on your mark" command the runner kneels and places the toe of her front foot about six to twelve inches behind the starting line (fig. 24.2a). The front foot is normally the opposite foot to the "kicking

Figure 24.2 Sprint Start

a. "On your mark" b. "Set" c. "Go"

Figure 24.3 Sprinting Form

Figure 24.4 Distance Running Form

foot." She extends her arms straight down, with the weight on the fingertips. (If children do not have adequate arm and shoulder girdle strength, allow them to support their weight on their knuckles.) The runner squeezes her fingers together to make a "bridge" with the thumb. On "set" she raises her lower knee and buttocks until her back is straight and parallel to the ground (fig. 24.2b). Her weight should be evenly distributed between her hands and her front foot. Her head is not raised as she should be looking at a spot on the ground a few feet in front of the starting line. On "go" she drives forward with her lead leg and, at the same instant, brings her rear leg forward (fig. 24.2c).

Running

There are several types of running positions, each with its own body lean, arm action, and foot contact. The elementary school track program, however, involves only two types, sprinting form and distance running form. In the sprinting form (fig. 24.3), the runner's body leans well forward and contact is made with the ball or front of the foot. The arms are bent at the elbows and swing vigorously from the shoulders. In distance running (fig. 24.4), the body is more erect and the weight is taken on the heel, then rocked forward. The elbows are bent slightly and the arm action is less vigorous than in sprinting.

Relay Running

Many teachers have observed that fast runners lose relay races to slower competitors simply because of poor passing techniques. It is quite possible to teach upper elementary children the correct "upswing" method of passing in a short period of time, because this method is perhaps the easiest for the beginner to master.

The runner who is to receive the baton draws her right hand straight back toward the approaching runner. She holds her fingers together, pointing to the side, while she points her thumb toward her body. This forms a V into which the approaching runner places the baton (fig. 24.5). The approaching runner brings the baton up into the receiving runner's hand (fig. 24.6). As soon as the front runner receives the baton, she brings it forward into her left hand in preparation for the next pass.

When students are ready to practice baton passing at full speed, it is important that they establish their own check marks—when they should start to run. As a general rule, have the runner place a mark on the ground five yards back of his starting point.

The incoming runner starts fifty yards back of the passing zone and runs as fast as possible. When he passes the check mark, the outgoing runner turns and runs as fast as possible. When the outgoing runner reaches the passing zone, he puts his hand back for the baton. He must be inside the passing zone before he receives the baton or his team is disqualified. If the incoming runner cannot catch up to the outgoing runner, the check mark should be moved closer to the outgoing runner's starting point. If the incoming runner runs past the outgoing runner, the check mark should be moved farther back from the outgoing runner's starting point.

Figure 24.5 Relay Receiver Form a V

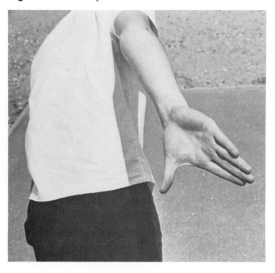

Figure 24.6 Passing the Baton Upward into the Hand

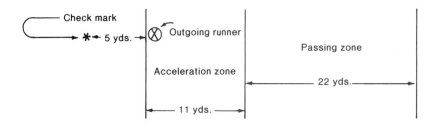

Standing Long Jump

The performer stands with his toes just behind the starting line, his feet comfortably spread, his knees bent, and his trunk well forward (fig. 24.7a). After several preliminary swings with the arms, he swings his arms forward and upward vigorously and extends his legs. As soon as his feet leave the ground, he begins to flex his knees, keeping his arms forward (fig. 24.7b). He lands with his feet parallel and his trunk and arms extended in a forward direction (fig. 24.7c).

Long Jump

A successful long jumper must be able to combine jumping and speed. Elementary school children have sufficient speed for this event and can execute the approach flight and landing relatively well. The performer begins several yards back from the takeoff board, runs forward, and places her takeoff foot on the board (fig. 24.8a). As soon as she leaves the board, she brings her rear leg and both arms forward and upward (fig. 24.8b). Her heels contact the ground and she immediately thrusts both arms back (fig. 24.8c), forcing her body well forward.

Figure 24.7 Standing Long Jump

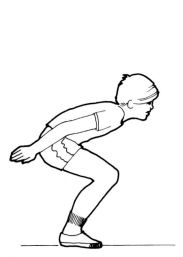  

a. Ready for jump   b. Knees bent   c. Trunk flexed

Figure 24.8 Long Jump

a   b   c

An effective technique to help students gain height in the jump is to suspend a hat from a crossbar or on the end of a rope attached to a stick (fig. 24.9). The height of the hat should be adjusted so that the student jumps to maximum height in order to put the hat on his head. The distance from the takeoff point varies, but it should be a little more than half of the total jump.

Hurdles

Elementary school children can run the hurdles with speed and efficiency. The main reason they usually do not learn the proper form is because the hurdles are set too high and/or too far apart.

Figure 24.9 Technique for Gaining Height

When the runner is approximately seven feet from the hurdle, she lifts her lead leg and extends it forward (fig. 24.10a). The arm opposite to the lead leg should also extend forward (fig. 24.10b). She continues moving her lead leg forward and upward until it clears the hurdle (fig. 24.10c). The rear leg then starts forward, with the toes turned up. Note the important forward body lean as the runner prepares for the next stage. She draws her lead leg down and thrusts her trailing leg forward. Throughout this whole movement the shoulders should be parallel to the finish line.

The following stages should be followed when introducing hurdles.

1. Begin by having the children sprint about twenty-five yards.
2. Place an obstacle (a cane or an old broom handle) on the ground approximately halfway or between thirty to forty-five feet from the starting line. Again, the children sprint the full length; however, they should make no attempt to hurdle the obstacle.
3. Place a second obstacle on the ground so that it is midway between the third and fourth strides. The teacher can check whether runners are taking the correct three strides between hurdles by observing if they are taking very short steps (usually five) or if they land on a different foot after each hurdle (usually four steps). In order to assist the runner in developing the three-step sequence between hurdles, set up numerous courses (see diagram) so that each runner can select the one that fits his step pattern.
4. The obstacles should now be raised nine to twelve inches. Use shoe boxes, bricks, small stands, or adjustable hurdles. Let the children practice and then gradually raise the hurdle

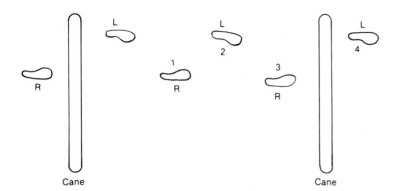

height to thirty inches. When the obstacle approaches twenty-four inches, the children should be taught what to do with the trailing leg. Have them walk down beside the hurdle. As they approach it, have them step in front and slightly to the side of the hurdle with their lead leg and then take the trailing leg over the hurdle. The thigh of the trailing leg should be parallel to the top of the hurdle; then it should be brought through quickly into the next stride. Once the correct technique is acquired, the children should jog down beside the hurdles doing the same drill. Finally, have them run from the starting position and hurdle in the center of each hurdle.

1. The takeoff must be between five and seven feet from the hurdle. The actual distance depends upon the child's size and strength. This seems like a long way when standing and looking at it, but it is very easy to negotiate the hurdle from this distance when in motion.

2. Bring the knee of the lead leg up quickly toward the hurdle.

3. Lean forward into the hurdle to acquire good balance.

4. Bring the lead leg down quickly.

5. Snap the trailing leg through quickly into the next running stride.

6. Always lean forward on the hurdle, never backward.

Table 24.3   Recommended Competitive Hurdles*

	Height of Hurdles (inches)	Number of Hurdles	Start to First Hurdle	Between Hurdles	Last Hurdle to Finish Line	Total Distance
12 and under	20 to 30"	6	33'4"	22'3"	35'5"	60 yards

*Adjust the height of the hurdle to meet the performer's level of ability.

Figure 24.10   Jumping Hurdles

a. Lift lead leg   b. Lean body forward   c. Thrust trailing leg down

Figure 24.11   High Jump—Scissors Style

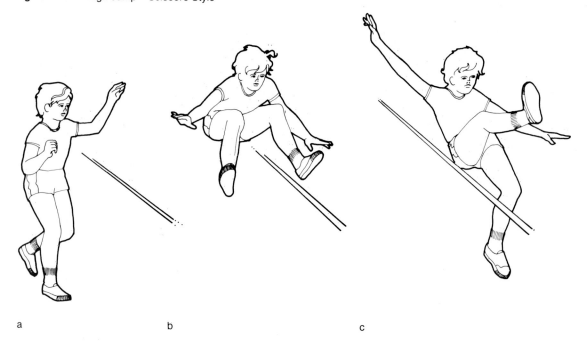

a   b   c

High Jump

Two types of jumping styles are described here. The "scissors style" is the easier of the two and should be learned first. The "straddle roll," although more difficult to learn, is the better of the two in terms of heights that can be reached. Regardless of the method taught, it is imperative that a good landing surface be provided. Children will not learn to jump correctly if they are afraid to land in the pit. Although foam rubber is more acceptable, shavings or an improvised rubber tube pit provide a satisfactory landing surface.

A very inexpensive jumping pit can be constructed by using discarded automobile tire inner tubes. Place tubes on the ground, as shown in appendix B, and tie them together. Then place a tumbling mat on top of the tubes. This provides a safe and comfortable landing surface that can be used both indoors and outdoors.

Scissors Method

The jumper approaches from the left at a slight angle to the bar—fifteen to twenty degrees (fig. 24.11a). He takes a few steps, plants his right, or "takeoff," foot, then swings his left foot high into the air. The left leg continues over the bar (fig. 24.11b), followed by the right in a scissors action. At the same time, the arms swing forward and upward, assisting the upward lift of the body (fig. 24.11c). The right foot lands first, followed by the left, completing the scissors action.

Straddle Method

Proper technique must be stressed when introducing this method of jumping. Poor technique leads to little or no improvement and a disillusioned jumper. The jumper approaches from the left side approximately forty-five degrees to the bar. He takes a few steps, plants his left, or "takeoff," foot, swings his right leg forward and upward and raises his arms (fig. 24.12a). He continues the upward and forward movement, extending his body and lifting his leg upward (fig. 24.12b). At the height of the jump, his body is parallel to the bar (fig. 24.12c). He continues "rolling" over the bar, landing on his hands and right foot (fig. 24.12d).

Triple Jump: Hop, Step, and Jump

This event is a very popular event among boys and girls alike. The appeal seems to be both the distance that is traveled and the immediate improvement once the proper techniques are learned. The runner starts thirty to forty yards back to gain maximum speed at the takeoff mark. The first stage is a hop on the right foot from the takeoff board (fig. 24.13a). To maintain forward speed, the hop is kept low. The left leg drives forward and the jumper lands on his right foot (fig. 24.13b). He continues forward with a thrust of the left leg (fig. 24.13c), lands on the heel of his left foot, and rocks forward toward the toe. He continues the forward action by pushing off from his left foot (fig. 24.13d) and landing on both feet in the pit.

Figure 24.12   Straddle Roll

a   b   c   d

Figure 24.13   Hop, Step, and Jump

a. Hop right   b. Land right   c. Step left   d. Jump

Shot Put

The six-pound shot put event has proved to be an extremely safe and enjoyable activity for boys and girls in the upper elementary school. Too often, however, this event is neglected in the upper elementary school track and field program. Various reasons are given for this, but most of the arguments prove invalid upon close investigation.

The performer stands near the back of the circle with his weight on his right leg and his left toe touching the ground. He holds the shot in a "cradled" position on the side of his neck. He extends his left arm upward for balance (fig. 24.15a). He then lowers his trunk over his right leg and raises his left leg upward and toward the front of the circle (fig. 24.15b). In a simultaneous action, he drives his right leg toward the front of the circle and shifts his left leg in the same direction. Throughout this shifting movement, the body should be kept low (fig. 24.15c). At the end of this shifting movement, he begins to extend his right leg upward, rotates his trunk toward the front, and extends his right arm forward and upward. The shot is released with a final push off the fingertips (fig. 24.15d). The body continues to move around to the left side.

To construct a throwing area for shot putting, take a piece of rope approximately five feet long and tape the ends. Drive two nails through the rope exactly three and a half feet apart. Hold one nail stationary and scribe an arc with the other end.

Figure 24.15 Throwing the Shot

a. Weight on right foot

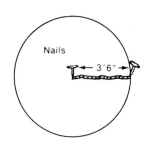

Nails

← 3′6″ →

Figure 24.14 Holding the Shot

a. Gripshot with fingers spread

b. Cradle shot on side of neck; lift opposite arm for balance.

380   *Chapter 24*

b. Lower trunk   c. Shift forward   d. Push shot off fingertips

Practice Activities

Track and field skills require a great deal of individual attention by the teacher and extensive practice by the student. The following practice activities should be used throughout the track and field unit to supplement individualized instruction and to encourage a competitive spirit among all members of the class. Several relays described in previous chapters are also suitable for track and field. They are the circle post relay, page 243; the zigzag relay, page 243; the rescue relay, page 243; and the obstacle relay, page 244.

Continuous Running

A set distance is established. For example, the children could be asked to run one mile on the track or to run from the school to a point one mile away. Each child runs as far as he can, then walks the rest of the mile. With practice, the children should gradually increase the distance they run. Enjoyable courses can be set up on the school ground or in a nearby park or wilderness area.

Interval Training

This is the most commonly used training method among track and field athletes. This form of training has three components: (1) the distance covered on each interval; (2) the recovery period between intervals; and (3) the number of repetitions performed. The following example illustrates this form of training.

A group of children are training for a 440-yard race. The best time for the group is seventy seconds. Since the length of the interval is 220 yards, the time is

reduced to thirty-five seconds expected for each 220-yard run. Each child attempts to run the first 220 yards within thirty-five seconds, rests or walks for three minutes, then attempts to run the next 220 yards within thirty-five seconds. This procedure continues to the end of the fifth 220-yard run. When a runner can complete the five 220-yard runs in the time allotment, the training can be increased in three different ways. These are to (1) reduce the running time, (2) reduce the recovery period, or (3) require more repetitions (increase to six or seven 220-yard runs).

Walk, Jog, Run

Make a small track out of traffic cones or any other type of markers.

Teach the children the difference between walking, jogging, and running. A jog is about half speed and a run is full speed. To start, students are allowed to walk at their own speed around the markers. The first blow of the whistle means that everyone jogs. The second blow means that everyone runs at top speed. The third blow means that everyone jogs, and the fourth blow means everyone walks. Continue this sequence.

Teaching Suggestions

At the beginning of the unit, allow more time between the walk and jog phases and short periods at top speed. Gradually increase the time at full speed.

Start and Pass

Arrange class into a line formation, with six to eight on each team. Put half the team behind each of two starting lines twenty-five feet apart.

This is essentially a starting drill. The teacher should use the following commands: "Take your marks," "Set," and "Go," or blow a whistle. On the whistle, two runners on each team behind opposite lines make fast starts and run until they pass each other. At the passing point each player slows down to a walk and goes to the rear of the line.

Teaching Suggestions

1. Each player runs all the way over the opposite line, then slows down to a walk back to the rear of the line.
2. Use standing and kneeling starts.

Call Race

Arrange two teams of five to ten runners on a starting line. Draw a turning line thirty feet in front of the starting line.

Line up each team along the starting line. Number the players on each team. The teacher calls out any number, such as "four." Both number four players run to the turning line and back across the starting line. Continue calling numbers at random until all runners have had a turn.

Teaching Suggestions

Call out "Take your mark," "Set," and then the number. Only players whose numbers were called should run. The remaining players stand up and wait. This is an excellent starting drill.

Number of Jumps

Arrange class in a long line formation, with the children's toes touching the starting line. Draw a finish line twenty to thirty feet in front of the starting line.

Each child begins on the starting line and makes a standing broad jump as far as possible. His subsequent jumps start from where his heels touched. The object is to see who can make it across the finish line in the fewest number of jumps.

Teaching Suggestions

Use partners to mark landing positions and to count jumps.

Over the Rope

Arrange teams of five to eight in a line formation facing a mat.

This high jumping activity can be used outside on grass or indoors on mats. Two players hold a long skipping rope at various heights while the remainder of the squad practices the scissors or straddle roll over the rope.

Baton Passing

The class is divided into groups of four to eight runners placed in a single line approximately four feet apart as shown in the diagram below.

From a stationary position the children start passing the baton from the end of each line. The first runner passes with his left hand to the runner in front, who takes the baton in his right hand. He immediately brings it forward into his left hand in preparation for the next pass. The baton should be brought up into the receiving runner's right hand. When the baton reaches the front of the line, everyone turns around and the drill is repeated.

After the students have the feel of passing the baton in a stationary position, have them do it in a slow jog. Therefore, the distance between runners will have to be increased. Repeat the drill, gradually increasing the speed, and the distance between runners.

X Baton ⟶	X ⟶	X ⟶	X ⟶	X
Pass with left	Take with right and pass with left			
X Baton	X	X	X	X
X Baton	X	X	X	X
X Baton	X	X	X	X

Hash Running

Hash running is a team race in which markers are located along the route, hidden directions are located near the markers, and a total team effort is required in order to finish the race in the shortest period of time. The following example provides a basic format that can be used in any rural or urban school. See the diagram to the right.

Before the class arrives for physical education, set up your "hash course." In the sample course the starting position is in front of the school. Each team (the size is optional) starts here (stagger the starting times) and is told it will find the first marker—a red ribbon placed on a goalpost—within fifty yards of the starting position. As soon as the marker is found by any member of the team, he calls to his teammates and they all come to the marker. They know that the first hidden directions will be somewhere within fifty yards (keep this distance constant) of the marker. The teammates move in different directions until one finds the directions, located on the school wall. As soon as a player finds the directions, he calls his team together. This pattern continues throughout the course. The team that returns in the shortest time wins the race.

Some Considerations

1. Since the majority of physical education periods are approximately thirty minutes, begin with three to four markers, then increase the number and difficulty as experience dictates.

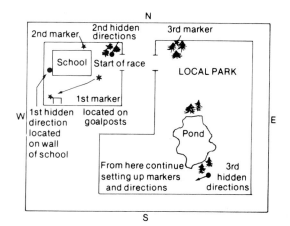

2. Make a rule that markers must be located before the directions, because some children may find directions first.
3. Although teams are staggered, one team may catch up to another, and thus vital information may be "given away." Encourage teams to make up diversionary signals if this occurs.
4. If you have taught orienteering and compass directions, use these skills in hash running.
5. Since schools in urban areas have problems with traffic and restrictive park areas, take care in planning hash courses to ensure the children's safety and the protection of public gardens.

Track and Field Meet: Rules and Regulations

The organization and general rules and regulations of any elementary school track and field meet will depend upon the children's general interest, the available time, and the facilities. The following information, although not complete, will assist in developing the facilities, meet rules, and order of events for most elementary school track meets.

I. Track dimensions: The 220-yard running track illustrated on page 384 can be constructed on most outdoor playing areas.

II. High jump pit: The pit should be twelve feet long and ten feet wide. Sawdust or shavings should be used to fill the pit, which should be boarded with straw bales. (Also see appendix B for an improvised pit constructed of rubber tubes).

III. Long jump pit: The runway to the pit should be approximately thirty yards long, with an eight-inch takeoff mark five feet from the pit. The pit should be ten feet wide and twenty feet long. It should be filled with fine sand.

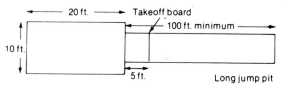

IV. Order and number of events: Each school, of course, may vary the length of dashes and include additional events. The following order of events should provide a format for scheduling.
   A. 50-yard dash
   B. Shot put
   C. Standing long jump
   D. Long jump
   E. 220-yard relay
   F. High jump
   G. 220-yard run
   H. Triple jump
   I. Softball throw
   J. Hurdles
   K. Obstacle race
   L. Tug-of-war

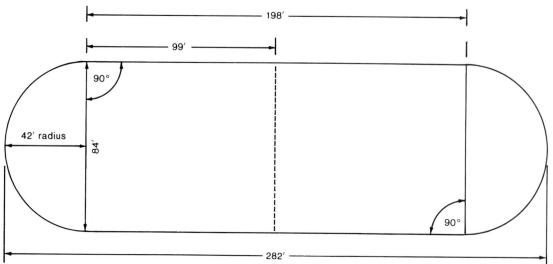

Plan for a 220–Yard Running Track

V. Track and field officials: The following jobs should be allocated to teachers or dependable students.
  A. Meet director
  B. Starters, same for all track events
  C. Finish judges—head finish judge and first-, second-, and third-place judges, and additional place judges, if desired
  D. Field judges—one judge and one helper for the high jump, standing long jump, triple jump and running long jump
  E. Announcer and head recorder with assistants for running messages and obtaining results of the events.
VI. Meet requirements: Each school should establish its own eligibility requirements for the following situations.
  A. Number of events each participant may enter. For example, perhaps each child could enter two track events and one field event.

  B. Classification of participants. Several methods can be used to classify participants, such as age, grade, or a classification index.
  C. Number of places and point awards. For example, the first four places could be recorded with five, four, three, and two points respectively.

Many other questions need to be answered if the track meet is to be successful. Give some thought to type of awards, methods of keeping school records, and required practice before a participant is eligible for the track and field meet. Once you and the students agree on the basic rules and regulations of the track meet, take time to explain them to the students, and post rules in the classroom and gymnasium.

Evaluative Techniques

Although performance in track and field events would appear to be easy to evaluate, quite the contrary is true. Each event is scored on the basis of either distance or time. The problem lies in placing a value on improvement rather than merely awarding an arbitrary number of points for the student's ranking in each event. This is further complicated by the philosophy underlying a track and field unit. At this age level, boys and girls should be free from excessive competitive pressure and should not have to judge themselves against the standards set by the exceptional athlete.

The solution is to allow each student to select a certain number of events and then record his initial and final scores. This approach to evaluating performance and improvement thus becomes a personal assessment. A child who is a low achiever can set a realistic goal for himself without worrying about who is the best in each event. Similarly, the outstanding performer can set a high standard, which motivates him to work at his maximum capacity.

6 Gymnastic and Movement Activities

Part 6 has been organized to meet the conditions existing in the majority of elementary schools. Many classroom teachers are still teaching gymnastic activities through a reasonably structured approach. At the same time, however, they are attempting to apply movement education concepts and skills into various parts of their gymnastic programs.

The three chapters in this section attempt to bridge the gap between the structured and movement education approaches to teaching gymnastic activities. Chapter 25 provides the basic stunts and tumbling activities. At the end of this chapter the concepts and skills of movement education are introduced in a systematic fashion. Numerous examples show how to incorporate these new movement ideas into stunt and tumbling lessons or units of instruction. Similarly, Chapters 26 and 27 present the structured skills that are performed with small equipment and large apparatus while providing additional suggestions for applying movement concepts and skills.

Teaching Gymnastic Activities

Each elementary grade presents unique organization and teaching problems. The children's age and maturity dictate the amount of material that can be covered within the allocated time in the gymnasium or activity room. The number of mats available may very well become the reason for organizing a class in a particular way. And the teacher's own ability and confidence in handling this type of physical activity may become the central reason for organizing a class in a certain fashion and for selecting particular activities. Regardless of such individual conditions, the following general teaching suggestions apply to all grade levels.

1. Children should be taught to listen to your normal conversational voice for all directions and commands. Once they learn to move and listen to your voice, there is no need to rely upon a loud whistle.

2. Teach children standard procedures for (a) changing their clothes and entering the gymnasium, (b) using their free time before the lesson begins, and (c) lining up in a specific way or place before the lesson begins or at any time you want to speak to all of the class.

3. Try to provide maximum participation and movement for each child during the instructional period. If a limited number of mats and other equipment means that the children must wait in long lines, the program should be changed. Techniques such as station work, task cards, and rotation procedures can be adapted to any grade level.

4. Establish a stunts and tumbling program based upon the children's individual abilities and progress. Do not establish a set number of skills for every child to accomplish. Some children simply are physically incapable of performing certain stunts. This obviously means that a wide variety of activities should be presented to each grade level.

5. Establish and consistently maintain a basic list of safety rules and regulations. These should include the following:

   a. If children are permitted to wear street clothes during this activity, do not allow bulky sweaters or watches and other jewelry.

   b. Children should not be allowed to practice any stunt or tumbling activity unless the teacher is in the gymnasium.

   c. When a stunt requires a spotter, children should be taught the proper spotting techniques. Once the techniques are learned, children should be permitted to perform stunts with the assistance of the required number of spotters.

Purposes and Techniques of Spotting

Spotting in stunts and tumbling or other gymnastic movements is defined as providing assistance in the performance of a skill. Spotting is both a teaching technique and a safety device. The teaching aspect is accomplished by the teacher or a classmate holding the performer or positioning himself in a way to assist the performer. The spotter helps the performer maintain his balance, or gently pushes or lifts him at

the strategic moment, helping him to get the "feel" of the movement before he attempts it on his own. The safety aspect of spotting involves positioning one or two helpers near the performer to provide additional support and to prevent a loss of balance, a fall, or an accident.

It is difficult to say which stunts and gymnastic skills require the use of spotters. Furthermore, the teacher and the child must judge when to remove close spotting so the child can attempt the skill on his own. As a general guideline for elementary school children, be overcautious until you are completely sure that the performer can execute the skill with relative ease.

The following suggestions may also help you find a safe procedure and environment for teaching the more difficult and challenging stunts and tumbling and gymnastic skills.

1. Analyze each stunt's points of difficulty and teach spotters the correct positions and movements.

2. Teach spotters to stay close to the performer but not to hamper his movement.

3. Use the strongest and most reliable children for the most difficult stunts.

4. Teach children not to "over spot." Instruct spotters to help only when the performer needs the extra lift or push so he does not come to rely too much on the assistance.

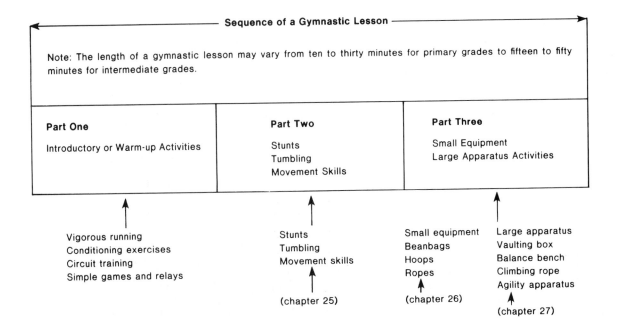

Note: The length of a gymnastic lesson may vary from ten to thirty minutes for primary grades to fifteen to fifty minutes for intermediate grades.

Part One	**Part Two**	**Part Three**
Introductory or Warm-up Activities	Stunts Tumbling Movement Skills	Small Equipment Large Apparatus Activities

Vigorous running
Conditioning exercises
Circuit training
Simple games and relays

Stunts
Tumbling
Movement skills

(chapter 25)

Small equipment
Beanbags
Hoops
Ropes

(chapter 26)

Large apparatus
Vaulting box
Balance bench
Climbing rope
Agility apparatus

(chapter 27)

Developing Units and Lesson Plans

There are several methods of organizing units and teaching individual or sequential lesson plans involving stunts and tumbling, small equipment, or large apparatus activities. The approach you decide to use will depend on such factors as the children's age, time and equipment available, and the emphasis the teacher wishes to give to one or more activities or movement skills. Thus, a standard unit or lesson plan suitable for any grade level would be of little value. The reader should review chapter 8 for a detailed presentation of the process of developing a variety of units, themes, and individual lesson plans.

The accompanying chart provides a basic guideline for the selection of appropriate activities from the next three chapters.

As a general guideline, begin each lesson with some type of vigorous warm-up activity such as running, jumping, and landing followed by exercises designed to increase the child's general strength and fitness (see chapter 9). Circuit training and vigorous

tag and team games are also appropriate warm-up activities. The rest of the lesson should include a mixture of balance, tumbling stunts, movement skills (chapter 25), and small and large apparatus activities (chapters 26 and 27). When time does not allow all three types of activities in a lesson, it is quite acceptable to teach stunts, tumbling, and movement skills on the first day and then begin with a short warm-up period the next day and move directly to small equipment and/or large apparatus activities. This procedure can be followed throughout a series of lessons. The essential point is to provide every child with an opportunity to experience and enjoy all the available gymnastic equipment and apparatus.

25 Stunts, Tumbling, and Movement Skills

The gymnastic activities most familiar to elementary school children are probably stunts and tumbling. For generations, children have learned to mimic animal walks, to balance on their heads, hands, and other parts of their bodies, and to perform a variety of agile tumbling skills. The purposes of these activities have remained the same. Children learn to move their bodies safely and gracefully. They improve their strength, agility, balance, and other important aspects of physical fitness, and they learn the importance of safety and perseverance when attempting a difficult stunt or tumbling skill.

One of the most recent and exciting additions to this program has been the introduction of movement concepts and skills developed in the movement education approach. These unstructured skills and movement concepts, coupled with the use of exploratory teaching methods and techniques, have provided an effective way for every child, regardless of physical ability or prior gymnastic experience, to experience success and enjoyment.

This chapter has been organized to cope with the varying programs and conditions that exist in elementary schools. The first two sections illustrate a variety of stunts and tumbling skills that are appropriate for primary and intermediate children. It is almost impossible to arrange skills by grade level, since children vary in their physical ability and previous stunt and tumbling experiences. Therefore, this chapter's grouping according to primary or intermediate levels is a very rough guideline.

The last section of this chapter describes movement concepts and skills and shows how they can be incorporated into a stunts and tumbling program. It is an extremely important section. Once children learn this new movement vocabulary, they can enrich their own experiences in stunts and tumbling activities. And, just as important, these concepts and skills provide a means of exploring and testing each child's physical and creative abilities with a wide variety of small equipment and large apparatus, such as vaulting boxes, climbing ropes, and the new, specially designed agility apparatus.

Stunts and Tumbling Activities for Kindergarten to Grade Three

The primary stunts and tumbling activities contained in this section (figs. 25.1 to 25.42) include numerous animal movements, balance stunts, simple partner activities, and several tumbling and safety skills. These activities are the foundations upon which the more advanced stunts and tumbling skills are built. As the reader will note in the last section of this chapter, there is a very close relationship between the activities described here and many movement education skills. Each complements the other in a very natural way.

The suggested levels for introducing each skill are only rough guidelines. If the class's skill level is high, move on to more advanced skills. As children progress to the third grade, they will be ready for more challenging skills. In this case refer to the next section on stunts and tumbling for intermediate grades (p. 406).

Stunts and Tumbling Activities K–3

Activity	Type of Skill	Appropriate Level	Page
Agility Stunts and Movement Patterns			
Wicket Walk	Agility, traveling	K–3	392
Bouncing Ball	Agility	K–3	392
Camel Walk	Agility, animal movement	K–3	392
Lame Puppy Walk	Agility, animal movement	K–3	392
Bear Walk	Agility, animal movement	K–3	393
Kangaroo Hop	Agility, animal movement	K–3	393
Knee Jump	Agility	K–3	393
Crab Walk	Agility, animal movement	K–3	393
Log Roll	Agility, tumbling	K–3	394
Side Roll	Agility, tumbling	K–3	394
Forward Roll	Agility, tumbling	K–3	395
Backward Diagonal Roll	Agility, tumbling	K–3	395
Wring the Dishrag	Agility, partner	K–3	397
Leap Frog	Agility, partner	K–3	397
Wheelbarrow	Agility, partner	K–3	397
Rocking Chair	Agility, partner	K–3	398
Rabbit Jump	Agility, animal movement	2–3	398
Elephant Walk	Agility, partner	2–3	398
Seal Walk	Agility, animal movement	2–3	398
Measuring Worm	Agility, animal movement	2–3	399
Heel Slap	Agility	2–3	399
Backward Roll	Agility, tumbling	2–3	399
Chinese Get-up	Agility, partner	2–3	400
Bear Hug Walk	Agility, partner	2–3	400
Twister	Agility, partner	2–3	401
Rooster Fight	Agility, partner	2–3	401
Mule Kick	Agility	2–3	401
Crab Fight	Agility, partner	2–3	402
Balance Stunts			
Tightrope Walk	Balance, traveling	K–3	402
Knee Walk	Balance, traveling	K–3	402
Turk Stand	Balance	K–3	403
Single Leg Balance	Balance	K–3	403
Frog Stand	Balance	2–3	403
Knee Dip	Balance	2–3	403
Thread the Needle	Balance	2–3	404
Headstand	Balance	2–3	404

Figure 25.1 Wicket Walk. Bend forward and grasp the legs just above the ankles. Take short steps without releasing the grip.

Variations:
1. Walk backward, sideward, and in a circle.
2. Place hands on opposite ankles and repeat.
3. Keep legs straight and repeat.
4. "Can you hold your ankles and find a new way to move your feet?" (jump, hop, etc.)

Figure 25.2 Bouncing Ball. Stand erect with arms at the sides and feet approximately shoulder-width apart. Take short jumps and gradually lower the body. Continue jumping and lowering the body until the hands touch the floor. This should simulate a ball coming to rest. Repeat action upward until the standing position is again reached.

Variations:
1. Repeat stunt, turning body as stunt is performed.
2. "Try to change the position of your hands or feet as you perform your stunt."

Figure 25.3 Camel Walk. Place one foot in front of the other, bend over from the waist, and lock hands behind back to represent the camel's hump. Walk slowly, raising the head and chest with each step.

Variations:
1. Walk backwards or sideways.
2. "See if you can keep your arms in the same position and sit down . . . then stand up."
3. "Can a camel run or gallop?"

Figure 25.4 Lame Puppy Walk. Begin with both hands and one foot on the floor. Keep the head up and walk or run "on all threes" like a lame puppy.

Variations:
1. Move in different directions—sideways, backward, and so on.
2. Change the position of the hands—farther apart, facing inward like a monkey, and so on.
3. Do a double lame puppy walk, with one hand and one foot on the floor.
4. "Show me how you can lie down, roll over right back to the same lame puppy position."

Figure 25.5 Bear Walk. Begin in a crouched position with hands and feet spread sideways. Simultaneously raise right hand and foot and shift in a forward direction. Repeat with left hand and foot.

Variations:
1. Move backwards or sideways.
2. Repeat above movements with arms and legs spread farther apart.
3. "Show me how a lame bear would walk."
4. "Can you balance a beanbag on your head as you walk?"

Figure 25.6 Kangaroo Hop. Begin in a squat position with the arms folded across the chest and the body weight over the toes. Jump up and forward, land on the toes, and gradually lower the body to the starting position.

Variations:
1. Move backward or sideways.
2. Repeat above with a beanbag on head or between knees.
3. "Find another part of your body to rest a beanbag on as you hop."
4. "Can you show me how a lame kangaroo would hop?"

Figure 25.7 Knee Jump. Stand with the feet about shoulder-width apart, the knees slightly bent, and the arms raised forward and sideways. Jump up, pull the knees up to the chest, wrap the hands around the lower legs, release grip, and land on the toes. Landing should be made with the knees bent.

Variations:
1. Jump up, straddle legs.
2. Jump up, slap seat, feet, or other parts.
3. "Invent a new position in the air."

Figure 25.8 Crab Walk. Start with the hands and feet on the ground. The back should be fairly straight to keep the seat off the ground. Walk forward by lifting the left hand and right leg up and forward.

Variations:
1. Walk backwards and sideways.
2. Walk with one foot in the air.
3. Balance a ball (or small object) on your tummy and walk.
4. "Can you hold one hand on your head, or tummy, and walk?"

Figure 25.9 Log Roll. This is the easiest roll to perform. Lie on the back with the arms extended over the head and the hands locked together. Keep the body in a straight line and roll to the side and then around to the starting position.

Variations:
1. Children should also learn to roll toward either side, stop halfway through, and change directions.
2. Combine log rolls with other stunts, such as from a long roll, change to a crab walk, to a long roll, to a bear walk.

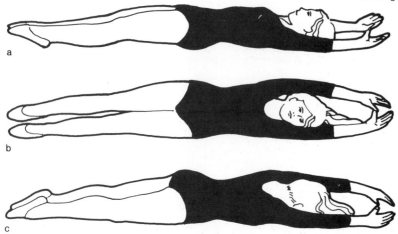

Figure 25.10 Side Roll. Begin in a back-lying position. Perform the roll with elbows, knees, and nose "hidden" or tucked in. Explain to young children that hiding these parts of the body helps them to roll in a ball-like fashion and to protect vulnerable parts.

Variations:
1. Roll towards either side.
2. "See if you can roll from a log to a side to a log roll."
3. "See if you can combine a side roll, a long roll, and a balance stunt."

Figure 25.11 Forward Roll. Most children have already learned the forward roll before the first grade and can usually demonstrate many variations involving different leg and arm positions. Begin in a squat position with the head up, the arms extended forward slightly, and the fingers pointing straight ahead. Push off from the toes, raise the seat, and tuck the chin to the chest. Continue forward movement, landing on the base of the neck and the top of the shoulders. Push off with the hands and continue forward motion to a crouching or standing position.

Variations:
1. Start from a standing position and end in a standing position.
2. "Try three different ways to change your leg position as you perform the roll."
3. "See if you can perform a forward, log, and side roll in any order you like."

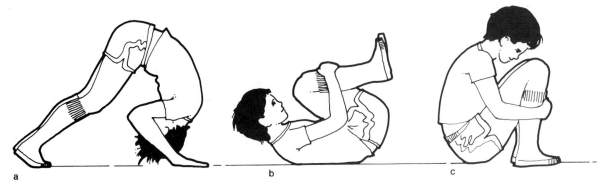

a

b

c

Figure 25.12 Forward Roll Spotting. Kneel on the left side of the performer, place the left hand on back of her head and the right hand on the back of the left thigh. As the child rolls forward, lift with the left hand and push forward with the right hand against the thigh.

Figure 25.13 Backward Diagonal Roll. This is one of the most important safety rolls. It is a means of rolling backward with a gradual dissipation of speed, thus preventing injury as well as providing an effective and graceful means of shifting from one movement to another. The roll is performed by rolling backward and bringing both legs to the side of one ear. This takes the weight off the neck and allows the child to roll off the shoulder. It is an appropriate skill for children who are not strong enough to perform the backward roll.

Variations:
1. Roll to both sides.
2. "Can you combine a log, side, and backward diagonal roll?"

a

b

c

Figure 25.14 Backward Diagonal Roll Spotting. Kneel on the performer's left side and face in the direction of the backward diagonal roll. Place the right hand under his left shoulder with fingers spread and hold the right hand ready to assist the performer in his backward movement.

Figure 25.15

Figure 25.16

Incorporating Rolling Skills

If children have learned to run in different directions without colliding, it is time to incorporate a rolling skill into their movement patterns. This can be accomplished in the following stages.

Step 1: Scatter all available mats on the floor. Assign four children around each mat as illustrated. Number each child in each group. On your command of "number 1," child 1 in each group approaches the mat from any direction, bends down, touches the floor, and performs a roll across the mat. He then gets up, moves to a new position and performs another roll across the mat. Next, call "number 2." Child 2 must wait for an open space across the mat before attempting to bend and perform a roll. When 1 and 2 develop the ability to wait and then roll, call "number three," who joins in the process. Continue to the last performer. It is important at this stage to encourage children to keep moving to new positions, then to bend and roll across the mat (fig. 25.15).

Step 2: Join two groups but do not shift the mats (fig. 25.16). Start each group on its own mat. When all the children are moving, call out "number one." Child 1 from each group then shifts to the other mat and joins that group. Once he is on the other mat, he may elect to stay there or shift back and forth as space dictates. Continue calling numbers 2, 3, and 4.

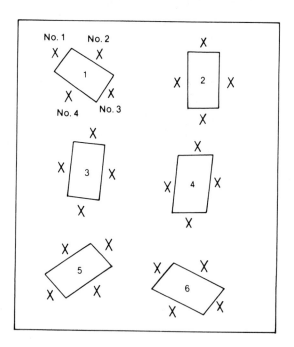

Step 3: Join three groups and continue the process.

Step 4: When three or four mats are being used by all the children, stop the class. Have half the class stand on the side of the gymnasium while the other children scatter on the floor. On command, the children on the floor run, stop, bend, and roll across any mat. Allow time for practice, then rotate the groups.

Step 5: Allow all children to run, bend, and roll. Then have them run, jump, land, and roll.

Balance Stunts

Figure 25.17 Wring the Dishrag. Partners face each other and join hands. With hands joined, each partner raises one arm (right for one partner and left for the other), and they turn back to back. Repeat with the other arms to return to the original position.

Variations:
1. When in a back-to-back position, both raise one leg as high as possible.
2. "When in this back-to-back position, can you do something different?" (bend down, twist to one side, etc.)

Figure 25.18 Leap Frog. One partner squats, keeping her head down. The other partner assumes a semicrouched position about two feet behind, with his hands resting on his partner's shoulders. Back partner spreads his legs and leaps over his partner. Continue sequence for several jumps.

Variations:
1. Raise the height of lower performer.
2. After performing a vault, land and roll.
3. Add two or more performers. Last peformer in the row leap frogs over all performers before next person begins his sequence.

Figure 25.19 Wheelbarrow. One partner lies on the floor, with legs spread and arms extended. The other partner stands between the extended legs and grasps her partner's lower legs. The lead partner takes short steps with his hands while the other player follows with short walking steps.

Variations:
1. Walk backwards or sideways.
2. Standing partner remains stationary while lower partner begins to move in a circle.
3. "How can you change the wheelbarrow to make it more fun?"

Figure 25.20 Rocking Chair. One partner lies on the floor on her back with her knees bent and her arms extended upward. The other partner stands at her feet, bends forward, and grabs her hands. One partner rocks back, pulling the other up and forward until they have changed positions.

Variation:

1. "Try the same stunt with both performers keeping one foot off the ground at all times."

Figure 25.21 Rabbit Jump. Begin in a squat position with the body weight over the toes. Leap forward and land on the hands and then the feet to simulate a rabbit hop.

Variations:

1. Hop backwards.
2. "Try to kick your feet high as you land on your hands."
3. "How many different directions can a rabbit hop?" (examples—circle, zigzag)

Figure 25.22 Elephant Walk. One partner sits on the floor with her legs extended sideward while the upper partner bends down and places his hands between her legs (his feet are opposite the sitting partner's shoulders). The lower partner wraps her legs around the upper partner's trunk and places her hands over his seat. The lower partner rises off the floor and the upper partner takes short, "elephantlike" steps while the lower partner holds on.

Variations:

1. Walk backwards and sideways.
2. "Can you and your partner make up a new animal walk? Give it a name!"

Figure 25.23 Seal Walk. Begin in a prone position with the belly down, the body and legs straight, and the toes pointed. Keep the arms straight to support the body and move the right hand forward. Shift the left hand forward and drag the legs, simulating the walking action of a seal.

Variations:

1. Use elbows instead of hands.
2. Crawl holding one leg in the air.
3. "See if you can find another part of your body to drag you forward."

Figure 25.24 Measuring Worm. Begin in a squat position with the arms shoulder-width apart and the hands on the floor. Without moving the feet, take short steps with the hands until the legs and the back are straight. Now, without moving the arms, take short steps with the feet until the toes touch the back of the hands.

Variations:
1. Keep one leg in the air at all times and repeat measuring worm.
2. "Can you perform the measuring worm with a partner or in threes?"

Figure 25.25 Heel Slap. Stand with the feet about shoulder-width apart. Jump up, slap heels, and return to starting position.

Variations:
1. Jump and make a half or full turn in the air.
2. Jump, slap heels, and clap hands over head.
3. Jump and slap heels twice.
4. "Find a new way to jump up and a new part of your body to slap."

Figure 25.26 Backward Roll. This is the most difficult roll to perform because it requires the weight to be taken on the arms during the roll. Begin in a squat position with the body weight evenly distributed on the fingers and toes. The back should be toward the mat. Push off the hands and roll backward, keeping the knees to the chest and the chin down (a). Continue backward roll until the body weight is well over the shoulders (b). At this point, push off with the hands, and land on the knees and toes (c).

Variations:
1. Perform backward roll with legs straight.
2. "Change position of legs as you perform a backward roll."

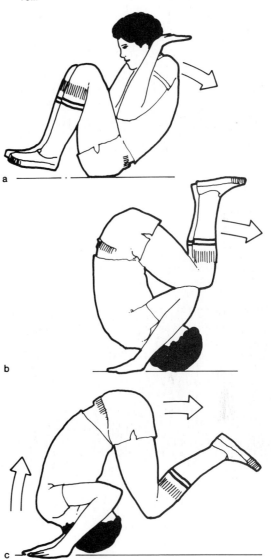

Figure 25.27 Backward Roll Spotting. Stand on the right side of the performer, and place hands on the hips. As he rolls onto his shoulders, gently lift performer upward and backward.

a

b

Figure 25.28 Chinese Get-up. Partners sit back to back with their elbows locked, knees bent and together, and feet flat on the floor. Both rise off the floor by pushing against each other and, if necessary, taking short backward steps.

Variations:
1. Stop when halfway up and walk forwards, sideways and backwards.
2. When all the way up, one pulls partner off floor. Repeat to other side.
3. "Can you think up a way to add or to change this stunt?" (add a third person, etc.)

Figure 25.29 Bear Hug Walk. Partner lies on floor facing upward. Other partner straddles him with legs spread, and bends forward placing hands on mat facing the first partner. Lower partner places his legs around partner's waist and hands around his neck. Upper partner begins to move forward on all fours carrying his partner.

Variations:
1. Walk backwards and sideways.
2. "Try and change the position of one arm or one leg but still perform the bear hug walk."

Figure 25.30 Twister. Partners stand back to back with legs apart and left hand on left knee. Each partner reaches through his legs with his right hand and grasps his partner's hand. Keeping the hand grip, one partner swings to the right and lifts his left leg over his partner's back. They return to the original position by reversing the movement.

Variations:
1. When both face each other, switch hands and return to a back-to-back position.
2. "Place a beanbag on your head and repeat the twister."

Figure 25.31 Rooster Fight. Stand on one leg with the arms folded across the chest. On "go" command, attempt to push opponent off balance, do not hit. As soon as one player touches the floor with her free foot, the other player is declared the winner.

Variations:
1. Place hands behind back and repeat stunt.
2. Place beanbag on head. If one player drops the beanbag, opposite player is declared the winner.
3. "Can you find another part of your body to rest the beanbag on and repeat your stunt?"

Figure 25.32 Mule Kick. Begin in a semicrouched position with hands about shoulder-width apart, knees bent, and feet together. In a simultaneous movement, shift weight over hands and vigorously thrust legs upward and backward.

Variations:
1. Thrust backward, upward, and apart.
2. Twist body to side as legs extend backward and upward.
3. "Can you add your own variation to this stunt?"

a

b

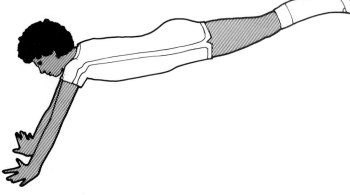

c

Figure 25.33 Crab Fight. Partners assume a crab walk position with hands and feet on the mat and seats off the mat. On signal "go," each attempts to push the other off balance. As soon as one player touches the mat with her seat or falls over, the other is declared the winner.

Variations:
1. Keep outside foot off ground.
2. Place utility ball on stomach. If a player drops the ball, the other is declared the winner.
3. "Invent a new rule for this game."

Balance Stunts

Figure 25.34 Tightrope Walk. Draw a line on the floor. Stand with arms extended sideward, head up, and both feet on the line. Walk forward placing the toe, then the heel, on the floor.

Variations:
1. Change position of arms.
2. Walk backward.
3. Make a half knee-bend and repeat.
4. "Can you walk on just part of your foot—heels, toes, side?"

Figure 25.35 Knee Walk. Start with the hands and knees on the mat. Reach back and grasp the feet or ankles. Shift the weight to the left side and take a short step with the right knee. Continue movement with short steps forward.

Variations:
1. Walk backwards and sideways.
2. "See if you can balance on one knee for three seconds."

Figure 25.36 Turk Stand. Begin in a cross-legged sitting position, with the arms folded across the chest and the body leaning forward slightly. Without releasing the grip, lean forward and extend the legs to a standing position. Return to the cross-legged sitting position.

Variation:
1. Lower yourself all the way down, roll on to your back without uncrossing your arms. Return to a standing position.

Figure 25.37 Single Leg Balance. Stand on one leg with the knee slightly bent, lower the trunk, and raise the arms and other leg until they are parallel to the floor.

Variations:
1. Extend the elevated leg to the side.
2. Place the arms in different directions—pointing forward or downward or holding against the sides.
3. Place sole of elevated leg against side of other leg (stork stand).
4. "Can you balance on one leg and twist your body?"
5. "See if you can swing your free leg forward and turn around and face the other way."
6. "Can you balance on one leg, jump and change to balancing on the opposite leg?"

Figure 25.38 Frog Stand. Squat with the arms straight, hands resting on the floor, and knees outside the elbows. The fingers should be pointing forward and spread apart for balance. Lean forward slowly, pressing the inside of the thighs against the elbows. As the feet rise off the ground, lower the head and trunk. Return to the starting position.

Variations:
1. Shift forward and perform a forward roll.
2. Shift forward, place head on mat, and perform a headstand.

Figure 25.39 Knee Dip. Stand on the left foot, bend the right leg back and up, grasping the foot with the right hand. Gradually bend the left leg until the right knee touches the floor. Return to the starting position without releasing the grip.

Variations:
1. Place hands on hips, extend right leg forward, bend and return.
2. "Can you invent a new way to perform the knee dip?"

Figure 25.40 Thread the Needle. Begin in a standing position, arms straight in front with hands grasping. Keeping hands touching, bend forward, raise right foot up and through arms. Return to starting position.

Variations:
1. Repeat with opposite foot.
2. Change hand position (interlocking fingers, grasping wrists, etc.) and repeat.
3. "Can you add your own variation to this stunt?"

Figure 25.41 Headstand. Form a triangle with the hands and forehead. Push off the mat with the toes of both feet, flex the knees, and raise the body to a halfway position. Once the body is in a stable, balanced position, continue raising the legs until the body forms a straight line. Note: Too much arch in the back tends to cause the body to fall forward.

Suggested progression in learning this stunt:
1. Begin in position *a,* walk forward on toes, shift to position *b,* and return.
2. Repeat *a* to full headstand.
3. Kick up from position *a.*
4. Perform stunt as shown.

Variations:
1. Change the position of the legs, such as straddle, one forward and one backward, etc.
2. Hold a ball or beanbag between legs.
3. "See if you can balance on your head and change the position of any other part of your body."

Stunts, Tumbling, and Pyramid Activities for Grades Four to Six

The stunts and tumbling program for intermediate children is essentially a continuation of the primary program. As children progress to the more advanced balance and agility stunts, more strength and control are required. More spotters also are needed because of difficulty and potential hazards in the improper performance of several balance and tumbling movements. The spotters should be given adequate training to ensure a safe performance.

Figure 25.42 Headstand Spotting. Kneel on the left side of the performer and place left hand under performer's shoulder. As she lifts her legs, grasp the shin of the left leg with right hand. Once she is in the headstand position, gradually release the hands, but keep them a few inches away and ready for support. A second spotter can be added to the other side.

Pyramid building has been included in the latter part of this section (p. 423). These activities require strength, balance, and teamwork, and are thoroughly enjoyed by children of this age level.

It is recognized that many of the stunts and tumbling activities suggested here (figs. 25.43 to 25.89) are structured or formal gymnastic movements. Therefore, it may appear to be a contradiction to suggest that the unstructured movement skills described on pages 428–34 be incorporated with these highly structured stunts and tumbling skills. But when a child learns such movement concepts as weight bearing, transfer of weight, direction and pathways, and the various qualities of movement, he can enrich all the structured stunts and tumbling skills. Several examples will be provided to show how formal stunts can be joined with one or more movement concepts.

Figure 25.43 Rolling the Log. Begin in a front-leaning position. Keeping the right hand on the floor and the legs, feet, and back straight, swing the left arm up and over the turning body. When the left hand returns to the floor, swing the right arm up and toward the left side, turning the body back to the original position.

Variations:
1. Perform stunt towards right and left sides.
2. "Can you change a part of this stunt to make it more challenging?"

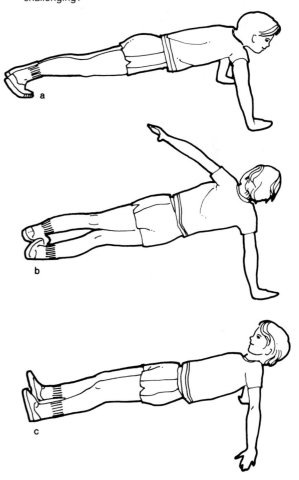

Activity	Type of Skill	Appropriate Level	Page

Agility Stunts and Movement Patterns

The agility and tumbling stunts described in the primary section may be reviewed before attempting the following stunts.

Activity	Type of Skill	Appropriate Level	Page
Rolling the Log	Agility	4–6	407
Bear Dance	Agility	4–6	407
Pig Walk	Agility	4–6	407
Shoulder Wrestling	Agility	4–6	407
Elbow Wrestling	Agility	4–6	407
Leg Wrestling	Agility	4–6	408
Going Down	Agility	4–6	408
Centipede	Agility	4–6	408
Push War	Agility	4–6	408
Seal Slap	Agility	4–6	409
Upswing	Agility	4–6	409
Forward Roll Variations	Tumbling	4–6	409
Egg Roll	Tumbling	4–6	410
Backward Roll Variations	Tumbling	4–6	410
Jackknife	Tumbling	4–6	410
Heel Click	Tumbling	4–6	411
Judo Roll	Tumbling	4–6	411
Triple Roll	Tumbling	4–6	411
Jump Through	Tumbling	4–6	412
Kip	Tumbling	4–6	412
Cartwheel	Tumbling	4–6	413
Handspring Over Partner	Tumbling	4–6	413
Knee Handspring	Tumbling	4–6	414
Handspring	Tumbling	4–6	414
Round-off	Tumbling	4–6	415
Forward Drop	Tumbling	4–6	415
Neckspring	Tumbling	4–6	416
Headspring	Tumbling	4–6	416

Balance Stunts

The balance stunts described in the primary section may be reviewed before attempting the following skills.

Activity	Type of Skill	Appropriate Level	Page
V-Sit	Balance	4–6	417
The Bridge	Balance	4–6	417
Knee and Shoulder Stand	Partner, balance	4–6	417
Side Stand	Partner, balance	4–6	418
Knee Stand	Partner, balance	4–6	418
Back Layout	Partner, balance	4–6	419
Flying Dutchman	Partner, balance	4–6	419
Table	Partner, balance	4–6	420
Forearm Headstand	Partner	4–6	420
Walking Down the Wall	Partner	4–6	420
Handstand	Partner	4–6	421
L-Support	Partner	4–6	422
Elbow Balance	Partner	4–6	422

Figure 25.44 Bear Dance. Squat on the right foot and extend the left leg forward. Extend arms from the sides. Simultaneously jump forward, draw the right leg back, and extend the left leg forward.

Variations:
1. Change position of arms—folded across chest, behind back, on head, etc.
2. Turn body towards right or left on each leg exchange.
3. "See if you can wrap inside arm around partner's waist and perform a double bear dance."

Figure 25.45 Pig Walk. One partner assumes a partial push-up position with his legs apart and his seat up. The lower partner faces the opposite direction and shifts backward until his arms are opposite his partner's ankles. The lower partner wraps his legs around his partner's trunk and grasps his partner's ankles. The upper partner takes short, "piglike" steps.

Variations:
1. Keep in pig walk position, lower towards mat, roll sideways, and return to original position.
2. "Try to modify this stunt in any way possible."
3. "Is it possible to design a three-person pig walk?"

Figure 25.46 Shoulder Wrestling. Partners kneel side by side facing in opposite directions with their hands locked behind their backs and their shoulders touching. On signal, and without losing shoulder contact, partners attempt to push each other off balance.

Variations:
1. Change position of hands—extend overhead, hold knees, etc.
2. Repeat shoulder wrestling, however, back must be parallel to the floor.
3. Repeat shoulder wrestling with both players holding a large utility or basketball.

Figure 25.47 Elbow Wrestling. Partners lie with their right elbows on the floor and holding hands. Their left forearms should be in contact with the floor. On signal, and without taking their elbows off the floor, partners attempt to push each other's hands to the floor.

Variations:
1. Change hands.
2. Repeat stunt, allow players to use both hands.
3. Repeat elbow wrestling, however, players must have knees off the mat (or one leg in the air, etc.).

Stunts, Tumbling, and Movement Skills   **407**

Figure 25.48 Leg Wrestling. Partners lie side by side on their backs facing opposite directions. On the signal "go", both raise their inside legs so that their knees are crossed. From this position, each partner tries to force his opponent's leg down to the mat.

Variations:
1. Repeat stunt, keeping outside leg off the mat.
2. "Modify any part of this stunt to make it more difficult and more fun for each performer."

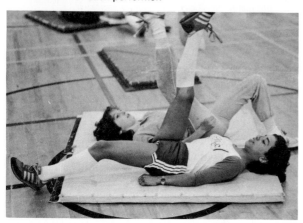

Figure 25.50 Centipede. This stunt should be performed by three children of equal size and strength. First performer gets down on his hands and knees. Second performer places his hands about two feet in front of the first performer, then his legs and hips on top of the first performer. Third performer repeats the same steps as the second performer. The centipede now walks with the first performer using hands and feet while the other two use only their hands.

Variations:
1. Walk backward and sideways.
2. Try turning around.

Figure 25.49 Going Down. Players sit side by side with their arms linked. On the signal "go", each player tries to force the other to roll backward. Players are not allowed to touch the floor with their free hands.

Variations:
1. Keep outside leg off the mat and repeat stunt.
2. Place outside hand on head (or grasp partner's hand above head) and repeat stunt.
3. "Think up a new way to hold inside hands and repeat stunt."

Figure 25.51 Push War. Draw three lines twenty to thirty feet apart. Players stand at the center line and place their hands on each other's shoulders. On the signal "go," each player attempts to push his opponent back over the end lines.

Variations:
1. Start in push-war position, then, on command, try to pull partner over line.
2. Grasp knee of partner with both hands. On command try to pull opponent over the line.
3. "Make up your own variation of this stunt."

Figure 25.52 Seal Slap. Begin in a front-lying position with the toes on the mat and the hands directly under the shoulders. Simultaneously push off from the hands and toes, clap the hands in the air, and return to the starting position.

Variations:
1. Attempt a double clap before returning to the starting position.
2. Instead of pushing off, see how far you can extend arms forward without touching the floor with your stomach (long bridge).
3. "Repeat seal slap and invent a new position of the arms and head when in the air."

Figure 25.53 Upswing. Kneel with arms extended sideward and backward. Swing arms forward and upward vigorously and at the same time push off from the feet. Finish in a partially crouched position.

Variations:
1. Repeat stunt with a quarter or half turn in the air.
2. "Can you modify this stunt in any way?"

Figure 25.54 Forward Roll Variations. Begin in a cross-legged position. Keeping legs crossed, shift forward, push off from toes, raise seat, and tuck chin onto chest. Continue forward movement to starting position.

Variations:
1. Do a one-foot takeoff.
2. Run to a two-foot takeoff.
3. Roll with the legs in a straddle position.
4. Roll while grasping the toes or ankles.
5. Roll with crossed arms or crossed legs.
6. Perform two or more rolls in succession.
7. Combine a forward roll with other rolls and balance stunts.

Spotting:
Use the same spotting technique described for the forward roll (p. 395).

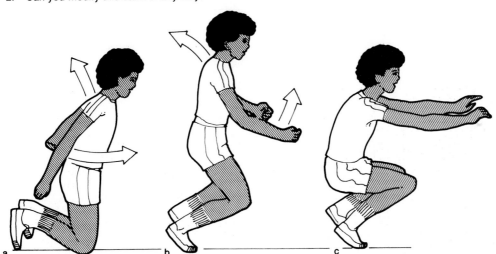

Figure 25.55 Egg Roll. Begin in a squat position. Place the arms on the inside of the knees, then stretch the hands around the lower legs and overlap them over the feet. Roll sideways, on the shoulder, to the back, to the shoulder, and then back to a sitting position. Continue the action around the circle to the starting position.

Variations:
1. Roll towards right then left side.
2. "See if you can vary your leg and hand position and repeat this stunt."

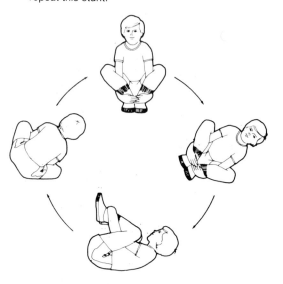

Figure 25.57 Jackknife. Begin in a partially crouched position with arm extended forward and sideways. Jump upwards and raise legs touching toes with hands and return to starting position.

Variations:
1. Repeat stunt with a run and a two-foot takeoff.
2. Run, jump, perform a tuck, straddle, twisted or other shapes, and land.

Figure 25.56 Backward Roll Variations. This roll starts with the same backward rolling action as the backward roll. As soon as the hands begin to press against the mat, the legs begin to extend upward. At the moment the legs are vertical, vigorously push off from the hands and snap the feet downward toward the mat, landing in a partially crouched position.

Variations:
1. Roll backwards with legs in a straddle position, crossed, or one foot in front of the other.
2. "Invent your own modification of the backward roll."

Spotting:
Use the same spotting technique described for the backward diagonal roll (p. 396).

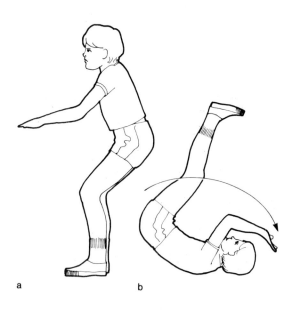

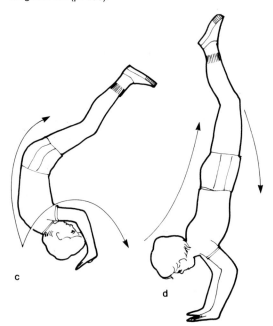

a   b   c   d

Figure 25.58 Heel Click. Start in a partially crouched position with arms sideways and slightly backwards. Jump up, click heels together, and return to the starting position.

Variations:
1. Start on one foot, jump up, click heels, and return to starting position.
2. Run, jump, click heels, and land on both feet.
3. Make up a sequence of three heel clicks, each starting from a different position.

Figure 25.60 Triple Roll. This is a continuous log roll involving three performers. As the center performer (#3) begins to roll to his right, the outside performer (#1) begins to thrust himself upward, over, and toward the center performer's previous position. The new center performer (#1) continues to roll toward the other side. As soon as he starts his roll, performer 2 thrusts himself up, over, and toward the center position. This action is then continued for several rotations. The important aspects of this triple stunt are the timing of each performer and the quick recovery of the outside performer.

Figure 25.59 Judo Roll. Start this roll from a standing position. Bend forward, extend the right arm and turn the head toward the left side. As the body moves forward and downward, swing the right arm toward the left and contact the mat with the top of the right shoulder. Continue the forward rolling action over the back and side, then move forward and upward.

Variations:
1. Perform roll to opposite side.
2. Run, then perform a judo roll from a one-foot takeoff.

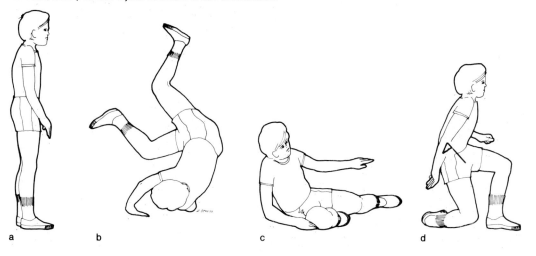

a   b   c   d

Figure 25.61   Jump Through. Begin in a front-leaning support position with the hands about shoulder-width apart. In one continuous movement, shift the legs forward between the arms to a back-leaning support position.

Variations:
1. Walk Through: Same as above but walk through the movement.
2. Side shift: Same as the walk through, except that as the performer moves forward, he tilts slightly to one side, raises the opposite arm off the floor, and brings his legs through.

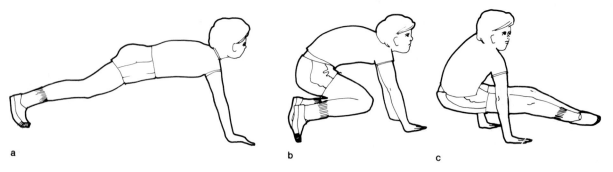

a   b   c

Figure 25.62   Kip. Begin in a back-lying position with arms at sides and legs extended. From this position, raise the legs and rock back until the knees are above the head (a). Note: The fingers should be pointing toward the body. Vigorously thrust the legs forward and upward and push off with both hands (b). Continue raising trunk forward and upward (c), and land in a partially crouched position (d).

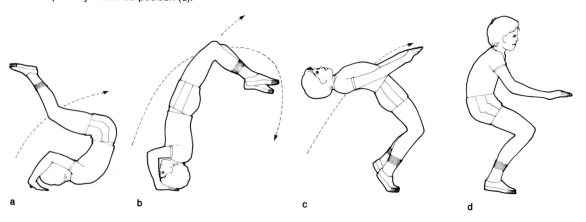

a   b   c   d

Figure 25.63   Kip Spotting. Kneel on the right knee on the performer's left side. Place the left hand on the performer's left upper arm and the right hand around the performer's lower arm. As the performer kips, pull with your left hand and lift upwards with the right hand.

Figure 25.64 Cartwheel. Begin with the back straight, the arms extended sideward, and the legs approximately shoulder-width apart. Bend toward the left, placing the left hand, then the right on the mat and, at the same time, raising the side. Note: In the middle of this stunt, the legs and arms should be fully extended and the body in a straight line. Continue sideways, placing right, then left leg on the mat and ending in the starting position.

a   b   c

Figure 25.65 Cartwheel Spotting. Stand opposite the spot where the performer's hands will be placed. Cross the right arm over the left, then place both hands on the performer's hips as she pushes off from her lead foot. Aid the performer in her sideward motion and vertical balance position when indicated.

Figure 25.66 Handspring over Partner. This is a lead-up stunt to the handspring. One partner kneels on the mat, places his hands well apart, and tucks his head toward his chest. The standing partner places his hands opposite the trunk of the kneeling partner, keeping his arm straight, and raises one leg off the mat. Still keeping his arms straight, he kicks upward with his free leg, pushes off with his back leg, and rolls over the kneeling partner.

Figure 25.67 Knee Handspring. The knee handspring can also serve as a lead-up stunt to the handspring. One partner lies on his back with his knees bent and together and his arms extended forward. The standing partner places his hands on his partner's knees, lowers his body forward, and raises one leg slightly off the mat. The top partner then swings top leg up, pushes off his lower leg, and continues the forward movement, placing his shoulders against the lower partner's hands. The lower partner keeps his arms extended to assist the top partner's forward motion.

Figure 25.69 Handspring Spotting. Kneel on the right side of the performer at the spot where his hands will land. Place your left hand on his right upper arm near the shoulder. As the performer shifts forward and upward, lift with the right hand and guide the forward action with your left hand. A second spotter may be required on the other side of the performer.

Figure 25.68 Handspring. Begin in a standing position. Run forward, skip on the left foot, place the right foot on the mat and then the hands, with the arms extended. Continue the upward and forward thrust of the right leg, followed by the left leg. When the body is in front of the head, push off from the hands and land on both feet with the knees partially bent.

a   b   c

Figure 25.70 Round-off. The first part of the round-off is the same as the cartwheel. As soon as both feet are off the ground, bring them together, then make a half turn toward the left (counterclockwise). Bend at the hips, and land on both feet facing the opposite direction.

Spotting:
Stand on the left side of the performer and opposite the spot where his hands will be placed. As the performer places his right hand on the mat, place your left hand under his right shoulder. Lift as he pushes off from his hands when indicated.

a   b   c

Figure 25.71 Forward Drop. Stand with the arms extended downward beside the body. In a simultaneous action, begin to fall forward, allowing the hands and arms to gradually absorb the downward momentum.

Variations:
1. Knee drop: Begin in a kneeling position with arms extended over the head. Fall forward in a similar manner as the forward drop.
2. Repeat forward drop but raise one leg and keep it off the ground as you drop.

a   b   c

Figure 25.72 Neckspring. This stunt should be taught from a stationary position over a rolled mat. Once the performer can execute the kipping action, he should be allowed to attempt the skill with a running approach to the rolled mat. Run toward the rolled mat, take off with both feet, place the hands on the mat, bend the arms, and place the back of head on the mat. Roll forward, dropping the legs, then extend the legs forward and upward vigorously and push off the hands.

Spotting:
Use same technique as for the kip, p. 412.

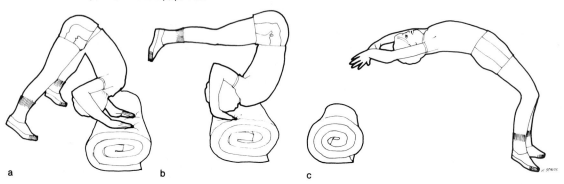

a   b   c

Figure 25.73 Headspring. This stunt is similar to the neckspring and should also be taught from a stationary position over a rolled mat. Once the performer can execute a kipping action, he should be allowed to attempt the headspring with a running approach. Run toward the rolled mat, take off with both feet, place the hands, then the top of the head, on the rolled mat. Keep the head and hands on the mat and bring the extended legs forward until an "overbalanced" position is reached. Then extend the legs up and forward vigorously and push off with the hands. Land on both feet, swing the arms forward, and bend the knees to regain a forward balanced position.

Spotting:
Use the same spotting technique described for the forward handspring (p. 414).

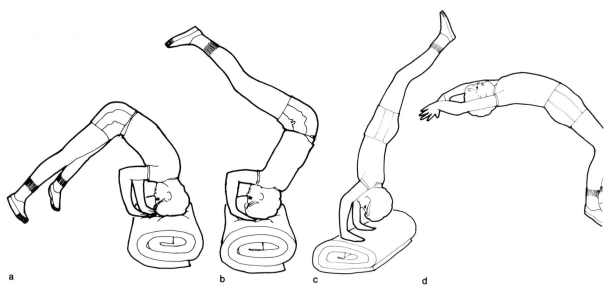

a   b   c   d

Balance Stunts

Figure 25.74 V-Sit. Sit with the knees bent, feet flat on the floor, and the hands grasping the sides of the ankles. Still grasping the ankles, extend the knees and balance on the seat.

Variations:
1. Repeat stunt holding toes.
2. When in the V-sit position, release grip and extend arms and legs sideways.
3. "Can you modify this stunt while still emphasizing a balance on the seat?"

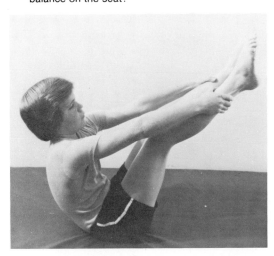

Figure 25.75 The Bridge. Sit on the edge of the mat holding the elbows high and the palms of hands facing up. Lower the back and place the palms on the mat, then arch the body.

Variations:
1. When in the arched position, raise and extend one leg.
2. Lower body, place head on mat, and extend arms sideways (wrestler's bridge).
3. "Can you perform a bridge with a variation in the arm, leg, or trunk position?"

Figure 25.76 Knee and Shoulder Stand. The base partner lies on his back with his knees bent and his arms up. The top performer stands facing her partner and places her hands on her partner's knees as she brings her shoulders forward. The base partner places his hands on the top performer's shoulders. As soon as the top performer's shoulders are held in a fixed position, she begins to raise her legs until they are in a vertical position.

Variations:
1. Top performer places one leg forward and one extending backwards.
2. "Find a new position for your legs." (sideways, knees flexed, etc.)
3. "What other way can you modify this stunt?"

Figure 25.77 Side Stand. Base partner assumes a wide, kneeling position with his weight evenly distributed on his arms and legs. Top performer stands on the side and curls his arm around his partner's trunk. The palms of both hands face up. The top performer leans across his partner and gradually raises his knees to a partially bent position above his partner's back. Then he extends his legs fully.

Variations:
1. "See how many ways the top performer can change the position of his legs."
2. "Is it possible for one or both performers to add a twist to their balanced position?"

Figure 25.78 Knee Stand. Base partner stands with his legs about shoulder-width apart, bends forward, and places his head between his partner's legs. Top partner places his hands on base partner's shoulders, and base partner grasps upper partner's thighs. Base partner begins to stand up, while top partner places his feet on base partner's thighs, releases his hands from his partner's shoulders, and begins to arch forward.

Variation:
1. "Can you redesign this stunt so that the final balance position of the top performer is facing the reversed direction?"

Figure 25.79 Back Layout. The base partner lies on her back, extends her arms up, and bends both knees. The soles of her feet should face her partner's back. The top partner rests the small of her back against her partner's feet and slowly extends back as her partner straightens her legs. The base partner can give support to the top partner by holding her arms just above the wrists.

Variation:
1. Repeat stunt and release hand grip as balance is achieved.

Spotting:
Stand near the top of the base performer's right shoulder, assist in placing the feet, and maintain balance when indicated.

Figure 25.80 Back Layout Spotting

Figure 25.81 Flying Dutchman. Base performer lies on her back, extends her arms up, and bends both knees. Top performer faces the base performer, grasps her hands, and places her stomach against the support's feet. Base performer extends her legs, then the top performer arches her back, releases her hands, and extends arms sideways. Note: Begin with a spotter to find balance position and as a standby safety person.

Figure 25.82 Table. Base partner assumes a crab-walk position with his thighs and trunk in a straight line. Top partner straddles base, places her hands on base's shoulders and feet on her knees. Top performer then raises seat until thighs and trunk are in a straight line. Both heads are facing the ceiling.

Variations:
1. When balance is reached, base partner raises right foot and top partner raises left foot into the air.
2. "Try to invent a new double balance stunt with both facing the ceiling."

Figure 25.83 Forearm Stand. Kneel with the elbows, hands and forehead on the mat. Gradually begin to rise upward until the legs are fully extended and the toes are pointed.

Variations:
1. Change position of legs after balance has been achieved.
2. "Can you change the position of your legs and twist your body?"

Spotting:
Use the same spotting technique described for the headstand (p. 405).

Figure 25.84 Walking Down Wall. Stand facing away from the wall with the feet about two feet away from the wall, the elbows high, and the palms facing up and toward the wall. Arch the head and shoulders back and place the hands on the wall. Walk the hands down the wall and touch the head to the mat. This movement should be performed without moving the feet; however, most children will have to move their feet a little farther away from the wall as they reach the lower phase of the arched position.

Variations:
1. Keep one foot in the air throughout movement.
2. Walk up the wall. Start in push-up position with heels touching the wall. Gradually move backward to a handstand position with feet resting on wall.

Figure 25.85 Handstand. Begin this stunt with the arms approximately shoulder-width apart, hands on the mat, and the fingers slightly bent (this aids in maintaining balance). Both feet should also be on the mat in the starting position with the right knee slightly bent. With the body weight well forward on the arms, kick the right leg up and follow with the left. Continue the upward movement of the legs, ending with the legs, body, and arms in a nearly straight line. The head should be well forward to assist in maintaining balance.

Variations:
1. Handstand against the wall, then bend elbow (about half way), and straighten to original position.
2. Walk on hands.

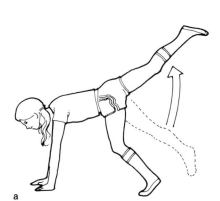
a

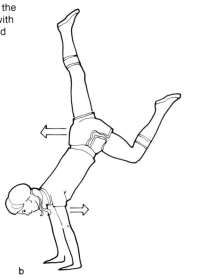
b

c

Figure 25.86 Handstand Spotting. This is similar to the spotting technique described for the headstand (p. 405). Both spotters kneel on the sides of the performer and place their hands under his shoulders. As the performer lifts his legs, each spotter grasps the thigh of the nearest leg. Once in the handstand position, spotter should gradually release the hands but keep them a few inches away and ready to give support.

Figure 25.87 Handstand Spotting. Use the same spotting technique described for the headstand (p. 405). An alternate method is to stand just in front of the spot where the performer's hands will be placed. The spotter's left leg should be extended back to provide a firmly balanced position. As the performer shifts her legs upward, the spotter should brace the performer's right shoulder against his own right leg and catch her legs as they come up.

Stunts, Tumbling, and Movement Skills   421

Figure 25.88 L-Support. Sit on the floor with the legs together and pointing straight ahead. Rest the hands on the floor below the shoulders. Keep the shoulders slightly forward of the hips, press down, and raise the hips and legs off the floor.

Figure 25.89 Elbow Balance. Begin this stunt in a partially front-lying position with the elbows bent and touching the sides of the body, and the fingers spread apart. Keep the elbows close to the sides and shift the trunk slightly downward and forward as the legs are raised.

Developing Individual and Partner Routines

The previous two sections have emphasized the acquisition of individual balance or agility skills. In addition, suggestions and challenges were provided to encourage children to modify these stunts or to invent new ones. Once children have acquired a repertoire of stunts and can practice in an independent and safe manner, a further challenge can be presented. The next task is to encourage children to perform two or more stunts or movement skills in a sequence. The following examples illustrate the types of challenges that can be presented to children of this age range. As a basic guideline, begin with simple, structured challenges involving known and previously practiced stunts and progress to more creative challenges that allow maximum freedom to interpret and create individual or partner routines.

Individual Agility Routines

1. "Make up a routine beginning with a rolling the log (p. 407), shift to a seal slap (p. 409), and finish with a jump through (p. 412)."
2. "Select three agility stunts that can be performed on the floor. Arrange your own sequence of these stunts and practice until you can move smoothly from one movement to the other."
3. "You may use the floor, a mat, or a combination of both. Design a sequence that has modified agility stunts, a change of direction, and one other stunt that you have created."

Individual Balance Routines

1. "Make up a sequence using the following stunts: bridge (p. 417), V-Sit (p. 417), and L-Support (p. 422)."
2. "Using a mat, make up a sequence that has a headstand and two other balance stunts."

Individual Balance and Agility Routines

1. "Design a routine that moves from an agility movement to a balance stunt to a new agility movement."
2. "Create a sequence of balance and agility stunts that also shows a change in direction and level."

Partner Routines

1. Partners have one mat to share. "Make up a matching routine (facing each other, side by side, or follow the leader) that includes a balance, a roll, and a new balance stunt."
2. "In partners, design a matching routine on the floor that has a cartwheel and at least three other agility stunts."

Pyramid Building

A human pyramid is usually considered to be a group of students forming a pyramidlike structure with one child at the top and the others gradually tapering to the sides. This is known as a true pyramid; however, other kinds of pyramids have high points somewhere within the pyramid or even at the ends. The block illustrations may be used as basic guides in constructing pyramids with two or more students.

The first stage of pyramid building is to learn to create individual poses that can be used for the center, side, or end positions. Many balance stunts, such as the headstand and the V-sit, can be used for these positions. Other poses shown can be added to these basic poses (fig. 25.90). It is also important to allow the class to design its own individual positions.

The next stage in pyramid building is the development of dual stunts. Again, many of the dual balance stunts described in the previous section can become the nucleus of a pyramid. Require the heaviest and strongest students to form the base of the pyramid and lighter students to be on top.

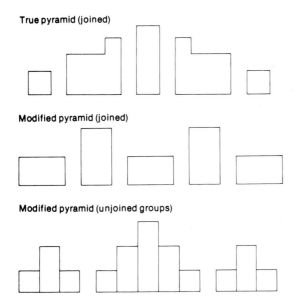

True pyramid (joined)

Modified pyramid (joined)

Modified pyramid (unjoined groups)

Once the dual stunts are learned, combine these positions. A symmetrical, six-person pyramid can be formed with two facing base stands and one individual pose such as the dog stand on each end facing the center. Beyond this point, the teacher and students can use their imaginations to design and construct an unlimited variety of pyramids. Examples are shown in figure 25.92.

Since pyramid building involves teamwork and timing, a standard procedure or set of whistle cues should be developed by the teacher. The first cue could mean that all stand at attention and face one direction. The second cue could signal all participants to move into the ready or primary position. A third blow might be necessary in two- and three-person high pyramids for the upper participants to shift into final position. A similar procedure should then be followed when dismounting.

Movement Concepts and Skills

The stunts and tumbling skills described in the previous sections are classified as structured skills or movement patterns. Each skill is performed in a particular way. While variations are allowed in the approach or the position of the hands or legs, the skill cannot be changed from its basic form. In order to overcome the structured limitations of formal stunts and tumbling activities, many of the movement concepts and skills developed in the movement education approach are being incorporated into stunts and tumbling and into activities with small equipment and large apparatus. These new movement concepts and skills allow the child to perform a movement according to his own level of physical and creative ability.

However, the problems encountered when introducing these unstructured movement concepts and skills to stunts and tumbling, small equipment activities, and large apparatus activities are not dissimilar to those encountered when introducing the problem-solving method in games programs. Introducing the new movement concepts and skills to primary children, particularly those in the first two grades, is relatively easy because primary children do not have a wide background of stunts and tumbling skills. Instead, many of their skills involve imitative movements rather than the complex skills of balance and agility taught in later grades. Also, primary children are normally taught through more informal methods both in the classroom and in the gymnasium. As a consequence, primary teachers have little difficulty incorporating movement concepts and skills into their stunts and tumbling program. Once the teacher understands this new movement vocabulary, she usually gives more emphasis to movement concepts and skills and less to structured stunts activities.

Figure 25.90 Individual Balance and Poses

a

b

c

d

e

f

Figure 25.91 Dual Balance and Poses

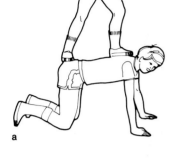

a

b

c

d

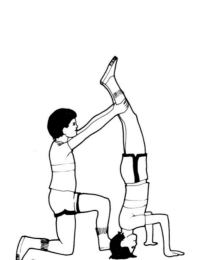

e

f

Figure 25.92

a   b

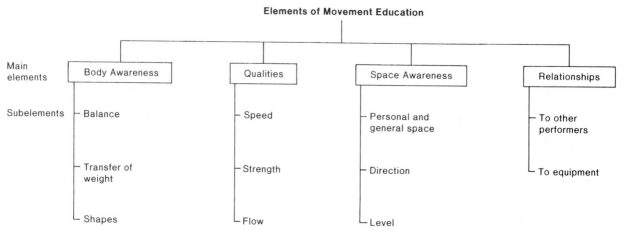

Elements of Movement Education

Main elements	Body Awareness	Qualities	Space Awareness	Relationships
Subelements	Balance	Speed	Personal and general space	To other performers
	Transfer of weight	Strength	Direction	To equipment
	Shapes	Flow	Level	

As with the problem-solving method, introducing the new movement concepts and skills is more difficult for intermediate teachers. By the time boys and girls reach the fourth or fifth grade, they have learned many stunts and tumbling skills, normally through a process of explanation, demonstration, and practice. It would be difficult and unwise to change this process completely and adopt a new movement vocabulary and a new way of learning. A more profitable approach is for the intermediate teacher to acquire an understanding of the basic movement concepts and skills described in this section and then to introduce them gradually into the regular stunts and tumbling activities. If the class is receptive to these ideas and demonstrates the ability to work independently and safely, greater emphasis can be given to the movement concepts and skills.

The main movement education elements of body awareness, qualities, space awareness, and relationships, outlined in the accompanying chart, are described on the following pages. Wherever possible, suggestions for teaching the movement skills of each element are offered, along with ideas for relating or incorporating them into the stunts and tumbling activities of the primary or intermediate program.

c

d

Body Awareness (What the Body Can Do)

Body awareness describes the ways in which the body or its parts can be controlled, balanced upon, or moved from one position to another. Skills involved in body awareness fall into the following three groups.

Balancing or "Weight Bearing"

A child is capable of balancing or "taking the weight" on different parts of his body. He can balance on one foot, on his head, or on all "threes" such as in the lame puppy walk. In order to help the child learn what parts of his body he can balance upon, it is necessary to present a challenge in the form of a movement problem and then let him answer the challenge in his own way. The question should begin with such phrases as "See if you can . . ."; "How many ways . . ."; "Can you . . ."; or "Try to discover . . ."—rather than a direct command such as "I want you to. . . ." The following questions show how to use the problem-solving method to assist the child in finding his own way of balancing on one or more parts of his body.

1. "Can you show me the one-leg balance?" Children may have already learned this balance stunt, so they should be capable of performing it.

2. "See if you can balance on your seat." This is still somewhat structured, yet the question allows each child to put his arms and legs in any position he wishes. A series of similar questions directing the child to balance on other parts—side, back, stomach—could follow.

3. Present a series of questions involving two or more parts of the body—"Can you balance on one foot and two other parts of your body?" "See if you can balance on three (or four) different parts of your body." "Can you find another way of balancing on three parts of your body?"

The main task within this sub-element of body awareness is to help children become aware of the many different ways in which they can balance their bodies. The movement challenges began with a familiar stunt (the one-leg balance), then shifted to specific parts of the body. The final challenge mentioned only a certain number of "points of contact," thus providing more freedom for the child to discover other ways that his body or its parts can be balanced.

Transfer of Weight

Transfer of weight, the second sub-element of body awareness, is the ability to shift from one balanced position to another. This skill can be developed as a logical extension of balancing on different parts of the body. The following questions illustrate how this progression can occur.

Figure 25.93

1. From one known skill to another: "Can you show me the measuring worm stunt, then change to a headstand?" (This is shifting from one three-point balance to another three-point balance.)

2. From a known part to three unknown parts: "See if you can balance on your seat, then shift to balancing on three different parts of your body." (From a one-point balance to a three-point balance.)

3. From unknown parts to unknown parts: "Can you show me a three-point balance, then shift to a new two-point balance?"

Shapes

Shape, the third sub-element of body awareness, includes the ways the human body can make stretched, curled, wide, narrow, and twisted shapes. The task is similar to balancing or weight bearing in that questions must be presented to help the child discover what shapes he can perform.

Stretch and curl shapes should involve the whole body first, then progress to individual parts. Questions should encourage the children to make the following shapes from various starting positions.

1. *Curled Shapes* (fig. 25.95)
   a. From a sitting position
   b. From a standing position
   c. While in flight
   d. From a front, back, or side lying position
   e. From a curled position to another curled position

2. *Stretched Shapes* (fig. 25.96)
   a. From a standing position
   b. While in flight
   c. From a sitting position
   d. From a front, back, or side lying position
   e. From a stretched position to another stretched position

Figure 25.94 Transfer of Weight

a   b   c

Figure 25.95 "Can you make a curled shape?"

Figure 25.96 "See if you can show me a stretched shape."

Progression should be from a stationary position into a curled or stretched shape. Begin with questions directed at curled shapes (from a–e), then try the same with stretched shapes (a–e), or switch from one to the other. Following are sample questions:

"Can you curl up and make a very small, ball-like shape?"

"Can you make a stretched shape from a standing position?"

"See if you can repeat your stretched shape or find a new one and then change into a curled shape."

"See if you can start with the turk stand and when you are low to the ground roll to a very curled-up shape."

Allow the class sufficient time for experimentation. During this time look for unusual shapes and provide encouragement and praise wherever necessary. Choose one or two shapes and let the children show them to the rest of the class; don't always choose the same children.

Once the class has a general understanding of stretch and curl, introduce wide and narrow and twisted shapes in a similar way. Wide and narrow shapes, like curl and stretch shapes, are contrasting. A wide shape (fig. 25.97) requires the legs or arms or both to be away from the trunk in some way. In contrast, a narrow shape is characterized by its thinness, which means the arms or legs must be close together or in line with the trunk.

A twisted shape can be performed in two ways. The first is by holding one part of the body in a fixed or stabilized position, such as on the floor, and then turning the body or any part of it away from the fixed base. In figure 25.98 the body is fixed or stabilized as the feet restrict the degree of twisting. A twisted shape can also be made when the body is in flight. In this case, one part of the body is held in a fixed position while the other part turns away from the *fixed* part, producing a twisted shape. Although it could be argued that the latter is a *turn* (usually defined as rotation of the body

Figure 25.97 Wide Shapes

Figure 25.99

Figure 25.98 Twisting—Body Stabilized

Figure 25.100

Qualities (How the Body Moves)

The element of qualities describes how the body moves from one position to another in relation to speed, force, and flow.

Speed
Speed is the ability to move quickly or slowly from one position to another (fig. 25.99).

Force
Force is the effort involved in a single movement or throughout a series of related movements. A child may leap high into the air, demonstrating a strong and forceful movement of the leg muscles (fig. 25.100). In contrast, a gentle shift from a high stretch to a low curl illustrates a light or gentle movement.

and loss of a fixed contact), with younger children the synonymous use of *twist* and *turn* is quite acceptable. The refinement in meaning can be made later.

At this stage in the introduction of movement skills and concepts, children should have learned the meaning of balance and shape. They should also be able to develop simple sequences involving a variety of shapes and balance skills.

Figure 25.101 Flow

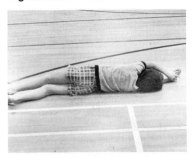

a. A smooth transition from one position . . .

b. . . . to another position . . .

c. . . . and to another position.

Flow

Flow is the smooth transition or linking of one movement pattern to another (fig. 25.101).

These aspects of qualities can be integrated into previously learned stunts, tumbling and safety skills, and the three components of body awareness. The following examples show a few of the many applications of speed, force, and flow to a single skill or a sequence of skills.

1. *Stunts:* Ask the class to perform the measuring worm stunt. After one or two practices, ask the class to perform part of the stunt very slowly and part very quickly (fig. 25.102).
2. *Tumbling Skills:* Pose a challenge such as "See if you can move slowly from a log roll to a side roll, then quickly from a side roll back to a log roll."
3. *Shapes:* Ask the class to make up a sequence of stretched, curled, and wide shapes. After each child knows his sequence, pose the following suggestion: "As you practice your sequence, try very hard to make each movement link smoothly to the next with no sudden stops or jerky movements between each skill." The stress here is on flow, or the ease and efficiency of moving from one shape or position to another.

Space Awareness (Where the Body Moves)

The third main element, known as space awareness, includes movement skills relating to use of general or limited space, direction, and levels of movement.

General or Limited Space

All the space in a gymnasium that can be used by a child constitutes his *general space* (fig. 25.103). In contrast, *limited,* or *personal,* space is the immediate

Figure 25.102 Measuring-Worm Stunt

Figure 25.103 General Space

Figure 25.104   Limited Space

Figure 25.105   Matching Shapes

Figure 25.106   Contrasting Shapes

area a child can use around him to perform a movement or series of movements. When a child is challenged to perform a series of different balance positions while remaining inside his hoop, he is using his personal, or limited, space (fig. 25.104).

Direction

Direction is the ability to move safely and purposely in a variety of pathways, such as forward, backward, or sideways, and to trace out pathways such as over, under, around, and through.

Levels

Levels concerns the ability to perform a movement or series of movements that require the body to be low to the ground, as when performing series of rolls, at a medium level, as in moving on all fours, or at a high level, as when performing a cartwheel or a leap from the floor.

Many of these aspects of space awareness have been stressed in teaching stunts and tumbling and, to a lesser degree, when teaching the movement skills of body awareness and qualities. For example, when each of the tumbling skills was introduced, each child began on his own mat. This was his personal, or limited, space. Gradually, his space was expanded to two mats, then to three, and finally to all the mats available in the general space of the gymnasium. Each child was also asked to move to an open space on the mat. His rolling movement may have been forward, sideways, or diagonal.

Relationships

The fourth element of movement education is the relationship of the individual or group to other performers or objects.

Partner Relationships

Movements with a partner can involve matching shapes (fig. 25.105), contrasting shapes (fig. 25.106), or one child acting as the leader while the other acts as the follower through a sequence of movements.

Many useful and enjoyable partner activities can be applied to a stunts and tumbling program. All of the partner activities described under the stunts sections for primary and intermediate children are essentially dual balance stunts or tandem-type agility walks. With "matching," "contrasting," and "following" challenges, partner activities can be greatly enriched. Following are examples of the many ways that partners can develop structured and unstructured movement sequences.

1. *Matching Movements Using Structured Skills:* "See if you can make up a sequence (or routine) with your partner that begins with a headstand, includes a roll, and ends with both in a balancing position (fig. 25.107)."

Figure 25.107 Partner Relationships

a. . . . that begin with a
headstand. . .

b. . . . include a roll. . .

c. . . . and end in a balance
position.

2. *Contrasting Movements Using Unstructured Skills:* "One partner makes a stretched shape and the other partner makes a contrasting curled shape. Next, the first partner makes another stretched shape and his partner makes a contrasting curled shape." Repeat again with two new stretched and curled shapes. Allow time to practice the contrasting shapes in a smooth sequence.

3. *Follow the Leader:* One partner leads and the other copies each movement. Challenges can be "Make a shape, change direction, make another shape, change direction," and so on. "Develop a sequence of balancing and rolling with one following the other." Or, "Make up a sequence with your partner that includes a change of direction and a change in speed."

Figure 25.108 In a Manipulative Way

Equipment Relationships

Equipment relationships involve the ability to perform a movement in a manipulative way, such as balancing or rolling with a hoop (fig. 25.108), or in a nonmanipulative manner, such as leaping over a hoop (fig. 25.109). Numerous examples of these types of relationships are described in the next two chapters.

This introduction to the four movement elements has simply opened the door to a new range of movement skills. Each of the skills within body awareness, qualities, space awareness, and relationships are unstructured and thus allow each child to perform each

Figure 25.109   In a Nonmanipulative Way

movement in his own unique way. Since these new movement skills can be mixed with stunts or tumbling skills, they enrich a child's movement experience.

The next two chapters deal with a wide variety of small equipment and large apparatus. Structured skills such as individual rope skipping, vaulting over boxes, and balancing on a beam will be presented. If the children have developed a basic understanding of the four movement elements, they will be able to apply these new movement skills to each piece of equipment and to the large apparatus in a very exciting and creative way.

26 Stunts and Movement Skills with Small Equipment

This chapter should be considered as a logical extension of stunts and tumbling activities. Adding a variety of small equipment to the gymnastic program provides an opportunity for each child to develop strength, balance, and coordination. Each piece of equipment included in this chapter can be used in a structured manner, such as teaching basic rope-skipping skills. And when the movement concepts and skills described in the previous chapter are applied, many additional uses can be found for the equipment. By presenting movement challenges or tasks, the equipment may be used in a manipulative manner or as an obstacle to maneuver around or over.

The material in this chapter has been organized to provide both primary and intermediate teachers with sufficient information to teach a wide variety of structured skills or to combine these skills with movement concepts and skills in an interesting and challenging way.

Teaching Procedures

The addition of small equipment activities to a gymnastic lesson presents several organizational and instructional problems. The following suggestions will assist you in incorporating small equipment into your gymnastic program.

Routine Procedures

Perhaps the most frustrating aspect of using small equipment is getting it out and putting it away in an orderly manner. One of the most successful and efficient ways of handling equipment is to have each type of equipment that is going to be used in a lesson placed in boxes or containers near the instructional area. The teacher can then give instructions about who will be using what type of equipment and where their working areas will be. When the equipment is not being used, it is returned to the appropriate container. Suggestions for carrying and placing equipment such as wands and hoops are given in the sections on each type of equipment.

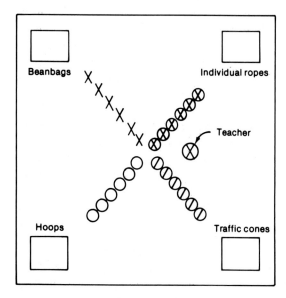

Using Small Equipment

It was stated in the previous chapter that small equipment should be used to provide additional challenges to stunts, tumbling skills, and movement skills (see lesson outline on p. 389). Since each class and grade level varies according to the time and equipment available and the students' background of skill, no standard application of this equipment can be recommended. Each of this chapter's sections includes a suggested list of individual and partner skills and a list of ideas and challenges to develop movement concepts.

Beanbag Activities

Beanbags are the most common type of small equipment and are available to virtually every classroom teacher. The beanbag should be at least six inches square for the activities suggested in this program. Cloth covers rather than smooth plastic or nylon ones are preferred for homemade beanbags.

Although beanbags traditionally have been used by primary teachers for simple games and manipulative activities, they have many applications at the intermediate level. The more familiar, structured beanbag activities are presented first to illustrate the contemporary use of the beanbag in the gymnastic program. Following that is a section on how the beanbag can be used as an obstacle or focus point in developing movement concepts and skills.

Individual Activities

The beanbag can be used to increase the difficulty of many previously acquired stunts and tumbling skills, as well as with many new balance and stunt activities. The following examples illustrate the beanbag's versatility.

1. *Stunts and Tumbling Skills:*
   a. Wicket walk (p. 392), beanbag behind neck.
   b. Tightrope walk (p. 402), beanbag on head.
   c. Bouncing ball (p. 392), beanbag on head.
   d. Single leg balance (p. 403), beanbag on head or arm.
   e. Forward roll (p. 395) and side roll (p. 409), beanbag under chin.
   f. Knee dip (p. 403), beanbag on head.
   g. L-support (p. 422), beanbag between knees.

2. *Throwing and Catching Skills:* The wide surface and lack of rebound property make the beanbag a valuable tool in helping young children learn how to throw and catch. Following are a few examples of how primary teachers can use the beanbag to develop hand–eye coordination:
   a. Toss the beanbag into the air and catch it with both hands, then with the left hand, and then with the right.
   b. Toss the beanbag into the air, change direction, or perform a hand movement (clap hands, touch the floor), and then catch the beanbag.
   c. Place targets on floor (hoops, milk cartons) and throw the beanbag into the target. Change throwing skill and distance.
   d. Move, throw, and catch. Have the children use a variety of locomotor skills (running, skipping, and so on) and throw and catch beanbags as they move about the instructional area.

Figure 26.1 "Balance the beanbag on your head . . .

Figure 26.2 . . . on your foot."

3. *Balance the Beanbag on Different Parts of the Body* (figs. 26.1 and 26.2): Designate specific parts of the body—head, elbow, and so on. Change body position and continue. For example, "Put beanbag on your back and balance on one foot."

4. *Move the Beanbag with Different Parts of the Body:* Ask the class to propel the beanbags with their knees and catch them; then designate other parts of the body, such as the head, foot, elbow, and shoulder.

Partner Activities

Many of the previous individual skills can be performed with two performers, and several new partner activities can be presented. Several examples follow.

1. *Throwing and Catching:*
   a. Throw the beanbag back and forth, changing the type of throw, distance, and position and angle of throw.
   b. Throw and catch with two beanbags.
   c. Throw and catch with one or both performers on the move.

Figure 26.3 Throw and catch the beanbag.

2. *Pass and Catch the Beanbag with Different Parts of the Body:* Propel with the feet and catch with the hands or feet. Propel with the head and catch with the stomach or another part of the body.

Applying Movement Skills

The individual and partner activities that have been previously described indicate the value and potential of beanbag activities in developing throwing, catching, balancing, and agility skills. If children have been taught through the problem-solving method and have acquired a basic understanding of movement concepts and skills, the next step is to use beanbag activities in a much more creative and challenging way. The following examples illustrate how the beanbag can be used as an obstacle to balance on or with, and to maneuver on or over. By posing tasks or challenges using movement skills, children discover through their own exploration the various ways their bodies or body parts can manipulate and control small obstacles.

Although the same challenge can be presented to primary and intermediate children, the movement response should be quite different. As children progress through the grades, they acquire more skill and movement understanding, which is revealed in the complexity and quality of their movement patterns. Following are examples of the types of questions that should be asked and the types of responses that can be expected from primary and intermediate children. Each teacher, however, should present challenges according to her class' previous gymnastic background and receptiveness to this exploratory approach.

1. *Balance and Transfer of Weight:*
   a. "How many different parts of your body can you balance the beanbag on?"

Figure 26.4   Balance on one part of the beanbag.

Figure 26.5   "How many different ways can you balance over the beanbag?"

Figure 26.6   "How many different ways can you cross the beanbag?"

   b. "Place the beanbag on the floor. Can you balance with one part of your body on the beanbag (fig. 26.4)?"
   c. "Place the beanbag on your seat and see how many ways you can balance on three different parts of your body."
   d. "Place a beanbag on the floor. How many different ways can you balance over the beanbag (fig. 26.5)?"
   e. "How many different ways can you cross your beanbag (fig. 26.6)?"

2. *Direction and Speed:* Scatter beanbags around the floor area and pose these challenge activities illustrating how the beanbag acts as an obstacle or focus point in the development of directional movements and the quality of speed.
   a. "Move around as many beanbags as possible, but do not jump over any."
   b. "Run in any direction and when you come to a beanbag, run completely around it, then move to another beanbag."
   c. "Move in any direction and as you approach a beanbag, jump over it, land, and then change directions to find another beanbag (fig. 26.7)."
   d. "Can you run in different directions showing a change of speed every time you jump over a beanbag?"
   e. Run and jump over a beanbag.

3. *Shapes:*
   a. "Can you make a stretched shape with the beanbag on the highest part of your body?"
   b. "See if you can keep the beanbag on one part of your body while you try to make two different curled shapes."

Figure 26.8   Follow your partner.

a. "Place beanbag on your head . . .

b. . . . one child leads. . .

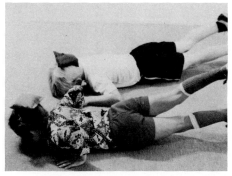

c. . . . and the other child must match her movements."

4. *Relationships:* Each partner has a beanbag.
   a. "Place the beanbags on the floor and make up a matching sequence that shows a change of direction and a change of speed."
   b. "Keep the beanbag between your feet and make up a matching sequence that includes moving forward, backward, and sideways."
   c. "Place the beanbags on your heads. One child leads and the other must match her movements (fig. 26.8)."

Figure 26.9   Rope Jumping

Rope-Jumping Activities

Children perform three basic types of rope-jumping activities in the primary and intermediate grades. One is rope jumping that involves light, graceful leaps over a rope turned by an individual or with a partner. The second is long rope jumping, which involves jumping over a long rope turned by two performers. Finally, ropes are used in a variety of ways to enhance movement concepts and skills.

Children of all ages enjoy performing individual rope-jumping skills with or without musical accompaniment. In the primary grades the level of interest or skill varies little between boys and girls. For many years, the trend has been for girls to continue this activity through the intermediate grades and for boys to shift their interests to other types of activities. However, recent physical fitness programs, such as "Jump for Heart," have created a very positive change in the attitude of boys towards all types of rope-jumping activities. Today this activity is enjoyed equally by boys and girls and with virtually no difference in skill level.

Individual Activities

Several kinds and thicknesses of rope can be used for individual rope jumping. A three-eighths-inch sash cord is probably the best; however, any rope, either sash or plastic, up to one-half inch in thickness is quite acceptable. It is equally important to have the proper length of rope for each child. To determine the correct

Figure 26.10 Having the correct length of rope is important for the child to jump properly.

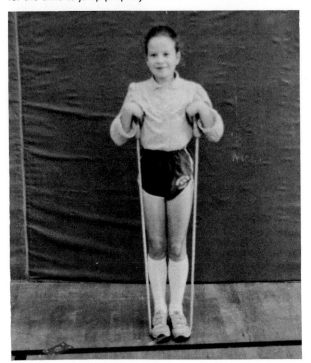

Figure 26.11 Correct Jumping Form

length, have the child stand in the center of the rope; it should extend from armpit to armpit (fig. 26.10). An incorrect length will adversely affect the rope-jumping performance.

The correct rope-jumping form is to hold the ends of the rope loosely in the fingers, with the thumbs placed on top of the rope and pointing to the sides. The elbows are held close to the sides, with the forearms and hands pointing slightly forward and away from the body (fig. 26.11). To start the rope turning, swing the arms and shoulders in a circular motion; once the rope begins to follow the circular motion, all further action should be initiated from the wrists and fingers. The jumping action should be a slight push off the toes, just high enough to allow the rope to pass under the feet.

Basic Rope-Jumping Skills

The following rope-jumping skills are listed in approximate order of difficulty. It is helpful to begin each new step without a rope. Once the child can execute the foot movements, let him try with a rope. At this stage, a musical background will help the child keep up a steady rhythm. Any folk-dance record such as "Shoo Fly" or "Pop Goes the Weasel" with a 4/4 rhythm works very well. All popular tunes with a similar beat will work as well and, in fact, are enjoyed more than folk dance records by upper elementary school children.

Many of the basic steps shown in figures 26.12 to 26.23 can be performed in slow or fast time and with the rope turned forward or backward. With slow

rhythm, the performer jumps over the rope, takes a rebound jump in place as the rope passes overhead, and then performs the original step or shifts to a new movement. The pattern is jump-rebound-jump. With slow rhythm musical accompaniment, the performer jumps over the rope on every other beat. With a fast rhythm, the rope is turned twice as fast so the performer executes a step only as the rope passes under his feet. With fast rhythm musical accompaniment, the performer jumps over the rope on every beat.

Once the children have learned two or more basic steps, they can begin to create many interesting and enjoyable routines. A few suggestions follow; however, each child should have an opportunity to develop his own routine.

1. Combine a change of speed with the alternate step.
2. Make up a sequence involving three different steps.
3. Make up a sequence involving a hop, an alternate step, and a change of direction.
4. Perform three different steps in a cross-arm position.
5. Move in different directions using hopping, jumping, and rocking-step skills.
6. Make up a sequence with the rope turning backward.

Figure 26.12 Two-Foot Basic. The two-foot basic step includes two jumps for each complete turn of the rope. Pull the rope around and jump over it, and take a second "rebound" jump as the rope passes backward and upward.

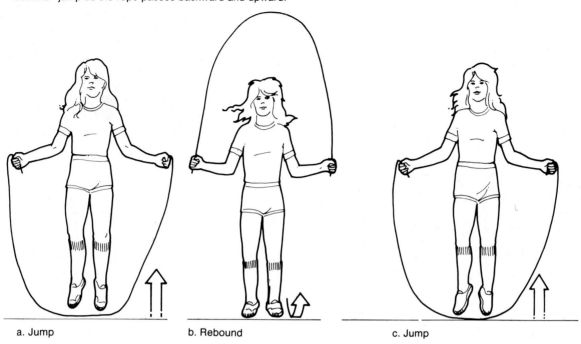

a. Jump   b. Rebound   c. Jump

Figure 26.13 Skier. A double foot jump represents the leg actions of a skier. Stand with feet together on one side of a line (a). Use a two foot basic action, jump over rope, and land about one and one-half feet on the other side of the line (b). Take a rebound jump, then jump and shift both feet back to the other side of the line (c). Once the skill is learned, try shifting feet forward and backward.

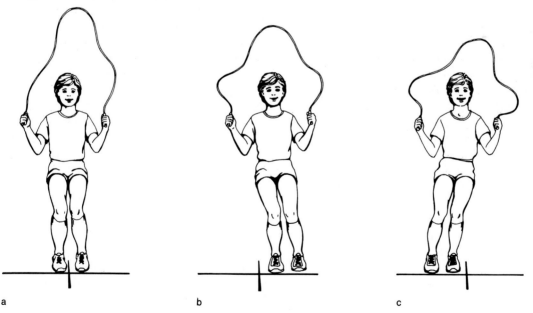

a   b   c

Figure 26.14 Alternate Step. Jump over rope with the right foot (jump), hop on same foot (rebound), then jump over rope with left foot (jump), and hop on the same foot (rebound). Pass the rope overhead.

a. Jump right

b. Rebound right

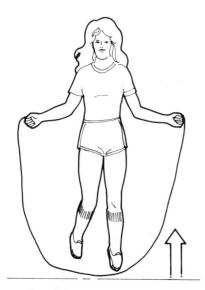

c. Jump left

d. Rebound left

Figure 26.15 Swing Step. This is basically the same as the alternate step, except swing the "free leg" forward, backward, or to the side during the rebound step.

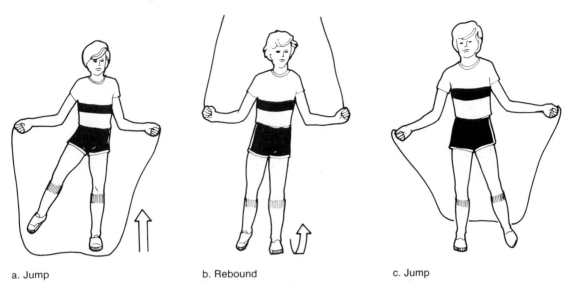

a. Jump   b. Rebound   c. Jump

Figure 26.16 Heel Toe. This is a combination of the "heel to heel" and "toe to toe" steps. Begin by standing on left foot, then jump on left foot, and place heel of right foot forward (a). Take a rebound jump (b) on the left foot. Jump and land on left foot and place right toe to back of left heel (c). Jump on right, land on right and place heel of left foot forward (d). Continue pattern.

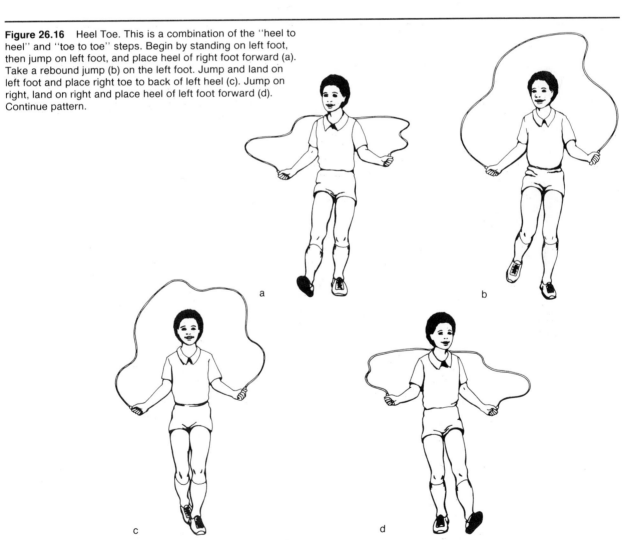

Figure 26.17 Can Can. Stand on the left foot. Jump on left foot and bring right knee up, pointing toe down (a). Rebound on left foot (b). Jump on left and kick right leg as high as you can (c). Jump on right foot and bring left knee up (d). Continue pattern.

a   b   c   d

Figure 26.18 One-Foot Hop. Perform the one-foot hop with each turn of the rope or with a rebound step after each jump over the rope. However, continue hopping on one foot for several rotations of the rope before transferring to hopping on the opposite foot.

a. Hop left

b. Rebound left

Figure 26.19 Rocker. When performing the rocker step, one leg is always forward and the weight shifts from the back to the front, or lead, foot. As the rope passes under the front foot, transfer the weight forward, allowing the back foot to raise and the rope to pass under it. After the rope passes under the back foot and begins its upward and forward arch, "rock" back, transferring the weight to the back foot.

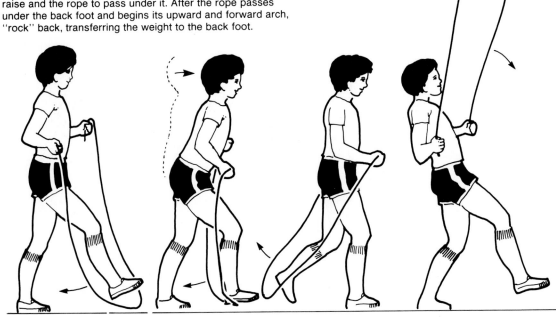

a. Pass rope under front foot   b. Rock forward   c. Pass rope under back foot   d. Rock backward

Figure 26.20 Spread Legs. Begin the spread-legs step in a front stride position with the weight evenly distributed on both feet. Pull the rope around, jump, and as it passes under, change the position of the feet. Continue pattern.

a. Begin in a stride position   b. Jump and change   c. Land in a stride position

Figure 26.21 Crossed Legs. Begin the cross-leg step with the right leg crossed in front of the left leg and the weight evenly distributed on both feet. Pull the rope around, jump, and as it passes under, cross the left leg over the right. Continue the pattern, alternating the front leg position.

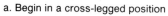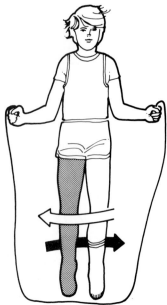

a. Begin in a cross-legged position   b. Jump and cross   c. Left leg over right

Figure 26.22 Cross Arms. Crossing arms should take place during an ongoing rope-jumping movement. As the rope begins its forward and downward movement, cross the left arm over the right, and bring the right hand up and under the left armpit. Make the next jump in this position. Continue in the crossed-arm position or alternate the crossed-arm position on each turn of the rope.

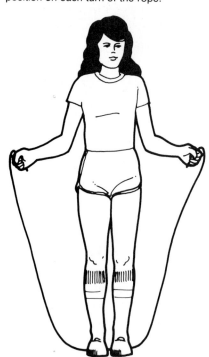

a. From a regular rope-skipping position . . .   b. . . . to cross left over right . . .   c. . . . right hand up under left armpit.

Figure 26.23 Pepper. The pepper step is two full turns of the rope while the performer's feet are off the ground.

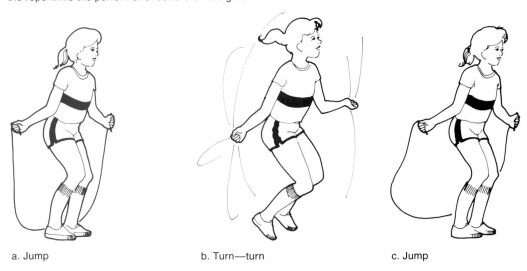

a. Jump

b. Turn—turn

c. Jump

Figure 26.24 Begin with a two-foot basic . . .

Figure 26.25 . . . partner enters front.

Partner Activities

Children can perform several enjoyable partner activities with an individual rope. Many variations and routines can be developed from the following basic starting positions. One partner begins with a two-foot basic step. As the rope comes forward and down, the outside partner enters and places her hands on her partner's waist (figs. 26.24 and 26.25).

Figure 26.26   Face each other.

Figure 26.27   One partner moves in.

Variations:

1. Partners perform mirror images, hopping, jumping, or other basic rope-jumping steps.
2. Outside partner turns her back to her partner and they continue jumping.
3. Outside partner keeps the same jumping cadence as her partner but begins to make a quarter or a half turn, then jumps back to her original position.

Partners stand facing each other with the rope held on the same side.

Variations:

1. One partner moves in, then out (fig. 26.27).
2. One partner moves in, followed by his partner.
3. When both are inside, they make up a sequence of matching steps.

Long Rope-Jumping Activities

Long rope-jumping is performed with one or more children jumping over a rope turned by two other children. The rope can be turned two different ways for jumping activities. Teach the "front door" first, then introduce the "back door" skill (fig. 26.28). To assist in teaching both types of jumping skills, use the suggested list of rope-jumping rhymes that begin on page 449.

Figure 26.28   Front Door. The children turn the rope toward the jumper (clockwise), and the jumper waits until the rope is moving away from her before she runs in. Back Door. The turners turn the rope away from the jumper (counterclockwise), and the jumper waits until the rope has passed its highest peak and is moving downward before he runs in.

The following progression of rope-jumping activities can be performed by entering through either the front or back door.

1. Run under the rope.
2. Run in, jump once, run out.
3. Run in, jump several times, run out.
4. Run in, jump once on one foot, run out.
5. Run in, jump several times on one foot, run out.
6. Run in, jump making quarter, half, three-quarter, or full turns with each jump, run out.

Figure 26.29 . . . arms over partner's shoulders.

7. Run in, jump on alternate feet, run out.

8. Run in, touch the floor with the hands on every other jump, run out.

9. Run in, squat (on all fours), jump in this position, run out.

10. Run in, jump up and touch toes, land, run out.

11. Run in, turners gradually increase speed to "hot pepper," slow down, run out.

12. Run in, turners gradually raise rope off the ground ("high water").

13. Run in with a ball, bounce the ball several times, run out.

14. Repeat these skills with a partner.

15. Place arm over partner's shoulder, run in, jump several times, run out (fig. 26.29).

16. With partner, run in, stand back to back, jump several times, run out.

17. With partner, run in, face partner, hold partner's right leg, jump several times, run out.

18. Follow the leader with four or five players and one chosen to be the leader. The leader runs in and performs any skill or stunt, then runs out. Each player follows and repeats the leader's stunt.

Rope-Jumping Rhymes

Rope-jumping rhymes, like singing games, are centuries old and belong to people of many nations. The first four rhymes are perhaps the most popular in North America. Each region may also have slight variations in words. Encourage children to use their own version, to adapt the version of the following favorites.

Down by the Meadow

Down by the meadow where the green grass grows,
There sits (call the name of jumper) sweet as a rose.
She sang, she sang, she sang, she sang so sweet,
And along came (jumper's sweetheart's name), and
Kissed her on the cheek.
How many kisses did she get?
1, 2, 3, 4, etc.
(Child keeps jumping until she misses.)

Teddy Bear, Teddy Bear

Teddy Bear, Teddy Bear, turn around.
Teddy Bear, Teddy Bear, touch the ground.
Teddy Bear, Teddy Bear, shine your shoes.
Teddy Bear, Teddy Bear, that will do.
Teddy Bear, Teddy Bear, go upstairs.
Teddy Bear, Teddy Bear, say your prayers.
Teddy Bear, Teddy Bear, turn out the light.
Teddy Bear, Teddy Bear, say good night.
Teddy Bear, hop on one foot, one foot.
Teddy Bear, hop on two feet, two feet.
Teddy Bear, hop on three feet, three feet.
Teddy Bear, hop right out.

Johnny On the Ocean

Johnny on the ocean,
Johnny on the sea,
Johnny broke a bottle,
And blamed it on me.
I told ma,
Ma told pa.
Johnny got a whipping
And a ha! ha! ha!
How many whippings did he get?
1, 2, 3, etc. (Child keeps jumping until she misses).

I'm a Little Dutch Girl

Charlie Chaplin went to France
To teach the pretty girls
The hula dance.
First on the heel,
Then the toe,
Do the splits,
And around you go.
Salute to the captain,
Curtsey the Queen,
Touch the bottom of the submarine.

All in Together

All in together, this fine weather,
January, February, March, etc.
(Jumper runs in on the month of his birthday.)
All out together, this fine weather,
January, February, March, etc.
(Jumper runs out on the month of his birthday.)

I Love Coffee

I love coffee, I love tea, I love (name).
I dislike coffee, I dislike tea, I dislike (name).
So go away from me.
(Child who is jumping calls the name of another child,
    who comes in, then goes out.)

Mabel, Mabel

Mabel, Mabel, set the table,
Don't forget the salt, vinegar, pepper. . . .
(Turners turn "pepper" on the last word.)

Fudge, Fudge

Fudge, Fudge, tell the judge,
Mama's got a newborn baby.
Wrap it up in tissue paper,
Send it down the elevator,
Elevator one, splits . . . elevator two . . . splits, and
    so on until the jumper misses. (Jumper performs
    the splits on the word "splits.")

Apple, Apple

Apple, Apple, up in the tree,
Tell me who my lover shall be,
A, B, C, D, E, etc. (Jump to each letter until the jumper
    reaches his sweetheart's first initial.)

Mama, Mama

Mama, Mama, I am sick,
Send for the doctor, quick, quick, quick.
Mama, Mama, turn around,
Mama, Mama, touch the ground.
Mama, Mama, are you through?
Mama, Mama, spell your name.
(Child performs actions indicated in the verse.)

Playground Ideas with Long Ropes

Long ropes have traditionally been used for jumping activities. The following examples illustrate other enjoyable uses of one or two long ropes.

1. *Jumping over One Rope:* Two performers hold a long rope approximately two feet off the ground (vary the height according to the ability of the group). Activities may include:
   a. High jumping (fig. 26.30).
   b. Jumping and making shapes in the air.
   c. Jumping and turning in the air.
   d. Crossing the rope with a cartwheel movement (fig. 26.31).
   e. Follow the leader activities.
2. *Jumping over Two Ropes:* Two performers hold two ropes about two feet off the ground. Repeat the same skills (fig. 26.32). Then have the rope holders hold one rope low and the other high; repeat the skills.

Figure 26.30   High Jumping

Figure 26.31   Crossing with a Cartwheel

Figure 26.32   Jumping over Two Ropes

These few examples should provide the teacher with a starting point. The creative teacher and class will come up with other ideas, such as jumping over one rope, then crawling under the other, or hopping, jumping, or performing some other locomotor movement from one end to the other.

Applying Movement Skills

Several basic rope-jumping skills that can be performed by an individual or with a partner have been described. The individual rope can also be used in many other interesting and challenging ways. For example, it can become an obstacle to manipulate, as when tying a knot using only the feet (fig. 26.33). And it can become an obstacle to maneuver around or over, such as finding many ways of crossing a rope.

It is now possible to apply the problem-solving method and the movement skills described in the previous chapter to individual rope activities. The individual rope thus becomes a means of further challenging the physical and creative abilities of the child. The four movement concepts and the various movement skills become the framework for developing a series of tasks or challenges. Following are some examples.

1. *Balance or Weight Bearing:* "See if you can hold the rope with both hands and balance on both knees and one elbow." This is a manipulating activity.
2. *Shapes:* "Can you make a twisted shape with your rope?" This is another manipulating activity.
3. *Direction:* "Place the rope on the floor in any pattern you like and make up a sequence that involves three changes in direction (fig. 26.34)." This is a maneuvering activity.
4. *Force and Rolling:* "Place the rope on the floor, then move a few steps away from it. See if you can run, leap over the rope, land, and roll."
5. *Relationships and Force:* "Make up a sequence with your partner and one rope that has three different pulling actions."
6. *Relationships and Shapes:* "Can you make up a sequence of matching shapes with your partner?"

Hoop Activities

The introduction of hoop activities will add challenge and variety to any gymnastic program. Hoops are inexpensive, easily stored, and, most important, a very versatile piece of equipment. It is strongly recommended that a class set, plus six to eight extra hoops,

Figure 26.33   Tie a knot with your feet.

Figure 26.34   "How many ways can you cross the rope?"

Figure 26.35 Hula Hooping

Figure 26.36 Hula Jumping

be purchased. A mixture of the standard forty-two-inch hoops and the smaller thirty-six-inch hoops is adequate for any elementary grade.

Since hoops can be extremely noisy, establish a strict routine for getting them out of the equipment room and carrying them to instructional areas. Require the children to place their hoops on the floor gently and to sit inside them while listening to instructions.

A few of the more common activities will be presented, followed by several suggestions for applying movement skills to hoop activities.

The following hoop individual and partner activities can be presented as a direct challenge. However, variations occur in the way the children attempt to perform the skills.

Figure 26.37 Jump over it.

Individual Activities

1. Hula Hooping: This skill is normally performed around the waist; however, other areas of the body, such as the arm, leg, wrist, and ankles can also be used (fig. 26.35).
2. Hula Jumping: The hoop can be used as a jumping rope (fig. 26.36). This is an effective substitute, particularly for primary children.
3. Place the hoop on the floor, then jump over it (fig. 26.37), or jump across it.
4. Roll the hoop with a reverse spin and as it returns repeat 3.
5. Spin the hoop. While it is spinning, try to run around it or jump over it before it falls.
6. Place the hoop on the floor. Walk around the edge of the hoop or run and jump into the center and then out.

Partner Activities

1. Play catch with one or two hoops.
2. Target throwing with partner: One partner throws the hoop at a designated part of his partner, such as his arm, right leg, or head. Vary the distance according to the level of skill.
3. One partner holds the hoop in a horizontal position while the other tries to run and jump over it or crawl under it (fig. 26.38).
4. One partner rolls the hoop while the other partner attempts to crawl through it.

Figure 26.38 Jump over and through.

Figure 26.39 Balance while holding your hoop.

Applying Movement Skills

The hoop has become one of the most popular pieces of small equipment for use with movement skills. The following challenges illustrate the scope and versatility of this piece of equipment.

1. *Balance or Weight Bearing:* "Can you balance over the hoop? (fig. 26.39)." "Can you balance with three parts on the hoop?" "See if you can balance on four parts and hold the hoop off the ground." "On how many different parts of your body can you balance the hoop?"

Figure 26.40 Make up a sequence with one holding.

2. *Shapes and Flow:* "Make up a sequence of three different shapes while holding your hoop."
3. *Rolling and Flow:* "Can you roll while holding onto your hoop?"
4. *Direction:* "Place four hoops on the floor in any pattern you wish, then make up a sequence that shows four changes in direction." After the sequence is developed, "Now add a change of speed or level to your sequence."
5. *Relationships and Shapes:* "Make up a sequence with your partner in which one partner holds the hoop and the other moves from shape to shape (fig. 26.40)."

Wand Activities

The initial lack of commercial equipment in many elementary schools forced teachers to improvise with what was available or to make their own equipment. The wand is an example of the latter. Discarded broom handles or three-quarter inch to one and one-half inch doweling cut into thirty-six-inch or forty-two-inch lengths are adequate for elementary school children. Wands present the same noise problem as hoops, so establish a similar procedure as suggested for hoops.

Numerous structured stunts can be performed with a wand. In addition, a wide variety of movement tasks or challenges can be designed to use the wand in a manipulative way or as an obstacle to maneuver around or over. The following activities should begin in the second or third grade. However, movement challenges using the wand can begin in the first grade.

Individual and Partner Activities

The stunts in figures 26.41 to 26.49 are a few of the many individual and partner activities children can perform with wands.

Figure 26.41 Finger Balance. Hold wand with one hand, then place the index finger of the opposite hand under the end of the wand. Release grip and balance the wand on the end of the finger. After practice, try balancing wand while walking forward and backward and then running.

Figure 26.42 Foot Balance. Place wand near the big toe, raise the foot off the floor, release grip, and try to balance the wand on the foot.

Figure 26.43 Back Touch. Begin with the legs straight and the feet approximately shoulder-width apart. Grasp the wand close to one end. Arch back, place the end of the wand on the mat, and continue arching back and down.

Figure 26.44 Double Foot Balance. Begin in a back-lying position, hold the wand above the head, and place the feet under the wand. Release hands and extend the legs upward, keeping the wand balanced across the feet.

Figure 26.45 Jump Through Stick. Stand with the knees partially bent and the feet about twelve inches apart. Hold the wand with the palms face down and the arms spread apart and the fingers grasping it. While keeping the arms straight, jump up and over the wand, landing in front with the knees slightly bent.

Figure 26.46 Thread the Needle. Begin in a back-lying position, knees bent, and hold the wand in front of the body. Without losing balance or touching the wand, bend the knees, pass the feet up and under the wand, and return to the original position.

Figure 26.47 Twist Away. Partners stand with their feet about shoulder-width apart. They grasp the wand with palms facing down. Each partner attempts to twist to his or her right. As soon as one partner releases his or her grip, the other is declared the winner.

Figure 26.48 Floor Touch. Partners sit on the floor in a cross-legged position. They grasp the wand with their palms facing down and their arms partially flexed. The wand must be parallel to the floor. On a signal from the teacher, each child tries to touch the wand to the floor on his or her right side. Change sides after each contest.

Figure 26.49 Dishrag. This is similar to wring the dishrag, described on page 397. Both partners must maintain their grips throughout the movement.

Applying Movement Skills

The wand can be as useful and usable as a hoop or a rope in developing movement concepts and skills. The following examples illustrate how balance, levels, and relationships can be further enhanced by a wand.

1. *Balance or Weight Bearing:* If the class has had prior experience with a wand, try these: "See how many different parts of your body you can balance the wand on." "Is it possible to balance the wand on your elbow (or knee or stomach, and so on)?"

2. *Transfer of Weight and Flow:* "Can you hold the wand with both hands and roll along the floor?" "Place the wand on the floor and see how many ways you can cross it using your hands and feet."

3. *Levels and Shapes:* "See if you can show me three stretched shapes—one low, one halfway up, and a high stretch—while holding a wand with both hands." "Can you make a twisted shape over your wand? Now under your wand?"

4. *Relationships:* Each partner has a wand. "Make up a sequence of matching (or contrasting) shapes with your partner (fig. 26.50)."

Figure 26.50 Matching Shapes

Parachute Activities

Parachute activities have become an integral part of many elementary school physical education programs. Children from grades two to six thoroughly enjoy performing a variety of stunts, games, and rhythmic activities while holding the parachute and moving in a variety of ways. The accompanying sections outline the basic teaching procedures and illustrate how parachute activities can contribute to fitness, skill development, and cooperative behavior. Without question, this type of activity is one of the most "fun-type" group experiences for all children—from the highly skilled to the severely handicapped.

Circle Sitting

During the first lesson, have the children begin by sitting in a circle with each child about two feet from the edge (skirt) of the parachute (canopy). From here, gradually introduce the following positions and turns.

1. *Overhand Grip:* Gripping the edge of the parachute with the palms facing down.

2. *Underhand Grip:* Gripping the edge of the parachute with the palms facing up.

Figure 26.51 Circle Sitting

Figure 26.52 Umbrella Games. Children begin with feet about shoulder-width apart, arms downward, and hands grasping parachute with an overhand grip (fruit basket position).

3. *Mixed Grip:* Gripping the edge of the parachute with the palm of one hand facing up and the palm of the opposite hand facing down.

4. *Fruit Basket:* This is a resting position. Children begin with feet about shoulder-width apart, arms downward, and hands grasping the parachute with an overhand grip. To coordinate all future group movements, begin with a preparatory signal such as "Ready," then a command such as "Go" or "Begin."

5. *Making Waves:* Begin in the fruit basket position. All children begin to gently shake the parachute (small waves) up and down. An increase in arm movements and speed increases the wave action. Other variations, such as odd numbers moving up while even numbers move down, or half the class up, the other half down, will produce different wave effects.

Figure 26.53 Making Waves

Figure 26.54 Umbrella

Figure 26.55 Mushroom

6. *Umbrella:* Begin in the fruit basket position. On command, lift the chute overhead. A slow count of 1, 2, 3 is normally needed to lift the chute into an umbrella position.

7. *Mushroom:* Begin in the fruit basket position. On signal, lift the chute to an umbrella position, then quickly take one step in and pull the chute down, holding the edge firmly to the floor.

Exercise Activities

The ultimate value of the following exercises is derived when the child is required to hold the chute taut and stretch, pull, or twist with an "overload" effort. Repetitions within exercises should be adjusted to the number that is appropriate for each child.

Side Stretcher

All students hold the chute taut with the left hand. The left knee is on the floor, and the right leg extends sideways with the right hand resting on the right leg. On command, the chute is pulled toward the right side. Repeat to opposite leg.

Row the Boat

All children sit with legs extended under the chute. The canopy is held with an overhand grip, arms bent, and chute touching the chest. On command, bend forward, extend arms, and touch hands to toes. Return to an upright position. Continue rowing action.

Variations

1. Place right arm backwards and repeat exercise.
2. Cross arm in front of chest and repeat exercise.

Curl-ups

Begin with the body under the parachute in a curl-up position. In this position, the chute is held with an overhand grip and held taut under the chin. Hold this grip and sit up to an upright position, then return to starting position.

Push-ups

Children first make a mushroom, keeping their hands and knees on the edge of the chute. Extend legs backward, perform one or more push-ups, then return to a starting position.

Chest Raiser

Children begin front-lying position, facing parachute, arms extended forward, and grasping chute with an overhand grip. Have all move backward until chute is taut. On signal, raise arm upward, hold for a few seconds, then return to starting position.

Variations

1. Raise arms and legs at the same time.
2. Hold chute with one hand and repeat exercise.
3. Begin lying on your side with a mixed grip and repeat exercise.

V-Sit

Children begin in a back-lying position, top of head facing the chute, and palms facing upward grasping the chute. Keep chute taut, then raise chest and straighten legs to a V-sit position. Return to starting position.

Game Activities

Number Exchange

Children are numbered from one to five around the circle. When the parachute is in the umbrella position, the leader calls one or two numbers. Players with these numbers exchange positions.

Snatch Club

Divide class into two groups then number each player in each group. Place a pin in the middle of the circle. When the chute is in an umbrella position call a number. Each player then tries to snatch the club and return to his position before the other tags him.

Circus Tent

From an umbrella position, all move under, turn around, kneel down, and hold chute to floor, then scramble out before chute falls on them.

Dance Activities

The parachute is extremely useful in teaching a variety of dance activities. All locomotor steps can be taught to children while holding the chute in the fruit basket, umbrella, or other positions. Changing directions, such as forwards, sideways, and backwards, as well as position exchanges can also be done while performing movements with the parachute. Rhythmic activities described in chapter 28 can be performed with the parachute. Marches, dixieland tunes, and many current hits can be used as musical accompaniments for these rhythmic activities. Several folk dances such as Pop Goes the Weasel, Seven Jumps and Csheborgar can also be performed with modification while holding the parachute.

Applying Movement Skills

Several movement skills, creative games, and inventive rhythmic sequences can be performed with a parachute. The following suggested challenges provide a basic starting point for most teachers.

Figure 26.56 Circus Tent. From an umbrella position, all move under, turn around, kneel down, and hold chute to floor, then scramble out before chute falls on them.

Movement Skills

1. "Hold the chute in the fruit basket position and make a stretched, curled, and twisted shape." Hold in the same position and balance on two parts, three parts, one knee and one elbow, and so on.
2. Hold chute with one hand and change direction and level.

Creative Games

Divide class into four working groups. Each group invents a game, then teaches the whole class.

1. "Design a game that starts with the parachute in the fruit basket position and uses one ball and four beanbags."
2. "Can you make up a game for the class that uses the parachute, one ball, and four bowling pins?"

Rhythmic Skills

1. Use same approach as in creative games.
2. "Make up a sequence that has a run, hop, and jump while holding on to the parachute."
3. "Can you design a routine that has a skip, slide, a change in direction, and a change in level?"

Figure 26.57 Parachute Golf. Place five or six balls on the chute. All players try to get the balls to drop through the hole.

Variations:

1. On and off: Designate two teams on each half of the circle. Each team has three balls (three white and three red balls). On signal, each team tries to get opponent's balls off the chute.
2. Repeat game, but try to get your own balls through the hole first. If a ball rolls over outer edge, it is placed back on the chute.

Chair Activities

The use of chairs as gymnastic equipment seems to have followed the same historical course as wands. The lack of equipment, coupled with the combined creative talents of teachers and children, produced numerous creative and challenging individual and dual activities using standard classroom chairs. A few of the most popular activities are described, and several ideas for using chairs in developing movement skills will be presented.

Individual Activities

The chair exercises and stunts in figures 26.60 to 22.64 contribute to strength, flexibility, balance, and agility. They were created by classroom teachers and children from various grades and schools. To prevent the chair from slipping, place it on a mat or have one child perform the stunt while a partner holds the base of the chair.

Figure 26.58 Dance with the parachute.

Figure 26.59   Chair Activities

Applying Movement Skills

A chair can be one of the most exciting pieces of small equipment if it is used safely and in a variety of positions. Too often the chair is used only in its normal upright position. However, when children learn to place it with the back or side on the floor, the potential for developing such movement skills as balance, shapes, and

Figure 26.61   Jump to Seat. Stand approximately one foot away from the chair and extend arms backward and upward. Simultaneously swing arms forward and upward and push off the toes. Land on the seat of the chair with knees bent and arms sideward for balance.

Figure 26.60   Side Balance. Lie across the chair with the left arm extended down and the right arm resting on the right side. Simultaneously raise the right arm and leg.

Figure 26.62   Bridge. Sit on the floor with the arms extended back and the fingers pointing toward the chair. The heels rest on the near edge of the chair. Raise the seat up until the trunk and legs form a straight line. At the top of this movement, the shoulders should be over the hands.

levels are greatly enhanced. Following are examples of creative and challenging ways to use this piece of equipment.

1. *Balance and Transfer of Weight:* "Can you balance with two parts on the seat of the chair and one part on the floor?" "See if you can balance on three parts on the seat of the chair, then shift to three new parts on the floor." "Place the chair in any position you like and see how many ways you can balance on it."

2. *Shapes and Levels:* "Make up a sequence of shapes on or off the chair." "Can you make a shape as you leap off the chair, then land and roll?"

3. *Relationships:* "With your partner and one chair develop a contrasting sequence of shapes." "Do the same with two chairs." "Can you make up a sequence that shows a change of balance and a change in level (fig. 26.65)?"

Figure 26.63 Dip. Stand on the chair, bend forward, reach back, and grasp the top of the chair. Simultaneously bend the right knee and extend the left leg forward.

Figure 26.64 Squat and Stretch. Begin in a squat position with the arms extended forward, and grasp the lower back legs of the chair. Keeping the hands on the chair, shift forward and upward until the upper trunk touches the back of the chair and the legs are extended.

Figure 26.65 Chair Activities with a Partner

a. Make up a sequence . . .

b. . . . that shows a change of balance . . .

c. . . . and a change of level.

Indian Club, Milk Carton, and Traffic Cone Activities

The success of any gymnastic program is very closely related to the amount and variety of small equipment available to each child. Since most elementary schools lack sets of the previously described equipment, the following "bits and pieces" can serve a very useful purpose. Discarded bowling pins, which can usually be obtained from local bowling alleys, make excellent substitutes for Indian clubs. Plastic-coated milk cartons are also readily available. And traffic cones, which are extensively used in the games program as field markers and goals, are also a valuable addition to the gymnastic program.

These types of small equipment are basically used as obstacles to maneuver around or over. They are also used in combination with other small equipment such as individual ropes, hoops, and wands to provide more complex and creative challenges. Following are examples of their use.

1. *Direction, Speed, and Force:* Scatter all available Indian clubs, milk cartons, and traffic cones around the floor area. The following challenges can be used to develop directional movements and a change of speed:
   a. "Run in different directions around the equipment."
   b. "Repeat with a change in speed."
   c. "Run sideways, diagonally, and backward around the equipment."
   d. "Run, jump over any piece of equipment, land, move to a new piece of equipment, and repeat (fig. 26.66)."
   e. "Repeat with a land and roll."

2. *Shape and Balance:*
   a. "How many ways can you balance over your equipment?"
   b. "Can you balance with one part on your equipment and one part on the floor?"
   c. "Make three different shapes over your equipment (fig. 26.67)."
   d. "Run, jump, and make a shape over your equipment."

3. *Relationships:* Each partner has one piece of equipment.
   a. "Make three matching shapes over your equipment."
   b. "Develop a matching sequence that includes a balance, a shape, and a change of direction (fig. 26.68)."

Figure 26.66 Run and jump over a cone, then over a hoop.

Figure 26.67 Make shapes over your equipment.

Figure 26.68

a. Make up a sequence that includes balance, . . .

b. . . . a shape, and . . .

c. . . . a change of direction.

Juggling Activities (3–6)

Juggling with scarves, bags, balls, and clubs has become another very popular activity within the elementary school physical education program. It's an activity that boys and girls can learn within a short period of time, and can become equally adept at. It's an excellent hand–eye coordination skill, allows every child to be active, and is inexpensive. Perhaps its real value lies in its noncompetitive and lifelong recreational use. Once the basic "cascade" or figure eight pattern is learned, a child's juggling repertoire can be expanded to include different throwing items and an unlimited number of exciting and challenging routines.

When introducing a juggling program, make sure every child has three items to juggle. Light scarves, (fig. 26.69) are extremely useful in demonstrating the basic "cascade" pattern shown in the accompanying pages. Juggling bags, which are easier to use than balls, may be purchased commercially or made by children. Balls of various sizes and weights are the third choice when teaching basic juggling. Once children have acquired the basic juggling skill, they will seek more challenging routines using discs, clubs, or other objects.

The basic juggling skill is performed in a figure eight pattern in an area roughly between the waist and top of head (fig. 26.70). Once proficiency has been acquired in this basic skill, a performer may throw high, to the side, or under one leg, but the basic figure eight movement is always maintained. Follow the next four steps to learn how to juggle with three bags. Master each step before moving to the next one.

Figure 26.69 Juggling

Figure 26.70 Figure Eight Pattern

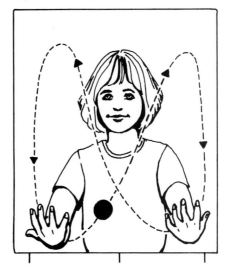

Figure 26.71 One-Bag Throwing

 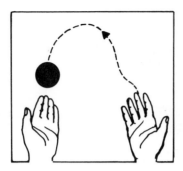 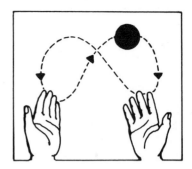

Figure 26.72 Hold and throw.

 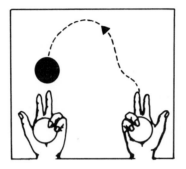 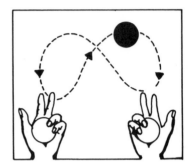

Step One: One Bag Throwing. Hold the bag with the fingertips and thumb of your dominant hand (fig. 26.71a). Scoop right hand towards left and release bag at about the middle of your body. Let the bag rise, then catch it as it descends down the left side (fig. 26.71b). Scoop left hand towards the middle and throw the bag upward towards the right side (fig. 26.71c). Continue practicing this figure eight pattern until it is a smooth wrist and fingerlike action.

Step Two: Hold and Throw. Pick up two bags and hold them on the heels of your hands. Pick up the third bag and hold it, with fingertips and thumb (fig. 26.72a). Throw the third bag from hand to hand in the figure eight pattern (fig. 26.72b and 26.72c).

Step Three: Exchange Two Bags. Hold two bags in your dominant hand and one in the other hand. Throw the bag from the fingertips of your dominant hand and call out "1" (fig. 26.73a). When the bag reaches its highest point, call out "2", then scoop the bag from your less dominant hand upward and under the other bag (fig. 26.73b). The bag coming to the less dominant hand should land on the palm. The bag coming to the dominant hand should be caught with the fingertips and thumb (fig. 26.73c).

Step Four: Three Bag Juggling. Throw the bag from your dominant hand and call "1" (fig. 26.74a). When the bag peaks, scoop the bag from the less dominant hand and call "2" (fig. 26.74b). When bag 2 peaks, scoop the bag from your dominant hand and call "3" (fig. 26.74c). When bag 3 peaks, throw the bag from your less dominant hand and call "4" (fig. 26.74d). When bag 4 peaks, throw the bag from your dominant hand and call "5" (figure 26.74e). Keep throwing and counting in this figure eight pattern.

Note: If children have difficulty, have them repeat to the end of figure 26.74c, ending with two bags in the left hand and one in the right. Repeat figures 26.74 a, b and c several times, then start from the first figure and continue on through figure 26.74e. Once children master to the end of figure 26.74e, they have learned to juggle. See appendix A for reference books about juggling and for inexpensive ways of making juggling clubs.

The central theme of this chapter has been to provide as many ideas as possible for using small equipment in both structured and exploratory ways. The next chapter continues this theme with large apparatus.

Figure 26.73   Exchange two bags.

Figure 26.74   Three-bag Juggling

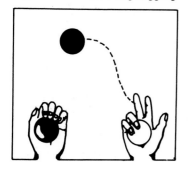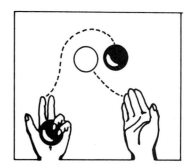

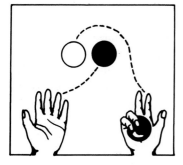

27 Stunts and Movement Skills with Large Apparatus

Teaching Procedures

Balance Beam and Bench
Individual Activities
Applying Movement Skills

Hanging Ropes
Safety Procedures
Suggested Conditioning Exercises
Individual Skills
Applying Movement Skills

Springboard, Beatboard, Minitramp, and Vaulting Box
Vaulting Stunts over Box
Applying Movement Skills

Horizontal Bar and Ladder
Horizontal Bar (Chinning Bar)
Horizontal Ladder

Climbing Frames and Portable Agility Apparatus
Climbing Frame
Portable Agility Apparatus

Outdoor Apparatus

The fundamental purpose of large apparatus in any gymnastic program is to provide an opportunity for the child to test his ability on more challenging apparatus. This chapter continues the central theme of the previous chapter. The basic skills that can be performed on such apparatus as the balance beam, vaulting box, and climbing rope are described and illustrated first. Then numerous suggestions are given for applying movement skills to this apparatus or integrating them with many of the traditional climbing, balancing, and vaulting movements performed on or over large apparatus.

Teaching Procedures

Large apparatus is normally used during the latter part of a gymnastic lesson. The following suggestions will assist the teacher in organizing and teaching both structured and movement skills with a variety of large apparatus.

1. Children of all ages should learn to carry and arrange apparatus with a concern for their own safety—the position of the body when lifting a heavy piece of equipment—and that of the class.

2. The arrangement of individual and multiple pieces of equipment and apparatus should complement the main theme of the lesson. For example, if the theme is "change of direction" and four benches are used, they should be scattered to encourage movements in a variety of directions. If the benches are placed in a row, the children will usually follow one or two classmates around each bench.

3. Since there is never enough large apparatus, adopt station work, using both small and large apparatus, coupled with a rotation system. In the accompanying diagram, the lesson stresses force (jumping and landing) and change of direction.

Figure 27.1

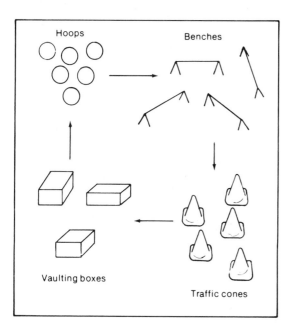

Figure 27.2 Performing Stunts across the Long Axis of the Balance Beam

The hoops, benches, traffic cones, and vaulting boxes are arranged to complement this theme. Each group practices at a station for a few minutes and then rotates to the next station. This gives each child an opportunity to use both small and large apparatus during an average lesson.

4. Whenever a stunt or movement pattern requires a spotter or spotters, proper instruction should be given to the children prior to and during the time they act as spotters. This is particularly important with vaulting skills over a box or bench.

5. Task or challenge cards described in chapter 5 can be used effectively with large apparatus activities.

Balance Beam and Bench

The balance beam or bench has been used in gymnastic programs for a number of years. However, it has been used in a very limited way, usually flat on the ground with children performing stunts on or across the long axis (fig. 27.2). When the balance beam or bench—now fitted with a hook or connector on one end, as illustrated—is placed at different angles or used in combination with other apparatus, the variety of movements and challenges becomes infinitely greater (fig. 27.3). This applies to teaching structured skills as well as the movement concepts and skills described in the previous two chapters.

A wide variety of structured skills are presented first in their relative order of difficulty, followed by suggestions for applying movement skills to the balance beam or bench.

Figure 27.3 Combining the Balance Beam with Other Apparatus

Figure 27.4 Locomotor Skills. Begin by walking forward and backward with arms extended sideways. Repeat with other locomotor skills—running, hopping, and so on.

Variations to each locomotor skill:
1. Change position of hands.
2. Place a beanbag on head or other part of body while performing locomotor skill.
3. Repeat skills with narrow surface or with bench on an incline.
4. Walk, run, or hop to middle, pick up beanbag, walk forward and off.

Individual Activities

Activities performed on the balance beam or bench require two types of balance skill: (1) static balance and (2) dynamic balance. *Static balance* is the ability to maintain a fixed stationary position, such as in the foot and knee balance (fig. 27.4). *Dynamic balance* is the ability to maintain correct body position while moving, as when walking forward and backward or when performing the one-foot hop. Most primary level balance skills are basically dynamic. As the children's strength and skill increase, the more advanced static balance activities can be introduced. Each of the suggested skills can be made more challenging by varying the angle of the beam or bench.

The skills in figures 27.4 to 27.12 can be performed on the broad surface of the bench or on the narrow beam. Reference is made to numerous stunts and tumbling skills that can be performed on a beam or bench. To assist in learning, have the children practice all the stunts on the floor, then move to the broad surface of the bench, and finally advance to the narrow surface of a beam. Any fixed line on the floor will serve as an imaginary balance beam or bench.

Figure 27.5 Foot and Knee Balance. Begin with the left foot well in front of the right, the knees bent, and the arms extended sideways. Bend the knees until the right knee rests on the beam. Hold this position for a few seconds, then extend and return to the starting position.

Variations:
1. "Can you repeat this stunt with a change in arm position?"
2. "Can you add another variation to the stunt?"

Figure 27.6 Side Balance. Walk to the center of the balance beam and stop, with the left foot in front of the right. Turn the right foot sideways, shift weight to the ball of the foot, and lift the right foot off the beam. Continue shifting sideways, arch the back, and raise the right leg.

Variations:
1. Hop to center, then perform the side balance.
2. Repeat stunt, turn sideways, and change the position of your right leg.
3. See if you can perform a front knee balance, shift to a side balance, then back to a front knee balance facing the opposite direction.

Figure 27.7 Squat on One Leg. Stand on the left foot with the arms extended sideways and the right foot off the beam. Bend the left knee, and raise the extended right leg forward and upward. Lower the body until the left knee is fully flexed.

Variations:
1. Repeat on opposite leg.
2. "In how many positions can you place the right leg while balancing on your left foot?"
3. "Can you shift from your balance position to the same position facing the opposite direction?"
4. "Can you shift from a squat on one leg to a side-balance position?"

Figure 27.8 Jackknife. Sit on the beam with the legs extended, the heels of both feet resting on the beam, and the hands holding the top edge of the beam. Bend the knees, and raise the feet off the beam. Continue the upward movement of the feet, lower the trunk backward, and straighten the legs. After practice, raise the legs without bending the knees and touch the feet with fingertips.

Variations:
1. Repeat stunt raising right leg and left arm.
2. "Can you repeat this stunt and twist your body in some way?"
3. "See if you can add your own variation to this stunt."

Figure 27.9 Swing Turn. Walk to the center of the beam. Shift weight to the left foot, and swing the right leg forward. Continue swinging the right leg forward, lift up on the ball of the left foot, and make a half turn, facing the opposite direction.

Variations:
1. Hop forward and repeat stunt.
2. Combine the swing turn with a side balance and a squat on one leg.
3. Make up your own routine with a swing turn and two other stunts.

a

b

c

Figure 27.10 Squat Mount. Stand with the feet about shoulder-width apart, the body erect, and the hands resting on the balance beam. While keeping the hands on the beam, jump up slightly forward, placing the feet on the beam.

Variations:
1. Straddle mount. Mount, placing feet outside of hands.
2. Squat mount. Perform a balance stunt, leap off, and land with flexed knees.
3. Leap off, make a tuck shape, and land with flexed knees.

Figure 27.11 Front Dismount. Begin in a crouched position with the arms straight and the hands grasping the outside edges of the balance beam. Extend the legs back until the head, trunk, and legs form a straight line. Lift the legs up and sideways, push off with the hands, and land on both feet beside the balance beam.

Figure 27.12 Forward Roll

Figure 27.13 Small Equipment Activities on the Balance Beam

The following animal movements and stunts can be performed on the bench or beam:

Movement or Stunt	Page
Lame Puppy	392
Crab Walk	393
Forward Roll	395
Backward Roll	399
Rabbit Jump	398
Seal Walk	398
Measuring Worm	399
Turk Stand	403
Frog Stand	403
Heel Slap	399
Cartwheel	413
Bridge	417
L-Support	422

Figure 27.14 Twisted Shapes on the Balance Beam

Several small equipment activities described in the previous chapter also can be performed on the beam or bench. It may be wise to require students to perform the skill on the bench before they attempt it on the narrower surface of the balance beam.

1. *Beanbag Activities:*
   a. Throw and catch to self
   b. Balance beanbags on different parts of the body and perform a series of balance stunts.
2. *Rope-Skipping Activities:*
   a. Basic skills, particularly the two-foot basic, one-foot hop, and rocker step
3. *Hoop Activities:*
   a. Hula hooping
   b. Hula jumping
4. *Wand Activities:*
   a. Foot balance
   b. Thread the needle

Applying Movement Skills

Several examples of the application of movement skills to the balance beam or bench are described and illustrated here. This should provide a starting point for the teacher.

One of the teacher's first tasks is to help children use the balance beam or bench in a variety of ways when performing a single movement skill or a sequence of movements. A movement task such as "See if you can make a twisted shape on the balance bench (or beam)" usually produces something like the shape illustrated in figure 27.14. The parallel arrangement of the benches

Figure 27.15 "Can you make a series of twisted shapes?"

Figure 27.16 Flight and Rolling

lacks imagination. Also, the use of the word *on* encourages all children to begin their movements from the same starting position. Questions should be presented in such a way that children begin to see the apparatus in a much wider perspective. Rephrasing the question to "Can you make a series of twisted shapes using various parts of the balance bench?" allows for greater scope, as illustrated in figure 27.15. Thus, when applying movement ideas to the balance beam or bench, think of the apparatus as either a point of contact or an obstacle to move around, across, or over (in flight). The following movement challenges illustrate this application.

1. *Direction and Speed:* Move around the benches showing a quick change of direction.
2. *Balance and Transfer of Weight:* Travel across the benches by changing from two to three to two points of balance.
3. *Balance, Shape, and Direction:* Develop a sequence traveling across the bench including a twisted shape, balancing on the side, and a change of direction.
4. *Flight and Rolling:* Beginning anywhere on the floor, run, jump onto a bench, leap off, land, and perform a safety roll. The roll may be a sideways, diagonal, or forward roll (fig. 27.16). Repeat and perform a stretch, twisted, or curled shape before landing.
5. *Relationships:* The balance beam or bench can be one of the most effective and versatile apparatus for developing the concept of relationships. The following examples illustrate how matching and contrasting can be integrated with other concepts and skills such as levels, direction, and speed:

a. "Develop a sequence of matching shapes with your partner on the top surface of your bench." "Repeat with one partner on the bench and the other on the floor (fig. 27.17)." "Repeat with both touching the bench."
b. "With one partner leading and the other following, make up a sequence of balance positions as you move from one end of the bench to the other."

At this stage in the development of movement concepts and skills, the angle of the bench or its combination with other types of apparatus adds to the challenge. These variations provide a greater opportunity for the children to test and expand their physical and creative abilities. A challenge such as "Make up a sequence that shows a change in level," is complemented by the angle of the bench. Also, adding chairs to the same challenge creates new dimensions for partners as they develop a matching sequence.

Hanging Ropes

A variety of climbing, swinging, and movement skills can be performed with a hanging rope. With proper instruction, including strengthening exercises for the arm and shoulder muscles, as well as following a sequential progression of skills, children can develop a high level of skill on the hanging ropes.

Suggestions for safety procedures and conditioning exercises are presented first, followed by a description of the basic climbing skills and ideas for applying movement skills to this apparatus.

Figure 27.17 Patterns on and off the Floor

a. Matching shapes . . .

b. . . . with one on the floor. . .

c. . . . and one on the bench.

Safety Procedures

Many school districts require that a mat be placed under the climbing rope when a child is performing a climbing or swinging skill. But it must be recognized that the mat has very little resilience and thus may have little value in preventing an injury. The following suggestions and procedures contribute far more to a child's safety than a mat.

1. Teach the proper hand and foot grip techniques for climbing and descending the rope.
2. Set individual goals rather than an arbitrary standard for every child to accomplish.

Figure 27.18 Climbing Ropes

3. Use spotters for difficult stunts, particularly those involving inverted hangs.
4. Establish safe and sensible rules for children. These may include the following:
   a. Never use ropes when a teacher is not present.
   b. Always climb down a rope; never slide.
   c. Never leave a rope swinging when you have finished with it.
   d. Never touch other performers on the rope unless you are spotting.
   e. Never climb a swinging rope.

Figure 27.19 One-Rope Exercises

Figure 27.20 Two-Rope Exercises

Suggested Conditioning Exercises

Climbing skills require sufficient arm and shoulder strength to raise and support the full weight of the body. The abdominal muscles also play a very important role in both climbing and descending skills. The following types of exercises will help increase the general strength and endurance of these muscle groups.

1. *Floor Exercises:* Pull-ups, push-ups, coffee grinder, measuring worm, sit-ups, curl-ups, and V-sit.
2. *Rope Exercises with One Rope:*
   a. Lie under the rope with the hands grasping it (fig. 27.19). Gradually raise the body upward. As strength increases, repeat exercise but keep the body straight throughout the movement.
   b. Sitting under the rope with the arms extended over the head and grasping the rope, pull body up. As strength increases, keep the legs extended and parallel to the floor.
   c. Stand facing the rope, reach up and grasp it, pull body up and hold position for a number of seconds.

   ### Variations
   1. Hold legs in different positions—pike, tuck, straddle.
   2. As body is pulled up, draw knees up to chest and hold.
   3. Draw legs upward until toes are above head.
3. *Rope Exercises with Two Ropes:*
   a. Hang between two ropes and make shapes of letters (Y, X, L, etc.), skin the cat, birds nest, tuck, pike or straddle positions, reverse hang, and swing forward or backwards and beat the floor each time you touch the center spot.
   b. Lie on back and grasp ropes with arms extended. Perform a backward roll with legs tucked, straddled, or in other positions.

Individual Skills

The following three basic rope-climbing skills should be performed with a mat below each rope. As soon as a child has acquired each climbing skill, monitor the distance he climbs each succeeding day. For example, allow an increase of two feet each day with a gradual, hand-over-hand *controlled* descent on each and every attempt.

Figure 27.21 Backward Roll

Figure 27.22 Scissors Method of Rope Climbing. Grasp the rope with one hand slightly above the other. Pull the body up with the right leg slightly in front of the left. Place rope inside the right knee and around the outside of the left foot. Cross the left leg over the back of the right leg, and press the inside of the left foot against the rope (a). Release the pressure on the ropes with the feet, then raise knees towards the chest (b). Lock the feet firmly against the rope, straighten legs, and reset hands above the head (c). To descend, keep pressure against feet and lower body in hand-under-hand position until knees are bent. Hold hands firmly and lower legs to new position, then lock feet again. Continue pattern.

a   b   c

Figure 27.23 Foot and Leg Lock Method of Rope Climbing. Grasp the rope with one hand slightly above the other. Pull the body up and loop the rope over the top of the right foot. Place the left foot on top of the rope, thus "locking" the foot position (a). Pull the body up to a new position (b). Repeat upward movement (c). Descend by maintaining the locked position of the legs, then move the hands down in a "hand-under-hand" fashion until the knees are against the chest. Hold the hand grip and slowly lower the legs to an extended position. Continue action to the floor.

a   b   c

Figure 27.24 Stirrup Method. Grasp the rope with one hand slightly above the other. Pull the body up and let the rope rest against the left side of the body. The rope then passes under the left foot and over the right foot (a). Release pressure of feet and raise body up (b). Lock grip of feet, raise hand to higher position, and continue action (c). To descend, move hand under hand and control pressure against the feet.

a   b   c

Figure 27.25 Balance three parts on the rope.

Figure 27.26 Swinging. Allow the children to grasp the rope at their own desired heights. Gradually introduce additional body movements and positions while swinging—twist, chin, legs straddle, etc.

Applying Movement Skills

The hanging rope can be used to develop movement skills in three basic ways: (1) movement challenges relating to shapes and weight bearing with a stationary rope; (2) movement challenges while the rope is swinging; and (3) movement challenges with the rope associated with another type of large apparatus.

The following movement tasks illustrate each type of challenge: "Can you balance with one part of your body on the floor and three parts on the rope (fig. 27.25)?" "How many different shapes can you make while holding the rope?" "Can you make different shapes while holding the rope and with both feet off the ground?" "Repeat previous challenge while the rope is swinging." Place one bench near both ends of the rope swing. "Swing and land on each bench." "Swing, make a half turn, and land on the opposite bench."

Springboard, Beatboard, Minitramp, and Vaulting Box

The springboard and vaulting box are two of the oldest apparatus in the gymnastic program. In this chapter the term *vaulting box* includes other similar apparatus, such as the vaulting bench, the jumping box, and the long horse, since they are used in much the same way. Teachers who do not have a vaulting box should refer to the diagrams of inexpensive equipment in appendix B. The latter can be constructed at a minimum cost.

The majority of vaulting stunts are usually performed from the springboard or minitramp onto a mat. Once children have developed sufficient skill in using the springboard and controlling their bodies while in flight, the vaulting box can be added to provide greater challenge and versatility of movements. The approach, takeoff, and landing are essentially the same for all vaulting activities, so children should practice these movements until they become almost automatic. A well-executed and consistent takeoff allows the child to concentrate on height and the execution of a specific vault.

Vaulting Stunts over Box

The standard or structured vaults illustrated in figures 27.28 to 27.34 can be performed over a box or long horse with a takeoff from the floor or off a springboard or minitramp.

Figure 27.27 Approach and Takeoff. The hurdle step is used to change running speed into a two-foot takeoff roll. Begin with a few short running steps, then take off with the right foot and (a) swing the opposite leg and arms forward and upward. Land with arms swinging downward and backward and knees slightly bent (b). When the performer's toes touch the board (or minitramp), the body should be just behind a vertical line drawn through the performer's toes. This position allows the performer to gain maximum height and control (c) rather than a rapid and uncontrolled low forward shifting action.

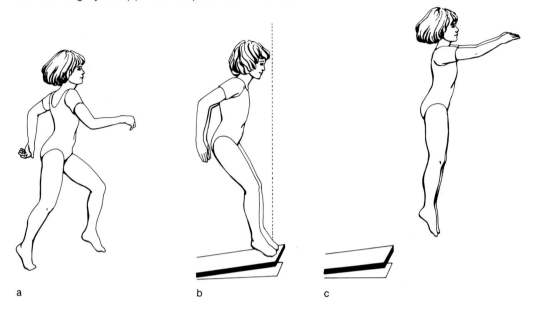

a   b   c

Figure 27.28 Squat Vault. From a two-foot takeoff (a) reach up, leaning slightly forward, and touch hands on top of the box (b). Simultaneously tuck the knees close to the chest (c) and continue forward and upward. Land with a gradual bending of the knees (d).

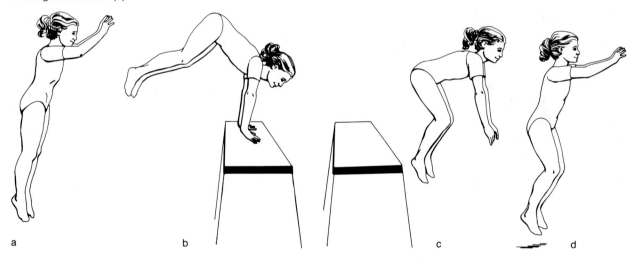

a   b   c   d

Figure 27.29 Spotting. Stand on the opposite side of the vaulting box and to the right of the oncoming performer. As she moves over the box, grasp her right wrist with your right hand. As she shifts forward, supply additional support to her upper body with your left hand.

Figure 27.31 Spotting. Stand close to the box directly in front of the oncoming performer. If she catches her toes or has too much forward momentum, place your hands on her shoulders to break the fall. If the performer clears the box and does not have too much forward momentum, step to the side quickly.

Figure 27.30 Straddle Vault. From a two-foot takeoff (a) reach forward with straight arms and extend legs sideward (b). Continue forward and upward, raising chest upward, bringing legs together (c). Land with a gradual bending of the knees (d).

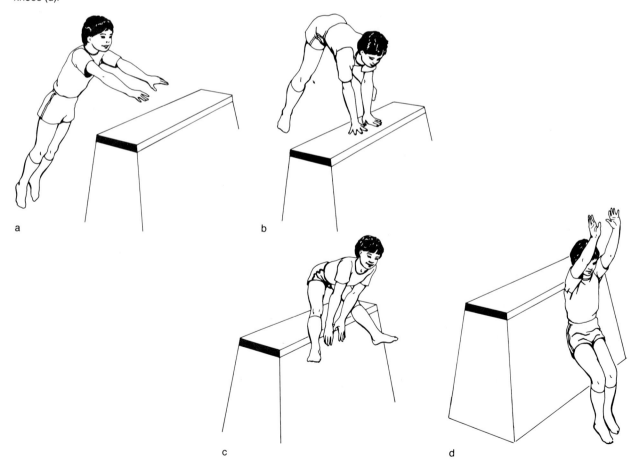

a

b

c

d

Figure 27.32 Head Spring. From a two-foot takeoff, place the hands and then the head on top of the box as the body extends upward and over. When the body is in a forward "overbalanced" position, push off from the fingertips and land with a gradual bending of the knees. Note: Most children tend to push off before they reach the overbalanced position, which causes them to "drop" onto the box rather than gradually arch and land.

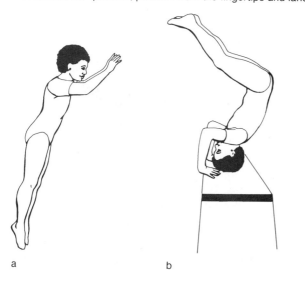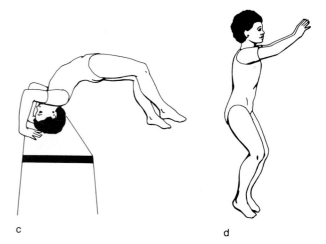

a   b   c   d

Figure 27.33 Spotting. Use one spotter. As the performer's hands contact the top of the horse, place your left hand on the performer's neck and support her through the movement to a safe landing position.

Figure 27.34 Hand Spring. From a two-foot takeoff (a), extend body upward and touch hands on top of horse (b). Keeping body straight, continue forward and push off as body loses point of balance (c). Continue arching forward and land with knees slightly bent (d). Note: Beginners bend at the hips as they touch the top of the horse, then "flip" and arch as they leave the horse. With practice a full body extension is maintained throughout the movement.

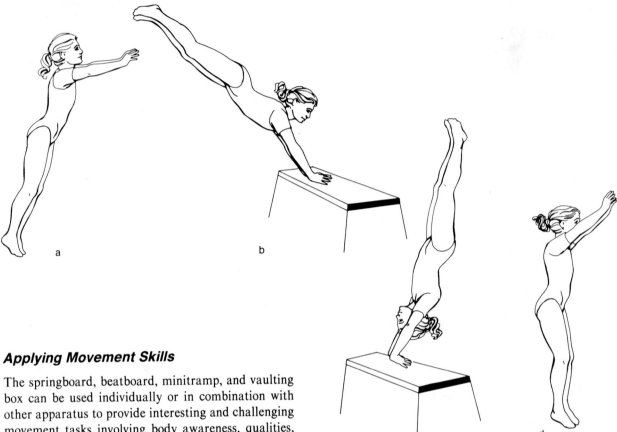

a   b   c   d

Applying Movement Skills

The springboard, beatboard, minitramp, and vaulting box can be used individually or in combination with other apparatus to provide interesting and challenging movement tasks involving body awareness, qualities, space awareness, and relationships. For example, all the individual shapes performed in flight from the floor can now be applied to the springboard, beatboard, or minitramp. These provide additional height and time necessary for executing curled or stretched, wide or narrow, and twisted shapes. In addition, since children have learned safety rolls—sideward, backward, and forward—they should be able to land and roll with grace and ease. The movement task shown in figure 27.35 illustrates the additional challenge and increased quality of movements performed from the springboard, beatboard, or minitramp. Similar movements can also be performed from the vaulting box.

The vaulting box should also be used as an additional challenge for the development of other movement concepts and skills. Here it is important to present challenges in such a way that all surfaces—particularly the sides and ends—are used when answering movement tasks. The following examples illustrate the variable use of the vaulting box.

1. *Shapes and Balance:*
   a. "Make a stretched (or wide or twisted) shape on the side, end, and top of the box."
   b. "Can you balance with one part on the apparatus and two parts off?"
   c. "See if you can balance with part of your body on top of the apparatus and part on the side or end of the apparatus."
   d. "Move from one side of the apparatus to the other (fig. 27.36)."

2. *Relationships:*
   a. "Make up a matching (or contrasting) sequence of shapes with one partner on top of the apparatus and the other on the floor."
   b. "How many different balance positions can you make with your partner on the side or top of the apparatus?"
   c. "Make up a sequence with your partner on the apparatus and show a change in balance."

Figure 27.35

Figure 27.36 Move from one side to the other side of the apparatus.

Sequences involving body awareness, qualities, space awareness, and relationships can now be designed to include the springboard and vaulting box individually or in combination with other small and large apparatus. The selection and arrangement of the apparatus should complement the movements of the sequence. Excessive rearrangement of apparatus serves little purpose in the development of movement skills, so teachers should caution children if they tend to waste time in arranging apparatus. One arrangement of apparatus should last for several lessons.

Figure 27.37 Hang Like a Monkey. Jump up, grasp the bar with the palms forward and the hands about twelve inches apart. Swing the right leg up and over the bar, resting the heel on top. Bring the left leg up and over the right leg and rest the back of the left leg on top of the right foot.

Variations:
1. Pull chest to bar.
2. Shift leg to side, pointing to the floor, etc.
3. Travel forward and backward by sliding hands and feet along the bar.

Horizontal Bar and Ladder

Many of the skills listed under horizontal bar and horizontal ladder can also be performed on other types of apparatus, including the new agility apparatus and existing outdoor play equipment such as the climbing cube and Swedish gym.

Horizontal Bar (Chinning Bar)

Since stunts performed on the horizontal bar require a great deal of arm and shoulder strength and endurance, teachers should begin with only one or two repetitions of each skill. When a child is able to perform five or six repetitions of a stunt, allow him to progress to the next one. The stunts are illustrated in figures 27.37 to 27.43.

Teaching Suggestions

In comparison with stunts on other indoor apparatus, stunts performed on the horizontal bar are extremely difficult for elementary school children. Thus, a great deal of encouragement must be shown by the teacher. In most cases, the initial disinterest in this apparatus is the result of insufficient arm and shoulder strength rather than an inherent absence of skill. The following

Figure 27.38 Body Swing. Jump up and grasp bar with palms facing forward. Swing body backward and forward.

Variations:
1. Grip bar with palms facing away or use a mixed grip.
2. Swing and reverse directions by gradually changing grips and direction.

Figure 27.39 Pull-ups. Jump up and grasp the bar with a front (palms facing forward) or reverse (palms facing backward) grip. Pull body up until chin is above the bar.

Variations:
1. Change grip and repeat.
2. Chin with legs in various positions: with knees bent, with legs straight, with legs parallel to the ground, or with toes above the bar.

Figure 27.40 Roll over Barrow. Jump up and take a front support position with arms straight and hands on top of bar. Bend at the waist, drop head forward, roll over the bar, bring legs down, and release grip.

Variations:
1. From front support position, bring right and then left leg over bar, balancing on top ("scramble over fence").
2. Roll over with one leg leading the other.
3. From front support position, adjust body to balance on stomach with arms extended sideways.

suggestions will not make the teacher's task any easier, but they will help prevent unnecessary accidents.

1. Check equipment before allowing children to perform any stunt.

2. Make sure you are in the proper position to spot for safety.

3. Begin with simple stunts and progress to the more difficult.

Figure 27.41 Rocking Chair Swing. Jump up and grasp the bar with the palms facing forward and the hands about shoulder-width apart. Draw both legs up and through the bar, drop the knees over it, and rest the back of knees firmly against the bar. Keep the knees bent, release grip, and swing back and forth. Reach up, grasp bar, and return to the starting position.

Variations:
1. Twist body toward each side.
2. Change position of arms.
3. With a spotter, swing back and forth, then dismount at the height of the forward swing.

Figure 27.42 Bird's Nest. Jump up and grasp bar with palms facing forward. Draw both legs up and through arms. Drop legs over the bar, resting back of knees firmly against the bar. Simultaneously shift lower legs backward and fully arch the back until the back of the heels rest against the bar and arms are extended.

Variations:
1. Remove one leg and extend it backward.
2. Bring legs back through the arms, then extend legs upward into an inverted hang.

Figure 27.43 Single Leg Swing. Jump up, grasp bar with palms facing forward. Draw one leg through arms and around the bar. Point opposite leg towards the ceiling. Swing forward and backward.

Variations:
1. Change legs and repeat.
2. Swing up to a sitting position on the bar. (Use a spotter until performer demonstrates control throughout movement.)
3. Shift forward from sitting to hanging position.

Horizontal Ladder

Activities performed on the horizontal ladder are similar to chinning bar activities. Both require a great deal of strength and endurance of the arm and shoulder girdle muscles. Therefore, follow the progression of skills in figures 27.44 and 27.45 and do not require *full travels,* that is, all the way across the ladder, until sufficient strength and endurance are developed. As a starting point, require the children to make it one-quarter of the distance. Increase the number of rungs each day until the children reach the full distance without undue stress.

Teaching Suggestions

The following safety hints require continuous reinforcement. Before the children begin to play or practice stunts on the apparatus take a few minutes to stress the following.

1. Check the apparatus before pupils are allowed to perform stunts.
2. Stand close to the performer while he is attempting a difficult stunt in order to help him and to prevent accidents.
3. Require each pupil to stand at least five feet from the apparatus while waiting for his turn.
4. Allow only two pupils on the ladder at the same time.
5. Require that the second pupil not begin his stunt until the first child is at least halfway across the ladder.
6. Require pupils to travel in the same direction.
7. Require that two parts of the body be in contact with the apparatus during the performance of all movements.
8. Do not permit children to touch or hinder a child who is performing a stunt.

The following skills performed on the horizontal bar may be performed on the horizontal ladder:

1. Body Swing, page 482
2. Pull-ups, page 482
3. Rocking Chair Swing, page 483.

Figure 27.44 Single Rung Traveling. Climb up one end of the ladder, rest feet on the top step, and grasp each side pole with one hand. Reach forward and grasp the second rung with one hand, palms facing forward, and the third rung with the other hand. Simultaneously shift the body forward toward the forward hand, and release the back hand. Continue forward, grasping the next rung. Repeat the movement with the opposite hand and continue traveling forward to the opposite end.

Variations:

1. Change position of legs as you travel—knees tucked, legs straddled, or one leg in front of the other.
2. Double rung travel. Begin with both hands on one rung. Swing forward and backward, and at end of a forward swing, release both hands and regrasp the next rung with both hands.
3. Rung travel sideways. Begin with hands on separate rungs and body facing sideways. Shift right hand to same rung as left hand, then shift left hand to next rung. Continue pattern to end of ladder.

Climbing Frames and Portable Agility Apparatus

One of the most significant contributions to the elementary school gymnastic program has been the development of new agility apparatus. This apparatus has been specifically designed to provide more challenging tasks than the traditional gymnastic apparatus can provide. Generally speaking, this new apparatus falls into two categories: (1) a climbing frame mounted on

Figure 27.45 Side Rail Traveling. Travel along one side rail using a hand-over-hand movement.

Variations:
1. Change position of legs as you travel.
2. Double rail traveling. Grasp both side rails with the palms of both hands facing in, and swing to a hanging position. Travel forward by sliding one hand forward, then the other. Do not release the grip. Slide the hands the full length of the ladder.

Figure 27.46 Agility Apparatus

Figure 27.47 Nissen Wall Gym

a wall with a variety of supplementary attachments and (2) a portable and modular apparatus with a variety of attachments such as balance beams, poles, ladders, and planks. Some of the portable agility apparatus is light enough to be carried and assembled by primary children. An example of each type is provided in the accompanying pages to illustrate their potential use in the gymnastic and movement education programs.

Climbing Frame

This climbing frame is a modification of the original Southhampton apparatus developed in England. It may be purchased in two or more sections and is permanently mounted on a gymnasium wall. The sections (fig. 27.47) are pulled out for use during the gymnastic lesson.

Portable Agility Apparatus

Agility apparatus (figs. 27.48 and 27.49) was designed to develop both structured and movement education skills. It consists of a modular turret system that permits two or more interconnecting turrets to be stacked in any desired height. A resilient plastic top is placed on the top frame. The turret provides a framework or building block to which poles, ladders, planks, beams, or benches can be connected at a variety of levels and angles.

The flexible design of this apparatus allows it to be used for developing such structured skills as balancing, vaulting, and climbing. And its portability, coupled with the numerous designs that can be created, makes the equipment extremely useful in developing movement concepts and skills. Since it is very light and durable, it can be moved by primary children to the classroom or outdoors with relative ease. The following examples will illustrate the application of this apparatus.

Outdoor Apparatus

There has been a major change during the past few years in the type of outdoor apparatus that is being constructed on elementary school playgrounds. New commercial equipment such as Big Toys are replacing the more traditional swings, steel climbing frames, and horizontal ladders. This new apparatus has been designed to complement the creative and exploratory natures of young children. The general design provides more levels, angles, and holes for young children to jump off, balance upon, and crawl through. Creative playgrounds described in chapter 6 are also part of this trend. Natural materials, such as large tree roots and boulders, and discarded building materials or equipment, such as giant sewer pipes and old trucks, are now seen on numerous playgrounds throughout North America.

This new and exciting outdoor apparatus should also be seen as a logical extension of the gymnasium in developing moving concepts and skills. The following examples illustrate how this apparatus can be used as an effective instructional laboratory. The skills learned through the teacher's movement challenges will help the child learn to use the apparatus in a constructive, safe, and creative way.

Figure 27.48

Figure 27.49

Figure 27.50 "How many ways can you get on and off your apparatus?"

Figure 27.51 "Show me how many ways you can balance on your apparatus."

1. *Balance and Weight Bearing:*
   a. "Find a place on the apparatus and show me how many different ways you can balance on your spot."
   b. "Can you move across the apparatus using different parts of your body?"
2. *Direction and Levels:*
   a. "See if you can climb up and down the apparatus using your hands and feet."
   b. "Can you move through the apparatus and show a low, medium, and high position?"
3. *Relationships:*
   a. "One partner leads and the other follows. Make up a sequence involving a transfer of weight and a change of direction."
   b. "Find a spot on the apparatus with your partner. Can you develop a matching sequence including a stretch, curl, and twisted shape (fig. 27.54)?"

Figure 27.52 "Can you move across the apparatus using different parts of the body?"

Figure 27.53 "See if you can climb up and down the apparatus using your hands and feet."

Figure 27.54 Matching Sequence

Teachers who are hesitant to use the indoor and outdoor apparatus suggested in this chapter should recognize one of the basic characteristics of the movement education approach: A child taught through this approach will not attempt a movement task on any apparatus until he feels he is mentally and physically ready. If this approach is followed by the teacher, accidents should be a rare occurrence.

7 Dance and Movement Activities

Part 7 has been organized in a slightly different way than the games and gymnastics sections. Chapter 28 describes the basic rhythmic skills that are used in game, gymnastic, and dance activities. This chapter has been placed in this section rather than just before the games section largely on the basis of convenience. Chapter 29 includes the most popular singing games and folk dance activities for primary and intermediate children. And chapter 30 describes several approaches that can be used to teach creative dance activities to children in the primary and intermediate grades.

28 Rhythmic and Movement Activities

Understanding the Elements of Rhythm
Underlying Beat
Meter, or Time Signature
Tempo
Rhythmic Pattern
Phrase
Intensity

Teaching Procedures
Sample Lesson: Beat, Measure, and Accent

Rhythmic Activities with Small Equipment
Inflated Balls
Individual Ropes
Rhythm or Lummi Sticks
Hoops

Task Cards

Rhythm is the ability to repeat an action or movement with regularity and in time to a particular rhythmic pattern. It is an essential ingredient of all movement, whether throwing a ball, dodging a player, or dancing a polka. Rhythm can be spontaneous, as when a young child makes up his own jumping pattern without any musical background or directions imposed by the teacher. The rhythmic activities described in this chapter, however, are more structured in nature and direction, relating to the performance of a variety of body movements in time to a specific musical accompaniment. (See film *Rhythmics in Movement,* appendix A.)

The material in this chapter has been arranged to assist children (ages seven to twelve) in acquiring a basic understanding of the elements of rhythm and how they can be combined with a variety of game, dance, and gymnastic movements. Once a child understands the elements of rhythm, other dance activities can be learned with greater speed and usually with a very positive attitude, particularly by older elementary school children. The basic approach of gradually moving from individual to partner to group activities is used. This gradual process of joining younger children together in a relaxed and creative manner provides the necessary stepping-stone for folk and creative dance activities for upper elementary school boys and girls. Once the teacher has read this chapter, she will also be able to incorporate many of the ideas into future folk and creative dance units. In addition, rhythmic activities may also be integrated into numerous game and gymnastic activities.

Understanding the Elements of Rhythm

Music and dance have one basic element in common—both are performed within rhythmic structure. Within this structure, the underlying beat, meter, and tempo are used to provide direction and emphasis to the song or dance movements. All of the following elements of rhythm are interrelated and have an effect on dance movements. They can be introduced to children in a meaningful way through the rhythmic activities described in this chapter.

Underlying Beat

Perhaps the simplest and most important element of rhythm to learn is the *underlying beat* of the musical accompaniment. If we ask children to feel their own pulse, they feel a steady pulsation of their heartbeat. Each beat of the heart has the same strength, or intensity, and recurs with the same amount of time between each beat. If the child is at rest, his normal heartbeat is about seventy-two beats per minute; each beat is spaced evenly throughout the one-minute period. After a vigorous activity the child's pulse rate increases to one hundred and twenty beats per minute. The heart is still beating with an even rhythm but faster and with a shorter interval between each underlying beat. Like a person's heartbeat, the *underlying beat in music* is the steady sound or pulsation that is heard or felt as the music is played. The underlying beat may be slow with long and even intervals between each beat or very fast with corresponding shorter intervals.

In dance, we move "in time" with the musical accompaniment when each foot, hand, or body movement synchronizes with each successive beat of the music. For example, when a child claps his hands or stamps his foot to each beat in the song "Row, Row, Row Your Boat," he is "keeping in time" to the rhythm of the song. Moving in time to the underlying beat is perhaps the most important prerequisite to all dance activities.

Measure

A measure is an equal grouping of underlying beats. As illustrated below, four identical quarter notes are grouped between two bar lines and repeated for three measures.

Accent

Accent is the extra force or stress given to certain beats in a measure. In the example, the *accent* is on the first beat in each measure. To children, the *accent* is heard as a louder beat of the first note or as singing the first word of the measure louder than the other words in the measure. The purpose of accenting music and movement is to provide variety and excitement to all types of dance activities. Accenting is also used to help children change direction, such as "change direction after

every fourth step" or shift to another movement pattern, such as, "alternately shift from a walk to a run after every fourth beat." In these examples the special stress or emphasis given to the first beat in each measure provides a signal for children to shift to the next movement.

Meter, or Time Signature

The meter, or time signature, is the numerical symbol placed in front of the written music to explain the underlying rhythm within a measure. The top number of this symbol indicates the number of counts to a measure while the bottom number denotes the kind of note that will receive *one beat*. Four of the most common meters used in the elementary dance program are described here.

4/4 METER: *Denotes four beats in each measure.*

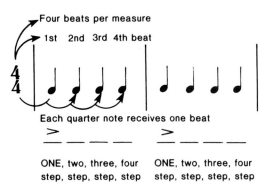

In the above 4/4 meter, each quarter note receives *one* beat, producing an even four-count meter rhythm. If a child was walking "in time" to this 4/4 meter he would *step, step, step, step* evenly within each measure in a moderate walking speed. Since there are four beats, the child would always start each new measure on the same foot.

The 4/4 meter is an *even rhythm* with each underlying beat receiving full note value. This meter can be used with the following steps: walk, run, hop, jump, leap, and schottische.

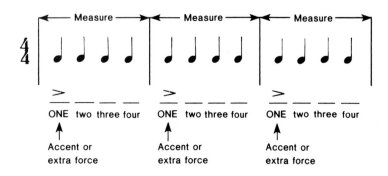

2/4 METER: *Denotes two beats in each measure.* The accent is on the first and third beat, and quarter notes get one beat.

The 2/4 meter is an *uneven rhythm* and is a combination of a *long* and a *short* beat. This meter is used with the following steps: skip, slide, gallop, polka, two step, and bleking step.

3/4 METER: *Denotes three beats in each measure.* The accent is on the first beat, and quarter notes get one beat.

The 3/4 meter is an *even rhythm* with each underlying beat receiving full note value. This meter is used for the following steps: waltz, mazurka, and varsoviana.

6/8 METER: *Denotes six beats in each measure.* The accent is on the first and fourth beats, and eighth notes receive one beat.

The 6/8 meter is an *uneven rhythm* and is a combination of a long and a short beat followed by another long and short beat within each measure. This meter is used for the following steps: skip and gallop.

Tempo

Tempo is the rate of speed of the music or movement. In musical accompaniment, the tempo can be slow, moderate, or fast, or it may increase gradually from slow to fast.

In folk and creative dance activities, it is important for children to feel and understand the difference between moving slowly, moderately, or very quickly. It is also important for each child to sense different speeds of the same music and learn to adjust his own movements to the new "tempo" of the music.

Rhythmic Pattern

The rhythm pattern is the grouping of sounds of the song or instrumental music to correspond to the underlying beat of the music. To illustrate in the song "Ten

Little Indians" the sounds of the music are of different durations in order to provide the rhythmic pattern. The words follow the rhythmic pattern and the rhythmic pattern corresponds to the underlying beat of the 2/4 meter of this music.

Phrase

In music, a phrase is a natural grouping of two or more measures that cling together in a natural way to give a feeling of a complete musical thought or idea. The rhyme "Baa Baa Black Sheep" extends through the second measure in order to give children a complete "musical sentence." Musical phrases are used in folk and creative dance activities to complete a series of movements before repeating them over or before starting a new series of movements.

Intensity

Intensity refers to the amount of force exerted in a movement or a sound. In movement, intensity is recognized as the feeling of heaviness or lightness. In sound, children hear loud and soft sounds in the musical accompaniment.

Teaching Procedures

The structure of a rhythmics lesson is similar to that of the game or gymnastic lesson described in previous chapters. Each rhythmic lesson normally has an introductory activity, a second skill development or movement training activity, and a third and final group

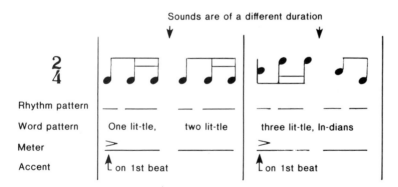

activity. The basic progression used to teach the elements of rhythm is from individual to partner to group activities. The following sample lesson illustrates how to introduce the underlying beat, measure, and accent.

Figure 28.1 Clap to the beat.

Sample Lesson:
Beat, Measure, and Accent

Main Theme: Moving to the underlying beat
Subthemes: Measures and accents
Progression: Individual to partner to group activities
Music: "Thriller" (or any fast popular record with a good 4/4 beat)

Part 1: Introductory Activity
Class members sit in a scattered formation on the floor with their legs crossed.

1. Have the children clap in the following ways (without music).
   a. Clap knees four times, repeating measure (1,2,3,4; 1,2,3,4; etc.).
   b. Clap hands four times, repeating measure.
   c. Tap the floor four times, repeating measure.
   d. Make up combinations of four claps on knees, then four taps on the floor, and four claps with the hands (fig. 28.1).
2. Have the children listen to "Thriller" for the 4/4 meter (four beats per measure) and the accent on the first beat.
3. Repeat a to d with music.

Additional Ideas: Once the class understands the meaning of the underlying beat and can clap four times within each measure according to this musical accompaniment, other combinations can be attempted in this introductory part of the lesson or at the beginning of a second, third, or fourth lesson stressing these elements of rhythm. These are:

1. Snap fingers.
2. From a standing position, slap different parts of the body.
3. From a standing position, shake one part of the body. Shake the right hand 1,2,3, and 4. Add other parts of the body; shake the right hand and the right leg.
4. Move parts of the body to the rhythm of the music. This could include bending, stretching, swinging, or twisting.
5. Perform locomotor movements to the rhythm of the music—walk, run, hop, jump, or leap (fig. 28.2).

Figure 28.2 Hop to the rhythm.

Part 2: Partner and Small Equipment Activities
In the second part of the lesson partners develop simple matching routines with the movements learned in the first part of the lesson.

1. Partners start on the floor facing each other. One child begins with four claps on whatever part of his body he chooses; his partner follows. The first performer chooses another part of his body and repeats, with his partner copying him. Continue with two more parts of the body. After the fourth part of the body, ask the partners to work together and perform the four clapping movements simultaneously on the four parts of their bodies.

Figure 28.3 Clap four times on the floor . . .

Figure 28.4 . . . then four times to each others' hands.

Figure 28.5 Include a twist . . .

Figure 28.6 . . . or shift of the body.

2. Join partner clapping: Partners sit cross-legged facing each other and tap four times on the floor (fig. 28.3), then four times to each other's hands (fig. 28.4), then back to four times on the floor.

3. Repeat 2 from a standing position, substituting tapping the floor with tapping or shaking one's own body parts or snapping fingers.

During the various activities of this part of the lesson, consciously stress *accenting* the first beat of each measure. That accent should also be used to signify the start of a new movement or a change in position or direction. If the latter two elements are emphasized, the meaning of a measure also becomes clear to each student.

Additional Ideas: As soon as the class understands the idea of matching clapping movements, the number of combinations becomes almost unlimited. Following are some possibilities to try here or leave until the next lesson.

1. Alternative hand clapping—tap the floor, clap one opposite hand, clap two hands.

2. Alternate a hand clap and a finger snap.

3. Include a turn, twist, or shift of the body after each measure (fig. 28.5 and 28.6). This might include four clapping movements followed by four steps around in a circle, then back to four clapping movements.

Rhythmic and Movement Activities   **497**

4. Develop matching routines (side by side or one behind the other) with a walk, run, hop, jump, or leap step.

5. Combine locomotor movements with clapping, shaking, or snapping fingers.

6. Include a change of direction or level in the above routines.

Part 3: Group Activities

Arrange the class into groups of four. Since this may be the first group experience with this type of rhythmic exercise, it is wise to go slow at the start to allow each child to feel comfortable and to be successful with your challenges. The first challenges should be similar to the ones first presented to individuals, then to partners. These are as follows:

1. In your group of four, sit cross-legged facing the center of the group. Without music, clap hands four times, tap floor four times, then hands again for four counts.

2. Repeat with music.

3. Make up a routine with each child tapping the floor, then all clapping hands, then tapping the floor again. "Next time when you clap hands, place your hands to the side and clap hands with the players on your right and your left." This should be enough to get each group started on its own routine.

If the children are receptive and "at ease," allow them to make up their own sitting, standing, or moving routines in their own group of four. If more help is needed, pose challenges keeping them sitting on the floor, then from a standing position, and finally involving locomotor movements.

The previous sample lesson was included to illustrate how children can learn to keep in time to the underlying beat of the music and to use the accent on the first beat of each measure as a signal to begin a new movement or direction. The next section illustrates how small equipment such as balls and individual ropes can be used within each part of a rhythmic lesson to stress the basic elements of rhythm.

Rhythmic Activities with Small Equipment

Small equipment is used with rhythmic activities in two basic ways. First, the equipment, such as a rope or hoop, can be used as a focal point or obstacle to move in and out of, around, or over. Second, when the equipment, such as a hoop or ball, is held or manipulated, it is used as an extension of the rhythmic movements of the body. Swinging a hoop and bouncing a ball to a rhythm are examples of the latter.

Begin by teaching hand or foot movements without equipment so that the children learn the basic movements and rhythmic patterns. Once these are acquired, introduce equipment to the routine or movement pattern.

Inflated Balls

Ball bouncing is particularly useful in helping children learn to move in time to the underlying beat of music. Any inflated ball can be used. Slow and fast tunes can be used in all of the following individual, partner, and group tasks.

Individual Tasks

Begin bouncing with one hand to the underlying beat of the music. Add the following challenges.

1. Change hands.
2. Bounce to one knee.
3. Bounce the ball around your body.
4. Bounce the ball with another part of your body (elbow, foot, etc.).
5. Bounce the ball and change direction—forward, backward, and sideways.
6. Bounce the ball and change levels—high, medium, and low.
7. Bounce, clap hands, bounce, and turn around.
8. Introduce a skipping rope. Place the rope on the floor in a curved or zigzag pattern. Develop tasks that require a bounce and a change of direction around or across the rope.

Partner and Group Tasks

The children can participate in various partner routines, such as (1) matching bounces, (2) follow the leader, (3) contrasting routines (one high and one low), and (4) bouncing and exchanging the ball on certain beats of the music.

Group routines involving four or more players can also be developed by most children in the intermediate grades. For example, "Make up a routine with four players that includes four different bounces, a change of direction, and a change in level" (fig. 28.7).

Figure 28.7 Make up a bouncing routine that includes four different bounces.

Figure 28.8 Move back and forth over the rope.

Figure 28.9 Include a two foot basic and hop step.

Individual Ropes

Basic rope-jumping skills and several ideas relating to the development of individual and partner routines were presented in chapter 26; however, no reference was made to musical accompaniment. The challenges on page 440 can now be presented with musical accompaniment, such as Michael Jackson's "Thriller" or any current popular tune that has a good beat.

The following examples illustrate the variety of ways an individual rope can be used in rhythmic activities by an individual or by two or more players.

Individual Tasks

Choose a record with a good 4/4 meter for the following individual tasks.

1. Place the rope on the floor in any pattern desired (straight, curled, or zigzag). Make up a routine of moving back and forth over your rope (fig. 28.8). If the children feel the 4/4 even rhythm they should use a walk, run, jump, hop, or leap step in their routine.

2. Keep the same rope pattern but change the record or tape to a 2/4 or 6/8 meter. Pose the challenge, "Now make up a new routine moving back and forth or around your rope." The uneven 2/4 or 6/8 rhythm should encourage children to use a skipping or sliding step in their routine.

Partner and Group Tasks

1. Develop a matching routine with your partner using even rhythm and including a two-foot basic and a hop step (fig. 28.9).

2. Make up a rope-skipping routine with one partner following the other. (Use uneven rhythm.)

3. Place one rope on the ground and make up a matching routine with your partner using a 2/4 meter (fig. 28.10).

4. Have the children place two ropes on the floor and repeat task 1.

5. In groups of four, make up a matching routine in any pattern you like.

Figure 28.10 Place one rope on the ground and make up a matching routine.

Figure 28.11 Lummi Sticks

Figure 28.12 Hold sticks between the thumb and fingers.

Rhythm or Lummi Sticks

Rhythm or lummi sticks* are extremely useful in developing the elements of rhythm. The sticks are approximately ten to twelve inches long and can be made from one-inch doweling or old broomsticks. The sticks are held between the thumb and fingers near the lower third of the stick (figs. 28.11 and 28.12).

Individual Tasks

The first tasks presented should give each child an opportunity to learn how to tap the sticks to the rhythm of the music and how to shift from one tapping movement to another. Challenges can include the following simple routines.

Sitting Cross-Legged

1. Tap the floor four times, tap the sticks together four times, tap the right on left four times, and so on (fig. 28.13).

2. Make up a routine tapping the floor in front, to the side, and behind you.

3. Make up a routine that includes tapping, throwing, and catching the sticks, and then another tapping movement.

4. Repeat 1, 2, and 3 to a 4/4 musical accompaniment.

Once the children can tap the sticks together, on part of the body, or on the floor, they can be used to teach accent, intensity, and different meters in a very enjoyable way. Try the following challenges.

*Lummi sticks and records can be purchased from Educational Activities, Inc., Box 392, Freeport, New York, 11520.

Figure 28.13 Tap sticks together four times.

Figure 28.14 From a standing position develop a routine tapping the sticks in front.

Sitting Cross-Legged

5. Repeat 1 and 2 making the first beat in each measure louder than the next three beats.

6. Tap the sticks together on the first beat, then tap the body (thighs, stomach, etc.) the next three times. Continue pattern.

7. Repeat 5 and 6 with the same musical accompaniment as 4 above.

8. Repeat 5 and 6 with a 2/4 musical accompaniment, tapping the first beat with the two sticks and the second against the body.

From a Standing Position

9. Develop a routine of tapping the sticks in front, to the side, behind the back, and against the body (fig. 28.14). Use 4/4 and a 2/4 or 6/8 musical accompaniment to emphasize even and uneven rhythms.

10. Develop a routine involving walking, running, hopping, or jumping and tapping the sticks to the 4/4 even rhythm of the musical accompaniment.

11. Develop a routine involving skipping or sliding and tapping the sticks to a 2/4 or 6/8 uneven rhythm of the musical accompaniment.

Partner and Group Tasks

The first partner activities should begin with both players sitting about two feet apart in a cross-legged position facing each other. This position encourages the players to develop routines using the floor for tapping as well as the partner's sticks. Following are a few sample routines.

1. Without music, hit sticks on the floor, hit both sticks together in front, hit with both arms sideways, hit floor.

2. Without music, partners hit sticks to the floor, hit their own sticks together, exchange right sticks, then exchange left sticks.

3. Repeat 1 and 2 above with a 4/4 or 2/4 musical accompaniment.

4. Without music, numerous calistheniclike and other rhythmic routines can be developed with two players standing face to face, side by side, or back to back.

5. Repeat 4 with same musical accompaniment used in 3.

6. Group activities can also be developed with sets of three or more children. Once the children have learned the basic tapping skills and have had rhythmic experience with hoops, balls, and skipping ropes, they will develop creative rhythmic routines with lummi sticks quickly and enthusiastically.

Hoops

The hoop can be used in two basic ways with rhythmic activities: (1) when placed on the floor, it becomes an obstacle or focal point to maneuver in and out of, around, or over, and (2) when held or manipulated, it can help the child move his body or parts of it to the rhythm of a drumbeat or music.

There are several standardized movement skills described in chapter 26 that can be performed in time to musical accompaniment. These skills and the ones provided in the accompanying paragraphs illustrate the versatility of hoops as well as their effectiveness in teaching the elements of rhythm.

Individual Tasks

Have each child place his hoop flat on the floor. Present challenges such as the following that involve locomotor skills and a change of direction.

1. "Make up a jumping routine moving in and out of your hoop." Later, add other challenges, such as "in and out, around, and over." (Use even rhythm, 4/4 or 3/4 music.)
2. Use two or more hoops on the floor and repeat challenge 1.
3. Introduce ball bouncing with a hoop.

Many twirling and movement skills can be done with a hoop. The following provide a basic starting point. Use uneven rhythm—2/4 or 6/8 music.

4. "Can you twirl the hoop on your body to the rhythm of the music ('Summer Place')?" Later, substitute back, arm, wrist, leg, or foot.
5. "Can you throw and catch the hoop, keeping in time to the rhythm of the music?"
6. "Develop a routine of swinging, jumping, and twisting."

Partner and Group Tasks

In partners: Twirling, throwing, catching, and nonlocomotor skills can be incorporated into a variety of interesting and challenging matching, contrasting, and follow-the-leader routines.

1. Develop a series of challenges involving partners using one or more hoops and using musical accompaniment with an uneven rhythm.
2. Repeat the challenge using partners, one or more hoops, and locomotor skills performed with an even rhythm accompaniment. (Run, walk, hop, jump, and leap.)
3. Repeat 1 or 2 adding a ball or other small equipment to the original challenge.

Group activities: The previous partner activities can be easily modified to add one or more children to each task.

Task Cards

The application of task or challenge cards can be used in rhythmic activities with individual, partner, or group activities with equal success. The following example illustrates the type of information that should be written on the card.

It is suggested that six to eight cards with different tasks but the same music be used. Divide the class into small groups. Each child reads the challenge and then proceeds to develop his own routine. Thus, there will be several different types of routines rather than variations of one task. Various levels of ability can be coped with by designing cards ranging from very simple tasks to challenges requiring greater skill and creative ability.

When equipment is unavailable for every child to perform a particular activity, use task cards and the station work technique. In the accompanying illustration, the class is divided into four groups and then subdivided into partners. Each set of partners reads the challenge, then proceeds to develop a matching routine. Any marching record can be used for all stations. Allow four to five minutes for the partners to develop their routines, then put on the record. If time permits, rotate the groups to the next station and repeat the process.

Station 1: Hoops. Make up a matching sequence with your partner that includes three different twirling movements, a pause in your routine, and a change in direction.

Station 2: Individual Ropes. Make up a matching routine that includes three different steps.

Station 3: Utility Balls. Develop a bouncing routine with one partner leading and the other following.

Station 4: Lummi Sticks. Make up a matching routine that includes a change of direction and a change in level.

The activities presented in this chapter should not be seen as a separate unit of dance. Rather, as was stated earlier, rhythmic activities should be integrated into games, gymnastics, and dance units. This can be done through periodic rhythmic warm-up activities and an occasional complete lesson of rhythmics interspersed within a games or gymnastic unit.

29 Traditional and Contemporary Dances

All structured dances performed in the elementary school can be broadly classified as traditional and contemporary dances. The classification includes singing games and traditional dances of past cultures as well as the contemporary dances of this generation.

In this chapter, two general sections have been organized to cope with the unique differences existing between primary and intermediate dance programs. The first section includes a wide selection of the more popular singing games and folk dances enjoyed by children in the primary grades (K–3). The next section, "Intermediate Folk Dance Program" (4–6), has been organized to allow teachers to introduce the elements of folk dance in a relaxed and creative manner. This is followed by suggestions related to teaching folk and square dance activities using both structured and exploratory methods of instruction. This section also includes descriptions of traditional and contemporary dances for the age level. A glossary of terms is included in the final section of this chapter, and information about record companies and musical equipment is provided in appendixes A and B.

Primary Folk Dance Program

Singing games are part of the dance heritage of every country. They are, in essence, the forerunners of the more complicated traditional and contemporary dances. As such, they provide a foundation upon which the more advanced dances can be built. Because of the cultural and historical significance of folk-singing games, primary teachers should take time to provide interesting materials relating to their origin, the customs of the people, and the meaning of various dance movements. This information can be presented in many ways, such as reading stories and poems about the people, displaying pictures, dolls, and other articles, and showing a film about the country.

Name of Dance	Skills	Formation	Origin	Page	Grade Level		
Approximate Order of Difficulty					K	1 2	3
Baa, Baa, Black Sheep	Walk, stamp, turn, bow, and curtsey	Circle	English	506	x		
Bluebird	Skip	Circle	American	506	x		
Twinkle, Twinkle, Little Star	Walk, swing	Circle	English	506	x		
Ring Around the Rosy	Walk, skip	Circle	English	507	x	x	
Farmer in the Dell	Walk, clap	Circle	English	507	x	x	
Sally Go Round the Moon	Walk, run, skip, slide	Circle	English	507	x	x	
The Muffin Man	Walk, clap, skater's position	Circle	English	508	x	x	
Loobie Loo	Walk, skip, slide	Circle	English	508	x	x	
Did You Ever See a Lassie	Walk, pantomime	Circle	Scottish	509	x	x	
How D'ye Do My Partner	Skip, bow, curtsey	Circle	Swedish	509		x x	
Oats, Peas, Beans, and Barley	Walk, skip, pantomime	Circle	English	510		x x	
Round and Round the Village	Skip, bow, curtsey	Circle	English	510		x	x
A-Hunting We Will Go	Skip, arching	Line	English	511		x	x
Jolly Is the Miller	Walk, pantomime	Circle	English	511		x	x
Shoo Fly	Walk, swing, turn	Circle	American	511		x	x
Children's Polka	Run, slide, hop	Circle	German	512		x	x
Danish Dance of Greeting	Run, stamp, bow, curtsey	Circle	Danish	512		x	x
Paw Paw Patch	Walk, skip, cast-off	Columns	American	513			x
Skip to My Lou	Walk, skip, swing, promenade	Circle	American	513			x
Pop Goes the Weasel	Walk, skip	Circle	American	514			x
Bleking	Step, hop, bleking step	Circle	Swedish	514			x

Note: Addresses of all record companies are listed in appendix A.

Most primary singing games are individual or partner activities; however, both types are performed within a group situation. Since five-, six-, and seven-year-olds are basically individualistic, the singing games presented in the following pages can be performed individually while the children are in a line, circle, or scattered pattern. With practice and maturity, children in the second and third grades progress to more advanced folk dances involving intricate patterns and group participation.

Teaching singing games to children in the primary grades, particularly to five- and six-year-olds, should be an enjoyable experience for teachers and a creative experience for children. The children's uninhibited behavior and joy of movement make singing games an appropriate activity. Once they learn the words, they will provide their own accompaniment and an infinite variety of interesting and creative versions of each singing game.

Since early primary children vary widely in maturity, motor ability, and interests, no single method of teaching will prove successful with this type of activity.

Each teacher should experiment with several approaches until she finds the one most suitable to her own style of teaching. Usually this is a combination of methods and techniques rather than one "special approach." The following suggestions may be helpful:

1. Use musical accompaniment that permits you to work freely with the children, such as commercial records or a tape recording of your own piano accompaniment.

2. Give the name of the folk dance or singing game and its origin, and mention something about the customs of the people. Illustrate by showing motion pictures, slides, or photographs of the people.

3. Teach the words of the singing game first. Children should practice singing the song until they have nearly memorized it.

4. Teach the basic steps of the singing game after the children have learned the verses.

5. Combine the basic steps with the words and music.

Additional Games and Folk Dances for Primary Grades

Name of Dance	Skills	Formation	Origin	Grade Level K 1 2 3				Record Source
Let Your Feet Go Tap	Tap, clap, skip	Circle	German	x	x			Folkcraft 1184
Mulberry Bush	Walk, skip, turn, pantomime	Circle	English	x	x			Bowman A–1, Folkcraft 1183
Ten Little Indians	Walk	Circle	American	x	x			Folkcraft 1197
London Bridge	Walk	Lines	English	x	x			Bowmar 36–A1(2) RCA 45–5056
Hickory, Dickory, Dock	Run, stamp	Circle	English	x	x			Victor 22760
Little Miss Muffet	Walk	Circle	English	x	x			Childhood Rhythms Series 7, No. 703
I Should Like to Go to Shetland	Gallop	Circle	English	x	x			Folkcraft 1190
Shoemaker's Dance	Skip, pantomime	Circle	Danish		x	x		Folkcraft 1187 RCA 45–6171
Ach ja	Walk, slide	Circle	German		x	x		Childhood Rhythms No. 7
Chimes of Dunkirk	Skip	Circle	French		x	x		Folkcraft 1185 RCA 45–6176
Thread Follows the Needle	Walk	Line	English		x	x		RCA 22760 (E–87) Pioneer 3017
Rig-a-Jig-Jig	Walk, skip	Circle	American			x	x	Folkcraft 1199
Sing a Song of Sixpence	Walk	Circle	English			x	x	Folkcraft 1180 RCA Victor 22760
Carousel	Slide, draw, step, stamp	Circle	Swedish			x	x	RCA 45–6179 Pioneer 3044–A
Hansel and Gretel	Heel-toe step, skip	Circle	German			x	x	Folkcraft 1193 RCA 45–6182
Jingle Bells	Skip, slide	Circle	Dutch			x	x	Folkcraft 1080
Jump Jim Joe	Run, jump	Circle	American			x	x	Folkcraft 1180 Bowman Album 3
Hokey Pokey	Turn, shake	Circle	American				x	McGregor 6995
Gustaf's Skoal	Walk, skip	Square	Swedish				x	Folkcraft 1175
Hinky, Dinky, Parlez Vous	Walk, do-si-do, promenade	Square	American				x	Folkcraft 1059

6. Attempt to create a permissive atmosphere in which children feel free to express their own ideas and movements.

Through singing games, children learn to walk, run, skip, or perform a combination of these basic dance steps to musical accompaniment. And when they can move rhythmically to music, they can create their own singing games. Allow them to develop their own dances to favorite nursery rhymes or songs. For example, "Sing a Song of Sixpence" or "I Saw a Ship a Sailing" have simple phrases and rhythmic melodies that provide the necessary ingredients for new singing games. In addition, children may wish to write their own verses about animals, spaceships, or special events, and then try to apply them to musical accompaniment. Finding the appropriate music usually becomes a joint venture for the teacher and class. The supplementary list of singing games and available records will be of some assistance.

Children should also be encouraged to create their own music. Perhaps, too, some children may be fortunate enough to have a teacher with a musical background and the talent to write musical accompaniments to fit the verses written by them.

Teachers of grades two and three should refer to the suggested "creative folk dance" approach for intermediate children (p. 515) for additional ideas. The creative folk dance approach can work equally well with seven- and eight-year-old children.

Baa, Baa, Black Sheep (K)

Musical Accompaniment
Childhood Rhythms, Series 7, No. 701
Folkcraft 1191

Formation: Single circle, with girls to right of boys and all facing center

Skills: Stamp, bow and curtsey, turn, and walk

Song

Baa, baa, black sheep,
Have you any wool?
Yes sir, yes sir,
Three bags full.
One for my master,
One for my dame,
And one for the little boy
Who lives in the lane.

Chorus:

Action

Stamp three times.
Shake fingers.
Nod head twice.
Hold three fingers up.
Turn right and bow or curtsey.
Turn left and bow or curtsey.
Turn around.
Face center and bow or curtsey.

Join inside hands and take sixteen steps counterclockwise.

Variations

All join hands and take eight slides to the right, then eight slides left. Raise hands and take four steps into the circle and four steps out. Repeat four in and four out. Drop hands and skip sixteen steps counterclockwise.

Bluebird (K)

Musical Accompaniment
Folkcraft 1180

Formation: Single circle facing center with hands joined forming arches, and one child standing under one arch as the "bluebird"

Skills: Skip

Song

Bluebird, bluebird through my window,

Bluebird, bluebird through my window,

Bluebird, bluebird through my window,
Oh Mary* I am tired.

*Substitute name of each chosen child.

Action

The bluebird skips in and out of the arches all around the circle, and at the end of the song stops behind a circle player.

During next chorus, bluebird taps both hands lightly on the front child's shoulders.

Old bluebird keeps hands on new bluebird's shoulders as *she* repeats the skipping action in a trainlike fashion in and out of the arches. Repeat action tapping and skipping action on each chorus.

Twinkle, Twinkle, Little Star (K)

Musical Accompaniment
Childcraft Ep–C4

Formation: Single circle facing center
Skills: Walking and swinging

Song

Twinkle, twinkle, little star,
How I wonder what you are.
Up above the world so high,
Like a diamond in the sky.
Twinkle, twinkle, little star,
How I wonder what you are.

Action

All children hold arms in front and wiggle fingers.
Turn right, raise and circle arms overhead for seven steps.
Face center, arms forward, wiggle fingers.

Ring Around the Rosy (K–1)

Musical Accompaniment
Folkcraft 1199

Song

Ring around a rosy
A pocket full of posies,
At choo, at choo*
All fall down.
The cow's in the middle
Lying down to rest.
Around the king, around the queen
We call jump up.
*Other words, such as *tish-a, tisher-a;
hush-a, hush-a; ashes, ashes;*
or *one two three,* can be substituted.

Formation: Single circle, girls to right of boys, facing
center with hands joined
Skills: Walking and skipping

Action

Keeping hands joined, circle left. All stop, face center, sneeze
twice, then drop to squatting position on word *down.*

All stay in squat position, sing verse and jump up at end of
verse.

Farmer in the Dell (K–1)

Musical Accompaniment
Folkcraft 1182
Victor 21618
Bowmar Singing Games, Album II

Song

The farmer in the dell,
The farmer in the dell,
Heigh-ho! the cherry-o,*
The farmer in the dell.
The farmer takes a wife,
The farmer takes a wife,
Heigh-ho! the cherry-o,
The farmer takes a wife.
The wife takes a child, etc.
The child takes a nurse, etc.
The nurse takes a dog, etc.
The dog takes a cat, etc.
The cat takes a rat, etc.
The rat takes the cheese, etc.
The cheese stands alone.

The farmer runs away, etc.
(Repeat for each player as he leaves center of circle.)

Teaching Suggestions

*This song may be sung "derry-o," "dairy-o," or
"the dearie-o."

Formation: Single circle facing center with hands joined.
One child, the "farmer," is in the center of the circle.
Skills: Walking and clapping

Action

All walk right around the circle, singing verse while the farmer
looks about for a wife.

Continue to walk around the circle as the farmer chooses a
wife, who joins him at the center of the circle.

Repeat procedure as directed.
Repeat procedure as directed.
Repeat procedure as directed.
Repeat procedure as directed.
Repeat procedure as directed.
Repeat procedure as directed.
Repeat procedure as directed.
Repeat procedure as directed.

Children in the center crowd around the "cheese" and clap
their hands over the cheese's head, while circle players stand
still, clap hands, and sing verse.

Continue walking as the farmer, then wife, etc., leave the
center of the circle.

Note: Cheese remains and becomes the new farmer.

Sally Go Round the Moon (K–1)

Musical Accompaniment
Folkcraft 1198
Victor 45–5064

Song

Sally, go round the moon,
Sally, go round the stars,
Sally, go round the chimneypots,
On a Sunday afternoon—Boom!
Repeat above.

Formation: Single circle facing center with hands joined
Skills: Walking, running, skipping, or sliding

Action

Walk, run, skip, or slide around the circle. On the word
"boom," all jump into the air and clap hands or perform any
movement they wish.

Repeat action in opposite direction.

The Muffin Man (K–1)

Musical Accompaniment
Folkcraft 1188

Song

Oh, have you seen the muffin man,
The muffin man, the muffin man,
Oh, have you seen the muffin man,
Who lives across the way.
Oh, yes, we've seen the muffin man
The muffin man, the muffin man
Oh, yes, we've seen the muffin man,
Who lives across the way.

Teaching Suggestions

With large numbers of children start with two
muffin men in the center of the circle. Substitute
"Drury Lane" as an English version.

Formation: Single circle facing center with one child (the
"muffin man") in the center

Skills: Walk, clap, skaters' position

Pattern

Children join hands and circle to the left using a walk or a
slow skip step and singing the first verse.

Children in circle stand facing center and clap hands while
singing "The Muffin Man." The child in center chooses a
partner from circle and brings him or her back to center (in
skaters' position). This child becomes the new muffin man
while the old partner returns to circle.

Loobie Loo (K–1)

Musical Accompaniment
Folkcraft 1184
Childhood Rhythms,
Series 7, No. 706
Bowmar Singing Games,
Album I, No. 1514

Song

Chorus:
Here we go Loobie Loo,
Here we go Loobie Light,
Here we go Loobie Loo,
All on a Saturday night.

Verse No. 1
I put my right hand in,
I put my right hand out,
I give my hand a shake, shake, shake
And turn myself about.
Repeat chorus after each verse.
I put my left hand in, etc.
I put my both hands in, etc.
I put my right foot in, etc.
I put my left foot in, etc.
I put my elbows in, etc.
I put my shoulder in, etc.
I put my big head in, etc.
I put my whole self in, etc.

Formation: Single circle facing center with hands joined

Skills: Walking, skipping, sliding, and pantomime activities

Action

Circle left using eight walking, skipping, or sliding steps.
Circle right eight steps.
Everyone drops hands and faces the center.

Place right hand toward center of circle.
Turn, place right hand away from circle.
Shake hand.
Turn in place.
Repeat action of chorus.
Repeat each verse according to the movement suggested.

Did you Ever See a Lassie (K–1)

Musical Accompaniment
Folkcraft 1183
Victor 45–5066
Pioneer 3012–B
Columbia 10008D

Song

Did you ever see a lassie,
("laddie" when boy is in center)
A lassie, a lassie,
Did you ever see a lassie
Go this way and that?

Chorus:

Go this way and that way.
Go this way and that way.
Did you ever see a lassie
Go this way and that?

Teaching Suggestions

Once the children have learned the basic movements, have them create impressions such as birds, animals, and mechanical toys. And instead of walking, have them walk using swinging and swaying, stamping, and clapping.

Formation: Single circle facing center with hands joined. One child is in the center of the circle.
Skills: Walking and pantomime activities

Action

All join hands and walk eight steps to the left, swinging joined hands, then eight steps back.

All stop, release hands, face the child in center and imitate her or his movements. Repeat singing game with a new leader in the center.

How D'ye Do My Partner (1–2)

Musical Accompaniment
Folkcraft 1190
Pioneer 3012
RCA Victor 21685
Bowmar, Album I. No. 1513 A

Song

How d'ye do my partner,
How d'ye do today?
Will you dance in a circle?
I will show you the way.

Chorus:

Tra,la,la,la,la,
Tra,la,la,la,la,
Tra,la,la,la,la,
Tra,la,la,la,la.
Repeat song.

Formation: Double circle with partners facing. Girls are on the outside circle.
Skills: Bowing, curtseying, skipping

Pattern

Boys bow to partners.
Girls curtsey to partners.
Boy offers hand to partner.
Join inside hands and turn counterclockwise.

With joined hands, skip around the circle. At the end of the chorus, girls move one position forward to new partners.

Oats, Peas, Beans, and Barley (1–2)

Musical Accompaniment
Folkcraft 1182
Folk Dancer MH 1110–A
Pioneer 3012

Song

Oats, peas, beans, and barley grow,
Oats, peas, beans, and barley grow,
Do you or I or anyone know
How oats, peas, beans, and barley grow?
First the farmer sows his seed,
Then he stands and takes his ease.
Stamps his foot and claps his hand.
And turns around to view the land.
Waiting for a partner,
Waiting for a partner,
Open the ring and choose one in.
While we all gladly dance and sing.

Chorus:
Tra,la,la,la,la,la,
Tra,la,la,la,la,la,
Tra,la,la,la,la,la,la,
Tra,la,la,la,la,la.

Formation: Single circle facing center with hands joined.
One child in the center of the circle is the "farmer."

Skills: Walking, skipping and pantomime actions

Pattern

Farmer in center stands while children in circle walk left, taking small steps. Circle players stop, point to the farmer, shrug, turn right, and stamp their feet.

Children in circle stop, face the center, and all dramatize the words of the song.

Children in the circle skip left as the farmer skips around inside the circle and picks a new partner. The farmer and new partner skip around inside the circle.

The two farmers continue to skip inside the circle while the others join hands and circle left. "Old farmer" joins the ring and "new farmer" repeats pattern.

Round and Round the Village (2–3)
(Go in and out the Windows)

Musical Accompaniment
Folkcraft 1191
Pioneer 3001–B

Song

Go round and round the village,
Go round and round the village,
Go round and round the village,
As we have done before.
Go in and out the windows,
Go in and out the windows,
Go in and out the windows,
As we have done before.
Now go and choose a partner,
Now go and choose a partner,
Now go and choose a partner,
As we have done before.
Now follow me to London,
Now follow me to London,
Now follow me to London,
As we have done before.
Shake hands before you leave me,
Shake hands before you leave me,
Shake hands before you leave me,
As we have done before.

Formation: Single circle with all facing center and hands joined. One or more players are outside the circle.

Skills: Skipping, bowing, and curtseying

Action

Circle children join hands and walk clockwise while outside players skip counterclockwise.

Children in circle stand and raise arms to form arches (windows) while outside players weave in and out.

"It" skips around the inside of the circle, stops, and bows or curtseys in front of a partner he or she has chosen.

"It" skips around inside the circle, followed by the new partner. Circle players skip in the opposite direction.

The circle players remain in place, clap their hands, and sing while inside players shake hands and bow or curtsey. The chosen player(s) then goes to the outside of the circle while other players return to the circle.

A-Hunting We Will Go (2–3)

Musical Accompaniment
Folkcraft 1191
Victor 45–5064
Childhood Rhythms,
Series 7, No. 705

Song

Oh, a-hunting we will go,
A-hunting we will go,
We'll catch a fox and put him in a box,
And then we'll let him go.

Chorus:
Tra,la,la,la,la,la,la,
Tra,la,la,la,la,la,
Tra,la,la,la,la,la,
la,la,la,la,
Tra,la,la,la,la,la.

Formation: Two parallel lines (longways set) facing each other, with girls on one side and boys on the other

Skills: Skipping, arching

Action

Head couple joins inside hands and skips down between the lines to the foot of the set.

Head couple turns around, changes hands, and skips back to the head of the set.

All other players clap hands while head couple skips down and back.

Head couple skips around the left side of the set, followed by other couples. When the head couple reaches the foot of the line, it forms an arch under which all other couples pass. Head couple remains while the second couple becomes the head couple.

Repeat dance with new head couple.

Jolly Is the Miller (2–3)

Musical Accompaniment
Folkcraft 1192
Victor 45–5067

Song

Jolly is the miller who lives by the mill,
The wheel turns around of its own free will,
One hand in the hopper and
the other in the sack,
The hop steps forward and the rim steps back.

Formation: Partners form a double circle facing counterclockwise with girls on the inside. One player, the "miller," stands in the center.

Skills: Walking and pantomime actions

Action

Couples join inside hands and walk counterclockwise while singing the song. During the second line, children in the inner circle extend left arms sideward to form a mill wheel. On the last word of the song ("back"), partners drop hands and the inner circle steps forward while the outer circle steps backward. The extra player tries to secure a partner during this exchange. The child without a partner goes to the center.

Repeat dance with new partner.

Shoo Fly (2–3)

Musical Accompaniment
Folkcraft 1185

Song

Shoo, fly, don't bother me,
Shoo, fly, don't bother me,
Shoo, fly, don't bother me,
For I belong to somebody.

Chorus
I feel, I feel,
I feel like a morning star,
I feel, I feel,
I feel like a morning star.

Formation: Single circle with girls on the boys' right. Hands are joined and all face the center of the circle.

Skills: Walking, swinging, and turning

Action

Walk four steps forward, swinging arms.
Walk four steps backward.
Walk four steps forward, swinging arms.
Walk four steps backward.

Partners join hands and walk around each other in a clockwise direction. Repeat. On the last "morning star," the boy raises his left hand and turns his partner under his arm. The girl is now on the boy's left. The girl on the boy's right becomes his new partner.

Join hands and repeat dance.

Children's Polka (Kinderpolka) (2–3)

Musical Accompaniment
Victor 45–6179
Folkcraft 1187
Pioneer 3004–B

Formation: Single circle with partners facing, both arms extended sideward and hands joined

Skills: Sliding, hopping, and running

Measure	Action
1–2	Take two slides toward center and step lightly three times.
3–4	Take two slides away from center; step lightly three times.
5–8	Repeat action of measures 1–4.
9–10	Slap own knees once, clap own hands once, and clap partner's hands three times.
11–12	Repeat action of measures 9–10.
13	Hop, placing right heel forward, place right elbow in left hand, and shake finger three times.
14	Repeat action of measure 13 with left foot.
15–16	Turn in place with four running steps and step lightly three times.

Teaching Suggestions

To help children learn the dance pattern, count in this manner:

Step, step, tap, tap, tap. Repeat.

Slap, clap, clap, clap, clap. Repeat.

Hop, one, two, three. Repeat.

Turn around now, tap, tap, tap.

Danish Dance of Greeting (2–3)

Musical Accompaniment
Folkcraft 1187
Victor 41–6183
Pioneer 3014–B
Burns, Evans, and Wheeler,
Album 1, No. 126 (with words)

Formation: Single circle of couples facing center. The girl is on the right side of the boy.

Skills: Clapping, stamping, bowing, curtseying, turning, and running

Song	Action
Clap, clap, bow.	Clap hands twice, turn and bow, or curtsey, to partner.
Clap, clap, bow.	Clap hands twice and bow, or curtsey, to child on the other side (neighbor).
Stamp, stamp.	Stamp on the right foot and then on the left.
Turn yourself around.	Turn around in place with four running steps.
Chorus:	
Tra,la,la,la,la,etc.	All join hands and circle to the right with sixteen short running steps. Repeat action to the left.
Tra,la,la,la,la,etc.	

Paw Paw Patch (3)

Musical Accompaniment
Folkcraft 1181
Victor 45–5066

Song

Where, O where is sweet little Sally?
Where, O where is sweet little Sally?
Where, O where is sweet little Sally?
Way down yonder in the paw paw patch.
Come on, boys, let's go find her,
Come on, boys, let's go find her,
Come on, boys, let's go find her,
Way down yonder in the paw paw patch.
Pickin' up paw paws, putting 'em in her pocket,
Pickin' up paw paws, putting 'em in her pocket,
Pickin' up paw paws, putting 'em in her pocket.
Way down yonder in the paw paw patch.

Formation: Columns of four to six couples with partners facing forward (to the head of hall)

Skills: Walking, skipping, clapping, and casting off

Action

First girl turns right, casts off, circles clockwise, and goes once around the set with sixteen skipping steps, and back to place. Everyone else remains in place, clapping and singing the song.

First girl takes the first boy's left hand and leads line of boys around the set. Boys may join hands. Girls in line clap hands. All finish in place facing the front.

Partners join hands and follow first couple once around to the right. First couple turns away from each other, with the boy going left and the girl going right, and skips to the foot of the line. The rest of the line moves one place forward.
Repeat entire dance with each new "first" girl leading.

Skip to My Lou (3)

Musical Accompaniment
Bowmar Singing Games Album 3, No. 1522–A
Folkcraft 1192
Folk Dancers MH 111–A
Pioneer 3003–A

Song

Verse No. 1
Boys to the center, Skip to my Lou,
Boys to the outside, Skip to my Lou,
Boys to the center, Skip to my Lou.
Skip to my Lou, my darling.

Verse No. 2
Girls to the center, Skip to my Lou,
Girls to outside, Skip to my Lou,
Girls to the center, Skip to my Lou,
Skip to my Lou, my darling.

Verse No. 3
Swing your partner, Skip to my Lou, (three times)
Skip to my Lou, my darling.

Verse No. 4
I've lost my partner now what'll I do, (three times)
Skip to my Lou, my darling.

Verse No. 5
I've got another one, prettier too, (three times)
Skip to my Lou, my darling.

Formation: Single circle with partners side by side and the girls on the boy's right

Skills: Walking, skipping, swinging, and promenading

Action

Boys walk four steps forward and four steps backward.

Repeat.

Girls repeat patterns as described above.

Partners join hands and swing or skip in place.

Release hands. Girls walk forward, boys turn and walk in the opposite direction.

New partners promenade counterclockwise to original position, with the girl on the boy's right.
Repeat dance with new partner.

Pop Goes the Weasel (3)

Musical Accompaniment
World of Fun, M–104–B
Folkcraft 1329
Victor 45–6180

Formation: Double circle in sets of four children. Girl is on partner's right. Couples facing clockwise are couples number 1, while couples facing counterclockwise are couples number 2.

Skills: Walking and skipping

Measure	*Action*
1–4	Join hands in a circle of four and circle left with eight skipping or sliding steps.
5–6	Walk two steps forward, raising joined hands, then walk two steps backward, lowering hands.
7–8	Number one couples raise their joined hands to form an arch as number two couples pass under. Number two couples continue forward to meet new partners. Repeat dance

Variation

Formation: Three children form a set, with two children joining inside hands. The third child stands in front with his back to the other two, extends his hands back, and holds the outside hands of the other two. All three face counterclockwise in a large circle.

Measure	*Action*
1–6	All sets skip around in a large circle.
7–8	On "pop" the child in front skips backward under the raised inside hands of the back couple and continues backward, meeting the couple behind him.
9–14	Repeat measures 1–6.
15–16	Repeat measures 7–8.

Bleking (3)

Musical Accompaniment
Pioneer 3016
Folkcraft 1188
Victor 45–6169

Formation: Single circle with partners facing. Boys face counterclockwise; girls face clockwise. Partners extend their arms forward at shoulder height and join hands.

Skills: Bleking step, stepping and hopping

Measure	*Action*
1–8	Hop on left foot, extend the right heel forward, keeping the right leg straight. As this movement takes place, thrust the right arm forward and pull the left arm back (count one). Continue for seven more counts, changing the lead foot on each count.
9–12	Partners face each other, extending arms sideways and joining hands. Boy begins with his right foot, girl with her left foot. Partners begin to turn in place by taking seven step-hops in a clockwise direction and end with a stamp on the last count. As the children turn in place, their arms move in a windmill action up and down with each step-hop.
13–16	Repeat action counterclockwise.

Intermediate Folk Dance Program

The traditional and contemporary folk dances that have been taught to upper elementary school children are rich in cultural heritage. These dances have normally been taught to children in a formal way, with the steps, formations, and gestures of each dance introduced systematically. However, contemporary approaches to teaching elementary school physical activities use more individualized instructional techniques and more exploratory and problem-solving methods to cope with the characteristics, needs, and interests of this age group. The material that follows is an attempt to introduce a more creative approach to teaching folk dance activities.

The next section describes the five basic elements of folk dance, followed by a suggested approach for teaching each of these elements in a systematic yet creative manner. The latter section of this chapter contains descriptions of some of the more popular folk and square dances for children of grades four through six.

Elements of Folk Dance

Although there are obviously marked differences in the steps, body gestures, and styles from one dance to another, all dances, regardless of age or cultural origin, are made up of five basic elements. The first element as illustrated includes the *steps* performed in the dance. Second, dancers move in a specified *direction*. Third, dancers move through a particular *pathway*. Fourth, dancers have a certain *relationship* to each other as they move through the dance. Finally, all dances are performed from a line, square, or circle *formation*. Each element is clarified in the accompanying pages.

Element 1: Steps
The following seven locomotor steps represent the basic ways children move in folk dance activities. Most of these skills are acquired long before children reach the intermediate grades. The emphasis therefore in this

Figure 29.1

dance program is to acquire different styles of performing each locomotor movement, to move gracefully and in time to the rhythm of the music, and to shift tempo, intensity, or other rhythmical skills to meet the challenge and enjoyable subtleties of each dance activity.

Walk A walk may vary from a basic heel-toe walking action to a shuffling movement from ball of foot to ball of foot.

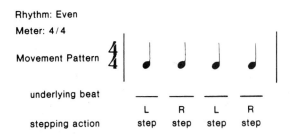

Rhythm: Even

Meter: 4/4

Movement Pattern

underlying beat

stepping action: L step, R step, L step, R step

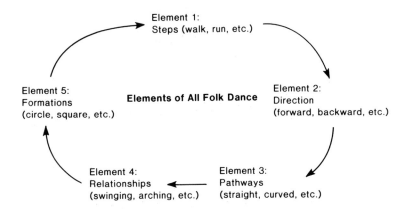

Element 1:
Steps (walk, run, etc.)

Element 2:
Direction
(forward, backward, etc.)

Element 3:
Pathways
(straight, curved, etc.)

Element 4:
Relationships
(swinging, arching, etc.)

Element 5:
Formations
(circle, square, etc.)

Elements of All Folk Dance

Run A run may vary from a slow heel-toe run to a
fast and vigorous running action from ball or toe of foot
to the opposite ball or toe.

Rhythm: Even

Meter: 4/4

Movement Pattern

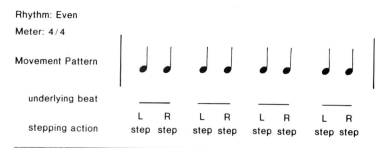

underlying beat

stepping action

Hop The hop is a basic springing action from the ball
of one foot to the ball of the same foot.

Rhythm: Even

Meter: 4/4

Movement Pattern

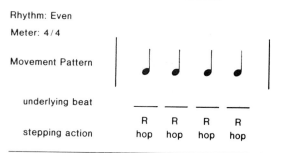

underlying beat

stepping action

Skip A skip is a step and a short hop on the same foot
shifting to a step and a hop on the opposite foot.

Rhythm: Uneven

Meter: 2/4 or 6/8

Movement Pattern

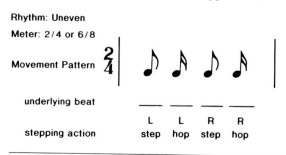

underlying beat

stepping action

Leap A leap is a basic springing action from the ball
of one foot to a landing on the ball of the opposite foot.
A slight or exaggerated knee bend on each landing is
followed by a lowering of the heel.

Rhythm: Even

Meter: 4/4

Movement Pattern

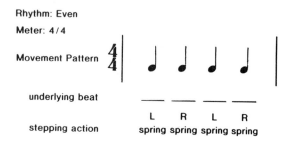

underlying beat

stepping action

Slide (or Gallop) A slide and a gallop are basically the
same steps with a slide performed in a sideward direction and the gallop performed in a forward direction.
A slide is a combination of a step on one foot followed
by a shifting of weight and a closing action on the opposite foot. One foot always leads while performing the
slide or gallop.

Rhythm: Uneven

Meter: 2/4 or 6/8

Movement Pattern

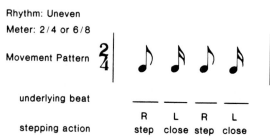

underlying beat

stepping action

Jump The jump is a basic springing action from the
balls of both feet to the balls of both feet with a slight
overexaggerated knee bend. The heel normally comes
down after the ball of the foot has made contact with
the floor.

Rhythm: Even

Meter: 4/4

Movement Pattern

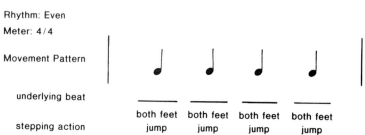

underlying beat

stepping action

Combination of Basic Steps

The following four basic dance steps are actually a combination of one or more of the individual locomotor steps.

Schottische Step The schottische dance step is a combination of three brisk walking steps followed by a hop. After the third three steps and a hop, the fourth measure may include a step hop, step hop, allowing performers to hop, hold, turn, or swing the free leg on the fourth count.

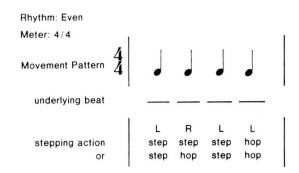

Rhythm: Even
Meter: 4/4

Movement Pattern

underlying beat

stepping action	L	R	L	L
	step	step	step	hop
or	step	hop	step	hop

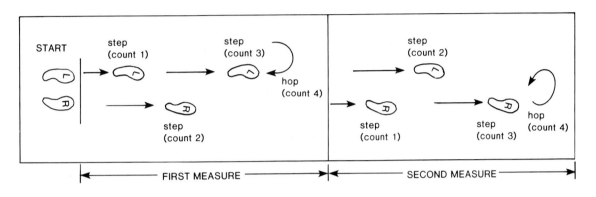

Waltz Step The waltz step consists of a graceful step forward on the left foot (count one), a step forward and sideward on the right foot (count two), followed by a closing action of the left foot and simultaneous shifting of weight to this foot (count three). Children will say "forward" (one), "side" (two), "together" (three).

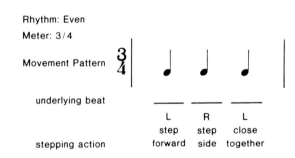

Rhythm: Even
Meter: 3/4

Movement Pattern

underlying beat

	L	R	L
stepping action	step	step	close
	forward	side	together

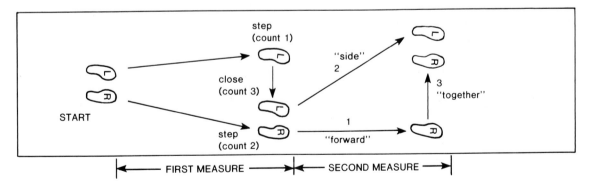

Two-Step   The two-step is a combination of a step forward on the ball of the left foot, then a closing action of the right foot (weight is briefly placed on the right foot), a step forward on the left foot, and a pause. The first two steps have the same short timing while the third step is twice as long as the first two. The pause allows the weight to stay over the left foot to allow the right foot to shift forward in order to begin the first step of the next measure. As children learn this dance step they will say "walk" placing left foot forward, "together" (bringing right foot up and beside the left foot), "walk" (placing left foot forward), "pause" (allowing weight to shift to left foot in preparation for the next step right).

Rhythm: Uneven

Meter: 2/4

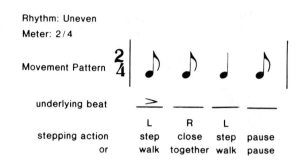

Movement Pattern

underlying beat

	L	R	L	
stepping action	step	close	step	pause
or	walk	together	walk	pause

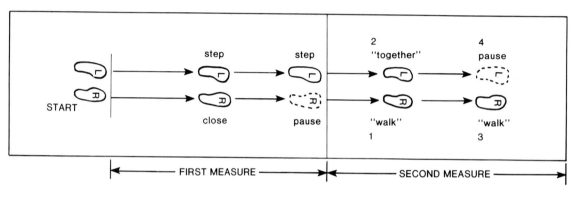

step   step   2 "together"   4 pause

START   close   pause   "walk" 1   "walk" 3

|←——— FIRST MEASURE ———→|←——— SECOND MEASURE ———→|

Polka   The polka step is similar to the two-step with the addition of a hop in the combined sequence of steps. The first measure begins with stepping left while the next begins with stepping right, alternating this action throughout the dance.

Rhythm: Uneven

Meter: 2/4

Movement Pattern

underlying beat

	L	R	L	L
stepping action	step	close	step	hop

Polka begins with a hop on last beat of previous measure.

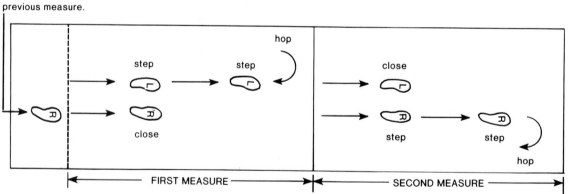

hop   step   step   close

close   step   step   hop

|←——— FIRST MEASURE ———→|←——— SECOND MEASURE ———→|

Directions

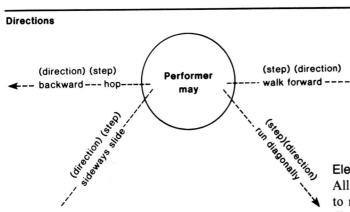

(direction) (step)
← -- backward --- hop---

(step) (direction)
-- walk forward ----- →

(direction) (step)
sideways slide

(step)(direction)
run diagonally ----

Element 2: Directions

All folk and square dance activities require performers to move in either a forward, backward, sideward, or diagonal direction. These are the simplest directions children may move in while performing the basic dance steps.

Pathways

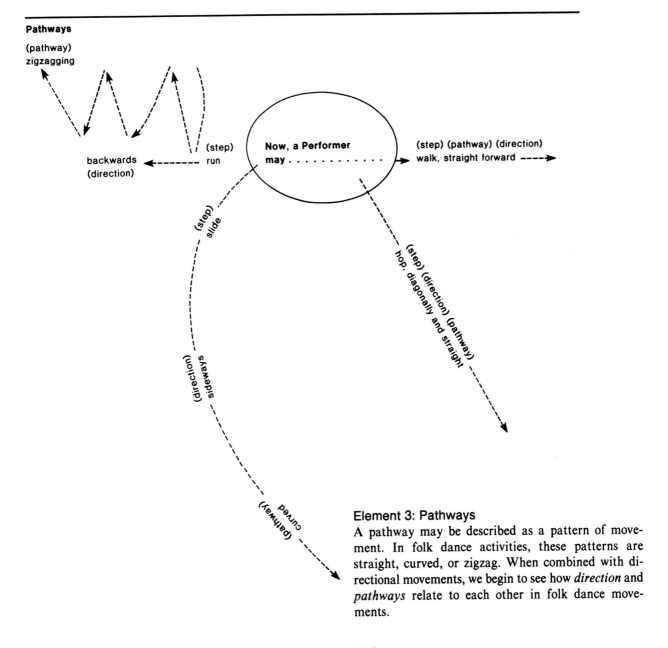

(pathway)
zigzagging

backwards
(direction)

(step)
-- run

Now, a Performer
may . . . .

(step) (pathway) (direction)
walk, straight forward ----→

(step)
slide

(step) (direction) (pathway)
hop, diagonally and straight

(direction)
sideways

(pathway)
curved

Element 3: Pathways

A pathway may be described as a pattern of movement. In folk dance activities, these patterns are straight, curved, or zigzag. When combined with directional movements, we begin to see how *direction* and *pathways* relate to each other in folk dance movements.

Figure 29.2 Open

Figure 29.3 Closed

Figure 29.4 Shoulder-Waist

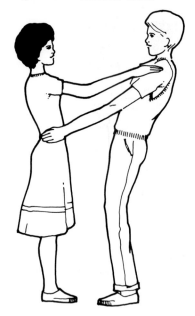

Element 4: Relationships

Relationships include the dance positions and the movement designs of two or more dancers.

Folk dance positions include: open (fig. 29.2), closed (fig. 29.3), shoulder-waist (fig. 29.4), skaters (fig. 29.5), two-hand (fig. 29.6), couple (fig. 29.7).

Movement designs include: bridging, starring, arching, turning, swinging, passing, meeting and parting, and weaving.

                                                    (relationships)
Now, performers may . . . in a skaters position,

  (step)   *(pathway)* *(direction)*
walk eight steps straight forward, change to shoulder-

  (relationships)   *(relationships)*
waist position and swing your partner.

Element 5: Formations

Folk and square dances are performed in either a *line, circle,* or *square formation*. These formations are quite familiar to the elementary school children, hence can be incorporated with their dances with relative ease.

                                            (relationships)
Now performers may . . . in promenade position,

(step) (pathway)   *(direction)*
walk straight forward for eight counts, then prome-

  (relationship)   *(formation)*
nade around the hall.

Teaching the Elements of Folk Dance

The approach suggested here is a continuation of the rhythmic approach presented in the previous chapter. Hence, it is assumed that children understand the elements of rhythm, such as *even and uneven rhythm, accent,* and *underlying beat,* and can recognize and apply these rhythmic elements to a variety of game, dance, and gymnastic movement skills.

In the previous section, the five elements of folk dance were described. These elements, as illustrated, can be *sequentially* introduced to children in an informal and relaxed manner through five interrelated stages. To illustrate, in lesson 1, which follows, the central theme of the lesson is to move (walk, run, hop, jump, or leap) in time to an even musical accompaniment. Individual, partner, and group activities focus on this central theme from the beginning to the end of the lesson. Subthemes such as changing speed or level provide a little variety and a review of previously acquired movement skills. Although children may change direction within each movement task, specific references to directional movements are deliberately left out of this lesson.

Figure 29.5 Skaters (or promenade)

Figure 29.6 Two-Hand (or facing)

Figure 29.7 Couple

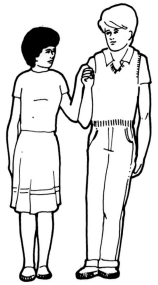

Introducing the Elements of Folk Dance

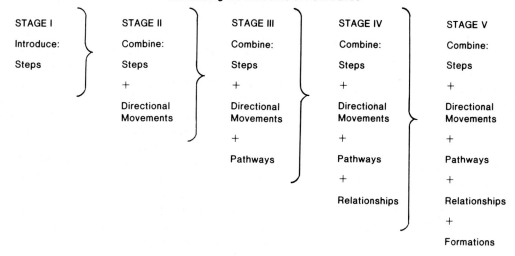

STAGE I	STAGE II	STAGE III	STAGE IV	STAGE V
Introduce:	Combine:	Combine:	Combine:	Combine:
Steps	Steps	Steps	Steps	Steps
	+	+	+	+
	Directional Movements	Directional Movements	Directional Movements	Directional Movements
		+	+	+
		Pathways	Pathways	Pathways
			+	+
			Relationships	Relationships
				+
				Formations

NOTE: Each of the five stages above progress from:

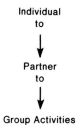

Individual
to

Partner
to

Group Activities

Lesson 1: Steps
Main Theme: Moving to even rhythm
Subtheme: Change of speed and level

I. Introductory Activities
   A. Individual walking, running, hopping, jumping, and leaping to 4/4 musical accompaniment.
   B. Add change of speed and level to above challenge.
II. Development
   A. In partners: "Make up a matching sequence that includes a run, hop, and jump and two changes in level." Use 4/4 musical accompaniment.
   B. In partners: "Develop a routine that includes clapping, twisting, shaking, running, and hopping steps." Use 4/4 musical accompaniment.
III. Group Activities (Culmination)
   A. In groups of four: Repeat B above with four children in each group standing in a line for both challenges.

In lesson 2, the central theme of the lesson emphasizes the second element, *directional movements.* This lesson follows the same pattern established in lesson 1, beginning with individual, shifting to partner, then to larger group activities. Subthemes of even and uneven rhythm and changing speed again provide variety as well as a review of previously introduced skills.

Lesson 2: Directional Movements
Main Theme: Directional movements
Subthemes: Moving to even and uneven rhythm, change of speed

I. Introductory Activities
   A. Repeat A and B, of lesson 1, adding a change of direction to each respective challenge.
II. Development
   A. "Make up a sequence that includes a run and a hop, two changes of direction, and a clapping and shaking movement." Use 4/4 musical accompaniment.
   B. In partners: "Begin with one standing behind the other. Create a routine that includes a skip and slide, moving sideways and diagonally, and a change in speed." Use 2/4 musical accompaniment.

III. Group Activities
   A. In groups of three: "See if you can make a routine that includes one locomotor skill performed to an even musical accompaniment and three changes in direction." Use 4/4 musical accompaniment.
   B. In groups of four: "Make up a routine that includes uneven rhythm and a change of direction." Use a 2/4 musical accompaniment.

At the completion of lesson 2, each teacher should consider such factors as the tone of the class, segregated or voluntary mixing of boys and girls for partner and group activities, and level of skill before planning the next four lessons. Some classes may need one or two more lessons stressing directional movements and to develop more positive interpersonal relationships before progressing to stage III. Hence, the number of lessons required to reach and complete the challenges in stage V really depends upon the above factors and the progress that is made from one lesson to the next.

Once the basic elements of folk dance have been learned through this informal and creative approach, a very positive attitude towards folk dance activities is also developed among boys and girls of this age range.

Teaching Traditional and Contemporary Folk Dances

Traditional and contemporary dances are dance patterns of past and present cultures. Generally speaking, when a dance such as Gustaf's Skoal has been handed down for many generations, it is designated as a traditional folk dance. On the other hand, a dance that originates within our own generation and is performed to recent or popular music is usually designated as a contemporary dance. Examples of the latter are the Patty Cake dance, the Hitchhiker, and the Twist. Both types of dances, however, express some aspect of the culture from which they originated. The Danish Dance of Greeting and the Sicilian Circle are examples of how dances can be used as a method of greeting or meeting others. Other dances, such as the Sailor's Hornpipe and our American Indian dance, are part of ceremonial or religious customs.

Methods of Teaching Folk Dances
If a teacher has followed a more exploratory approach when teaching rhythmic skills and the elements of folk dance, she should continue teaching traditional folk dance with a similar approach. For example, a class with this type of background experience could be taught any one of the accompanying folk or square dances in

its entirety, then be allowed to modify or, in their own way, enrich the dance by adding new relationships, directions, or pathways of movement. Introducing a traditional or contemporary dance according to the following suggestions provides an opportunity for the children to understand and appreciate the cultural background associated with the dance. Then, allowing the class to add its own creative ideas, in turn, enriches the dance experience of every child in class.

1. Acquire a general background of the people from which the dance originated and their customs for presentation to the class.

2. Present the background information about the dance in relation to the class's interest and maturity. Make it meaningful to the children.

3. Use audiovisual aids such as costumes, scenery, and folk songs to stimulate interest in and a deeper understanding of the people and customs represented in the dance.

4. Allow the children to hear the music before they learn the dance pattern.

5. Teach the dance by phrases rather than by counts.

6. When teaching the steps use a slower tempo until they are learned; then, increase the tempo to the appropriate speed of the dance.

7. Look for general problems, such as starting off on the wrong foot, and correct these difficulties; later, provide individual assistance.

8. Indicate any change in dance formation just before the beginning of the new phase.

9. Encourage creative expression within the pattern of the dance. Many of the older, traditional dances require movements that are uncomfortable or too rigid for children to perform.

10. Avoid spending too much time on one dance.

Square Dances

American folk dances include mixers, couples, longways, circles, and square dances that have been developed in this country during the past few hundred years. Of all these American folk dances, square dances have become the most popular with upper elementary school children. There is no single reason for this growth in popularity, although the simplicity of the steps and the enjoyment of participation could well be two important reasons.

The following suggestions will help teachers present various types of square-dance patterns. A list of basic terms used in square dance is provided in the glossary at the end of this chapter.

1. Emphasize fun and enjoyment rather than perfection of each and every skill.

2. Teach all square-dance movements from a circle formation, with each girl standing to the right side of her partner.

3. Select square dances that involve simple patterns, and introduce them at a slower speed.

4. Teach the dance by calling the dance patterns first without music, and then with musical accompaniment. Once the dance is learned, you may continue to call your own dance or use a record with the calls included.

5. The majority of square dancing is done with a shuffle step rather than a run or a hop. Emphasize a smooth and graceful slipping action, landing on the ball of the foot rather than on the heel.

6. The success of square dancing depends, in part, upon keeping the square of four couples symmetrical and the partners parallel. Constantly check to see that children maintain the square and partners do not wander away from each other.

7. Encourage children not only to call their own dances but also to create their own sequences of square-dance figures.

Folk and Square Dances for Intermediate Grades

Name of Dance	Skills	Formation	Origin	Page	Grade Level		
					4	5	6
Cshebogar	Walk, skip, slide, turn	Circle	Hungarian	524	x	x	
Glowworm Mixer	Walk, run, do-si-do	Circle	American	525	x	x	
Little Brown Jug	Slide, swing	Circle	American	526	x	x	
Hora	Side step, step swing	Circle	Israeli	526	x	x	
Troika	Run, stamp, arch	Circle	Russian	526	x	x	
Oh Susanna	Walk, slide, do-si-do, promenade	Circle	American	527	x	x	
Schottische	Schottische step	Circle	Scottish	527	x	x	
Badger Gavotte	Slide, two-step, dance	Circle	American	528	x	x	
Grand March	Walk	Line	American	528	x	x	x
Sicilian Circle	Walk, chain, right and left through	Circle	American	529	x	x	x
Virginia Reel	Walk, swing, do-si-do, cast-off skipping	Longways	American	529	x	x	x
Solomon Levi	Walk, swing, allemande left	Square	American	530	x	x	x
Oh Johnny	Walk, swing, allemande, do-si-do	Square	American	530	x	x	x
Ace of Diamonds	Walk, swing	Circle	American	530	x	x	x
Seven Jumps	Step hop	Circle	Danish	531	x	x	x
Norwegian Mountain March	Waltz, turn	Circle	Norwegian	531		x	x
Heel and Toe Polka	Polka step	Circle	American	532		x	x
Oklahoma Mixer	Walk, two-step, heel-toe	Circle	American	532		x	x
Rye Waltz	Slide, waltz step	Circle	American	532		x	x
Red River Valley	Walk, swing, do-si-do	Square	American	533		x	x
Tinikling	Tinikling step	Line	Philippine	533		x	x

Note: Addresses of all recording companies are listed in appendix A.

Cshebogar (4–5)

Musical Accompaniment
Folkcraft 1196

Formation: Single circle of couples with hands joined. Couples face the center with the girl on the boy's right side.

Skills: Walking, skipping, sliding, and the Hungarian turn

Measure	Action
1–4	Take eight slide steps to the left, and end with a jump on both feet.
5–8	Take eight slide steps to the right, and end with a jump on both feet.
9–12	Take four walking steps to the center, raising your hands high as you go. Take four walking steps backward to place in circle, lowering your hands as you return.
13–16	Face partner and place right hand on his or her waist. Raise left arm, pull away from partner, and skip around him or her. (This is a Hungarian turn.)
17–20	Face partner, join hands with arms held at shoulder height. Slide four steps slowly toward the center of the circle, bending toward the center as you slide. Boys start with left foot and girls with right foot.
21–24	Four step-draw steps outward (step-close-step).
25–28	Two draw steps in and two draw steps out.
29–32	Do the Hungarian turn again.

Additional Folk and Square Dances

Name	Skills	Formation	Origin	Grade Level 4	5	6	Record Source
Greensleeves	Walk	Circle	English	x	x		Victor 45–6175
Gustaf's Skoal	Walk, skip, turn	Square	Swedish	x	x		Victor 45–6170
Tennessee Wig Walk	Walk, side step	Circle	American	x	x		Decca 28846
Teton Mountain Stomp	Walk	Circle	American	x	x		Windsor 4615 Victor 45–6172
Bingo	Walk, R. grand	Circle	American	x	x		Folkcraft 1189
Alley Cat	Grapevine step	Free	American	x	x		Columbia IL 2500
La Raspa	Bleking, turn	Free	Mexican	x	x		Folkcraft 1119
Mayim	Walk, hop, grapevine	Circle	Israeli	x	x	x	Folkcraft 1108
Hop Morr Anika		Circle	Swedish	x	x	x	Victor 4142
Road to the Isles	Walk, schottische	Couples	Scottish	x	x	x	Imperial 1005A
Hinkey Dinkey Parlez Vous	Swing, promenade	Square	French	x	x	x	Folkcraft 1023 (with call)
Let's Square Dance	Walk	Square	American	x	x	x	Victor 3001
Hohsey Square Dance	Walk	Square	American	x	x	x	MacGregor (Album 4618)
Chester Schottische	Schottische	Circle	American	x	x	x	Folkcraft 1101
Road to the Isles	Schottische	Free	Scottish	x	x	x	Folkcraft 1095
Miserlou	Walk, grapevine	Circle	Greek	x	x	x	Victor 1620
Crested Hen	Step, hop	Threes	Danish		x	x	Victor 6176
Jessie Polka	Two step, polka step	Couples	American		x	x	Folkcraft 1071
Put Your Little Foot	Varsovienne	Couples	American		x	x	Folkcraft 1165
Varsovienne	Varsovienne step	Circle	American			x	Folkcraft 1034
Hot Time	Walk, swing, allemande	Square	American		x	x	Folkcraft 1037
Ten Pretty Girls	Walk	Circle	American		x	x	World of Fun 113
Cotton Eye Joe	Polka	Free	American		x	x	World of Fun 118
Brown Eye Mary	Walk, skip, promenade, allemande	Circle	American		x	x	Folkcraft 1186

Glowworm Mixer (4–5)

Musical Accompaniment
MacGregor 310-B
Windsor 4613–B

Formation: Players form a double circle and all face counterclockwise. Boy on inside circle holding the girl's left hand in his right.

Skills: Walking, running, and do-si-do

Measure

1–4

5–8

9–12

13–16

Action

Promenade counterclockwise with eight walking steps.

Promenade clockwise with eight walking steps.

Pass right shoulders, back-to-back, then step back to place (do-si-do).

Turn to the right, face new partner, and do-si-do with eight running steps.

Little Brown Jug (4–5)

Musical Accompaniment
Columbia 52007
Folkcraft 130-;A
Imperial 1213

Formation: Double circle with partners facing each other, girls on the outside circle. Hands are joined and raised to shoulder height.

Skills: Sliding and swinging

Measure	Action
1–8	Boy touches his left heel to side, then his left toe next to his right foot. Repeat movement. Take four slide steps to the left. Girls start with outside foot and do the same.
9–16	Repeat measures one through eight with four slides to the right.
17–24	Clap own thighs four times, then own hands together four times.
25–32	Partners clap right hands together four times, then left hands together four times.
33–40	Hook right elbows with partner and skip around in a circle with eight skipping steps.
41–56	Repeat clapping sequence of measures 17 to 24 and 25 to 32.
57–64	Hook left elbows and repeat turns.

Hora (4–5)

Musical Accompaniment
Folkcraft 1110
Folk Dancers MH 1052

Formation: Single circle with arms straight and hands on shoulders of dancers on either side

Skills: Side step, step swing

Measures	Action
1. "Right, cross"	Step sideward with the right foot. Step sideward with left foot and place behind the right foot.
2. "Right, swing"	Step sideward with the right foot. Hop on the right foot and swing left foot forward across the front.
3. "Left swing"	Step sideward with the left foot. Hop on the left foot and swing right forward and across the front.

Teaching cues: Moving towards the left.

```
   R      L      R      L      L      R
Right, Cross, Right, Swing, Left, Swing
```

Troika (4–5)

Musical Accompaniment
World of Fun M105
Folkcraft 1170

Formation: Circle of "threes," (one boy in middle of two girls, one girl in middle of two boys, or all boys and all girls) facing counterclockwise

Skills: Running, stamping, and arching

Measure		Action
1–4	Run Forward	Run sixteen steps forward.
5–6	Outside Under	Center and inside partner raise joined hands forming an arch and run in place while the outside dancer, with eight running steps, moves in front of center dancer, under the arch, back around the center dancer to starting position. Center dancer unwinds by turning under the arch.
7–8	Inside Under	Repeat above with inside dancer turning under.
9–12	Circle Left	Sets of three join hands and take twelve running steps ending with three stamps in place.

13–16

As a Mixer:
During the last figure, the center dancer moves forward while the other dancers stamp three times in place.

Repeat twelve running steps to the right, ending in a re-formed line and with three stamps in place.

Oh Susanna (4–5)

Musical Accompaniment
Victor 45–6178
Folkcraft 1186

Formation: Partners standing in a single circle facing center, with hands joined. The girl is on the boy's right side.

Skills: Walking, sliding, do-si-do, promenade

Measure	Call	Action
1–8	Slide to the left and slide to the right.	All take eight sliding steps to the right and eight sliding steps to the left.
9–12	Forward and back.	All take four steps to the center and four steps back.
13–16	Girls forward and back.	Release hands. Girls walk four steps toward the center of the circle and four steps back. Boys stand in place and clap hands.
17–20	Boys forward and back.	Boys go to center while girls clap hands.
21–24		Do-si-do with partners.
25–28		Do-si-do with corner girls.
29–32		Everyone promenades around the circle.

Schottische (4–5)

Musical Accompaniment
MacGregor 4005
Folkcraft 1101
Imperial 1046

Formation: Double circle with partners facing counterclockwise. Boys are on the inside circle and hold partners in an open dance position.

Skills: Schottische step

Measure	Action
1–2	Partners start with outside feet (boy's left, girl's right), run forward three steps, and hop on outside foot and extend inside foot forward.
3–4	Begin with inside foot and repeat action.
5–6	All perform four step-hops in place.

Repeat the first six measures as often as desired or substitute the following variations for measures 5 and 6.

Variation 1: Ladies Turn
Boys take four step-hops in place and girls turn under their arms. On the next turn, reverse movements, with the boys turning under the girls' raised arms.

Variation 2: Both Turn
Partners drop hands and dance four skip-hops in place, turning away from each other (boy turns left, girl turns right) on the first step, and ending in the starting position on the fourth step-hop.

Variation 3: Wring the Dishrag
Partners join hands about waist high and both turn under raised arms and continue around and back to the starting position.

Badger Gavotte (4–5)

Musical Accompaniment
MacGregor 610B
Folkcraft 1094

Formation: Double circle with couples facing counterclockwise. Partners join hands. Girl is on the boy's right side.

Skills: Sliding, two-step, and closed dance position

Measure	Action
1–2	Begin with the outside foot (boy's left, girl's right), walk forward four steps, face partner, join hands, take three sliding steps to the boy's left, and touch the right toe behind the left foot.
3–4	Repeat measures 1 and 2 in the opposite direction.
5–8	Change to a closed dance position and take eight two-steps progressing counterclockwise, with the boys starting with the left foot and the girls with the right foot.
	Repeat dance until music ends.

Grand March (4–6)

Musical Accompaniment
Any marching record

Formation: Boys line up on one side of the room and girls on the other side. All face the foot of the room. The teacher stands in the center of the end line at the head of the room.

Skills: Walking

Call	Action
Come down the center in twos.	March to meet partners at the foot of the room. As the couples meet, they turn, join hands, and march down the center to the head of the room, where the teacher is standing to give directions.
Two right and two left.	The first couple turns to the right, the second to the left, and so on.
Come down the center in fours.	When the two head couples meet at the foot of the room, they hold hands and walk four abreast down the center.
Four right and four left.	When children reach the front of the room, they divide again, with four going to the right and four going to the left, and so on.
Come down the center in eights.	When the lines of four meet at the front of the room, they join hands to form a line of eight abreast. The lines of eight march to the head of the room and halt.

Note:

This process may be reversed, with lines of eight dividing into columns of four. The columns of four march back to the other end of the room, where the two columns merge into one column of fours. The fours divide at the head of the room, and so on, until all are back to the original position of one couple.

Variations

From "Come down the center in fours," separate into twos, then call: "Form arches," or "Over and under."

First couple forms an arch and the second couple tunnels under. Third couple forms an arch and the fourth couple tunnels under. Continue this pattern.

First odd couple arches over the last couple in line and then under the next and so on down to the front of the line.

Sicilian Circle (4–6)

Musical Accompaniment
Windsor A7S4A
Folkcraft 1115, 1242 (with calls)
Methodist 104

Formation: Circle of "sets of four" with couple facing couple. The girl should be on the boy's right side.

Skills: Walking, ladies chain, right and left through

Measure	Call	Action
1–4	Now everybody forward and back.	Join inside hands with partner. Take four steps forward toward the opposite couple and four steps backward to place.
5–8	Circle four hands around.	Join hands and circle left with eight walking steps and finish in original places.
1–4	Ladies chain.	Ladies chain across and back with the two girls changing places. The boy takes the approaching girl's left hand in his left, places his right arm around her waist, and pivots backward to reface the opposite couple.
5–8	Chain the ladies back again.	The girls return to their original positions with the same movement.
1–4	Right and left through.	Right and left with opposite couple, over and back. Walk forward to opposite couple's place, passing right shoulders, then, keeping side by side as though inside hands were joined, turn half around as a couple (man turns backward while lady turns forward), and reface opposite.
5–8	Right and left back.	Repeat the same movement, returning to original place.
1–4	Forward and back.	Forward and back.
5–8	Forward again, pass through.	All walk forward eight steps, passing opposite by right shoulder, to meet new couple. Repeat dance with new couple.

Virginia Reel (4–6)

Musical Accompaniment
Burns, Album J. No. 558
Victor 45–6180
Folkcraft 1249

Formation: Six couples in file formation with partners facing each other. Boys are on the caller's right.

Skills: Walking, skipping, swinging, do-si-do, and cast-off

Measure	Call	Action
1–8	Bow to your partner, go forward and back. Go forward and back again.	Players take three skips forward, curtsey or bow, then skip back. Repeat.
9–12	Now forward again with right hand swing, and all the way back.	Partners hold right hands, turn once around, and then back.
13–16	Now forward again with left hand swing, and all the way back.	Partners join left hands, turn once around, then back.
1–4	Now forward again with a two-hand swing, and all the way back.	Partners join both hands and turn clockwise and back.
5–8	Forward again with a do-si-do.	All partners do a do-si-do.
9–16	The head two sashay down the middle and all the way back to the head of the set.	Head couple joins hands and slides down the center of the set and back.
17–24	Cast off, with boys going left and girls going right.	All face the caller, with the boys' line skipping left and the girls' line skipping right, ending at the foot of the set.
25–32	Form an arch and all pass through.	The head couple meets at the foot of the set, joins hands, and raises them to form an arch. The second couple leads the other couples through the arch and moves to the head of the line to become the new head couple.
		Repeat dance with each new head couple.

Solomon Levi (4–6)

Musical Accompaniment
MacGregor 007–4A (with calls)

Formation: Square of four couples who are numbered counterclockwise. Girl is on the boy's right side.

Skills: Walking, swinging, and allemande left

Measure	Call	Action
1–4	Everyone swing your honey; swing her high and low.	Swing partner.
5–16	Allemande left with left hand, and around the ring you go. A grand old right and left. Walk on your heel and toe and meet your honey, give her a twirl, and around the ring you go. Sing chorus.	Left hand to corner, walk around corner back to partner. Extend right hand to partner, left to next girl, alternating right and left hands until partners meet. Give partner a swing and promenade.
1–8	Oh Solomon Levi, tra la la la la la Oh Solomon Levi, tra la la la la la.	Promenade around set. Repeat dance with couples two, three, and four leading. After couple number four completes its turn, have all four couples separate and repeat dance.

Oh Johnny (4–6)

Musical Accompaniment
MacGregor 652A (with calls)
Folkcraft 1037

Formation: Square dance set with girls on boys' right. All join hands.

Skills: Walking, swinging, allemande left, do-si-do

Measure	Call	Action
1–4	All join hands and circle the ring.	All couples move to the right in walking steps.
5–8	Stop where you are and give your honey a swing.	In closed dance position, swing partners.
9–12	Swing that little gal behind you.	Boy swings girl on his left.
13–16	Now swing your own.	Boy swings girl on his right.
1–4	Allemande left with the corner gal.	Turn to corners, give left hand to corner girl, walk around her, and return to partner.
5–8	Do-si-do your own.	Fold arms and pass right shoulder to right shoulder around partner and back to corner girl, who becomes new partner.
9–16	Now you all promenade with your sweet corner maid, Singing, "Oh, Johnny, oh, Johnny, oh."	Everyone promenade. Repeat dance.

Ace of Diamonds (4–6)

Musical Accompaniment
Folkcraft 1176
Victor 45–6169
Methodist M–102

Formation: Double circle with partners facing

Skills: Walking, and swinging

Measure	Action
1–4	Clap hands once, stamp on left foot, then hook right elbows with three polka or six skipping steps.
5–8	Clap hands once, stamp on right foot, hook left elbows, and repeat swing.
9–12	Partners face each other with hands on hips. Inside dancers start backward with left foot; outside dancers move forward with right foot. Both take four steps.
13–16	Partners reverse directions for four steps.
17–24	Join inside hands, hop on inside foot, and polka counterclockwise around the circle.

Seven Jumps (4–6)

Musical Accompaniment
Victor 45–6172
Methodist M–108

Formation: Single circle with hands joined.

Skills: Step hop

Measure	Action
1–8	Beginning with left foot, take seven step hops, then jump and land with feet together on the eighth beat.
9–16	Face clockwise, start with right foot and take seven step hops, then jump and land on both feet, facing the center.
17–18	Drop hand, place hands on hips and raise right knee high, then stamp foot on floor and join hands.
1–18	Repeat measures 1 to 18; however, do not join hands.
19	Raise left knee, stamp foot, and join hands.
1–19	Repeat measures 1 to 19, but do not join hands.
20	Kneel on right knee, stand and join hands.
1–20	Repeat measures 1 to 20, but do not join hands.
21	Kneel on left knee, stand and join hands.
1–21	Repeat measures 1 to 21, but do not join hands.
22	Place right elbow on floor and cheek on right fist, then stand and join hands.
1–22	Repeat measures 1 to 22, but do not join hands.
23	Place left elbow on floor, and cheek on left fist, then stand and join hands.
1–23	Repeat measures 1 to 23, but do not join hands.
24	Place forehead on floor, stand and join hands.
1–16	Repeat measures 1 to 16.

Norwegian Mountain March (5–6)

Musical Accompaniment
Folkcraft 1177
Victor 45–6173

Formation: Circle in sets of three children, all facing counterclockwise. The "set" is composed of one boy in the center and slightly in front of two side girls. The boy holds the girls' inside hands and the girls join outside hands, forming a triangle.

Skills: Waltzing and turning under

Measure	Call	Action
1–8	Waltz run.	Start on the right foot and take eight running waltz steps (twenty-four steps). All should accent the first step of each measure, and the leader should occasionally glance over his right and left shoulders at his partners.
9–10	Boys under.	Boy moves backward with six running steps under the arch formed by the girls' raised arms.
11–12	Left girl under.	Girl on the boy's left takes six steps to cross in front of and under the boy's raised right arm.
13–14	Right girl turns.	Girl on the boy's right takes six steps to turn under the boy's right arm.
15–16	Boy turns.	Boy turns under his own right arm to original position. Repeat dance.

Heel and Toe Polka (5–6)

Musical Accompaniment
Burns, Evans, and Wheeler
Album 2, No. 225
Folkcraft 1166
MacGregor 400B

Formation: Double circle, with partners facing counterclockwise. Open dance position with girl on boy's right side.

Skills: Polka step

Measure	Call	Action
1–2	Heel and toe.	Partners touch outside heels forward and bend backward slightly. Touch toes of outside feet backward, bend forward slightly, and take three running steps forward. (Heel and toe, and step, step, step.)
3–4	Heel and toe.	Repeat 1–2 with inside foot.
5–8	Heel and toe.	Repeat measures 1–4.
9–16		Partners face each other, the boy places his hands at the girl's waist and the girl places her hands on the boy's shoulders. All polka around the circle in a counterclockwise direction.

Oklahoma Mixer (5–6)

Musical Accompaniment
Folkcraft 1035
Methodist World of Fun 102
MacGregor 400

Formation: Double circle of couples, with girl on boy's right. Take the Varsovienne position, with the left foot free.

Skills: Walking, heel-toe, and two-step

Measure	Action
1–2	Begin with the left foot and take two, two-steps.
3–4	Begin with the left foot and take four walking steps forward.
5–8	Repeat measures 1–4.
9–12	Place the left heel forward and to the left, then the left toe opposite the right foot. Hold left hand, release right. Girls walk to the center of the circle in front of the boys as the boys move to the outside of the circle. The girls finish facing clockwise; the boys, counterclockwise.
13–16	The boy does a right heel and toe and takes three steps in place. The girl does a right heel and toe and walks to the boy behind.

Repeat dance with new partner. |

Rye Waltz (5–6)

Musical Accompaniment
Folkcraft 1103
Imperial 1044

Formation: Double circle with boys in the center facing girls. Partners take an open dance position.

Skills: Sliding and waltz step

Measure	Action
1–4	Boys extend left toe to the side and return to inside of right foot. Repeat point and close. Girls perform the same movement with the right foot. Girls take three slide steps to the boys' left and touch right toe behind left foot.
5–8	Repeat in opposite direction.
9–16	Waltz around the room, with boys using their right shoulders to lead.

Red River Valley (5–6)

Musical Accompaniment
Imperial 1096
MacGregor Album 8 (with calls)
Folkcraft 1056

Formation: Square of four couples, who are numbered counterclockwise. Girl is on the boy's right.

Skills: Walking, swinging, and do-si-do

Measure	Call	Action
1–4	All join hands in the valley.	Everyone joins hands.
5–8	And circle to the left and to the right.	With joined hands, walk four steps left and back four steps to the right.
1–4	And you swing the girl in the valley.	Boys swing corner girls (girl on the boy's left).
5–8	Now swing that Red River Gal.	Boys return to their own partners and swing them.
1–4	Now you lead right down the valley.	Number one and number three couples walk to couples on their right and join hands in a circle.
5–8	And you circle to the left, then to the right.	Walk four steps to the left and back four steps to the right.
9–12	Two ladies star in the valley.	Girls star with right hands (join right hands) in the center of the set and walk once around clockwise.
13–16	Now swing with the Red River Gal.	Boys swing partners.
1–4	Same couples to the left down the valley.	Couples number one and three walk to their left and join hands with new couples.
5–8	And you circle to the left and to the right.	Walk four steps to the left and back four steps to the right.
9–12	Now two gents star in the valley.	Boys star with their right hands and turn once around clockwise.
13–16	And you swing that Red River Gal.	Everyone swings with his partner. Repeat entire dance with two side couples taking the active part. Instead of a star, do-si-do the second time, elbow swing the third, etc.

Tinikling (5–6)

Tinikling is a very exciting Philippine folk dance depicting the movements of the long-legged, long-necked tinikling bird, which is similar in appearance to the crane, heron, and flamingo. In the tinikling dance the "bird" moves around two persons who sit on the floor and manipulate two nine-foot-long bamboo poles in an attempt to trap the bird's legs. The poles are placed about two feet apart on two blocks of wood.* The players holding the bamboo poles slide them across the boards and strike them together on count one. On counts two and three, they lift the poles about an inch off the boards, open them about one foot apart and tap them twice against the boards. The musical accompaniment is a 3/4 waltz meter with a distinct "strike, tap, tap" rhythm throughout the dance.

Figure 29.8

*Bamboo poles or 1- to 1½-inch wooden dowels can be used. Standard two-by-four lumber can be used for the blocks.

Tinikling Steps

Several basic tinikling steps can be performed individually or in combination. Once children learn to perform the following stepping movements, they soon will develop combinations and routines. (See end of chapter for suggested records and films.)

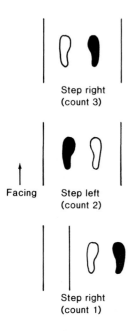

Step right
(count 3)

Facing   Step left
             (count 2)

Step right
(count 1)

Basic Step

Two dancers begin in a standing position, facing each other on opposite sides of the poles. Each dancer's left side is closest to his pole. With the 3/4 rhythm, one step is performed outside the poles as they are hit together and two steps inside the poles as they are tapped twice on the blocks. The rhythm pattern is step right, (outside poles); step left, (inside poles); step right, (inside poles).

After the basic side step is learned, the following variations can be attempted.

Straddle Step

The dancer performs two jumps with feet together inside the poles and a straddle jump when the poles are brought together (fig. 29.9). The rhythm pattern is out-in-in, out-in-in, etc.

Forward and Back

The dancer stands facing the poles. The movement consists of a step forward with the right foot inside the poles, followed by a step forward on the left foot. As the poles are brought together, the dancer takes a step forward on the left foot to the opposite side. The pattern is reversed on the next measure, with a step back on the right foot, a step back on the left foot, and a step back to the original position on the right foot.

Figure 29.9   Straddle Jump

Figure 29.10   Forward and Back

When the class has learned the basic steps and pole movements, the poles can be arranged in a variety of patterns to allow the children to move in different directions. A few examples are shown in the accompanying diagrams.

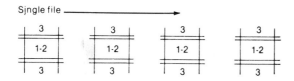

Single file

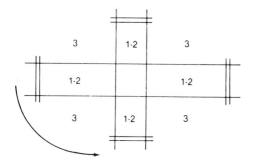

Crossed formation

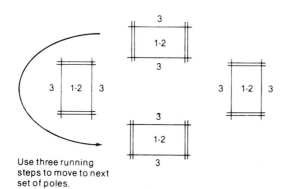

Square formation

Use three running steps to move to next set of poles.

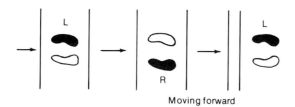

Moving forward

Resource Information

1. *Suggested Records*
   a. "Special Folk Dances" ("Tinikling," Carinosa, Czardas, Vengorka and Tarantella in 3/4 meter), RCA Victor, EPA–4126
   b. "Alley Cat," ATCA 45–6226
   c. "No Matter What Shape," Liberty Records, 55836
2. *Film*
   Tinikling—the Bamboo Dance (16 mm), Martin Moyer Productions, 900 Federal Avenue East, Seattle, Washington

Glossary of Terms

The following words and phrases occur frequently in folk and square dances for children in the intermediate grades.

Active couple(s)
The couple(s) designated to start a dance or to whom a part of the dance is addressed.

Advance
To move forward, usually with walking steps.

Allemande left
Form a circle or square formation with all dancers facing the center, the boy joins his left hand with the girl on his left and walks around counterclockwise and back to his starting position.

Allemande right
Same as allemande left but toward the opposite direction.

Arch
Two dancers join inside hands and raise arms to form an arch.

Balance
In square dancing the usual movement following a "swing your partner." Partners face each other, join right hands, and step back with weight on the left foot and the right heel touching in front. Both partners may also bow slightly.

Bow and curtsey
The bow, performed by the boys, may be a simple nod of the head or an elaborate and pronounced deep bend of the trunk. The curtsey, performed by the girls, may be a simple nod of the head or an elaborate and pronounced deep bend of the knees and a graceful sideward extension of the dancing costume.

Break
Release hands.

Chain (ladies chain)
In square dancing, the girls move across to the opposite couple, extending their right hands to each other as they pass, then their left hands to the opposite boy. The boy places his right hand behind the girl's back, grasping her right hand, and turns her one full turn counterclockwise.

Clockwise
Moving in the same direction as the hands of a clock.

Corner
When facing the center, the boy's corner is the girl on his left and the girl's corner is the boy on her right.

Counterclockwise
Moving in the opposite direction as the hands of a clock.

Divide or split the ring
Active couples pass through the opposite couples.

Do-si-do
These words mean ''back to back'' and usually involve two persons who are facing each other. The two dancers walk forward, pass right shoulders and without turning move to the right, passing back to back, and then walk backward to the starting position.

Forward and back
This figure involves dancers facing each other. Both sides advance four steps forward (or three steps and a bow) and take four steps backward.

Grand right and left
This is a weaving pattern and usually follows an allemande left. Face partner and join right hands, pass and give left hand to the next dancer, and continue weaving around set.

Head couple
In square dancing, the couple nearest the music or caller.

Home
The starting place at the beginning of a dance.

Honor
Salute or bow to partner or other dancers.

Opposite
The person or couple directly across the square.

Promenade
This is the skater's position in which partners stand side by side and face the same direction. The girl stands on the boy's right. Partners join left hands about waist high, then join right hands above the left arms.

Sashay
The American term for the French term ''chasse.'' These are sliding steps sideward.

Separate
Partners leave each other and move in opposite directions.

Square
Four couples, with each forming one side of a square.

Star or wheel
Two or more dancers join right hands in the center of the set and walk forward or backward as directed.

Swing
This is a rhythmic rotation of a couple with a walking step, buzz step, two-step, or skip. The swing may be a one-hand, two-hand, elbow, or waist swing.

Varsovienne position
The boy stands slightly behind and to the left of his partner. While both are facing the same direction, the girl raises both hands to about shoulder height and the boy joins his right hand with the girl's right hand and his left hand with the girl's left hand.

30 Creative Dance Activities

The Body
Lesson Plans

Stimuli
Additional Suggestions
Additional Resource Material

Sound Accompaniment
Teacher's Voice
Percussion Instruments
Recorded Music
"Classmade" Instruments

Creativity, according to Jack Wiener (1969), cannot exist in the abstract, and neither can creative teaching. As teachers, we want children to be able to feel and express their ideas through movement; we want them to be creative. However, no child can be imaginative or creative without a vocabulary of words, concepts, and ideas. Nor can a child express a creative movement without a vocabulary of movement skills and an awareness of various forms of internal and external stimuli.

Our task in enhancing the child's creative process is twofold. First, we must recognize the level of cognitive and motor development of the age group we are teaching. Primary children, for example, have a limited vocabulary and capacity for abstract thinking. Their world of ideas is still very small; they normally demonstrate "being like" or "imitation of" in their first attempts at creative movements. But boys and girls in the intermediate grades have acquired a rich vocabulary, as well as an interest in exploring abstract ideas and the capacity to carry out these ideas. Their movement vocabulary has also expanded far beyond the basic locomotor skills to personal reservoirs of numerous complex movement skills and motor patterns.

Our second task in enhancing the creative process is developing an approach or format that can be used to encourage each child to develop his own creative ideas and to express them through movement. This chapter provides such an approach. It begins with a discussion of the movements of the body using Laban's movement classification system. Lesson plans are provided for illustrating how creative movements can be built from movements of the body, the efforts or qualities of movement, the space and directional patterns of each dance movement, and the relationship of dancers to each other. The latter two sections of this chapter discuss the various types of stimuli and sound accompaniment essential to the development of creativity.

The elements of creative dance can be grouped under three broad headings. Perhaps the most important is the body itself—what it is capable of doing, how it moves, and its relationship to other objects or performers. These are the body's essential tools for creative movement. They are similar to the manipulative skills of a painter, the vocabulary of a poet, and the vocal control of an opera singer. The second element of creative dance is the individual's reaction to a stimulus. The stimulus may be internal, such as a feeling, or it may be external, communicated to the child's mind through his senses. It may be a picture, sound, or story that stimulates the thinking process to produce movement. Sound, however, is a stimulus in a broader sense; it acts almost like a third element of creative dance. For example, sound, in the form of voice, percussion, or other musical accompaniment, enhances the creative process, when a child with a movement vocabulary is stimulated by a poem or picture to express his reaction.

The Body

Movements of the body have been classified in dance in a variety of ways. Folk dance, for example, has a series of stylized or standardized steps, such as the schottische, polka, and waltz step. Similarly, ballet and modern dance have unique vocabularies. Only Laban's system of analyzing all movement is comprehensive enough to cover all body movements. His movement classification was used in previous chapters and is used in this chapter as a basic system to describe the movements of the body and as a format for teaching creative dance.

All movements performed by a child can be analyzed according to the specific body parts that are involved (body awareness), the effort of the movement (qualities), the space (space awareness) within which a movement takes place, and the relationship of the body to equipment or other performers. This is illustrated in table 30.1. In gymnastics, as described in chapters 25, 26, and 27, all movements can be taught according to this classification system. However, since the emphasis in gymnastics is primarily directed toward the efficiency and utility of movement, descriptive terminology such as *swirl, hasty,* and *retreating* are not used. In creative dance the emphasis of movement is directed toward self-expression that is demonstrated through movement. This necessitates the use of additional expressive words that can explain and stimulate creative movements. Several new descriptive words are included under each of four broad headings and can be used within each creative dance lesson to clarify and stimulate creative movements.

Figure 30.1

The four elements of movement used to teach creative dance are body awareness, qualities, space awareness, and relationships. In the accompanying paragraphs, additional expressive words are listed under each element. When these words are expressively stated by the teacher and accompanied by other creative movements or gestures, she can effectively and enjoyably create new modes, feelings, and exciting expressive movements by each child within her charge.

Lesson Plans

A lesson plan should be considered a flexible guideline that can be modified to meet many factors. The experienced classroom teacher with an extensive background in teaching creative dance can structure an environment that produces maximum creative responses from each child. This is a rare talent not possessed by many teachers. Consequently, some basic lesson structure should be followed when beginning to teach creative dance using Laban's basic elements; a suggested format follows.

Suggested Lesson Structure

Main Emphasis One aspect of the main elements of movement—body movements, effort, space, or relationships—should be chosen as the *main theme* of the lesson. In addition to the main theme, one or more subsidiary themes should be selected from the other three elements.

Part 1: Introductory Activity During this portion of the lesson, stress vigorous body activity that relates to the main theme or subthemes. This part of the lesson is identical to the lesson format suggested in chapters 25, 26, and 27.

Table 30.1 Expressive Words for Developing Creative Movements

Body Awareness (What the Body Can Do)

Shapes	**Additional Expressive Words**
Curl	Bend, ball-like, round, circular
Stretch	Straight, arrowlike, gigantic
Twist	Knarled, knotted, screwed, crooked

Balance

Balance	Standing, sitting, kneeling, lying, holding, stable, solid, steady, stick, anchor, settle

Transfer of Weight

Traveling Actions—Using Locomotor Skills

Walk	Stamp, creep, waddle, totter
Run	Dash, dart, flee, scurry
Hop	Spring
Jump	Bounce, spring
Skip	Skate, romp, frolic
Slide	Shift, glide, slip, skid, slither
Gallop	Stamp, prance
Leap	Spring, lunge, soar, fly, spring, vaulting, hurdling

Traveling Actions—
Using Different Parts of the Body

Roll	Tumbling, revolving, gyrating, bowling
Crawl	Creep, swim, streak
Slide	Slither, slipping
Stop	Freeze, pause, anchor, hold, settle
Turn	Spin, whip, swivel, pivot, swirl, twist, twirl, whirl
Rise	Float, pop, lift, ascent, evaporate
Sink	Melt, flop, drop, collapse, squash, settle, lower, plunk
Expand	Grow, blossom, reach, open, inflate, swell, spread, explode
Contract	Shrink, shrivel, close, curl
Vibrate	Shake, quiver, tremble, wobble, shudder, wiggle
Strike	Stamp, punch, pound, kick, hammer, splatter, batter, flick, jerk, slash, chop, slap, poke, jab

Qualities (How the Body Can Move)

Speed	**Additional Expressive Words**
Quick	Sudden, hasty, hurried, swift, presto
Slow	Sustained, prolonged, leisurely, unhurried, poky, snaillike, crawl, dawdling, linger, mosey, plod

Force

Strong	Firm, gripped, sturdy, stoutness, heavy, stomping
Light	Fine, delicate, buoyant, feather, fluff, fly, float, tiptoe, drifting

Flow

Free	Gliding, flying, slithering, moving, traveling, sailing
Bound	Static, jerky, darting, twitching

Space Awareness (Where the Body Can Move)

Space	**Additional Expressive Words**
Personal	Limited, near, cramped, close, cosy, little, puny
General	Open, far, everywhere

Direction

Forward	Advancing, straight
Backward	Retreat, recoil, rebound, flinch, shrink, cringe
Sideward	Right, left, beside, abreast
Diagonal	Cornerwise, across
Upwards	Ascending, rising, climbing, skyward, uphill
Downward	Descent, dropping, falling, sinking, lowering, declining, slumping

Levels

High	Top
Medium	Middle
Low	Bottom, deep

Relationships (What the Body Relates With)

With People	**Additional Expressive Words**
Individuals, partner, or groups	Near, away from, meeting, parting, mirroring, contrasting, following, leading, reacting, together, apart, above, below, independent, friendly, aggressive, fearful, happy, sad, copying

With Objects

Near to, away from, over, under, adjacent

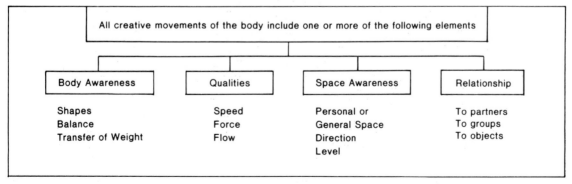

Additional Expressive Words

Part 2: Theme Development This part of the lesson should be devoted to developing the main theme by stimulating the child to explore, discover, and select movements relating to it.

Part 3: Final Activity In this part of the lesson, the child or group of children should develop a sequence of movements from the previous part of the lesson. The sequence may stand alone or develop into a creative dance through the addition of music. The central theme should be emphasized and the subtheme should play a lesser role.

A teacher cannot anticipate the success of any creative dance lesson. If the class has not had experience in this type of activity and if the classroom teacher is also trying this type of lesson for the first time, each lesson at first will appear to be isolated. Gradually, however, as children build a repertoire of movements and learn to think and move in creative patterns, each lesson will appear to be too short. The teacher, too, will develop greater powers of observation and more effective uses of her voice, percussion instruments, and all other forms of musical accompaniment. The consequence will likely be a central theme beginning with the first lesson and carried throughout the second, third, and subsequent lessons. When this occurs, the format will emphasize the latter portion of the lesson to allow the children maximum freedom for creating, refining, and expressing their feelings and ideas through their own creative dance movements.

The following sample lessons should be seen as a starting point, not something that should be duplicated each lesson.

Primary Program

One of the most difficult tasks for a primary teacher is choosing the appropriate main themes. There is no standard format for introducing these themes. It depends upon the capabilities of the teacher and the potential creative abilities of her class. The length of time within a lesson or for several lessons that a theme or subtheme is stressed will depend upon the success and interest of the class. The following sample lesson may assist the teacher in planning her first few lessons. Several themes appropriate for primary children are suggested at the end of the lesson.

Sample Lesson (Grades 1–2)
Main Theme Locomotor skills—running and walking
Subtheme Change of direction
Music Bowmar, B1 507 "Rhythm is Fun," Side 1

Part 1: Introductory Activity Begin with the children sitting down near the record player. Explain that when you play the music, they should try to run with "light feet" in any direction and without touching anyone.

When the music stops, they should stop and listen to you. Use the expression "Off you go" or a similar informal phrase.

Observe: Are they moving in different directions or simply in a circular fashion around the gymnasium? Are they moving lightly or very heavily on their feet? Are they bumping into each other?

After a few minutes stop the music and say in a normal conversation voice, "Some moved very softly and used all the space. Let's try it again and this time see if you can run lightly and move into all the open spaces. Off you go." Allow time for the children to practice, then stop the music and gather them around the record player.

Part 2: Theme Development Explain to the children that this time, without music, they are to see if they can walk very lightly and change directions as they walk. "Off you go." As they are walking in various directions, stimulate awareness and change of direction by saying, "Can you move sideways, backward, forward, and turn?"

Observe: Lightness on feet, change of direction, patterns being established.

After a few moments stop the children and then pose the following challenges: "See if you can make up your own *movement sentence* or sequence that has three different ways of moving—a walk or run and a turn. You may put these movements together any way you like. Ready, away you go."

Observe: Different patterns.

Help any child who does not understand.

Wait a few moments, then stop the children and tell them to watch one or two children demonstrate their sequences. Select one or two for demonstration, emphasizing variety. Praise any child who has performed for the class. Now tell the whole class to practice the sequences again, but this time to music. Play music and observe.

Part 3: Final Activity Arrange children in partners. Have each child teach the other his sequence. See if they can perform it together, side by side. If the children work together successfully, ask them to make up a new sequence they can do side by side or with one following the other. Allow them a few minutes to plan and practice; then, without telling them, simply turn on the music and observe.

Before the end of the lesson, praise the class and point out the main aspects of the lesson—lightness, change of direction, and sequence. This will help the children build a movement vocabulary.

Suggested Themes The following themes are appropriate for primary children. Recognize that the same theme can be presented to grades one to three by varying the words. More sophisticated movements and a more sustained interest in the theme are expected as the children progress through grades two and three.

1. Traveling: All types of locomotor movements—walking, running, and jumping. Begin using descriptive words such as *swirling, creeping,* and *bouncing.*

2. Shapes: Total body shapes—curled, stretched, and twisted. Use the descriptive words shown in table 30.1.

3. Parts of body: Develop themes in which parts of the body are used as a dance form—the hands (clapping, following, shaping), feet (moving, stamping, lightness, and patterns of movement).

4. Effort: Introduce the main differences between strong and light, quick and slow, and static or free-flowing movements.

5. Space: Stress use of all space, moving with awareness of self and others. Simple directions—right and left, forward and backward.

6. Relationships: All creative dance should show a relationship of the individual to others or to objects. Begin with relationships of the individual to the whole group, then to another individual, and then from group to group.

Intermediate Program

Several fundamental considerations must be made when introducing creative dance activities to intermediate children. The vast majority of children in these grades have not been exposed to creative dance. Consequently, they are usually inhibited and negative toward this type of activity. However, on the positive side, their vocabulary is extensive. They know the meaning of and shades of difference between such words as *delicate, fluent,* and *angular.* And they can concentrate longer on a subject. Finally, their ability to produce shapes, sequences, and group dances is far beyond that of primary children. These factors indicate that the initial creative dance lessons for "beginners" should start with structure and gradually move to more indirect forms as the children demonstrate their ability and interest in pursuing more creative challenges.

The following lesson plan is designed for intermediate children with limited experience in creative dance. Additional lesson themes are provided at the conclusion of the lesson.

Sample Lesson (Grades 4–5)

Main Theme Body actions—running and body shapes
Subtheme Effort—quick and slow and strong and light
Music Drum

Part 1: Introductory Activity Ask the class to find a space on the floor and sit down. Stress good scatter formation. When they are seated, tell them that when you beat the drum, they are to run quickly around the room. When the drum stops, they should stop and listen for the next challenge. Without telling the children what to do simply say, "Let's repeat." Then begin varying the speed of your drumbeats and the length of the phrases.

Observe: Are they capable of moving about the room without colliding? Can they vary their speed according to the variations in speed and phrases?

Repeat, the running challenge. However, when the drum stops, ask them to assume a very low position. Repeat, and each time require a new position, such as high, stretched, V-shaped, twisted, and so on. Repeat the running challenge, but ask them to jump in the air as high as they can at any time while the drum is beating. Tell them to touch the floor with the fingertips of both hands when they land. This ensures good control of landing.

Observe: Height of jumps and control on landing. Notice if any child naturally performs a different type of movement while in the air (twisted, curled, or wide shape).

Following this, have the children find a new space on the floor, sit down, and wait for the next part of the lesson.

Part 2: Theme Development Ask the children to get into low ball-shape positions.

Without drum: When you give the signal, they begin to rise slowly, ending in some form of stretched position, pointing upward, backward, or sideward. Repeat, but this time rise as fast as possible.

With drum: Tell them to rise toward any shape they desire while you beat the drum with a slow, even beat. When you change the beat to a faster tempo, they begin collapsing to their standing position. Repeat several times.

With drum: Have children rise, turning in a spirallike fashion as you beat a slow, steady pulse.

Observe and comment: Look for good movements and select one or two children to demonstrate. The children may be shy initially, particularly if they are experiencing this type of dance lesson for the first time.

Without drum: Repeat similar movements; however, this time ask children to begin in the original position and lift a heavy object as high as possible in an upward and spirallike fashion. Stress slowness and the strength or force that must be exerted.

Part 3: Final Activity Up to this point all movements have been performed as an answer to one or more challenges and with or without a drum. No attempt has been made to build up a sequence of movements involving various elements, or with a partner or group. The central theme was taken from body actions emphasizing running and body shapes, with subthemes emphasizing strong, light, quick, and slow movements.

Without drum: Review the elements you have stressed in the lesson, pointing out running, leaping, shapes, quick–slow, and strong–light. Ask the children to develop a series of movements that includes (1) a run, (2) a twisted shape, and (3) quick and slow movements. By providing the initial structure, each child, regardless of his inhibitions or "free spirit," has something in common with the class to explore. Allow time to practice.

Observe: While the class is practicing, see how many are working out a sequence with the elements suggested. If the challenge is too difficult, inject more verbal direction, such as, "All right, let's all begin with a run, then a leap, and land on four parts of the body. . . . See if you can continue building your sequence from here."

After the children have had time to practice, have them find a partner to demonstrate their sequences. Allow them time to share their sequences, then suggest they work together and develop a new matching sequence. Tell them that they may include and arrange their movements as they wish.

General Comment

If the class seems to be at ease and enjoying the lesson, have one or two partners demonstrate to the class. Also, experiment with other musical accompaniments, such as a popular song or other available records.

Depending upon the class's reaction, and your own background, plan the next lesson to include a brief review of this lesson and then go on to more challenging questions, always including some form of partner activity. Gradually move toward sequences and dances performed by small groups of three, four, or five children.

Suggested Themes

Several themes suggested for primary children may also be appropriate for intermediate children. In addition, the following themes are appropriate for grades four through six.

1. *Traveling:* Combining all forms of locomotor movements, with stress on control, and change of pace, direction, and movements.
2. *Body Actions:* Use of individual parts as well as the whole body in leading, matching, contrasting, and showing relationships in abstract and concrete ways.
3. *Effort:* Stress the combination of force, speed, and flow as well as the shades of difference between strong and light or quick and slow.

Figure 30.2

Stimuli

The previous section provided one way of approaching the teaching of creative dance. An imaginative creative dance program can also be developed using Laban's basic elements of body movements, body effort, space, and relationships. These aspects of movement are the paints of the painter or the notes of the musician. How body movements are joined together by the individual, partners, or groups should result both from the teacher's guidance and the children's creativity. Creative movements can be further enhanced by the effective use of a wide variety of meaningful stimuli, such as objects, stories, and paintings. Whatever external stimulus a teacher uses should be within the bounds of the children's understanding and potentially rich in numerous forms of expression. The examples in table 30.2 have proved appropriate for elementary school children. The sample lesson also illustrates how a teacher can approach the class and build several creative dance lessons from one central idea.

Primary Program
Sample Lesson (Grades 2–3)
Lesson Clouds and nature
Basic Theme Interpretive movements
Formation Multiple (scattered, line, and circle)

The purpose of this lesson is to stimulate light and heavy movements, with emphasis on the quality rather than the direction of the response. A short discussion should precede this lesson to familiarize children with new words and concepts of clouds as part of nature. This can be done through class discussion or stories and poems about clouds.

Table 30.2 Stimuli for Creative Movements

Stimuli	Grade Level						
	K	1	2	3	4	5	6
Balloons	X	X	X				
Fairy tales	X	X	X	X			
Animals	X	X	X	X	X		
Pictures	X	X	X	X			
Witches	X	X	X	X			
Fire			X	X	X	X	X
Weather (snow, wind, etc.)	X	X	X	X	X	X	X
Trees and plants	X	X	X	X	X	X	X
Stories and poems	X	X	X	X	X	X	X
Journeys	X	X	X	X	X	X	X
Marionettes	X	X	X	X	X	X	X
Mechanical objects (robots)	X	X	X	X	X	X	X
Rubber Bands	X	X	X	X	X	X	X
Clay	X	X	X	X	X	X	X
Wire	X	X	X	X	X	X	X
Sports	X	X	X	X	X	X	X
Astronauts	X	X	X	X	X	X	X

Suggested Teaching Procedure

1. Movement introduction

   Have children sit in a scattered formation on the floor. The following questions and discussion will provide the stimulus for the interpretive movements.
   a. Think of coming to school on a nice warm day when the sky is filled with pretty white clouds. What do the clouds look like?
   b. If you could touch a cloud, what do you think it would feel like?
   c. If you were a big cloud, what would you do on a nice warm day?

2. Interpretive movements
   a. Let's all move about the room as if we were clouds in the sky.
   b. To indicate light movements: "Can you run very lightly on your tiptoes?"
   c. What else is soft and light and makes you feel like moving as you did?
      Introduce musical accompaniment: tambourine, triangle, or song bells.
   d. Can you move your arms and your whole body very softly and lightly while I play the triangle? (Vary the speed but always keep the intensity very soft.)
   e. Seated in scattered formation: We have talked about light and soft things and moved so we felt that way. What is very different from softness?

f. What can you think of that is just the opposite of soft, fluffy clouds?
g. Move around the room again, but this time we will be heavy and hard. (Use drum or blocks for accompaniment.)

Possible Responses from Children

1. Movement introduction

   The responses you get to your questions will be tangible objects that are familiar to this age group.
   a. Mashed potatoes, cotton candy, or cotton balls.
   b. Soft and fluffy like whipped cream or daddy's shaving cream.
   c. Sleep, fly around and look at everyone, ride with the wind.

2. Interpretive movement
   a. Running, romping, moving on tiptoes, or heavy pronounced steps.
   b. Running lightly, swinging or swaying, and so on.
   c. Kitten, bunny, feathers.
   d. Children may remain in the same spot or shift about the room with light, expressive movements.
   e. Stones, big and fat, heavy, rough.
   f. Giants, elephants, sledgehammer.
   g. Heavy pounding with feet and clenched fists, dragging arms to imitate elephant walk.

Additional Suggestions

Reorganize the class into partners or small groups and pose questions that require a group effort to express the movement. For example, ask partners to interpret two thunderclouds moving toward each other. Continue the lesson, emphasizing soft and heavy movements. For the conclusion, discuss the movements, or play a record and allow the children to interpret the music.

Additional Resource Material

The sample lesson will assist in developing a basic approach to teaching creative or interpretive movements. Numerous other methods and techniques can be used with equal success. Table 30.3 contains possible animal, mechanical, and nature movements that can be used as an additional source of creative movements.

The suggested movements can be performed with the musical accompaniment listed. The records and instrumental accompaniments listed should be considered as illustrative samples. Each teacher, therefore, should develop a similar resource chart and list records that have proved successful in creating various types of creative responses.

Table 30.3 Resources for Developing Creative Movements

	Suggested Types of Movement	Musical Accompaniment	
		Record	*Instrument*
Animal Movements			
Bear	Heavy, slow walk, running, climbing	Childhood Rhy. Series 5, Re. 501, Bears Bowmar, Rhythm Time #1 and 2	Drum (slow) Woodblocks Claves
Camel	Slow, bouncy walk, carrying object	Childhood Rhy. Series 1, Re. 103, Camels Bowmar, Rhythm Time #1 and 2	Drum (uneven)
Elephant	Heavy, slow, rocking walk, lifting object	Childhood Rhy. Series 1, Re. 103, Elephants Bowmar, Rhythm Time #1 and 2	Drum (slow heavy)
Frog	Hopping, jumping, bouncing, bending	Childhood Rhy. Series 5, Re. 501, Frongs	Drum (short, quick)
Worm	Curling, bending, stretching		Scraper
Monkey	Fast crawl, bent-knee jumps		Woodblock
Rabbit	Jumping, bending, running, sniffing	RCA Rhy. Ser. Vol. 2, 45–5007 Harry and Light of Heart	Woodblock
Soldier	Crawling, running, marching	RCA Rhy. Ser. Vol. 2, 45–5007 Soldiers March	Drum Drum rolls
Tall Man–Short Man	Bending and stretching, bent-knee walk, tiptoe walk	Childhood Rhy. Series 2, Re. 201, Fast and Slow	Drum (fast and light, heavy and slow)
Cat	Cautious walking, running, playing, stretching	Cap. 2 Pussy Cat Parade	Woodblock Sticks
Chicken	Choppy, quick walk, scratching, pecking, flapping arms	Rhythm Time ES—102	Woodblock (short, quick)
Raggedy Andy	Loose, floppy walk, swinging, bending	RCA, Dance a Story LE 106	Drum Tambourine
Giant	Slow, heavy walk and run, exaggerated movements	Childhood Rhy. Series 1, Re. 106, Giants	Drum (heavy and slow) Cymbal
Horse	Galloping, prancing (knees high), walking, carrying rider	Childhood Rhy. Series 1 Re. 102, Horse	Woodblock
Butterflies	Light, sustained movements, use of arms, soft runs, and skips	RCA Rhy. Ser. Vol. 2, 45–5005 Waltz	Gong Cymbal
Mechanical Movements			
Bulldozer	Pushing, bending, walking, show effort	Rhythm Productions, Adventures in Rhythm Vol. 1 Young People's Records, 10014	Drum Scrapers
Dump truck	Bending and stretching, lifting, locomotion, show effort	Childhood Rhy. Series 2, Re. 201, Up and Down	Drum
Lumber loader	Bending and stretching, lifting, slow and sustained, show effort	Childhood Rhy. Series 1, Re. 104, Elevators	Drum
Washing machine	Twisting, rolling, bouncing	RCA Rhy. Ser. Vol. 2, 45–5004 March from Nut.	Scraper Drum

Table 30.3 Continued

	Suggested Types of Movement	**Musical Accompaniment**	
		Record	*Instrument*
Ditchdigger	Bend and stretch, push and lift, show effort	Phoebe James Productions, Elementary Rhythms AED 6	Drum
Lawn sprinkler	Twisting, turning, bending, stretching	Childhood Rhy. Series 2, Re. 201, Round and Round	Shakers Maracas
Top	Twisting, turning, running, skipping, walking, falling	Childhood Rhy. Series 1, Re. 104, Top	Scraper Cymbal Gong
Clocks	Locomotion (percussive), swing and sway (stiff)	RCA Rhy. Ser. Vol. 3, Clock	Woodblock
Percolator	Rising and falling, jiggling and bobbing (loose and floppy)	Phoebe James Productions, Elementary Rhythms AED 6	Woodblock (accelerating beat)
Pop-up Toaster	Rising and falling, bending and stretching, hopping, jumping	Childhood Rhy. Series 2, Re. 205, Jumping Jacks	Woodblock Drum
Airplanes	Rising and falling, sustained arm movements with running	Childhood Rhy. Series 1, Re. 104, Airplanes	Drum (vibratory beats)
Typewriter	Walking, hopping, jumping, (short, quick) bending, stretching	Phoebe James Productions, Elementary Rhythms AED 6	Woodblock Triangle Bell

Nature Movements

Wind	Use of arms, turning and smooth run, bending and stretching while running	Let's Play Kagortman Ser. 2 P.J.	Drum Tambourine
Rain	Rising and falling, bending and stretching, shaking	Garden Varieties AED 4	Drum Maracas
Flowers	Bending and stretching, swinging and swaying	Garden Varieties AED 4	Drum Tambourine
Bees	Swinging and swaying, whipping and slashing with arms and trunk	Garden Varieties AED 4	Drum Tambourine
Sun	Rising and falling, bending and stretching, big and small movements	Garden Varieties AED 4	Gong Cymbal
Clouds	Sustained, smooth movements, tiptoe walks and runs, swinging and swaying	Rhythm Time 104	Cymbal Drum
Shadows	Darting walks and runs, bending and stretching, striking and dodging	Rhythm Time 104	Drum Woodblock
Moon	Rising and falling, bending and stretching, sustained locomotion	Rhythm Time 104	Drum
Waves	Rising and falling, skipping, swinging and swaying, dynamic falls	RCA Rhy. Ser. RCA, Dance a Story, L 108 Vol. 2, 45–5006	Drum (loud and soft) Cymbal
Fire	Striking and dodging, jumping, turning, hopping, stretching	Phoebe James Productions, Elementary Rhythms AED 11	Drum (first slow, loud and soft)
Smoke	Rising, turning, swinging, swaying, running, skipping, stretching	Phoebe James Productions, Elementary Rhythms, AED 5	Cymbal Tambourine

Sound Accompaniment

The value of any form of sound accompaniment to a creative movement is judged on how it can further stimulate and enhance a child's imagination and creative movements. Proper selection and application of sound accompaniment is critical to the success of a creative dance program. Some of the more important considerations relating to the teacher's voice, percussion instruments, and other forms of recorded music follow.

Teacher's Voice

All teachers are aware of their voices in the classroom, the activity room, and the gymnasium. In creative dance, however, the manner and tone of a teacher's speaking voice can become an important stimulus in evoking creative movements. Simply speaking softly to children can create slower and lighter movements. Similarly, speaking sharply in a loud voice or drawing out the words will provide sufficient stimulus for another type of movement response. When a teacher adds other characteristics to her voice, such as hissing, clicking, or humming sounds, the mood and action of the dance is directed in a variety of ways. And the reservoir of sounds a young performer is capable of making should be exploited to the fullest, since they provide an equally important stimulus.

Percussion Instruments

Various percussion instruments are very useful in a creative dance program. The drum, tambourine, and cymbals are ideal when teaching children to move in time to the beat and tempo of a musical accompaniment. Perhaps the drum is the most useful to the teacher in the initial stages of teaching creative dance; however, the following percussion instruments are also valuable.

1. Banjo drums
2. Improvised drums—large and small containers such as coffee tins and plastic containers with plastic or cloth covers
3. Tambourine
4. Woodblocks—solid or hollow
5. Rhythm sticks—varying in size from ½-inch by 6 inches to ½-inch by 12 inches
6. Castanets
7. Coconut shells
8. Cymbals
9. Triangle
10. Bells—assorted sizes, individual and on a strip of cloth
11. Shakers—may be made with gravel, beans, or sand

Figure 30.3

Recorded Music

The use of recorded music in any creative dance program needs little elaboration. What a teacher and class select depends upon the availability of records or tapes. It is suggested that teachers write to the record companies listed in appendix A for catalogues and attempt to build up a school record library. In addition, the general availability of tape recorders suggests another inexpensive and flexible way of adding musical accompaniment to the dance program. If tape recorders are used, a format should be established for recording taped music and for classifying and storing school tapes.

"Classmade" Instruments

When a teacher or class make inexpensive equipment, it is normally due to financial reasons. Simply, no money—no equipment! The suggestions that follow are based, to a very minor degree, on available finances and, to a major degree, on the positive effects of making one's own musical instrument.

Getting children interested in creative dance is a difficult task for many classroom teachers. No simple list of teaching suggestions will work for each and every teacher. However, it has been shown that when children make their own musical instruments, a very positive attitude develops, both toward the instruments and toward using them to accompany their creative dance movements.

The instruments shown in figures 30.4 to 30.6 can be made by children from grades two to six. In the process of making their own instruments, children learn to

Figure 30.4

Figure 30.6

use a variety of tools and materials. Each child's instrument must make a sound that is pleasing to himself, to his peers, and to the teacher. The value and enjoyment children receive from creating their own percussion instruments varies from one child to another. Some enjoy making and decorating while others simply like to hear their own musical accompaniment. Whatever the reasons, the "homemade" instruments shown in appendix B are easy and fun to construct and provide a reservoir of enjoyable and useful instruments for every child in the class.

Figure 30.5

Appendixes

A
**Bibliography and
Audiovisual Materials**

B
**Inexpensive
Equipment**

C
**Apparatus, Equipment,
and Supply Companies**

A Bibliography and Audiovisual Materials

The following bibliography and related audiovisual materials are organized according to general subject areas. Specific written references and films may be located under the following headings.

1. Curriculum and Instruction

2. Facilities, Apparatus, and Equipment

3. Basic Mechanics and Motor Learning

4. Health, Posture, and Physical Fitness

5. Integrating Physical Education with Other Subjects

6. Exceptional Children

7. Games and Sports

8. Stunts, Tumbling, and Gymnastic Activities

9. Rhythmics and Dance

10. Movement Education

1. Curriculum and Instruction

Written Material

American Alliance for Health, Physical Education, Recreation and Dance. *Basic Stuff Series.* Reston, Va.: AAHPERD, 1981.
Series 1: Psycho-Social Aspects of Physical Education.
Series 1: Humanities in Physical Education.
Series 2: Early Childhood (ages 3–8).
Series 2: Childhood (ages 9–12).

——. *Curriculum Design: Purposes and Processes in Physical Education Teaching-Learning.* Reston, Va.: AAHPERD, (no published date).

——. *Desirable Athletics Competition for Children of Elementary Age.* Reston, Va.: AAHPERD, 1968.

——. *Echoes of Influence for Elementary School Physical Education.* Reston, Va.: AAHPERD, 1977.

——. *Essentials of a Quality Elementary School Physical Education Program.* Reston, Va.: AAHPERD, 1981.

——. *Guidelines for Children's Sports.* Reston, Va.: AAHPERD, 1979.

——. Personalized Learning in Physical Education. Reston, Va.: AAHPERD, 1976.

——. *Promising Practices in Elementary School Physical Education.* Reston, Va.: AAHPERD, 1969.

Arnheim, D. D., and Pestolesi, R. A. *Elementary Physical Education: A Developmental Approach.* 2d ed. St. Louis: C. V. Mosby Co., 1978.

Arnold, P. J. *Education, Physical Education and Personality Development.* London: Heinemann Educational Books, 1968.

Ashlock, R. B., and Humphrey, J. H. *Teaching Elementary School Mathematics through Motor Learning.* Springfield, Ill.: Charles C Thomas, 1976.

Boyer, M. H. *The Teaching of Elementary School Physical Education.* New York: J. Lowell Pratt and Co., 1965.

Bruner, J. S. *Towards a Theory of Instruction.* Cambridge: Harvard University Press, Belknap Press, 1966.

Bucher, C. A., and Thaxton, N. A. *Physical Education for Children: Movement Foundations and Experiences.* N.Y.: Macmillan Publishing Co., 1979.

Burton, E. C. *The New Physical Education for Elementary School Children.* Boston: Houghton Mifflin Co., 1977.

——. *Physical Activities for the Developing Child.* Springfield, Ill.: Charles C Thomas, 1980.

Canadian Association for Health, Physical Education and Recreation. *New Perspectives for Elementary School Physical Education Programs in Canada.* Ottawa, 1976.

Capon, J. *Successful Movement Challenges: Movement Activities for the Developing Child.* Byron, Calif.: Front Row Experience, 1981.

Clarke, H. H. *Application of Measurement to Health and Physical Education.* 4th ed. Englewood Cliffs, N.J.: Prentice-Hall, 1967.

Cochran, N.; Wilkinson, L. C.; and Furlow, J. J. *A Teacher's Guide to Elementary School Physical Education.* 3d ed. Dubuque, Ia.: Kendall-Hunt, 1976.

Corbin, C. B. *Becoming Physically Educated in the Elementary School.* 2d ed. Philadelphia: Lea and Febiger, 1976.

Cowell, C. B., and Hazelton, H. W. *Curriculum Designs in Physical Education.* Englewood Cliffs, N.J.: Prentice-Hall, 1955.

Dauer, V. P., and Pangrazi, R. P. *Dynamic Physical Education for Elementary School Children.* 7th ed. Minneapolis: Burgess Publishing Co., 1983.

Elliot, M. E.; Anderson, M. H.; and LaBerge, J. *Play with a Purpose.* 3d ed. New York: Harper and Row Publishers, 1978.

Fabricius, H. *Physical Education for the Classroom Teacher.* 2d ed. Dubuque, Ia.: Wm. C. Brown Publishers, 1971.

Fait, H. F. *Experiences in Movement: P.E. for the Elementary Child.* 3d ed. Philadelphia: W. B. Saunders Co., 1976.

Fowler, J. S. *Movement Education.* Philadelphia: Saunders College Publishing, 1981.

Gage, N. L. "Theories of Teaching." *Theories of Learning and Instruction.* 63d Yearbook of the National Society for the Study of Education, Part 1. Edited by E. Hilgard. Chicago: University of Chicago Press, 1964.

Gallahue, D. L. *Developmental Movement Experiences for Children.* New York: John Wiley and Sons, 1982.

——. *Motor Development and Movement Experiences for Young Children (3–7).* New York: John Wiley and Sons, 1976.

——. *Understanding Motor Development in Children.* New York: John Wiley and Sons, 1982.

Graham, G.; Holt/Hale, S. A.; McEwen, T.; and Parker, M. *Children Moving: A Reflective Approach to Teaching Physical Education.* Palo Alto, Calif.: Mayfield Publishing Co., 1980.

Halsey, E., and Porter, L. *Physical Education for Children.* rev. ed. New York: Holt, Rinehart & Winston, 1967.

Harrison, J. M. *Instructional Strategies in Physical Education.* Dubuque, Ia.: Wm. C. Brown Publishers, 1983.

Heitmann, H. M., and Kneer, M. E. *Physical Education Instructional Techniques: An Individualized and Humanistic Approach.* Englewood Cliffs, N.J.: Prentice-Hall, 1976.

Hellison, D. *Beyond Bats and Balls.* Reston, Va.: AAHPERD, 1978.

Hoffman, H. A., Young, J., and Klesius, S. E. *Meaningful Movement for Children: A Developmental Theme Approach to Physical Education.* Rockleigh, N.J.: Allyn and Bacon, 1980.

Humphrey, J. H. *Child Development through Physical Education.* Springfield, Ill.: Charles C Thomas, 1980.

Jackson, J. J., and Turkington, H. D. *Quality Programming,* Vol. I. In H.PED., Victoria, B.C.: University of Victoria, 1981.

———. *Quality Programming,* Vol. II. In H.PED., Victoria, B.C.: University of Victoria, 1981.

Jarvis, O. T., and Rice, M. *An Introduction to Teaching in the Elementary School.* Dubuque, Ia.: Wm. C. Brown Publishers, 1972.

Jarvis, O. T., and Wootton, L. R. *The Transitional Elementary School and Its Curriculum.* Dubuque, Ia.: Wm. C. Brown Publishers, 1966.

Kirkendall, D. R.; Gruber, J. J.; and Johnson, R. E. *Measurement and Evaluation for Physical Education.* Dubuque, Ia.: Wm. C. Brown Publishers, 1980.

Kozman, H. C.; Cassidy, R.; and Jackson, C. O. *Methods in Physical Education.* 4th ed. Dubuque, Ia.: Wm. C. Brown Publishers, 1967.

Lien, A. J. *Measurement and Evaluation of Learning.* Dubuque, Ia.: Wm. C. Brown Publishers, 1967.

Logsdon, B. J., et al. *Physical Education for Children: A Focus on the Teaching Process.* Philadelphia: Lea and Febiger, 1977.

MacKenzie, M. M. *Towards a New Curriculum in Physical Education.* New York: McGraw-Hill Book Co., 1969.

Magill, R. A.; Ash, M. J.; and Smoll, F. L. *Children in Sport.* Champaign, Ill.: Human Kinetics Publishers, 1982.

Means, L. E., and Applequist, H. A. *Dynamic Movement Experiences for Elementary School Children.* Springfield, Ill.: Charles C Thomas, 1974.

Metheny, E. *Movement and Meaning.* New York: McGraw-Hill Book Co., 1968.

Metzger, P. A. *Elementary School Physical Education Readings.* Dubuque, Ia.: Wm. C. Brown Publishers, 1972.

Miller, A. C.; Cheffer, T. F.; and Whitcomb, V. *Physical Education: Teaching Human Movement in the Elementary Schools.* rev. ed. Englewood Cliffs, N.J.: Prentice-Hall, 1974.

Morris, G. S. D. *Elementary Physical Education: Towards Inclusion.* Salt Lake City: Brighton Publishing Co., 1980.

Moston, M. *Teaching Physical Education.* 2d ed. Columbus: Charles E. Merrill Publishing Co., 1981.

National Conference on Physical Education for Children of Elementary School Age. *Physical Education for Children of Elementary School Age.* Chicago: The Athletic Institute, 1951.

Rich, J. M. *Humanistic Foundations in Education.* Worthington, Ohio: Charles A. Jones Publishing Co., 1971.

Schmuck, R. A., and Schmuck, P. A. *A Humanistic Psychology of Education.* Palo Alto, Calif.: National Press Books, 1974.

Schurr, E. L. *Movement Experiences for Children: A Humanistic Approach to Elementary School Physical Education.* 3d ed. Englewood Cliffs, N.J.: Prentice-Hall, 1980.

Siedentop, D. *Physical Education Introductory Analysis.* 2d ed. Dubuque, Ia.: Wm. C. Brown Publishers, 1976.

Singer, R. N. *Teaching Physical Education: A Systems Approach.* Boston: Houghton Mifflin Co., 1974.

Torbert, M. *Follow Me: A Handbook of Movement Activities for Children.* Englewood Cliffs, N.J.: Prentice-Hall, 1980.

Turner, L. F., and Turner, S. L. *Creative Experiences Through Sport.* Palo Alto, Calif.: Peek Publications, 1979.

———. *Elementary Physical Education: More Than Just Games.* Palo Alto, Calif.: Peek Publications, 1976.

Vannier, M., and Gallahue, D. L. *Teaching Physical Education in Elementary Schools.* 6th ed. Philadelphia: W. B. Saunders Co., 1978.

Willgoose, C. E. *Evaluation of Health Education and Physical Education.* New York: McGraw-Hill Book Co., 1967.

———. *The Curriculum in Physical Education.* Englewood Cliffs, N.J.: Prentice-Hall, 1969.

Films

Title: All the Self There Is
Details: 16mm, 13½ minutes, sound, color
Distributor: AAHPERD, c/o NEA Sound Studios, 1201 16th Street, N.W., Washington, D.C. 20036
Description: This film is designed to interpret physical education to teachers, administrators, and parents. It depicts new approaches in physical education and focuses on the importance of sports and activity in developing self-concept and self-confidence.
Purchase Price: $90; rental, $15

Title: Physical Education for Children
Details: 16mm, 21 minutes, sound, color
Distributor: Thomas Howe Associates Ltd., No. 1, 1226 Homer Street, Vancouver, B.C., Canada V6B2Y5
Description: Physical Education for Children is an interpretive film for teachers and the general public. It illustrates how the basic needs and interests of elementary school-age children are translated into a physical education program. The nature and role of intramural activities and programs for exceptional children are also covered in this film.
Purchase Price: $315

Title: Physical Education in Elementary Schools
Details: 16mm, 20 minutes, color
Distributor: Stuart Finley, 3428 Mansfield Road, Falls Church, Virginia
Description: Illustrates physical education from kindergarten through the elementary grades.
Purchase Price: $200

Title: They Grow Up So Fast
Details: 16mm, 28 minutes, sound, color
Distributor: The Athletic Institute
Description: Interprets physical education to the public.
Purchase Price: $135

Title: *Profiles of Elementary Physical Education*
Details: 3 reels, 16mm, 32 minutes, color, and black and white
Distributor: Coronet Films
Description: Stresses successful methods of teaching physical education to elementary school children.
Purchase Price: $360

2. Facilities, Apparatus, and Equipment

Written Material

Aaron D., and Winawer, R. P. *Child's Play.* New York: Harper & Row, 1965.

Aitken, M. H. *Play Environments for Children: Play, Space, Improvised Equipment and Facilities.* Bellingham, Wash.: Educational Designs and Consultants, 1972.

Athletic Institute. *Planning Facilities for Athletics, Physical Education and Recreation.* Washington, D.C.: American Alliance for Health, Physical Education, Recreation and Dance, 1979.

Beckwith, J., and Hewes, J. J. *Build Your Own Playground.* Boston: Houghton Mifflin Co., 1974.

Corbin, C. B. *Inexpensive Equipment for Games, Play, and Physical Activity.* Dubuque, Ia.: Wm. C. Brown Publishers, 1972.

Cowan, J. C.; Torrance, G. D.; and Torrance, P. E. *Creativity: Its Educational Implications.* New York: John Wiley and Sons, 1967.

Daltner, R. *Design for Play.* Toronto: Van Nostrand Reinhold Co., 1969.

Frost, J. L., and Klein, B. L. *Children's Play and Playgrounds.* Boston: Allyn and Bacon, 1979.

Gabrielsen, M. A., and Caswell, M. M. *Sports and Recreation Facilities for School and Community.* Englewood Cliffs, N.J.: Prentice-Hall, 1958.

Hurtwood, A. *Planning for Play.* London: Jarrold and Sons, 1969.

Ledermann, A., and Trachsel, A. *Creative Playgrounds and Recreation Centers.* 2d ed. New York: Praeger Publishers, 1968.

3. Basic Mechanics and Motor Learning

Written Material

Abernathy, R., and Waltz, M. "Towards a Discipline: A First Step." *Quest,* 2 April 1964.

American Alliance for Health, Physical Education, Recreation and Dance. *Basic Stuff Series 1: Kinesiology.* Reston, Va.: AAHPERD, 1981.

———. *Basic Stuff Series 1: Motor Development.* Reston, Va.: AAHPERD, 1981.

Arnold, P. J. *Education, Physical Education and Personality Development.* London: Heinemann Educational Books, 1968.

Barratt, M. et al. *Foundations for Movement.* 2d ed. Dubuque, Iowa: Wm. C. Brown Publishers, 1968.

Broer, M. R. *Efficiency of Human Movement.* 3d ed. Philadelphia: W. B. Saunders, 1973.

Brown, C., and Cassidy, R. *Theory in Physical Education.* Philadelphia: Lea and Febiger, 1963.

Bunn, J. W. *Scientific Principles of Coaching.* Englewood Cliffs, N.J.: Prentice-Hall, 1955.

Corbin, C. B. *A Textbook on Motor Development.* Dubuque, Iowa: Wm. C. Brown Publishers, 1973.

Cratty, B. J. *Movement Behavior and Motor Learning.* 2d ed. Philadelphia: Lea and Febiger, 1967.

Davis, E. C., and Wallis, E. L. *Towards Better Teaching in Physical Education.* Englewood Cliffs, N.J.: Prentice-Hall, 1961.

Day, R. H. *Perception.* Dubuque, Iowa: Wm. C. Brown Publishers, 1966.

Drowatzky, J. N. *Motor Learning: Principles and Practices.* Minneapolis: Burgess Publishing Co., 1975.

Espenschade, A., and Eckhart, H. M. *Motor Development.* Columbus: C. E. Merrill Books, 1967.

Gage, N. L. "Theories of Teaching." *Theories of Learning and Instruction.* 63d Yearbook of the National Society for the Study of Education, Part I. Edited by E. Hilgard. Chicago: University of Chicago Press, 1964.

Gallahue, D. L. *Developmental Movement Experiences for Children.* New York: John Wiley and Sons, 1982.

Johnson, G. B. "Motor Learning." *Science and Exercise of Medicine and Sports.* Edited by W. R. Johnson. New York: Harper & Row, 1960.

Kephart, N. C. *The Slow Learner in the Classroom.* Columbus: C. E. Merrill Books, 1960.

Knapp, B. *Skill in Sport.* London: Routledge and Kegan Paul, 1967.

Laban, R. von, and Lawrence, F. C. *Effort.* London: Macdonald and Evans, 1947.

McClenaghan, B. A., and Gallahue, D. L. *Fundamental Movement: A Developmental and Remedial Approach.* Philadelphia: W. B. Saunders, 1978.

Magill, R. A. *Motor Learning Concepts and Applications.* Dubuque, Ia.: Wm. C. Brown Publishers, 1980.

Northrip, J. W.; Logan, G. A.; and McKinney, W. C. *Analysis of Sport Motion,* 3d ed. Dubuque, Iowa: Wm. C. Brown Publishers, 1983.

Rarick, G. L. *Physical Activity and Human Growth and Development.* New York: Academic Press, 1973.

Robb, M. D. *The Dynamics of Motor Skill Acquisition.* Englewood Cliffs, N.J.: Prentice-Hall, 1972.

Robertson, M. A., and Halverson, L. E. *Developing Children—Their Changing Movement: A Guide for Teachers.* Washington Square, Philadelphia: Lea and Febiger, 1983.

Signer, N. C. *The Psychomotor Domain: Movement Behavior.* Philadelphia: Lea and Febiger, 1972.

Stallings, L. M. *Motor Skills Development and Learning.* Dubuque, Ia.: Wm. C. Brown Publishers, 1973.

Torbert, M. *Secrets to Success in Sport and Play.* Englewood Cliffs, N.J.: Prentice-Hall, 1982.

Turner, L. F., and Turner, S. L. *Elementary Physical Education: More Than Just Games.* Palo Alto, Calif.: 1976.

Wickstrom, R. L. *Fundamental Motor Patterns.* Philadelphia: Lea and Febiger, 1970.

Wissell, J. *Movement Fundamentals.* 2d ed. Englewood Cliffs, N.J.: Prentice-Hall, 1961.

Ziachkowsky, L. D.; Ziachkowsky, L. B.; and Martinek, T. W. *Growth and Development.* St. Louis: C.V. Mosby Co., 1980.

4. Health, Posture, and Physical Fitness

Written Material

Albinson, J. G., and Andrews, G. M. *Child in Sport and Physical Activity.* Baltimore: University Park Press, 1976.

A.M.A. *Heartbook.* AMA National Center, 7320 Greenville Ave., Dallas, Texas 75231.

American Alliance for Health, Physical Education, Recreation and Dance. *Basic Stuff Series 1: Exercise, Physiology.* Reston, Va.: AAHPERD, 1981.

———. *AAHPERD Health Related Physical Fitness Test.* Reston, Va.: AAHPERD, 1980.

———. *AAHPERD Youth Fitness Test Manual.* rev. ed. Reston, Va.: AAHPERD, 1976.

———. *Special Fitness Test Manual for Mildly Mentally Retarded Persons.* Reston, Va.: AAHPERD, 1968.

Carr, W. *Fit for Kids.* Menlo Park, Calif.: Addison-Wesley, 1981.

Kraus, H., and Hirschland, R. P. "Muscular Fitness and Health." *Journal of the American Association for Health, Physical Education and Recreation,* 24 December 1953.

Mott, J. A. *Conditioning and Basic Movement Concepts.* 2d ed. Dubuque, Ia.: Wm. C. Brown Publishers, 1977.

President's Council on Youth Fitness. "Youth Physical Fitness: Suggested Elements of a School-Centered Program." Washington, D.C.: U.S. Government Printing Office, 1961.

Royal Canadian Air Force Exercise Plans for Physical Fitness. rev. U.S. ed. Pocket Books, 1962.

Sorani, R. P. *Circuit Training.* Dubuque, Iowa: Wm. C. Brown Publishers, 1966.

Steen, D. *Aerobic Fun for Kids.* Toronto, Ontario: Fitzhenry and Whiteside, 1982.

Stone, D. B.; O'Reilly, L. B.; and Brown, J. D. *Elementary School Health Education.* 2d ed. Dubuque: Wm. C. Brown Publishers, 1980.

Wallis, E. L., and Logan, G. A. *Figure Movement and Body Conditioning through Exercise.* Englewood Cliffs, N.J.: Prentice-Hall, 1964.

Williams, M. H. *Nutrition for Fitness and Sport.* Dubuque, Ia.: Wm. C. Brown Publishers, 1983.

Films

Title: How Your Heart and Circulatory System Works
Details: 16 mm, 19 minutes, sound, color
Distributor: Thomas Howe Associates, Ltd., 1226 Homer Street, Vancouver, B.C., Canada V6B 2Y9.
Description: This film is designed for upper elementary school children. It describes how the heart and circulation works, explains the function of blood, then describes how to monitor heart rate and blood pressure. The film also illustrates how various factors such as exercise, fear, and excitement affect heart rate. The latter section of the film briefly explains various diseases and disorders of the heart.
Note: An interactive videodisc, covering the same material, is also available through the Faculty of Education, Simon Fraser University, Burnaby, B.C., Canada V5A 1S6.
Purchase Price: $475; rental, $47; video price, $350.

Title: The Time of Our Lives
Details: 16mm, 28 minutes, sound, color
Distributor: Association Films
Description: For family audiences, this film is designed to encourage interest in physical fitness and emphasize relaxation.
Purchase Price: $145, free loan

Title: Vigorous Physical Fitness Activities
Details: 16mm, 13½ minutes, color, and black and white
Distributor: President's Council on Physical Fitness, Washington, D.C.
Description: Shows how to get maximum participation in the physical activity period through proper use of time, equipment, and facilities.
Purchase Price: Color, $55; black and white, $30

Title: Youth Physical Fitness—A Basic School Program
Details: 16mm, 13 minutes, color, and black and white
Distributor: President's Council on Physical Fitness, Washington, D.C.
Description: Overviews an elementary school physical education program and illustrates techniques of physical fitness testing.
Purchase Price: Color, $65; black and white, $30

Title: Youth Physical Fitness, A Report to the Nation
Details: 16mm, 28 minutes, sound, color
Distributor: Equitable Life Assurance, 1285 Avenue of Americas, New York
Description: Demonstrates how school and community groups benefit from a well-rounded physical education program.
Purchase Price: Free loan

Title: Why Exercise?
Details: 16mm, 14 minutes, color
Distributor: Association Films, 3419 Magnolia Boulevard, Burbank, California
Description: Demonstrates types of activities that develop strength, endurance, and flexibility.
Purchase Price: $152; rental, $54.33

5. Integrating Physical Education with Other Subjects

Written Material

Ashlock, R. B., and Humphrey, J. H. *Teaching Elementary School Mathematics through Motor Learning.* Springfield, Ill.: Charles C Thomas, 1976.

Barlin, A., and Barlin, P. *The Art of Learning through Movement.* Los Angeles: Fearson Publishers, 1974.

Blatt, G. T., and Cunningham, J. *It's Your Move: Expressive Movement Activities for the Language Arts Class.* New York: Teacher College Press, 1981.

Cratty, B. J. *Active Learning.* Englewood Cliffs, N.J.: Prentice-Hall, 1971.

———. *Learning about Human Behavior.* Englewood Cliffs, N.J.: Prentice-Hall, 1975.

Dienes, Z. D., *Mathematics through the Senses, Games, Dance and Art.* Atlantic Highlands, N.J.: Humanities Press, 1973.

Doray, M. *J Is for Jumping: Moving into Language Arts.* Belmont, Calif.: Pitman Learning Inc., 1982.

Dorran, M., and Gulland, F. *Telling Stories through Movement.* Los Angeles: Fearson Publishers, 1974.

Gilbert, A. G., *Teaching the Three Rs through Movement Experiences.* Minneapolis, Minn.: Burgess Publishing Co., 1977.

Hall, T. *Academic Ropes.* Byron, Calif.: Front Row Experience, 1981.

Humphrey, J. H. *Education of Children through Motor Activity.* Springfield, Ill.: Charles C Thomas, 1975.

———. *Improving Learning through Compensatory Physical Education.* Springfield, Ill.: Charles C Thomas, 1976.

Werner, P. H., and Burton, E. C. *Learning through Movement: Teaching Cognitive Content through Physical Activities.* St. Louis: C. V. Mosby Co., 1979.

6. Exceptional Children

Written Material

American Alliance for Health, Physical Education, Recreation and Dance. *Annotated Bibliography on Perceptual-Motor Development.* Reston, Va.: AAHPERD, 1973.

———. *Approaches to Perceptual-Motor Experiences.* Reston, Va.: AAHPERD, 1970.

———. *Foundations and Practices in Perceptual-Motor Learning.* Reston, Va.: AAHPERD, 1971.

———. *Guide for Programs in Recreation and Physical Education for the Mentally Retarded.* Reston, Va.: AAHPERD, 1968.

———. *Physical Activities for the Mentally Retarded* Reston, Va.: AAHPERD, 1968.

———. *Questions and Answers About P.L. 94–1142 and Section 504 Update.* Reston, Va.: AAHPERD, 1979.

———. *Special Fitness Test Manual for Mildly Mentally Retarded Persons.* Reston, Va.: AAHPERD, 1976.

Arnheim, D. D.; Auxter, D.; and Crowe, W. C. *Principles and Methods of Adaptive Physical Education and Recreation.* 3d ed. St. Louis: C. V. Mosby Co., 1977.

Capon, J. *Perceptual Motor Lesson Plans, Level I.* Front Row Experience, 564 Central Ave., Alameda, Calif. 94501, 1975.

———. *Perceptual Motor Lesson Plans, Level II.* Front Row Experience, 564 Central Ave., Alameda, Calif. 94501, 1977.

Cipriano, R. E. *Readings in Special Olympics.* Boston: Special Learning Corporation, 42 Boston Rd., Guilford, Conn. 06437, 1980.

Cratty, B. J. *Adapted Physical Education for Handicapped Children and Youth.* Denver: Love Publishing Co., 1980.

———. *Developmental Games for Handicapped Children.* Palo Alto: Peek Publications, 1969.

———. *Motor Activity and the Education of Retardates.* 2d ed. Philadelphia: Lea and Febiger, 1974.

———. *Remedial Motor Activity for Children.* Philadelphia: Lea and Febiger, 1975.

Cratty, B. J., and Martin, M. M. *Perceptual-Motor Efficiency in Children.* Philadelphia: Lea and Febiger, 1969.

Cruikshank, W. M., and Johnson, O. G. *Education of Exceptional Children and Youth.* 3d ed. Englewood Cliffs, N.J.: Prentice-Hall, 1965.

Daniels, A. S., and Davies, E. A. *Adapted Physical Education.* New York: Harper and Row, 1975.

Delacato, C. *The Treatment and Prevention of Reading Problems.* Springfield, Ill.: Charles C Thomas, 1959.

Fait, H. F. *Special Physical Education.* Philadelphia: W. B. Saunders Co., 1966.

Geddes, D. *Physical Activities for Individuals with Handicapping Conditions.* 2d ed. St. Louis, Mo.: C. V. Mosby Co., 1978.

Hackett, L. C. *Movement Exploration and Games for the Mentally Retarded.* Palo Alto, Calif.: Peek Publications, 1970.

I.R.V.C. *Adapted Physical Education Guidelines: Theory and Practice for the Seventies and Eighties.* Reston, Va.: AAHPERD, 1976.

Kephart, N. C. *The Slow Learner in the Classroom.* Columbus: Charles E. Merrill, 1960.

Klappholz, L. *Physical Education for the Physically Handicapped and Mentally Retarded.* New London: Croft Educational Services, 1957.

Kratz, L. E. *Movement without Sight.* Palo Alto, Calif.: Peek Publications, 1977.

Larson, S. C., and Poplin, M. S., *Methods for Educating the Handicapped: An Individualized Education Program Approach.* Boston: Allyn and Bacon, 1973.

Lerch, H. A.; Becker, J. E.; Ward, B. M.; and Nelson, J. A. *Perceptual-Motor Learning Practices.* Palo Alto, Calif.: Peek Publications, 1974.

Logan, G. A. *Adapted Physical Education.* Dubuque, Ia.: Wm. C. Brown Publishers, 1972.

Miller, A. G., and Sullivan, J. V. *Teaching Physical Activities to Impaired Youth.* New York: John Wiley and Sons, 1982.

Price, R. J. *Physical Education and the Physically Handicapped Child.* London: Lepos Books, 1980.

Sherrill, C. *Adapted Physical Education and Recreation.* Dubuque, Ia.: Wm. C. Brown Publishers, 1976.

Smith, P. *Perceptual Motor Test.* Palo Alto, Calif.: Peek Publications, 1973.

Turnbull, A. P., and Schultz, J. R. *Mainstreaming Handicapped Students: A Guide for Classroom Teachers.* Boston: Allyn and Bacon, 1979.

Vannier, M. *Physical Activities for the Handicapped.* Englewood Cliffs, N.J.: Prentice-Hall, 1977.

Watkinson, E. J., and Wall, A. E. *The P.R.E.P. Program: Play Skill Instruction for Mentally Handicapped Children.* Ottawa: CAAHPER, 333 River Road, Ottawa, Ont. K1L 8B9, 1982.

Films

Title: A Child Is a Child
Details: 16 mm, 8 minutes, sound, color
Distributor: Aims Instructional Media Services, Box 1010, Hollywood, Calif. 90028
Description: Stresses that all children have similar needs. Shows how to integrate mentally retarded, blind, and emotionally disturbed children with nonhandicapped children.

Title: And So They Move
Details: 16 mm, 19 minutes, sound, black and white
Distributor: Audio-Visual Center, Michigan State University, East Lansing, Mich. 48824
Description: Describes appropriate activities for mentally retarded and physically handicapped persons.

Title: Just for the Fun of It
Details: 16 mm, 18 minutes, sound, color
Distributor: Educational Media Center, Orange County Dept. of Education, Civic Center Drive, Santa Anna, California.
Description: Illustrates a variety of activities for mentally retarded children.

Title: Those Other Kids
Details: 16 mm, 25 minutes, sound, color
Description: Describes legal developments and basic information about special education programs.

Title: If *Those Were Your Children*
Details: 16 mm, sound, black and white
Distributor: Metropolitan Life Insurance Co., 1 Madison Avenue, New York
Description: A child study with emphasis on the detection of early signs of emotional disturbance in day-to-day behavior patterns.
Purchase Price: Free loan

7. Games and Sports

Written Material

American Alliance for Health, Physical Education, Recreation and Dance. *ICHPER Book of Worldwide Games and Dances.* Reston, Va.: AAHPERD, 1976.

———. *Sports Safety.* Reston, Va.: AAHPERD, 1977.

———. *Sports Safety Monograph Series.* Reston, Va.: AAHPERD, 1978.

———. *Sport Skills Test Manuals.* ("Basketball," "Football," "Softball," and "Volleyball.") Reston, Va.: AAHPERD, 1976.

Avedon, E. M., and Sutton-Smith, B. *The Study of Games.* New York: John Wiley and Sons, 1971.

Blake, O. W. *Lead-Up Games to Team Sports.* Englewood Cliffs, N.J.: Prentice-Hall, 1964.

Boyer, M. H. *The Teaching of Elementary School Physical Education Games and Related Activities.* New York: J. Lowell Pratt & Co., 1965.

Bresnahan, G. W.; Tuttle, W. W.; and Cretzmeyer, F. *Track and Field Athletics.* St. Louis: C. V. Mosby Co., 1960.

Campbell, W. R., and Tucker, N. M. *An Introduction to Tests and Measurements.* London: G. Bell and Sons, 1967.

Cooke, D. C. *Better Basketball for Boys.* New York: Dodd, Mead & Co., 1960.

Coquitlam Park and Recreation Department. *Coquitlam Aquatic Program 1972.* Coquitlam, British Columbia, 1972.

Council for National Cooperation in Aquatics. *Water Fun for Everyone.* New York: Associated Press, 1965.

Delano, A. L. *Field Hockey.* Dubuque, Ia.: Wm. C. Brown Publishers, 1964.

Egstrom, G. H., and Schaafsma, F. *Volleyball.* Dubuque, Ia.: Wm. C. Brown Publishers, 1968.

Fluegleman, A. *More New Games.* New York: Doubleday and Co., Inc., 1981.

———. *The New Games Book.* New York: Doubleday and Co., 1976.

Foreman, K. E., and Husted, V. *Track and Field for Girls and Women.* 2d ed. Dubuque, Ia.: Wm. C. Brown Publishers, 1971.

Gibbon, A., and Cartwright, J. *Teaching Soccer.* London: Bell and Hyman, 1981.

Gomme, A. B. *The Traditional Games of England, Scotland and Ireland.* vol. 2. New York: Dover Publications, 1964.

Hale, P. et al. *Individual Sports: A Textbook for Classroom Teachers.* Dubuque, Ia.: Wm. C. Brown Publishers, 1974.

Kneer, M.; Lipinski, D.; and Walsh, J. *How to Improve your Softball.* Chicago: The Athletic Institute, 1963.

Kneer, M., and McCord, C. L. *Softball.* Dubuque, Ia.: Wm. C. Brown Publishers, 1966.

Lane, E. C.; Obrecht, D.; and Wienke, P. *Track and Field for Elementary School Children and Junior High Girls.* Chicago: The Athletic Institute, 1964.

Lenel, R. M. *Games in the Primary School.* London: University of London Press Ltd., St. Paul's House, Warwick Lane, E.C. 4, 1970.

Magill, R.; Ash, M. V.; and Ash, F. L. *Small Children in Sports: A Contemporary Anthology.* Champaign, Ill.: Human Kinetics Publishers, 1978.

Mauldon, E., and Redfern, H. B. *Games Teaching.* London: Macdonald and Evans Ltd., 8 John Street, W.C.I., 1981.

Mitchell, D. B. K. *Hawaiian Games for Today.* Honolulu: Kamehameha School Press, 1975.

Mitler, K., ed. *Physical Education Activities.* Dubuque, Ia.: Wm. C. Brown Publishers, 1966.

Morris, D. *How to Change the Games Children Play.* Minneapolis: Burgess Publishing Co., 1976.

National Collegiate Athletic Association. *Official N.C.A.A. Soccer Guide.* New York: The National Collegiate Athletic Bureau (publishes annually) Soccer Instruction Guide, The Athletic Institute, 1961.

Nelson, R. L. *Soccer for Men.* 4th ed. Dubuque, Ia.: Wm. C. Brown Publishers, 1981.

Newell, P., and Bennington, J. *Basketball Methods.* New York: Ronald Press Co., 1962.

Orlick, T. *The Cooperative Sports and Game Book.* New York: Pantheon Books, 1978.

——. *The Second Cooperative Sports and Game Book.* New York: Pantheon Books, 1982.

——. *Winning through Cooperation.* Washington D.C.: Acropolis Books, 1978.

Powell, J. T. *Track and Field Fundamentals for Teacher and Coach.* 3d ed. Champaign, Ill.: Stipes Publishing Co., 1962.

Richardson, H. A. *Games for the Elementary School Grades.* Minneapolis: Burgess Publishing Co., 1951.

Robb, G. *Soccer.* London: Weidenfelf and Nicolson, 1964.

Schaanning, C. *Hints on Orienteering.* London: B. J. Ward, 1965.

Seidel, B. L., et al. *Sports Skills: A Conceptual Approach to Meaningful Movement.* Dubuque, Ia.: Wm. C. Brown Publishers, 1975.

Smale, R.; Barlee, J.; and Scott, E. J. *Swimming . . . Do It This Way.* London: John Murray Publishers, 1967.

Stuart, F. R. *Classroom Activities.* Reston, Va.: AAHPERD, 1963.

Turkington, D., and Kirchner, G. *Basketball for Intermediate Grades.* Burnaby, British Columbia: Simon Fraser University, 1969.

——. *Volleyball for Intermediate Grades.* Burnaby, British Columbia: Simon Fraser University, 1969.

Weiner, P. H. *A Movement Approach to Games for Children.* St. Louis: C. V. Mosby Co., 1979.

Weinstein, M., and Goodman, J. *Playfair.* San Luis Obispo, Calif.: Impact Publishers, 1980.

Wiley, R. C. *Soccer: A Syllabus for Teachers.* Eugene, Oregon: The University of Oregon Cooperative Store, 1962.

Winterbottom, W. *Training for Soccer.* London: William Heinemann, 1960.

Wooden, J. R. *Practical Modern Basketball.* New York: Ronald Press Co., 1966.

Yost, C. P. *Teaching Safety in the Elementary School.* Reston, Va.: AAHPERD, 1972.

Films

Title: Teaching Games to Primary Children
Details: 16mm, 16 minutes, sound, color
Distributor: Thomas Howe Associates LTD, No. 1, 1226 Homer Street, Vancouver, B.C. V6B2Y5
Description: This film describes how to plan and organize a primary games program that will develop skills through individual, partner, and group activities. Numerous suggestions relating to class organization, lesson planning, and teaching methods are provided. The problem-solving method and creative games approach are given major emphasis.
Purchase Price: $240

Title: Teaching Games to Intermediate Children
Details: 16mm, 17 minutes, sound, color
Distributor: Thomas Howe Associates LTD, No. 1, 1226 Homer Street, Vancouver, B.C. V6B2Y5
Description: A companion film to *Teaching Games to Primary Children.* It illustrates how individual, partner, and group activities can be used to teach games such as soccer, basketball, and softball. Numerous examples are provided to show how to apply the problem-solving method and the inventive games approach to upper elementary school children.
Purchase Price: $255

Title: Participation for All
Details: 16mm, 21 minutes, sound, color
Distributor: Thomas Howe Associates LTD, No. 1, 1226 Homer Street, Vancouver, B.C. V6B2Y5
Description: Participation for All is the central theme of this comprehensive film describing an elementary school intramural program for all grade levels, how to develop student leadership, and ways of modifying a variety of indoor and outdoor activities to maximize the use of all available space and equipment.
Purchase Price: $315

Title: Classroom Physical Education
Details: 16mm, 22 minutes, sound, color
Distributor: Thomas Howe Associates LTD, No. 1, 1226 Homer Street, Vancouver, B.C. V6B2Y5
Description: A most useful and informative film for classroom teachers who do not have daily access to the gymnasium or playing field. It illustrates how the classroom can be effectively used to conduct fitness activities, yoga exercises, modified games, folk and creative dance, and many other exciting and challenging activities.
Purchase Price: $330

Title: *Lifetime Sports in Education*
Details: 16mm, 17 minutes, color, sound
Distributor: NEA, Washington, D.C.
Description: Demonstrates methods and techniques of organizing and teaching large groups.
Purchase Price: $80

Volleyball

Volleyball for Boys, 11 minutes, Cornet Films

Volleyball for Intermediate Grades, 26 minutes, Thomas Howe Associates LTD., No. 1, 1226 Homer Street, Vancouver, B.C. V6B2Y5

Volleyball Techniques for Girls, 9 minutes, McGraw-Hill Book Co.

Touch Football

Ball Handling in Football, 11 minutes, Encyclopaedia Britannica Films

Basketball

Ball Handling in Basketball, 10 minutes, Encyclopaedia Britannica Films

Basketball for Intermediate Grades, 28 minutes, Thomas Howe Associates LTD., No. 1, 1226 Homer Street, Vancouver, B.C. V6B2Y5

Basketball for Girls—Fundamental Techniques, 10 minutes, Cornet Films

Soccer

Soccer for Boys, 16mm, 23 minutes, color, sound Thomas Howe Associates LTD., No. 1, 1226 Homer Street, Vancouver, B.C. V6B2Y5

Soccer for Girls, 11 minutes, Cornet Films

Softball

Softball for Boys, 10 minutes, Cornet Films
Softball for Girls, 11 minutes, Cornet Films

Track and Field

Fundamentals in Track and Field, 26 minutes, Encyclopaedia Britannica Films

The High Jump, 16mm, 12 minutes, Educational Foundation for Visual Aids, 33 Queen Anne Street, London, W. 1

Hold High the Torch, 16mm, 29 minutes, color, sound, Association Films. (Story of the Olympics as carried out in the U.S.A. Shows how athletes are selected and trained.)

Long Jump, 16mm, 10 minutes, Rank Audio-Visual, Ltd., Woodger Road, Shepherds Bush, London, W. 12

Shot Putting, 16mm, 10 minutes, Rank Audio-Visual, Ltd., Woodger Road, Shepherds Bush, London, W. 12

Sprinting and Hurdling: Young Athlete, 16mm, 17 minutes, Educational Foundation for Visual Aids, 33 Queen Anne Street, London, W. 1

Track and Field, filmstrip (sound or silent), Athletic Institution, 805 Merchandise Mart, Chicago, Illinois

Track and Field for Intermediate Grades, Thomas Howe Associates LTD., No. 1, 1226 Homer Street, Vancouver, B.C. V6B2Y5

Triple Jump, 16mm, 10 minutes, Rank Audio-Visual, Ltd., Woodger Road, Shepherds Bush, London, W. 12

Outdoor Recreation

Title: *Canoeing*
Details: 16mm, 13½ minutes, color, sound
Distributor: Thomas Howe Associates, LTD., No. 1, 1226 Homer Street, Vancouver, B.C. V6B2Y5
Description: Canoeing has become a very popular activity in the elementary school outdoor recreation program. This film describes the basic canoeing and safety skills and instructional techniques appropriate to upper elementary school-age children. Special features include animated illustrations of all major strokes and a boat-over-boat rescue.
Purchase Price: $202.50

Title: *Orienteering*
Details: 16mm, 18 minutes, color, sound
Distributor: Thomas Howe Associates, LTD., No. 1, 1226 Homer Street, Vancouver, B.C. V6B2Y5
Description: Orienteering is finding one's way across country using a map and compass. This film illustrates how children are taught to use a compass, read a map, and follow a designated course. Numerous orienteering games and activities are also included along with many helpful teaching suggestions.
Purchase Price: $270

8. Stunts, Tumbling, and Gymnastic Activities

Written Material

Bailie, S., and Bailie, A. *Elementary School Gymnastics.* St. Louis: Atlas Athletic Equipment Co., 1969.

Baley, J. A. *An Illustrated Guide to Tumbling.* Boston: Allyn and Bacon, 1968.

Boone, W. T. *Better Gymnastics: How to Spot the Performer.* Mountain View, Calif.: World Publishing Inc., 1979.

Cassidy, J., and Rimbeaux, B. C. *Juggling for the Complete Klutz.* Stanford, Calif.: Klutz Press, 1977.

Dreham, V. L. *Head over Heels Gymnastics for Children.* New York: Harper & Row, 1967.

Evans, D. *Oh, Chute!* Sioux Falls, South Dakota, Raven Industries, Applied Technology Division, 1970.

Fisher, H.; Shawbold, D. R.; and Wohlford, P. R. *Individual and Dual Stunts.* Minneapolis: Burgess Publishing Co., 1960.

Keeney, C. J. *Fundamental Tumbling Skills Illustrated.* New York: Ronald Press, 1966.

Loken, N., and Willoughby, R. *Complete Book of Gymnastics.* 3d ed. Englewood Cliffs, N.J.: Prentice-Hall, 1977.

Norman, R. *Gymnastics for Girls and Women.* Dubuque, Ia.: Wm. C. Brown Publishers, 1965.

O'Quinn, G. *Gymnastics for Elementary School Children.* Dubuque, Ia.: Wm. C. Brown Publishers, 1967.

Ruff, W. K. *Gymnastics Beginner to Competitor.* Dubuque, Ia.: Wm. C. Brown Publishers, 1968.

Ryer, O. E. and Brown, J. R. *A Manual for Tumbling and Apparatus Stunts.* 7th ed. Dubuque, Ia.: Wm. C. Brown Publishers, 1980.

Skolnik, P. L. *Jump Rope.* New York: W. P. Workman Publishing Co., 1974.

Szypula, G. *Tumbling and Balancing for All.* 2d ed. Dubuque, Ia.: Wm. C. Brown Publishers, 1968.

Films

Title: Movement Experiences—Parachutes
Details: 16 mm, color, sound
Distributor: Pan-Dau Films, 108 West Fairmont, Tempe, Ariz.
Description: This film illustrates a variety of parachute activities by children in the fifth grade.

9. Rhythmics and Dance

Written Material

Traditional Dance

American Alliance for Health, Physical Education, Recreation and Dance. *Children's Dance.* Reston, Va.: AAHPERD, 1973.

Ellefeldt, L. *Folk Dance.* Dubuque, Ia.: Wm. C. Brown Publishers, 1969.

Evans, J. *Let's Dance.* Toronto: Can. Ed. Media, 1981.

Farina, A. M. *Developmental Games and Rhythms for Children.* Springfield, Ill.: Charles C Thomas, 1980.

Harris, J. A.; Pittman, A.; and Waller, M. S. *Dance a While.* 4th ed. Minneapolis: Burgess Publishing Co., 1968.

Kadman, G., and Hodes, T. *Israeli Folk Dance.* Tel Aviv: Education and Culture Center, 1959.

Kraus, R. *A Pocket Guide of Folk and Square Dances and Singing Games.* Englewood Cliffs, N.J.: Prentice-Hall, 1966.

Kulbitsky, O., and Kaltman, F. L. *Teacher's Dance Handbook, Number One, Kindergarten to Sixth Year.* Newark: Bluebird Publishing Co., 1960.

Latchaw, M., and Pyatt, J. *Folk and Square Dances and Singing Games for Elementary Schools.* Englewood Cliffs, N.J.: Prentice-Hall, 1966.

Melamed, L. *All Join Hands.* Montreal: Lanie Melamed, 494 Victoria Ave., Montreal, P.Q. H2Y 2R4., 1977.

Monsour, S.; Cohen, M. C.; and Lindell, P. E. *Rhythm in Music and Dance for Children.* Belmont, Calif.: Wadsworth Publishing Co., 1966.

Murray, R. L. *Dance in Elementary Education.* 3d ed. New York: Harper & Row, 1975.

Mynatt, C. V., and Kaiman, B. D. *Folk Dancing for Students and Teachers.* 2d ed. Dubuque, Ia.: Wm. C. Brown Publishers, 1975.

O'Rafferty, P. *The Irish Folk Dance Book* (with music). London: Peterson Publications.

Phillips, P. A. *Contemporary Square Dance.* Dubuque, Ia.: Wm. C. Brown Publishers, 1968.

Robins, F. J. *Educational Rhythmics for Mentally and Physically Handicapped Children.* New York: Associated Press, 1968.

The Royal Scottish Country Dance Society. *Twenty-four Favorite Scottish Country Dances* (with music). London: Peterson Publications.

Snider, M. *Folk Dance Handbook.* North Vancouver, B.C.: Hancock House Publishers Ltd., 1980.

Society for International Folk Dancing. *A Selection of European Folk Dances* (with music). 2 vols. New York: Pergamon Press, 1964.

Stuart, F. R., and Gibson, V. L. *Rhythmic Activities: Series III.* Minneapolis: Burgess Publishing Co., 1961.

Vick, M., and McLaughlin, C. R. *A Collection of Dances for Children* (card file). Minneapolis: Burgess Publishing Co., 1970.

Wakefield, E. E. *Folk Dancing in America.* New York: J. Lowell Pratt & Co., 1966.

Creative Dance

Barlin, A. L. *Teaching Your Wings to Fly.* Santa Monica, Calif.: Goodyear Publishing Co., Inc., 1979.

Boorman, J. *Creative Dance in the First Three Grades.* Don Mills, Ontario: Longman Canada, 1969.

———. *Creative Dance in Grades Four to Six.* Don Mills, Ontario: Longman Canada, 1971.

———. *Dance and Language Experiences with Children.* Don Mills, Ontario: Longman Canada, 1973.

Carroll, J., and Lofthouse, P. *Creative Dance for Boys.* New York: International Publications Services, 1969.

Eastman, M. *Creative Dance for Children.* Tucson, Ariz.: Mettler Studios, 1965.

Fleming, G. A. *Creative Rhythmic Movement: Boys and Girls Dancing.* Englewood Cliffs, N.J.: Prentice-Hall, 1976.

Joyce, M. *First Steps in Teaching Creative Dance to Children.* 2d ed. Palo Alto, Calif.: Mayfield Publishing Co., 1980.

Monsour, S.; Cohen, M. C.; and Lindell, P. E. *Rhythm in Music and Dance for Children.* Belmont, Calif.: Wadsworth Publishing Co., 1966.

Murray, Ruth L. *Dance in Elementary Education.* 3d ed. New York: Harper & Row, 1975.

Russell, J. *Creative Dance in the Primary School.* London: Macdonald and Evans, 1965.

Stanley, S. *Physical Education: A Movement Orientation.* 2d ed. New York: McGraw-Hill Book Co., 1977.

Taylor, C. *Rhythm: A Guide for Creative Movement.* Palo Alto, Calif.: Peek Publications, 1974.

Thackery, R. M. *Music and Physical Education.* rev. ed. New York: Harper & Row, 1963.

Wiener, J., and Lidstone, J. *Creative Movements for Children.* New York: Van Nostrand Reinhold Co., 1969.

Winters, S. J. *Creative Rhythmic Movement for Children of Elementary School Age.* Dubuque, Ia.: Wm. C. Brown Publishers, 1975.

Films

Title: Rhythmics in Movement
Details: 16mm, 18 minutes, color, sound
Distributor: Thomas Howe Associates, LTD., No. 1, 1226 Homer Street, Vancouver, B.C. V6B2Y5
Description: *Rhythmics in Movement* describes how the basic movement skills relating to games, dance, and gymnastic activities are taught to the accompaniment of music. The film illustrates how moving to rhythm begins with simple hand clapping and foot movements and progresses to partner and group routines. Numerous ideas relating to teaching strategies, use of small equipment, and selection of music are also provided.
Purchase Price: $270

Title: Creative Folk Dance
Details: 16mm, 17 minutes, color, sound
Distributor: Thomas Howe Associates, LTD., No. 1, 1226 Homer Street, Vancouver, B.C. V6B2Y5
Description: This film illustrates how folk dance activities can be taught using creative teaching strategies. Children are gradually introduced to each basic step and pathway through progress from individual to partner to group dance patterns. Numerous ideas relating to lesson plans, musical accompaniment, and teaching techniques are also provided.
Purchase Price: $225

Title: Building Children's Personalities with Creative Dancing
Details: 16mm, 30 minutes, color
Distributor: Bailey Films, 6509 Lonpre Avenue, Hollywood, Calif.
Description: Shows how a skillful teacher can lead children through the phases of creative dance expression.

Title: Learning through Movement
Details: 16mm, 32 minutes, black and white, sound
Distributor: S. L. Film Productions, 5126 Nartwick Street, Los Angeles, Calif.
Description: Explores the multiplicity of learning concepts that a child can experience in a creative dance class.

Title: Creative Dance in the Junior School
Details: 16mm, 40 minutes, color, sound
Distributor: County Film Library, 2 Walton's Parade, Preston, Lancashire, England
Description: Illustrates progression of dance through the junior school (intermediate level); shows dances composed by children.

Title: Music and Movement
Details: 16mm, 13 minutes, color, sound
Distributor: Rank Audio-Visual, Woodger Road, Shepherds Bush, London, W. 12
Description: A high standard of work from six-year-olds showing response to music and how the use of percussion and visual stimuli develop quality of movement.

Title: Free to Move
Details: 16mm, 34½ minutes, color
Distributor: Southern Film Production, Brockenhurst, Hampshire, England
Description: The film illustrates the way children move and the relevance of this understanding to a child's total education. Shows excellent relationships to classroom and gymnastic activities.

Title: Tinikling
Details: 16 mm, 11 minutes, color, sound
Distributor: General Learning Cooperation, 3 East 54th Street, New York, N.Y.
Description: Instructions and teaching techniques for Philippine stick dances.

Title: Discovering Rhythm
Details: 16 mm, 11 minutes, color, sound
Distributor: Universal Education and Visual Arts, 221 Park Avenue South, New York, N.Y. 10003.

Source of Records and Tapes

Several outstanding record companies have a wide variety of records and tapes for elementary school traditional, contemporary, and creative dance programs. Unless you are purchasing a specific record, it is wise to write to several of the following companies, indicating your area of interest and requesting a catalog. It is also important that you request that your name be kept on the mailing list in order to keep up with new releases.

Bowmar Records, 622 Rodier Drive, Glendale, Calif. 91201.

Burns Record Co., 755 Chickadee Lane, Stratford, Conn.

Canadian Folk Dance Record Service, 605 King Street, West, Toronto 2B, Ontario.

Can. Ed. Media Ltd., 185 Spadina Ave., Suite 1, Toronto, Ont. M5T 2C6.

Childhood Rhythms, 326 East Forest Park Avenue, Springfield, Mass.

Children's Music Center, 5373 West Pico Blvd., Los Angeles, Calif. 90019

Columbia Records, 1473 Barnum Avenue, Bridgeport, Conn.

Educational Activities, Box 392, Freeport, N.Y. 11520

Educational Recordings of America Inc., Box 6062, Bridgeport, Conn.

Folkcraft Record Co., 10 Fenwick, Newark, N.J. 07714

Folk Dancer, Box 201, Flushing, Long Island, N.Y.

Imperial Records, 137 North Western Avenue, Los Angeles, Calif.

Israeli Music Foundation, 931 Broadway, New York, N.Y.

McGregor Records, 729 South Western Avenue, Hollywood, Calif.

RCA Victor Education Dept. J, 133 Ave. of the Americas, New York, N.Y. 10036

Square Dance Square, Box 689, Santa Barbara, Calif.

Windsor Records, 5530 N. Rosemead Boulevard, Temple City, Calif. 91780

World of Fun Records, Cokesbury Regional Service Center, 1600 Queen Anne Rd., Teaneck, N.J. 07666

10. Movement Education

Written Material

Bilborough, A., and Jones, P. *Physical Education in the Primary Schools.** London: University of London Press, 1969.

Buckland, D. *Gymnastics.* London: Heinemann Educational Books, 1970.

Cameron, W. McD., and Pleasance, P. *Education in Movement.* Oxford: Basil Blackwell & Mott, 1965.

Cope, J. *Discovery Methods in Physical Education.* London: Thomas Nelson and Sons, 1967.

Hackett, L. C., and Jensen, R. G. *A Guide to Movement Exploration.* Palo Alto, Calif.: Peek Publications, 1966.

Halsey, E. *Inquiry and Invention on Physical Education.* Philadelphia: Lea & Febiger, 1964.

Howard, S. "The Movement Education Approach to Teaching in English Elementary Schools." *American Journal for Health, Physical Education and Recreation,* January 1967.

Inner London Educational Authority, *Educational Gymnastics.** London: 1966.

Kane, J. E. *Movement Studies in Physical Education.* London: Routledge and Kegan Paul, 1977.

Kirchner, G.; Cunningham, J.; and Warrell, E. *Introduction to Movement Education.* 2d ed. Dubuque, Ia.: Wm. C. Brown Publishers, 1978.

Kruger, H., and Kruger, J. M. *Movement Education in Physical Education: A Guide to Teaching and Planning.* Dubuque, Ia.: Wm. C. Brown Co., Publishers, 1977.

Laban, R. *Modern Educational Dance.** London: Macdonald and Evans, 1948.

Laban, R., and Ullmann, L. *The Mastery of Movement.** London: Macdonald and Evans, 1960.

Locks, L. F. "The Movement Movement." *American Journal for Health, Physical Education and Recreation,* January 1966.

Ludwig, E. A. "Towards an Understanding of Basic Movement Education in the Elementary Schools." *American Journal for Health, Physical Education and Recreation,* March 1968.

Mauldin, E., and Layson, J. *Teaching Gymnastics.** London: Macdonald and Evans, 1965.

Ministry of Education. *Moving and Growing.** London: Her Majesty's Stationary Office, 1952.

Ministry of Education. *Planning the Program.** London: Her Majesty's Stationary Office, 1965.

Morison, R. *A Movement Approach to Educational Gymnastics.* London: J. M. Dent and Sons, 1969.

Rizzitiello, T. G. *An Annotated Bibliography on Movement Education.* Washington, D.C.: AAHPER, 1977.

Simons, W. M. M. "Educational Gymnastics—Its Meaning, Uses and Abuses." *Canadian Journal of Health, Physical Education and Recreation.*

Stanley, S. *Physical Education: A Movement Orientation.* New York: 2d ed. McGraw-Hill Book Co., 1977.

Films

Series C contains four films that sequentially introduce the movement education approach. This series is specifically designed to be used as in-service films for teachers of grades one through six or for use in teacher training programs (produced in 1978).

Title (Film No. 1): Introducing the Elements of Movement Education

Details: 16mm, 16 minutes, color, sound

Distributor: Thomas Howe Associates, No. 1, 1226 Homer Street, Vancouver, B.C. V6B2Y5

Description: This film represents stage one in introducing the movement education approach. It describes how the safety skills and vocabulary of movement education are progressively introduced to primary and intermediate children. Brief sample lessons, problem-solving techniques, and numerous teaching ideas are provided.

Purchase Price: $240

Title (Film No. 2): Using Small Equipment in Movement Education

Details: 16mm, 16 minutes, color, sound

Distributor: Thomas Howe Associates, No. 1, 1226 Homer Street, Vancouver, B.C. V6B2Y5

Description: The first part of the film describes how small equipment such as hoops, beanbags, and individual ropes are used in a movement education lesson. The second part shows how small equipment should be used to extend a child's movement potential and creative response. Ideas relating to task cards, station work, and a variety of instructional techniques are also included.

Purchase Price: $240

Title (Film No. 3): Using Large Apparatus in Movement Education

Details: 16mm, 15 minutes, color, sound

Distributor: Thomas Howe Associates, No. 1, 1226 Homer Street, Vancouver, B.C. V6B2Y5

Description: This film describes how large apparatus such as vaulting boxes, climbing ropes, and balance benches are used to challenge and extend a child's physical and creative abilities. It also illustrates how to combine large apparatus with small equipment, how to use task cards in an effective and enjoyable way, and how to arrange a variety of large apparatus.

Purchase price: $225

Title (Film No. 4): Theme Development in Movement Education

Details: 16mm, 16 minutes, color, sound

Distributor: Thomas Howe Associates, No. 1, 1226 Homer Street, Vancouver, B.C. V6B2Y5

Description: This film begins with a brief explanation of how to plan a short theme in a progressive and systematic way. In the second part, an extended theme of matching shapes is developed with a fourth-grade class through a series of nine lessons. Shows excellent use of small and large equipment.

Purchase Price: $240

Title: Movement Education—From Primary to College Level Programs

Details: 16mm, 22 minutes, color, sound

Distributor: Thomas Howe Associates, No. 1, 1226 Homer Street, Vancouver, B.C. V6B2Y5

Description: This film illustrates the role and emphasis of movement education in elementary, high school, and college programs. In the majority of scenes, typical programs are shown to illustrate the methods used, levels of performance, and differences in facilities and equipment. The film also shows a few advanced movement education programs to illustrate the quality of performance that can be reached through this type of program.

*All books with an asterisk may be purchased from the Ling Book Shop, Ling House, 10, Nottingham Place, London W C 1.

B Inexpensive Equipment

1. Skipping Ropes
2. Horizontal Bar
3. Balance Beam
4. Balance Bench
5. Scooters
6. Wands
7. Vaulting Box
8. Sawhorse
9. Jumping Boxes
10. Jumping Pit
11. All-Purpose Game Bat
12. Sand Blocks
13. Tambourines
14. Wooden Nail Keg Drum
15. Metal Drum
16. Plastic Plant Pot Drum
17. Rattlers
18. Jingle Bats, Bands, Pin-ons, and Sticks

1. Skipping Ropes

To Cut Ropes

1. Measure off the desired length of rope.
2. Wrap five inches above and below the cut mark with tape (plastic preferred; adhesive acceptable).
3. Place rope on small wooden block and cut rope in middle of taped area.

To Store Ropes

1. Since there may be three or four different lengths of rope, dip the ends of the ropes in different colored paint to represent short, medium, and long lengths. (Dip about six inches.)
2. A simple way to store ropes is across or over a bar as shown. The standard can be of any design with the top bar about four feet off the floor.

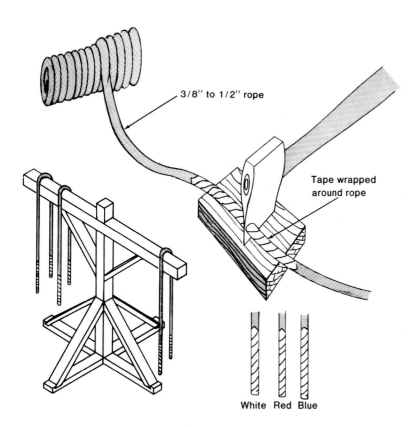

3/8″ to 1/2″ rope

Tape wrapped around rope

White Red Blue

2. Horizontal Bar

General Features

The following horizontal bar can be made for an approximate cost of fifteen to twenty dollars. It is designed for efficient assemblage and storage. The bolt as shown in detail B prevents the bar from rotating while performing stunts. The bar is held firmly to the upright standard with a fixed 2¾'' washer on the inside and a washer and bolt shown in detail D. For efficient storage, the side support shown in detail A may be drawn upward.

Designed by Bill Bressler
Drawn by Gary Sciuchetti

Detail B

See Detail B

3,16'' × 2'' bolt

1, 4'' hole   Weld

Height of bar
72''—66''—59''

1, 1/8'' solid steel bar
76'' long

11, 2'' pipe
Wing nut
Lag bolt

Detail D

23, 4'' diameter washer
welded to bar

See Detail A

Detail A

Hinges   Dado joint

3. Balance Beam

General Information

The diagram of the intermediate level balance beam is basically a 12' 4" beam mounted on two sawhorses. Standard competition height for a beam is four feet; however, for intermediate level children, the height may range from 3½' to a maximum of 4'. It is also desirable to make the grooves for the low and high balance beams the same in order to mount the same beam on both standards.

A. Intermediate Level

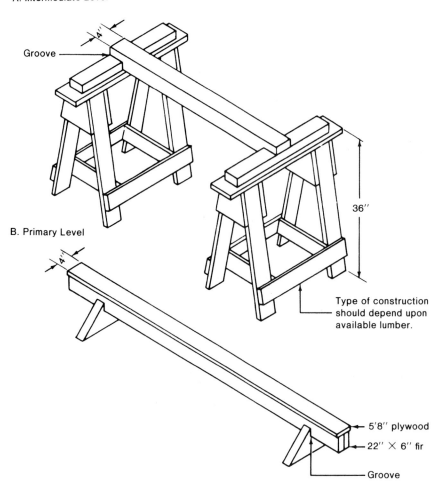

Groove

4"

36"

B. Primary Level

4"

Type of construction should depend upon available lumber.

5'8" plywood

22" × 6" fir

Groove

4. Balance Bench

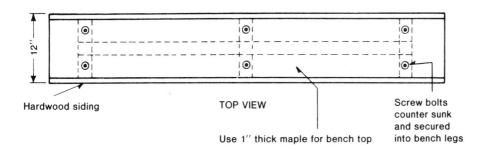

Hardwood siding

TOP VIEW

Use 1″ thick maple for bench top

Screw bolts
counter sunk
and secured
into bench legs

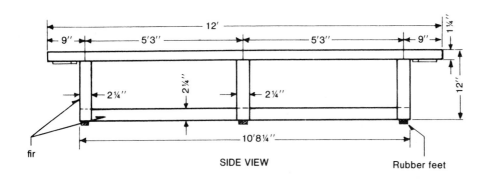

fir

SIDE VIEW

Rubber feet

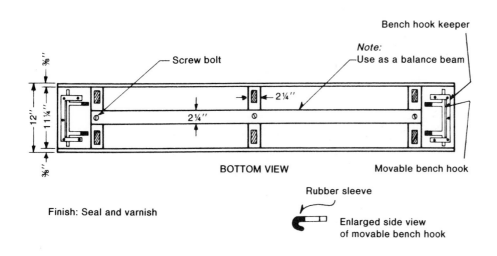

Screw bolt

Bench hook keeper

Note:
Use as a balance beam

BOTTOM VIEW

Movable bench hook

Finish: Seal and varnish

Rubber sleeve

Enlarged side view
of movable bench hook

5. Scooters

General Information

An inexpensive set of floor scooters may be made from ¾'' plywood and plastic casters. Cut 12'' squares, round the edges and attach a strip of rubber around the outside edge. The latter strip prevents the edges from splintering and lessens the noise when scooters hit. A simple way to store scooters is illustrated here. The pole should be at least ¾'' thick and firmly attached to the base.

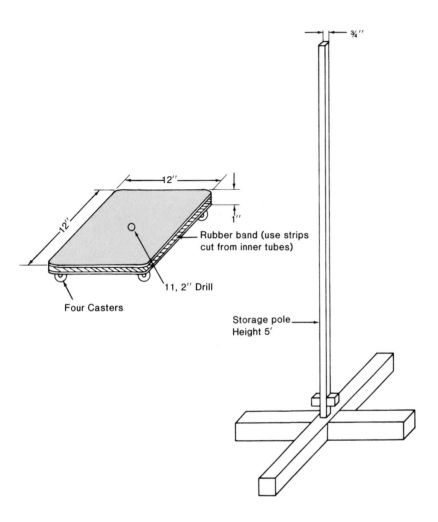

¾''

12''

12''

1''

Rubber band (use strips cut from inner tubes)

11, 2'' Drill

Four Casters

Storage pole
Height 5'

6. Wands

General Information

A set of wands (see chapter 6 for appropriate lengths) may be made from old broomsticks. Cut each broomstick off at the desired length and round both ends. Dip the end of each set of wands in different colored paint to facilitate each selection.

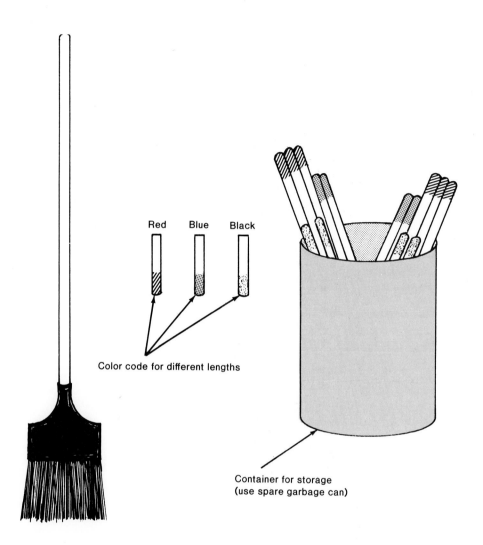

Red Blue Black

Color code for different lengths

Container for storage
(use spare garbage can)

7. Vaulting Box

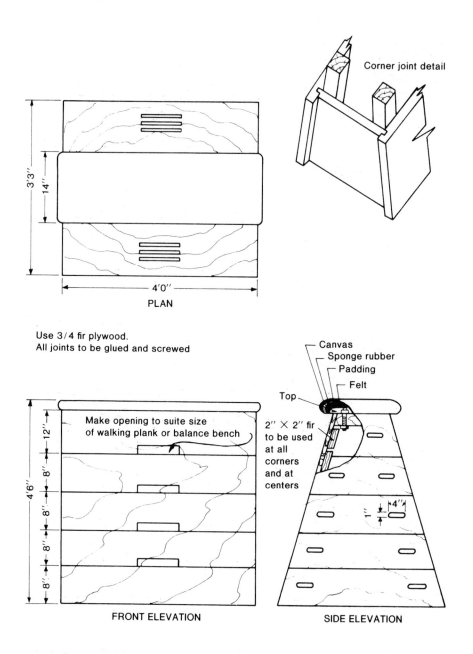

Corner joint detail

3'3"

14"

4'0"

PLAN

Use 3/4 fir plywood.
All joints to be glued and screwed

Make opening to suite size
of walking plank or balance bench

4'6"

12"

8"

8"

8"

8"

FRONT ELEVATION

Canvas
Sponge rubber
Padding
Felt

Top

2" X 2" fir
to be used
at all
corners
and at
centers

1"

4"

SIDE ELEVATION

Finish: Wiped white rez stain-shellacked and varnished

8. Sawhorse

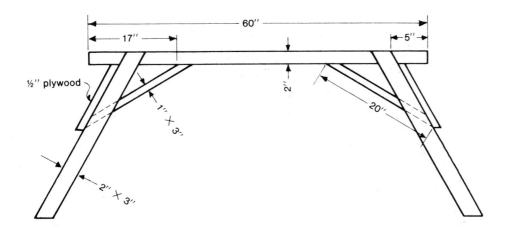

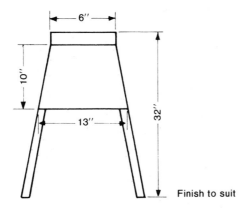

Finish to suit

9. Jumping Boxes

General Features

The jumping boxes shown here can be made for approximately fifty dollars, depending upon the number and size of each box. A minimum of three for each set is recommended. *Do not* cover top with rubber matting or cloth material. Sand all corners and, if desired, paint or varnish.

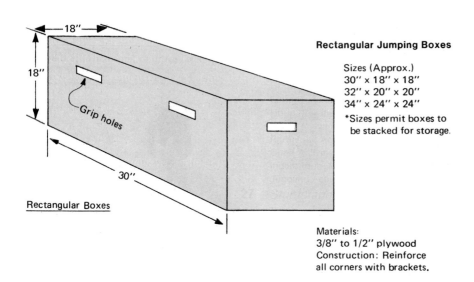

Rectangular Boxes

Rectangular Jumping Boxes

Sizes (Approx.)
30" x 18" x 18"
32" x 20" x 20"
34" x 24" x 24"
*Sizes permit boxes to be stacked for storage.

Materials:
3/8" to 1/2" plywood
Construction: Reinforce all corners with brackets.

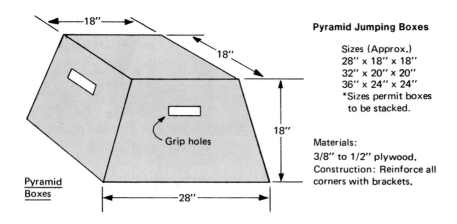

Pyramid Boxes

Pyramid Jumping Boxes

Sizes (Approx.)
28" x 18" x 18"
32" x 20" x 20"
36" x 24" x 24"
*Sizes permit boxes to be stacked.

Materials:
3/8" to 1/2" plywood.
Construction: Reinforce all corners with brackets.

10. Jumping Pit

How To Make

The rubber tubes are placed on the ground as shown in the diagram and tied together. A tumbling mat is then placed on top of the tubes. This provides a safe and comfortable landing surface. It can also be used indoors and outdoors.

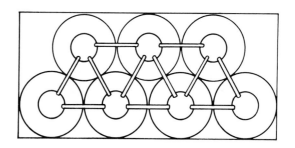

---

11. All-Purpose Game Bat

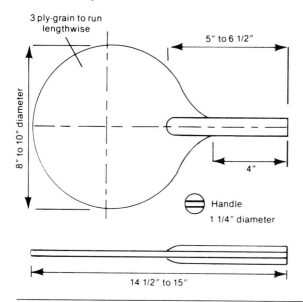

3 ply-grain to run lengthwise

8" to 10" diameter

5" to 6 1/2"

4"

Handle
1 1/4" diameter

14 1/2" to 15"

---

12. Sand Blocks

Materials

1. Two blocks of wood (approx. 4" × 6" × 1")
2. Sandpaper or emery paper (different grades)
3. Thumbtacks, glue or screws
4. Thread spools or knobs

How To Make

1. Cut blocks of wood.
2. Sand surfaces and round edges.
3. Glue or screw on handle.
4. Cover bottom surface with sandpaper and tack each end. Use different grades of sandpaper or emery paper to make different sounds.
5. Decorate as desired.

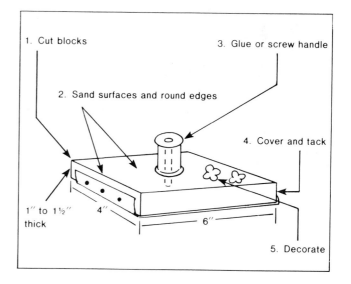

1. Cut blocks

2. Sand surfaces and round edges

3. Glue or screw handle

4. Cover and tack

1" to 1½" thick

4"

6"

5. Decorate

13. Tambourines

Materials
1. *Pie Plate Tambourine:* Old pie plate, safety pins, bells or strings, and bottle caps or roofing discs
2. *Ping Pong Bat Tambourine:* Old table tennis bat, nails and bottle caps, or roofing discs
3. *Stick Tambourine:* Stick 6″ × 1½″ × ¾″ and bottle caps or roofing discs

How To Make A Pie Plate Tambourine
1. Make nail holes around outer edge of pie plate. Sand rough side of nail hole.
2. Attach safety pin and bell to each hole, or attach string and bottle caps (two per string) to each hole.
3. Decorate as desired.

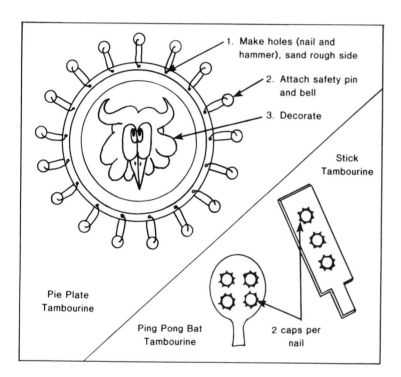

1. Make holes (nail and hammer), sand rough side

2. Attach safety pin and bell

3. Decorate

Pie Plate Tambourine

Stick Tambourine

Ping Pong Bat Tambourine

2 caps per nail

14. Wooden Nail Keg Drum

Materials

1. Nail keg (or any wooden container that has not been waterproofed or sealed)
2. Medium and fine sandpaper
3. Tacks (upholstery tacks)
4. Paints
5. Floor seal
6. Muslin, nitrate solution

How To Make

1. Sand with medium, then fine sandpaper.
2. Paint outside surface of keg with floor seal. Add a second coat after twenty-four hours.
3. Apply one coat of flat white. (If still darkish, add another coat after twenty-four hours.)
4. Decorate keg with bright enamel paints.
5. Cut muslin (or sailcloth) about two inches larger than top of nail keg.
6. Place muslin on top, drawing evenly down sides, and place thumbtacks 1'' below top rim.
7. Start above tacks and wind colored yarn around keg and work down to cover ends of muslin. Tuck yarn under last row and tie.
8. Apply five to six coats of nitrate solution to muslin and yarn. Allow each coat to dry thoroughly.

Note: Drum beaters—A drum stick can be made by wrapping a soft cloth (cotton, wool) around end of dowel. Cover with leather, muslin, or sailcloth and wrap with heavy cord.

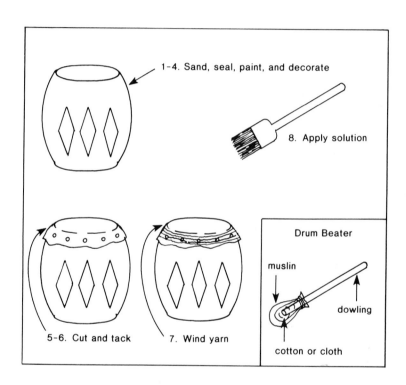

1-4. Sand, seal, paint, and decorate

8. Apply solution

5-6. Cut and tack   7. Wind yarn

Drum Beater

muslin

dowling

cotton or cloth

15. Metal Drum

Materials
1. Metal can (paint, coffee, etc.)
2. Inner tubing or rubber sheeting
3. Wire and yarn
4. Paints

How To Make
1. Remove top and bottom lids; remove any paper and soak to dissolve dirt and/or glue.
2. Apply one or two coats of flat white paint then decorate with bright enamel paint (keep decoration towards the middle as the outside two inches will be covered with tubing).
3. Cut two rubber sheets two inches larger than opening. Puncture holes one inch in from outer edge and about two inches apart. Lace twine through holes.
4. Place first sheet over top end and wrap twine one inch below top of rim. Repeat on bottom.
5. Pull top and bottom laces tight and tie.
6. Tie a twine to top lace then to bottom and zigzag lace around drum. This will hold both ends tight.

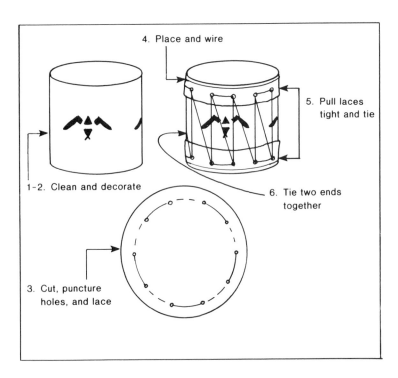

4. Place and wire

5. Pull laces tight and tie

1-2. Clean and decorate

6. Tie two ends together

3. Cut, puncture holes, and lace

16. Plastic Plant Pot Drum

Materials
1. Various size plastic plant pots
2. Masking tape
3. Muslin or sailcloth
4. Paint and yarn

How To Make
1. Seal drain holes with masking tape. Apply two or three strips over each hole.
2. Apply one or two coats of flat white paint.
3. Cut a circle of muslin to cover top plus sides, and one inch under bottom edge.
4. Cut out triangles evenly spaced around circumference of cloth circle. Fold remaining ends down ½″ and sew to form ½″ hem open at both ends.
5. Lay cloth over top, down sides, and under bottom edge. Lace heavy twine through hems of the ends, pull, secure, and tie.
6. Wrap yarn around upper edge and just below vertical lines.
7. Apply five or six coats of nitrate solution to all muslin and yarn. Allow each coat to dry thoroughly.
8. Decorate as desired with enamel paint.

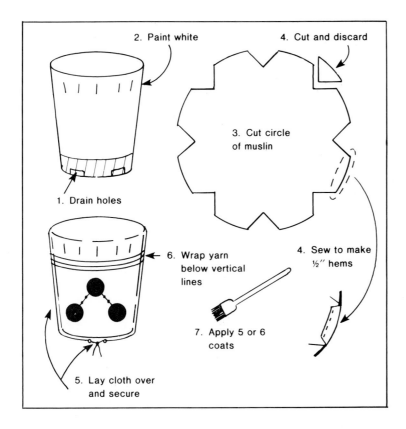

2. Paint white

4. Cut and discard

3. Cut circle of muslin

1. Drain holes

6. Wrap yarn below vertical lines

4. Sew to make ½″ hems

7. Apply 5 or 6 coats

5. Lay cloth over and secure

17. Rattlers

Materials

A rattle can be made from any container that can be easily sealed and permits a variety of material to move freely inside the container. Some examples are—

1. A tennis ball container with rice or dried peas.
2. A wooden match box with peas, rice, or sand.
3. A plastic vinegar bottle with marbles or nuts with shells on.
4. Plastic tubing (1½'') with seeds.

Note: The rattling sound of any container is determined by a combination of the size, shape, and material of the container combined with the nature of the rattling material. Experiment with different materials in each container to find the most appealing sound.

How to Make

1. Where necessary, clean container and remove all labels.
2. Place materials inside and seal opening. For tubes, cover ends with plastic or cloth and wrap with masking tape.
3. Decorate with paper, string, or paint.

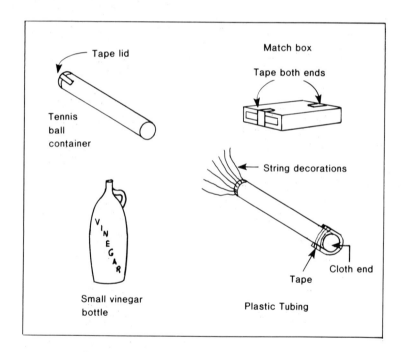

18. Jingle Bats, Bands, Pin-ons, and Sticks

Materials
1. *Jingle Bats:* Coat hanger, tongue depressors, masking tape, six to eight bells, string
2. *Jingle Bands:* Six- to eight-inch cloth bands, four or five bells and string
3. *Jingle Pins:* Bells in sets of three or four, string, and safety pin
4. *Jingle Sticks:* Eight-inch stick, two circle head screws, six bells, and string

How To Make
See diagrams and modify each type of jingle instrument to the available materials and creative abilities of the children.

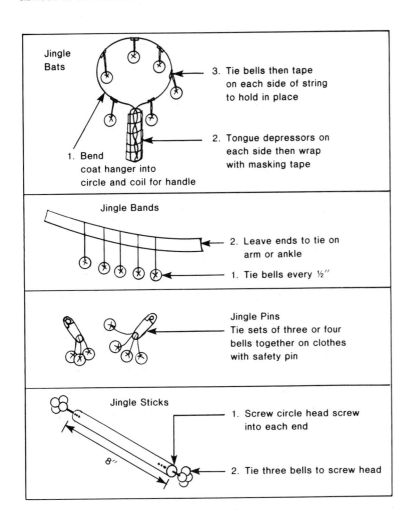

Jingle Bats

3. Tie bells then tape on each side of string to hold in place

2. Tongue depressors on each side then wrap with masking tape

1. Bend coat hanger into circle and coil for handle

Jingle Bands

2. Leave ends to tie on arm or ankle

1. Tie bells every ½″

Jingle Pins
Tie sets of three or four bells together on clothes with safety pin

Jingle Sticks

1. Screw circle head screw into each end

2. Tie three bells to screw head

8″

C Apparatus, Equipment, and Supply Companies

The following companies are listed on the basis of manufacturing and/or selling agility apparatus (indoor and outdoor), equipment (large tumbling mats, springboard, etc.) and supplies (hoops, beanbags, etc.).

Big Toys
2601 South Hood
Tacoma, Washington 98409
or 11940 Mitchell Road
Richmond, B.C.
Canada V6VIT4
Telephone (800) 663–5973

Agility Apparatus and Outdoor Apparatus

American Athletic Equipment Co.
Box 111
Jefferson, Iowa 50129

Equipment

American Gym Company, Inc.
Box 131
Monroeville, Pennsylvania 15146

Equipment and Agility Apparatus

Atlas Athletic Equipment Co.
2339 Hampton
St. Louis, Missouri 63139

Equipment

Mr. J. A. McLaughlin
Director of Industries for
Commissioner
Ottawa 4, Canada

Agility Apparatus

Game-Time, Inc.
Litchfield, Michigan

Agility Apparatus

Gym Master Co.
3200 So. Zuni
Englewood, Colorado 80110

Equipment

Gymnastic Supply Co.
247 West Sixth Street
San Pedro, California 90733

Equipment and Supplies

The Delmer F. Harris Co.
P.O. Box 288, Dept. J
Concordia, Kansas 66901

Agility Apparatus

Lind Climber Company
807 Reba Place
Evanston, Illinois 60202

Agility Apparatus

Madsen Gymnastic Equipment Ltd.
Unionville, Ontario   *Agility Apparatus*

The Mexico-Forge Climbers
R.D. 1, Reedsville,
Pennsylvania   *Outdoor Apparatus*

Murray Anderson-Olympic Gymnastic Equipment
128 Dunedin Street
Orillia, Ontario   *Agility Apparatus*

National Sports Company
360 North Marquette Street
Fond du Lac, Wisconsin 54935   *Equipment*

Nissen Corp.
930 27th Avenue, S.W.
Cedar Rapids, Iowa 52406   *Agility Apparatus and Equipment*

Porter Athletic Equipment
Porter-Leavitt Co. MFGR
9555 Irving Park Road
Schiller Park, Illinois 60176   *Equipment*

A. G. Spalding & Bros. Inc.
Chicopee, Massachusetts 01014   *Equipment and Supplies*

W. J. Volt Rubber Corp.
Subsidiary of American Machine
and Foundry Co., New York
3801 South Harbor Boulevard
Santa Ana, California 92704   *Equipment and Supplies*

R. W. Whittle, Ltd.
P. V. Works
Monton, Eccles
Manchester, England   *Agility Apparatus*

Creative Playthings Inc.
Princeton, New Jersey   *Playground Apparatus*

Childcraft
155 East 23rd Street   *Climbing Ropes and Gymnasium*
New York, N.Y. 10010   *Apparatus and Equipment*

Glossary

The following words and phrases occur frequently in the instructional and extraclass physical education programs. Separate glossaries are arranged alphabetically according to the following general categories.

Curriculum and Teaching

Accident
An unforeseen event occurring without the will or design of the person whose act caused it.

Apparatus work
The third part of a gymnastic lesson.

Classification index
A method of arranging equal groups for competitive purposes.

Classroom games
Games, relays, and contests that can be played in the classroom.

Concept
The degree of meaning a person possesses about something he has experienced.

Correlation
Relating one subject area to another.

Creative games
Games that are invented by children.

Creative playgrounds
A unique arrangement of outdoor apparatus (commercial or locally constructed).

Creativity
The degree of inventiveness of a movement.

Cumulative record
A method of plotting a child's performance (skill or physical fitness items) at the beginning and end of each year.

Curriculum
The total experience within the physical education program that is provided for all children.

Direct method
A teaching method in which the choice of the activity and how it is performed is entirely that of the teacher.

Dual activities
Cooperative and competitive activities between two children.

Equipment
Material or apparatus that is of a relatively permanent nature and would last, with repeated use, from five to ten years.

Evaluation
The subjective and objective assessment of program effectiveness and student progress.

Extraclass program
Cooperative and competitive programs between two or more schools.

Field theory
A theory that stresses that learning proceeds from comprehension of the whole to the identification of smaller parts.

Games of low organization
Activities such as relays, tag, and simple team games that involve one or more basic skills and a minimum of roles and playing strategies.

Humanism
A philosophy that asserts the dignity and worth of man and his capacity for self-realization through reason.

Indirect method
A teaching method that allows the children to choose the activity, as well as how and what they wish to perform within the activity.

Individual games
Low-organization games played by one person with or without small equipment.

Individualized learning
A system of teaching that adapts to each learner's individual abilities, needs, and interests.

In loco parentis
Acting in the place of the parent.

Instructional unit
The organization of material around a central activity or theme of instruction.

Intramural program
Competitive or club activities that are offered during nonclass time, on a voluntary basis, and within the jurisdiction of one school.

Introductory activity
The first part of a physical education lesson.

Limitation method
A teaching method in which the choice of the activity or how it is performed is limited in some way by the teacher.

Method
A general way of guiding and controlling the learning experiences of children.

Modified teaching unit
A unit of instruction that emphasizes one type of activity and provides a minor emphasis in one or more other activities.

Movement training
The second part of a dance or gymnastic lesson.

Multiple teaching unit
A unit of instruction that includes two or more activities.

Negligence
An act, or absence of it, that falls below the standard established by law for the protection of others against unreasonable risk or harm.

Obstacle course
An arrangement of small and large equipment designed to improve physical fitness and skill development.

Physical education
That part of the educational process that contributes to the physical, emotional, social, and mental development of each child through the medium of physical activity.

Play day
An interschool event in which children from two or more schools play on the same team.

Relay activities
Activities that involve a race between two or more participants or teams.

Self-image
The feeling and/or opinion a child has about himself.

Sociogram
A technique used to study the relationships within groups.

Solid teaching unit
An extensive period of instruction that is devoted exclusively to one type of activity.

Specificity of skill
The differential ability of an individual to acquire and perform physical skills and movement patterns.

Sports day
An interschool competitive event in which teams represent their own schools.

Spotting
A method of assisting a performer in the execution of a difficult stunt or movement.

Station work
A technique of organizing the class into small working units.

Stimulus response theory
A theory that stresses that learning consists of strengthening of the connections (bonds) between the stimulus and the response.

Supplies
Material that is expendable within one or two years.

Teaching formation
A specific way of organizing the class, such as line, circle, or shuttle patterns.

Team teaching
The organization of teachers and students into instructional groups that permit maximum utilization of staff abilities.

Technique
A smaller part of a method.

Tournament
A method of organizing small and large groups for competition.

Structure, Growth, and Mechanics

Agility
The ability to shift the body in different directions quickly and efficiently.

Asthma
A condition of the lungs that causes labored breathing and wheezing.

Balance
The ability to maintain a stationary position or to perform purposeful movements while resisting the force of gravity.

Calisthenics
Conditioning exercises designed to improve physical fitness.

Circuit training
Repeating one or more exercises as many times as possible within a set time limit.

Diaphysis
The center of bone growth located in the middle of the long bones.

Endurance
The ability to continue a muscular effort or movement over a prolonged period of time.

Epilepsy
A disease of the nervous system that is characterized by seizures and convulsions.

Epiphysis
Center of growth located near the end of the long bones.

Exceptional child
A child who deviates from the normal intelligence, physical health, motor ability, or behavioral characteristics of the average or typical child.

Flexibility
The range of movement of a joint.

Force
The push or pull exerted against something.

Growth
An increase in size.

Hyperopia
Farsightedness, resulting in a condition in which distant objects can be seen clearly but nearby objects appear blurred.

Isometric exercise
Contraction of muscles involving a push, pull, or twist against an object that does not move.

Isotonic exercise
Contraction of muscles that involves both shortening and lengthening the muscle fibers.

Kyphosis
Marked curve of the upper back.

Linear motion
A movement in which the body or an object as a whole moves in a straight line.

Locomotor skills
Basic motor skills involving a change of position of the feet and/or a change of direction of the body.

Lordosis
An exaggerated forward curve of the lower back.

Maturation
The general progress from one stage to a higher and more complex stage of development. Maturation occurs as a function of time and is independent of experience.

Myopia
Nearsightedness, resulting in a condition in which distant objects appear blurred while nearby objects are seen clearly.

Neuromuscular skills
All motor skills that are under the voluntary control of the brain.

Nonlocomotor skills
Movements of the body that are performed from a relatively stable base.

Obesity
A condition characterized by excessive bodily fat tissue.

Overload
A performance of an exercise or activity that requires the individual to exert more than a normal effort.

Perceptual-motor responses
The process of perceiving a stimulus and translating the stimulus into a motor response.

Physical fitness
The state that characterizes the degree to which a person is able to function.

Physically gifted
To possess a unique talent or ability in physical activities.

Physically handicapped
A child who suffers from a disease or physical handicap.

Posture
The relative alignment of the body segments.

Power
The ability of the body to apply a maximum muscular contraction with the quickest possible speed.

Rotary motion
A movement that traces out an arc or circle around an axis or fixed point.

Scoliosis
A lateral curvature of the spinal column.

Slow learner
A child whose IQ is between seventy and ninety.

Spatial awareness
The ability to move the body or its parts in specified directions.

Speed
The ability to perform successive movements of the same pattern in the shortest period of time.

Strength
The amount of force a muscle or group of muscles can exert.

Yoga exercise
An ancient Indian system of exercise performed slowly.

Movement Education

Agility apparatus
All types of indoor and outdoor climbing apparatus.

Apparatus work
The third part of a movement education lesson, concerned with the application of movement ideas to large and small apparatus.

Asymmetry
A position or movement that is characterized by unevenness of one part of the body to its opposite side. Using a line drawn through the vertebral column, all twisting, curling, or held positions where greater stress is given to the limbs on one side, would be asymmetrical positions.

Balance
The ability to hold the body in a fixed position. (The common expression is "weight bearing.")

Body awareness
The way in which the body or parts of it can move (stretch, bend, twist, and turn).

Continuity
Movements following each other in succession.

Curl
An action that flexes or bends the body or its parts.

Flight
The ability to propel the body into the air.

Flow
The ability to link one movement to another with control and harmony.

Force
The degree of effort or tension involved in a movement.

General space
The physical area in which a movement takes place.

Introductory activity
The first part of a movement education lesson involves general warm-up, lasting approximately five minutes.

Level
The relative position of the body or any of its parts to the floor or apparatus. Level may be applied to either stationary activity or position.

Movement ideas
A movement concept related to one or more of the basic elements of qualities, body awareness, space awareness, or relationships.

Movement training
The second part of a movement education lesson, concerned with the development of movement themes and activities.

Pattern
The arrangement of a series of movements in relation to shape, level, and pathway.

Personal space
The area around an individual that can be used while he keeps one part of his body in a fixed position on the floor or apparatus; also known as limited space.

Qualities
Refers to how the body can move. It is the ability to move quickly or slowly, to perform light or heavy movements, and the flow with which one movement is linked to another.

Relationship
Refers to the position of the body in relationship to the floor, apparatus, or other performers.

Safety training
The ability of children to move and land safely and efficiently. In a broader context, it refers to the individual's safety on or around apparatus and to his concern for the safety of other participants.

Sequence
A series of movements performed in succession.

Shape
The image presented by the position of the body when traveling or stationary.

Space
The area in which a movement takes place.

Stretch
Moving the body or parts of it from a flexed to an extended position.

Symmetry
In movement education, symmetry describes a movement or balance position in which both sides of the body would look identical if an imaginary line were drawn through the middle of the body.

Theme
A central movement idea.

Time
The speed with which a movement takes place (quick, slow, sudden, or sustained).

Traveling
Moving in various directions by transferring the weight from one part of the body to another.

Turn
Rotation of the body and loss of the initial fixed point of contact (e.g., turning in a full arch).

Twist
One part of the body is held in a fixed position on the floor or apparatus and the rest of the body is turned away from the fixed position (e.g., twisting the trunk to the side and back).

Weight
The degree of muscle tension involved in the production of a movement, or the maintenance of a static position involving tension.

Wide
An action that moves the arms or legs away from the trunk.

Dance

Accent
The emphasis given to a beat in a series of beats in a measure.

Active couple(s)
The couple(s) who is designated to start the dance or to whom a part of the dance is addressed.

Advance
To move forward, usually with walking steps.

Allemande left
From a circle or square formation with all dancers facing the center, the boy joins his left hand with the girl on his left and walks once around counterclockwise and back to the starting position.

Allemande right
Same as allemande left only toward the opposite direction.

Arch
Two dancers join inside hands and raise their arms to form an arch.

Balance
In square dancing the usual movement following a "swing your partner." Partners face each other, join right hands, step back with the weight on the left foot and the right heel touching in front. Both partners may also bow slightly.

Beat
The constant steady pulsation that exists in a movement or a musical accompaniment.

Bow and curtsey
The bow, performed by the boy, may be a simple nod of the head or an elaborate and pronounced deep bend of the trunk. The curtsey, performed by the girl, may be a simple nod of the head or an elaborate and pronounced deep bend of the knees and a graceful sideward extension of the dancing costume.

Break
Release hands.

Buzz
The weight is held on one foot while pushing with the other foot.

Chain (ladies chain)
In square dancing, the girls move across to the opposite couple, extending right hands to each other as they pass, then left hands to the opposite boy. The boy places his right hand behind the girl's back, grasping her right hand, and turns her one full turn counterclockwise.

Clockwise
Move in the same direction as the hands of a clock.

Contra or longways
Couples standing in a long line with boys on one side and girls on the other.

Corner
When facing the center, the boy's corner is the girl on his left and the girl's corner is the boy on her right.

Counterclockwise
Moving in the opposite direction as the hands of a clock.

Creative dance
The expression of ideas and feelings through unstructured movement.

Divide or split the ring
Active couples pass through the opposite couples.

Do-si-do
These words mean "back to back" and usually involve two persons facing each other. Two dancers walk forward, pass right shoulders and, without turning, move to the right passing back to back, then walk backward to their starting positions.

Folk dance
Dance patterns of past cultures.

Forward and back
This figure may involve one or more dancers facing each other. Both advance four steps forward (or three steps and a bow) and four steps backward.

Gallop
A sliding movement performed in a forward direction.

Grand right and left
This is a weaving pattern and usually follows an allemande left. Face partner and join right hands, pass, give left hand to the next dancer, and continue weaving around set.

Head couple
In square dancing, the head couple is the couple nearest to the music or caller.

Home
The original starting place at the beginning of a dance.

Honor
Salute or bow to the partner or other dancers.

Hop
Transfer of weight from one foot to the same foot.

Intensity
The quality or force of music or movement.

Jump
A light transfer of weight from one foot or from both feet to both feet.

Leap
A light transfer of weight from one foot to the other foot.

Measure
An identical repetitive grouping of underlying beats.

Open
Partners stand side by side with their inside hands joined. Girls stand to the boys' right.

Opposite
The person or couple directly across the square.

Phrase
A group of measures that fit together into a meaningful whole.

Promenade
Partners join hands in a skater's position and walk counterclockwise around the set.

Reel
In a longways dance, the head couple moves to the center of the set and performs an elbow turn. The girl goes to the first boy and the boy goes to the first girl, performs an elbow swing, returns, and repeats action with partner. Pattern continues to the end of the line.

Rhythmic
Performing a variety of body movements in time to a specific rhythmic accompaniment.

Run
A transfer of weight from one foot to the other with a momentary loss of contact with the floor by both feet.

Sashay
This is the American term for the French term "chasse." These are sliding steps sideward.

Separate
Partners leave each other and move in opposite directions.

Singing games
A form of folk dance considered forerunners to the more complicated traditional dances.

Skip
A combination of a long step and a short hop, with the lead foot alternating after each hop.

Slide
A combination of a step and a short leap, which can be performed forward, sideways, or backward.

Square
Four couples, with each forming one side of a square.

Square dance
A type of American folk dance.

Star or wheel
Two or more dancers join right hands in the center of the set and walk forward or backward as directed.

Swing
A rhythmic rotation of a couple with a walking step, buzz step, two-step, or skip. The swing may be a one-hand, two-hand, elbow, or waist swing.

Tempo
The rate of speed of music or movement.

Varsovienne position
The boy stands slightly behind and to the left of his partner. While both are facing the same direction, the girl raises both hands to about shoulder height and the boy joins his right hand with girl's right hand and his left hand with the girl's left hand.

Walk
A rhythmic transfer of weight from one foot to the other. One foot is always in contact with the ground.

Basketball

Backcourt
The half of the basketball court that is the farthest from the offensive basket.

Baseball pass
An overhand pass that employs the same basic techniques used when throwing an overhand baseball pass.

Baseline
The end line of a basketball court.

Basket
The circular goal located on the backboard.

Center
The middle position on the forward line, usually played by the tallest player on the team.

Defense
The team that does not have possession of the ball.

Drive
A quick dribbling movement toward the opponent's basket.

Fast break
A situation where the defensive team gains possession of the ball and moves the ball into a scoring position before the opposing team can recover into a defensive position.

Free throw
An unguarded shot that is taken from the free throw line. If successful, the team shooting scores one point.

Frontcourt
The part of the basketball court that is nearest the team's goal.

Jump ball
A situation in which two opposing players simultaneously gain possession of the ball and the referee tosses it up between the two players.

Jump shot
A shot that is taken while the player has both feet off the floor.

Lay-up
A shot that is taken close to the backboard. The ball is released off one hand and is gently placed over the rim or against the backboard to allow it to rebound into the basket.

Offense
The team that has possession of the ball.

One-on-one
A situation in which one offensive player tries to outmaneuver one defensive player.

Pivot
A player who has possession of the ball may move one foot while keeping the other foot in contact with the floor.

Post
The post player is normally a pivot player positioned near the key with his back toward the basket.

Rebound
A shot attempted at the basket, which falls back into the court area.

Set shot
A shot taken from a stationary position.

Traveling
A player who takes more than one step with the ball without dribbling it.

Zone defense
A type of defense in which the defensive players are assigned a specific area of the court to guard.

Field and Floor Hockey

Attack
Players who are designated as forward line players.

Boarding
Holding a player against the wall.

Bully
A method of starting the game, after each goal, and after halftime.

Corner
When the defending team causes the ball to go over the end line, the attacking team is awarded a free hit from the nearest corner of the field.

Crease
The semicircular area around the goal area.

Defensive team
The team that does not have possession of the ball.

Dodge
A means of evading an oncoming tackler.

Dribble
A means of advancing the ball or puck with a series of short taps.

Drive
Hitting the ball from a moderate to a long distance.

Fielding
Gaining possession of the ball or puck.

Flick
A method of putting the ball or puck into the air.

Free hit
A free hit awarded to the opposing team after a breach of the rules.

High sticking
Raising the stick above shoulder level.

Obstruction
When a player runs between an opponent and the ball.

Offensive team
The team that has possession of the ball.

Offside
A situation in which an offensive player is in his opponent's half of the field and does not have possession of the ball as well as not having opponents between him and the goal line.

Roll-in
When the opponent causes the ball to cross the side line, a player on the nonoffending team is awarded a free roll-in at the point of infraction.

Scoop
A method of raising the ball into the air.

Tackle
A method of getting the ball away from an opponent.

Flag and Touch Football

Blocking
A legal method of stopping an opponent.

Down
A method of starting play after the ball has been stopped. In football, each team is given four downs to advance the ball ten yards.

Hike
The movement of the ball from the center player to the quarterback.

Lateral
A sideways pass of the ball.

Safety
When a defensive player in possession of the ball is trapped behind his own goal line. The attacking team is awarded two points.

Scrimmage line
The line on which each down begins. The defending team must remain behind this line until the ball has left the center's hands.

Spiral
A forward pass in which the football moves with a spirallike action, with the point of the ball leading.

Stance
The starting position of a football player.

Touchback
When a defensive player intercepts a ball behind his own goal line and places it on the ground rather than attempting to run it out over the goal line. One point is awarded to the attacking team.

Touchdown
When a member of the attacking team carries the ball over the goal line or a teammate catches a ball while in the end zone. The attacking team is awarded six points.

Soccer

Attacking team
The team that has possession of the ball; also known as the offensive team.

Corner kick
A placekick awarded to the attacking team after the defending team has sent the ball over its own goal line.

Defending team
The team that does not have possession of the ball.

Direct free kick
A free kick from which a goal may be scored directly.

Feint
A deceptive movement to mislead an opponent.

Foul
An illegal act, such as tripping or holding an opponent, that results in a direct free kick being awarded the nonoffending team.

Heading
Playing the ball by striking it with the head.

Indirect free kick
A free kick from which a goal may not be scored directly.

Infringement
An illegal act, such as being offside, that results in an indirect free kick being awarded the nonoffending team.

Kickoff
A short kick taken by the center forward at the center of the field. The kickoff is used to start the game, at halftime, and after each goal is scored.

Offside
An illegal position of a player that occurs when he is in his opponent's half of the field and when there are fewer than two opposing players in front of him at the moment the ball is played by one of his teammates.

Penalty kick
If a foul is committed by the defending team within the penalty area, the attacking team is given a direct free kick from the twelve-yard mark and directly in front of the goal. All other players must be outside the penalty area until the kick is taken.

Punt
A kick that is performed by dropping the ball and contacting it with the top of the foot before it touches the ground.

Throw-in
A two-hand overhand free throw awarded to the team that did not cause the ball to cross over the sideline.

Trapping
A method of stopping the ball using any part of the body other than the hands.

Volley
A type of kick in which the ball is contacted while it is in the air.

Softball

Away
The number of players who have been put out ("one away").

Bag
Base.

Bases loaded
Runners on every base.

Box
The specific area marked and designated as the catcher's area, the batter's area, or the coach's area.

Clean the bases
A player who hits a home run with one or more teammates on bases.

Cleanup
The fourth, and usually the strongest, hitter in the batting order.

Diamond
The area inside the four bases.

Double play
A defensive play by the fielding team resulting in two outs.

Earned run
A run that is scored as a result of an offensive play and not as a result of an error committed by the defensive team.

Error
A mistake committed by the defensive team.

Fair ball
Any legally batted ball that is touched or lands in the fair territory.

Fan
A player who misses his third strike.

Forced out
A defensive player in possession of the ball touches a base before a runner, who is forced to move to that base.

Foul ball
A hit ball that lands outside of fair territory.

Infield
The playing area within and immediately adjacent to the diamond.

Innings
A division of the game in which both teams play until each has three players out.

Out
The retirement of a batter after he has three strikes or a base runner who is caught or forced out.

Outfield
The fair territory that is located beyond the infield.

Pinch hitter
Any substitute hitter.

Pop-up
A high fly ball that lands in or near the infield.

RBI
An abbreviated term to indicate the number of runs batted in by a player.

Steal
A player who advances to another base after the ball leaves the pitcher's hand and before the infield player can tag him with the ball.

Walk
This occurs when four balls are called on the batter. The batter advances to first base.

Track and Field

Baton
A short round stick that is passed between members of a relay team.

Float
An interval or period during a long run in which the runner has a relaxed stride with no increase or decrease in speed.

Front runner
A runner who performs best when he is ahead of his opponents.

Hash running
A team race with markers and hidden directions located along a route.

Heats
Preliminary track-and-field events to determine who will compete in the final events.

Jogging
A slow, easy run.

Lap
One complete circuit around the track.

Pace
The rate of speed the runner sets for a particular distance run.

Passing zone
An area on the track within which the baton must be passed.

Pole position
A runner who is assigned the inside, or curb, lane of the track.

Scratch
A foul committed by stepping over the scratch line.

Stride
The distance between the right and left foot imprints on a track. The measurement is made from the toe of the back foot to the heel imprint of the lead foot.

Volleyball

Block
One or two defensive players jump up at the same time as the spiker with their hands raised and facing the oncoming ball.

Dink
A deception drop volley that is executed from a spiked position.

Hitter
Another term used for a spiker.

Illegal contact
Any contact of the ball in which it comes to a visible resting position.

Net recovery
A fair move by a player to play the ball after it has been hit into the net by one of his teammates.

Setup
This is normally the second hit by a team and is directed to a forward player, who then may attempt a spike or a volley over the net.

Side out
A violation that is committed by the serving team.

Spike
A ball that is hit in a downward direction into the opponent's court.

Index

Game Activities

Classroom Games

Balloon hit, 187
Beanbag Basket Relay, 184
Beanbag Pile, 186
Charades, 190
Circle Spot, 186
Clothespin Drop, 189
Crambo, 189
Crumble and Toss, 187
Follow the Leader, 186
Fox and Rabbit, 184
Go Go Stop, 186
Hat Race, 189
Hens and Chickens, 188
Hide the Thimble, 189
Human Checkers, 189
I'm Tall, I'm Small, 184
I Saw, 187
My Ship Is Loaded, 187
Poorhouse, 187
Puzzled Words, 190
Rattlesnake and Bumblebee, 189
Ring, Ring, Bell, 188
Ringmaster, 185
Simon Says, 186
Spell Act, 190
Tic-Tac-Toe, 189
Vis-a-Vis, 186
Who Moves?, 188
Who's Leading?, 187

Cooperative Games

Airplanes, 262
Blind Chariot Race, 270
Co-op tag, 267
Copy Cat, 268
Cross-Over Blanket Volleyball, 263
Cross the City Bridge, 268
Doubles Hopscotch, 261

Eight-Legged Caterpillar, 264
Four-legged Obstacle, 269
Hoopscotch, 268
Hula Pass, 270
Juggle a Number, 262
Merry-Go-Round, 264
Modified Musical Chairs, 265
Nine-Person Skip, 264
One Hole Parachute Golf, 266
Pass a Person, 266
Perpetual Motion Machine, 261
Piggy-Back Earthball, 271
Recycled Snakeskins, 262
Rope Ball, 270
Tug-O-Peace, 266
Twister, 262

Individual and Partner Games

Alphabet Game, 253
American Hopscotch, 249
Barnyard Golf, 253
Beanbag Horseshoes, 251
Chair Bowling, 250
Deck Tennis, 255
Four Square, 254
French Hopscotch, 250
Frisbee, 259
Italian Hopscotch, 250
Jacks, 251
Marbles, 251
Orienteering, 257
Paddleball, 254
Shuffleboard, 256
Shufflecurl, 256
Sidewalk Tennis, 256
Softball Croquet, 252
Tetherball, 253

Relay Activities

Animal Walk Relay, 243
Back-to-Back Relay, 244
Caterpillar Race, 245
Chariot Race, 245
Circle Post Relay, 243
Leapfrog Relay, 242
Locomotor Skill Relay, 242
Obstacle Relay, 244
Paul Revere, 245
Piggyback Relay, 245
Rescue Relay, 242
Row-a-Boat Relay, 246
Scooter Relay, 244
Shuttle Relay, 243
Siamese Twins, 245
Skin-the-Snake Relay, 245
Skipping Rope Relay, 243
Sports Skill Relay, 246
Stick and Ball Relay, 243
Stunt Relay, 243
Two-Legged Relay, 244
Wheelbarrow Relay, 244
Zigzag Relay, 243

Running and Tag Games

Animal Tag, 227
Automobiles, 224
Ball Stand, 229
Bat Ball, 234
Battle Ball, 234
Beanbag Basket, 225
Birds and Cats, 224
Bombardment, 235
Borden Ball, 236
Bounce Net Ball, 235
Boundary Ball, 230
Brownies and Fairies, 223

Dance Activities

Gymnastic Activities

Small Equipment

Large Apparatus